PAMELA DAVIES   PETER FRANCIS

DOING CRIMINOLOGICAL RESEARCH

THIRD EDITION

SAGE

Los Angeles | London | New Delhi
Singapore | Washington DC | Melbourne

Los Angeles | London | New Delhi
Singapore | Washington DC | Melbourne

SAGE Publications Ltd
1 Oliver's Yard
55 City Road
London EC1Y 1SP

SAGE Publications Inc.
2455 Teller Road
Thousand Oaks, California 91320

SAGE Publications India Pvt Ltd
B 1/I 1 Mohan Cooperative Industrial Area
Mathura Road
New Delhi 110 044

SAGE Publications Asia-Pacific Pte Ltd
3 Church Street
#10–04 Samsung Hub
Singapore 049483

Editor: Natalie Aguilera
Assistant editor: Delayna Spencer
Production editor: Sarah Cooke
Copyeditor: Sharon Cawood
Proofreader: William Baginsky
Indexer: Judith Lavender
Marketing manager: Susheel Gokarakonda
Cover design: Stephanie Guyaz
Typeset by: C&M Digitals (P) Ltd, Chennai, India
Printed in the UK

© Pamela Davies and Peter Francis 2018

First edition © Victor Jupp, Pamela Davies and Peter Francis 2000
Second edition revisions © Pamela Davies and Peter Francis 2011
This edition published 2018

Chapter 1 © Peter Francis and Pamela Davies 2018, Chapter 2 © Peter Francis 2018, Chapter 3 © Alison Wakefield 2018, Chapter 4 © Hannah Bows 2018, Chapter 5 © Vicky Heap and Jaime Waters 2018, Chapter 6 © David Scott 2018, Chapter 7 © Alexandra Hall 2018, Chapter 8 © Pam Cox, Heather Shore and Barry Godfrey 2018, Chapter 9 © Jo Deakin and Jon Spencer 2018, Chapter 10 © Nick Tilley, Graham Farrell and Andromachi Tseloni 2018, Chapter 11 © Lyria Bennett Moses and Janet Chan 2018, Chapter 12 © Pamela Davies 2018, Chapter 13 © Jerzy Sarnecki and Christoffer Carlsson 2018, Chapter 14 © Elizabeth Stanley 2018, Chapter 15 © Marie Segrave and Sanja Milivojevic 2018, Chapter 16 © Ross McGarry and Zoe Alker 2018, Chapter 17 © Steve Hall 2018, Chapter 18 © Majid Yar 2018, Chapter 19 © Ronnie Lippens 2018, Chapter 20 © Matthew Hall, Chapter 21 © Kathleen Daly 2018, Chapter 22 © Rob White 2018

Library of Congress Control Number: 2018932232

British Library Cataloguing in Publication data

A catalogue record for this book is available from the British Library

ISBN 978-1-4739-0272-5
ISBN 978-1-4739-0273-2 (pbk)
Printed and bound by CPI Group (UK) Ltd, Croydon, CR0 4YY

At SAGE we take sustainability seriously. Most of our products are printed in the UK using responsibly sourced papers and boards. When we print overseas we ensure sustainable papers are used as measured by the PREPS grading system. We undertake an annual audit to monitor our sustainability.

CONTENTS

EXTENDED CONTENTS

LIST OF FIGURES AND TABLES

FIGURES

TABLES

LIST OF BOXES

NOTES ON CONTRIBUTORS

Zoe Alker is Lecturer in Criminology, University of Liverpool.

Lyria Bennett Moses is Associate Professor, Faculty of Law, UNSW Sydney.

Hannah Bows is Assistant Professor of Criminal Law, Durham University.

Christoffer Carlsson is Lecturer in Criminology, Department of Criminology, Stockholm University.

Janet Chan is Professor, Faculty of Law, UNSW Sydney.

Pam Cox is Professor of Sociology, Department of Sociology, University of Essex.

Pamela Davies is Professor of Criminology, Northumbria University.

Kathleen Daly is Professor of Criminology and Criminal Justice, Griffith University.

Jo Deakin is Senior Lecturer of Criminology and Criminal Justice, University of Manchester.

Graham Farrell is Professor of Criminology, Leeds University.

Peter Francis is Professor of Criminology and Deputy Vice-Chancellor, Northumbria University.

Barry Godfrey is Professor of Social Justice, University of Liverpool.

Alexandra Hall is Senior Lecturer in Criminology, Northumbria University.

Matthew Hall is Professor of Law and Criminal Justice, University of Lincoln.

Steve Hall is Emeritus Professor of Criminology, Teesside University.

Vicky Heap is Senior Lecturer in Criminology, Sheffield Hallam University.

Ronnie Lippens is Professor of Criminology, Keele University.

Ross McGarry is Senior Lecturer, University of Liverpool.

Sanja Milivojevic is Senior Lecturer in Criminology, La Trobe University.

Jerzy Sarnecki is Professor of Criminology, Stockholm University.

David Scott is Senior Lecturer in Criminology, The Open University.

Marie Segrave is Associate Professor of Criminology, Monash University.

Heather Shore is Professor of History, Leeds Beckett University.

Jon Spencer is Reader in Criminology and Criminal Justice, University of Manchester.

Elizabeth Stanley is Reader in Criminology, Victoria University of Wellington.

Nick Tilley is Professor of Criminology, University College London.

Andromachi Tseloni is Professor of Criminology, Nottingham Trent University.

Alison Wakefield is Senior Lecturer in Security Risk Management, University of Portsmouth.

Jaime Waters is Senior Lecturer in Criminology, Sheffield Hallam University.

Rob White is Professor of Criminology, University of Tasmania.

Majid Yar is Professor of Criminology, Lancaster University.

ACKNOWLEDGEMENTS

This is the third edition of *Doing Criminological Research*, and the first one that does not have the name of Victor Jupp on the cover. Victor sadly passed away in 2012, and, although his name was listed as part of the editorial team for the second edition, Victor was not involved in its compilation, writing and production. In the six years since his death, we have concluded that the time is right to move forward with just the two of us as named co-editors. Yet, although Victor's name does not adorn the cover, his influence continues to shape our thinking about doing criminological research. Victor's book, *Methods of Criminological Research*, originally published in 1989 and reprinted on numerous occasions, remains, for us, one of the best research methods texts in criminology. Whilst dated, its quality lies, first, in its originality – it was one of the first published textbooks on methods in criminology; second, in the accessibility of its writing; third, in its depth of ideas and use of illustrations; and, finally, in its application of concepts, theories and methods to real-world examples.

These qualities, we hope, continue to shape iterations of *Doing Criminological Research*. It has been our intention to produce a third edition that is as relevant today as it can be to students and academic colleagues studying and working in Higher Education, as well as to practitioners working in the criminal justice, voluntary and charitable sectors, and to those working in business and corporate institutions. We have broadened its reach and scope, deepened its examination of particular methods and methodologies, and located discussion of their application in a wider range of contemporary criminological topics. Feedback on earlier editions has consistently been excellent; and in writing this edition we have also tried to incorporate the helpful observations and recommendations from the various anonymous reviewers of the second edition. We would like to thank them for their helpful and thoughtful comments.

Of course, the key marker of any textbook is the quality, relevance and accessibility of the content. As we have done for every other edition of *Doing Criminological Research*, we identified a long list of researchers whose work we admired greatly, and whom we knew were involved in doing interesting, novel and high-quality research that is challenging, critical and reflective in equal measure, and importantly impactful both on the discipline and on wider society. In simple terms, we wanted to showcase some of the best work being carried out by criminologists from a range of countries. Each chapter demonstrates the power of having a criminological imagination and confirms the expertise of each contributor in crafting accessible, exciting and impactful chapters that are not only insightful, but also tell it like it is. We would like to take this opportunity to thank each and every one of them for their personal engagement with us as editors, for their belief in the importance of telling their story in *Doing Criminological Research* (third edition), and for delivering chapters on time.

We would also like to take this opportunity to again thank Natalie Aguilera and Delayna Spencer at SAGE, both of whom have shown enormous belief in and commitment to us as academics. We would also like to extend our thanks to Sarah Cooke, Production Editor at SAGE, who has managed the process efficiently and effectively. We have had the pleasure of working with SAGE for 20 years now, and we look forward to extending our relationship into a third decade. Finally, we would like to extend our thanks to Gillian Howie, at Northumbria University, our colleague and friend, who has supported us in bringing *Doing Criminological Research* to a successful conclusion, liaising with contributors, managing the compilation of the manuscript and working with SAGE.

Pamela Davies and Peter Francis
Newcastle upon Tyne
May 2018

CHAPTER CONTENTS

GLOSSARY TERMS

decision making	primary data
research questions	secondary data
reflexivity	interview
generalizability	participant observation
research design	ethnography
validity	case study
research proposal	

1 DECISION MAKING AND REFLEXIVITY IN DOING CRIMINOLOGICAL RESEARCH

PAMELA DAVIES AND PETER FRANCIS

INTRODUCTION

Criminology as a subject of study is diverse, wide-ranging, international and frag-mented. It is carried out by a variety of researchers (for example, students, academics, policy analysts and practitioners) who study and work within a variety of institutions (for example, universities, central and local government, criminal justice agencies, voluntary and third-sector bodies), working with a variety of dif-ferent discipline bases (for example, sociology, politics, psychology, geography, economics, history, law and business). Criminologists are likely to ask questions about the following: the nature of crime and its extent; the perpetrators of crime; victims of crime; institutions of the criminal justice system and their workings; and how each of these interacts with wider social structural dimensions such as power, inequality, age, social class, gender, sexuality, race and ethnicity. Typical research questions might include 'How much crime is there and how is it geo-graphically and socially distributed?'; 'What kinds of people commit crimes?'; 'Are there any patterns to victimization in society?'; 'In what ways does the crim-inal justice system discriminate against categories of people?'. Such research questions are broad but are an essential element in decisions about what to study and what to research.

Your criminological imagination can be stimulated in all manner of ways and yet, for some of us, turning ideas into research projects can be quite daunting, and difficult. Starting to do criminological research may be individualized, but, more likely than not, it often starts as a collaborative effort, whether working alongside a supervisor, with co-investigators as part of a wider research team, or with research partners, sometimes stretching across geographical boundaries and sometimes across strategic corporate organizations and businesses. Doing crimi-nological research is something we can all do, but it does require particular disciplinary knowledge, abilities and skills, and we all need to engage in critical reflection and continue to grow and develop our own thinking and approach to doing it. Often, that can be done by learning from the mistakes and errors that we make in doing research – it does not always go as planned. We can also learn from what our peers – supervisors, colleagues, reviewers, markers, etc. – say about it. You may find yourself taking risks that pay off or that lead to disappointing results. Your criminological imagination may sometimes need to be reined in and tempered as you realize the practical considerations, and ethical and professional standards that are demanded and expected by your supervisors, peers and pro-fessional bodies.

In putting together this book, we have been keen to address the needs of those of you who are fairly new to doing criminological research, but whose criminological imagination is flourishing. You may well be an undergraduate criminology student or a postgraduate researcher. However, you may also be an academic lecturer who is teaching doing criminological research or supervising masters or postgraduate researchers. And we have also been keen to acknowledge that much criminological research is now conducted within organizations, third-sector bodies and public and private institutions. We have therefore attempted to acknowledge that there are a variety of researchers who would find a book on doing criminological research helpful and useful. With that in mind, we have not only tried to bring together the end-to-end cycle of doing criminological research within a single volume, we have also been keen to build on the real strengths of earlier editions of this book – that is, bringing together some of the best researchers doing criminology and letting them tell it like it is – warts and all. For us, this is the best way to learn – from the best there are, and from honest and reflective accounts of doing criminological research in the field. There is no better way – apart from doing it yourself. In delivering our vision for the book, we kept in mind a number of golden threads – or cross-cutting themes – that we wanted the book and its contributors to address. These are discussed below.

Golden threads and cross-cutting themes

The first golden thread that runs throughout the book and its chapters is that doing research involves engaging in a process of decision making. *Doing Criminological Research* commences by stressing the importance of: preparing and planning your research; designing your research project such that it will shed a light on your research questions; reflective thinking about decisions you have made and are making; and forward thinking about how you will undertake the research and analyse, write up and present it. Focusing on decision making at the preparation and planning stage encourages you to take decisions to rule out, as far as possible, potential risks and threats to the validity of your conclusions (see more below). One key initial decision concerns the choice of subject matter of research, or what is sometimes referred to as the research problem. This decision is pivotal because the research subject or problem provides the main focus for your research project and is a major influence on subsequent decisions about the ways in which your project is to be accomplished.

Another key decision that the book is concerned with is the kinds of methods to use and the sorts of data to collect. Crucially, each decision must be properly reasoned and justified to ensure that the research is as valid, reliable and robust as it can be. All of the chapters explore the many ways in which criminological research is entered into and carried out. They consider the exciting and innovative ways in which criminological researchers execute their research. This book assembles a collection of chapters that illustrate the importance of planning, preparing, doing and presenting criminological research, with each of the contributors giving some thought to these various stages. Importantly, they do this by drawing on their own experiences of doing criminology in the field, and by describing and reflecting on the decisions they made throughout that process.

The second golden thread that runs throughout the book and its chapters is that of the excitement, fun and reward of doing high-quality criminological research. Despite the need for good decision making, in what is often an uncertain and messy environment of working, doing criminological research is really exciting. Whether you are a third-year undergraduate student embarking on your dissertation; a postdoctoral researcher undertaking a funding council fellowship; an associate professor or a professor of criminology leading a collaborative research project, outlining the topic and the reasons for the research, developing your thinking and ideas as the evidence unfolds against a research question that you have formulated in light of an identified problem, can be hugely rewarding. Why wouldn't it be – after all, it involves doing what you want to do, in an area that you are interested in, with the intention of generating new and original research outputs and outcomes. Done well, it can stoke the criminological imagination; certainly it can ensure curiosity, challenge and criticality remain central to your thinking and practice – essential for being a good researcher. With this in mind, central to this book is the importance of the criminological imagination to doing criminological research. Indeed, each contributor focuses on how criminological research is accomplished. Each chapter does so through illustrations and exemplifications from those who have experienced doing criminological research in the field – even when their field is an office, library, archive and desk!

A third golden thread that runs throughout the book and its chapters is that despite the best-laid plans, the practice and experience of doing criminological research can be, and often is, different to that envisaged. That is, whilst decision making is key, sometimes those decisions may turn out to be wrong, or sometimes you may well need to make additional decisions that run counter to those you first made, to address errors in previous thinking or issues that have arisen in practice. Research is a social activity often influenced by factors external to and outside the control of the investigator. It is not possible to escape the reality that even the best-laid plans and designs have to be actualized in social, institutional, economic, cultural and political contexts. Many of these factors, often in different combinations, can be constraints and can have a profound effect on the outcome of research. Feminist scholars have long argued that 'methodology matters' (Stanley, 1993), yet it remains usual for the messiness of research to be sanitized, de-emotionalized and glossed over in published reports. Following Stanley and Wise (1993), Letherby (2003: 79) reminds us of the '"dirtiness" of so-called "hygienic" research'. The untold hours of personal, ethical and reflexive pondering that goes on in preparing for and planning criminological research, around research design and operationalization, entry to the field, during fieldwork, on exiting the field and in the analysis, writing up, dissemination, conclusion and impact of research, are rarely acknowledged. This is often hard and challenging emotional toil and labour which researchers do and experience, yet often they are encouraged to pretend they do not. Contributors to this volume dwell on some of these details and reflect, where possible, on how they might have overcome them.

The fourth and final golden thread that runs throughout the book and its chapters is the importance of reflexivity. In the main, social and criminological researchers are concerned with individuals – although not always at first hand – and these are people with feelings, opinions, motives, likes and dislikes. What is more, typically, criminological research is a form of interaction and what comes to pass as 'knowledge' can be the result of interactions in the research process. We have already noted that decision making is a theme that we see as key to conducting criminological research from start to finish. Reflecting on the decisions which have been taken in research and on the problems which have been encountered is an essential element of doing research. In fact, it is often the case that a reflexive account is published as part of a research report or a book; indeed, whole articles, chapters and even books have been written on this very topic. Typically, such an account covers all phases and aspects of the research process. For example, it will outline and discuss how a research problem came to take the shape that it did, how and why certain cases were selected for study and not others, the difficulties faced in data collection, and the various influences on the formulation of conclusions and their publication. Reflexive accounts should not be solely descriptive but should also be analytical and evaluative. Reflexivity is not a self-indulgent exercise akin to showing photographs to others to illustrate the 'highs' and 'lows' of a recent holiday. Rather, it is a vital part of demonstrating the factors which have contributed to the social production of knowledge. The contributors to this book reflect on, and offer transparent accounts of, the various constraints and impediments to research, the decisions they made, the operational rules they followed and the methodological choices they often had to continuously 'make up' during the research process, in order to ensure their research stands up to ethical scrutiny and is valid.

Reading and using *Doing Criminological Research*

Doing Criminological Research is a hugely successful book. This third edition is completely new and refocused. Of course, the previous two editions had strengths, namely:

- the focus on decision making and reflexivity throughout the research process
- the range of examples and case studies used to demonstrate different methods in practice
- the accessibility of the book and the learning features used throughout.

However, this new edition offers much more than those previous volumes, builds further on their strengths, by expanding the scope and depth of methodological interrogation and breadth of contributors doing criminological research in new, innovative, dynamic and novel ways. It is our belief that this third edition represents a single point of reference and a comprehensive resource. We have been keen to identify a common format for each chapter that helps your reading and understanding in order to:

- ensure consistency in approach and to secure a thorough review of all aspects of the academic and scholarly research literature
- strengthen the student-centred nature of the book, allowing for a focused, accessible and user-friendly approach
- provide a more useful and 'ready-made' teaching and learning tool
- signpost theoretical, research, practical and reflective aspects of the book.

Where relevant, each chapter offers:

- a concise critical overview and review of the academic and scholarly research on particular related topics
- a robust discussion of the literature on the methodology and methods used
- an examination of the use of the methods in practice
- judicious use of presenting visual material (lists, bullet points, tables, boxes, etc.)
- summary/review sections, questions/activities, suggested further readings, creating a more interactive internal structure generally.

Chapters variously also incorporate the following features:

- enhanced and consistent use of definitions and explanations, key themes, concepts, terminologies, etc.
- greater and more specific cross-referencing for ease and speed of use within and between chapters – signposts (jigsaws) throughout the text direct you to the glossary
- textual illustration and exemplification/case studies
- good use of diagrammatic illustration and visual imagery, such as tables, boxes, extracts
- questions within each chapter as well as tasks to complete.

Doing Criminological Research (third edition) is a book that can be read from start to finish, yet it is also a book that can be dipped into, with individual chapters serving as resources in their own right and relating to specific and particular aspects of doing criminological research. We hope that you enjoy it.

THINKING CRITICALLY ABOUT DOING CRIMINOLOGICAL RESEARCH

Here, we pull out the salient structural elements of the book and its chapters, and offer new and additional material that we think will help you develop not only your approach to doing criminological research, but also your criminological imagination.

Defining the topic, cases, context and time

Deciding 'what to study' and what your research problem is together form the first important decision you have to make. There must be some initial statement of the territory to be examined. This acts as a benchmark against which progress is measured. One of the hallmarks of effective research is the clear formulation of research problems and questions. These will guide you as the researcher to constantly return to key issues, whilst not acting as strait-jackets to inhibit creative inquiry (and possibly reformulation of the research problem) as the project progresses. One of the hallmarks of ineffective research is a research problem which allows an investigator to lose his or her way, with the outcome that conclusions do not address what was intended. A key decision, then, concerns topic – what to study? For most criminologists, the starting point for a research topic is an idea or a topic that is of interest to them, the source of which may be many and varied and can include personal interest, the research literature, social problems or a new development in society.

Typically, research questions begin by being broad and unfocused. What is more, they form a platform for making decisions about who to study, where and when. That is, there are decisions not just about topic but also about cases, context, and time. Broad research questions can be refined and reformulated to be more incisive and penetrative to take the form of, for example, 'How do urban and rural areas (context) differ in terms of victimization of racially motivated crimes (cases) in the period between 1980 and 2010 (time)?' In this way, decisions are taken to open up some dimensions of a broad topic to inquiry and not others. Peter Francis in Chapter 2 describes the process of formulating research questions.

End purpose of research

Many factors influence decisions about the topic, cases, context and time, one of the most important of which is the end purpose of research. For example, where an investigator is commissioned to evaluate the introduction of some aspect of crime prevention policy, or a particular initiative, the selection of topic, cases, context and time will typically be specified in advance by the sponsor. Rob White, in Chapter 22, explores in detail the process and opportunities that come with doing criminological evaluation, and, importantly, he offers some reflection on the similarities and differences between criminological research and evaluation research. Box 1.1 details an example of an evaluation project that was designed by the police. This new approach to tackling domestic abuse by serial perpetrators had five key objectives, and the evaluation needed to be designed such that it could report on the outcomes with respect to these after one year and then again at the end of a two-year period.

Even where there is a commitment to a broad academic aim of making some contribution to knowledge and to theory, it will be necessary to ground empirical inquiry in specific cases, contexts and time periods. The significance of decisions about such 'grounding' lies in the limits of generalizability. That is, all research takes place in particular contexts, studying particular cases at specific times, and yet aims to make broad claims beyond the particularistic scope of inquiry. The extent to which it can do so depends on the representativeness and typicality of the contexts, cases and times which have been chosen. The project referred to in Box 1.1 was confined to a northern police region. The evaluation was case (domestic abuse), context (the MATAC), area (northern area) and time specific (over two years). Though there are general principles that might be replicated in other areas and thus there may be some aspects of the approach that are generalizable, it is not possible to claim that the results can be generalized. The end purpose of this research was for the local commissioners and project team.

International, cross-cultural and comparative research

Sometimes, the research is much broader in outlook, reach and scope. With the forces of globalization impacting more readily in late modern society on crime, victimization and criminal justice (see, for example, Loader and Sparks, 2007), criminologists have become much more open to exploring doing criminological research in a comparative, cross-cultural and global context. That has required different approaches to doing criminological research, in order to address the many challenges that arise once the focus of the research becomes wider, broader and bigger. In some instances, you might be wondering what these problems are – much of the world is similar and offers similar approaches to the control and regulation of crime. Crime in one country is similar to that in another. And, yes, some are. But, as the International Crime Victims Survey (ICVS) identifies, there remains significant variation within and between countries relating to crime, victimization and experiences of criminal justice (see van Dijk, 2015; van Kesteren et al., 2014). Indeed, language challenges aside, criminal justice approaches differ significantly, as do definitional and conceptual understandings, not least with regards what we may see as simple terms such as crime and victims. Thus, alongside social, political and economic factors, globalization can and does impact considerably on how criminological research is carried out, with what tools and methodological approaches, and with what success. Matthew Hall, in Chapter 20, provides a good overview of the various approaches, challenges and opportunities of doing criminological research in a globalized, late modern world.

Anticipating conclusions

When formulating research problems, you must not just consider what to study, where and when, but also anticipate the answer to the question, 'What do I want to say?' This is not to suggest that you can write a final paper or report before carrying out the research. Rather, it is to indicate that there needs to be some anticipation of the kind of conclusion that may be reached and the kind of evidence required to support it. For example, where the aim is to evaluate the effectiveness of the introduction of some form of criminal justice policy (for example, MATAC or the new law of 'coercive control'), it is necessary to formulate research problems and questions in such a way that some conclusion can be reached about the effectiveness of the policy (see Rob White in Chapter 22). There are other ways in which researchers anticipate outcomes when formulating research questions. In a more radical and critical vein, what is sometimes termed standpoint research seeks to pose problems and address them from a particular standpoint (for example, a feminist, or gender-sensitive, perspective) and anticipates reaching conclusions which reflect that standpoint. Such research may be less likely to be concerned with questions about the effectiveness of specific policies and more concerned with addressing fundamental issues such as discrimination, inequality, oppression and justice (see, for example, Walklate et al., 2018).

It is not just about anticipating the conclusions that need some thought from the outset. It is also useful to think through the writing up and presenting of the research findings. Often, the findings will be written up for publication in a journal article and, sometimes, as a manuscript for publication by one of the leading academic book publishers, such as SAGE. During the research process itself, conference papers and presentations may well be delivered as well, providing a useful opportunity to share initial findings and thoughts and reflections on what the research is starting to uncover. Where the research is for a funding council or an organization that has, for example, funded a piece of evaluation, often a research report will need to be produced. Students will be expected to produce a dissertation or a PhD thesis, and again these may form the basis for further publications, such as journal articles and book chapters. Anticipating these from the outset of the research can help in the process of doing the research itself, a point well made by Alexandra Hall in Chapter 7, who explores the writing up and presentation of criminological research.

Audiences of research

When thinking of your research, you need to pose not just the question 'What do I want to say?' but also 'To whom do I want to say it?' The audiences of research findings include academic supervisors and peers, policy-makers who have commissioned research, practitioners who are interested in applying the findings in their day to day work, pressure groups who want to put forward a particular viewpoint and politicians who want to formulate or justify policies. Increasingly, researchers are building 'impact' into their research from the outset. Delivering impacts from research is increasingly important in research bidding and grant applications and in assessments of research excellence. The Economic and Social Research Council (ESRC) define research impact as 'the demonstrable contribution that excellent research makes to society and the economy' (ESRC 2018). Impact then, is about beneficial changes that will happen in the real world, as a result of research. This can involve academic impact, economic and societal impact or both. Impacts occur through processes of knowledge exchange and the co-production of knowledge. Most researchers and funders tend to focus on instrumental impacts such as actual changes in policy or practice, though there can also be 'negative impacts', such as evidence that prevents the introduction of a new and potentially harmful piece of legislation. Conceptual impact is impact that contributes to the understanding of policy issues or refames debates or alters attitudes, whereas capacity building impacts can be achieved through technical and personal skill or training development. Other types of impact include attitudinal or cultural impacts and enduring connectivity impacts. The former might involve people's increased willingness to engage in new collaborations. The latter might include follow-on interactions such as collaborative workshops, reciprocal visits and joint proposals (Reed, 2016). The nature of the intended audience – and where impact is intended – should be anticipated when formulating research problems. The effect on, change or benefit tends to be viewed as impactful if it goes beyond the world of researchers. The likelihood of achieving impact is therefore in part dependent on the way in which we formulate our research questions.

There is, therefore, a strong connection between the way in which a research problem is expressed and the types of findings and conclusions which are eventually presented. Different audiences give credibility to evidence and arguments presented in certain ways. For example, most articles in academic journals are expected to be presented in a very formal way. Further, there is a wealth of experience which indicates that policy-makers give greater credence to statistical as opposed to non-quantitative evidence, whereas pressure groups often favour detailed studies of 'deviant' cases or *causes célèbres* so as to make maximum impact. There is also some evidence to suggest that research undertaken with overseas collaborators has a bigger potential impact. In Box 1.2, different types of impact are outlined. The ways in which arguments and conclusions emerge and are presented are very much influenced by early decisions about the nature of the research problem and how it is expressed.

BOX 1.2   TYPES OF RESEARCH IMPACT

- Academic impact is the demonstrable contribution that excellent social and economic research makes in shifting understanding and advancing scientific method, theory and application across and within disciplines.
- Economic and societal impact is the demonstrable contribution that excellent social and economic research makes to society and the economy, and its benefits to individuals, organizations and/or nations.

The impact of research, be it academic, economic or social, can include:

- instrumental: influencing the development of policy, practice or service provision, shaping legislation, altering behaviour
- conceptual: contributing to the understanding of policy issues, reframing debates
- capacity building: through technical and personal skill development.

Source: Economic and Social Research Council (ESRC) at www.esrc.ac.uk/research/impact-toolkit/what-is-impact (accessed 09/12/17)

The research literature

As a researcher, you also need to be aware of what has been said before, by whom and in what ways. Preparing an area for research involves making sense of that which has been undertaken before, how, why and with what results. In making decisions about what to study, you will draw on an initial review of the academic and scholarly literature. After all, the objective here is to discover relevant material published on the topic area in order to help support the framing of the research questions. Alison Wakefield, in Chapter 3, provides a thorough discussion of the various types of research literature. Yet reviewing the research literature continues throughout the process of doing criminological research. The purpose of reviewing the literature is to identify the key issues and problems and controversies surrounding the proposed research area. This may be by identifying a gap in existing knowledge, articulating the weakness of argument of a particular approach, or assessing the evidence against competing perspectives. Thus, a literature review allows you to locate your research within the work of others. In doing so, you will explore the conceptual literature on the topic area, written by the leading researchers and which gives insight into theories, concepts and ideas, as well as the research literature, offering specific accounts and findings of other research projects carried out in the field.

METHODOLOGICAL APPROACHES TO DOING CRIMINOLOGICAL RESEARCH

Decision making does not just occur at the outset of doing criminological research. It continues throughout the process. Thus, in preparing criminological research, you will also make decisions about the kinds of methods to use and the sorts of data to collect.

1. You will need to develop a research strategy and research design.
2. You will need to identify what data to collect and how to collect it.
3. You will have to make a number of decisions regarding the operationalization of the approach and methods chosen, and include sampling, access and ethical issues.

Hannah Bows gives an overview of the broad approaches and distinctions between qualitative and quantitative approaches in Chapter 4, though she, Vicky Heap and Jaime Waters, in Chapter 5, and Jerzy Sarnecki and Christoffer Carlsson, in Chapter 13, make it clear that triangulation and mixed methods approaches mean that separating qualitative from quantitative research is often an artificial exercise.

Decisions will therefore be taken in the context of the purpose of the research and the time and resources available. Crucially, each decision must be properly reasoned and justified to ensure that the research is as valid, reliable and robust as it can be. Green (2008) asks the following in relation to the connections between research questions and research design:

- Are your approaches and research strategies commensurate with the question you are asking?
- Is your proposed sample consistent with the groups, organizations, relationships or processes specified in the question?
- What methodological strategies are implied by the purposes and objectives of your research question?

- What methods of data collection are most consistent with the objectives of the research, as they are embedded in the question?
- Does the question need adjusting in light of your proposed research design, or could you rework your research design on the basis of your reconsidered question?

Validity

A primary factor in determining the content of a research project is the research problem: you will seek to design a strategy of research that will reach conclusions which are as valid as possible to the research problem. There are two aspects of validity which need to be emphasized. The first concerns whether the conclusions you reach are credible for the particular cases, context and time period under investigation. Conclusions are neither 'right' nor 'wrong'; they are more or less credible. The extent to which they are credible is the extent to which they are said to be internally valid. For example, if you are investigating the effects of security improvements on levels of crime in a particular area, the strength of validity will depend on whether there is evidence that a drop in crime levels followed the introduction of security measures and also evidence that no other factor could have produced or affected the change (such as the introduction of police beat patrols). Nick Tilley, Graham Farrell and Andromachi Tseloni touch on this in Chapter 10. A second aspect of validity concerns whether it is possible to generalize the conclusions to other cases, contexts and time periods. The extent to which this is possible is the extent to which conclusions are said to be externally valid. External validity is very much dependent on the cases, contexts and time periods which form part of the research design having representativeness and typicality.

The hallmark of a sound research proposal is the extent to which the research deci- sions which comprise it anticipate the potential threats to validity. This aspect of validity is concerned with the degree of 'fit' between a research problem and the strategy proposed to investigate it – is the proposed design likely to produce valid conclusions in relation to the research problem? Several factors are likely to influence the degree of fit between research problem and research design and are therefore likely to affect validity. For example, decisions about research design have to be taken in the context of constraints imposed by cost and time, and there are many forms of research which cannot be justified on the grounds of ethics. Also, it is not possible to anticipate threats to validity which may occur unexpectedly and when research is under way. So, all research, whether in the planning stage or in the operational stage, is a compromise between what is desirable in pursuit of validity and what is practicable in terms of cost, time, politics and ethics. This can be termed the validity 'trade-off'.

All of this underlies the value of viewing research as a form of decision making. Focusing on decisions taken when research is under way helps us evaluate the ways in which the validity of conclusions has been affected in ways which were not – and perhaps could not be – anticipated. This is vital to the evaluation of research which has already been completed.

As criminological researchers, we can collect data from existing resources, including using other people's data. This is generally known as secondary research or secondary analysis. Or, we can collect data from the subjects of research first hand. This is generally known as primary research or primary analysis. These categories can overlap and research designs will often triangulate methods to ensure that validity of measurement and valid conclusions are arrived at. Broad distinctions between primary and secondary research, alongside a range of common operational themes, allow us to consider some of the ways that criminological research takes shape. Here, we follow these broad distinctions and the initial discussion is divided into two:

- existing resources
- data from subjects/primary data collection – in particular, a number of key operational themes are addressed including sources and types of data, surveys, sampling, interviews, observations and ethnography.

Existing resources as data

There are several ways in which existing resources can be used as valid research data by criminologists and victimologists. Typically, advice and guidance in criminological research texts would refer here to the use of secondary analysis of official statistics and we too discuss the use of crime data in criminological research.

Secondary analysis of official statistics

Secondary analysis is a form of investigation which is based on existing sources of data and can be distinguished from primary research and analysis where you would collect the data for yourself at first hand. Secondary data refers to any existing source of information which has been collected by someone other than you and with some purpose other than the current research question. There is a wide range of secondary sources potentially available, such as police or Crown Prosecution Service or youth justice data, institutional records, diaries and letters and other documentary and mediated resources. Pam Cox, Heather Shore and Barry Godfrey, in Chapter 8, discuss doing historical analysis of crime, victims and justice. In Chapter 10, Nick Tilley, Graham Farrell and Andromachi Tseloni explore the use of secondary data to explain the crime drop in England and Wales since 1995.

The forms of data that are routinely used for criminological research are official statistics on crime. Crime in England and Wales has, since the early 2000s, been annually reported on in a complementary series that combines the reporting of police-recorded crime and the British Crime Survey (BCS)/Crime Survey for England and Wales (CSEW). There remain three key stages in the crime-recording process:

1. Reporting a crime – someone reports a crime to the police or the police themselves discover a crime. The police register these reports as a crime-related incident and then decide whether or not it is a 'notifiable' (recorded crime) offence and whether to record it as a crime.
2. Recording a crime – the police decide to record the report or their discovery of a crime and need to determine how many crimes to record and what the offence type(s) is/are.
3. Detecting a crime – once a crime is recorded and investigated, and evidence is collected to link the crime to a suspect, it can be detected.

Thus, these 'counting rules' need to be thoroughly understood, together with how they have changed over time, as this affects comparisons and trends. Also, despite there being more consistency and better quality of crime recording over time, there is still the problem of 'attrition' and the mismatch between what people report and what is recorded by the police. The discrepancy in some areas and for some crimes remains worryingly disparate. Nevertheless, such statistics provide a good measure of trends in well-reported crimes. They are an important indicator of police workload and can be used for local crime pattern analysis.

The Crime Survey for England and Wales (CSEW) is an important monitor of the extent of crime in England and Wales. It is used by the government to evaluate and develop crime-reduction policies as well as providing vital information about the changing levels of crime over the last 30 years. The survey measures crime by asking members of the public, such as you, about their experiences of crime over the last 12 months. In this way, the survey records all types of crime experienced by people, including those crimes that may not have been reported to the police. The value of the survey is its ability to find out about crimes which do not get reported to, or recorded by, the police. It has previously shown that only 4 in 10 crimes are actually reported to the police, so conducting the survey is very valuable in understanding all of the other crimes which go unreported. Typically, the Crime Survey records a higher number of crimes than police figures because it includes these unreported crimes. As well as measuring crime, the Crime Survey for England and Wales looks at:

- identifying those most at risk of crime, which is used in designing crime-prevention programmes
- people's attitudes to crime and the Criminal Justice System, including the police and the courts
- people's experiences of anti-social behaviour and how this has affected their quality of life.

In 2015/16, around 50,000 households across England and Wales were invited to participate in the survey. In previous years, three quarters of the households invited to take part agreed to participate. Data from the CSEW and other large data sets can be used by researchers and teachers. In 2017, the Office for National Statistics (ONS) announced a consultation on a proposal that, in the context of public sector financial constraints, the future level of funding for the CSEW would be reduced with effect from October 2017. Further to this, the ONS put forward a range of proposals to reduce the cost of the CSEW in 2017/18 and future years. See Box 1.3 for a summary of the proposed changes.

BOX 1.3   CHANGES TO THE CRIME SURVEY FOR ENGLAND AND WALES

ONS CONSULTATION 2017

The consultation asked for responses to the following questions:

- What are your views on the proposed cost savings?
- Of the proposed cost-saving options, which would you prefer ONS to adopt?

Option A: Reduce target response rate (to 69%)
Option B: Reduce sample size (by 1,800 interviews)
Option C: Remove additional questions from CSEW to reduce survey to core questions required to produce quarterly crime estimates

The consultation proposes that all the following will be removed from the CSEW questionnaire from October 2017:

- all questions in the 'Performance of the Criminal Justice System' module, excepting those related to the performance of the police
- all questions in the 'Experiences of the Criminal Justice System' module
- all questions in the 'Attitudes to the Criminal Justice System' module
- Questions relating to victims' experiences of the court system and use of victim services from the 'Victimization' module.

Option D: Mixed approach – reduce target response rate (to 71%) and reduce sample size

Questions:

- What are your views on the proposed cost savings?
- Of the proposed cost-saving options, which would you prefer ONS to adopt?
- Is there a particular reason for your stated preference?
- What impact would these potential options have on your use of CSEW data?
- Do you have any other comments?

Outcome:
The main feedback was:

- A majority of respondents (40%) identified Option D – reducing the response rate to 71% and the sample size by 600 – as the best option of those available for achieving the required cost savings.
- Many respondents raised concerns regarding the removal of questions related to victims' experiences of the court system and use of victim services.
- In particular, 34 respondents (28%) specifically identified the removal of the questions on restorative justice from the 'Victimisation' module as a major concern.

The ONS:

- Reduced CSEW sample size for the 2017/18 survey year by 600 households and reduced the survey response rate to 71% from October 2017 (Option D).
- Removed the three modules of questions asked of respondents about the performance of, their experiences of and their attitudes to the criminal justice system from October 2017.
- Retained questions related to victims' experiences of the court system and use of victim services included in the 'Victimisation' module of the CSEW that were previously proposed for removal.

Such large-scale data sets are invaluable sources and resources that enable researchers to confront real-life research. The consultation by the ONS described in Box 1.3 received a total of 123 responses from academics, police forces and police and crime commissioners, local or regional government organisations, other government departments, charities and voluntary organisations. These responses were impactful in terms of influencing the outcome. Data collections such as the CSEW, the Young People and Crime Survey, and the Youth Lifestyles Survey constitute well-documented examples of real-life data collection and allow students as researchers to engage critically with methods and methodologies. They are rich sources of raw material for data analysis and can be used to engage in secondary analysis. They are sources of evidence that can be interrogated.

In Chapter 11, Lyria Bennett Moses and Janet Chan explore the emerging use of Big Data in criminology and criminal justice, and highlight some of the challenges and issues that Big Data bring to those wishing to undertake criminological research with and/or on it. They note that there are two main areas where Big Data has been used for researching crime and justice: first, the use of Big Data such as social media streams as *data* in criminological research; and, second, the use of Big Data for real-time monitoring or to make predictions that can be used for law enforcement or criminal justice purposes, such as increasing situational awareness, preventing crime and enhancing efficiency. These categories obviously overlap, and research in the first category may be applied in the second.

Primary data collection

Above, we considered data arising from secondary sources and secondary analysis. Often, such data will be used in conjunction with other data collected first hand in order to achieve triangulation and increased validity. Primary research and analysis can be conducted in several ways by criminologists and victimologists. Here, we note a number of common methodological issues that relate to obtaining data from subjects first hand. We focus on surveys and samples, interviews, observations and ethnography.

Surveys and samples

One important method of collecting data from subjects is the social survey. Social surveys have been used extensively in criminological research, and crime/victim surveys typically use structured questions as a means of collecting data from individual respondents first hand. This can be done by interviewing them or by requesting that respondents fill in a self-completion questionnaire. The CSEW mentioned above is one such survey. Survey research lends itself to the collection of both quantitative and qualitative data. The cases surveyed in criminological research can include a wide range of units of analysis, including interactions or documents. Individuals and categories of individuals are popular as primary and supplementary sources of data for criminological researchers. Whilst questions posed are typically structured, allowing the researcher to present the same stimuli and thereby collect the same kinds of data from a large number of people quickly, cheaply and with comparability of response, such questions in surveys run the risk of being too structured. Clearly, as you can already see, survey research involves complex issues (see Jo Deakin and Jon Spencer, Chapter 9).

It is very rare to collect data from the whole of the population in which a researcher is interested: this is a very costly and time-consuming exercise. For this reason, social surveys are usually sample surveys. A sample survey is a form of research design which involves collecting data from, or about, a subset of the population with a view to making inferences from, and drawing conclusions about, that population (the term 'census' is generally used when all members of a population are included in a study). There are skills in selecting a sample which is representative of the wider population and several chapters in this volume refer to sampling issues, some in the context of gathering data from respondents first hand (see for example Chapter 2 by Peter Francis).

Several contributions in the chapters that follow discuss doing criminological research that involves gathering data first hand from respondents. Whether their work has involved surveying sample populations, interviewing individual respondents and/or conducting focus groups, all have sought to avoid being overly structured, impersonal, and inflexible in their approach to gathering data first hand in order to demonstrate how these techniques can be used to produce valid, ethical, effective, rigorous and comprehensive data. Victim-oriented surveys inevitably deal with sensitive and emotive issues. Respondents are asked to reflect on personal and intimately harmful topics and experiences that they may not have disclosed previously, with strangers or via keying in data, albeit in a confidential manner. Hannah Bows in Chapter 4 and Vicky Heap and Jaime Waters in Chapter 5 illustrate how surveys can be employed when mixing methods. A persistent criticism of traditional crime surveys is that they tend to be confined to restricted ages of the population. Those under the age of 16 and those living in institutions as well as the homeless – all of whom might be deemed 'vulnerable populations' – are often excluded from national and supra-national/international surveys. From 2009 the CSEW has included a separate survey to record the experiences of young people aged 10–15. This interview is shorter than the adult one. Young people are selected to take part from the same households selected to take part in the adult survey. Permission from a parent or guardian is always obtained before an interview is conducted with anyone aged 10–15 (Francis, 2007). Both the sensitive topic and age-restriction critique are addressed head on in Chapter 9 by Jo Deakin and Jon Spencer, who discuss tackling difficult subjects and gathering sensitive data with vulnerable populations through large-scale national surveys.

Interviews

Interviews can be defined as a method of data collection, information or opinion gathering that specifically involves asking a series of questions. Typically, interviews represent a formal meeting or dialogue between people where personal and social interaction occurs (Davies, 2006). They are typically associated with qualitative social research and are often used alongside other methods. They can vary enormously in terms of the context or setting in which they are carried out, the purpose they serve as well as how they are structured and conducted. This means they are a flexible and adaptable tool and there are many different types of interview. Most commonly, interviews are conducted on a face-to-face basis and they can include one or more interviewers who are normally in control of the questions that are put to one or more interviewees or respondents. However, interviews can be informal, unstructured, naturalistic, or in-depth discussions in which the shape of the interview is largely determined by the individual respondent, through to very structured discussions according to a format with answers offered from a prescribed list in a questionnaire or ideal standardized interview schedule. An example of an interview with little interaction between the researcher and the researched is Computer Assisted Personal Interviewing (CAPI) where interviewers enter responses into a laptop computer, self-keying, to answer questions themselves. Since 1994 this mode of interviewing has been used in the BCS/CSEW for more sensitive topics. The type, nature and range of interviews used within criminology are explored by various contributors to this book, including Pamela Davies in Chapter 12, Elizabeth Stanley in Chapter 14, Marie Segrave and Sanja Milivojevic in Chapter 15, Ross McGarry and Zoe Alker in Chapter 16 and Majid Yar in Chapter 18.

Sometimes interviews may be conducted by telephone, Skype or by way of electronic communication such as e-mail. Interviews of this nature are popular for reasons of cost-effectiveness and the speed of data collection. Telephone interviews are routinely used for the conducting of opinion polls by market researchers. Political opinion polls are some of the most well-known types of interview conducted by this method.

As a means of collecting data first hand, interviews can be an invaluable source of information that generate valid, representative and reliable data. They enable you to follow up and probe responses, motives and feelings and in many of their forms, non-verbal communications, facial expressions and gestures, for example, can enrich the qualitative aspects of the data. However, assuming the use of the interview as the obvious method of choice for qualitative research can generate inappropriate or unmanageable data unfit for specific contexts and for specific purposes. In addition to this, there are skills to the practice of interviewing itself. Every aspect of the interview process can invite critique, for example over whether they are generating valid, sound and reliable data, and whether there is bias (including unconscious bias) surrounding the interviewer–respondent relationship.

Alternative types of interviews are associated with distinct advantages and disadvantages. Unstructured interviews, where the respondent talks freely around a topic, can produce rich grounded data but can be very time-consuming to analyse and the potential for bias on behalf of the interviewer might be increased. The more guided or focused the interview, generally speaking, the less time-consuming and less problematic is the analysis due to the more standardized nature of the responses. In opting for the latter form of interview, there is generally an increased likelihood that the researcher might not be asking the most significant questions.

Observations and ethnography

Participant observations and ethnography are among the most common methodological traditions in criminological research (see Dolman and Francis, 2010). Observational research can probably best be described as the 'hanging out' school of research. Observations can be used in various criminal justice settings, including the prison, and might well be used in conjunction with other methods such as interviews. In the pilot stages of research it is desirable and often necessary to spend some time among the research populations and/or in the institutional setting, particularly if this happens to be a prison, before embarking on interviews or survey work (Martin, 2000).

The ethnographic researcher will enter the field as soon as possible and is likely to undertake other tasks such as a literature review and conceptualization during and on completion of fieldwork (Silverman, 2007). Participant observation and ethnographic methods, conversational and discourse analysis, documentary analysis, film and photography and life histories, can attract criticism. Often, they are seen as producing 'soft' data rather than 'hard' factual data (Hollands, 2000) and certainly 'thick', 'rich' and 'intense' are three strong words to describe the data produced from ethnographic research. Steve Hall and Simon Winlow (Winlow and Hall, 2009), the former a contributor to this current book, have long been involved in ethnographic research and readers are encouraged to see for themselves the intense meanings and understandings that are derived from such inquiry. See Chapter 17 by Steve Hall and Chapter 18 by Majid Yar.

BOX 1.4   ETHNOGRAPHIC AND QUALITATIVE RESEARCH THAT ADDRESSES THE CHANGING NATURE OF YOUTH IDENTITIES IN CONTEMPORARY BRITAIN

Winlow, S. and Hall, S. (2009) 'Living for the weekend: youth identities in northeast England', *Ethnography*, 10(1): 91–113. The author's empirical data comes from ethnographic and qualitative research that addresses the changing nature of youth identities in contemporary Britain. To whet the reader's appetite, a brief description of the methodology is given here:

- 43 young people between the ages of 18 and 25 were interviewed.
- Interviews were conducted in order to gain some insight into their attitudes towards:

  - marriage
  - relationships and kids
  - work
  - leisure
  - body image
  - fashion
  - consumerism
  - friendship and life course.

- Interviews were unstructured and included friendship cohorts.
- Key research contacts and snowball sampling were used,

Case study research

Case study research is also an important approach to doing criminological research. Kathleen Daly, in Chapter 21, begins by stating that despite its long and varied history in social science related research, case study research is not well understood amongst social scientists. Case study research is a complex and far-reaching approach to doing criminological research and there is no one way to deliver it. It has a background in the Chicago School of Criminology, utilizing a range of data, methods of investigation and approaches to analysis and interpretation. Case study research usually focuses on a case or cases, and utilizes a range of methods and types of data collection and analysis to bring depth and breadth to the topic area under review. It can be both quantitative and qualitative in nature.

Visual Methodologies

Ronnie Lippens in Chapter 19 provides a robust overview of the development and use of visual methodologies in criminological research. As such, he begins his assessment honestly by noting that the 'emerging field of visual criminology is quite varied and many criminologists have their own ideas about what it should comprise'. Certainly, there is no one definition of what visual criminology comprises. For us, given its emergent status (despite being around longer than you would initially think, dating back to the late nineteenth century in one form or another), such methodologies can involve both secondary and primary research approaches, and are used for a variety of reasons. For some, it can involve social media, participatory diagramming and the use of visual research tools, and visual media. You may use images already available in archives or galleries, or in individual collections (such as the photographs that you or I take with our families and friends, or on holiday). Here, your key aim is to make sense of the image, use the image and understand what the image is about and why. The image can also be used as method – to allow for a discussion or to tease out specific reflections or thoughts from a research subject. And the image can also be an outcome of the research itself. For example, you could use this as part of a research project looking at the way in which the image, rather than the voice, can be a means through which individual actions, behaviours, thoughts and ideas can be captured and presented. For example, one of us, Peter Francis, along with Rachel Pain (Pain and Francis, 2003), used the visual image alongside participatory research methods to capture the ideas and lifestyles of a range of young people in a northern city (see also Francis, 2007).

BOX 1.5   EXAMPLE OF AN ABSTRACT

Pain, R. and Francis, P. (2003) 'Reflections on participatory research', *Area*, 35(1): 46–54.

ABSTRACT

Participatory research approaches are increasingly popular with geographers in developed as well as developing countries, as critical qualitative methodologies which, at their best, work with participants to effect change. This article adds to recent debates over the methodologies, practices, philosophical and political issues involved. Drawing on a project on young people, exclusion and crime victimization in Newcastle upon Tyne, England, we discuss the limitations of participatory diagramming and illustrate some of the social and political barriers to meaningful participation in, and action from, this type of research.

Methodological choices

There are a number of concerns and issues often encountered during the research process which a scrupulous, ethical and effective researcher should grapple with. In terms of data collection, many key issues will arise from the way in which you operationalize your research. Operationalization refers to the laying down of rules which stipulate when instances of a concept have occurred. Operational rules link abstract concepts to observations. Such observations are sometimes also known as indicators. The extent to which you, the research designer and investigator, can devise a means of observing and measuring the concepts that lie at the heart of a research problem is the extent to which there is measurement validity. General and abstract non-directly measurable concepts are the building blocks of theories. The researcher needs to operationalize these concepts after careful clarification of them. Whilst there are various checks that can be used to assess validity, including criterion validity, content validity and construct validity, we would draw attention to your ability as a researcher to engage in creative decision making. Many of you will be doing criminological research yourself, whilst others will be managing a research project. In both instances, you will face significant moments when you must make important methodological choices. When such decision-making moments are upon you, we suggest you foreground power and give due consideration to unequal relationships between the researcher and the researched.

So, you should be continuously checking and ensuring that you are studying what you want to study, that you are measuring what you should be measuring and what you intended to measure.

Research proposals

Ultimately, the aim of research is to bring forward evidence to make an argument in relation to the research problem(s). The means by which this is to be accomplished is stipulated in a research proposal, which is a statement of preliminary decisions about the ways in which such evidence will be collected, analysed and presented. A research proposal can have varying degrees of formality, as Peter Francis describes in Chapter 2. In the Appendix to his classic book, *The Sociological Imagination*, C. Wright Mills (Wright Mills, 1959) describes the early stages of research as involving the collecting of notes, cuttings, extracts and personal thoughts. These are organized and categorized to formulate research ideas and plans, but in a manner which is constantly under review and reformation. For Mills, the writing of research proposals is a continuous process of reflection and of stimulating the 'sociological imagination'. However, at the more formal end of the spectrum, grant-awarding bodies and other sponsors of research require precise written statements which address specific headings and must be submitted by a stipulated deadline. There are variations in the context of a proposal but typically it will address the following:

1. There will be a statement about the mechanisms by which cases will be selected. Such cases may be individuals selected to be interviewed as part of a survey but they may also be documents be analysed or interactions to be observed.
2. The means by which data will be collected should be outlined. This may be, for example, by interviewing, using observational methods or by the use of secondary sources such as documents to be analysed or official government statistics.
3. It is necessary to detail the ways in which data will be analysed, for example by using one or more of the computer packages which are available for this purpose.

When research is stimulated through a tendering process or is commissioned, there are likely to be research criteria already set out. The research aims, objectives and questions may already be determined by the funder. An example of how the National Rural Crime Network (NCRN) invited tenders and instructed potential bidders to develop their proposal is reproduced in Box 1.6. Other issues also need to be addressed, for instance timescale and budget; anticipated problems, such as gaining access to data; ethical dilemmas; confidentiality issues; and policy implications. A research proposal is a statement of intent about the ways in which it is anticipated the research will progress, although, as most researchers will attest to, the reality of how the project is actually accomplished is often somewhat different.

BOX 1.6   EXAMPLE OF THE REQUIREMENTS FOR
A RESEARCH PROPOSAL

NCRN seeks research partner to understand domestic abuse in rural areas
Title: Understanding domestic abuse in rural areas
The call: The National Rural Crime Network is looking for a research partner to help it understand the barriers to reporting domestic abuse in rural areas,

---

improve reporting and improve services to victims to help them to cope and recover.

Evidence suggests there is under-reporting of domestic abuse in rural areas. Analysis of police data shows that the number of reported domestic abuse incidents from rural areas is about half that of urban areas, despite there being no evidence that the occurrence of domestic abuse is any different in rural areas than urban.

Instruction for proposals – Your proposal should include the following information:

- your understanding of the NRCN and how this would shape your approach to the brief
- three case studies of similar work for public sector clients
- your proposed process, stages of work, methodologies and a project schedule/timings, working to the deadlines set out above
- any potential barriers and issues you anticipate and how they might be overcome
- a breakdown of your financial quote – how you will allocate the fees and any expenses within the total you are quoting as your standard day rates for the people who will deliver this project and the number of days each person will spend on the job
- your proposed project team and their biographies demonstrating why they have the skills and experience to fulfil the brief
- details of your approach to quality assurance and how you will guarantee quality research tools, analysis and deliverables
- any discounts/added value you are prepared to offer, bearing in mind that value for money will be important during the evaluation process.

REFLECTING ON DOING CRIMINOLOGICAL RESEARCH

The importance of reflexivity

Research findings and conclusions are not 'things' that are lying around waiting to be picked up by the criminologist; as we have articulated throughout this chapter, they are the outcome of research decisions which are taken at different stages (and of the factors that influence these, including factors external to and out of the control of the investigator). As Peter Francis articulates in Chapter 2, research design is an exercise in compromise whereby the investigator seeks to trade off the strengths and weaknesses of different methods when making connections with research questions. But it is not possible to escape the reality that even the best laid plans and designs have to be actualized in social, institutional and political contexts, which can have a profound effect on the outcome of research. Giving recognition to this is important on three counts: first, it allows some assessment to be made of the likely validity of conclusions; second it ensures we are reminded of the messiness of research; and third it encourages us to reflect critically on what comes to pass as 'knowledge', how and why. This latter aspect is one hallmark of critical social research. The contribution of reflexivity to the assessment of validity and also to critical social research will be discussed later.

Research as a social activity

A number of assumptions underpin this particular concern about doing criminological research. The first is that research is a social activity. Criminology is not like those physical sciences in which researchers study and engage inanimate objects. In the main, you will be concerned with individuals, and social research is a form of interaction. You should easily recognize this because one influential theoretical approach within the discipline – interactionism – emphasizes that what comes to be recognized as 'criminal' can be the outcome of interactions in the processes of the criminal justice system. What therefore, comes to pass as 'knowledge' is also the outcome of interactions in the research process.

Research and emotion

Social scientists have tended often to emulate the pure sciences in striving for objectivity in their research. This has meant that emotive writing tends to be the exception rather than the rule. Writing in the first person is often actively discouraged though when you are engaged in research for a dissertation or PhD this seems an odd way to proceed. Pretending we are not the author through a thinly disguised use of the term 'the researcher' can make your writing feel stilted and laboured. One of us – Davies (2012) – has written about the use of the first person in academic writing. See Box 1.7 for an abstract of this article.

BOX 1.7   EXAMPLE OF AN ABSTRACT

Davies, P. (2012) '"Me", "me", "me": the use of the first person in academic writing and some reflections on subjective analyses of personal experiences', *Sociology*, 6(4): 744–52.

ABSTRACT

This research note discusses being self-conscious methodologically. It illustrates my pains to be deeply reflexive about research and academic writing. It does so with reference to a personal experience that raised, as feminist research often does, emotional as well as intellectual issues. It specifically explores the use of the first person in academic writing. Writing as 'I' forced comparisons between the personal and impersonal which, in turn, have caused me to reflect more deeply on emotive, individual and subjective analyses of personal experiences. With reference to a case study of 'me', this note is a reminder of the materiality and sociality of writing. It shows how social scientists have emotions about the subjects they study. Furthermore, it demonstrates implications for parental experience studies research and policy and practice in child and family social work.

Keywords: emotions, experience, 'I', individual, personal, reflexivity, subjective

Research and politics

Criminological research is not just a social activity; it is also a political activity. It involves some form of relationship between the subjects of research and the investigators, but there are also others who have an interest. The range of stakeholders typically includes sponsors of research, gatekeepers who control access to sources of data and the various audiences of research findings. These audiences include the media, policy-makers and professionals working in the criminal justice system, politicians and academics. Gatekeepers may have a formal role and legal powers to restrict access (for example, a prison governor) or they may be able to deny access by informal means (for example, by continually cancelling appointments). Sponsors of research include government departments, the Home Office, the Ministry of Justice, institutions of criminal justice, such as the police and charitable bodies or pressure groups such as the Howard League or Prison Reform Trust. Each of these stakeholders has interests to promote and to protect. Also, each has differential levels of power with which to promote and protect such interests. The exercise of such power is ingrained in the research process, from the formulation of problems through to the publication of results.

Research and politics connect in differing ways. For example, politics can have an impact on the doing of criminological research and also on its outcome. The kind of research which is funded and the ways in which research problems and questions are framed are very much influenced by sponsors. Often, they are interested in policy relevance (in their terms) and insist on a formal customer–contractor relationship in which 'deliverables' are clearly specified. Research is often also dependent on whether gatekeepers give access to subjects – or other data sources – in the first place.

A second way in which politics and research connect is in the differing ways in which the activity of research and its outputs contribute to politics. One important way in which this occurs in criminology is in the conduct of policy-related research. Such research can take a variety of forms but one which has contributed substantially to the formulation and implementation of criminal justice policy is evaluation research. Sometimes this kind of work is known as administrative criminology because of its contribution to the administration and management of the criminal justice system. However, criminologists who represent a critical approach see such work not solely as contributing to policy, but, more importantly, as also justifying policy. In this sense, they look on policy-related research as playing a political role in mechanisms of social control and not as benign, value-free contributions to administration and management. David Scott, in Chapter 6, explores the politics of doing criminological research from a critical criminological perspective, while Rob White, in Chapter 22, explores evaluation research.

Research and ethics

Research is not just a social and political activity but also an ethical activity, as David Scott further describes in Chapter 6. Ethics is about the standards to be adopted towards others in carrying out research. Sometimes these standards are mandatory to the practice of research, for example in certain kinds of medical research, whereas in other contexts and disciplines they are merely guidelines. Sometimes they are formally expressed in professional codes of conduct such as in the ethical codes of the British Society of Criminology, the British Sociological Association and the British Psychological Society, whereas in other disciplines there is a much less formal body of custom and practice.

One ethical principle which is often expressed in social research is that of informed consent. This can be rather elastic but basically it refers to the principle that the subjects of research should be informed of their participation in research, which may be taken to include giving information about possible consequences of participation. Further, it includes the belief that subjects should give their consent to participation, and its possible consequences, prior to their inclusion. Another principle which is sometimes propounded is that no person should be harmed by research, for example that the introduction of 'experimental treatment' in some styles of research should not cause physical or psychological damage to subjects or, perhaps, disadvantage some individuals in comparison with others.

Matters of ethics interact with the pursuit of validity and also with the political dimensions of research. If the principle of informed consent is applied in full and in such a way that subjects are aware of all aspects of research, including its purpose, it is highly likely that they will behave or react in ways in which they would not normally do. Such reactivity on the part of subjects is a threat to the validity of findings. Further, the challenging of the ideological positions of certain groups in society – perhaps with a view to replacing them with others – is a central aim of some forms of research, especially critical research. However, this inevitably involves doing harm to the interests of such groups. In this way, the fundamental aims of critical research can come face to face with the ethical principle that research should not harm or damage individuals or groups of individuals.

The case for reflexivity

It has been emphasized that your reflexivity is a vital part of planning and doing criminological research. This is because criminological research is a social, political and ethical activity. There are several roles which reflexivity can play in research, for example the assessment of validity. Validity is the extent to which conclusions drawn from a study are plausible and credible and the extent to which they can be generalized to other contexts and to other people. Validity is always relative, being dependent on the decisions which have had to be taken in the planning and doing of research. Making such decisions explicit and, more importantly, assessing the probable effect on validity is the main purpose of a reflexive account (which is sometimes published alongside conclusions).

SUMMARY AND REVIEW

Throughout this book, we suggest that the conduct of research can be expressed in terms of decision making. Such decision making inevitably involves trade-offs, for example trading off the weaknesses of one course of action against the strengths of another. Some decisions have to be taken about the minutiae of research, say in deciding whether to have a sample of 100 or of 1200. Such technical issues matter, but so do the fundamental principles of criminological inquiry. These include validity (the pursuit of credible and plausible knowledge); politics (whose side am I on, if any?); and ethics (what standards should I adopt and in relation to what?). Unfortunately, as noted earlier, the pursuit of one principle may inhibit the pursuit of another. So, the most fundamental decision you must make is how to position yourself in relation to the validity, the politics and the ethics of research and the trade-offs which may have to be made between these.

1. Read this chapter and Chapter 2 and then write a sentence describing each of the following terms: research proposal; research focus; research problem; research question; research hypothesis.

2. Read Chapters 3, 4 and 5 and then write a sentence describing each of the following terms: research strategy; research design; quantitative research; qualitative research; systematic literature review; narrative review.

3. Read Chapter 10 and then answer the following:

   a. What are the challenges and opportunities of doing quantitative criminological research?

4. Read Chapters 12, 14 and 17 and then answer the following:

   a. What are the challenges and opportunities of doing qualitative criminological research?

5. Read Chapters 4 and 5 and then answer the following:

   a. What are the challenges and opportunities of doing mixed method criminological research?

6. Read Chapters 14, 16 and 17 and then compare the strengths and weaknesses of each of the following:

   o semi-structured interviews
   o biographical interviews
   o participant observation
   o appreciative ethnography.

7. Read Chapters 11, 13 and 15 and then, drawing on the innovative ways of doing criminological research that these chapters discuss, plan a strategy to conduct research on your chosen topic. You should aim for methodological triangulation in your research design.

8. As you read Chapters 6, 15, 17 and 22, write down the differing ways in which politics intrudes into social research.

9. Reflecting on Chapters 1, 4, 6, 15 and 17, describe the main ethical issues facing criminology research.

10. What are the ways in which people can be harmed by criminological research? Are there some categories of people (e.g. corrupt police officers) who should not be protected against the harmful effects of criminological research?

11. What distinguishes critical research from policy-related research, if anything?

12. Write down the issues which you think should be addressed in a reflexive account.

SUGGESTIONS FOR FURTHER READING

There are a number of texts on social research methods and on doing criminological research, many of varying quality and content. The two, in our view, that offer authoritative, clear and well-authored overviews of doing criminological research for students are:

Caulfield, L. and Hill, J. (2014) *Criminological Research for Beginners: A Student's Guide*. London: Routledge.

Crowther-Duffy, C. and Fussey, P. (2013) *Researching Crime*. Basingstoke: Palgrave Macmillan.

In relation to understanding the detail, breadth and scope of doing criminological research, we would still recommend our ex-colleague, Victor Jupp's classic criminological text-book: Jupp, V. (1989) *Researching Crime*. London: Routledge; and the first two editions of this book, namely: Jupp, V., Davies, P. and Francis, P. (eds) (2000) *Doing Criminological Research*, 1st edition. London: Sage; and Jupp, V., Davies, P. and Francis, P. (eds) (2010) *Doing Criminological Research*, 2nd edition. London: Sage.

REFERENCES

Davies, P. (2006) 'Interviews': entry in V. Jupp (ed.), *The Sage Dictionary of Social Research*. London: Sage.

Davies, P. (2012) '"Me", "me", "me": the use of the first person in academic writing and some reflections on subjective analyses of personal experiences', *Sociology*, 6(4): 744–52.

Dolman, F. and Francis, P. (2010) 'Doing ethnography in the context of policing', in P. Davies, P. Francis and V. Jupp (eds), *Doing Criminological Research*. London: Sage.

Economic and Social Research Council (2018) https://esrc.ukri.org/research/impact-toolkit/what-is-impact/ (accessed 2 August 2018).

Francis, P. (2007) 'Young people, victims and crime', in P. Davies, P. Francis and C. Greer (eds), *Victims, Crime and Society*. London: Sage.

Green, N. (2008) 'Formulating and Refining a Research Question', in N. Gilbert, *Researching Social Life* (third edition). London: Sage.

HEFCE (2014) Research Excellence Framework 2014: The Results. Available at: www.ref. ac.uk/2014/media/ref/content/pub/REF%2001%202014%20-%20full%20document. pdf (accessed 18 March 2018).

Hollands, R.G. (2000) '"Lager louts, tarts, and hooligans": the criminalisation of young adults in a study of Newcastle night-life', in V. Jupp, P. Davies and P. Francis (eds), *Doing Criminological Research*. London: Sage.

Letherby, G. (2003) *Feminist Research in Theory and Practice*. Milton Keynes: Open University Press.

Loader, I. and Sparks, R. (2007) 'Contemporary landscapes of crime, order and control: governance, risk and globalization', in M. Maguire, R. Morgan and R. Reiner (eds), *The Oxford Handbook of Criminology*, 3rd edition. Oxford: Oxford University Press, pp. 78–101.

Martin, C. (2000) 'Doing research in a prison setting', in V. Jupp, P. Davies and P. Francis (eds), *Doing Criminological Research*. London: Sage.

Pain, R. and Francis, P. (2003) 'Reflections on participatory research', *Area*, 35(1): 46–54.

Reed, M.S. (2016) *The Research Impact Handbook*. Fast Track Impact.

Silverman, D. (2007) *Doing Qualitative Research*. London: Sage.

Stanley, L. (1993) 'On auto/biography in sociology', *Sociology*, 27(1): 41–52.

Stanley, L. and Wise, S. (1993) *Breaking Out Again: Feminist Ontology and Epistemology*. London: Routledge.

van Dijk, J. (2015) 'The case for survey-based comparative measures of crime', *European Journal of Criminology*, 12(4): 437–45.

van Kesteren, J., van Dijk, J. and Mayhew, P. (2014) 'The international crime victims surveys: a retrospective', *International Review of Victimology*, 20(1): 49–69.

Walklate, S., Fitz-Gibbon, K. and McCulloch, J. (2018) 'Is more law the answer? Seeking justice for victims of intimate partner violence through the reform of legal categories', *Criminology and Criminal Justice*, 18(1): 115–31.

Wright Mills, C. (1959) *The Sociological Imagination*. New York: Oxford University Press.

CHAPTER CONTENTS

GLOSSARY TERMS

research questions

research proposal

inductive

deductive

research objectives

research design

secondary data

primary data

quantitative

qualitative

quantitative research

qualitative research

probability sampling

reflexivity

2 PLANNING AND PROPOSING CRIMINOLOGICAL RESEARCH

PETER FRANCIS

INTRODUCTION

This chapter outlines the stages involved in planning and proposing criminological research. Once you have read it, you will be confident about what to do and why, and eager to get started on planning and proposing your own project. Whilst it can be frustrating and certainly hard work, planning criminological research is a source of considerable pleasure and satisfaction, especially if you end with a proposal for research that is feasible, manageable and deliverable. It can engender a real enthusiasm for a topic and harness your intellectual excitement!

The chapter is structured into three sections. The first section explores how you might identify a topic area and formulate a research question, drawing on your interests, what you may have studied as part of your course and the research literature. The second section examines the process of planning the connections between what it is you want to study and how you will actually study it. It explores research design and the importance of making informed decisions about your methodology and methods of data collection and analysis. The third section outlines one way in which you may wish to write up your ideas in a research proposal. It also discusses the importance of talking through your ideas with peers and supervisors, and of engaging reflexively in the process. Being able to reflect critically is a key element of planning criminological research – knowing when to execute certain stages; reflecting on when they have worked; and, importantly, learning when and why they did not. To bring alive the various stages, I have used, by way of illustration, the final year dissertation project, as it is my view that the stages described in the pages that follow, if not the final research outcome, are similar for both under-graduate and postgraduate levels of study.

Whilst the chapter has been written to help you plan your research, it has not been written as a step-by-step guide. Nor is it meant to convey simple linear steps to planning and completing your proposal. In some instances, the stages described may well appear to operate in parallel. Sometimes you may be able to bring stages forward and push other steps back. And, throughout, you will make mistakes, even before you finalise the proposal. But don't worry. Take risks and enjoy the process. Be adventurous and ambitious, as the chapter will then serve in equal measure as an exacting yet fulsome resource to challenge and support you through the process. With these points in mind, please read this chapter with curiosity and imagination about what it is you wish to study, why and how.

GETTING STARTED: PLANNING CRIMINOLOGICAL RESEARCH

Undergraduate and postgraduate degree courses provide numerous opportunities for criminological research to be undertaken. These can occur in specific modules where you are tasked with formulating a research question, applying a specific data collection method, analysing a particular data set, or developing a research proposal, with the key learning outcomes assessed as part of the final summative assignment. However, the first real opportunity that many of you will get to undertake a substantial piece of criminological research on your own is for your final-year dissertation project.

Planning dissertation research

For undergraduate and postgraduate study, the dissertation is the capstone project, the end point of your learning, one that brings together everything you have learnt into a single piece of self-directed work, initiated, planned, undertaken and written up by you. That is why it is viewed as a major piece of independent study. Whilst you will have a supervisor, ultimately it is down to you to plan and propose the research, as well as to carry it out in the time frame set. Criminological dissertations usually involve one of two approaches: either they involve undertaking a literature-based study, by way of a narrative review or a systematic review; or they involve undertaking a primary piece of research. Sometimes the approach is determined by the university or college where you are studying; often, it is up to you to define which is best suited to what you wish to achieve. Box 2.1 identifies the key approaches to doing a criminological dissertation.

BOX 2.1   APPROACHES TO DOING A CRIMINOLOGICAL
RESEARCH DISSERTATION

Literature-based dissertation		Primary-research-based dissertation
Narrative literature review	Systematic review of the research literature	Involves the use of qualitative and/or quantitative research methods
• Involves analysing existing literature and developing an argument about it • The literature will be embedded throughout the dissertation in a series of chapters	• Involves a formulaic and prescriptive review process that employs transparent and systematic criteria for identifying, searching and reviewing the literature	• Involves undertaking an original piece of research on your chosen topic area, ensuring the validity, reliability and ethical nature of the work undertaken

(Continued)

(Continued)

- You may wish to discuss the way in which you searched and reviewed the literature under a methodology heading in your introductory chapter
- You will identify the relevant databases that you will use to search for relevant material, alongside key search terms and phrases to use to identify appropriate research material

- It concerns evaluating the suitability of each source and synthesizing results
- You will discuss the methodological approach to doing the SR in a separate methods section that will confirm the research question, sift criteria, databases used, search terminology (primary, secondary, etc.), approach to sifting and evaluating the literature

- Usually, given the time and resources available to you, you will have fairly small sample sizes and thus your findings will be illustrative only, and the focus is on your ability to operationalize the data collection methods and their analysis
- Will involve a separate literature review chapter that critically reviews the literature on your chosen topic
- Contains a separate methodology chapter that details what you did, how you did it and any issues and developments along the way

Because of its relative importance to your degree classification, it is all too easy to become stricken with anxiety, uncertainty, desperation and panic when confronted with doing a dissertation. It may feel as though everything you have learned during your course about doing social research has drained away. You may feel a sense of loss as to what it is you wish to research, as you cannot think of a topic or you are unable to formulate an idea. Or, the wealth of literature may appear overwhelming, or the lack of existing research may seem a barrier to developing your own research ideas. Or you might not know how to connect what it is you are interested in with how you would go about researching it. These thoughts are understandable. Yet, don't panic and don't despair! Studying for an undergraduate or postgraduate degree is about challenge, curiosity and criticality. When planned well, with foresight and imagination, the dissertation can prove to be one of the most rewarding assignments that you will undertake, one that you will wish to tell others about, including potential employers on graduation. Often, it will have pride of place on your CV. After all, it can define who you are and what you are interested in.

To help you cope with the pressures of planning and organizing your criminological research, you may wish to read, alongside this chapter, some of the sources of guidance on dissertation preparation and academic writing detailed in Box 2.2.

BOX 2.2 USEFUL LITERATURE ON ACADEMIC WRITING AND PLANNING A DISSERTATION

Bonnett, A. (2016) *How to Argue: A Student's Guide*, 3rd edition. London: Prentice Hall.

Cottrell, S. (2013) *The Study Skills Handbook*, 4th edition. Basingstoke: Palgrave.

Francis, P. (2010) 'Planning criminological research', in V. Jupp, P. Davies and P. Francis (eds), *Doing Criminological Research*, 2nd edition. London: Sage.

Hart, C. (1998) *Doing a Literature Review: Releasing the Social Science Imagination*. London: Sage.

Jupp, V., Davies, P. and Francis, P. (2010) *Doing Criminological Research*, 2nd edition. London: Sage.

Levin, P. (2017) *Excellent Dissertations*, 2nd edition. Maidenhead: Open University Press.

Punch, K. (2016) *Developing Effective Research Proposals*, 3rd edition. London: Sage.

Redman, P. (2017) *Good Essay Writing*, 5th edition. London: Sage.

Walliman, N. (2013) *Your Undergraduate Dissertation: The Essential Guide for Success*. London: Sage.

Identifying a research topic or idea

All research projects start with a topic and a research problem – an area for study and an initial statement of the overall territory to be studied – not least because both are a major influence on the subsequent decisions that you will make about the ways in which the dissertation is to be accomplished (Davies, 2010). Some of the best research projects derive from some of the simplest topic areas and so don't get caught up in trying to be different, or the most original or unique. For example, at this stage, broader areas will do, such as drug use in prison, or policing domestic violence, or age-related criminality, so long as you are suitably interested in them to focus your thinking at subsequent stages, and to carry out and write up your research. Simply put, you have to be interested in what it is you wish to study for your dissertation.

As a consequence, it is best if the topic area you choose derives from a subject area that has captured your imagination over the course of your studies and which lends itself to being researched (Davies, 2007). One of the best ways to begin to capture your thoughts is to look back at what you have studied in specific modules, or read in particular textbooks or journal articles, that has excited you or caught your imagination. Ask yourself, which essay did you really enjoy completing? Talk to your guidance tutor or module tutors for inspiration, along with friends and family. If they are available in your library or online, read the dissertations of previous graduates on your course to get a feel for the work that other students have carried out. During this stage, you may actually identify more than one topic and, if you do, you will need to work systematically through each one to decide the most appropriate one to research. In doing so, talk to your supervisor, as s/he will help. Davies (2007: 26) suggests that you should approach defining the topic logically by thinking about:

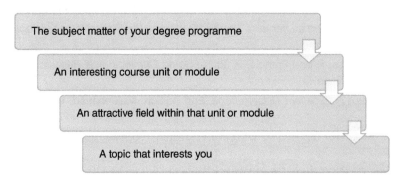

The subject matter of your degree programme

An interesting course unit or module

An attractive field within that unit or module

A topic that interests you

FIGURE 2.1   **Defining your topic**

Bryman (2015) suggests the topic usually arises because it is of interest to you, and comes from many interrelated sources:

- personal interest or experience
- the research literature that you have read as part of another module
- a wish to test or explore the validity of a particular theoretical perspective or model
- an ambition to 'solve' a puzzle
- new developments in policy, legislation or practice
- specific social problems.

In addition, your choice of topic may be informed by your career aspirations and employment/placement experiences to date; and/or specific issues that have received significant media interest.

In most cases, the source of a topic derives from a combination of factors, as Robert Reiner (1991: 39–40) makes clear in his classic research study on Chief Constables of England and Wales:

A number of factors ... made it an attractive and interesting project. Above all, there was the growing prominence of some Chief Constables as vocal and controversial public figures ... At the same time, a study of Chief Constables seemed a logical progression to plug a gap in the burgeoning field of police studies ... Having previously published a study of the backgrounds, careers and occupational perspectives of the federated ranks of the police (Reiner 1978), it seemed a logical step to attempt to conduct similar research on the elite levels.

Reiner's quote identifies how the choice of topic does not emerge in a vacuum. Criminological research is social research and by its very nature it is constructed in a context where a variety of elements can influence what is proposed, by whom and with what intention (Hughes, 2010; Morgan, 2000). In addition, think carefully about the way in which your own values, ethics and politics influence your own decision-making processes. Acknowledgement of this for May (1997: 45–6) 'enables an understanding of the context in which research takes place and the influences upon it, as well as countering the tendency to see the production and design of research as a technical issue uncontaminated by political and ethical questions'.

Formulating a research question

Once you have identified the broad topic area you wish to study, and have reflected on the factors that have influenced your choice, the next step is to bring focus to it. While, for example, 'drug use in prison', 'mental illness and crime', 'policing domestic violence', 'violence in the media', 'globalization of criminal justice', 'transnational crime', 'age-related criminality' and 'youth crime' are good initial topic ideas, they are too broad. The criminological research that you end up proposing must be achievable in the time constraints available, and able to produce valid conclusions. If it does not, then I would hazard a guess that it will only serve to confirm that your question(s) was too broad, lacked depth or was too hard to manage within the confines of time and resources. So now is the time to focus in on what it is you wish to research.

The formulation of a research question(s) involves narrowing the focus of the initial topic idea so that it is 'researchable' (Green, 2008: 47), achievable, feasible and manageable (Bryman, 2008; Davies, 2014; Davies, 2010) within the time frame given. You should be looking to develop a question that is answerable, and that also provides a clear signpost as to what you are looking for from the research (Davies and Francis, 2011). The formulation of the question(s) should be articulated in such a way that conclusions can be drawn from it/them. As Jupp (2000: 14–15) notes:

The conclusions of research will be credible and plausible only to the extent to which the questions and problems they address are clearly formulated and expressed and followed through in a consistent manner during the inquiry. Above all, research problems and questions should be capable of being answered by some form of social inquiry.

Formulating research questions involves bring clarity to your initial ideas, and focus to the planning of your research.

Good research questions set the scope; articulate the specificity and complexity; define the direction; and provide the frame of reference for any assessment of your work (O'Leary, 2005). They can involve questions about topic (what is it about the topic that I am really interested in?), cases (who is the focus of the research?), contexts (what is the context of the research – geography, people, groupings, etc.?) and time periods (what period of time will the research cover?) (Davies, 2010). They can involve sub-questions and subsidiary problems. They can be framed as questions, as propositions or as hypotheses. And they differ from one to another:

> Some research questions can be very narrow and explicit in terms of units of analysis and contexts, perhaps grounding questions in particular contexts and in relation to particular kinds of people. Other social research questions are broad, merely acting as 'signposts' to the direction in which an inquiry might proceed. Such research questions – as signposts – tend to typify qualitative, ethnographic-type research. (Davies, 2010: 38)

Green (2008: 47–50) details six properties that a research question or problem should have, and these are detailed in Box 2.3.

BOX 2.3   SIX PROPERTIES OF A RESEARCHABLE QUESTION

Criminological research questions should be:

1. Interesting – to the curious, passionate and enthusiastic researcher
2. Relevant – makes a contribution through being significant, novel or original to the research community of which the research forms a part
3. Feasible – with specific and limited boundaries which are mindful of practicalities and resources including costs, time frames, skills, access and safety
4. Ethical – ethical considerations should be embedded from the outset in the research planning and formulation stages
5. Concise – well articulated, with the terms, concepts and objects of research clearly defined
6. Answerable – interrogative questions that ask who, what, when, where, how, which and why.

Source: Adapted from Green, 2008: 47–50 and cited in Davies, 2010

Being clear about the purpose of your research

In moving from topic area to formulating a research question, it is important to be mindful of the purpose of the research you wish to undertake. Davies (2010) distinguishes between:

- policy-related research – the purpose of which is to aid policy formulation or revision/assessment
- intervention-based research – the purpose of which is to aid understanding of the effectiveness of specific interventions against stated outcomes
- theory-based research – the purpose of which is to benefit understanding and explanations regarding human agency, social institutions and social structures
- critical research – the purpose of which is to get behind the mere appearance of things to offer an outsider view of human agency, social institutions and social structures.

Whilst some of the above may not be directly relevant to doing criminological dissertation research, I introduce you to them here in order to help raise some of the key questions that you should be thinking about at this stage, namely:

- What is it that you actually want to study and why?
- What is the purpose of your research?
- What do you want to achieve from it?
- How will it differ from that which has already been written?
- What are the gaps in our existing knowledge to which it might contribute?
- What insights do you hope to gain from completing the dissertation?
- Is it likely to be of interest to others?

In working through these questions, think about the distinctions between inductive and deductive approaches to doing criminological research. The former is the process of moving from observation to theory building; the latter involves theory testing. Similarly, be careful to differentiate between descriptive and explanatory type questions. The former relates to wanting to describe a particular phenomenon; the latter concerns wanting to explain (see Davies and Francis in Chapter 1).

There is no easy way of defining and specifying your research question and the process involves trial and error. Interrogating your initial topic area involves teasing out the criminological problem you wish to address, the perspective from which you want to approach it, the questions that you wish to answer as part of doing the research, and the purpose of doing the research.

Formulating the research question can be messy and sometimes mentally painful. You may wish to capture your thoughts in a mind map – in which you can visualize both the overall topic area and the fine detail, including the possible focus and questions. There are some good apps and software that can help you to do this digitally with ease, quickly and effectively such as FreeMind and Freeplane, both of which are open-source cross-platform. This can be a great help when you are planning the structure of your dissertation. Box 2.4 offers summary guidance on moving from a topic area to a research question.

Reviewing the research literature

Immersing yourself in the research and scholarly literature is an essential aspect of interrogating the topic you have chosen and bringing focus to it through your research question(s), although the literature review is something that you will continue to do well into the period of fieldwork itself (Walliman, 2013). It is therefore important that you critically review everything of relevance to your chosen topic area. This is, in part, to demonstrate that you are aware of and understand that which is already published, and that you are able to interpret it in relation to your study. As Alison Wakefield details in Chapter 3, the process of doing a literature review enables you to identify relevant questions to ask, themes to include, methodologies to follow, as well as allowing for the development of conceptual or theoretical frameworks and the framing of empirical research findings.

Literature reviews can take several forms. These can include a systematic review, a rapid evidence assessment and a narrative review (Bryman, 2008; Hart, 1998), and the choice of literature review that criminologists adopt as part of the research process is determined by their research questions and overall ambitions for the project. As Box 2.1 notes, sometimes the literature review will form the substantive basis upon which the research will be based, while in projects that propose to deliver primary research, the literature review will be used to support the development of the research strategy, will act as your springboard into the field and will be drawn on when making sense of the data collected. In systematic literature reviews, the approach to searching and assessing the literature is in its own right sophisticated, and the methodology is written up and presented as a separate section.

At an early stage of planning your dissertation, your approach to reviewing the literature will most likely resemble that of a narrative review. Narrative reviews are used much more to develop understanding of a topic area and can involve more of a developmental and uncertain process. While they may have a starting point, they do not always have an identifiable end point, and your searching and reading might take you to places that you had not anticipated at the outset. Narrative reviews offer less specific criteria for the inclusion and exclusion of studies, and are by their very nature much more wide-ranging and fluid pieces of work.

Most of you will start by reading textbook overviews and summary articles on your particular chosen topic area, scanning their bibliographies for relevant further sources. In doing so, however, remember that summary and textbook overviews will have been written with a particular emphasis in mind, and that a textbook author's take on a particular research study may differ from that of someone else's (including your own, and that of the author of the study), so it is important to read the original research study if you can. Nevertheless, what textbook and summary articles do allow is for you to get started quickly, developing your understanding of the key issues that arise from a review of your topic area. After all, the objective here is to discover relevant material published on the topic area in order to help support the framing of the research question(s). After a while, you will start to build up a succinct overview of the proposed subject area, detailing what the literature has to say about the topic area, identifying gaps in the literature, areas of informed debate and specific research studies and key themes.

Reading and note taking

As part of your degree programme, you will already have developed skills in critical reading. It is a process which is much slower than reading for pleasure and involves absorption and reflection of the material being read within a questioning/critical framework to ensure that you understand what you are reading and how it relates to your topic, and that you are able to draw out the key points of relevance. A critical analysis of any text (book, article etc) should begin with an acknowledgement that different perspectives exist on any given topic. Acknowledging this will ensure that you make yourself aware of the perspective from which specific authors you are reading are working from. In this way, you will be then able to explore the evidence presented and how, assess the authority of the author(s) to make the claims being made, and identify any biases or other issues in the argument as presented. You should then be able to identify the strengths and limitations of the research discussed, and assess its implications and significance for your own study. Furthermore, you should examine the connections between each particular piece of work you have read and the work of others on the same topic.

It is essential that you make good notes as part of the literature review. Remember, you will come back to these at some point in the future. Your notes must be succinct and detail the page numbers of any quotes listed. Don't just copy but summarize and critically evaluate the text that you read. In addition, always note the full bibliographical details of all the sources you use in your dissertation. You may wish to teach yourself how to use Endnote bibliographic software. Endnote can help you to manage your references, insert citations into your text and, at the same time, create a reference list in your selected reference style, such as Harvard.

Making time and marking milestones

Any piece of criminological research, including a dissertation, requires good time management. At the outset, you will feel as though you have lots of time as dissertations tend to have long lead in times with the hand-in date a considerable way off. This time should be used well to undertake the things detailed in the paragraphs and sections above, including identifyting the topic, formulating your question(s), reviewing the literature, and, as the next section details, exploring access, sampling and data collection approaches. Setting yourself a timetable is useful in providing an understanding of the key tasks that need doing and by when. You will need to allow for slippage by identifying periods of extra time in your planning.

It is also essential to get into good habits from the beginning, for example by keeping a research diary. A research diary can be used to record your first thoughts, day-to-day activities, insights, decision making and anxieties as the research unfolds and progresses. The diary can also be used as a reflective tool and as a source of data, filling in elements of the research context, reminding you of particular incidents and aspects of fieldwork, sampling and data collection (Bowen, 1997; Meloy, 2002). Reflecting at the end of each week using your timetable and research diary will enable you to identify or anticipate problems in each of these areas. Table 2.1 provides an example of a simple research timetable.

TABLE 2.1   **Research timetable**

Month	S	O	N	D	J	F	M	A	M
Define topic/formulate research questions									
Undertake literature search and review									
Develop data collection tools and data analysis approaches									
Enter the field									
Identify and contact participants for research purposes									
Engage in carrying out the research									
Undertake data write-up (transcription of interviews etc.)									
Analyse data and search further the literature									
Write up the dissertation and ensure university guidelines are met									
Hand in the dissertation with time for it to be printed and bound									

MAKING CONNECTIONS: PROPOSING DATA COLLECTION METHODS

You will by now have a good idea of what it is you want to research for your dissertation and why. You may have also started to think about how you want to achieve it. That is, you may well have started to make connections between getting started – planning criminological research, and research design – proposing data collection methods.

For some of you, given the formulation of your research question and the purpose and outcome of your research, your dissertation will take the form of a literature review. Your aim will be to develop further your knowledge and understanding of the literature on your chosen topic and research question, identifying the relevant databases that you will search and constructing a range of search terms and phrases to identify appropriate research material. Your dissertation research proposal or plan will articulate the way in which you will search, sift and review the literature (see Alison Wakefield in Chapter 3).

Proposing secondary or primary research

For those of you drawn to the excitement of doing research in the field, or because it is stipulated in your dissertation guidelines, whilst you will continue to review the research literature, your research question(s) will be formulated with the intention of doing fieldwork. You will therefore also have to think carefully about your approach to data collection and analysis. Secondary data analysis or primary research can add important elements to your research but only if they are appropriate to your proposed research questions (see Chapter 4 by Hannah Bows). In making connections between the what (topic area and research question(s)) and the how (research design and methods of data collection), you should be starting to think about the following questions:

- Will the approach adopted help answer the question that is the subject of your dissertation?
- Is it feasible to undertake, given the time and resources available to you as an undergraduate/postgraduate student?
- Can you ensure that it will be methodologically sound?
- Does it conform to School or Faculty and university ethics policies?

You may decide to use data that is already available. Much of this will be secondary data in that it has been collected and collated by someone else. For Jupp et al. (2000: 62), secondary data and analysis:

refer to a form of inquiry and analysis based entirely on pre-existing data sources …
A secondary source is an existing source of information which has been collected by
someone other than the researcher and with some purpose other than the current
research problem in mind.

Data that is not available from a secondary source, or which is available but is inaccurate, unreliable or invalid, will have to be collected using primary research
techniques. This is often called primary data collection and refers to the process
whereby you collect the data yourself. When primary data collection is deemed an
appropriate option for data collection, validity, reliability and accuracy are also
important factors that you will need to take into account. Primary data can be collected in many ways including through the use of questionnaires, activity diaries,
interviews, focus groups and by means of observation.

The key questions that you will be faced with at this stage of planning your research
are what type of data do you wish to collect, and what is the most appropriate way to
do so. The quantitative approach to collecting data is about counting, ranking and
ordering in a systematic way (Denscombe, 2017). It is used to answer predetermined
questions, such as the percentage of people who are satisfied with the police or are
fearful of crime (see, for example, Deakin and Spencer in Chapter 9 of this book).
Quantitative data collection generally involves statistics and seeks to be reliable (that
is, the same results would be produced if the data was collected again). Qualitative data
is about people's attitudes, motives and behaviours. This is useful if, for example, you
are interested in exploring the views of drug users or the views of students in relation
to their offending behaviour. If you have focused your research topic and have developed a degree of specificity as outlined above, the questions that you have already
identified should help inform selection of the most appropriate data that you need and
point you towards the methodological approaches (and methods) relevant for their collection and analysis. Davies (2007: 26) suggests that where your dissertation aims to:

- describe, monitor and investigate: both qualitative and quantitative research can
  provide evidence, although with different descriptions
- explore: it depends on the form of exploration, but both quantitative and qualitative research can be used, but will produce different exploratory material
- interpret: qualitative research is especially strong here
- look beyond the surface: this is usually undertaken using qualitative research
- evaluate: if it concerns replication and quantification, then quantitative research
  is appropriate, although if the aim is to evaluate perspectives then qualitative
  forms can be used
- explain: both quantitative and qualitative approaches can be used
- prove: it is mostly a quantitative approach, but can involve qualitative approaches.

Quantitative data and qualitative data are available from many sources. Box 2.5 sets
out some approaches to data collection that you may wish to consider in planning
your research.

BOX 2.5 WAYS OF COLLECTING DATA

- **Observation**: indirect, overt, covert observing and participant observation where the researcher is implicit in the activity being observed; while observation may seem casual and informal, it is often a structured activity where the researcher will usually have a plan or ticksheet that enables the observations to be recorded and annotated
- **Interviewing**: face to face, by email, questionnaire, telephone and can take the form of structured and semi-structured questions; conversations with a purpose discovering information from the individual's own perspective (Lauder, 1993 cited in Robson, 1993)
- **Questionnaires**: can be completed on mass as a survey at a distance or one to one with the researcher present
- **Documents and artefacts**: internal to an organization, individual or in the public domain
- **Content analysis**: extracting content from web pages, radio, television programmes, text within books, visual images.

Source: Adapted from Robson (1993)

However, remember that each source of data and collection method outlined in Box 2.5 has particular strengths and weaknesses (see Box 2.6).

BOX 2.6 SOME STRENGTHS AND WEAKNESSES OF DATA COLLECTION METHODS

Data source	Strength	Weakness
Observation	- Reality – covers events in real time - Contextual – covers event's context and meaning - Insightful into interpersonal behaviour	- Time-consuming - Selectivity, might miss facts - Reflexivity, observer's presence might cause change - Bias due to researcher's actions
Interviewing	- Depth – interviewing allows for a deep understanding of meaning and emotion	- Bias due to poor questions - Response bias

Data source	Strength	Weakness
	• Targeted focus on case study phenomena • Allows for the voice of the researched to be heard in their own words • Insightful – provides perceived causal inferences	• Incomplete recollection and/ or interviewee unwilling to explore depth of issues • Can be less representative due to sample sizes • Reflexivity – the interviewee expresses what the interviewer wants to hear
Questionnaires	• User anonymity • Practical – they are a fairly simple way to gather large data sets • Scale – able to cover a large sample • Systematic and quantifiable • Generalizable – able to generalize findings to a wider population	• Bias due to questions posed • Cost of administration and data analysis • Response rates often difficult to secure • Often difficult to provide context and meaning (they often count incidence and prevalence rather than research the dynamic processes)
Documents and artefacts	• Stable repeated review • Unobtrusive, exist prior to case study • Exact names etc. • Broad coverage – extended time span • Insightful into cultural features • Insightful into technical operations	• Retrievability difficult • Biased selectivity • Reporting bias, author bias • Access may be blocked • Privacy may inhibit access • Selectivity, availability
Content analysis	• Able to capture meaning and terminology through assessment of words, sounds and images • Focuses on communication and thus social interaction in an unobtrusive manner • Cheap to administer • Easy access to material • Systematic and reliable	• Biased selectivity • Reporting bias, author bias • Difficult sometimes to assess context appropriately • Can lack a theoretical underpinning • Time consuming, especially relating to coding and inputting of data

Source: Adapted from Yin (1993) in Tellis (1997)

And, do not forget, as Vicky Heap and Jaime Waters detail in Chapter 5, mixed methodologies and methods are also appropriate means through which criminological research can be undertaken; the key benefit of using a mixed approach is that by delivering qualitative and quantitative methods alongside each other, the problems of one method can be ameliorated by the use of another.

Access and sampling

Blaxter et al. (2006) identify that in choosing and then refining your research approach during the planning stage you will need to give some thought to issues of access. You may require access to:

- people: in the community, their place of work, the home, particular groups
- organizations or institutions: government/public departments, public institutions, private organizations
- documents: held in public or private institutions, libraries and archives
- data: as detailed above, not all secondary data will be made available to you and when it is, it may not be delivered to you in a form that you want.

Access may prove difficult to secure for you as a researcher. With regard to data or documentation, they may not be made available to you. If available, it may involve negotiating access in a format that is suitable and appropriate. It is also important to be aware of issues relating to data reliability, accuracy and availability. Just because the data has already been collected does not mean that it will be accurate or reliable. Certainly, you will have to think about how you will ensure the reliability and validity of the data that you wish to use. Access to people and organisations will often need to be negotiated, primarily through face-to-face meetings and written correspondence, which can be time consuming and not always successful, and in some cases additional security clearance may well be required. And you will need to think of the impact your research may have on people and organisations and how you will mitigate that risk. Moreover, for all forms of access, you will need to think carefully about how long you will need access for, and why, and in doing so, you should think about whether you will be able to secure access in the time that you have. That is, securing access can sometimes be a very long and drawn-out process.

Access also involves making decisions about sampling, and selecting a sample will be dependent on your research design:

- A quantitative approach determines that a statistical level of confidence is required. It is crucial in maintaining confidence and rigour in the findings and you should think carefully about the number of respondents you can attract and provide adequate time to analyse the data that you secure. You may wish to consider having between 50 and 150 respondents for an undergraduate dissertation.

- If your approach is qualitative, then a richer understanding of the issue is required and a small number of respondents is acceptable. In qualitative studies, a relatively small sample can produce great diversity, detailed information and rich descriptions. Lincoln and Guba (1985) estimate that a relatively small sample can reach saturation point (where the greatest possible amount of data or information is obtained). You may wish to look at having between 4 and 10 respondents for an undergraduate dissertation.

There are various approaches to sampling, some more appropriate to a quantitative approach and some more to a qualitative approach, and as part of planning your research, and connecting your research questions to how you will do it, you must design and develop a sampling strategy. Kumar (2005: 169) considers the aims of selecting a sample to be:

- 'to achieve maximum precision within a given sample size
- avoid bias in the selection of your sample'.

Sampling strategies can be identified in two broad categories: probability sampling which involves *randomization*; and non-probability sampling that involve *non-randomization*. Box 2.7 identifies some of the more familiar sampling strategies.

BOX 2.7   TYPES OF SAMPLING STRATEGIES

Type of sample	Definition
Probability sample – randomized	
Cluster	Sampling whole clusters of the population at random
Random	Sampling at random, where each individual has an equal chance of selection
Stratified	Sampling within groups of the population, e.g. by gender, social class, education level, religion, and then the population is randomly sampled *within* each category
Systematic	Sampling through selection of every *xth* case from a list of cases
Non-probability sample – non-randomized	
Convenience	Sampling those most convenient
Purposive	Sample is handpicked, constructed to serve a very specific case and/or issue

(Continued)

(Continued)

Type of sample	Definition
Quota	Sampling is convenience by type within groups, e.g. 75 young people aged between 18 and 21 years of age
Self-selecting	Sample is voluntary and self-selecting
Snowball or chain	Sample develops through interaction, relying on one respondent leading to another

Source: Adapted from Blaxter et al. (2006), Neill (2003) and Trochim (2006)

Data processing and analysis

Quantitative and qualitative data have particular characteristics in the approach taken, the form the data takes and the analysis methods used. You might plan to use mixed methods, that is, a combination of both quantitative and qualitative approaches. And, if you have chosen mixed methods, you will need to be confident about delivering data processing and analysis on both quantitative and qualitative data. Some data, particularly secondary data produced by others, may need a lesser form of analysis than, say, primary data. Primary data collected by you will definitely need to be analysed and it is important from the outset that you make yourself aware of the analytical facilities available to you. Quantitative data analysis can involve inputting the data into a spreadsheet or an IT statistical package that will allow for calculations and their presentation in the form of tables and charts. Qualitative data is undertaken in a different way. Although there are IT packages that can help in the analysis of qualitative data such as NVivo, ATLAS.ti, Quirkos or Provalis, many students analyse qualitative data derived from interviews or observations by identifying themes, patterns and trends, and then illustrating them with quotations drawn from the transcripts or field notes.

Thinking about how you will analyse the data, whether you actually have the knowledge and skills to do it, what you need to learn in order to do it, and how long it will take are four key considerations that you will need to reflect on as part of the planning of your research project, making connections between what you want to do and how you will do it. Box 2.8 provides detail on approaches to data analysis.

Ethical considerations

As David Scott details in Chapter 6 of this book, ethical considerations are an essential ingredient in planning your research project and require careful thought,

BOX 2.8   APPROACHES TO DATA ANALYSIS

Quantitative	Qualitative data
In taking a quantitative approach, you will know in advance what you are looking for (hypothesis), you will try to remain objective and distinct from the focus of the research and will use the data to count, classify or construct statistical models to explain your observations. What does the data look like and how is it explored and analysed?	In taking a qualitative approach, the aim is understanding. You may know only roughly in advance what you are looking for; the design emerges as the study unfolds, enabling a responsive approach to data collection and analysis, and, as researcher, you will often play a subjective role in data collection and analysis. What does the data look like and how is it explored and analysed?

Data:

Data:

* Numbers and statistics
* Efficient in testing hypothesis
* Misses contextual detail

* Words, pictures, objects, sounds
* Activities, behaviour, attitudes
* In-depth interviews
* Direct observation
* Documentation
* Artefacts
* Time-consuming
* Less able to generalize

Exploring the data:

Exploring the data:

* graphs and charts
* cross-tabulations
* seeking patterns and relationships in the data
* comparing means, exploring correlations.

* seek relationships between identified and emerging themes
* relate behaviour or ideas to biographical characteristics of respondents.

Steps in analysis method:

Steps in analysis method:

1. Identifying a data entry and analysis manager (e.g. IBM SPSS, MS Excel, R, Python)
2. Reviewing data (e.g. working with surveys, questionnaires)
3. Coding data
4. Data entry

1. Familiarization with the data through repeated reading, listening, etc.
2. Transcription of interview, etc. material
3. Organization and indexing of data for easy retrieval and identification (e.g. by hand or computerized program such as NVivo, ATLAS.ti, Quirkos or Provalis)

(Continued)

(Continued)

Quantitative	Qualitative data
5. Analysing data (e.g. descriptive statistics, statistical tests). 6. Presentation of data	4. Anonymising of sensitive data 5. Coding (may be called indexing) 6. Identification of themes 7. Development of provisional categories 8. Exploration of relationships between categories 9. Refinement of themes and categories 10. Development of theory and incorporation of pre-existing knowledge.

negotiation and agreement, particularly if the research involves human participants or data on individuals. Often, ethical considerations are formalized as guidelines (see the British Sociological Association's statement of ethical practice at: www.britsoc.co.uk/ethics (accessed 25 May 2018) as well as the British Society of Criminology's statement at: www.britsoccrim.org/documents/BSCEthics2015.pdf (accessed 29 May 2018). Ethical implications usually occur around five main areas, as detailed in Box 2.9.

BOX 2.9   ETHICAL CONSIDERATIONS

1. Data – there should be agreement about the use and storage of the data.
2. Vulnerability – you will need to consider how you will work with vulnerable groups, e.g. young children, asylum seekers and those unable to give informed consent.
3. Confidentiality – this must be honoured and material collected under this agreement should remain in confidence.
4. Anonymity – participants or organizations may request and have been assured that they will not be identifiable in the dissertation, and you will need to give consideration to how this will be achieved, e.g. by removing names and referring to participants as participant 1 etc., and removing biographical or some contextual information.
5. Informed consent – this process confirms that the participant has been supplied with sufficient information regarding the research and has had time to decide whether or not to participate.

Undertaking research for your dissertation requires that you also work within your own university's guidelines and ethical regulations. As with every aspect of your dissertation, it is very important that you consult your supervisor about the proposed research that you plan to undertake.

Supervision, peer support and critical reflection

Doing criminological research can be either individual or collaborative, although dissertation research is more likely to be an independent piece of work. Whatever the nature of it, your research will be enhanced by talking to others about what you plan to do, how and why, using a given approach and timescale.

Supervision is an essential ingredient of doing a dissertation and you should draw on the expertise and knowledge of your supervisor regularly. This is particularly so when getting started and making connections between your research questions and research design. The initial role of the supervisor is to facilitate discussion about planning and then doing the dissertation, and to make general points about proposed topic areas where warranted. S/he will support you in your search for a topic area, help you focus the research question and will constantly prompt you to think about the context and consequences of what you are proposing to do through critical and challenging feedback. They will raise questions about the manageability and feasibility of what you have proposed and offer constructive advice regarding your research design. Discussion might also focus on the process and timetable of the dissertation, as well as on preparation, note taking and writing. In addition, issues surrounding presentation, referencing and bibliographic construction will be reinforced. This will ensure that s/he can give feedback on your proposal and you can either adjust your plans, or implement the proposed research, with plenty of time. Supervision also allows for an early discussion about the politics and ethics of what you are proposing.

When engaging with your supervisor, however, remember that the dissertation is your piece of work based on your independent study. Your supervisor will not tell you how to do your dissertation or what to put in it. Supervisor/supervisee relationships are interpersonal ones and hence cannot be precisely defined beforehand. The amount and type of tutorial assistance requested/provided should be agreed by both parties at the earliest possible time. Contact at regular intervals is important, based on a discussion of draft chapters as the dissertation progresses – it is no good seeking guidance a week before supervision concludes.

In addition to formal supervision, peer support is also a useful mechanism through which to gain feedback on your proposed research. Sharing ideas with peers, talking through each other's plans and reading each other's proposals are all useful in helping structure and focus your proposed research activity as well as your proposal.

Also essential to the successful planning of research is, as Davies and Francis describe in Chapter 1, reflexivity. The idea of critical reflection – the process whereby you reflect on what you have done, as well as engaging in constructive dialogue with others about the nature of what you have proposed and/or undertaken, and why – is a crucial ingredient in planning your research. It allows you to reflect critically on the assumptions and approaches you have adopted and why, with a view to making adjustments to what you have proposed or wish to do, or to justifying why you wish to do the things you have proposed.

BRINGING IT TOGETHER: WRITING AND PRESENTING YOUR RESEARCH PROPOSAL

Having completed the various stages described above, and feeling confident that you have a research project in mind, a good way of presenting your research ambitions is to write a short proposal that describes what it is you wish to undertake, how and why. A research proposal is a written document which outlines your proposed research, including what it aims to do, how it will be undertaken and the anticipated outcome(s), along with the timescale and milestones proposed. Your proposal will also outline why the research is important and will justify the research design, including how it connects your research questions to the data collection methods. In combining description and argument, your research proposal should emphasize internal cohesiveness and consistency in your planning of the research. Throughout, the proposal will make connections to the wider literature on the subject/topic area under scrutiny.

In some dissertation modules, the proposal is the first of two summative assessment points. Even when a proposal is not a formal requirement, its usefulness outweighs the time it takes to write it. It offers you an opportunity to structure and formalize what it is you want to do. When done well, the proposal can act as a firm foundation upon which to prepare and implement the research activity, a stage-by-stage guide to carrying out your research.

A good proposal should answer a series of interrelated questions about the research that you are proposing, and these are detailed in the left-hand column of Box 2.10. In writing your proposal, you should also consider a series of further questions detailed in the right-hand column of Box 2.10 that will allow you to continue to reflect on, interrogate and refine what you have proposed.

Francis (2000) details a number of key elements of a research proposal:

- *Title page, title and your name*: the front page provides the title of the study along with your name and course.
- *Introduction and statement of purpose*: the aim of this section is to outline the topic area, highlight the importance of the study, identify its relation to what is already known about the topic area, and provide a concise statement of purpose.

BOX 2.10   THE RESEARCH PROPOSAL

A proposal must answer the following questions:	Ask yourself the following questions when writing the proposal:
• What is the topic area under review and why is it important? • What is your research question or what are your research questions?	• Why are you interested in this topic? • Will your interest last over the length of the dissertation? • Is it a topic question and, if so, why? • Is/are the research question(s) focused and does it/do they offer a feasible, manageable piece of work?
• What does the research literature have to say about the topic and how does your proposed research 'fit' with that which has already been done?	• Is there research literature on your chosen topic? • Have you started to gather together the relevant material contained in books, journals, eBooks and eJournals, and are you able to say something about what it says about your chosen research area? • Have you reflected on your research question(s) as a result of what you have read so far? • Do you still need to access some literature via interlibrary loan and online? • Do you have the time left to access it? • Have you kept records of what you have read?
• How do you intend to carry out the research? • What data collection and analysis techniques do you propose using?	• Have you given due consideration to the design of the dissertation? • Are the methods that you have chosen appropriate for the research question asked? • Are you comfortable in designing and delivering the methods chosen or do you need to undertake some more reading and piloting of them? • How will you analyse the data? • How do you intend to handle the dissertation?
• What is your timetable and what resources do you need to carry it out?	• Have you left yourself enough time to undertake the fieldwork and write up the results?
• What political and ethical issues, if any, may arise during your proposed research?	• Are there likely to be any political or ethical issues that you will need to address as part of your dissertation?

The discussion may also detail your research strategy and whether a tightly structured or more evolving piece of research is proposed.

- *Topic area, research aims and objectives*: under this section, conceptual frameworks are identified together with the specific aims of your proposed research and the means by which they are to be secured – the objectives.
- *Background literature review*: in drawing on the research literature to frame your research, ensure that it does not just become a description of what others have done in the area, but rather use it to develop your research questions and demonstrate their importance. This may be by identifying a gap in existing knowledge, articulating the weakness of argument of a particular approach, or assessing the evidence against competing perspectives.
- *Theoretical and practical significance*: it is essential your proposal addresses the question of how and why the proposed research aims to contribute and in what way.
- *Research strategy and data collection methods*: discussion of the rationale for the research design together with a description of the particular methods chosen is an essential part of any research proposal. It is important you show how the research methodology is appropriate and to ensure that the research design connects the questions to the data.
- *Sampling, data processing and analysis*: the proposed sampling frame must be outlined with discussion of how it relates to the research strategies and methods. Additionally, you should describe, outline and justify the procedures for data processing and analysis, including the use of computer-assisted mechanisms.
- *Political, ethical and practical issues*: any limitations to the study which you foresee, or any issues that you belive need to be overcome, should be dealt with in this section. The proposal should show how all ethical issues have been given due consideration and reflection.
- *Timetable*: a detailed research timetable or timeline must be outlined.

SUMMARY AND REVIEW

This chapter has described the key decision-making stages involved in planning and proposing criminological research for a dissertation, at undergraduate or postgraduate level. From the outset, you will need to identify a topic area to research, one that interests you and one that is suitable in terms of ethics and in terms of the resources that you have available to you. Of particular importance is narrowing your topic area and formulating a research question that focuses your ideas and demonstrates specificity. This process allows you to capture case, context and time pressures and is also informed by an initial review of the research literature which will continue through the identification of the data to collect and the methods to be used. In some cases, the literature review will form the main element of the dissertation. Having focused your research ambitions and harnessed your imagination into a researchable question(s), you will then need to plan how you wish to carry out your proposed research, making decisions about the type of approach you will wish to follow. This process of research design will allow you to connect what you want to study with how you will achieve it in the time frame and resources available to you. To help bring your ideas together, it is useful to write a research proposal that structures what it is you wish to study, why, how, with what resources and in what time frame. Having completed all of this, it is now time to do your research. Good luck and enjoy.

STUDY QUESTIONS AND ACTIVITIES FOR STUDENTS

1. Think about a criminological topic that you are interested in undertaking research on. Write down what it is and where the idea came from.

2. Think again about the research you would like to undertake and brainstorm the various areas of interest that relate to this broad topic.

3. Begin to formulate a research question that you would like to study (think of the process – the funnelling of ideas, from large to narrow). Is it interesting, relevant, feasible, ethical, concise, answerable?

4. Identify the core characteristics of qualitative and quantitative research design. Make a list of the key methods relating to quantitative and qualitative research. Against each method, identify the key strengths and key weaknesses of each method and how these connect to the broader approaches (qualitative/quantitative).

5. Think about how you would go about researching the topic that you have identified. What data collection methods would you choose? Qualitative? Quantitative? Which is the most appropriate in answering your research question?

    a. A statistical confidence
    b. A rich understanding

6. How do you propose to secure access to the data? Are there key individuals or a gatekeeper that will assist you in accessing the documents, people and places of an organization?

7. Using the template from Box 2.10:

    a. Choose a topic of criminological interest and express it in terms of the title of your research project, your research focus, your research problem or question/hypothesis.

(Continued)

(Continued)

b. Build up a 1000-word research proposal of your own by considering how each component (research question, literature review, data collection and analysis and politics and ethics of research) could address your chosen research topic.

8. Reflect on your own draft proposal and ask yourself the question, 'Are there any threats to validity?'

SUGGESTIONS FOR FURTHER READING

Two texts will allow you to explore planning and proposing research:

Caulfield, L. and Hill, J. (2014) *Criminological Research for Beginners: A Student's Guide*. London: Routledge, especially Part 2: Getting Going with Criminological Research and Chapters 4–7.

Crowther-Dowey, C. and Fussey, P. (2013) *Researching Crime: Approaches, Methods and Application*. Basingstoke: Palgrave Macmillan, especially Part 1: The Principles of Research and Chapters 1–3.

Also of relevance are:

Crowe, I. and Semmens, N. (2008) *Researching Criminology*. London: McGraw-Hill.

Davies, M.D. (2007) *Doing a Successful Research Project Using Qualitative and Quantitative Methods*. Basingstoke: Palgrave.

In relation to formulating research questions, read:

Booth, W.C. (2003) Chapter 3, 'From topic to questions', in *The Craft of Research*, 2nd edition. Chicago: University of Chicago Press. This includes examples of ways to find the makings of a problem and how to turn it into a problem that guides your research.

De Vaus, D. (2002) Chapter 3, 'Formulating and clarifying research questions', in *Surveys in Social Research*, 5th edition. London: Routledge. The first half of this chapter is especially useful for considering the type of research question that you are formulating and the scope of your research.

O'Leary, Z. (2004) Chapter 3, 'Developing your research question', in *The Essential Guide to Doing Research*. London: Sage, especially the section on moving from ideas to researchable question using insights from personal experience, theory, observations, contemporary issues and engagement with the literature; and also the section on narrowing, clarifying and redefining your research question.

Tashakkori, A. and Creswell, J.W. (2007) 'Exploring the nature of research questions in mixed method research', Editorial, *Journal of Mixed Methods Research*, 1(3): 207–11.

REFERENCES

Blaxter, L., Hughes, C., Tight, M. (2006) *How to Research.* Buckingham: Open University Press.

Blaxter, L., Hughes, C. and Tight, M. (2010) *How to Research*, 4th edition. Milton Keynes: Open University Press.

Bonnett, A. (2011) *How to Argue: Essential Skills for Writing and Speaking Convincingly.* London: Prentice Hall.

Bowen, T.J. (1997) 'Understanding qualitative research: a review of Judith Meloy's *Writing the qualitative dissertation – understanding by doing*', *The Qualitative Report*, 3(3), September. Available at: www.nova.edu/ssss/QR/QR3-3/bowen.html (accessed May 2018).

Bryman, A. (2016) *Social Research Methods*, 5th edition. Oxford: Oxford University Press.

Cottrell, S. (2013) *The Study Skills Handbook*, 4th edition. Basingstoke: Palgrave.

Davies, M.D. (2007) *Doing a Successful Research Project Using Qualitative and Quantitative Methods.* Basingstoke: Palgrave.

Davies, M.D. (2014) *Doing a Successful Research Project, Using Qualitative and Quantitative Methods*, 2nd edition. Basingstoke: Palgrave.

Davies, P. (2010) 'Formulating research problems', in V. Jupp, P. Davies and P. Francis (eds), *Doing Criminological Research*, 2nd edition. London: Sage.

Davies, P. and Francis P. (2011) Part One. Preparing Criminological Research in P. Davies and P Francis (eds). *Doing Criminological Research* (Second Edition). London: Sage.

Denscombe, M. (2017) *The Good Research Guide for Small Scale Social Research Projects*, 6th edition. Buckingham: Open University Press.

Francis, P. (2000) 'Getting criminological research started', in V. Jupp, P. Davies and P. Francis (eds), *Doing Criminological Research*. London: Sage.

Green, N. (2008) 'Formulating and refining a research question', in N. Gilbert (ed.), *Researching Social Life*, 3rd edition. London: Sage.

Hart, C. (1998) *Doing a Literature Review: Releasing the Social Science Imagination*. London: Sage.

Hay, C. (2002) *Political Analysis: A Critical Introduction*. Basingstoke: Palgrave.

Hughes, G. (2010) 'Understanding the politics of criminological research', in V. Jupp, P. Davies and P. Francis (eds), *Doing Criminological Research*, 2nd edition. London: Sage.

Jupp, V. (2000) Formulating Research Problems in Jupp, V. Davies, P. and Francis, P. (eds) *Doing Criminological Research* (First Edition). London: Sage.

Jupp, V., Davies, P. and Francis, P. (eds) (2010) *Doing Criminological Research*, 2nd edition. London: Sage.

Kumar, R. (2005) *Research Methodology A Step by Step Guide for Beginners*. London: Sage.

Kumar, R. (2014) *Research Methodology: A Step-by-Step Guide for Beginners*, 4th edition. London: Sage.

Levin, P. (2011) *Excellent Dissertations*, 2nd edition. Maidenhead: Open University Press.

Lincoln, Y. and Guba, E. (1985) *Naturalistic Inquiry*. London: Sage.

May, T. (1997) *Social Research Issues, Methods and Processes*, 2nd edition. Buckingham: Open University Press.

Meloy, J.M. (2002) *Writing the Qualitative Dissertation: Understanding by Doing*, 2nd edition. Hillsdale, NJ: Lawrence Erlbaum Associates.

Morgan, R. (2000) 'The politics of criminological research', in R.D. King and E. Wincup (eds), *Doing Research on Crime and Justice*. Oxford: Oxford University Press.

Neill, J. (2003) *Quantitative Research Design: Sampling & Measurement*. Available at: http://wilderdom.com/OEcourses/PROFLIT/Class5QuantitativeResearchDesign SamplingMeasurement.htm (accessed May 2018).

O'Leary, Z. (2004) *The Essential Guide to Doing Research*. London: Sage.

O'Leary, Z. (2005) *Researching Real-World Problems: A Guide to Methods of Inquiry*. London: Sage.

Punch, K. (2016) *Developing Effective Research Proposals*, 3rd edition. London: Sage.

Redman, P. (2017) *Good Essay Writing*, 5th edition. London: Sage.

Reiner, R. (1991) *Chief Constables*. Oxford: Oxford University Press.

Robson, C. (1993) *Real World Research*. London: Blackwell.

Robson, C. and McCartin, K. (2016) *Real World Research*. London: Blackwell.

Tellis, W. (1997) *Introduction to Case Study*. Available at: www.nova.edu/ssss/QR/QR3-2/tellis1.html (accessed May 2018).

Trochim, W. (2006) *The Research Methods Knowledge Base*. Available at: www.social researchmethods.net/kb/sampling.php (accessed May 2018).

Walliman, N. (2013) *Your Undergraduate Dissertation: The Essential Guide for Success*. London: Sage.

Yin, R.K. (1994) *Case Study Research: Design Methods*. Thousand Oaks, CA: Sage.

Yin, R.K. (1993) *Applications of Case Study Research*. Thousand Oaks, CA: Sage.

CHAPTER CONTENTS

GLOSSARY TERMS

literature review
narrative literature review
systematic review
positivism
inductive

deductive
research question
grounded theory
inductive research
research design

3

UNDERTAKING A CRIMINOLOGICAL LITERATURE REVIEW

ALISON WAKEFIELD

INTRODUCTION

A literature review is an evaluative overview of the state of academic knowledge on a research topic. It is often the first stage in a research project because the researcher needs to establish the nature and extent of what is already known in order to justify and contextualize any empirical work, although there is likely to be a continuing engagement with the research literature right through the research process.

The chapter is a detailed guide to doing a criminological literature review. It begins with a definition and explanation, and then goes on to describe the two main types of literature review and how they are applied within criminology. The steps in doing a literature review are then outlined, with guidance on each and criminological examples provided. Breaking the task down in this way should reassure any inexperienced researcher that an apparently daunting task is actually quite straightforward and, with the right choice of topic, can be a fascinating and illuminating undertaking, generating valuable new ideas and knowledge.

WHAT IS A LITERATURE REVIEW?

 A literature review provides a survey and discussion of the main published work in a given topic or field. According to Denney and Tewksbury (2013: 218):

> Learning how to effectively write a literature review is a critical tool for success for an academic, and perhaps even professional career. Being able to summarize and synthesize prior research pertaining to a certain topic not only demonstrates having a good grasp on available information for a topic, but it also assists in the learning process.

A literature review is a key element of an empirical research project which conveys to the reader that you have:

- read widely around the chosen topic
- gained a good command of the issues
- acknowledged the work of others
- set the study in the context of the existing body of literature, highlighting any gaps in the research.

The process of doing your literature review enables you to identify relevant questions to ask, themes to include and methodologies to follow within your study. It also informs the development of your conceptual or theoretical framework and, when presented as a chapter in a student project, dissertation or thesis, should frame the empirical research findings. A literature review is much more than an annotated bibliography or set of descriptive summaries of previous work. It provides a critical, evaluative synthesis of the research literature on a given topic set out according to a number of organizing themes. Different models can be used, most notably the narrative literature review and the systematic review. Unlike an academic essay providing a general discussion on a particular subject, the literature review provides a synthesis of others' findings, arguments and ideas in your field of study. It should address the question 'how well does the extant literature address my research question and sub-questions?', and in doing so it will respond to a number of different considerations, some of which are summarized in Figure 3.1.

Two types of literature normally feature in such a review: theoretical literature and substantive literature. Theoretical literature is employed by the criminologist for the purpose of devising a theoretical framework to anchor the research within the discipline, give direction to the study and make explicit the *ontological* and *epistemological* assumptions that the researcher brings to the research. These latter concepts relate to how one sees the nature of society, institutions and relationships (ontology), and whether these can be assessed objectively or are socially constructed; and how human actors may go about making sense of the social world (epistemology), including the question as to whether its existence can be proven, or whether it can only be described and interpreted. Different perspectives, such as positivism and interpretivism, support more objective or more subjective views of the world and its interpretation, and thus favour different methods of research. In devising your theoretical framework, it is also important to note how the various criminological (and other) theories falling into these or other schools of thought operate at different levels of analysis. They may be divided into the following categories and used separately or in combination:

- *micro theories* – concerned with types of people, individual agency and interpersonal interactions, such as biological or rational choice perspectives
- *meso theories* – relating to communities, social movements or organizations, and to collective agency and organizational processes, such as ecological or subcultural perspectives
- *macro theories* – regarding social institutions, cultural systems and societies, such as critical criminology or feminist perspectives (adapted from Einstadter and Henry, 2006: 319).

Certain perspectives span more than one category, such as labelling or control theories (which, arguably, bridge the micro and meso levels), while others integrate theories either at the same level of analysis or across levels, such as cultural criminology's fusion of a number of perspectives, including labelling, subcultural theories and postmodernism. Criminological research might also look beyond criminology to engage with social, political or cultural theories, in order to consider crime and criminal justice topics in a broader context of political economy, social stratification, social capital or cultural change, for example.

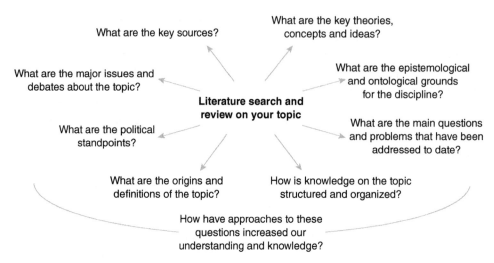

What are the key sources?

What are the key theories, concepts and ideas?

What are the major issues and debates about the topic?

What are the epistemological and ontological grounds for the discipline?

Literature search and review on your topic

What are the political standpoints?

What are the main questions and problems that have been addressed to date?

What are the origins and definitions of the topic?

How is knowledge on the topic structured and organized?

How have approaches to these questions increased our understanding and knowledge?

FIGURE 3.1 Some of the questions the literature review can answer

Source: Adapted from Hart (1998: 14)

Two main routes to theorizing are open to you. Research may be *theory-generating* or inductive, where theories are derived from the data collected, in which case the literature review will normally critically discuss previous theoretical and empirical works to highlight the lack of knowledge that is used to justify the study. Alternatively, it may be *theory-testing* or deductive, with the literature review outlining the concepts and propositions of theory to be tested (Fawcett, 1999; see also Harding, 2013 and May, 2011). The importance of theory to the research process cannot be overstated: May (2011: 27) stresses 'the constant relationship that exists between social research and social theory', with each influencing the other. He further points out that 'data are not collected, but produced' and 'facts do not exist independently of the medium through which they are interpreted, whether that is an explicit theoretical model, a set of assumptions, or interests that have led to the data being collected in the first instance' (2011: 26). In deciding your theoretical perspective, you will need to reflect carefully on your values, beliefs and assumptions to establish which theory will best represent these in your research.

The substantive literature is the general literature on the specific topic you are studying, including theory and research in similar or related areas. Most of this literature is published in academic books and peer-reviewed journals, but there is also what is known as 'grey literature' – information sources that are not controlled by commercial publishers. These include reports published directly by the organizations producing them, such as government agencies, as well as conference papers, student theses and newspaper articles.

In an ideal world, you would complete the literature review prior to the planning of the research, in order to establish whether the study is needed, to differentiate your work from past studies and add to the body of knowledge, and to build on the concepts, theories and methodologies that have already been created. Such a review may establish that the research question can be answered from the existing body of knowledge and that a research synthesis by means of systematic review, rather than an empirical study, would be the most appropriate strategy. For these reasons, the literature review is typically perceived as one of the first stages in the research process. But, in practice, the criminological researcher has to be alert to new research as it is published, and the completion of empirical research and comparison of findings with the extant literature may lead you into further avenues of reading. This is particularly the case when adopting a grounded theory methodology (Glaser and Strauss, 1967), an inductive research approach that operates more or less in a reverse direction to traditional research by starting with data collection, and, as data emerge, making constant comparisons between data and theory and accessing literature only as it becomes relevant.

BOX 3.1   TYPICAL STRUCTURE OF A STUDENT DISSERTATION

- Introduction
- Literature review
- Research methodology
- Findings and discussion (sometimes separated into two chapters)
- Conclusion

WHAT IS THE PURPOSE OF A LITERATURE REVIEW?

There are different purposes for writing a literature review. The most common are as:

- a *stand-alone literature review article* or assignment and hence a project in itself, giving an overview of the literature on a particular topic
- part of a *research proposal* – this could be a proposal for an undergraduate or postgraduate dissertation or research project, or an application for a grant. It should include a section summarizing the key issues and existing findings on a

given topic, in order to demonstrate how the proposed research will contribute to the field of study

- part of a *research report* – it may be an early chapter in an undergraduate or post-graduate dissertation or research project, providing the context to which an empirical study has contributed.

For the purposes of a student project, dissertation or thesis, it normally takes the form of a literature review chapter, although many students are required to submit a research proposal for assessment at an early stage in their studies. In a typical student dissertation, as shown in Box 3.1, a literature review is preceded by the introductory chapter and followed by a methodology chapter in which the empirical research design is explained and justified. In the social sciences, it might normally comprise 20–25% of the available words. Yet references to the academic literature should not be confined to the literature review chapter: they will help to introduce the topic in the introductory chapter, illustrate methodological issues in the methods chapter and form a basis for comparison and discussion in the latter chapters. There are several useful step-by-step guides for students seeking to write a successful literature review (see, for example, Booth et al., 2012; Caulfield and Hill, 2014; Denney and Tewksbury, 2013; Galvan and Galvan, 2017; Machi and McEvoy, 2016; Northey and Tepperman, 2015; Ridley, 2012).

WHAT DOES A LITERATURE REVIEW LOOK LIKE?

It is always helpful to find models to follow when undertaking an unfamiliar task. Other literature reviews in your topic area or discipline may reveal the sorts of theme you might explore in your own research, or show you ways of organizing your review. Numerous criminological examples are available online, or can be found by browsing libraries for bodies of literature such as those outlined in Box 3.2.

BOX 3.2   SOURCES OF EXAMPLE LITERATURE REVIEWS

- *Websites*, such as the research pages of the UK Home Office and Ministry of Justice hosted on the GOV.UK website, the Australian Institute of Criminology, the Swedish National Council for Crime Prevention, the US National Institute of Justice and the Campbell Collaboration
- *Dissertations* and theses by past students

- *Research monographs* (as opposed to student textbooks), many of which are based on doctoral research. 'Classic' texts have emerged in this tradition such as Howard Parker's (1974) *A View from the Boys*. More recent examples include Wakefield (2003) on private security, Grewcock (2010) on border crimes and Sergi (2017) on the mafia and organized crime.
- *Journal articles* based on reviews of literature, such as those published in the prestigious annual series of commissioned reviews, *Crime and Justice: A Review of Research*, Schauer and Wheaton (2006) on sex trafficking, Turchik and Wilson (2010) on sexual assault or Waddington (1999) on police culture (see also Chapter 8 in this volume for an example of a literature review on child sexual abuse and the media).

Two types of literature review are introduced in this section: the narrative review and the systematic review.

Narrative reviews

A 'traditional' literature review is increasingly known as a 'narrative' literature review, particularly among those who seek to distinguish it from the systematic review, of which more shortly. Narrative literature reviews are well suited to broad fields of study, being comprehensive in nature and covering a wide range of issues. They enable the researcher to contribute to the body of knowledge by bringing together disparate contributions to an emerging field, or updating an established field with new research findings and theoretical perspectives.

In preparing this type of literature review, criminological researchers need to be careful to go beyond providing a series of descriptions of past studies, offering an overarching critical perspective of the field. The researcher must identify categories for structuring the discussion, allowing the literature to be broken down into sections. Examples include a thematic or chronological approach, outlined in more detail later in the chapter.

Box 3.3 reproduces part of the table of contents of a thematic narrative review on police corruption, carried out by Newburn (1999) as a stand-alone report for the UK Home Office. The table of contents (p. vii) offers an overview of the key themes identified in the literature: definitions of police corruption (Chapter 2), its causes (Chapter 3) and control strategies (Chapter 4). These, in turn, are divided into sub-themes to sort and categorize the literature still further. The stated purpose of this report was 'to identify key issues in police integrity and corruption, with a specific emphasis on the causes of corruption and the efficacy of different prevention strategies' (Newburn, 1999: 2), providing a comprehensive overview of the topic at a time when, as the report states, a series of recent scandals had put the matter in the political spotlight.

1. **Introduction**

   Corruption in various jurisdictions
   Aim and methodology
   The report

2. **What is police corruption?**

   Corrupt activities
   The problem of definition
   A question of ethics?
   The 'slippery slope' to 'becoming bent'
   Summary

3. **The causes of police corruption**

   A few bad apples?
   The causes of corruption
   Drug-related police corruption

4. **Corruption control**

   Human resource management
   Anti-corruption policies
   Internal controls
   The external environment and external controls
   Possible unintended consequences of corruption control

5. **Conclusion: Toward 'ethical policing'**

In the first chapter, Newburn provides a brief outline of his methodology, reported to cover 'the main English language literature on the issues of police corruption and police ethics over the last 20 years', drawn from sociology, criminology and 'official inquiries from the US and Australia' (1999: 2). More recent literature reviews, such as Myhill's (2012) study of community engagement in policing, tend to have more detailed methodology sections, particularly with respect to sampling, setting out the literature search strategies in terms of keywords employed and databases searched, number of sources included and the inclusion criteria.

The main weakness of narrative reviews is their inability to demonstrate an absence of reviewer subjectivity or bias. In other words, because of their breadth, they do not necessarily state how sources have been identified, how fully the literature has been appraised or how sources have been included or excluded. In a student dissertation or thesis, it is good practice to include an overview of the literature review methodology employed.

A type of review that became popular in medical and health services research in the 1990s, and took hold in the social sciences this century, is the systematic review. Reflecting the growing popularity of systematic reviews in the social sciences, there are now several publications dedicated to this research methodology (see, for example, Boland et al., 2017 and Gough et al., 2017). Now preferred in some areas of criminology, it is typically used for the purpose of evaluating the effectiveness of an intervention as evidenced by past studies, in order to support future evidence-based policy making. Such reviews address common failures of social sciences and other disciplines to produce cumulative knowledge on given hypotheses, since studies carried out into a similar issue have frequently provided differing results, and literature reviews taking account of a range of separate studies have not always been systematic in their approach. According to Pawson (2006: 18), systematic reviews have also come to be favoured over evaluation studies as a means of feeding into policy-making, on the basis that 'in order to inform policy, the research must come before the policy'.

Systematic reviews are intended to bring together the most directly relevant and rigorous evaluations that have been conducted on a particular topic, employing transparent and systematic criteria for searching the available literature, evaluating the suitability of each source for inclusion in the review, and synthesizing the results. Such literature reviews are designed to offer a rigorous and replicable approach to reviewing the literature, for the purpose of eliminating the subjectivities of reviewer bias and addressing the uncertainty as to whether all the evidence has been identified and evaluated. The approach followed in the systematic review is described as fully and systematically as would be any empirical research.

The Campbell Collaboration is an international research network that produces systematic reviews of evaluation research on specific social policy interventions in order to inform policy making, and which has been instrumental in raising the status of the approach within criminology. It is a sibling organization to the longer-established and healthcare-focused Cochrane Collaboration, and includes a Crime and Justice Coordinating Group among its thematic subgroups. On its website, the Campbell Collaboration outlines four components of a systematic review:

1. Clear inclusion/exclusion criteria
2. An explicit search strategy
3. Systematic coding and analysis of included studies
4. Meta-analysis (where possible).

Box 3.4 provides a second extract from the contents page of a literature review, in this case a systematic review by Farrington and Welsh (2002: iii) of research evaluating the effects of street lighting on crime, once again conducted for the UK Home Office. In this example, the parameters of the literature were much narrower than those employed by Newburn (1999). Rather than interrogating general literature on street lighting and crime, the focus was on establishing the combined results of 13 American and British studies, selected by means of an exhaustive literature search process and the application of explicit and rigorous inclusion criteria. All of the chosen studies adopted the same general strategy of evaluating the direct relationship between interventions to improve street lighting in the study areas and crime levels in those areas, for the purpose of informing crime-prevention policy making. Aggregating the statistical results by means of a meta-analysis, Farrington and Welsh were able to draw the conclusion that 'improved street lighting was followed by a decrease in crime' (2002: 39).

BOX 3.4   WHAT DOES A SYSTEMATIC REVIEW OF THE EFFECTS OF IMPROVED STREET LIGHTING ON CRIME LOOK LIKE?

1. **Background**

   Research on street lighting and crime
   How might improved street lighting reduce crime?
   Causal links between street lighting and crime
   Determining what works to reduce crime
   Characteristics of systematic reviews
   Aims of this report

2. **Methods**

   Criteria for inclusion of evaluation studies
   Search strategies
   Programmes not meeting inclusion criteria

3. **Results**

   Key features of evaluations
   Results of American studies
   Results of British studies

4. **Conclusions**

   Summary of main findings
   Priorities for research
   Policy implications

The structure of this systematic review differs markedly from Newburn's (1999) narrative review. The general literature is briefly summarized in the introductory background chapter (Chapter 1) to provide a mini narrative review, and then the review methods are explained in much greater detail in a distinct methods chapter (Chapter 2). The findings in this much more focused study are set out in a single chapter (Chapter 3) and, like the Newburn review, it ends with a conclusion chapter (Chapter 4).

The strengths of the systematic review are also its limitations, emphasizing the very different purposes of the two types of literature review. The prescriptive approach required of a systematic review precludes the comprehensive coverage of the literature that, in the case of the Farrington and Welsh (2002) study, would include a detailed exposition of the relevant theoretical explanations, such as environmental and situational theories of crime, and a discussion of the causal links between street lighting and crime that are proposed within the literature. Both topics are discussed briefly by Farrington and Welsh in their introductory chapter, whereas a narrative review would give these themes far more weighting and serve as a more general appraisal of the topic area.

A systematic review can, however, be a huge undertaking, generating tens of thousands of sources that need to be filtered, depending on the scope of the topic. Joliffe (2008) describes using the approach in his doctoral research, which sought to establish whether there was empirical support for the relationship between empathy and offending. The field of study can of course be narrowed. Lösel (2008) gives the example of a broad definition (sex offender treatment) versus a narrow one (hormonal treatment of adult child molesters), the former of which will generate a large body of results and perhaps one that is *too* large. Yet, he argues, the latter approach may produce only a limited number of studies and present dilemmas of inclusion and exclusion of those identified, some of which may be limited in their methodological rigour. An alternative approach based on similar principles is a 'rapid evidence assessment', as employed by Joliffe and Farrington (2007) in relation to the impact of mentoring on re-offending, in which the methods used in a systematic review are applied within a restricted time frame.

Petrosino et al. (2003) and Farrington and Welsh (2005) offer guidance on employing a systematic review methodology in criminological research. Examples of systematic reviews can be found on the websites of the Campbell Collaboration, and the Swedish National Council for Crime Prevention (*Brottsförebyggande rådet – Brå*), on such topics as risk factors in terrorism radicalization, sex offender treatment, bullying prevention in schools and neighbourhood watch.

A 'meta-analysis' (a term coined by Glass in 1976) is an optional component of a systematic review, and comprises a statistical synthesis of the findings. This is achieved by identifying a common measure of effect size, such as a standardized mean difference (a way of standardizing a range of outcomes measured on different scales) or correlation coefficient (showing the relationship between variables demonstrated by the combined results). Criminological examples are provided by Andrews et al. (1990) on the effectiveness of correctional treatment and Gore and Drugs Survey Investigators' Consortium (1999) on young people's illicit drug use.

Finally, a related movement is the emergence of the 'qualitative meta-synthesis' (including its sub-genre, 'meta-ethnography'), advocating synoptic interrogations of literature according to systematic methods to ensure comprehensiveness and eliminate researcher bias. Like the systematic review, its origins are in health services research, with the objective of enhancing evidence-based decision making.

Can the two approaches influence each other?

There is no doubt that the systematic review has a wider influence. Within the UK Home Office, for example, an increasing proportion of the literature reviews published online are systematic reviews. Those that are not badged as such nonetheless now incorporate distinct methodology sections, outlining the search methods used, the bodies of literature consulted and the approaches to synthesis that have been employed. While the formulaic approach of systematic reviews can militate against the richness of language and creativity of style often found in narrative reviews, this does not have to be so. There is scope to bring some of these linguistic techniques into the systematic review. The debate within the social sciences over which method is 'best' has seen a proliferation of papers, coming particularly from the natural sciences, encouraging researchers to implement more systematic approaches to reviewing the literature. The most biting critiques of this approach point to the broader limitations of the policy context into which research findings are received, such as the fact that no policy 'happens from scratch' since other provisions will always be present and that 'synthetic recommendations cannot match the complexity of the policy systems that will host them' (Pawson, 2006: 12–13). They also point out the danger of political preference for 'evidence-based' research which legitimates a targeting of government research questions on narrowly focused and short-termist studies that support partisan objectives (Hope and Walters, 2008; Morgan and Hough, 2008). Further, Pawson has criticized the meta-analytic orientation of the Campbell Collaboration systematic reviews, questioning the assumption that past studies are directly relevant to future interventions and arguing that 'a more adaptive mode of knowledge management is required to cope with the vicissitudes of complex systems' (Pawson, 2006: 171). He provides an alternative model of 'realist review', incorporating analyses of the contexts in which interventions take place, including the staffing and implementation arrangements, institutional culture and political climate.

A summary of the strengths and weaknesses of both approaches is presented in Box 3.5.

BOX 3.5   NARRATIVE VERSUS SYSTEMATIC REVIEWS

Narrative reviews	Systematic reviews
Strengths	**Strengths**
1 Suit broad fields of study	1 Identify the cumulative knowledge on a given hypothesis
2 Provide holistic interpretations	2 Support evidence-based policy making
3 Cover topics comprehensively	3 Employ systematic and transparent literature search criteria
4 Bring together diverse perspectives	4 Seek to include only high-quality research
5 Can accommodate a richness of language and creativity of style	5 Provide a rigorous and replicable approach to reviewing the literature
6 Are flexible to different epistemological frameworks	6 Seek to eliminate reviewer bias
	7 Address uncertainties as to whether all the evidence has been identified and evaluated
Weaknesses	**Weaknesses**
1 Do not always clearly specify the review methodology	1 The prescriptive approach precludes comprehensive coverage of the literature
2 May not explicitly differentiate low- and high-quality research	2 Can generate an excess of sources, requiring extensive filtering
3 May have little practical application	3 Can be formulaic and dry in style
	4 Interventions' relevance and effectiveness may be undermined by the complexities of the policy process
	5 Are not impervious to political agendas despite claimed methodological rigour

HOW DO I GO ABOUT DOING A LITERATURE REVIEW?

The process of reviewing the literature begins as soon as you have a provisional research topic, and before you finally decide on the precise scope of your research. At this stage, you need to establish how much has already been written on your topic, what has been said – and not said – and the sorts of questions others have asked. Such an approach will help you determine the feasibility of your own ideas, identify knowledge gaps and decide the scope and parameters of your research, research question and sub-questions and research methods.

There are several social science research texts that devote a chapter to doing effective literature reviews (see, for example, Gray, 2017; Punch, 2014; Thomas, 2017) and others that discuss how to prepare your review (Pan, 2016), how to ensure your review is comprehensive (Onwuegbuzie and Frels, 2016) and traditional and systematic techniques for doing your literature review (Jesson, 2011). As a preliminary measure, it is best to skim the surface of the literature rather than undertake a full-scale literature search. Online facilities – library catalogues, databases and the internet – offer the best starting point.

Searching the literature

A literature strategy can be broken down into a series of steps, as follows.

Deciding what you are looking for

List your subject keywords, thinking about your topic and the key concepts associated with it.

What alternative terms are used to describe it?

Are there alternative spellings, such as British and American variants of a term? A search on the word paedophile (English UK spelling) will exclude resources that employ the English US spelling – pedophile – of the same term and vice versa.

Are common acronyms used?

Can a word be truncated to incorporate different words with the same stem (e.g. *rehabilit** to find *rehabilitate, rehabilitation* or *rehabilitative*)?

Are there any specific themes, cases or examples you are interested in?

Are there any terms that you should exclude?

Group these keywords using Boolean operators:

1. OR to group alternative terms (e.g. *police OR policing*)
2. AND to link words together (e.g. *crime AND prevention*)

3. Brackets to clarify a combination of terms (e.g. *(police OR policing) AND (crime AND prevention))*
4. NOT to exclude terms (e.g. police AND violence NOT domestic).

Boolean operators should be expressed in capital letters because this is required by some search tools.

Deciding where to look

A number of different electronic sources are available to help you search the literature:

- Many university libraries have *subject-specific guides* which provide a helpful starting point for literature searches in a given discipline. You may also have access to a subject librarian at your university who can help you.
- You can use *library catalogues* to find books and journals held within those libraries, but not their content. Use keywords to identify books and journals relevant to your topic.
- *Bibliographic databases* allow you to search the academic literature in more detail, some covering a wide range of disciplines and others being more focused. You can search these not only by subject but also by author, publication date and other features. Often, the search results will include short summaries or abstracts of the articles identified to help you assess their relevance, and some services are 'full text', providing you with the full document. Databases relevant to criminology include ASSIA, Criminal Justice Abstracts and SocINDEX.
- *Google Scholar* functions in a similar way to bibliographic databases, its main advantage being its accessibility to all internet users. It is important to note that some resources discovered via Google Scholar are behind paywalls. If using Google Scholar on campus, you should find direct links in the results to resources held in your university library.
- You can also supplement the information provided in this chapter with *study skills guides on literature reviews*. These may introduce you to new tools, as information resources are constantly evolving. At Northumbria University, for example, information on conducting a literature review is provided via their Skills Plus platform. Here, there are printable help guides and an online tutorial, which can be found at http://nuweb2.northumbria.ac.uk/library/skillsplus/.

Limiting or expanding your search

Make sure you are focused when choosing your sources, considering each in terms of its relevance to your research question and sub-questions. If your search produces too many sources, perhaps including many which seem irrelevant, you will need to narrow your search by including more search terms. If the amount of literature still seems infinite, it may be sensible to limit yourself to research published within a certain time frame or jurisdiction, or to identify other parameters for narrowing your scope.

On the other hand, for some emerging topics there may appear to be little literature or even none at all. If your search identifies too few sources, you will need to broaden your search by using more general words. For example, if your study is about corrosive substance attacks/acid throwing as a form of gang violence, the body of academic literature remains limited at the time of writing. You may find it helpful to draw on the broader literature on this type of attack, much of which is associated with gender violence in South Asia, as well as the general literature on gang violence. In turn, it may then be necessary to limit the literature search to work published in your own country in the past ten years.

Reading and note-taking

An initial appraisal of the literature will help clarify the key issues, controversies and debates and provide a basis for future readings. What are the main theoretical perspectives, major research studies and their methods and results? If there is an up-to-date student textbook or chapter among your sources that is directly relevant to your topic, start here for a comprehensive overview of the field, key texts and further readings.

In this initial phase, researchers can waste a lot of time reading in too much detail. Rather than reading a whole book, why not look for book reviews which summarize and evaluate the content for you? You should be able to get the measure of a book with thoughtful use of the contents and index pages and from the summaries provided in the introductory and concluding chapters, or of an article by reviewing the abstract (summary). Different reading techniques include *skimming*, where you look quickly through the text focusing only on these elements; *scanning*, which is searching rapidly for specific information, such as a keyword, and ignoring everything else; and *reading to understand*, which involves more detailed study of a key source (Freeman and Meed, 1999).

Once this initial appraisal is complete, you need to make a decision about which aspect of the topic to focus on. Hopefully certain themes within the literature will have intrigued you, and you will find it helpful at this stage to discuss your findings with your supervisor and agree a feasible research question and specific research sub-questions. Following this, a more extensive and thorough literature review is needed for the purpose of obtaining a detailed knowledge of the specialist area being studied, in order to devise an appropriate research design. As outlined earlier in the chapter, the approach to this will differ depending on whether you are carrying out a narrative review, a systematic review or a rapid evidence assessment.

As you conduct your detailed literature review, be sure to record the full bibliographic details of any texts you think will be relevant, using a consistent format. It is usual in the social sciences to employ the Harvard or APA systems of referencing, and to adopt a consistent approach to the recording of bibliographic information. Specialist bibliographic software such as EndNote is a useful aid in this process. Look for online study skills guides to help you with your referencing. The University of Portsmouth's *Referencing@Portsmouth* website (http://referencing.port.ac.uk), for example, provides a referencing tool as well as guidance pages to support student research.

It is also critical that you make sure any phrases copied directly into your notes are placed in quotation marks and page referenced, to avoid the risks of inadvertent plagiarism.

Annotated bibliographies

A useful way both of organizing your material and of making notes is to put together an annotated bibliography. Numerous online examples are available, many of which can be accessed via the bibliographies section of the World Criminal Justice Library Network website, although the quality and recency of the bibliographies are variable.

Box 3.6 provides an example of an annotation, which should include at the very least the full bibliographic citation; a brief summary of the content, including theoretical frameworks and methodological approaches; and a short evaluation or analysis. Other elements may include the background of the author, the target audience, the reliability of the text, and any special features (such as tables, diagrams or graphs) that are particularly useful. For each source, it is also a good idea to note how the material will address your research question and sub-questions.

Writing the literature review

Writing a literature review is an iterative process – you will find yourself going back to the literature many times. It is important, however, to begin with a plan setting out the progression of your literature review and indicating the depth of content required for each section in accordance with the overall word limit you have assigned to it. The following guidance is focused on how to write a narrative review, as opposed to the more specialized techniques and purpose of a systematic review.

The literature review should be written in such a way that no expert knowledge is assumed on the part of the reader. As with any essay or research paper, it needs to start with a clear introduction, outlining the structure of the review. The introduction may also give a general outline of the key features of the literature.

BOX 3.6   WHAT DOES AN ANNOTATION LOOK LIKE?

Annotation	Key
(1) Hayward, K. (2004) City Limits: Crime, Consumer Culture and the Urban Experience. London: Routledge-Cavendish.	1. Citation
(2) This book explores the 'crime–city nexus' within a cultural criminology framework. (3) Its aim is identifying the myriad forms of relationships that exist between the contemporary "urban experience", certain forms of criminal behaviour, and the particular social forces and cultural dynamics that one associates with *'late modern consumer culture'* (p. 1, emphasis in original), drawing on a multidisciplinary range of theoretical and cultural sources, including art and literature. (4) The article is useful to my research because of its application of theory to contemporary youth crime in the city. (5) Hayward builds on strain theory and the relative deprivation thesis to create a picture of the distinctive needs and desires of late modern youth, focusing on the insatiability of contemporary consumption, the risk-taking behaviours characteristic of today's urban lifestyles (from binge-drinking to adventure holidaying), and the construction of crime in popular culture as cool and exciting. (6) Criminologists will debate whether Hayward's thesis really offers important new insights or simply a synthesis of old perspectives on crime, but it is useful in its application of established sociological perspectives to the analysis of late-modern social change and urban crime. (7) The cultural criminological framework used by Hayward will help inform the theoretical framework I plan to develop in my study.	2. Introduction 3. Aims and research methods 4. Usefulness to your research 5. Summary 6. Evaluation 7. Reflection (how the work illuminates your topic or will add to your research)

Source: Based on guidance provided by the University of New South Wales (2018); extracts from Wakefield (2005: 671–3)

Your literature review should follow a coherent structure, engaging analytically with the assembled sources to group related items together and draw out key issues and trends. You may find it useful to consult others' work for examples as to how this can be done. Some make the mistake of doing little more than an annotated bibliography, which focuses on one source at a time. The most common ways of organizing the literature are as follows:

- *thematically*, grouped according to the main trends and categories in the field of scholarship, as shown in Newburn's (1999) corruption study (see Box 3.4)
- *chronologically* or historically, divided into historical or developmental phases, if the topic has a historical background or there have been discernable shifts in thinking over time
- *methodologically*, organized according to the research methods used across the field of literature, if the field is characterized by several main methodological approaches.

It may sometimes be appropriate to use more than one of these strategies, for example dividing the literature by themes and then chronologically within each section. Such groupings will help you move from reading and note-taking to producing a structured analysis of the literature, making it easier to compare and contrast different theoretical approaches, findings and methodologies, and to analyse the strengths and weaknesses as well as the gaps in previous research.

In the process of writing, your literature review ought to engage critically with the literature, rather than simply summarizing what others have said. The research question and sub-questions should frame the review and, in a thematic structure, the sections into which the literature review is divided are likely to be based on the research sub-questions. Your task is to show how the literature addresses your research question and sub-questions, supporting or extending existing knowledge. It is also important to ensure that your 'voice' or position is clearly identifiable and to use language that clarifies your position or that of others on a particular issue. Some examples relating to the subject of policing are provided in Box 3.7, drawn from Wakefield (2003).

The literature review should end with a conclusion, summarizing the main points, identifying the limitations and gaps in the literature, and making recommendations for future research (your empirical research). It should be noted that the review will only be finalized when your whole project is close to completion, because new research is constantly being published and any relevant studies will need to be added to the literature review throughout the research process.

BOX 3.7 SAMPLE TEXT FROM A LITERATURE REVIEW

The sociology of policing has persistently entertained the debate as to what constitutes 'policing'. Johnston argued that one of the major limitations of this area of criminology has been its tendency 'to conflate policing (a social function) with police (a specific body of personnel)' (1999: 176–7), leading to a preoccupation with the role and functions of the state police forces as opposed to the wide range of bodies engaged in policing activities …

} **relational marker** indicating the writer's relationship to the audience or scholarly community in which they are writing

Definitions of 'policing' have abounded in recent years, highlighting the difficulty in encapsulating in a few words the diversity of objectives it might encompass and the range of agencies engaged in their pursuit.

} **attitude marker** indicating the writer's assessment of an issue. An alternative would be to include 'Johnston **perceptively** argued'

… The first interpretation of policing as a 'regulatory process', formalized in the nineteenth century in Britain through the establishment of a public police force, encompasses the activities of multiple agencies, in common with the more recent conceptions of policing as 'governance' (Shearing, 1992), 'networked nodal governance' (Kempa et al., 1999) and the 'governance of security' (Johnston and Shearing, 2002). It may be argued … that as policing is becoming increasingly 'segmented', it is taking a form that appears less and less as an explicit and unified 'process' of regulation, in a reversal of nineteenth-century developments.
For the same reason, the usefulness of the interpretation of 'policing' as 'the work of the police' must also be called into question.

} **hedging expression** making a statement about the degree of certainty of a question, as contrasted with an **emphatic expression** relating to the strength of the claim or the writer's level of confidence in it

Source: Based on guidance provided by the University of New South Wales (2009); extracts from Wakefield (2003: 3, 4, 15)

SUMMARY AND REVIEW

A literature review is an evaluative overview of the state of knowledge on a research topic. In broad terms, its purpose is to show you have read widely around the chosen topic, gained a good command of the issues, acknowledged the work of others and set your study in the context of the existing body of literature, highlighting gaps in research. It provides a critical, evaluative synthesis of the research literature on the topic at hand set out according to a number of organizing themes. Examples of literature reviews include narrative reviews, in which the researcher seeks to identify trends and categories in a broad field of scholarship, and systematic reviews, used for the purpose of evaluating the effectiveness of an intervention in order to support evidence-based policy making.

The literature review process begins with the devising of an appropriate search strategy. Once gathered, a useful way both of organizing your research material and of making notes is to put together an annotated bibliography. In the process of writing, your literature review needs to engage critically with the literature, speaking directly to your research question and sub-questions. Your task is to show how the literature addresses these questions, supporting or extending existing knowledge.

STUDY QUESTIONS AND ACTIVITIES FOR STUDENTS

1. When might it be most appropriate to conduct a systematic review or rapid evidence assessment, as opposed to a narrative review?

2. What is the purpose of a theoretical framework for your research?

3. Contact a subject-specialist librarian for assistance in researching your topic, and register for any courses that are available.

4. Search the website of your university library for subject-specific resources, and practise using the search tools (e.g. the library catalogue, online databases and the search tools on the website of key subject journals) and exploring the types of resources available.

5. Compose a 'search string' using your subject keywords and Boolean operators. Type it into Google and Google Scholar, and note the number and quality of results returned. Widen or narrow your search as appropriate.

6. Analyse your approach to reading – are you managing your time effectively, employing techniques of skimming and scanning as much as possible? Are you

(Continued)

(Continued)

being selective in your note-taking, noting only the information that is relevant to your needs?

7. Devise a plan for your literature review, assigning a word limit to each of the main sections. Add to the sections of the plan as you develop your ideas until you and your supervisor are happy with the structure.

SUGGESTIONS FOR FURTHER READING

The definitive textbook on literature reviews is Hart's *Doing a Literature Review: Releasing the Social Science Research Imagination* (1998). Chapter 5 of *Criminological Research for Beginners: A Student's Guide* (2014) by Caulfield and Hill is focused on critiquing the literature and the process of writing the literature review, whilst Galvan and Galvan (2017) provide an easy to follow, sequential step-by-step guide on *Writing Literature Reviews* in the social and behavioural sciences. Additionally, Denney and Tewksbury (2013) outline 'How to write a literature review' specifically for students of criminology. Criminological researchers could also consult the annual journal *Crime and Justice: A Review of Research* for examples of authoritative literature reviews on a range of criminological topics.

Many examples of literature reviews carried out by and for government agencies can be found online, on such sites as:

- the research pages of the UK Home Office and Ministry of Justice hosted on the GOV. UK website (www.gov.uk/government/organisations/home-office/about/research and www.gov.uk/government/organisations/ministry-of-justice/about/research)
- the Australian Institute of Criminology (www.aic.gov.au)
- the Swedish National Council for Crime Prevention (www.bra.se/english)
- the US National Institute of Justice (https://www.nij.gov/)
- the World Criminal Justice Library Network, an excellent starting point for identifying annotated bibliographies and other subject reading lists, albeit of varying age and quality: http://andromeda.rutgers.edu/~wcjlen/WCJ.

Detailed information on systematic reviews can be found on the websites of the Campbell Collaboration (www.campbellcollaboration.org) and the Cochrane Collaboration (www.cochrane.org), and guidance on rapid evidence assessments is provided by the UK government's Social Research Unit. Some guidance is now archived at http://webarchive.nationalarchives.gov.uk/20140402164155/http://www.civilservice.gov.uk/networks/gsr/

resources-and-guidance/rapid-evidence-assessment A more easily accessed source is www.nfer.ac.uk Pawson provides details of his realist synthesis model at www.leeds.ac.uk/realist synthesis

Finally, there is a host of online guidance on literature reviews and annotated bibliographies provided on university websites. The University of New South Wales, Sydney, provides excellent resources at https://student.unsw.edu.au/annotated-bibliography

REFERENCES

Andrews, D.A., Zinger, I., Hoge, R.D., Bonta, J., Gendreau, P. and Cullen, F.T. (1990) 'Does correctional treatment work? A clinically relevant and psychologically informed meta-analysis', *Criminology, 28*(3): 369–404.

Boland, A., Cherry, G. and Dickson, R. (2017) *Doing a Systematic Review: A Student's Guide*. London: Sage.

Booth, A., Papaioannou, D. and Sutton, A. (2012) *Systematic Approaches to a Successful Literature Review*. London: Sage.

Caulfield, L. and Hill, J. (2014) *Criminological Research for Beginners: A Student's Guide*. Hoboken, NJ: Taylor & Francis.

Denney, A.S. and Tewksbury, R. (2013) 'How to write a literature review', *Journal of Criminal Justice Education, 24*(2): 218–34.

Einstadter, W.J. and Henry, S. (2006) *Criminological Theory: An Analysis of Its Underlying Assumptions*, 2nd edition. New York: Rowman and Littlefield.

Farrington, D.P. and Welsh, B.C. (2002) *Effects of Improved Street Lighting on Crime: A Systematic Review*, Home Office Research Study 251. London: Home Office. Available at: http://webarchive.nationalarchives.gov.uk/20130128103514/http://rds.homeoffice.gov.uk/rds/pdfs2/hors251.pdf (accessed 13/06/17).

Farrington, D.P. and Welsh, B.C. (2005) *What Works in Preventing Crime: Systematic Reviews of Experimental and Quasi-Experimental Research*. London: Sage.

Fawcett, J. (1999) *The Relationship Between Theory and Research*. Philadelphia: F.A. Davis Company.

Freeman, R. and Meed, J. (1999) *How to Study Effectively*. London: Collins Educational.

Galvan, J.L. and Galvan, M.C. (2017) *Writing Literature Reviews: A Guide for Students of the Social and Behavioural Sciences*, 7th edition. New York: Routledge.

Glaser, B.G. and Strauss, A.L. (1967) *The Discovery of Grounded Theory: Strategies for Qualitative Research*. Chicago: Aldine.

Glass, G. (1976) 'Primary, secondary, and meta-analysis of research', *Educational Researcher, 5*(10): 3–8.

Gore, S. and Drugs Survey Investigators' Consortium (1999) 'Effective monitoring of young people's use of illegal drugs', *British Journal of Criminology*, *39*(4): 575–603.

Gough, D., Oliver, S. and Thomas, J. (eds) (2017) *An Introduction to Systematic Reviews*, 2nd edition. London: Sage.

Gray, D.E. (2017) *Doing Research in the Real World*, 4th edition. London: Sage.

Grewcock, M. (2010) *Border Crimes: Australia's War on Illicit Migrants*. Sydney: Federation Press.

Harding, J. (2013) *Qualitative Data Analysis: From Start to Finish*. London: Sage.

Hart, C. (1998) *Doing a Literature Review: Releasing the Social Science Research Imagination*. London: Sage.

Hayward, K. (2004) *City Limits: Crime, Consumer Culture and the Urban Experience*. London: Routledge-Cavendish.

Hope, T. and Walters, R. (2008) *Critical Thinking about the Uses of Research*. London: Centre for Crime and Justice Studies. Available at: www.crimeandjustice.org.uk/sites/crimeandjustice.org.uk/files/Evidencebasedpolicyfinal.pdf (accessed 13 June 2017).

Jesson, J.K. (2011) *Doing Your Literature Review: Traditional and Systematic Techniques*. London: Sage.

Joliffe, D. (2008) 'Researching bullying in the classroom', in R. King and E. Wincup (eds), *Doing Research on Crime and Justice*, 2nd edition. Oxford: Oxford University Press.

Joliffe, D. and Farrington, D.P. (2007) *A Rapid Evidence Assessment of Mentoring*. London: Home Office.

Lösel, F. (2008) 'Doing evaluation research in criminology', in R. King and E. Wincup (eds), *Doing Research on Crime and Justice*, 2nd edition. Oxford: Oxford University Press.

Machi, L.A. and McEvoy, B.T. (2016) *The Literature Review: Six Steps to Success*, 3rd edition. Thousand Oaks, CA: Corwin Press.

May, T. (2011) *Social Research: Issues, Methods and Process*, 4th edition. Maidenhead: Open University Press.

Morgan, R. and Hough, M. (2008) 'The politics of criminological research', in R. King and E. Wincup (eds), *Doing Research on Crime and Justice*, 2nd edition. Oxford: Oxford University Press.

Myhill, A. (2012) *Community Engagement in Policing: Lessons from the Literature*. London: Home Office. Available at: http://whatworks.college.police.uk/Research/Documents/Community_engagement_lessons.pdf (accessed 13 June 2017).

Newburn, T. (1999) *Understanding and Preventing Police Corruption: Lessons from the Literature*, Police Research Series Paper 110. London: Home Office. Available at: http://webarchive.nationalarchives.gov.uk/20110218140731/http://rds.homeoffice.gov.uk/rds/prgpdfs/fprs110.pdf (accessed 13 June 2017).

Northey, M. and Tepperman, L. (2015) *Making Sense: A Student's Guide to Research and Writing – Social Sciences*. Maidenhead: Open University Press.

Onwuegbuzie, A. and Frels, R. (2016) *Seven Steps to a Comprehensive Literature Review*. London: Sage.

Pan, M.L. (2016) *Preparing Literature Reviews: Qualitative and Quantitative Approaches*, 5th edition. Glendale, CA: Pyrczak Publishing.

Parker, H. (1974) *A View from the Boys: Sociology of Downtown Adolescents (People, Plans & Problems)*. Newton Abbott: David & Charles.

Pawson, R. (2006) *Evidence-Based Policy: A Realist Perspective*. London: Sage.

Petrosino, A., Boruch, R., Farrington, D., Sherman, L. and Weisburd, D. (2003) 'Towards evidence-based criminology and criminal justice: systematic reviews and the Campbell Collaboration Crime and Justice Group', *The International Journal of Comparative Criminology*, 3(1): 18–41.

Punch, K.F. (2014) *Introduction to Social Research: Quantitative and Qualitative Approaches*, 3rd edition. Los Angeles, CA: Sage.

Ridley, D. (2012) *The Literature Review: A Step-by-Step Guide for Students*, 2nd edition. London: Sage.

Schauer, E.J. and Wheaton, E.M. (2006) 'Sex trafficking into the United States: a literature review', *Criminal Justice Review*, 31(2): 146–69.

Sergi, A. (2017) *From Mafia to Organized Crime: A Comparative Analysis of Policing Models*. London: Palgrave Macmillan.

Thomas, G. (2017) *How To Do Your Research Project: A Guide for Students*, 3rd edition. London: Sage.

Turchik, J.A. and Wilson, S.M. (2010) 'Sexual assault in the US military: a review of the literature and recommendations for the future', *Aggression and Violent Behaviour*, 15: 267–77.

University of New South Wales (UNSW) (2018) *Getting Started on Your Literature Review*. Sydney: The Learning Centre, UNSW. Available at: https://student.unsw.edu.au/getting-started-your-literature-review (accessed 13 June 2018).

Waddington, P.A.J. (1999) 'Police (canteen) sub-culture: an appreciation', *British Journal of Criminology*, 39(2): 286–308.

Wakefield, A. (2003) *Selling Security: The Private Policing of Public Space*. Cullompton: Willan Publishing.

Wakefield, A. (2005) 'Review of *City Limits: Crime, Consumer Culture and the Urban Experience* by Keith Hayward', *British Journal of Sociology*, 56(4): 671–3.

CHAPTER CONTENTS

GLOSSARY TERMS

descriptive research   qualitative research
methodology   quantitative research
ontology   method
epistemology   survey questionnaires
quantitative   interviews
qualitative

4 METHODOLOGICAL APPROACHES TO CRIMINOLOGICAL RESEARCH

HANNAH BOWS

INTRODUCTION

This chapter focuses on different methodological approaches in criminological research. Even before a research topic and question have been finalized, it is necessary to consider the research methodology, which provides the framework for the study and determines how the research will be conducted. The terms 'methodology' and 'method' will be used throughout this chapter, and it is important at the outset to explain what the terms mean. Despite often being used interchangeably, they actually refer to different things. Methodology concerns the process of examining methods and comparing the kinds of knowledge they produce (Greener, 2011). This process is underpinned by epistemological concerns, which are based on how the researcher views knowledge and the best way to gain knowledge about a particular social phenomenon. The end product is a particular method (or methods) which is/are adopted to conduct the research. The methodology can therefore be thought of as the *system* and methods as the *tools*. Figure 4.1 outlines how these core elements overlap and combine to create the methodology. This chapter begins by providing an overview of developing a research methodology before moving on to consider approaches to deciding on appropriate method(s). We then consider some of the most common methods in social research, broadly categorized as primary and secondary methods, and close with a discussion of the key ethical considerations in criminological research.

Ontology	**Epistemology**
Theory of 'reality' – whether reality exists independently of society or is constructed by people	Theory of knowledge and is concerned with the question of what counts as valid knowledge; broadly, epistemology is constructive or positivistic

Method
The tools used to collect data on a particular phenomenon, broadly categorised as quantitative or qualitative

FIGURE 4.1   Core elements of methodology

DEVELOPING A RESEARCH METHODOLOGY

There are three broad research strategies: descriptive research, explanatory research and exploratory research:

- Descriptive research describes people, situations or phenomena. Usually, there will be guiding questions underpinning the research but not a strict hypothesis.

This research is useful to provide contextual data which can then be developed into a hypothesis.

- Explanatory research intends to explain why a phenomenon occurs and is usually developed to test a particular hypothesis. It is concerned with producing conclusive answers.
- Exploratory research is often used when little is known about a phenomenon. This type of research seeks to create hypotheses rater than test one. It is not intended to produce final and conclusive answers, but instead focuses on developing some initial knowledge about an issue or phenomenon.

BOX 4.1   DECIDING ON A RESEARCH STRATEGY

When deciding which research stategy to adopt, it is important to consider what the focus of the research is (Robson, 2002). What is it you want to find out about? Once you have a topic, you will need to examine what is currently known about that topic – this usually involves conducting literature reviews. This review should help you identify existing knowledge and gaps, methodological issues in existing studies, and so on. From there, you have a grounding to develop your research questions, which will be rooted in your research approach. For example, if there is little or nothing known about your topic, you may wish to conduct exploratory research to examine experience. Taking burglary as an example, an exploratory research approach may seek to understand the experiences of victims of burglary. A descriptive research approach may be interested in examining the prevalence and nature of burglary offences during a particular year or in a particular geographical area. An explanatory research project may seek to examine burglary patterns and socio-economic variables across time and place (a longitudinal study) to explain who is most likely to be burgled.

The research strategy you choose is the foundation for your methodology – it will guide how you design and conduct your research, which is shaped by the type of knowledge you want to gain. The methodology provides the framework for your research and is the approach to studying the research topic and turns the research questions into projects (Robson, 2002). There are two broad approaches to research: qualitative and quantitative, although increasingly a third category of mixed methods is also used. Whilst some scholars have suggested other ways of categorizing research methodologies (e.g. Robson, 2002 who suggests using variance or process thinking as a starting point), these remain the two most commonly described and used. Each approach is steered by several sets of assumptions and these assumptions guide which approach is deemed the most appropriate for the research.

The assumptions are based on your ontological and epistemological positions. A good way of thinking about the differences in these positions is to use the 'tree in the forest' analogy. This philosophical question asks, if a tree falls in the forest but no one hears it, does it make a sound? The quantitative ontology would say it did – the tree fell and made a sound regardless of whether anyone knew about it or heard it. Qualitative ontology, however, would say that a sound can only be a sound if some-one hears it – the two cannot be separated, one is linked to the other. The way in which you view the world and reality (ontology) therefore shapes the type of knowl-edge (epistemology) you seek to gain and the way (qualitative or quantitative) you gain that knowledge.

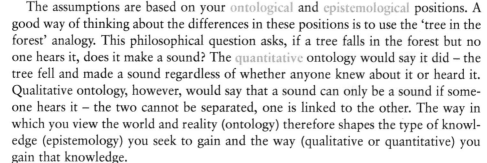

Qualitative methodology is concerned with exploring the behaviour, opinions or perspectives, feelings and experiences of people as individuals or groups. It lies in the *interpretive* approach to social reality: reality exists not independently of people, but rather is socially constructed, and meaning is developed through experience. Consequently, qualitative methodology is rooted in a *constructivist* epistemology. Who heard the tree fall, what sound did they hear? The methods most appropriate for this approach are inductive, meaning data is analysed to see if any patterns emerge and the findings are rooted in the data itself. Therefore, qualitative method-ology does not seek to test out preconceived ideas or theories (hypotheses). For example, research questions in qualitative research examining domestic violence might be:

- What are the emotional impacts of domestic violence on victims?
- What are victims' experiences of accessing support services?
- What does 'justice' look like for domestic violence victims?

In contrast, quantitative methodology is concerned with measuring or testing exist-ing ideas or theories (hypotheses) and generally assumes that reality exists independently of human construction and experience. This epistemology is *positiv-istic* and is concerned with scientific fact, which can be observed by rigorous, independent testing. Central to this methodological approach is validity and reliabil-ity and scientific methods are viewed as the 'best' methods to gain valid, reliable knowledge. Put another way, it is concerned with the accuracy of measurement. Reliability focuses on consistency of measurement and replication. In criminology, quantitative researchers are concerned with explaining crime and predicting future crime, what causes crime and how this can be prevented. For example, quantitative research examining burglary might ask:

- What characteristics of neighbourhoods are associated with high burglary crime levels?
- What socio-economic factors are associated with high levels of burglary?
- What effect do anti-burglary measures such as CCTV or alarms have on levels of burglary?

Traditionally, these two methodological approaches have been positioned as distinct and incompatible; however, increasingly researchers are realizing the benefits of combining quantitative and qualitative approaches. In particular, there is an increasing appreciation of the ability of mixed methods to 'triangulate' research and achieve internal validity. There are two types of methodological triangulation: 'across method' which combines both quantitative and qualitative data collection, and 'within method' which involves the use of different approaches within either qualitative or quantitative methods. In 1970 Denzin referred to 'triangulation' in research and outlined four broad types of triangulation:

1. Data triangulation involving time, space and people
2. Investigator triangulation involving multiple observers of the same object
3. Theoretical triangulation involving multiple perspectives on the same set of objects
4. Methodological triangulation, either within method (i.e. more than one quantitative method) or mixed method (i.e. combining quantitative and qualitative methods).

These are revisited later in the chapter to consider how different methods can produce different knowledge and be used in combination to examine specific phenomena.

DECIDING METHODS OF DATA COLLECTION

Once the vision of your research and the overall methodological framework have been established, the next stage is to decide which method(s) will be most appropriate for your research. It is useful to consider whether you need to collect 'primary' or 'secondary' data as this will influence the methods you use. Primary data collection involves collecting data which does not currently exist. Secondary data collection is the collection of materials, evidence or data which already exists but may not have been collected or analysed previously, or you intend to analyse it in a different way. Broadly, then, research methods can also be grouped into these categories. Both categories can be used to conduct empirical research (collection of new data), although primary research methods are more commonly associated with empirical data as this involves the collection of 'new' data.

Primary research methods

There are many different methods that are useful for collecting primary data, and the type of method used will depend on the nature of the research, the research question and the methodological framework. As noted, methods can be broadly categorized as either quantitative or qualitative, but in practice this distinction is not always reflective of the method. For example, surveys and questionnaires have been traditionally considered quantitative methods and usually involve closed questions; however, surveys or questionnaires that involve primarily open questions can elicit qualitative data. Other primary research methods include experiments, interviews and focus groups and creative or visual methods using props, art or photography which are associated with a qualitative methodology. Some of these methods are considered in the following sections of this chapter and many are given more consideration throughout the book.

Surveys and questionnaires

 Surveys are a popular method in criminological research and are often used by government officials, an obvious example being the Crime Survey for England and Wales (formerly the British Crime Survey) which is the primary national victimization survey. In a review of methods used across criminology and criminal justice, Kleck et al. (2006) found surveys were the most popular method. This was the method most often used to obtain information on crime, criminals and society's reaction to crime. Kleck and colleagues (2006) found that some type of formal survey was used to collect information in 45% of all the research reported.

A survey generally collects data on different variables, which can broadly be categorized into three groups (Aldridge and Levine, 2001: 5):

- Attributes – this includes demographic information and characteristics such as gender, age, sex, marital status, level of education.
- Behaviour – this generally includes questions on the what, when and how often.
- Opinions, beliefs or attitudes – these seek to examine the respondent's point of view.

Questions on surveys can be open or closed; however, they are commonly associated with closed questions. Open questions are usually broad how, what and why questions, for example:

- How does anti-social behaviour affect your community?
- What are the impacts of the new legislative changes to 'legal' highs?
- Why did you choose to take part in restorative justice?

Closed questions, in contrast, are usually yes/no questions or Likert scale questions (for example, strongly agree, agree, neutral, disagree, strongly disagree). Some questions might be:

- Do you worry about anti-social behaviour in your community? (yes/no)
- Has the change in legislation around 'legal' highs affected you? (yes//no)

- Cannabis should be made legal. (Likert scale)
- Prison sentences for violent offences should be longer. (Likert scale)
- Have you ever considered a restorative justice approach? (yes/no)

There are several benefits to using surveys. They allow researchers to gather a lot of information from a large sample of people in a single instrument, and they can be cost-effective and relatively quick. Surveys can be useful if the researcher is seeking to gather data which is generalizable. For example, a researcher seeking to examine how many people have experienced a particular crime (say burglary) and examine the social demographic characteristics of people who have been burgled to get an idea of who is most at risk, may choose the survey method to send to a representative sample of people living in England.

Box 4.2 contains a case study example of surveys in a recent study examining sexual violence against people aged 60 and over in the UK.

BOX 4.2 EXAMINING THE EXTENT OF SEXUAL VIOLENCE AGAINST OLDER PEOPLE – FREEDOM OF INFORMATION REQUESTS (BOWS AND WESTMARLAND, 2017)

Part of my PhD research involved using Freedom of Information legislation to make requests to all of the police forces in the UK to gather information and data on recorded sexual offences involving a victim aged 60 or over at the time of the offence. This involved designing two questionnaires which were used to collect the data held by the police forces:

1. The first questionnaire asked for: (a) the number of recorded sexual offences involving all victims recorded between 1 January 2009 and 31 December 2013; (b) the proportion of those cases involving a victim aged 60 or over.
2. The second questionnaire asked for demographic information (*variables*) on *each individual* case involving an older victim. This included the gender of the victim and perpetrator, the ethnicity of the victim and perpetrator, the age of the victim and perpetrator, the location of the sexual offence and the relationship between the victim and perpetrator.

In the study, using this questionnaire allowed for consistency across the forces and provided clear questions for the police force to address when collecting the data. The questionnaires were sent via email. Thus this method allowed for quick, easy and cheap access to the relevant data. This data was then inputted into SPSS and the *variables* were analysed.

The survey method has been criticized by a number of academics. Bryman notes that surveys have been criticized for their tendency to 'view events from the outside', and for imposing empirical concerns 'upon social reality with little reference to the meaning of the observations to the subject of investigation' (1984: 78). Bowling accuses crime survey methodology of 'attempting to convert a social process into a series of quantifiable moments which do not adequately reflect the experiences or feelings of those interviewed' (1993: 241). Furthermore, Farrall et al. (1997) argue that respondents may simply report generalized responses, which may not adequately represent their actual emotions on any one occasion. Surveys rely on the researcher knowing a significant amount about the social phenomenon he/she will be researching, in order to provide questions and responses that accurately measure the respondents' range of answers (Greener, 2011). As Mishler (1986) argues, 'the standard approach to interviewing [the survey interview] is demonstrably inappropriate for and inadequate to the study of the central questions in the social and behavioural sciences' (cited in Hollway and Jefferson, 2008: 297). The main reason for this is because the approach fails to address how respondents' meanings are related to circumstances. Reliance on coding-isolated responses strips them of any remaining context (Hollway and Jefferson, 2008).

Interviews

Usually associated with qualitative methodology, semi-structured or unstructured interviews are used to gain in-depth, 'rich' data about a particular social phenomenon (Pierre and Roulston, 2006). Pierre and Roulston note that qualitative research methods 'encourage richer, thicker description that might yield a true representation of authentic, real, lived experience' (2006: 677). Face-to-face semi-structured interviewing is commonly used in social research, particularly feminist research, in order to find out about people's experiences in context and the meanings these hold. Such interviews are usually conducted using a number of open-ended questions that allow interviewees to dictate how the interview progresses. Often, the interviewer will use probes to encourage further information from the interviewee (see Box 4.3). The purpose of the interview is to gain in-depth data, placing the interviewee at the heart of the research and inductively gleaning information in a natural setting. As Bryman (1984) notes, this type of methodology is committed to 'seeing the social world from the point of view of the actor, expressing preference for a contextual understanding so that behaviour is to be understood in the context of meaning systems employed by a particular group or society' (p. 77). This epistemology therefore lends itself to methods which facilitate an 'inside view' (p. 78). The purpose of interviews is to provide descriptions which can inform theory, based on the data collected, rather than testing predetermined hypotheses or theories. Rather than seeking to gain 'truth' about a reality that exists outside of human perception, this qualitative method seeks to investigate the participants' own reality. These concepts reflect an idealist, social constructionist ontological and epistemological position.

However, this does not mean that the interview method is without its limitations. One of the main problems is the difficulty in generalizing (Greener, 2011; Hammersley, 1991). Indeed, many researchers would agree with this view, particularly positivists who favour empirical quantitative data and analysis (Greener, 2011). However, it is arguable whether research of this nature necessarily needs to be generalizable. Taking the August riots in 2011 which began in Tottenham, London following the police killing of Mark Duggan and which spread across other parts of England as an example, the research suggests that the reasons why people participated in the riots were complex and multi-faceted, based on a number of political, economic and social conditions (Lewis, 2011). These specific conditions are arguably unlikely to present themselves in the same exact ways again, and, therefore, it is argued that what is important from a research perspective is to gain understanding of why people participated in these particular riots. Whilst themes and theories may be developed from interview-based research, it is not necessarily the priority of the research to do this. Its purpose is simply to develop understanding.

BOX 4.3 POLICE PERCEPTIONS OF 'RISK' IN RELATION TO OLDER SEX OFFENDERS

I recently conducted some research for Durham Constabulary to examine how public protection officers at six forces across England and Wales were responding to the growing number of 'older' sex offenders on their caseloads. In particular, the research was concerned with exploring the current practices around risk management where the older offender had care or support needs, for example dementia and/or needed residential care. In order to understand the issues and the practices of officers at these forces, semi-structured interviews were conducted over the telephone with officers working in public protection units. Interviews focused on:

1. The number of sex offenders aged 50+ and 60+ living in the community and currently being managed by the force.
2. Whether there had been an increase in the number of older offenders on the caseloads.
3. What issues, if any, age presented in terms of managing the offender in the community.
4. How 'risk' (to the public and the offender) was managed and whether age affected this.
5. Current practice around older sex offenders with care needs.

A semi-structured interview schedule allowed for these topics to be covered but allowed flexibility for participants to discuss other related issues as and when they

(Continued)

(Continued)

became relevant. It also allowed me to ask 'probing' questions to find out more or follow up on things the participants said. A questionnaire or survey would not allow for such probing, thus the data collected may have been less 'rich' or detailed. Examples of probing included asking 'why' or 'how' if the answer given was vague, in order to gain more detail. Alternatively, some probes involved asking about specific experiences. For example, for question 5, a follow-up question was 'Have you had to manage any older offender with care needs?' to stimulate further discussion.

Focus groups

There is no single definition of a focus group; however, the key characteristics are a collective, organized discussion and interaction between a group of people. They are distinguished from group interviews, where the researcher interviews more than one person at a time but the emphasis is on the researcher asking questions which the individual(s) respond to. In a focus group, participants interact with each other, asking each other questions or making statements which other participants respond to. In a study examining young women's responses to safety advice and associated safety behaviours in licensed venues, Brooks (2011) conducted focus groups with 35 women to examine their perceptions, understandings and responses to safety in bars, pubs and clubs.

One of the primary benefits of using focus groups is that participants help to stimulate and develop data through their discussions with each other. Focus groups are useful in analysing not only what the group say to each other, but also how they say it and how they interact. The attitudes and reactions may be independent of the focus group environment but are revealed in a particular way within the group gathering. Another strength of the focus group is that it allows the researcher to gather a large amount of data in a short period of time, compared to individual interviews or surveys. Furthermore, whilst observational methods require the researcher to wait for things to happen, the focus group is guided by interview schedules or questions which facilitate discussion around particular themes or topics.

The primary limitations of focus groups are that certain people in the group may be more vocal, or controlling, of the discussion than others. Some participants may not contribute much, or may feel they have to agree with comments made by other members. In some environments, people may not feel comfortable answering questions honestly and focus groups may not be appropriate for all research topics, for example those on sensitive issues such as domestic or sexual violence. However, some of the above issues can be mitigated by the researcher 'chairing' the discussion effectively. In particular, the role of the lead or Chair is to facilitate the discussion with open questions, keep the discussion going with prompts, to ensure the discussion does not veer off topic and to interrupt sessions if there appears to be any upset or distress in the group. Furthermore, by paying close attention to the dynamics of the group, the Chair can ensure each participant has the opportunity to contribute by inviting and encouraging individuals to share their thoughts or perceptions – this is particularly useful if a group session is being dominated by one or two individuals.

Ethnography

Ethnography is an umbrella term for a methodology which incorporates a number of different approaches, including observation, participant observation, autoethnography and interviews. Ethnography has a rich history, dating back to ancient times from when travellers and outsiders lived among strangers, or tribes, and recorded their way of life (Brewer, 2000). Consequently, ethnography is often associated with anthropology, where researchers would immerse themselves within the lives and cultures of particular people or groups in order to develop rich data on their everyday lives. However, in criminology, ethnography has its roots in the Chicago School, with scholars including Ernest Burgess, George Mead and Robert Park, emerging in the 1920s and 1930s.

One of the most common ethnographic methods is participant observation. Participant observation involves observation of individuals or groups of people in their natural setting to understand more about them, their lives and cultures. It is a form of 'fieldwork'. In the context of crime, that might mean observing a group of offenders, or victims, or indeed practitioners – for example, observing young people in youth offending institutions to examine what their everyday lives are like (see Box 4.4). Hammersley (1991) identifies this as a key issue, criticizing ethnography on the whole as producing data which merely provides descriptions of events and does not present generalizable data or theories.

BOX 4.4 YOUNG PEOPLE'S EVERYDAY LIVES IN YOUNG OFFENDERS INSTITUTIONS IN DENMARK (BENGTSSON, 2016)

Bengtsson (2016) conducted an ethnographic study to develop an understanding of what everyday life is like for young people who are in young offenders institutions in Denmark. As well as conducting interviews with young people, Bengtsson also carried out around 350 hours of fieldwork observation. During these observations, Bengtsson would watch the young people interacting with each other and staff and how they got involved in activities. Through these routine and everyday interactions, Bengtsson observed that the culture, and indeed relationships between the young people, were characterized by hypermasculinity. By using observation and interviews, Bengtsson was able to examine behaviours through interviews but also see them *in action*. By gathering data in this way, the author gained insights into how relationships and space were negotiated. The analysis made sense of this by reference to hypermasculinity scripts.

Creative methods

Whilst the methods described so far in this chapter are some of the most popular methods, a range of other research methods exist and are increasingly used to address research questions. One umbrella group of methods are referred to as 'creative' methods.

Such methods can be used alone but are often used in combination with other methods. These methods have been particularly useful in research with young people, but also those in 'hard to reach' groups. An example of one category of creative methods is discussed here but there are many more, including the use of art, drawings, craft and poetry (see also Chapter 19 by Lippens in this volume).

Photo elicitation and photo voice

Visual or 'image-based' methods using photo images are often considered a new technique; however, they have a track record of application in social research dating back to the 1970s (Balomenou and Garrod, 2016). These methods are increasingly used in criminology, leading some scholars to suggest the field is experiencing a visual turn. Specifically, within criminology, scholars have suggested that the field is experiencing a 'visual turn' (Rafter, 2014).

Photos can be used to stimulate discourse in interviews or focus groups (typically referred to as photo elicitation – see Matteucci, 2013) or can be used as part of a participatory-action approach to research. There are a number of ways this method can be utilized; however, one of the most common is to give participants cameras and ask them to take photos representing particular topic(s) (photo voice or photo documentation), with the resulting photographs either analysed (qualitatively or, occasionally, quantitatively) or used to stimulate discussion in focus groups or interviews (photo elicitation) (see Box 4.5). The latter provides researchers with laddering or multidimensional analysis (Balmoneou and Garrod, 2016).

These methods enable participants to be actively involved in constructing knowledge. They provide the researcher with an in-depth look into the lives of participants. Though the method often uses small sample sizes, the aim of qualitative methodology is not to produce generalizable findings and this criticism is not in itself a reason not to use these methods.

BOX 4.5   VISUAL METHODS IN PROBATION RESEARCH (CARR ET AL., 2015)

A study by Carr et al. used participant-generated photos (photo voice) in a study examining probation officers. Officers were asked to take images relating to their work, for example things that represented obstacles or something that would improve the nature of their work. This was followed up with interviews where respondents provided further information on the pictures they had generated. Participants generated a total of 389 images using their own digital devices (typically mobile phones). This generated a large amount of data in a short space of time, at minimum cost, and provided researchers with visual insights into the daily lives of probation officers and the difficulties, and opportunities, they had in relation to their work. It provided participants with the freedom and flexibility to decide what was and was not important and, as such, they were co-creators in the research project. However, the authors found that some participants contributed a large number of photographs (nearly 150) whereas others only provided a small number, which meant the data was potentially skewed and reflected the opinions and decisions of a minority of participants. However, the researchers felt the main limitation, or difficulty, in using this method was how to interpret and analyse the images and there were concerns about misinterpreting the meaning behind the images.

Mixing methods

As discussed earlier in this chapter, the two primary approaches to research (qualitative and quantitative) were traditionally seen as distinct and incompatible with each other. There was something of a 'paradigm war' between the two approaches (Oakley, 1999). However, increasingly researchers are now using these methodologies in combination with each other and a variety of methods are being utilized to examine criminological issues. The benefits of combining methods, for example surveys with interviews, is that it allows researchers to examine both the extent and nature of a particular problem (for example, theft) by surveying a large number of people, as well as exploring how these crimes impact communities and victims, and the needs of victims following this type of offence through interviews with affected individuals. A more complete, rounded understanding is therefore possible where a combination of methods is used.

Secondary research methods

Secondary research involves the analysis of existing data and is often termed 'desk-based' research, as it does not involve the collection of primary empirical data. There are a number of secondary research methods: re-analysis of existing data (for example, crime surveys or published police data, newspaper or media articles) or analysis of existing literature (for example, policy documents, reports, peer-reviewed articles and books).

Secondary analysis of data

Secondary analysis of existing data is used to find answers to research questions that differ from the questions asked in the original research (Hinds et al., 1997). There are a number of benefits to this method. First, it is a cheap and relatively quick way of producing 'new' findings on a particular issue. The data has already been collected and this saves the researcher the time and effort of going through the primary data collection process. Bypassing these steps also cuts down on cost, as the data is available for analysis immediately and this limits the cost to researcher time.

Literature reviews and rapid evidence assessments

One of the most common forms of secondary analysis is a literature review. Reviewing existing literature (books, journal articles, policy documents) allows the researcher to examine what data and theory exist in relation to a particular topic or area of inquiry. The author of this chapter recently conducted a critical literature review of sexual violence against older people (Bows, 2017) to examine what is currently known about the prevalence, nature and characteristics of victims and offenders. This involved searching for, and analysis of, literature across elder abuse, sexual violence and domestic violence fields using a range of databases including EBSCOHOST, Ingenta-Ingenta connect and JSTOR. The review helped to identify existing knowledge but also gaps in knowledge.

Most researchers conduct literature reviews as part of a study, either at the proposal stage (to get an idea of what already exists and where the gaps are, in order to make a rationale for their study) or when they begin their study, to enable them to situate their findings within the broader literature. For the literature review described above (Bows, 2017), the review was conducted for the latter reason. However, literature reviews can be methods in themselves and can take a number of forms.

Systematic reviews are generally associated with quantitative methodology. Farrington et al. (2001: 340) describe systematic reviews as using 'rigorous methods for locating, appraising, and synthesizing evidence from prior evaluation studies. They contain a methods and results section and are reported with the same level of detail that characterizes high-quality reports of original research'.

Another form of literature review is the meta-analysis. Meta-analysis is a quantitative, formal, epidemiological study design used commonly in medical sciences, to systematically assess previous research studies to derive conclusions about that body of research (Haidich, 2010). Often, a meta-analysis will follow on from a systematic review.

Other forms of reviews include rapid evidence assessments (REA) and scoping reviews. RAEs are typically conducted over a very short period of time, involve assessing what is known about a policy or practice issue, usually by adopting a systematic approach but involving critical appraisal of the existing literature. A scoping review is usually a smaller review which attempts to assess the scope of available literature on a particular topic.

ETHICS

Ethical concerns are at the heart of social research and are the key principles which inform, and shape, research practice. Being aware of ethical issues in criminological research is critically important and it is essential that ethical issues are considered prior to, and throughout, the research process. Most disciplines have official ethical guidelines – in criminology, this is provided by the British Society of Criminology (BSC) (n.d.).

The BSC code of ethics categorizes the key ethical responsibilities into five groups: general responsibilities; responsibilities of researchers towards the discipline of criminology; researchers' responsibilities to colleagues; researchers' responsibilities towards research participants; and relationships with sponsors. The largest category concerns the responsibilities towards research participants and incorporates physical, social and psychological well-being as well as other concerns such as data protection.

All university-based projects have to go through internal ethical approval which usually involves completing an ethics form, detailing the project and identifying the key ethical concerns and how these will be addressed, which is scrutinized by a panel who decide whether enough consideration has been given to the full range of issues identified. In addition, many public sector institutions have their own ethical approval forms and processes. For example, if you want to conduct research in prisons, you will have to go through the National Offender Management Service (NOMS) ethical process for your project to be approved prior to you being allowed to conduct your research.

SUMMARY AND REVIEW

This chapter has introduced you to some of the methodological approaches in criminological research. You should now have an understanding of the different methodological frameworks that underpin research and how these shape the research design and methods utilized. Whilst this chapter has focused on quantitative and qualitative as two opposing approaches, in reality researchers are increasingly combining these approaches and realizing the benefits of mixed methods. In addition, this chapter has introduced you to some of the ethical principles that underpin all research projects. Each project will have specific ethical issues that require consideration, depending on the nature of the research, topic and the methods adopted.

The following chapters in this volume will provide you with insights into a range of methods utilized in different research contexts and develop your understanding of research in action, providing you with the foundations to begin your own criminological research project.

Choose and read one of the published studies listed below and then consider the following questions:

1. What is the research methodology?

   a. What ontological and epistemological assumptions underpin their methodology?
   b. What theory underpins the study?

2. Does the study use primary or secondary data (or both)?

3. What method(s) is/are used?

4. What type of data does this produce?

5. What were the key ethical considerations in this study and how were they negotiated?

SUGGESTIONS FOR FURTHER READING

Lewis, S., Crawford, A. and Traynor, P. (2016) 'Nipping crime in the bud? The use of anti-social behaviour interventions with young people in England and Wales', *British Journal of Criminology*, 57(5): 1230–48. This article reports on the findings from a study which utilized quantitative and qualitative data to examine the use of anti-social behaviour warning letters or orders and the various interventions utilized by different services.

Lewis, R., Rowe, M. and Wiper, C. (2017) 'Online abuse of feminists as an emerging form of violence against women and girls', *British Journal of Criminology*, 57(6): 1462–81. This study used a mixed-method approach combining an online survey with qualitative in-depth interviews to examine feminists' experiences of online abuse and harassment.

Pina-Sánchez, J., Lightowlers, C. and Roberts, J. (2017) 'Exploring the punitive surge: Crown Court sentencing practices before and after the 2011 English riots', *Criminology and Criminal Justice*, 17(3): 319–39. This article reports on findings from a secondary, quantitative analysis study on the Crown Court Survey.

Wistow, R., Kelly, L. and Westmarland, N. (2017) '"Time out": a strategy for reducing men's violence against women in relationships?', *Violence against Women*, 23(6): 730–48. This article reports on the findings from a mixed-method study which combined qualitative interviews and telephone surveys with victims and perpetrators of domestic violence.

REFERENCES

Aldridge, A. and Levine, K. (2001) *Surveying the Social World: Principles and Practice in Survey Research*. London: McGraw-Hill Education.

Balomenou, N. and Garrod, B. (2016) 'A review of participant-generated image methods in the social sciences', *Journal of Mixed Methods Research*, *10*(4): 335–51.

Bengtsson, T.T. (2016) 'Performing hypermasculinity: experiences with confined young offenders', *Men and Masculinities*, *19*(4): 410–28.

Bowling, B. (1993) 'Racial harassment and the process of victimization', *British Journal of Criminology*, *33*(2): 231–50.

Bows, H. (2017) 'Sexual violence against older people: a review of the empirical literature', *Trauma, Violence, & Abuse* [online]. Available at: http://journals.sagepub.com/doi/abs/10.1177/1524838016683455 (accessed 17 March 2018).

Bows, H. and Westmarland, N. (2017) 'Rape of older people in the United Kingdom: challenging the "real-rape" stereotype', *British Journal of Criminology*, *57*(1): 1–17.

Brewer, J. (2000) *Ethnography*. London: McGraw-Hill Education.

British Society of Criminology (n.d.) Code of Ethics for Researchers in the Field of Criminology [online]. Available at: www.britsoccrim.org/docs/CodeofEthics.pdf (accessed May 2018).

Brooks, O. (2011) '"Guys! Stop doing it!": Young women's adoption and rejection of safety advice when socializing in bars, pubs and clubs', *British Journal of Criminology*, *51*(4): 635–51.

Bryman, A. (1984) 'The debate about quantitative and qualitative research: a question of method or epistemology?', *British Journal of Sociology*, *35*(1): 75–92.

Carr, N., Bauwens, A., Bosker, J., Donker, A., Robinson, G., Sučić, I. and Worrall, A. (2015) 'Picturing probation: exploring the utility of visual methods in comparative research', *European Journal of Probation*, *7*(3): 179–200.

Denzin, N. (1970) *The Research Act in Sociology*. Chicago: Aldine.

Farrall, S., Bannister, J., Ditton, J. and Gilchrist, E. (1997) 'Questioning the measurement of the "fear of crime": findings from a major methodological study', *British Journal of Criminology*, *37*(4): 658–79.

Farrington, D.P., Petrosino, A. and Welsh, B.C. (2001) 'Systematic reviews and cost-benefit analyses of correctional interventions', *The Prison Journal*, *81*(3): 339–59.

Greener, I. (2011) *Designing Social Research: A Guide for the Bewildered*. London: Sage.

Haidich, A.B. (2010) 'Meta-analysis in medical research', *Hippokratia*, *14*(1): 29–37.

Hammersley, M. (1991) *What's Wrong with Ethnography?* London: Routledge.

Hinds, P.S., Vogel, R.J. and Clarke-Steffen, L. (1997) 'The possibilities and pitfalls of doing a secondary analysis of a qualitative dataset', *Qualitative Health Research*, *7*(3): 408–24.

Hollway, W. and Jefferson, T. (2008) 'The free association narrative interview method', in L. Given (ed.), *The SAGE Encyclopedia of Qualitative Research Methods*. Thousand Oaks, CA: Sage, pp. 296–315.

Kleck, G., Tark, J. and Bellows, J.J. (2006) 'What methods are most frequently used in research in criminology and criminal justice?', *Journal of Criminal Justice*, 34(2): 147–52.

Lewis, P. (2011) 'Reading the Riots study to examine causes and effects of August unrest', *The Guardian*, 5 September.

Matteucci, X. (2013) 'Photo elicitation: exploring tourist experiences with researcher-found images', *Tourism Management*, 35: 190–7.

Mishler, E.G. (1986) *Research Interviewing: Context and Narrative*. Cambridge, MA: Harvard University Press.

Oakley, A. (1999) 'Paradigm wars: some thoughts on a personal and public trajectory', *International Journal of Social Research Methodology*, 2(3): 247–54.

Pierre, E.A.S. and Roulston, K. (2006) 'The state of qualitative inquiry: a contested science', *International Journal of Qualitative Studies in Education*, 19(6): 673–84.

Rafter, N. (2014) 'Introduction to special issue on visual culture and the iconography of crime and punishment', *Theoretical Criminology*, 18(2): 127–33.

Robson, C. (2002) *Real World Research*, 2nd edition. Oxford: Blackwell.

CHAPTER CONTENTS

GLOSSARY TERMS

pragmatism
multiple realities
inductive
deductive
mixed methods design
inferences and meta
   inferences

triangulation
complementarity
development
initiation
expansion
inference quality

5

USING MIXED METHODS IN CRIMINOLOGICAL RESEARCH

VICKY HEAP AND JAIME WATERS

INTRODUCTION

The purpose of this chapter is to introduce you to mixed methods research, an approach where both quantitative and qualitative methods are utilized in the same research project. Mixed methods is a relatively new methodological strategy and has become increasingly prominent since the turn of the twenty-first century (Plano Clark and Creswell, 2008). It is a methodological approach often employed in situations where the use of both quantitative and qualitative methods can help provide a better understanding of the phenomena being studied, for example where the area of research is complex and multi-faceted. In the discipline of criminology, using a mixed methods strategy can be particularly advantageous because of the distinct issues and complexities that studying crime, deviance and victimization entails – for instance, combining national crime survey data (quantitative) with interviews or case studies (qualitative) to provide a more in-depth understanding of the topic.

This chapter provides a practical guide on how to approach and design your own criminological mixed methods research project. Its starting point is the research philosophy that underpins mixed methods (a combination of pragmatism, multiple realities and so-called abduction), before it goes on to consider the specifics of mixed methods research design (the sequence question and the priority question). It then goes on to discuss the processes of integration (covering triangulation, complementarity, development, initiation, expansion) and evaluation (covering inference quality and inference transferability). Finally, the chapter focuses on the actual creation of a mixed methods research project (which entails thinking about central research questions, creating a specific methodology and presentation). These themes are also highlighted in the two case studies (Boxes 5.1 and 5.2), which show how the application of mixed methods principles and procedures can work in real-life research situations. In addition, throughout the chapter you will be introduced to some of the terminology associated with mixed methods research. This is especially important because mixed methods research is still an emerging field in which terminologies and definitions are contested and often inconsistently used (Teddlie and Tashakkori, 2010).

THE PHILOSOPHY OF MIXED METHODS RESEARCH

This section covers the research philosophies that inform the mixed methods approach, specifically its epistemological and ontological underpinnings. As mixed methods is neither solely quantitative nor qualitative, the traditional (if contested) divisions between positivism and interpretivism and objectivism and constructivism are not especially useful in this setting. As such, the focus will be on pragmatism

(Tashakkori and Teddlie, 1998; Denscombe, 2002) as the most appropriate epistemological approach and the notion of multiple realities (Onwuegbuzie et al., 2009) as constituting the ontological framework for mixed methods. The section ends by suggesting how pragmatism and multiple realities can be brought together under the mixed methods banner into a coherent overall approach.

Pragmatism

Epistemology is the branch of philosophy concerned with the theory of knowledge, and as such investigates our methods of acquiring knowledge, how we come to 'know' things and what justifications we have for considering something as 'truth' and accepting it as valid 'knowledge' within a particular discipline such as criminology (Bryman, 2016). In terms of truth, it would be useful to think about what is meant by 'truth' and how we know something to be 'true'. For example, do you view the world as something that you can see and measure independently of your existence in it? Or, is the world something that you can interact with and influence? Criminologists often define valid knowledge as evidence produced by rigorous and systematic research (although the exact nature of this can be contested and is determined by one's epistemology), rather than hearsay or 'common sense' knowledge which could be based on supposition or rumour. What you see as truth and valid knowledge will reflect your epistemological stance (your understanding of the world). Pragmatism tends to be the preferred epistemological standpoint of mixed methods research – what Denscombe (2014: 158) calls its 'epistemological partner'. For the pragmatist, knowledge 'is both constructed and based on the reality of the world we experience and live in' (Onwuegbuzie et al., 2009: 122).

Pragmatism is not the only epistemology to be linked with mixed methods work. Researchers have shown how mixed methods can be related to phenomenology (Mayoh and Onwuegbuzie, 2015), critical realism (Denscombe, 2014; Harrits, 2011; Layder, 1993, 1998; Lipscomb, 2008; Pawson and Tilley, 1997), constructivism (Denzin, 2012) or 'transformative' and 'emancipatory' epistemologies (Mertens, 2009; Onwuegbuzie and Frels, 2013). However, pragmatism is the most commonly adopted epistemology in such work.

One advantage of pragmatism is that it assists us in moving beyond the 'paradigm wars' (Bryman, 2016; Hammersley, 1992; Oakley, 1999) that pitch qualitative against quantitative and positivism against interpretivism. Instead, pragmatism encourages the researcher to take a more practical approach to their work, driven primarily by the needs of the research question at hand. So, whilst 'the "theory" might say that positivism and interpretivism are incompatible in terms of their basic beliefs about social reality, in practice social researchers have tended to pick and choose from the array of methods at their disposal' (Denscombe, 2002: 23). Pragmatism takes the philosophical stance that 'good social research depends on [...] what it is practical to accomplish and what kind of data are required' (Denscombe,

2002: 24). For example, if you wanted to research female prisoners you could examine official statistics from the Ministry of Justice (quantitative), but this would only provide a partial picture. You could also carry out interviews with female prisoners (qualitative), but this alone would give limited insight. With pragmatism, combining quantitative and qualitative data gives you a fuller picture and a greater depth of understanding. Furthermore, the practicalities associated with completing an undergraduate dissertation differ greatly to a multi-million pound international research project. For both of these, you might use mixed methods and take a pragmatic approach, but these projects would look quite different due to the scale, scope and means (time and money) of the research questions being investigated. An undergraduate dissertation studying female prisoners might contain a small-scale non-probability questionnaire of people's perceptions of female prisoners, alongside a handful of interviews on the same topic. In contrast, a fully funded international research project could use Ministry of Justice statistics, as well as interviews with prisoners and prison officers, case studies and documentary analysis.

BOX 5.1   PRAGMATISM'S CORE PRINCIPLES (DENSCOMBE, 2014: 158)

- Knowledge is based on practical outcomes and 'what works'.
- Research should test what works through empirical inquiry.
- There is no single, best 'scientific' method that can lead the way to indisputable knowledge.
- Knowledge is provisional. It is the product of the historical era and the cultural context within which is it produced.

The guiding principle for pragmatists is not how well a piece of research adheres to 'its "positivistic" or "interpretivistic" epistemology, but how well it addresses the topic it is investigating' (Denscombe, 2002: 23). This is why pragmatism is so useful for mixed methods research: it puts the research question(s) at the heart of the research process and allows the researcher to move beyond the traditional qualitative/quantitative divide. It focuses on utilizing the best research tools for the problem at hand and how to get the most from them. It recognizes the strengths and weaknesses of different strategies and seeks to combine them in such a way as to accentuate their positives and compensate for their negatives, all the while being driven by a desire to provide an answer to the research question(s). Pragmatists therefore 'consider the research question to be more important than either the method they use or the worldview that is supposed to underlie the method' (Tashakkori and Teddlie, 1998: 21).

Multiple realities

Ontology is the study of the nature of reality, and in the social sciences an ontological position provides us with a 'theory of the nature of social entities', social phenomena and their meanings (Bryman, 2016: 693). The notion of multiple realities is an ontological position that can support the adoption of mixed methods. It suggests that there is no singular 'correct' ontological understanding of the social world, and that instead there are multiple ontologies or multiple understandings of reality and that each has validity. This acknowledgement can influence our understanding and measurement of social phenomena and the meanings we ascribe to them. More or less, this ontological stance means that good research practice, which best answers the central research question, is more important than getting bogged down in ontological considerations. Thinking again about researching female prisoners, there is legitimacy in looking at statistical data, as these will give you a certain truth. Interviewing the female prisoners will *also* give you a certain truth. Both of these truths are equally valid and multiple realities embrace this, bringing them together.

Much like pragmatism moves us away from the 'paradigm wars' in the realm of epistemology, so the notion of multiple realities moves us away from similar debates in the realm of ontology. It recognizes subjectivism, objectivism and intersubjectivism simultaneously and rejects the traditional dualisms of subjectivism versus objectivism/ constructionism and fact versus value (Onwuegbuzie et al., 2009). There is a 'high regard for the reality and influence of the inner world of human experience in action' (2009: 122) and, like pragmatism, the notion of multiple realities sees knowledge as inherently provisional; 'current truth, meaning and knowledge are tentative and changing' (2009: 122). Thus, attention is directed to the sense that ours is always a partial perspective, and the perspectives of others in different times, places and social situations may be very different but no less valid. In the absence of universally valid truth, there is no 'magic bullet' of a method that can uncover that which is applicable to all. Instead, the best research tools to use in a given situation are those that offer the best opportunity for a thorough investigation of the matter at hand. The similarity between this stance and that of pragmatism is clear.

Pragmatism, multiple realities and mixed methods

When creating research proposals, it is vital to make sure that there is a logical alignment between the different philosophical and methodological aspects. In terms of the research philosophy, it is important that the epistemology, ontology and research strategy all come together in a coherent whole which, in turn, underpins the actual process of the research project. The links between, say, positivism, objectivism and a quantitative research strategy are clear and much discussed, as are those between interpretivism, constructionism and a qualitative research strategy. Similarly, for our purposes it is quite evident that pragmatism links well with the notion of multiple realities and a mixed methods strategy. A 'what works' pragmatism (Denscombe, 2014) that considers knowledge to be provisional and based on practical outcomes clearly dovetails neatly with the sense that there are multiple realities and, in turn, with a mixed methods approach. In practice, pragmatism allows you to pick the best data collection methods to answer your central research question and multiple realities let you look at the world in a variety of different ways. This provides the foundation for combining quantitative and qualitative data and data collection methods in mixed methods. Continuing the example of researching female prisoners, this combination of pragmatism and multiple realities brings together the quantitative and qualitative data to provide a more complete picture of their experiences.

Mixed methods researchers have also sought to avoid the inductive/deductive dualism often associated with qualitative and quantitative research, and have thus developed an alternative in the guise of the 'abductive' approach. As Morse and Niehaus (2009: 39) put it, abduction is 'a third mode' of inquiry where the aim 'is to move back and forward between induction and deduction throughout the research by first developing conjectures and then systematically testing these conjectures'. Rather than the theory generation associated with inductive approaches, or the theory testing associated with deductive approaches, by blending the two the abductive approach is geared towards problem solving and thus fits in well with the pragmatic bent of mixed methods work.

Table 5.1 summarizes the epistemology, ontology, strategy and the role of theory across the three major epistemological positions in social (including criminological) research, namely positivism, interpretivism and pragmatism.

As Table 5.1 shows, the mixed methods strategy walks the line between qualitative and quantitative approaches. Mixed methods researchers look beyond the dualistic nature of the 'paradigm wars' and instead focus on determining what would be the best approach and the best methods to answer the research question(s) at hand; attention is turned to 'what works' given the circumstances of the project. Indeed, in an era where much criminological research is 'policy based' and funded by bodies that require easily digestible answers to very specific questions, there is a sense that the time has truly arrived for the mixed methods approach in the discipline of criminology.

TABLE 5.1 Three Major Epistemological Positions in Social Research

Epistemology	Positivism	Interpretivism	Pragmatism
Ontology	Objectivism	Constructivism	Multiple Realities
Strategy	Quantitative	Qualitative	Mixed Methods
Relationship between Theory & Research	Deductive Testing of Theory	Inductive Generation of Theory	Abductive Problem Solving

MIXED METHODS DESIGNS

This section discusses what to consider when designing your mixed methods research project. Two key questions will be covered: the priority question and the sequence question (Bryman, 2016; Denscombe, 2014). The priority question is concerned with the weighting of the qualitative and quantitative component(s) of the research and asks whether the components are to be equally weighted, or whether one component is more dominant than the other. The sequence question is related to the order in which you carry out the qualitative and quantitative component(s) of the research: which component should come first, second and so on, or is each component to be carried out simultaneously? The section ends by looking at how the answers to the sequence and priority questions combine to create the overall design of the research.

The priority question

The priority question will often be the first aspect of the research design that you need to make decisions about in a mixed methods project. Consideration will be given as to which aspect of the research, the qualitative or the quantitative, is the more important or dominant component of the project, or whether they are of equal status. Some authors refer to this as the 'status question' (Denscombe, 2014) and some, as we do here, as the 'priority question' (Bryman, 2016).

Your answer to the priority question will depend on your research question(s) and the aims and objectives of your research. You may feel that the quantitative and qualitative components of your research are of the same value and importance because they will help you answer your research question in the same measure. In this case, one component should not dominate the other, and the answer to the priority question is that the components are equal in priority. This can be shown through the use of notation: in this case it would be shown as 'QUANT' and 'QUAL', with both in capital letters. An example is Best et al. (2016). This research collected data about participants' substance use and recovery (QUANT) and carried out interviews (QUAL). Both data collection methods and subsequent data were of equal importance, therefore had equal priority (QUANT→QUAL).

If your quantitative and qualitative components are not of equal status, then you can denote which component is dominant. The notation for this is to show the dominant component in capital letters and the less dominant component in lower-case letters. So, if your research has a dominant quantitative component, the notation for this would be 'QUANT qual'. Alternatively, if the dominant component of your research is qualitative, the notation for this would be 'QUAL quant'. In Waters' (2009) research into older, illegal drug users, the quantitative component (secondary data analysis of the British Crime Survey) took precedence over the qualitative component (interviews). This meant that the quantitative component was of higher status (QUANT/qual}→).

Some research inquiries will demand a more intricate mixed methods design which incorporates more than one qualitative and one quantitative component. In this instance, you still need to decide if all the components are of equal status and priority, or if certain components are more or less dominant, and you would use the same approach to notation as above to show this. Maruna and King (2009) used this design in their public perceptions research about the 'redeemability' of offenders, consisting of three components of equal priority (QUANT → QUAL → QUANT).

The sequence question

The sequence question is concerned with the order in which the components of the research are organized. The two basic options are simultaneous and sequential. In a simultaneous design, the qualitative and quantitative components are carried out at roughly the same time. The two components resemble standalone 'silos' of work where the data from each is essentially collected independently of the other silo, although of course the silos ultimately remain part of a broader piece of research. The two components are then brought together and the findings are integrated. Crucially, in a simultaneous study, the components remain distinct and do not influence each other during the data collection phase. Of course, it may be the case that in a simultaneous study the data collection for each component does not take place at *exactly* the same time, but there is generally no interaction between the two processes of data collection which are carried out as close in time as is practical. Examples of a simultaneous piece of work might include conducting qualitative interviews whilst at the same time carrying out a quantitative questionnaire, or carrying out secondary analysis of a data set whilst working on a qualitative media analysis. Waters' (2009) study into older, illegal drug users also applies here, as she used a simultaneous design with data collection for both components being carried out at the same time (QUANT/qual}→). The simultaneous design is illustrated in Table 5.2, but can also be shown more simplistically with a forward slash between the components (for example, QUAL/QUANT}→).

In a sequential design, one component is carried out first. The data collection process, the data itself and the analysis of the data are then used to inform the design of the subsequent component(s). Either a qualitative or quantitative component can be used as the starting point, dependent once again on the research question(s) and the aims and objectives of the inquiry. This approach allows you to 'build' the research from one component to the next. The notation for a sequential design is shown in Table 5.2. One example of a sequential design is where you may conduct a number of qualitative interviews to inform a subsequent large quantitative questionnaire (qual→QUANT). Another example might be that you carry out a large-scale quantitative survey that is used to inform an additional method of data collection such as qualitative interviews (QUANT→QUAL). An example of this is where Best et al. (2016) used their survey (QUANT) not only to collect data, but also as a precursor to the creation of their interview schedule and qualitative data collection (QUAL), resulting in a sequential design, as the quantitative data collection came before the qualitative data collection (QUANT→QUAL).

TABLE 5.2 **Design Sequence Notation**

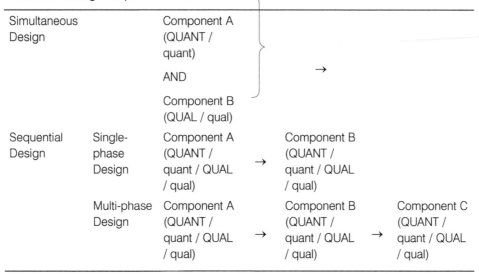

Simultaneous Design		Component A (QUANT / quant) AND Component B (QUAL / qual)	→			
Sequential Design	Single-phase Design	Component A (QUANT / quant / QUAL / qual)	→	Component B (QUANT / quant / QUAL / qual)		
	Multi-phase Design	Component A (QUANT / quant / QUAL / qual)	→	Component B (QUANT / quant / QUAL / qual)	→	Component C (QUANT / quant / QUAL / qual)

'Multi-phase' sequential designs are also options. This is where there is more than one quantitative or qualitative component. The notation for a sequential multi-phase design is shown in Table 5.2. You can include as many iterations as are necessary for the purposes of your research project. Examples might include a focus group (qual) to highlight key issues, followed by a representative questionnaire (QUANT) to measure the concept, followed by interviews (QUAL) to add further detail to the findings of the questionnaire. The notation of the resulting sequence would be 'qual→QUANT→QUANT'. In their evaluation of the Gateway Protection Programme (a refugee assistance scheme), Platts-Fowler and Robinson (2015) use this design, starting with interviews and focus groups with refugees (qual), followed by three waves of a survey (QUANT). The final 'multi-phase' sequential design looks like this: (qual→QUANT→QUANT→QUANT).

Priority, sequence and the overall design

Priority and sequence can be combined in any number of ways in your mixed methods design. When deciding how to answer the priority and sequence questions, you should consider a number of things: What is your research question(s) and what is it that you are seeking an answer to? What are your research aims and objectives (what are you planning to achieve with your project)? What is the purpose of and justification for the study? What data collection methods are being used and why? Are there any practical constraints on the research, such as limits on time and resources? It is important to be able to justify the decisions that you make. You should have good reasons for having a dominant component or for giving your components equal priority. There should be a clearly articulated rationale for your decision to adopt a simultaneous or sequential design. Ultimately, the answers to all these questions should come together to create a coherent piece of research that can be robustly defended.

Although there are multitudes of potential mixed method designs, Bryman (2016: 639) outlines four basic designs that will likely cover most circumstances. He calls these the 'convergent parallel design', the 'exploratory sequential design', the 'explanatory sequential design' and the 'embedded design' (see Table 5.3 for details). These four designs (themselves based on Creswell and Plano Clark, 2011) offer a good starting point for most projects and show you how answers to the priority and sequence questions feed into the overall design.

When you are presenting your research, be it in a report or dissertation, the decisions you make on priority and sequence, and how they relate to the purpose of the study, should be explicitly discussed and your justifications for the decisions made should be clearly outlined. Box 5.1 explores the PhD research carried out by Jaime Waters. The PhD research focused on illegal drug use among adults not involved in treatment programmes or the criminal justice system and over the age of 50. The experience of this research suggests the importance of the priority and sequence questions and, inadvertently, how mixed method approaches can offer a degree of flexibility that can be useful when problems arise in the data collection phase. Note how the aims and objectives of the project (in this case, the desire to produce an exploratory study of an under-researched area) fed into the design and informed the answers to the priority and sequence questions.

Name	Description	Diagram	Example
Convergent parallel design	Simultaneous collection of quantitative and qualitative data, typically of equal priority. The resulting analyses are then compared and/or merged to form an integrated whole. Typically associated with triangulation.	QUANT / QUAL → Compares / Merges → Findings	Waters (2009) (see Case Study 1)
Exploratory sequential design	Collection of qualitative data prior to the collection of quantitative data. Associated with the generation of qualitative based hypotheses or hunches that are then tested quantitatively.	QUAL / qual → Informs → QUANT / quant → Findings	Platts-Fowler and Robinson (2015)

TABLE 5.3 Basic Mixed Methods Designs

Name	Description	Diagram	Example
Explanatory sequential design	Collection and analysis of quantitative data followed by the collection and analysis of qualitative data in order to elaborate or explain the quantitative findings.	QUANT / quant ↓ Explains / Explores ↓ QUAL / qual ↓ Findings	Heap (2010) (see Case Study 2)
Embedded design	Either the quantitative or qualitative component can take priority, but the work draws on both approaches. Can be simultaneous or sequential. Typically used when quantitative or qualitative alone is felt insufficient for understanding the phenomenon of interest, and the supplementary component is used to buttress the dominant component.	QUANT / QUAL qual / quant ↓ Integrates ↓ Findings	Best et al. (2016)

(adapted from Bryman, 2016: 638-9)

BOX 5.2   JAIME WATERS' PHD RESEARCH (2009) – ILLEGAL DRUG USE AMONG OLDER ADULTS

This work started in 2003 when there was a real dearth of research on illegal drug use in the over-50s. Due to the lack of knowledge of this particular population at the time, the study was intended to be exploratory in nature. My intention was to try and show the extent of illegal drug use among older adults, and also paint a picture of the older illegal drug user and the reasons behind their drug use. This underpinned the decision to carry out mixed methods work. I adopted a pragmatic approach whereby the research would have a quantitative component – secondary data analysis of the British Crime Survey (now the Crime Survey for England and Wales); and a qualitative component – semi-structured interviews with members of the target population. This was designed so that each component supported the other in order to provide a robust overall picture of the field.

The design of the project was simultaneous (both the qualitative and quantitative components being carried out at approximately the same time) and the quantitative and

(Continued)

(Continued)

qualitative components were of equal status (QUANT/QUAL}→). Thus, the project was of what Bryman (2016) would call a 'convergent parallel design'. It was envisaged that this methodology would provide a good overview of illegal drug use in the over-50s in line with the aims and objectives of the study. Statistical evidence as to the extent and nature of illegal drug use would sit alongside rich or 'thick' qualitative knowledge.

When it came to operationalizing the research, I encountered serious difficulties in recruiting participants. The main difficulty was that potential interviewees were unwilling to speak on the record about their engagement in an illegal activity (Waters, 2015). As a result of this, I shifted priority towards the quantitative component. This meant undertaking a more detailed analysis and discussion of the British Crime Survey, so whilst the project remained simultaneous in nature, the quantitative component assumed a greater role in terms of priority. The PhD had changed from a 'QUANT/QUAL}→' design to a 'QUANT/qual}→' design. Thus, I inadvertently came to realize one of the strengths of the mixed methods approach: if something does not go to plan with one component of mixed methods research, all is not necessarily lost as in certain circumstances mixed methods allow for some degree of flexibility. Although certain aspects of the project, including some of the objectives, did need revising, I was still able to answer my central research question and address the broad aims of the study with this small adjustment. In my case, a simple change in priority enabled me to finish and make the most of my project.

COMBINING MIXED METHODS RESEARCH

The process of combining quantitative and qualitative results is perhaps one of the most challenging aspects of mixed methods research, particularly because this is often rooted in the philosophical approach adopted by the researcher, and linked to the overarching rationale for undertaking mixed methods research in the first place. Ultimately, how you intend to combine the results is something to consider when designing your mixed methods research project, in a similar way to how you would think about the type of analysis you are going to use for each component, although, due to the complexities and realities of real-world research, these intentions may have to be revised according to the prevailing circumstances, as illustrated in Box 5.1.

The 'mixing' in mixed methods

Fundamentally, the process of combining results from the quantitative and qualitative components of data collection is about examining the sets of results and discerning how they can contribute to answering the central research question(s). In mixed methods research, this process creates two types of findings that transcend the quantitative/ qualitative divide, which have been defined by Teddlie and Tashakkori (2009) as:

- inferences – the conclusions and interpretations from each component (quantitative or qualitative) of a mixed methods research project
- meta-inferences – the conclusions and interpretations drawn across the quantitative and qualitative components.

As mixed methods research has developed as a research strategy, the way in which meta-inferences are generated has evolved over time. This is contested terrain and numerous scholars have proposed different ways to combine quantitative and qualitative results (see Bryman, 2016: 641). You may also find that some researchers refer to this part of the process as the 'point of interface' (Morse and Niehaus, 2009). Bryman (2006) conducted a content analysis of mixed methods research studies and found that 16 different approaches had been used. Weighing up the merits of 16 different approaches to the combining of results is a heavy burden for those new to mixed methods research. However, Greene et al. (1989), on the basis of an analysis of 57 mixed methods research studies, suggest five ways that findings from each component can be combined: triangulation, complementarity, development, initiation and expansion. This serves as a very useful starting point when considering how to 'mix' your results:

Triangulation is where two or more methods are used to investigate the same phenomenon. The aim is to seek a convergence and corroboration of the inferences generated from each research component. For example, Maruna and King (2009) used three components (QUANT→QUAL→QUANT) to triangulate public perceptions about the 'redeemability' of offenders. The data was collected as part of the Cambridge University Public Opinion Project, which investigated public attitudes towards justice. The first component involved a postal survey (QUANT) of British households, which measured punitiveness. This was followed by exploratory interviews (QUAL) to understand perceptions of punishment and, finally, a series of small experiments (QUANT) to determine if punitive attitudes could be manipulated.

Complementarity is where two or more methods are used to investigate distinct, albeit often overlapping, aspects of a phenomenon. This contrasts with triangulation and focuses on enhancing the meaningfulness of the meta-inferences generated. Greene et al. (1989: 258) suggest that complementarity provides an 'enriched, elaborated understanding of the phenomenon'. For example, Waters (2009) used secondary data analysis of the British Crime Survey (now the Crime Survey for England and Wales) (QUANT) to look at the demographics of drug users aged over 50, and semi-structured interviews (qual) to understand their motivations and attitudes towards the use of illegal drugs (QUANT/qual}→).

Development is a technique of mixed methods research involving the employment of a sequential design, with the inferences drawn from the first component used to help inform the development of the second component. This approach is employed to increase the robustness of the findings and any concepts generated as a result. For example, Best et al. (2016) started with a survey (QUANT) that collected data about participants' substance use and recovery. This baseline data then informed the development of interviews (QUAL), which together evaluated a programme designed to help people discontinue their heroin use (QUANT→QUAL).

Initiation refers to mixed methods research where new perspectives or paradoxes emerge. This may not have been the purpose of the mixed methods design, but the inferences generated from each component of the research allow for further analysis to be undertaken to create new knowledge and ideas. For example, Platts-Fowler and Robinson (2015) evaluated the Gateway Protection Programme, which used interviews and focus groups with refugees (qual) to inform and develop three waves of a longitudinal survey (QUANT), based on newly discovered perspectives (qual→QUANT→QUANT→QUANT).

Expansion utilizes mixed methods research to provide breadth and depth to a study. For example, the distinct components of a single project might collect data about different aspects of a topic. This approach reflects the philosophically pragmatic notion of selecting the most appropriate tool for the job at hand. For example, Heap (2010) used a postal survey (quant) to measure public perceptions of anti-social behaviour, which then informed public focus groups (QUAL) and semi-structured interviews (QUAL) with anti-social behaviour practitioners (quant→QUAL/QUAL).

Aside from triangulation, which is narrowly concerned with exploring one phenomenon, the other types of mixed methods research elaborated by Greene et al. (1989) can be used quite flexibly and often in combination, allowing for some quite sophisticated 'mixing' of results (see Box 5.2 on Heap's PhD). This possibility should be considered at the design stage, but it can also emerge as the research project develops through the process of data collection and analysis.

I undertook an ESRC Collaborative Award Studentship that was part-funded by the Home Office, therefore the research agenda was broadly decided before I started. The Home Office wanted to develop a better understanding about the drivers of public perceptions of anti-social behaviour (ASB), as perceptions were used at that time as the proxy measure to determine the extent of ASB (the police now record incidents too). I was also tasked with exploring the variations in perceptions between different localities and investigating the different methods used by practitioners to reduce public perceptions of high levels of ASB in local areas, meaning I had three research questions to answer. Like many externally funded projects, my funder knew what they wanted and it was my job as the researcher to make the project work. As a result, I adopted a pragmatic approach to the research (both literally and philosophically).

I undertook an explanatory sequential mixed methods design, starting with a quantitative component to identify important themes (a public perception question-naire), followed by two qualitative components to investigate in some detail the themes that were generated (focus groups with members of the public and inter-views with ASB practitioners). The qualitative components were prioritized within my project because of the depth and originality they provided (quant→QUAL/QUAL). Also, my own small-scale questionnaire was not going to replicate the British Crime Survey (now the Crime Survey for England and Wales).

Component one involved collecting quantitative data, through a questionnaire, to measure public perceptions of ASB in the eight study areas. Due to concerns about respondents having access to the internet, I conducted a postal survey, sending out 500 questionnaires per study area. I posed mainly closed questions, with some core ASB perception questions that featured in the British Crime Survey, as well as new questions to investigate the drivers of perceptions. I did not expect a high response rate, despite including a pre-paid return envelope and offering respondents entry into a prize draw for completion. I was right to be cautious, with 422 usable questionnaires returned, a response rate of 10.6%. At the time I was disappointed, but the mixed methods design and the priority of the qualitative components meant this was not too much of a problem. The 422 responses were enough to conduct a logistic regression analysis in SPSS and generate the themes to be explored qualitatively (just not quite enough to obtain 50:50 variability and a 95% confidence level). Logistic regression is a predictive model used to explain the relationship between a dichotomous (two category) variable and one or more independent variables. For example, the analysis discovered that respondents who perceived ASB to be committed deliberately (opposed to thoughtlessly) were three times more likely to perceive high levels of ASB in their local area.

Components two and three were conducted simultaneously. Component two, focus groups with the public, was problematic. My aim was to conduct two focus groups per area (16 overall). The biggest hurdle was accessing people who would talk to me. In the end, I conducted ten focus groups, involving a total of 68 participants. Component three involved interviewing ASB practitioners from the police, registered providers of social housing, and both strategic and frontline officers from

(Continued)

local councils. Although my data collection did not go strictly according to plan, the flexibility and nature of conducting mixed methods allowed any weaknesses in one of the components to be compensated for by strengths in the other two.

I combined my results by using the techniques of complementarity (to measure the overlapping as well as the distinct aspects of the phenomenon), development (where one component informed the others), initiation (to uncover new perspectives) and expansion (to provide breadth and depth), which produced an overall set of meta-inferences. Ultimately, the ability to combine the results from each component allowed me to bring together all the components of the research and provide answers to my central research questions.

EVALUATING MIXED METHODS RESEARCH

Once the results from each component have been successfully combined to create a set of meta-inferences, it is important to evaluate the *quality* of the findings produced. However, this is not necessarily straightforward in mixed methods research, primarily because of the different epistemological and ontological positions associated with quantitative and qualitative research; Onwuegbuzie and Johnson (2006) call this 'the problem of integration'.

Creswell and Plano Clark (2011: 239) suggest that mixed methods researchers should aim for 'validity'. This is a term widely used by both quantitative and qualitative researchers, and as such represents common ground between the two. They characterize validity as the result of a process which involves 'employing strategies that address potential issues in data collection, data analysis and the interpretations that might compromise the merging or connecting of the quantitative and qualitative strands of the study and the conclusions drawn from the combination'. However, validity is a somewhat contentious term in mixed methods research because it is arguably overused, often rather meaninglessly, and is disliked by many qualitative researchers due to its strong associations with quantitative strategies (Creswell and Plano Clark, 2011). As a result, novel evaluative terminology has been created specifically for use in mixed methods research. Teddlie and Tashakkori (2003, 2010) use the concept of inference quality instead of validity to judge the value of the conclusions and interpretations that stem from the combination of inferences from each of the components. Greene (2007: 167) suggests that the process of assessing the quality of inferences should reflect a multiplistic stance that:

- focuses on the available data support for the inferences, using data of multiple and diverse kinds

- could include criteria or stances from different methodological traditions
- attends to the nature and extent of the better understanding that is reached with this mixed methods design, as this is the overall aim of mixed methods inquiry.

Furthermore, Teddlie and Tashakkori (2003) also use the term 'inference transferability', which reflects quantitative notions of generalizability and qualitative concerns with transferability.

All of this leads to a rather practical question: Which evaluative term(s) should you use in your mixed methods research project? There is clearly no single correct answer to this question. The terms you use will reflect a number of things, such as your own identity as a researcher, your own preferences and the nature of the project you are working on. They will be, in short, the product of your own academic judgement.

In practice, a sensible approach to evaluating mixed methods research is to:

1. Evaluate the research methodology and findings from each data collection component using an appropriate evaluative term for the strategy involved (e.g. reliability and validity for quantitative, and trustworthiness and authenticity (Guba and Lincoln, 1994) for qualitative).
2. Select which terminology you are going to adopt to evaluate the meta-inferences generated through the integration of your findings (validity OR inference quality/inference transferability). This will depend on:
   a. Your personal feelings towards the terms in question based on your perspectives of epistemology and ontology
   b. Your understanding of, and confidence in using, terminology that is specific to mixed methods
   c. The nature of your research project, which may grant priority to either the quantitative or qualitative components.
3. Justify your selection and be consistent in your application of terminology throughout your project and the associated written work.

CREATING A MIXED METHODS RESEARCH PROJECT

Developing a research project based on just a single research strategy can be a challenging enough endeavour, so planning a mixed methods research project with multiple components requires an additional level of preparatory thinking and planning. It makes sense to develop your project only once you have a sound grasp of mixed methods research philosophy, mixed methods designs, and how to combine and evaluate mixed methods research. This section will discuss the creation of a coherent proposal for a mixed methods research project, putting everything explored in the previous sections into practice. It will consider issues such as the composition of the central research question, how the central research question drives the research design, methodology and ethics, and the task of presenting your work.

Research questions and mixed methods

In Chapter 2 of this volume, Peter Francis explains the key principles involved in creating a clear, researchable question. When creating a mixed methods research project, the type of question(s) that you pose will influence the decisions you make about philosophy, design, combining the data and components. These decisions will ultimately shape what the overall mixed methods project looks like. The philosophical pragmatism that underpins mixed methods research, and the idea of using the best tools for the job at hand, will drive the decisions you make about which question(s) to pose in each component of your study. Ultimately, to a large extent, the central research question(s) can demand the selection of a mixed methods project, which, in turn, influences the sampling and data collection techniques (Onwuegbuzie and Leech, 2006). These interconnections highlight the complex and dynamic nature of mixed methods research questions (Plano Clark and Badiee, 2010).

For example, when considering how to combine the data, if you only have one central research question, you will likely employ triangulation (where two or more methods are used to investigate the same phenomenon). In your development stage, you will need to ensure that the research question is broad enough to cover both research strategies without privileging one above another (for example, ensuring the question is not too deductive or inductive in approach, allowing for the inclusion of both the quantitative and qualitative components). If your research warrants an overall central research question that is supplemented by subsidiary questions for each research component, the remaining four mixed methods approaches to combination (complementarity, development, initiation and expansion) will be appropriate. This is because the different components of the research will seek to answer different questions. The subsidiary questions can then reflect the quantitative component(s) and the qualitative component(s), with the freedom to decide whether to pose descriptive or explanatory questions (De Vaus, 2002). Subsequently, you will use the meta-inferences generated by the inferences produced by each component to answer the overarching central research question(s). In the end, if you focus on what you want to find out and how you plan to combine the data, creating a mixed methods central research question (or a set of research questions) should not prove to be too daunting a task.

Mixed methods methodology

Once you have created a suitable mixed methods central research question(s), the next step is to design the project. With a certain topic or research question in mind, and a commitment to pragmatism, it is useful to divide the topic up into its component parts. When undertaking a mixed methods research project for the first time, it might be difficult to think about all of these different elements at once. You may therefore find it useful to work through the following four areas of decision making:

Area 1:

- Central research question(s)
- Philosophical rationale

Area 2:

- Proposed method of combining the data
- Mixed methods design (sequencing and priority decisions)
- Research design

Area 3:

- Data collection methods
- Sampling
- Methods of data analysis

Area 4:

- Evaluative terminology decisions
- Ethical approval

However, once the philosophical rationale and central research question(s) have been settled on, consideration of the remaining issues is not necessarily a linear process and it does not have to occur in any particular order. In other words, the decisions made on each of the above points are not independent of each other, and decisions in one area will influence those in another, and vice versa. As you work through each area of decision making, you will see your project begin to 'build'. For example, if you intend to combine your data for the purposes of development (an 'Area 2' decision), you will need to undertake the data analysis sequentially (an 'Area 3' decision). Or, if you decide your data collection will consist of a questionnaire to uncover themes that will feed into a series of in-depth interviews (an 'Area 3' decision), then in terms of sequencing and priority (an 'Area 2' decision) you will be adopting a 'quant→QUAL' approach. The key is to come up with a robust and defensible overall methodology, where each decision makes sense in terms of the others, and in terms of the project as a whole.

Presenting mixed methods research

It goes without saying that it is important to present your research in a manner that reflects your research process and makes logical sense. Many mixed methods research projects utilize a fairly complex research methodology. Therefore, presentation often requires a little more thought. For sequential mixed methods designs, report the research components in the order that they were conducted. If you used a simultaneous design where one component was considered to have a higher priority, report the findings with the higher priority first. If, however, the components had equal status, you need to make a decision about which component to report first. This could be based on similar previous studies and their mode of presentation, or perhaps how each component relates to the literature. A suggested format for presenting your work can be seen in Box 5.3.

BOX 5.4   BASIC STRUCTURE

A basic structure for a mixed methods research project might look like this:

- Abstract
- Introduction
- Literature review
- Methodology
- Component 1/higher priority findings
- Component 2/lower priority findings (and so on...)
- Discussion of inferences and meta-inferences
- Conclusion
- References
- Appendices

The final stage of presenting your work is to thoroughly check each section to ensure that you are using the correct quantitative, qualitative and mixed methods terminology, as well as to uncover other errors such as typographical ones. Proofread carefully and ensure that the process you have reported is accurate and transparent.

SUMMARY AND REVIEW

This chapter has introduced you to the essential elements of mixed methods research and demonstrated how they can be utilized in the criminological arena. We began by looking at the philosophical underpinnings of mixed methods research, namely pragmatism and the notion of multiple realities, before moving on to consider the issue of mixed methods designs. We saw how the answers to two questions, the priority question and the sequence question, are integral to the design process in mixed methods work. Next, the focus shifted to combining the data and the five key techniques identified by Greene et al. (1989): triangulation, complementarity, development, initiation and expansion. We then discussed the evaluation of mixed methods research and outlined some of the terminological controversies that have developed in this area. Finally, we described some of the practicalities of actually creating a piece of mixed methods research, from devising a central research question, through developing a methodological approach, to presenting your project and its findings.

STUDY QUESTIONS AND ACTIVITIES FOR STUDENTS

1. How do pragmatism and the notion of multiple realities underpin mixed methods research?

2. What is the sequence question? What is the priority question? How do the answers to the sequence and priority questions inform the design of a mixed methods study?

3. Which of the five approaches to combining findings offers the least flexibility to researchers, and why?

4. What are the contentious issues relating to the evaluative terms used in mixed methods work, in particular the notion of 'validity'?

SUGGESTIONS FOR FURTHER READING

Two sets of co-authors have become central in the mixed methods field: Creswell and Plano Clark, and Tashakkori and Teddlie. Each has produced various textbooks and journal articles on the subject. They hold slightly differing views on issues such as the appropriate evaluative terminology, and therefore it is useful to read material from both to get a holistic overview of the mixed methods strategy. Two key texts to start with are:

Creswell, J.W. and Plano Clark, V.L. (2011) *Designing and Conducting Mixed Methods Research*, 2nd edition. London: Sage.
Tashakkori, A. and Teddlie, C. (2010) *Sage Handbook of Mixed Methods in Social and Behavioural Research*. London: Sage.

Furthermore, Alan Bryman has written a couple of dedicated mixed methods chapters in his *Social Research Methods* textbook (2016), now in its fifth edition (Oxford: Oxford University Press). This book also provides a comprehensive overview of quantitative and qualitative strategies, which you will need to understand thoroughly before attempting to use mixed methods

REFERENCES

Best, D., Irving, J., Cano, I., Andersson, C. and Edwards, M. (2016) *An Evaluation of Intuitive Recovery: Interim Report*. Sheffield: Helena Kennedy Centre for International Justice.

Bryman, A. (2006) 'Integrating quantitative and qualitative research: how is it done?', *Qualitative Research*, 6: 97–113.

Bryman, A. (2016) *Social Research Methods*, 5th edn. Oxford: Oxford University Press.

Creswell, J.W. and Plano Clark, V.L. (2011) *Designing and Conducting Mixed Methods Research*, 2nd edition. London: Sage.

Denscombe, M. (2002) *Ground Rules for Good Research: A 10 Point Guide for Social Researchers*. Buckingham: Open University Press.

Denscombe, M. (2014) *The Good Research Guide: For Small-Scale Social Research Projects*, 5th edn. Maidenhead: Open University Press.

Denzin, N.K. (2012) 'Triangulation 2.0', *Journal of Mixed Methods Research*, 6(2): 80–8.

De Vaus, D. (2002) *Surveys in Social Research*, 5th edn. London: Routledge.

Greene, J.C. (2007) *Mixed Methods in Social Inquiry*. San Francisco: Jossey-Bass.

Greene, J.C., Caracelli, V.J. and Graham, W.F. (1989) 'Toward a conceptual framework for mixed-method evaluation designs', *Educational Evaluation and Policy Analysis*, 11(3): 255–74.

Guba, E.G. and Lincoln, Y.S. (1994) 'Competing paradigms in qualitative research', in N.K. Denzin and Y.S. Lincoln (eds), *Handbook of Qualitative Research*. Thousand Oaks, CA: Sage, pp. 105–17.

Hammersley, M. (1992) 'The paradigm wars: reports from the front', *British Journal of Sociology of Education*, 13: 131–43.

Harrits, G.S. (2011) 'More than method? A discussion of paradigm differences within mixed methods research', *Journal of Mixed Methods Research*, 5(2): 150–66.

Heap, V. (2010) 'Understanding Public Perceptions of Anti-Social Behaviour: Problems and Policy Responses', PhD dissertation, University of Huddersfield, UK.

Layder, D. (1993) *New Strategies in Social Research*. Cambridge: Polity Press.

Layder, D. (1998) *Sociological Practice: Linking Theory and Social Research*. London: Sage.

Lipscomb, M. (2008) 'Mixed method nursing studies: a critical realist critique', *Nursing Philosophy*, 9(1): 32–45.

Maruna, S. and King, A. (2009) '"Once a criminal, always a criminal?" Redeemability and the psychology of punitive public attitudes', *European Journal of Criminal Policy and Research, 15*: 7–24.

Mayoh, J. and Onwuegbuzie, A.J. (2015) 'Toward a conceptualization of mixed methods phenomenological research', *Journal of Mixed Methods Research, 9*(1): 91–107.

Mertens, D.M. (2009) *Transformative Research and Education*. New York: Guilford.

Morse, J.M. and Niehaus, L. (2009) *Mixed Method Design: Principles and Procedures*. Walnut Creek, CA: Left Coast Press.

Oakley, A. (1999) 'Paradigm wars: some thoughts on a personal and public trajectory', *International Journal of Social Research Methodology, 2*: 247–54.

Onwuegbuzie, A.J. and Frels, R.K. (2013) 'Toward a new research philosophy for addressing social justice issues: critical dialectical pluralism', *International Journal of Multiple Research Approaches, 7*(1): 9–26.

Onwuegbuzie, A.J. and Johnson, R.B. (2006) 'The validity issue in mixed research', *Research in the Schools, 13*(1): 48–63.

Onwuegbuzie, A.J. and Leech, N.L. (2006) 'Linking research questions to mixed methods data analysis procedures', *The Qualitative Report, 11*(3): 474–98.

Onwuegbuzie, A.J., Johnson, R.B. and Mt Collins, K. (2009) 'Call for mixed analysis: a philosophical framework for combining qualitative and quantitative approaches', *International Journal of Multiple Research Approaches, 3*(2): 114–39.

Pawson, R. and Tilley, N. (1997) *Realistic Evaluation*. London: Sage.

Plano Clark, V.L. and Creswell, J.W. (2008) 'Methodological selections', in V.L. Plano Clark and J.W. Creswell (eds), *The Mixed Methods Reader*. Thousand Oaks, CA: Sage.

Plano Clark, V.L. and Badiee, M. (2010) 'Research questions in mixed methods research', in A. Tashakkori and C. Teddlie (eds), *Sage Handbook of Mixed Methods in Social and Behavioral Research*. Thousand Oaks, CA: Sage, pp. 275–304.

Platts-Fowler, D. and Robinson, D. (2015) 'A place for integration: refugee experiences in two English cities', *Population, Space and Place, 21*(5): 476–91.

Tashakkori, A. and Teddlie, C. (1998) *Mixed Methodology: Combining Qualitative and Quantitative Approaches*. Thousand Oaks, CA: Sage.

Teddlie, C. and Tashakkori, A. (2003) 'Major issues and controversies in the use of mixed methods in the social and behavioral sciences', in A. Tashakkori and C. Teddlie (eds), *Handbook of Mixed Methods in Social and Behavioral Research*. Thousand Oaks, CA: Sage, pp. 3–50.

Teddlie, C. and Tashakkori, A. (2009) *Foundations of Mixed Methods Research*. Thousand Oaks, CA: Sage.

Teddlie, C. and Tashakkori, A. (2010) 'Overview of contemporary issues in mixed methods research', in A. Tashakkori and C. Teddlie (eds), *Sage Handbook of Mixed Methods in Social and Behavioral Research*. Thousand Oaks, CA: Sage, pp. 1–41.

Waters, J. (2009) 'Illegal Drug Use Among Older Adults', PhD dissertation, University of Sheffield, UK.

Waters, J. (2015) 'Snowball sampling: a cautionary tale involving a study of older drug users', *International Journal of Social Research Methodology, 18*(4): 367–80. literature review

CHAPTER CONTENTS

GLOSSARY TERMS

ontology
epistemology
inquest
abolitionist
positivist
self-inflicted deaths (SIDs)

6

THE POLITICS AND ETHICS OF CRIMINOLOGICAL RESEARCH

DAVID SCOTT

INTRODUCTION

The ways in which we understand the world we live in and how we talk about social reality influence not only what we consider to be right or wrong but also whether we consider it important that this state of affairs continues or is brought to an end. Our current 'knowledge' about 'crime', harm and punishment come from a number of different sources, but one of the most significant is criminological research. But how is the knowledge generated, and what are the underlying assumptions that shape the questions and findings of such research? This chapter is about the politics and ethics of doing criminological research and it starts by introducing the philosophical conceptions of ontology and epistemology, two important ideas referred to throughout the chapter which bring to our attention competing interpretations of the nature of social reality and questions regarding the legitimacy of criminological knowledge. It is important that we think carefully about *how we know things (epistemology)* and *what things are (ontology)* as this shapes the way we act. Ultimately, *what* we know and *how* we know it are informed by our politics and ethics. To illustrate how political and ethical considerations shape the way we conceive and evidence social realities, the chapter refers to a number of critical studies on imprisonment, with particular focus on the competing ways of framing self-inflicted deaths. A self-inflicted death (SID) occurs when somebody takes their own life. This only becomes a suicide if the person *intended to die* and is officially defined as such by the Coroner's Court at an inquest. The distinction between a suicide and SID is very important because a number of prisoners in the past have died when acts of 'self-harm', intended only as a 'cry for help', have gone wrong and resulted in their death, and also because of the way in which prisoner deaths are recorded by the Prison Service.

Significantly, this chapter explores the politics and then the ethics of doing criminological research from an abolitionist perspective. When addressing the politics of criminological research, the chapter locates the 'search for truth' within the context of State power, social divisions and an increasing emphasis on research funding and sponsorship. It is argued that our current political climate has facilitated the (self)-policing of 'deviant' criminologists and the privileging of research projects which share the domain assumptions of the State. The ethics of criminological research are then surveyed, with four influential approaches considered: the justification of research on the grounds of its positive consequences; the promotion of close adherence to Research Ethics Boards' (REBs); emphasis on cultivating the virtues of the researcher; and a focus on ethical questions which arise during the research itself. The chapter concludes with some critical reflections on the challenges of doing criminological research ethically.

ONTOLOGY AND EPISTEMOLOGY

Different researchers have contrasting ideas about *what prison is* and *how we should understand prison life*. We can see in Table 6.1 some of the differences between two contrasting perspectives on the prison place: penal reform and penal abolition.

TABLE 6.1 Differences between penal reform and penal abolitionism

Penal reform – assumptions about the nature of prison reality (what prison is):	Examples from this perspective:
• Prison can be a humane and safe place • Healthy prisons can be a conduit for positive change/rehabilitation • Calls for change are primarily focused on the criminal process • As valid justifications of the deprivation of liberty are assumed to exist, the legitimacy of the State's power to punish is largely unquestioned	Andrew Rutherford (1986) *Prisons and the Process of Justice* London: Heinemann David Ramsbottom (2003*) Prisongate* London: Free Press John Podmore (2013) *Out of Sight, Out of Mind* London: Biteback Alison Liebling (2003) *Prisons and their Moral Performance* Oxford: OUP
The way knowledge is generated (how we should understand prison life):	HMCIP (2016) *HMCIP Annual Report* London: HMCIP
• Key sources include those from academics, policy makers, official reports and practitioners • Key informants can include prisoners, policy makers and practitioners • Key questions are often functional and policy orientated in nature and aimed at finding answers about improving penal practices	Vivien Stern (1984) *Bricks of Shame* Harmondsworth: Penguin Howard League for Penal Reform: http://howardleague.org Prison Reform Trust: www.prisonreformtrust.org.uk
Abolitionists – assumptions about the nature of prison reality (what prison is):	**Examples from this perspective:**
• Prisons are considered to be places of inherent harm, suffering and death • The pains of imprisonment may be ameliorated but not removed • People cannot be taught how to live freely whilst in captivity • Penal change must correspond with social change (moves beyond criminal process) • As prisons contradict basic human values, the legitimacy of the power to punish and the deprivation of liberty are questioned	Davis, A.Y. (2003) *Abolition Democracy* New York: Seven Stories Press Drake, D. (2010) *Prisons, Punishment and the Pursuit of Justice* London: Palgrave Moore, L. and Scraton P. (2014) *The Incarceration of Women* London: Palgrave Scott, D. (2018) *Against Imprisonment* Winchester: Waterside Press Scott, D. and Codd, H. (2010) *Controversial Issues in Prison* Buckingham: Open University Press
The way knowledge is generated (how we should understand prison life):	
• The view from below is emphasized and subjugated, (silenced) voices are given a platform to be heard and, if appropriate, the	Scraton, P. and McCulloch, J. (eds) (2009) *The Violence of Incarceration.* London: Routledge

(Continued)

TABLE 6.1 (Continued)

position of the most excluded and disadvantaged people/group should be carefully (and selectively) adopted to ensure that this worldview is represented • Key questions reflect the ethical and political priorities of human rights, democratic accountability and social justice	Sim, J. (1990) *Medical Power in Prisons* Buckingham: Open University Press Sim, J. (2009) *Punishment and Prisons* London: Sage

The discussion in Table 6.1 focuses on the 'what' and the 'how' questions of penal reform and abolitionism and how they impact on assumptions about penal realities and the legitimacy of knowledge generated by prison researchers. Such questions of legitimate knowledge are very important because they remind us that criminological research does not exist in a political or moral vacuum. When thinking about doing criminological research, it is essential that we first situate the (re)production of criminological knowledge within the everyday conflicts, moral dilemmas and power relations of the 'real world'. Of course, this immediately begs questions regarding how, in the first instance, we should understand and generate knowledge about human life (Haiven and Khasnabish, 2014; Mills, 1959). In the academic literature, the 'what' and the 'how' questions of criminological research are framed around the interlinked philosophical conceptions of ontology (the nature of social reality) and epistemology (the nature of knowledge).

BOX 6.1   ONTOLOGY (THE NATURE OF SOCIAL REALITY)

When criminologists talk of 'ontology', they are referring to:

1. A specific way of understanding the nature and reality of a given society/set of social conditions
2. What we can expect if certain social conditions remain the same as they are now
3. The manner in which such social conditions influence the possibility (or denial) of positive social change in the future.

Let us once again take the example of the prison to illustrate the three aspects of ontology (nature of social reality) highlighted in Box 6.1. The ontology of a liberal penal researcher who is committed to penal reform is that while the prison is a painful environment justified on the grounds of punishing offenders, it can also be a place that can generate positive human change. In other words, prisons can act as conduits for prisoner rehabilitation. Liberal penal researchers argue, however, that existing prison conditions often fail to meet the necessary requirements to achieve this goal, hence the need for prison reform. The prison's potential to bring about positive transformations of the human soul is only possible *if* the prison in the future is a good, healthy, virtuous and moral institution (Liebling, 1992). The ontology of a researcher who thinks prisons should be abolished is very different. For the abolitionist prison researcher, the prison is an inherently harmful place characterized by suffering and death. Although there have been times when the prison has facilitated positive human transformations, such instances are the exceptions that prove the rule. Prisons are places primarily of dehabilitation rather than rehabilitation. Further, the prison cannot be successfully reformed in the future because it is a place of harm, misery and denigration shaped by institutionally structured violence. Institutionally structured violence refers to the systematic denials of human need and the generation of injury, harm and death by the daily workings of a given State institution. As prisons will always be inhumane and immoral institutions, abolitionist researchers argue that they should be closed down and life-affirming alternatives promoted in their place (Scott, 2016a, 2018).

The ontological assumptions about the nature of social reality inevitably impact on 'epistemology' – that is, understandings of the nature of knowledge and how researchers attempt to distinguish between claims of what is true and what is false (i.e. legitimate knowledge).

BOX 6.2   EPISTEMOLOGY (HOW WE GO ABOUT KNOWING ABOUT THE WORLD AND HOW WE DISTINGUISH BETWEEN WHAT IS TRUE AND FALSE)

When criminologists talk of epistemology, they are referring to the way of defining, describing and evidencing the 'truth' of a given approach to social reality (ontology). This means thinking about:

- the basic assumptions underpinning the research project (and what is missing)
- which academic references and other sources are utilized in the study (and what research and data are not counted as appropriate evidence)
- who are the key informants/focus of the research (and who is excluded)
- what questions are to be asked (and what questions are not asked)
- whose voice is heard and given greatest credibility/authority (and which voices are not heard/are discredited).

Epistemology (the nature of knowledge) is important because the kind of questions researchers ask, and to whom, can lead to very different forms of evidence/knowledge about the kind of society that we live in and thus reaffirm or question previous ontological assumptions. Different researchers have different ontologies and epistemologies. Indeed, when reading prison research it can sometimes feel like two very different literatures exist. One would anticipate (correctly) that the sources approvingly cited, questions asked and focus of the research project of a liberal penal researcher are often very different to those of a researcher who thinks that prison should be abolished. A shorthand way of discovering a researcher's ontology is to read their list of references in a given publication. Whilst this is not always the case (some sources cited may be selectively presented or only used to indicate that the author is aware of their contribution to the field), it can often reveal their basic assumptions about the world/nature of social reality.

What the above discussion indicates is that to fully understand the tensions regarding how social research is conceived, supported, produced and disseminated, we need to consider the politics and ethics of doing criminological research.

THE POLITICS OF SOCIAL RESEARCH

We have discussed above the manner in which the researcher's approach to knowledge is shaped by their assumptions about social reality. Such ontological assumptions and epistemological priorities are inevitably tied to the political context of the research itself. We shall explore the politics of criminological research in four different sections:

- the search for truth
- scientific relevancy
- the policing of researchers
- funding fit.

The search for truth

There are contrasting views regarding the politics of criminological research. For some social scientists, like Hammersley (1995, 2015), it is possible to focus on an exclusive pursuit of the truth. For Hammersley (1995: 40), the meaning of 'value neutrality' is the commitment to uncovering things as they actually are and the generation of knowledge that is 'of value in itself and/or has desirable consequences in the world'. From this perspective, a scientifically pure form of research is thought to be achievable and, in this view, research can transcend social circumstances and be an objective study of the lived realities of participants. The ontological and epistemological assumptions are that the social world can be objectively analysed and that an untarnished and 'apolitical knowledge' can be produced so long as the researcher is focused on *the search for truth*. Knowledge production, however, is closely associated with power relations and the proposition that there can be 'value-free' knowledge has been strongly contested (Behr et al., 2013; Schumann, 2013). Specifically, critical thinkers like Walters (2003) have argued that social research is often used to reinforce existing power relations and social divisions and thus acts in the interests of the current social order rather than provide an objective analysis. In our time of 'market-led' (Walters, 2003) criminological research, the designs and methodologies of criminological studies often reflect the ontological assumptions of the State. The State is a configuration of alliances in a given historical moment which mediates power relations and intervenes in social life. It is a collection of different institutions, actors and partnerships working in alliance together. As a state is always in flux, with new and different partners potentially joining forces to exercise power, it can be a site for class struggle and resistance, meaning that engagement with the State can lead to progressive and emancipatory change, but such outcomes are by no means certain. Indeed, the research independence for those who closely align with State institutions can be fatally undermined by either the external constraints of government authorities or research funders. Whatever the aspirations of the researcher, considerable constraints can undoubtedly be placed on any apparently neutral *search for truth*.

Scientific relevancy

Schumann (2013) notes that the State has historically drawn a distinction between 'proper' criminologists – who advocate a 'pseudo-science' of criminology; and 'deviant' criminologists – who examine law, conflict and harm in their social contexts. He suggests that the former category play a central role in legitimizing the repressive practices of penal institutions such as the prison. Legitimacy refers to the correct, justified and valid way of doing something. As there are a number of different approaches regarding the 'right way' of doing research, the validity of certain research findings has been contested. Schumann dismisses claims to scientific objectivity prevalent within the positivist orientations of mainstream criminology as the work of 'charlatan scientists'. Positivist criminology is underscored by the belief that the methods and methodologies of the natural sciences can be applied to the study of human life. Schumann, however, identifies various 'deceptive practices' adopted by positivistic criminologists in order to demonstrate legitimation. First, there is a claim that criminology is a unique and coherent subject which is able to explain 'crime'. Noting that the only consistent feature of all 'crimes' is that they are labelled as such by actors within the criminal process, Schumann (2013) dismisses these claims as an 'illusion' designed to obscure the partial application of criminal law against the poor, marginalized and excluded. Second, there is the claim that 'legitimate' criminological research adopts the highest standards in research methodology. What is considered as legitimate research is often shackled to restrictive methodological practices. Schumann suggests that this attachment to scientific research standards (positivism) is problematic as it can lead to the rejection of critical research which falls foul of the scientific model.

This discussion is particularly important at a time when criminological knowledge has become commodified, transferred out of the public sphere and into the realm of the private sector, as researchers find themselves under increasing pressure to sell their services to the highest bidder (Walters, 2003). A culture of managerialism means that research which is not easily quantifiable, producing 'scientific' results that are immediately clear and implementable, is simply not considered 'relevant'. Whilst those who legitimate State agendas make a great deal of 'noise', those who propose alternative narratives are 'silenced, inaudible above the consensus of the technicians and the suffocating policy demands of the State' (Hillyard et al., 2004: 372). Here, the definition of 'relevant research' is research that serves the interests of the State by legitimating existing policy initiatives, especially those that encourage privatization and the growth of the penal apparatus (p. 374). It is important then that such understandings of 'relevancy' are contested and alternative formulations – grounded in what is *relevant* for ordinary people and the harms, problems and difficulties they encounter on a day-to-day basis – are at the forefront of criminological research. Accepting State definitions of a given set of social circumstances inevitably rules in and rules out certain realities (ontology), thus shaping legitimate knowledge (epistemology).

The policing of researchers

Schumann (2013) goes on to consider the growing prevalence of the patronage of criminological research by the State in terms of research funding. These developments have led to what Schumann describes as an 'access for loyalty bargain' – an understanding that the researcher will not report on her observations in a way that will harm the funder or the institution studied. The impact of disloyalty by 'deviant' criminologists is the rejection of research findings and a perceived incompatibility in terms of future research projects. This may result in the self-policing of researchers so they can continue to receive State funding – such as from the police service, the Ministry of Justice or the Home Office – for future studies. For Walters (2003), there are also other forms of policing researchers. The technocratic and pragmatic needs of government departments and funders/sponsors not only shape the parameters of what is researched (and what is not) but also place a straightjacket on academic independence by the monitoring of the research process itself:

> [Research] contracts may include legal requirements that the researcher meet monthly with the client to discuss progress, that the researcher notify the client in writing of any

changes to the original methodology, that the researcher submit one or two interim reports before the final report, that the principal researcher have all staff approved by the client, and that any changes to the research team be brought to the client's attention in writing. (Walters, 2003: 87)

The policing of researchers is nothing new. One of the most well-known examples is the study of long-term prisoners in Durham prison by Stan Cohen and Laurie Taylor in the early 1970s. Cohen and Taylor (1972) drew on an innovative methodology and proposed that the ontological assumptions of the research should be determined by prisoners themselves. The Home Office considered the research unscientific and after the Prison Department (now the Prison Service) had placed intolerable constraints upon the research methodology, the project was abandoned.

Today, there are specific requirements for undertaking research in prisons. The decision on access to research in prisons was made by Her Majesty's Prison and Probation Service (HMPPS) and there is a long and detailed application form (see Box 6.3).

BOX 6.3 HMPPS RESEARCH APPLICATION PROCESS

Anyone planning to conduct research in prisons must submit an HMPPS research application form. The HMPPS application is the process that covers all research projects requiring access to data, staff or offenders (and not just prisons). All research applications are reviewed on the following criteria:

- Are there enough links to HMPPS priorities?
- What are the likely demands on resources, e.g. staff time, office requirements, data providers?
- Is there an overlap with other current or recent research?
- How appropriate and able is the methodology?
- Are there any data protection/security issues?
- Are there any ethical considerations?
- What is the extent of the applicant's research skills and experience?

Source: Her Majesty's Prison and Probation Service (www.gov.uk/government/ organisations/her-majestys-prison-and-probation-service/about/research)

Funding fit

Funding fit refers to the level of correspondence between the ontological assumptions of the research funder and the researcher. Let us return to the running theme in this chapter around the ontological and epistemological assumptions of the prison place. In so doing we shall consider the framing of self-inflicted deaths in prison and 'funding fit'. A self-inflicted death (SID) occurs when someone takes their own life. In England and Wales, a prisoner kills themselves on average once every three days (INQUEST, 2016). Every five hours, a prisoner is officially recorded as attempting to take their own life and every 20 minutes a prisoner is officially recorded as having self-harmed. The likelihood of a prisoner taking their own life is between four and eleven times higher than the general population. For some liberal penal reformers (especially those closely associated with the Prison Research Centre at the Cambridge Institute of Criminology, such as Alison Liebling) and in much contemporary penal policy and practice, it is assumed that SIDs arise from a combination of 'risky prisoners', who may or may not be psychiatrically ill, and an inability to cope with the stress of confinement. A highly stressful environment for 'non-copers' is believed to turn already existing emotional disturbances into suicidal ideation (the idea of suicide). Suicidal prisoners simply do not have the personal resources to cope with the deprivations of an 'unhealthy' and poorly performing prison (Liebling, 1992). The ontological assumption is that the prison environment can be healthy and safe for people with vulnerabilities, but becomes deadly when it falls below certain standards.

For prison abolitionists, the idea of dividing prisoners between 'copers' and 'non-copers' is problematic because it creates false assumptions about who is and who is not 'suicide prone'. Indeed, as Cohen and Taylor (1972) pointed out many years ago, most prisoners only just about cope with prison life. The real pains of imprisonment are not to be found in the given quality of living conditions, relationships with staff or levels of crowding, but in the denial of personal autonomy, feelings of time consciousness and the lack of an effective vocabulary to express the hardship of watching life waste away. Prisons are institutions structured in such a way that they systematically deny human need and generate suicidal ideation. Deaths in prison should not then be considered as aberrations or malfunctions of the system but rather traced back to the daily processes of imprisonment itself (Scott, 2014).

BOX 6.4   THE HARRIS REVIEW

The Harris Review is an independent review into self-inflicted deaths in NOMS (National Offender Management Service) custody of 18–24-year-olds, which found:

- that all young people in custody are regarded as vulnerable
- a focus on the State duty to care for prisoners and the vulnerabilities generated by State confinement
- an importance of State accountability for deaths in prison
- a recognition of the devastating impact on prisoner families

- it was informed by evidence from lobby groups, practitioners, academics and families
- a key and explicit aim of learning lessons from previous self-inflicted deaths
- calls for a reconsideration of the purpose of prison and how it is currently used.

In one of the most radical analyses of SIDs in prison in recent times, Lord Toby Harris (2015), in his official independent inquiry (Box 6.4), noted that 'the prison environment is grim, bleak and demoralising to the spirit'. Drawing on the evidence of bereaved prisoner families, prisoners and a wider range of penological experts, the Harris Review (2015) moved beyond the ontological assumptions of the Prison Service and argued that rather than focusing on the individual failings, risks and vulnerabilities of prisoners who have died, we should instead acknowledge that responsibility for such deaths lies with the State. The government response to the report was disappointing, if not unsurprising: 33 of the 108 recommendations of the Harris Review (2015) were rejected outright. Further, only a few months after the publication of the Harris Review (2015) new research was commissioned on SIDs in prison. This invitation for tender (Box 6.5) asked for researchers to explore once again the relationship between SIDs and individual responsibility, risk factors and mental health, whereas broader concerns about State irresponsibility and structured violence are ignored (Department of Health, 2016).

BOX 6.5   DEATHS IN CUSTODY INVITATION FOR TENDER (DOH)

The Deaths in Custody project, up for tender, aimed to:

- look at how vulnerable individuals can be better identified
- identify gender and age-specific vulnerabilities
- identify how risks can be better anticipated and acted upon
- examine trends to establish changes in particular (vulnerable) groups over time
- examine environmental and clinical antecedents to SIDs' contribution of environment/ regimes/conditions to risk factors
- examine barriers to implementing procedures and information sharing
- examine emergency procedures
- review changes to health care and prison officer training to reduce SIDS.

Source: Department of Health (2016)

The Harris Review (Box 6.4) and DoH Tender (Box 6.5) are therefore based on different ontologies about prison (i.e. the assumption of the Harris Review that prison is a place of pain and harm that undermines the coping strategies of all prisoners compared with the assumption of the DoH Tender that prison only poses a life risk for those people that are considered as vulnerable); and about what can be achieved (i.e. the assumption of the Harris Review that as prison is inherently harmful the only plausible policy option that can reduce SIDs is to rethink imprisonment and radically reduce the prison population compared with the assumption of the DoH Tender that improved identification of at-risk and vulnerable prisoners, alongside improved training, emergency procedures and better information sharing can reduce SIDs); and different epistemologies (i.e. the generation of knowledge through the view from below and prisoner families in the Harris Review compared with the call by the DoH for research focused on the workings of the current Prison Service policies and practices). This comparison illustrates that how we think about a problem, the questions that are asked and who the informants are can perform a significant part in shaping the conclusions and recommendations of research on the same issue.

THE ETHICS OF SOCIAL RESEARCH

The previous section has explored some of the political factors shaping the ontological and epistemological dimensions of criminological research. These are important but research methodologies and designs are not shaped by politics alone. Criminological research must also be understood within its ethical context. Ethical questions provide a further set of considerations. I argue that such considerations are much more likely to be regulated by individual conscience or professional bodies than by the State or funders/sponsors. We shall explore the ethics of criminological research in four different sections:

1. Consequentialist ethics
2. Ethical guidelines, principles and duties
3. Virtuous researchers
4. Situational and relational ethics.

Consequentialist ethics

The 'consequentialist approach' is based on the assumption that the ends justify the means. Thus, a criminological research project should be judged on its results and not how the findings were ascertained. If a research project provides new insights, then the authors could argue that how this knowledge was gleaned is irrelevant: the positive consequences derived from the study mean the research should have been undertaken. There are a number of studies that have been criticized for adopting unethical research methods (Humphreys, 1970; Milgram, 1974) but here we focus on the infamous Stanford Prison Experiment (see Box 6.6 and Box 6.7), undertaken in the basement of Stanford University's Jordan Hall in the summer of 1971 (Haney, 2009; Haney et al., 1973; Zimbardo, 2009).

BOX 6.6   STANFORD PRISON EXPERIMENT 1971

In an attempt to understand how situational power relations impacted on individual identities, the social psychologists Phillip Zimbardo, Craig Haney, Curt Banks and David Jaffe created a simulated prison environment in the basement of their university psychology department; 18 men were recruited and randomly assigned to be either a prisoner or a guard in the experiment. At any one time, there were nine prisoners and three guards on duty, rotating on 8-hour shifts. The prisoners wore nylon stocking caps, ankle chains and had their prison number sewn on the back of their uniform. Within literally hours of the start of the experiment, which was originally planned for two weeks, significant behavioural changes were noted in both prisoners and guards. Perhaps overly influenced by cultural representations of prisons and prison officers in films such as *Cool Hand Luke* (released in 1967), a number of the guards became aggressive and abusive, effectively dehumanizing the prisoners and abusing their power in cruel and sadistic ways. Treatment of prisoners (especially those who rebelled) included being stripped naked; denial of sleep; solitary confinement; deprivation of meals and blankets; and being forced to do push-ups and other meaningless activities. After showing signs of depression, apathy and submissiveness, nearly half of the prisoners had to be released after only a few days. The experiment itself was terminated on day six because of serious concerns for the safety and wellbeing of all those participating.

Source: Haney (2009); Haney et al. (1973)

BOX 6.7   THE JOHN WAYNE SHIFT

John Wayne was the nickname for the guard who was the meanest and toughest of them all; his reputation had preceded him in various accounts I had heard. Of course, I was eager to see who he was and what he was doing that attracted so much attention. When I looked through the observation point, I was absolutely

(Continued)

(Continued)

stunned to see that their John Wayne was the 'really nice guy' with whom I had chatted earlier. Only now, he was transformed into someone else. … It was an amazing transformation from the person I had just spoken to – a transformation that had taken place in minutes just by stepping over the line from the outside world into that prison yard. With his military-style uniform, billy club in hand, and dark, silver-reflecting sunglasses to hide his eyes … this guy was an all-business, no-nonsense, really mean prison guard …

After a brief consultation between John Wayne and his little sidekick, Burdan, a new sexual game is devised: 'Okay, now pay attention. You three are going to be female camels. Get over here and bend over touching your hands to the floor.' (When they do, their naked butts are exposed since they are wearing no underwear beneath their smock-dresses.) Hellmann (guard John Wayne) continues with obvious glee, 'Now you two, you're male camels. Stand behind the female camels and *hump* them'.

Burdan giggles at this double entendre. Although their bodies never touch, the helpless prisoners are simulating sodomy by making thrusting motions of humping. They are dismissed back to their cells as the guards retreat to their quarters, clearly feeling that they have earned their night's salary. My nightmare from last night is coming true. I am glad that now I can control it by ending it all tomorrow.

Source: Zimbardo (2009: 169)

Although the Stanford Prison Experiment had some intellectual utility (see discussion in Box 6.6 and Box 6.7), it is on shaky grounds in terms of consequentialist ethics. This is because the second dimension of consequentialist ethics is that we should look to minimize harmful consequences. In this particular study, significant harm was inflicted on the research participants. Whilst this was most notably on the prisoners, the 'John Wayne' prison guard also experienced trauma and depression following the experiment as he came to terms with both his notorious exploits and the reactions of others. Although a small number of similar studies have been conducted (see, for example, the BBC prison study *The Experiment* in 2002), ethical concerns have largely closed down this type of research.

Ethical guidelines, principles and duties

The key principles of social research ethics were laid down by the *Belmont Report* (National Commission for the Protection of Human Subjects of Biomedical and Behavioural Research, 1979). Almost 40 years ago, the *Belmont Report* provided an early template for ethical guidelines of University Research Ethics Boards (REBs), emphasizing the importance of not harming research participants. Research participants should not suffer physical harm, loss of self-esteem or experience unnecessary stress. They should be protected by anonymity and confidentiality in analysis and dissemination (i.e. publication). Criminological research should also be guided by informed consent, provision of sufficient information for participants and voluntariness; a clear assessment of risks and benefits; and the selection of subjects by fair procedures (Israel, 2015). Haggerty (2016: 15), however, warns of how Research Ethics Boards (REBs) can also contribute to the policing of criminological research. REBs may promote risk reduction and protect the reputation of the university rather than seeking to reflect the intellectual or social importance of creating new knowledge. Ethics can be trumped by risk.

A number of the principles found in the *Belmont Report* are also to be found in the *2015 Code of Ethics of the British Society of Criminology* (BSC – see Box 6.8). Yet, reflections on the ethics of research lead us back to key questions around ontology and epistemology. As Walters (2003) has highlighted, criminological research funding has reached a new zenith in recent years and this pressure to conform is illustrated in the 2015 BSC ethics code. Sections 5.1 and 5.2 remind researchers that they should 'avoid damaging confrontations with funding agencies and the

---

BOX 6.8   BRITISH SOCIETY OF CRIMINOLOGY 2015 CODE OF ETHICS

SECTION 5: RELATIONSHIPS WITH SPONSORS

Researchers should:

1. seek to maintain good relationships with all funding and professional agencies in order to achieve the aim of advancing knowledge about criminological issues and to avoid bringing the wider criminological community into disrepute with these agencies. In particular, researchers should seek to avoid damaging confrontations with funding agencies and the participants of research which may reduce research possibilities for other researchers.
2. seek to clarify in advance the respective obligations of funders and researchers and their institutions and encourage written agreements wherever possible. They should recognise their obligations to funders whether contractually defined or only the subject of informal or unwritten agreements. They should attempt to complete research projects to the best of their ability within contractual or unwritten agreements. Researchers have a responsibility to notify the sponsor/funder of any proposed departure from the terms of reference.

Source: British Society of Criminology (2015) at www.britsoccrim.org/documents/BSCEthics2015.pdf

participants of research'. This could imply compliance so that future opportunities for funding are not damaged. As Schumann (2013), Behr et al. (2013) and Walters (2003) have warned, this could mean adopting methodologies and epistemologies which reflect the priorities and ontologies of the State.

This discussion of risk and rule-bound ethics raises important questions about undertaking interviews with 'vulnerable' research participants and asking questions on sensitive and emotive topic areas. Taking the example of self-harm and attempted SIDs in prison once again, it is possible that asking prisoners about their experience of coping/not coping with imprisonment may be traumatizing for participants. It may be deeply upsetting for some to talk about the harmful outcomes of the prison place. On the other hand, prisons are places that systematically generate hurt and injury and so any probing inquiry inevitably touches on such emotive issues. Indeed, by providing a sympathetic ear and a platform for their voice to be heard, the research may even be a cathartic and empowering experience. People react to research questions differently, but all participants who are talking about a harmful experience will probably find this painful to some extent. Researchers should not be silenced or prevented from asking difficult questions, though it is important they are sensitive and responsive to the emotional feelings of participants in that moment, recognizing that interviews may have to be prematurely ended if distressing for respondents.

Virtuous researchers

Research principles and guidelines are undoubtedly good things but they are not always helpful in the day-to-day situational context of doing research (Carlen, 2016). Many of the ethical decisions researchers need to make cannot be codified. For virtue ethicists like Fricker (2007), researchers should have good character and be committed to the *search for truth* (see also Hammersley, 1995; Gregory, 2003). Accepting that there can be no objective or value-free research, for Fricker (2007) problems arise when epistemology is either compromised by a bias or prejudice against the credibility of the worldview of research participants or when researchers do not have the appropriate social or cultural resources to understand participant worldviews. Consequently, the best guide for doing ethical research is to habituate researchers into the culture and practices of research excellence. By this she means training researchers in virtues around unprejudiced listening, ethical trust, respect, honesty, sensitivity and scholarship so that they can develop their own 'ethical consciousness' and a 'virtuous perception' of the world (Fricker, 2007: 74). In so doing, researchers will develop wise and virtuous judgements and become reflexive enough to recognize their own privileged position and personal prejudices.

For Fricker (2007) though, this individual pursuit of excellence is not always enough. There may also be collective (societal) failures of interpretation (how we understand). Here, whole social experiences may be 'obscured' from our collective understanding. The research subject is in effect silenced. If researchers cannot understand or frame an issue/harm appropriately, they therefore are unable to communicate it effectively to others. One example is the prisoner experience of the pains of imprisonment. On the surface, the daily prison regime seems mundane. Some have even gone as far as to claim that it is easy – a 'holiday camp' (Barrett, 2015). Yet one of the most insidious aspects of imprisonment is the manner in which the enforced boredom of prison life leads to an increased sense of time consciousness (Cohen and Taylor, 1972). There is no obvious language available to describe the sense of waste, longing and loss generated through the awareness of the passing of time, and this lack of understanding only exacerbates the pains of imprisonment (Scott, 2016a). Fricker (2007) suggests that what we need is a new common sense – a new shared interpretation – of the lived realities of the marginalized and excluded and a commitment to become a responsible and 'virtuous hearer' (Fricker, 2007: 5): that is, to be prepared to listen carefully, empathetically and without prejudice not only to what is said but also what is not said, thus identifying structural denials of voice (Cohen, 2001).

Situational and relational ethics

Relational and situational ethics locate a research participant's position within the broader structural power relations of advanced capitalist societies and are sensitive to how this can impact on perceptions of truth and credibility. Because we are dealing with human relationships, objectivity and value neutrality are considered impossible and constructions of social reality (ontology) are understood within the context of oppressive power relations and intersections between different social identities (Barton, 2006). Asymmetries of power are also important in shaping ethical commitments and obligations. For the ethicist Dussel (2013), the researcher's ethical responsibilities are tied to those participants who have the least power and/or ability to present an accurate representation of their lived realities.

Social and criminological researchers alike are tasked with the responsibility of illuminating the experiences of those people on the margins of society – those who have been exploited, dominated and oppressed. Epistemology should be directed to eliciting knowledge and understandings of worldviews that have been forgotten or erased in mainstream analysis. Significantly, for Dussel (2013) knowledge claims are shaped through the actual encounter (relationship) with the research participant. Rather than just being 'virtuous hearers', there is an ethical responsibility to move beyond existing ways of interpreting the world (ontologies) and to embrace the worldview of the Other (that is, the person who is considered as an outsider and does not belong in our sense of community and sometimes, in extreme circumstances, our 'moral universe' as someone who counts as a fellow human being). This process will always be aspirational and unfinished because it demands the continual search for new inclusionary visions of social reality which acknowledge difference and diversity whilst at the same time recognizing what we all share: a common humanity. The promoting of new epistemologies (knowledge claims) grounded in the ontological assumptions (worldview) of those placed on the margins of society is known in criminological research as the 'view from below' (Scraton, 2004; Sim et al., 1987).

The 'view from below' is a way of looking at the world through the eyes of those people who, because of social structures, have limited credibility or authority. It highlights the importance of hearing the voice of the poor, marginalized or disempowered. It is central to the ethical and political priorities of critical criminology.

The ethical responsibilities placed on the researcher are much more than simply calculations of harm and utility, adherence to ethical guidelines, or developing excellent research skills and value judgements. For relational ethicists such as Dussel (2013) and McCormack (2014), the researcher has a responsibility to ensure that *all* are heard, even when words are not spoken. This means looking at the world through the eyes of the Other, adopting or translating their language, meanings and understandings, and trying to read any unexpected forms of communication (McCormack, 2014):

> When words cannot be heard, the body becomes the only means of communication. Hunger strikes, silent marches and destruction or harm to the self can be political actions that make manifest the extreme violence and inequality of the ruling system, and thus the impossibility of communication and justice under the existing institutional parameters. (McCormack, 2014: 184)

Thus, self-harm and para-suicide (attempted self-inflicted deaths) in prison may be ways of trying to communicate the unspeakable and ungraspable pain and suffering generated by institutionally structured violence (Scott, 2016a). SIDs may well be a tragically sad way of expressing a prisoner's ontology (reality) of prison life. The prison researcher therefore needs to learn to feel and understand the experience of otherness, to excavate silences, acknowledge that which is normally denied and attempt to translate into narrative form currently unarticulated stories of human life (McCormack, 2014).

Yet, for Dussel (2013), even this is still not enough to be considered an ethical researcher. The researcher must also show solidarity to sufferers by taking responsibility for the *rebuilding of lives* alongside a political commitment to *transform existing asymmetrical power relations*. The *search for truth* is essential but not a sufficient condition in itself to be ethical. As Haiven and Khasnabish (2014) argue, social researchers should stand alongside the dominated and exploited, locate themselves as part of their struggle for justice and help to facilitate their critical and emancipatory potential for social transformation. In the spirit of the left-wing philosophy of 'commonism' (working with the common people, for common goals in the common interest), Haiven and Khasnabish (2014) maintain that social research should be a collective endeavour that we do *with and for* others. As such, the ethics and politics of criminological research intimately intertwine.

SUMMARY AND REVIEW

This chapter has argued that social research cannot be understood outside of the existing social divisions and power relations (Barton et al., 2007). It has foregrounded the philosophical concepts of ontology and epistemology. In so doing it has drawn on research on suffering and death in the prison place, highlighting some of the ethical and political dilemmas that shape prison studies. The very different ontologies and epistemologies of liberal penal reformers and abolitionists have been highlighted, as well as how certain forms of critical knowledge can be sidelined or excluded because their epistemologies are inconsistent with the ontological assumptions of those who fund research. Penal abolitionists argue that the 'ontology' of the prison place is fundamentally predicated on violence, exploitation, infringements of human dignity, unnecessary suffering and death. Thus, for abolitionist 'epistemology' it is important to draw on the experiences of prisoners, as well as prisoner families and prison staff, and to validate their knowledge and experience. For Sim et al. (1987), Scraton (2004) and Scott (2016b), it is only through (carefully and empathetically but critically) hearing the voice of prisoners that a full understanding of imprisonment can be achieved. It is not that we should always agree with the view from below, but that we should ensure that *all* voices are heard and acknowledged, even if they are later challenged and alternative viewpoints promoted.

Criminological research is not only shaped by political factors. Ethical considerations are also important and quite rightly question the legitimacy of certain research practices that generate harm, such as the Stanford Prison Experiment. Exploring different ethical frameworks, it has been shown that, sometimes, the researcher's own ontological assumptions need to be challenged by the worldviews of people on the margins, to ensure that ethical duties and responsibilities are fully met. Further, for abolitionists the ethics and politics of social research are directly tied to ongoing social struggles against the harms of imprisonment, the repair of human injury and the building of non-penal radical alternatives grounded in the principles of social justice. There is then an interplay between ontological and epistemological assumptions that requires considerable reflection. This places considerations of ethics and politics at the heart of the research process. One major challenge of doing criminological research for both students and professional researchers is finding a way of thinking about ontology and epistemology that can meet the ethico-political priorities and demands explored in this chapter.

STUDY QUESTIONS AND ACTIVITIES FOR STUDENTS

1. Choose a criminological topic of interest and then identify the ontological assumptions and epistemological priorities of:

   a. public opinion
   b. the mainstream media

(Continued)

(Continued)

   c. politicians

   d. criminal justice agents

   e. the main criminological perspectives that have explored this topic.

Think then about your own ontological assumptions and epistemological priorities. In what ways are they similar to or different from those of the above? In what ways have they changed (if any) since you started studying criminology?

2. Is it possible for social research to be simply about the 'search for truth'? What are the possible obstacles that can be placed in the way of such a pursuit of value free and objective knowledge? How might some of those obstacles be overcome?

3. You are planning to undertake a research project in a prison. What are the ethical implications of your study and how would you ensure that you undertake the research in a way which complies with the four different ethical frameworks discussed in this chapter? How would you aim to avoid some of the problems encountered by penal researchers discussed in this chapter?

4. Look up the ethical guidelines of one or more of the following:

   ○ British Society of Criminology Statement of Ethics 2015 at www.britsoccrim. org/documents/BSCEthics2015.pdf

   ○ Singapore Statement on Research Integrity at www.singaporestatement. org

   ○ Belmont Report: Ethical Principles and Guidelines for the Protection of Human Subjects of Research at www.hhs.gov/ohrp/regulations-and-policy/belmont-report/index.html

   ○ your university.

Ask the lecturers (and PhD students) at your university about their experience of Research Ethics Boards. What kinds of issues have they encountered in the research? Have they been focused on research ethics or risk? Why would this distinction between ethics and risk be important?

SUGGESTIONS FOR FURTHER READING

I would recommend the below sources for students wishing to explore further key themes on research values, hearing voice and reflecting critically on undertaking social research in state institutions like the prison.

Research values are central to the ethics and politics of criminological research, and the websites of the BBC programme *The Experiment* (BBC, 2002) and the Stanford Prison Experiment (2017) provide detailed yet critical reflections on the ethical consequences of undertaking social psychological experiments on prison life. For a contrasting ethical framework regarding research values, see the statements of ethics by the British Society of Criminology (2015) and the Singapore Statement on Research Integrity (2010), both of which highlight the importance of following rules and guidelines when undertaking social research. One of the most influential criminological accounts of why research values matter is 'Talking about prison blues' (Cohen and Taylor, 1977), which provides a candid and insightful discussion of the problems the authors encountered when undertaking research with high security prisoners in HMP Durham in the early 1970s. A more recent account drawing on ethnographic work, this time focused on research on prison officers to illustrate critical research values, is Scott (2015b).

Hearing voice is also of great importance in critical social research. Listening to the view from below has been championed by many researchers, and one recent defence of this approach drawing on an explicitly ethical framework is Scott (2016b). The view from below, however, should not be viewed uncritically, and in an important contribution to the debate Sim (2003) notes that it is essential that researchers also emphasize 'whose side we are not on'. One of the best ways to understand how the ontological and epistemological assumptions of the researcher impact on the generation of criminological knowledge is to read a first-hand reflective account by an experienced researcher. This not only inevitably adds a human element to the narrative but also shines a spotlight on some of the most pertinent ethical and political dilemmas confronting criminologists in the field. Scraton (2016) and Scott (2015a) provide good recent examples of this kind of autobiographical and reflexive account of doing prison research from an abolitionist perspective.

REFERENCES

Barrett, D. (2015) 'Concerns over "holiday camp" jails', *The Telegraph*, 11 February. Available at: www.telegraph.co.uk/news/uknews/crime/11406172/Concerns-over-holiday-camp-jails.html (accessed 2 May 2018).

Barton, A., Corteen, K., Scott, D. and Whyte, D. (eds) (2006) *Expanding the Criminological Imagination*. London: Routledge.

BBC (2002) *The Experiment*. London: BBC. Available at: www.bbcprisonstudy.org (accessed 2 May 2018).

Behr, C.-P., Gipsen, D., Klien-Sconnfeld, S., Naffin, K. and Zilmer, H. (2013) 'State control: the use of scientific discoveries', in J. Gilmore, J.M. Moore and D. Scott (eds), *Critique and Dissent*. Ottawa: Red Quill Books.

British Society of Criminology (2015) *British Society of Criminology Code of Ethics 2015*. London: British Society of Criminology.

Carlen, P. (2016) 'Ethics, politics and the limits of knowledge', in M. Adorjan and R. Ricciardelli (eds), *Engaging with Ethics in International Criminological Research*. London: Routledge.

Cohen, S. (2001) *States of Denial*. Cambridge: Polity Press.

Cohen, S. and Taylor, L. (1972) *Psychological Survival*. Harmondsworth: Penguin.

Cohen, S. and Taylor, L. (1977) 'Talking about prison blues', in C. Bell and H. Newby (eds), *Doing Sociological Research*. London: Allen and Unwin.

Department of Health (DoH) (2016) *Invitation to Tender: A Review of Self-inflicted Deaths in the Criminal Justice System – Exploring Contributory Factors and Identifying Approaches*. London: DoH.

Dussel, E. (2013) *The Ethics of Liberation*. Durham, NC: Duke.

Fricker, M. (2007) *Epistemic Injustice: Power and the Ethics of Knowing*. Oxford: Oxford University Press.

Gregory, I. (2003) *Ethics in Research*. London: Continuum.

Haggerty, K. (2016) 'Ethics creep: governing social science research in the name of ethics', in M. Adorjan and R. Ricciardelli (eds), *Engaging with Ethics in International Criminological Research*. London: Routledge.

Haiven, M. and Khasnabish, A. (2014) *The Radical Imagination*. London: Zed Books.

Hammersley, M. (1995) *The Politics of Social Research*. London: Sage.

Hammersley, M. (2015) 'Research "inside" viewed from "outside": reflections on prison ethnography', in D. Drake, R. Earle and J. Sloan (eds), *The Palgrave Handbook of Prison Ethnography*. London: Palgrave.

Haney, C. (2009) *Reforming Punishment*. Washington, DC: American Psychological Association.

Haney, C., Banks, C. and Zimbardo, P. (1973) 'Interpersonal dynamics in a simulated prison', *International Journal of Criminology and Penology*, 1(1): 69–97.

Harris, T. (2015) *'The Harris Review': Independent Review into Self-Inflicted Deaths in NOMS Custody of 18–24 year olds*. London: HMSO. Available at: http://iapdeathsincustody.independent.gov.uk/harris-review (accessed 2 May 2018).

Hillyard, P., Sim, J., Tombs, S. and Whyte, D. (2004) 'Leaving a "stain upon the silence": contemporary criminology and the politics of dissent', *British Journal of Criminology*, 44(3): 369–90.

Humphreys, L. (1970) *Tearoom Trade*. London: Duckworth.

INQUEST (2016) Deaths in Prison. Available at: www.inquest.org.uk/deaths-in-prison (accessed 8 September 2016).

Israel, M. (2015) *Research Ethics and Integrity for Social Scientists*. London: Sage.

Liebling, A. (1992) *Suicides in Prison*. London: Routledge.

McCormack, D. (2014) *Queer Postcolonial Narratives and the Ethics of Witnessing*. London: Bloomsbury.

Milgram, S. (1974) *Obedience to Authority*. London: Pinter & Martin.

Mills, C.W. (1959) *The Sociological Imagination*. Oxford: Oxford University Press.

National Commission for the Protection of Human Subjects of Biomedical and Behavioural Research (1979) *The Belmont Report: Ethical Principles and Guidelines for the Protection of Human Subjects of Research*. Detroit, MI: Department of Health, Education and Welfare. Available at: www.hhs.gov/ohrp/regulations-and-policy/belmont-report/read-the-belmont-report/index.html (accessed 2 May 2018).

Schumann, K. (2013) 'On proper and deviant criminology: varieties in the production of legitimation for penal law', in J. Gilmore, J.M. Moore and D. Scott (eds), *Critique and Dissent*. Ottawa: Red Quill Books.

Scott, D. (2014) *Self-inflicted Deaths: Official Submission to the Harris Review*, 29 October. Available at: http://iapdeathsincustody.independent.gov.uk/wp-content/uploads/2015/08/Submission-to-Harris-Review-from-Dr-David-Scott.pdf (accessed 2 May 2018).

Scott, D. (2015a) 'Walking among the graves of the living: reflections about doing prison research from an abolitionist perspective', in D. Drake, R. Earle and J. Sloan (eds), *The Palgrave Handbook of Prison Ethnography*. London: Palgrave.

Scott, D. (2015b) 'Critical research values and the sociological imagination: learning lessons from researching prison staff', in J. Frauley (ed.), *C. Wright Mills and the Criminological Imagination: Prospects for Creative Inquiry*. London: Routledge.

Scott, D. (2016a) *Emancipatory Politics and Praxis*. London: EG Press.

Scott, D. (2016b) 'Hearing the voice of the estranged Other: abolitionist ethical hermeneutics', *Kriminolosches Journal*, 48(3): 184–201.

Scott, D. (2018) *Against Imprisonment*. Winchester: Waterside Press.

Scraton, P. (2004) 'Speaking truth to power: experiencing critical research', in M. Smyth and E. Williamson (eds), *Researchers and their Subjects: Ethics, Power, Knowledge and Consent*. Bristol: Policy Press.

Scraton, P. (2016) 'Bearing witness to the pain of others: researching power, violence and resistance in a women's prison', *International Journal of Crime, Justice and Social Democracy*, 5(1): 5–20.

Sim, J. (2003) 'Whose side we are not on', in S. Tombs and D. Whyte (eds), *Unmasking the Crimes of the Powerful*. Bern: Peter Lang Publishing.

Sim, J., Scraton, P. and Gordon, P. (1987) 'Introduction', in P. Scraton (ed.), *Law, Order and the Authoritarian State*. Milton Keynes: Open University Press.

Singapore Statement on Research Integrity (2010) *2nd World Conference on Research Integrity*. Available at: www.singaporestatement.org (accessed 2 May 2018).

The Stanford Prison Experiment (2017) *The Story: An Overview of the Experiment*. Stanford: Social Psychology Network. Available at: www.prisonexp.org/the-story (accessed 2 May 2018).

Walters, R. (2003) *Deviant Knowledge: Criminology, Politics and Policy*. London: Routledge.

Zimbardo, P. (2009) *The Lucifer Effect: How Good People Turn Evil*. London: Ebury Publishing.

CHAPTER CONTENTS

GLOSSARY TERMS

literature review
methodology
summarizing
rehearsing
visual criminology
virtual ethnography

7 WRITING UP AND PRESENTING CRIMINOLOGICAL RESEARCH

ALEXANDRA HALL

INTRODUCTION

The final stage of any criminological research project is writing up and presenting findings. However, writing up, which follows a number of phases through formulation, data collection and analysis, is not just a technical exercise but also a space for the further development of the research. It is the opportunity to bring the distinct elements of the research together, to re-read the notes, literature review and data sets, to further analyse and theorize, and to begin to make a clear and sophisticated argument. Successfully writing up and presenting your research can be a very rewarding experience that brings with it a great feeling of accomplishment. It can also be a demanding, frustrating, nerve-wracking and, at times, tedious task.

Forms of reporting available to social researchers today include conventional and alternative possibilities, all of which involve particular processes requiring careful consideration and planning in terms of structure and style (Thody, 2006). Written and oral presentation remain the most common forms of dissemination in the social sciences, both of which comprise conventional and unconventional styles. In recent years, however, new methods of dissemination have begun to appear. In criminology, for instance, the recent 'visual turn' has paved the way for an increased use of images in criminological research, with photographs (see Carrabine, 2012), illustrations (e.g. Stephens Griffin, 2015) and documentary film (e.g. Redmon, 2005) growing in popularity.

This chapter focuses on writing up and presenting criminological research. While the primary focus is on writing up, the chapter also explores various other dissemination techniques. The chapter begins with writing up, outlining the traditional method and structure that can be followed by university students writing up a dissertation/ thesis or research report. This is followed by discussions of oral presentations and emerging visual and virtual forms of presentation. It finishes by offering some 'top tips' that might be of help during the process.

WRITING UP

This section focuses on the process of writing up criminological research. As Matthews and Ross suggest, '[a]ll academic writing starts with the same thing – *planning*' (2010: 436, original italics). Essentially, the plan should set out the purpose of the piece of academic writing and break it down into manageable sections. One of the first decisions to make before writing up is which particular sequence these sections should follow. Jotting down an initial plan with a list of headings can help with this process. Although a number of sequential formats exist and the chosen format may change during the process, particularly if an alternative presentation style is chosen, laying out a basic structure that orders the sections in a typical sequence can still be worthwhile, especially during the initial planning phases of writing.

A basic structure

The following is an indicative structure for a university dissertation/thesis or research report with a brief description of what should be included in each section:

1. Title page

This page includes the title of the study alongside the writer's name and the date. The title should include the most applicable keywords that reflect the main purpose and findings of the research. The writer should choose keywords that can be easily searched for online. Researchers regularly include a subtitle to clarify the basic purpose of the research. It is often a good idea to revise and finalize the title and subtitle at the very end of a research project.

2. Abstract

The abstract follows the title to summarize the overall content of the research and the researcher's basic argument. It should be no more than 250 words in length and include an introduction to the research problem, key findings and conclusion. It is often best to write the abstract at the end of the writing-up process.

3. Introduction

The introduction outlines the field of study and the research question to be investigated before summarizing the content and structure of the dissertation and its main arguments. It is also important to include a contents page and a list of tables and figures between the abstract and the introduction. This should be done at the very end and not in the initial planning stages because the order of the contents may change a number of times in the process of writing up.

4. Literature review

The literature review provides the context for the dissertation and evidences the researcher's background knowledge of the field. It can comprise one chapter or a number of chapters. The aim is to review and critically discuss existing work in the field that is relevant to the study. It should also include a discussion of the main theories and concepts that will eventually frame and attempt to explain findings. Depending on the nature of the research, some dissertations also include a separate chapter in which the theoretical framework will be established and explained in detail.

5. Methodology

The methodology section includes an account of how the researcher aims to answer the research question/hypothesis. This involves outlining and justifying the appropriateness of the chosen methods of investigation, as well as their limitations. The section should discuss both theoretical and practical methodological issues – from epistemological and ontological considerations to sampling and access. Research ethics are also an essential part of the discussion in this section.

6. Findings

This section presents a discussion of the main findings of your research. Findings and the relevant data on which they are based can be presented in various ways that depend on the methodological approach (see discussion below). This section might take up more than one chapter and, depending on the chosen approach and structure, can overlap with the discussion section.

7. Discussion

In this section, the researcher weaves together the data and the theory, relating the main findings to the theoretical and/or policy discussion in the literature review. This should include a critical evaluation of the findings and how well they answer the research question. The discussion should answer the following questions:

- Has the research question been adequately answered?
- Have the aims and objectives of the research been fulfilled?
- How has the research filled gaps in the current literature?

8. Conclusion

The conclusion is an opportunity for a succinct summary of what the researcher has found, an outline of the main points and arguments and a brief discussion of their implications for the field of study, which might be theoretical, methodological, policy oriented or some permutation of the three. The section can include specific policy recommendations that are supported by the research findings. The section often finishes with suggestions for further research.

9. Appendices

The appendices should include any supplementary material that is important to the research but which was too detailed to include in the main body of the text. This can include raw data, drawings, supplementary evidence relating to research participants, graphs and maps. Researchers should be sure to signpost and reference appendices correctly in the text.

10. Bibliography

The bibliography is a list of all of the sources referred to in all the previous sections. References should be included and correctly matched in the text (in-text citation) and the final bibliography. There are different ways to reference; therefore, it is important to use the accepted style. Follow university guidelines and, if necessary, refer to the booklet *Cite Them Right* (Pears and Shields, 2016).

Guiding principles

Alongside the format, there are a number of crucial factors to consider in the processes of planning and writing up. Some of these may seem obvious but, as Matthews and Ross (2010) point out, they can be easily forgotten. Important questions researchers should ask themselves as they write a research paper or essay include:

- What are the aims of the research and are they clearly outlined in the paper?
- Who will make up the audience?
- Does the paper include an appropriate introduction and conclusion?
- What is the word limit and has an appropriate amount of space been taken up by each section?
- Have relevant and clear signposts been included to break up different sections?
- Is the literature review adequately comprehensive and critical?
- What methods have been adopted and are they clearly outlined in the paper?
- Is the presentation of data appropriate and comprehensible?
- Is the argument reasoned and does it follow a logical sequence?
- Have appropriate links been made between data and theory?
- If images, tables, figures or graphs are presented in the text, are they formatted correctly?
- Have existing standards or guidelines been followed (e.g. university guidelines)?
- Have referenced source materials been cited accurately and consistently throughout, including both in-text citation and the final bibliography/reference list?

Thody (2006) offers a useful framework of principles to guide the selection of writing and presentation styles, which are summarized in the context of criminological research below and explain in more detail some of the crucial factors listed above. She begins by suggesting a dialogue with data that involves careful planning alongside writing from the start of a project. It is worth bearing in mind that, although the most significant chunk of writing comes at the end of the project, the writing process will have commenced during various earlier stages of the research. Writing the proposal – which includes an overview of the methodology – conducting the literature review, and note-taking during data collection and analysis will have involved some aspect of writing up. This leaves the researcher with a number of sources to draw on and incorporate into the final presentation. In other words, the researcher is not starting from scratch and will have been writing up various aspects of the research throughout the process (Chamberlain, 2013). According to Thody (2006), the main principles to consider during the writing and presenting stage include:

Whether or not to follow precedent. There are a number of conventional and alternative writing formats available to researchers. However, the choice is usually predetermined by the type of project on which the researcher is working. For example, undergraduate dissertations and chapters for edited collections usually have a required format, whereas a PhD thesis or research monograph can provide opportunities to break free from convention. It is often worthwhile consulting an experienced colleague, supervisor or book editor before an innovative approach is taken. As a general rule of thumb, it is important to follow the required rules and customs associated with a chosen form and style of written work, whether conventional or alternative. Consulting existing guidelines is therefore advisable before commencing the final write-up.

How much of your personality as a writer/presenter to admit. Reflexivity, autobiography and emotion are seen as increasingly significant in criminological research. The researcher must decide how much of her voice should appear and where those reflections should appear in the presentation and analysis of findings. Too much can seem self-indulgent and lead to the researcher/writer appearing as a dominant voice rather than the researched. However, there are occasions where this is necessary. For instance, Wakeman's (2014) autoethnography of drug use and drug dealing and Owens' (2012) prison survival guide provide examples of criminological researchers directly drawing on their personal histories and biographies as they reflect on crime, deviance and the criminal justice system. Moreover, when adopting an in-depth qualitative approach commonly found in the ethnographic method (see Hall, Chapter 17), the views and actions of the researcher become intertwined with those of the researched in quite complex ways. On these occasions, the researchers' voices and reflections on the process – personal commitments to the research, positionality, epistemological and ontological frameworks – can become indispensable to the text, adding richness and authenticity to its final presentation. Examples of pieces benefiting from an increased appearance of the researcher's voice include Hobbs' (1988) ethnography of criminal entrepreneurship and working-class life in the East End of London; Adler's (1993) six-year exploration of an upper-level drug-dealing community in Southern California; Bourgois' (1995) study of street-level dealing in East Harlem; Winlow's (2001) covert ethnography and discussion of his insider status as a nightclub doorman researching violence and professional crime in north-east England; Fleetwood's (2014) reflections on her time in Ecuadorian prisons interviewing and observing female drug traffickers; Fraser's (2015) experience as a youth worker and researcher over a prolonged period of time examining Glasgow's youth gangs; and Ellis' (2015) in-depth study of male violence in an English town.

The practicalities including time spent and word limit. Everyone begins writing up a project with the best intentions, and then things get in the way. Dealing with the practicalities of writing and being realistic about your own strengths and weaknesses can be difficult to manage. Realistically, when considering the time required for each stage of the writing process, or the word limit, it is worth knowing that more than the initial estimates will usually be required. However, when struggling to manage it is important that researchers try not to panic, because with help and consultation most find they can adapt to any given situation. If writing up is taking much longer to complete because of other work and family commitments, ask for an extension and, if possible, renegotiate a submission date, and make a note to plan work more effectively in the future and try not to take on too much.

Valuing and assessing readers and audiences. Alongside the methodological approach, the choice of the style of presentation depends on the target audience. Whether the audience is the examiners reading the dissertation or thesis, practitioners and policy makers reading a report prepared for a governmental agency, the general public reading a newspaper piece or watching a documentary film, or reviewers of the academic journal targeted for publication, considering who the target audience is and how best to present the research to suit their needs is of the utmost importance (Chamberlain, 2013). For some authors, their research aims to reach beyond academic, policymaking and practitioner communities. The methodology and subsequent presentation of research findings can therefore take on different and more accessible forms that are sensitive to the needs of general, non-specialist audiences. For instance, the purposeful use of everyday language in published work can benefit a broader audience outside of academia. However, for students, whose audience is a dissertation/thesis examiner, following university guidelines and academic regulations and complying with the rules of vocabulary, punctuation and grammar are both of the utmost importance (see Thody, 2006: 39).

Thinking about the overt and covert purposes of the presentation. If the format has been chosen and the researcher is ready to begin the process of writing up, it is advisable to revisit the data, methodological approach and theoretical framework and clarify the overall purpose of the piece. The researcher might be aiming to test an idea, enhance understanding, share information, gain acceptance, or simply to achieve a good result in an assessment in order to progress to the following year. Depending on the aim, there are a number of considerations that are important to think about, which include how to weave together data and theory in the text, and whether the chosen approach better suits analytical prose or narrative text. Different schools of thought in the social sciences emphasize different aspects of the research and require varying amounts of writing dedicated to the underlying aims of the research and the approach to it. Clare and Hamilton's (2003) collection on writing research offers chapters dedicated to linking data to text from feminist, interpretivist, poststructuralist and positivist-analytic approaches, among others. More recently in criminology, additions to the field include narrative criminology, which, drawing on symbolic interactionism, emphasizes the importance of storytelling to the lives of perpetrators and victims of crime (see Presser and Sandberg, 2015). Another is ultra-realism, which combines advanced ethnographic methods and networked data gathering with new philosophical and psychosocial conceptual frameworks (see Hall and Winlow, 2015). Adopting specific approaches such as these impacts not only on methods and theory, but also on the writing process and final presentation of the research. For example, if following a narrative approach, enough time should be spent introducing the research participants whose stories are being told. From the ultra-realist perspective, for instance, a sufficient amount of time should be spent contextualizing the data and theorization in the broader and deeper political, economic and psychosocial forces, processes and structures that underlie the criminal/harmful phenomena being examined.

The arts and craft of producing written work. As Thody points out, 'there's no magic formula and no choices about starting to write' during the final write-up stage (2006: 60). Therefore, the researcher can get started by writing anything. In other words, make a start, no matter how insignificant it may seem. The actual schedule can vary from person to person. Some might benefit from setting daily writing tasks (including word or paragraph limits) or by writing during predetermined times each day. Some find it more productive to write at weekends, in the evenings or during holidays, during the working week, or some combination of the above. The same is true when the researcher reaches the end. At some point, the writing must finish and the researcher must let go of the whole project. This can often be just as hard as beginning the process. It is extremely important to calculate roughly how long it will take to write various sections and stick to your own deadlines, so that the project can be completed to the required standard. As you develop your writing and presenting technique, try to work out and remember what works best for you at each stage of the writing process. Alongside the formula for beginning and finishing a piece of written work, style and tone are also significant issues. There is no space here to fully explore style and tone – appropriate language, correct tense, choice of voice, and so on – but useful overviews can be found in Thody (2006), Bryman (2012) and Kara (2015). Finally, the process of constantly refining writing to a high standard is important; therefore, a sequence of drafts is essential. There is no set number but a polished piece of academic writing will most likely have been drafted at least three or four times. As the work moves through the drafting stages – from first draft through middle draft(s) to final draft – not just the writing but the argument can be developed. Drafting presents an opportunity to review, evaluate and refine the research's themes and concepts and how they are presented. It is important to establish a flow from paragraph to paragraph using transitional devices, which are summative phrases at the beginning and end of paragraphs that tie together and signpost the overall argument, and clearly introduce theory and data where necessary in order to support interpretations. A final copyedit is also essential, which allows the researcher to check the structure, flow, grammar, spelling, word count and referencing before the final proofread and submission.

It is often only during the final write-up stage that a researcher fully endorses the argument they are trying to make. This follows constant reformulation and refinement throughout the numerous stages of writing and rewriting. Bearing this in mind, Ward makes the important point that the researcher should 'think about the dissertation process as a series of loops rather than a straight line' (2014: 157). This allows for additional feedback, reflection, literature and theory to be integrated into each section of the dissertation throughout the process. For example, sections of the research can be revisited and additional literature can be read and concepts integrated into the analysis as the writing up progresses and the argument develops. As Ward adds, this makes room for a 'series of iterations': leaving space for editing and moving text, images and figures in the document (2014: 158). This is necessary because, alongside text, written work in criminology often includes the presentation of data in various forms.

Data presentation

Data can be processed and presented in a number of ways in criminology, just as it can in social research more generally. The best way to present data depends on the audience, the methodological approach to the data collection and analysis, and the overall purpose of the research. Whether the approach is qualitative, quantitative or mixed methods, a number of considerations should be taken into account as the data is presented in the text. Tables, graphs, charts and figures are often used to enhance clarity and accessibility. Other techniques include the summarizing of findings and using stories, which can include the use of quotes and observations edited from field notes and transcriptions. Moreover, since the establishment of the visual turn in social science, images and extracts from media sources appear more regularly in criminological research. During the write-up, the researcher should think about where the data can be best placed in the document; for instance, in the main body of the text or an appendix. How best to weave together theory, analysis and data in the text – which is essential if the argument is to make sense to the reader – also requires careful thought and refinement in drafts. Whilst analysing the data and organizing thoughts around it, many choose a thematic approach, which is often also the best way to begin the process of presenting the data in the research. Thorough introductions to data processing and analysis can be found in Matthews and Ross (2010) and Chamberlain (2013).

ORAL PRESENTATIONS

Criminological research often involves oral presentations. These can be extremely daunting experiences. In a similar way to written work, there are a number of useful guiding principles and techniques the researcher can adopt during the process. The essential aspects to focus on as an oral presentation is planned are what the researcher wants to achieve from the presentation and how best to communicate this to the audience. An audience is different to a readership – the former can only hear the talk and read the slides in real time. It is therefore extremely important to be clear and concise in order to communicate the points and the overall argument effectively. Sometimes it is worthwhile handing out the paper the talk is based on. Whilst keeping in mind the overall purpose of the presentation and the audience, *brainstorming* is often a useful way to approach the topic. This involves randomly noting down the key points the oral presentation covers. This can be followed by a process of *organizing*, where the presentation is drafted as the researcher thinks about structure and what is to be said in each section. This includes the preparation of any visual aids such as PowerPoint slides, handouts, etc. Summarizing the presentation's key points concisely and clearly in an appropriate way that can be presented or distributed (on a notepad or notecards) is the next stage. Finally, rehearsing the presentation is important, if possible in front of an audience, which will give the researcher the opportunity to practise the approach and the timing and receive feedback. Timing is very important: don't try to fit in too much because this will only result in panic and a rushed presentation. On the day of the oral presentation, be sure to check the ICT and any other equipment needed in the allocated room.

VISUAL AND VIRTUAL TURNS: CONTEMPORARY FORMS OF PRESENTATION IN CRIMINOLOGICAL RESEARCH

Two important trends in criminology in recent years are the so-called visual and virtual turns (see Carrabine, 2012; Yar, 2013). Both criminology and ethnography methods have been explored in previous chapters. This section briefly discusses these developments in criminology and offers some key examples in the context of writing up and presenting.

As Carrabine (2012) suggests, our mediatized culture is saturated with images of crime, something that calls for the further analytical and presentational use of the image in criminological research. Indeed, media analysis in criminology is not new. Various examples can be found that analyse TV and film (see Campbell, 2016; Linnemann, 2016; Wakeman, 2017 for recent examples). However, criminological researchers now increasingly draw on images that they have both retrieved and produced – distinguished as natural or contrived/elicited data – as part of research projects conducted in various environments. This is evident in the growing use of photographic methods and the presentation of photographic material in texts. Notable examples from the field include Carrabine's (2014) historical work on criminology and photography, Young's (2016) groundbreaking book on street art and graffiti, Kindynis' (2017) images of recreational trespass and Linnemann's analysis of police trophy shots in the USA (2016).

In many ways, the increasing use of visual methods and forms of presentation in criminology has occurred in conjunction with the advancement and enhanced accessibility of various information and communication technologies, particularly the internet, since the inception of user-generated content and participatory networking online and the widespread use of high-grade cameras and handheld devices. Consequently, there is often a strong relationship between visual and virtual methods. This is clear in the recent work of scholars who have analysed images derived from social media: Hall and Antonopoulos (2015, 2016) on the supply and demand of illicit pharmaceuticals online, Wood (2018) on Facebook fight pages, and Vitis and Gilmour (2017) on the 'dick pic' phenomenon and female resistance to online harassment are just some examples of this new approach.

Taking the production of images in criminology a step further into the domain of the audio-visual is David Redmon, a criminologist and documentary filmmaker who has produced films alongside his written work. Redmon's documentary film *Mardi Gras: Made in China* (2005) and his accompanying book *Beads, Bodies, and Trash: Public Sex, Global Labor, and the Disposability of Mardi Gras* (2014) follow the commodity chain of Mardi Gras beads and the different meanings attached to them as they move through space and place, from production in China to consumption in New Orleans. These are exceptional examples of his developing body of work. The production of images in criminology can also be seen in a number of plays commissioned by arts and criminal justice organizations. One example is *Key Change*, an award-winning play commissioned by Open Clasp Theatre Company (2016) and devised with inmates of HMP Low Newton, a women's prison in England. The production aims to use the power of the image to represent prisons and prison life and to give a voice to those who have served prison sentences. Furthermore, illustrative presentations including graphic novels (Morris, 2012) and comics (Stephens Griffin, 2015) can be used as ways of creatively communicating research findings, analysis and theoretical explanations to an audience.

There is no space here to offer a thorough discussion of the processes involved in presenting all the types of research briefly outlined above (see Kara, 2015 for a practical guide). Instead, the purpose has been to draw the reader's attention to different and emerging ways of presenting research in criminology. It is important to point out that if the researcher plans to present visual data, careful consideration of the formatting, quality and placement, as well as copyright issues and ethical issues, are of utmost importance. In terms of copyright and ethics, approval should be sought for the use of images, or alternatively images should be appropriately anonymized before they are published (see Carrabine, 2015). However, to reiterate an earlier point, when considering an alternative method and form of presentation, seek guidance and approval from supervisors or editors beforehand.

TOP TIPS

Researchers can encounter many obstacles during the presentation phase. For many, no matter how experienced and confident they might be, writing up includes the experience of writers' block, a common condition that can rear its ugly head at any moment during the process. Oral presentations can also be nerve-wracking. In consideration of this, the following section outlines tips and techniques that can help during the process of preparing research for presentation.

Spark your interest. One of the most important tips for a criminological researcher – something some have learned the hard way – is to research and write about subjects that genuinely capture your interest. Choosing a topic of interest is not always possible from the outset. However, it is usually possible to adopt an approach that is interesting and at least of some value to future work. For example, a researcher might be writing up the final essay for an undergraduate module, having struggled to engage with the material, or starting out on a funded PhD initially written by the supervisors with their own research interests in mind. Although at first these tasks might seem uninteresting or difficult, adopting a carefully considered methodological approach and theoretical framework that spark your interest not only makes the task more interesting but also gives value to the development of your future research and writing.

Manage your time. The process of writing involves a number of stages that each require sufficient time to be set aside for. Recognizing how much time you need and giving yourself enough time to complete the writing up to the best of your ability will, more often than not, facilitate a less stressful experience and produce a better end product. As this chapter has shown, planning, drafting and copyediting are fundamental stages of the writing process and they require sufficient time as you approach a deadline. You should also bear in mind the time it will take to complete the abstract, referencing, tables and figures and any other additions to the piece beyond the substantive text.

Make a start and save everything. Once a project starts, write from the very beginning. Create a file and begin to write down anything you can and save everything that you write. It could be brief notes about ideas for the project in bullet points or more substantial notes that you can use during this or future projects. Revisiting notes made during past projects can jog your memory and inspire you.

Prepare. Preparing sufficiently is crucial for building confidence and improving presentation technique. Think about the periods in the day, the week and the month when you write and prepare for presentations most effectively, and factor this into the process. Finding a rhythm and being efficient help a lot. Prepare PowerPoint slides for a presentation well in advance, leaving time to revisit and reformulate them if necessary. The worst feeling is a last-minute rush to finish something when you are tired and frustrated. Try your best to avoid this situation as much as possible.

Sleep on it. If you're struggling, do something else that is important, or sleep on it and come back to your work the following day with a clear mind and fresh eyes. This is what is commonly referred to as a draft stop: leaving your writing for a day or two before returning to it feeling refreshed. This is another reason to leave yourself plenty of time during the process; you want enough time to take a break from writing, if necessary, before returning to it with the aim of improving on what you have already produced.

Practise, practise, practise. Developing your writing technique takes time and hard work. An increasing number of academics use social media, including blog posts, as a means not only of testing their ideas but also as a way of sharpening their thinking and improving their writing technique. Others set up writing retreats and support groups with fellow students and colleagues.

Seek feedback. Ask a friend or colleague to read (or watch) and review a draft of your work. Another set of eyes often works wonders and can highlight issues you may have missed yourself.

Manage the stress and anxiety. Learn how to express frustrations productively: make a to-do list; break down large pieces of writing into manageable chunks; organize your notes and/or documents on your computer; prioritize your time effectively; and work in a team if possible.

Learn from your mistakes. At the end of each project, think about which aspect you have struggled with most during the writing up and presenting stages and make a note of areas for improvement. Writing is a craft; everyone starts somewhere. Feeling out of your depth at times is natural. English may not be your first language, or you may not have been taught English particularly well in earlier education. Another tip here is to note down areas for improvement that are highlighted by reviewers and copyeditors to work on during future writing projects. Furthermore, if a style or format is not working well for you, try a new approach (see discussion of alternative techniques above).

SUMMARY AND REVIEW

This chapter has focused on important processes and issues that researchers will encounter when writing up and presenting criminological research. The first section dealt with writing up, providing an indicative dissertation/research report structure and offering some guiding principles and techniques that researchers in criminology can adopt as they plan and carry out their final write-up. This was followed by a brief discussion of oral presentations, again offering some guiding principles and techniques. The next section discussed emerging visual and virtual forms of presentation. The aims here were to provide recent examples of work based on the presentation of images and to outline the most basic issues to consider when presenting visual or virtual research. The chapter ended with some 'top tips' that can be used by criminological researchers during the writing up and presenting stages of their projects. Giving these processes and issues some attention when writing up research can help to increase confidence, enhance the experience and increase the quality of the end product.

1. Reflect on a previous experience of writing up or presenting.
   a. What did you struggle with most?
   b. How do you plan to implement changes to improve your technique in the future?

2. Look up various approaches to writing up and presenting.
   a. What are the key strengths and weaknesses of each?
   b. Which style better suits your research and why?

3. You have just finished a written piece of work. Ask yourself the following questions as you copyedit your work:
   a. What are the aims of the research and are they clearly outlined in the paper?
   b. Who will make up the audience?
   c. Does the paper include an appropriate introduction and conclusion?
   d. What is the word limit and has an appropriate amount of space been taken up by each section?
   e. Have relevant and clear signposts been included to break up different sections?
   f. Is the literature review adequately comprehensive and critical?
   g. What methods have been adopted and are they clearly outlined in the paper?
   h. Is the presentation of data appropriate and comprehensible?
   i. Is the argument reasoned and does it follow a logical sequence?
   j. Have appropriate links been made between data and theory?
   k. If images, tables, figures or graphs are presented in the text, are they formatted correctly?
   l. Have existing standards or guidelines been followed (e.g. university guidelines)?
   m. Have referenced source materials been cited accurately and consistently throughout, including both in-text citation and the final bibliography/reference list?

SUGGESTIONS FOR FURTHER READING

There are a number of resources available that will serve you well in developing your knowledge of how to present your research appropriately. Perhaps the best three that will allow you to understand the basics, and at the same time help you to think innovatively and creatively about the process and opportunities are:

Clare, J. and Hamilton, H. (2003) *Writing Research: Transforming Data into Text*. London: Churchill Livingstone.

Matthews, B. and Ross, L. (2010) *Research Methods: A practical guide for social sciences*. Essex: Pearson Education Ltd.

Kara, H. (2015) *Creative Research Methods in the Social Sciences*: A Practical Guide. Bristol: Policy Press.

REFERENCES

Adler, P.A. (1993) *Wheeling and Dealing: An Ethnography of an Upper-Level Drug Dealing and Smuggling Community*. New York: Colombia University Press.

Bourgois, P. (1995) *In Search of Respect: Selling Crack in El Barrio*. Cambridge: Cambridge University Press.

Bryman, A. (2012) *Social Research Methods*, 4th edition. Oxford: Oxford University Press.

Campbell, E. (2016) 'Policing paedophilia: assembling bodies, spaces and things', *Crime, Media, Culture, 12*(3): 345–65.

Carrabine, E. (2012) 'Just images: aesthetics, ethics and visual criminology', *British Journal of Criminology, 52*(3): 463–89.

Carrabine, E. (2014) 'Seeing things: violence, voyeurism and the camera', *Theoretical Criminology, 18*(2): 134–58.

Carrabine, E. (2015) 'Visual criminology: history, theory and method', in H. Copes and M. Miller (eds), *The Routledge Handbook of Qualitative Criminology*. New York: Routledge.

Chamberlain, J.M. (2013) *Understanding Criminological Research: A Guide to Data Analysis*. London: Sage.

Clare, J. and Hamilton, H. (2003) *Writing Research: Transforming Data into Text*. London: Churchill Livingstone.

Ellis, A. (2015) *Men, Masculinities and Violence: An Ethnographic Study*. London: Routledge.

Fleetwood, J. (2014) *Drug Mules: Women in the International Cocaine Trade*. Basingstoke: Palgrave Macmillan.

Fraser, A. (2015) *Urban Legends: Gang Identity in the Post-Industrial City*. Oxford: Oxford University Press.

Hall, A. and Antonopoulos, G.A. (2015) 'License to pill: illegal entrepreneurs' tactics in the online trade of medicines', in P.C. van Duyne, A. Maljevic, G.A. Antonopoulos, J. Harvey and K. von Lampe (eds), *The Relativity of Wrongdoing: Corruption, Organised Crime, Fraud and Money Laundering in Perspective*. Nijmegen: Wolf Legal Publishers.

Hall, A. and Antonopoulos, G.A. (2016) *Fake Meds Online: The Internet and the Transnational Market in Illicit Pharmaceuticals*. Basingstoke: Palgrave Macmillan.

Hall, S. and Winlow, S. (2015) *Revitalizing Criminological Theory: Towards a New Ultra-Realism*. London: Routledge.

Hobbs, D. (1988) *Doing the Business: Entrepreneurship, the Working Class and Detectives in the East End of London*. Oxford: Oxford University Press.

Kara, H. (2015) *Creative Research Methods in the Social Sciences: A Practical Guide*. Bristol: Policy Press.

Kindynis, T. (2017) 'Urban exploration: from subterranea to spectacle', *British Journal of Criminology*, *57*(4): 982–1001.

Linnemann, T. (2016) 'Proof of death: police power and the visual economies of seizure, accumulation and trophy', *Theoretical Criminology*, *21*(1): 57–77.

Matthews, B. and Ross, L. (2010) *Research Methods: A Practical Guide for Social Sciences*. Harlow: Pearson Education.

Morris, G. (2012) 'Can you picture this? Academic research published as a graphic novel!' *LSE Impact Blog*. Available at: http://blogs.lse.ac.uk/impactofsocialsciences/2012/07/23/academic-research-published-graphic-novel (accessed 5 April 2018).

Open Clasp Theatre Company (2016) Key Change. Available at: www.openclasp.org.uk/productions/key-change (accessed 5 April 2018).

Owens, F. (2012) *The Little Book of Prison: A Beginners Guide*. Hook, Hants: Waterside Press.

Pears, R. and Shields, G. (2016) *Cite them Right: The Essential Referencing Guide*, 10th edition. London: Palgrave Macmillan.

Presser, L. and Sandberg, S. (eds) (2015) *Narrative Criminology: Understanding Stories of Crime*. New York: New York University Press.

Redmon, D. (2005) *Mardi Gras: Made in China*. Available at: www.imdb.com/title/tt0436569 (accessed 9 July 2018).

Redmon, D. (2014) *Beads, Bodies, and Trash: Public Sex, Global Labour, and the Disposability of Mardi Gras*. London: Routledge.

Stephens Griffin, N. (2015) 'Combining biographical and visual methods in practice: a vegan comic case study', in M. O'Neill, B. Roberts and A.C. Sparkes (eds), *Advances in Biographical Methods: Creative Applications*. London: Routledge.

Thody, A. (2006) *Writing and Presenting Research*. London: Sage.

Vitis, L. and Gilmour, F. (2017) 'Dick pics on blast: a woman's resistance to online sexual harassment using humour, art and Instagram', *Crime, Media, Culture*, *13*(3): 335–55.

Wakeman, S. (2014) 'Fieldwork, biography and emotion: doing criminological autoethnography', *British Journal of Criminology*, *54*(5): 705–21.

Wakeman, S. (2017) 'The "one who knocks" and the "one who waits": gendered violence in *Breaking Bad*', *Crime, Media, Culture*. Available at: http://journals.sagepub.com/doi/abs/10.1177/1741659016684897?journalCode=cmca (accessed 20 March 2018).

Ward, K. (ed.) (2014) *Researching the City*. London: Sage.

Winlow, S. (2001) *Badfellas: Crime, Tradition and New Masculinities*. London: Berg.

Wood, M.A. (2018) '"I just wanna see someone get knocked the fuck out": spectating affray on Facebook fight pages', *Crime, Media, Culture*, 14(1): 23–40.

Yar, M. (2013) *Cybercrime and Society*, 2nd edition. London: Sage.

Young, A. (2016) *Street Art World*. London: Reaktion Books.

CHAPTER CONTENTS

GLOSSARY TERMS

complainant
Old Bailey
coining
victim-offender overlap
tagging
digital corpus linguistic methods
prosopography

8 USING HISTORICAL ARTEFACTS, RECORDS AND RESOURCES IN CRIMINOLOGICAL RESEARCH

PAM COX, HEATHER SHORE AND BARRY GODFREY

INTRODUCTION

In the past, victims had to drive prosecution processes themselves in order to access any kind of justice. They were central to the criminal justice system, particularly prior to the nineteenth century. However, there has been little research conducted on historical victims of crime. Most crime historians have focused on offenders, on the cultures of control employed to contain or reform them, and on public responses to particular kinds of crime committed by them. There is a large gap in our knowledge of those people who have pursued justice on their own behalf over the course of the last 300 years. As leading crime historian George Rudé put it (1985: 76): 'What do we know about the characters or attitudes of victims? The answer is very little.' More than half a century on, that is still the case. To that we could add the question 'Will knowing more about the history of victims tell us more about the criminal justice system as a whole and how well that system works?' In this chapter, then, we describe the importance of researching this topic. We then describe the research journey – giving examples of what has been done so far, including the methods used and results obtained, before going on to describe research that we would like to conduct in the future – research using new historical methods and sources to explore key questions about the history of victims of crime.

WHY IS RESEARCH ON THE HISTORY OF VICTIMS IMPORTANT?

Research on the victims of crime is important for three main reasons.

1. They are a central component of the criminal justice system. For a large range of offences, unless there is a victim there is no crime. They appear as witnesses (although much less than they ever did, as the number of trials per head of population has decreased markedly over time), and they are uppermost in the minds of magistrates and judges at the point of sentence (even if they didn't appear in the courtroom).
2. The ability of victims to have equal access to the courts is a central tenet of a democratic state. Securing fair and effective access to justice for victims of crime is a priority for many states around the world. It concerns citizens' ability, through the prior claiming or granting of rights, to seek formal acknowledgement and redress of wrongs committed against them within a given legal system (see Conklin, 2001; Cooper, 2009; Law Society, 1992; Mayo et al., 2014; Palmer et al., 2015; Sandefur, 2009).
3. Measuring the experience of victims allows us to measure the efficiency of the wider criminal justice system. For example, various initiatives have been put in

place in recent years to close 'justice gaps', where some groups or individuals in society have not had equal access to fair trials, or redress as victims of crime. These initiatives have included, amongst other things, the introduction of better legal protection and awareness of rights; available and affordable counsel through the increasing provision of legal aid (Brooke, 2016; Maguire, 1928; Morgan, 1994); procedural rules for trials and delivery of justice; and an unbiased judiciary.

Since the 1980s, victims have been placed firmly on the criminological and public policy map (Goodey, 2004; Gottfredson, 1984; Kirchengast, 2006; Newburn, 1993). However, we still know surprisingly little about past victims of crime. How has access to justice for victims changed? Who has sought access to justice and with what outcomes? How have victims' rights and needs been defined and met over time? What has been the result of changed levels of help for victims to gain justice? What has been the impact on prosecution patterns and outcomes of the introduction (and reform or withdrawal) of specific rights, resources and services for victims involved in criminal trials?

Which groups have had the most effective access to justice in what circumstances and how has that changed over time? Historians of the eighteenth century in the 1970s and 1980s believed that the criminal justice system was a tool for the rich to use against the poor (Hay, 1975; Linebaugh, 1991). Within that system, the rich prosecutor was assumed to hold the power of life or death over unrepresented ill-informed and uneducated labourers and tenants. However, more recent research, based on a study of the complainants in criminal trials, has proved that the power to prosecute was not solely within the purview of the powerful. Social inferiors used the law to call their 'betters' to account in public (Beattie, 1986: 8–10, 193–6; Hay, 1989: 354–60; King, 1984: 29–34, 2000: 35–9, 2004: 144–6). We do not know whether the law continued to be so widely used by all classes in the nineteenth century. We do know, however, that victims of crime in the eighteenth century *appeared* to be predominantly male. Was this true, or was it that certain groups in society – women, migrants, children – were prevented from reporting their victimization? When this changed – if it did – was this because of changing levels of aid for victims of crime or because of wider social changes? In the nineteenth and twentieth centuries, did victims have increased access to justice through legal representation, and, if they did, were they able to secure better results in court? How have people begun to investigate these questions?

WHAT METHODS ARE APPROPRIATE FOR A STUDY OF THE HISTORY OF VICTIMS?

Information about victims of crime can be found quite easily in local archives and records offices throughout the UK. The local court registers for most petty sessions' courts (magistrates' courts) give the name of the 'complainant' alongside that of the defendant, the offence and the sentence imposed. It is a relatively straightforward matter to create a data set (using Excel or SPSS) that records the victims and some information which is usually obvious (for example, the name of the complainant normally reveals the gender, but not always), as well as sometimes providing additional information – 'wife of accused', or 'child of 12', and so on. Transcribing a sufficiently large number of months of prosecutions in one town's petty sessions' courts will provide enough data to cross-tabulate gender of victim by offence, for example. This is meaningful data, which can reveal interesting results – how many women were victims of indecent assault compared to men, for example? How many children were victims of crime in any one place? Unfortunately, however, we usually want to know about *change* when we think about victims, and crime generally. That means collecting data over several years, and if we want to compare one town against another, then it means collecting details of tens of thousands, maybe hundreds of thousands, of prosecutions which can be entered into a single data set. For example, the database of 50,000 prosecutions taking place in the reasonably small town of Crewe in north-west England in the late nineteenth century, analysed by Godfrey, Cox and Farrall for their study *Criminal Lives* (2007), took nine months to construct.

TABLE 8.1 Defendant and victim data

Date	First name defendant		Surname defendant	Sex	Name victim	Surname victim	Sex vic
31/12/1888	Peter		Steadman	M	PC	Kerns	M
31/03/1891	Richard		Garner	M	Police		M
30/06/1891	Henry		Farmer	M	Alfred	Oldham	M
31/12/1895	Mary	Ann	Doyle	F	Police		M
31/03/1896	Agnes		Grady	F	Police		M
31/12/1896	Emma		Boston	F	Police		M
30/06/1899	Emma		Brockley	F	Police		M
30/09/1899	George	Henry	Wright	M	Rebecca	Edwards	F
31/03/1900	Henry		Mottram	M	Annie	Crank	F
30/06/1900	Emma		Boston	F	Police		M

An alternative to transcribing huge amounts of data is to focus on a smaller sample of cases involving a smaller number of victims. Past issues of local newspapers, which are usually kept on microfilm in local libraries, can provide detailed histories of individual cases of victimization. A trial can involve a number of weeks of reportage, and a detailed case study can easily be constructed, although, again, a small number of specific cases may not illustrate a general trend in the way that a large-scale quantitative study can:

> A policeman described a clearly very agitated woman as 'capering about like a mad dog' (*Crewe Chronicle*, 14 May 1881). The court had a titter at the language of a woman in a street brawl. She said that she and her 'daughter had had a little drink. They were slightly elevated (Laughter).' In fact five of the thirteen jokes surround drink and mark the ambiguous boundary between cultures of sociability and the drunkenness that framed so much violence. (Godfrey et al., 2009: 262)

The means of securing both a significant number of cases for a database, with a diversity of victims, and also a sufficiently deep and rich amount of data for the study of just a few cases of victimization, has recently been transformed. The digital delivery of eighteenth- and nineteenth-century court records and newspapers has now allowed researchers to quickly locate and transcribe criminal cases without needing to travel to archives. Crime historians have helped to pioneer Big Data digital humanities research. The Old Bailey proceedings was a pioneering project which allowed the interrogation of large numbers of court cases at the Central Criminal Court between 1674 and 1913. A more recent project, the AHRC-funded *Digital Panopticon*, is creating a substantial new resource which allows users of a freely available website to piece together the lives of people sentenced to either imprisonment or transportation in the eighteenth and nineteenth centuries. So, what have we learned about victims and criminal justice using traditional and digital methods and sources?

THE RESEARCH JOURNEY

Historians of crime and victimization use cutting-edge methods to analyse available sources of data, but those methods change over time, and so does access to available sources as the following sections will show. Research on victims, and on offenders for that matter, has been shaped by the type of historical sources that have been available to researchers. There is a research journey which takes us from basic research (counting the numbers of different types of victims over time in contemporary court registers) through to some quite detailed analysis of the interactions of gender and victimization (using newspapers and other, more qualitative sources), back to counting victims again (but with a quantum leap in scale this time around because of the availability of 'Big Data'). Let us start by describing some of the interesting issues that have been uncovered during the research 'journey'.

Change over time

Digital crime history projects have helped to transform crime history research and that of its parent disciplines, social and economic history (Hitchcock and Shoemaker, 2007). One of the most important of these is the Old Bailey Online (OBO) project that has made it possible to search the lives of the thousands of people involved in 202,000 trials at London's central criminal court over three and a half centuries. Using the online statistical tool embedded in the project's website, it is possible to obtain some 'headline' figures, such as the recorded number of complainants (who may be the victim of the crime, or someone who prosecutes on their behalf). For example, it is possible to see the rise in the recording of complainants involved in these cases up to the mid-nineteenth century, followed by a sharp fall and thereafter stabilising at between 500 and 1000 victims per year until the First World War (see Figure 8.1). This cliff-edge fall is intriguing, but this data tells us very little about why the fall took place, or how victims were affected by it.

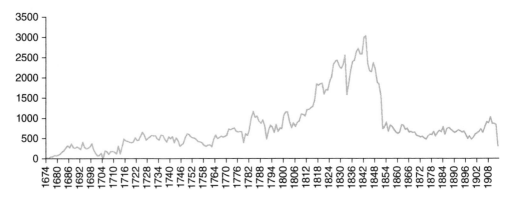

FIGURE 8.1 Number of complainants recorded at the Old Bailey, 1674–1913 (figures taken from Old Bailey Online)

What more do we know about these victims apart from their names? Old Bailey trial records in this period did not routinely record the ages of offenders or victims: the ages of only 662 of these victims are recorded – a tiny fraction of the total number. However, we know more about their gender and we can also break this down by offence (see Table 8.2).

Men were clearly the complainants in most cases, and appear most often to be the victims of certain kinds of offences prosecuted in the Old Bailey, such as pickpocketing, robbery and fraud. This may be because men held more wealth and were therefore greater targets for acquisitive crime. The percentage of female complainants was higher in cases of coining (although the reasons for this are not clear) and in cases of indecent

TABLE 8.2 Offence and gender of complainant, Old Bailey, 1674–1913

	Male complainant	Female complainant	Total	% male	% female
Pickpocketing	10819	926	11745	92	8
Robbery	3897	543	4440	88	12
Fraud	3194	459	3653	87	13
Assault	562	248	810	69	31
Coining	339	177	516	66	34
Indecent assault	98	351	449	22	78

assault, where young women and girls were more often the victims of men rather than the other way around. However, this kind of bald prosecution data tells us very little about the victims themselves. Things start to get a little more interesting when we look at the gender of victims across the whole of the period covered by the Old Bailey Online. Figure 8.2 shows us that not only did female complainants make up a small fraction of the total number, but also the percentage was steady between the late eighteenth and early twentieth centuries. This is despite the significant fall in the number of complainants from the 1850s. Changes in prosecution practice caused a dramatic fall in the numbers of male, rather than female, complainants, as can be seen in Figure 8.2.

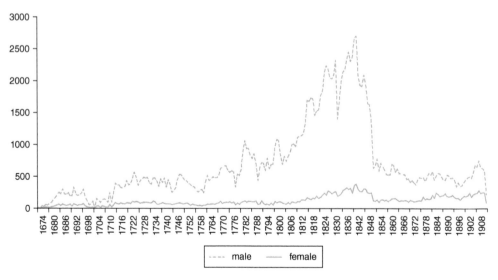

FIGURE 8.2 Victims, by gender, at the Old Bailey, 1674–1913 (figures taken from Old Bailey Online)

Even this limited data highlights some interesting – and as yet unanswered questions – around the gender of victims in the eighteenth to twentieth centuries.

GENDER

Feminist historians instigated some of the earliest historical research into victimization, notably through studies of the experiences of female victims of sexual violence and child abuse (Clarke, 1987, 1997; D'Cruze, 1998; D'Cruze and Jackson, 2009; Jackson, 1999, 2000; Tomes, 1978). In addition, local and regional studies have offered snapshots of male and female victims appearing in selected courts (Conley, 1991; Rudé, 1985). While these studies offer much in terms of empirical depth, they tend to offer less in terms of chronological breadth, with most focusing on a time span of a few decades at most. None of the authors of these studies were able to make use of digitized crime or census data. A broader view is offered by more recent historical studies that have more directly addressed victims over time. Recent internationally focused studies include Kirchengast's (2006) collection, *The Victim in Criminal Law and Justice*, which traces the development of the victim from feudal law to the present day in an international survey. Rock (2004) produced a very good analysis of the shifts in the historical power of the victim to prosecute and punish offenders, and their impact on the development of the modern criminal law and justice system. Large-scale empirical studies of victims are few and far between, however.

As part of a project on the meanings of violence carried out in 2000 ('Prosecutions for violent offences in selected English, Australian and New Zealand petty sessions' courts, 1880–1914', ESRC project R000223300), a database of 10,000 prosecutions for minor violence in ten English courts in the 1880–1914 period was constructed. The quantitative data collected for this project is archived at the Data History Data Service (ref. no. 4483). Because the court registers from which these statistics were drawn recorded the names of the victim and defendant, it was possible to carry out an analysis of the conviction rates and the penalties imposed by gender of the victim involved (see Table 8.3).

TABLE 8.3 Conviction by 'gendered context' (sex of victim and assailant) (%)

	Dismissed	Bound over	Convicted
Women assaulting women	35	10	56
Women assaulting men	50	5	45
Men assaulting women	24	11	65
Men assaulting men	28	3	69

In Table 8.3, we can see that men were always more likely than females to be convicted, regardless of the gender of their victim, with 69% of the men who attacked other men convicted, in contrast to 56% of the women who attacked another woman. The women who assaulted men had a considerably lower conviction rate (45%) than men who assaulted women (65%). If we rank the contexts, in terms of the likelihood of conviction, men were most vulnerable to conviction. The gender of the victim did not seem to alter this general position.

Turning now to consider the penalty imposed (Table 8.4), the majority of female offenders, regardless of the gender of the person they attacked, received a mid-ranking penalty. Male offenders received more serious penalties. The highest proportion of offenders receiving the most severe punishments was men assaulting women (57%).

TABLE 8.4 Penalty by 'gendered context' (sex of victim and assailant) (%)

	Low (costs/bound)	Mid (1–7 days)	High (+7 days)
Women assaulting women	19	62	19
Women assaulting men	18	64	18
Men assaulting women	18	25	57
Men assaulting men	6	50	44

As Godfrey et al. (2005: 717–18) found, 'Magistrates clearly targeted "male" contexts of violence, and handed down more convictions and harsher penalties to men involved in these, in contrast to women involved in "female" contexts ... magistrates downplayed ... the majority of assaults which involved females as both assailants and victims'. In order to arrive at this conclusion, the researchers on the project compared court outcomes, not only by the gender of the accused, but also by the amount of culpability they had for the offence, the severity of the assault, the social bond between offender and victim (spouses, strangers, and so on), and (through analysis of a subset of offenders in newspaper trial reports) demeanour, attitude, and 'performance' in court. What was missing (and looking back at this research again, it is still surprising that it was not carried out) was an analysis of the outcomes by gender of the victim.

What would also take this research forward is an analysis not only of the gender of victim or complainant, but also whether they were actually present in court during all or part of the prosecution. Given all we have said about the centrality of the victim in the prosecution process, this seems an odd thing to say, but as the nineteenth century entered its final quarter, the victim was disappearing from the courtroom.

THE DISAPPEARANCE OF THE VICTIM IN COURT

Available evidence on historical victims is limited but suggests that victims were highly active drivers of the criminal justice process in England in the past. For much of the eighteenth and nineteenth centuries, they brought prosecutions as complainants, acted as their own prosecution 'lawyers', gave evidence as witnesses and put up personal rewards for the recovery of lost goods. Before the introduction of the police force in the 1830s, many victims paid private prosecution associations to bring offenders to direct – and sometimes – indirect justice (Gray, 2016; King, 1989). However, from the later nineteenth century on, the role of victims as active drivers of justice was severely reduced. One consequence of the rise of the 'policeman state' was the increasing willingness of the police to act as prosecutors in court (Emsley, 2007: 272, 2013: 195). By the 1870s and 1880s, the police were prosecuting drunkenness, fighting, assaults, burglaries and some sexual offences *on behalf* of victims who could not, or would not or were discouraged from, prosecuting on their own behalf. Due to their power of detecting and apprehending suspects, and then determining whether those suspects 'should' be tried in court, the police slowly grew to exert a very powerful influence over recorded crime through the centrality of their role in the detection and prosecution process (Rock, 2004). It may be that, ironically, the professionalization of the justice system resulted in the erosion of wider public access to justice.

The ESRC 'meaning of violence' project inspired a further study funded by the Leverhulme Trust to explore the changing contours of crime in a single north-west English town, Crewe. The 'Crewe database' of 50,000 prosecutions was interrogated for evidence of the 'police take-over' of the prosecution process. In analysing prosecutions for assault by category of complainant (whether the person who took the case to court was the individual who was assaulted or a police officer, or someone else), fascinating patterns were revealed. It seemed that the number of police-led prosecutions remained steady between 1880 and 1940, whereas the number of individual-led prosecutions fell away over that period. The impact on recorded violent crime over this period, in Crewe at least, was considerable (the added trend-line indicates a flat-line for police prosecutions, and a falling trend-line for individuals; see Figure 8.3).

Kearon and Godfrey (2007) argue that, although victims were less often present in court, they retained a symbolic power, and the state and its agents often invoked absent individual victims as representative of the whole community. It became much easier for newspapers and social commentators to make claims for victims (and, by extension, for the community) when actual victims were not in court. Victims therefore became more easily idealized in the nineteenth century. More significantly, by the end of the century, victims and offenders were viewed as completely distinct and separate groups with their own characteristics. The real situation was much more complex.

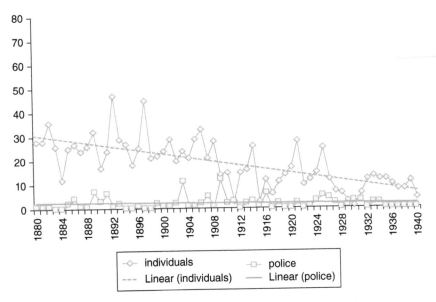

FIGURE 8.3 Prosecutions for assault, Crewe, 1880–1940, with added trend-line (graph taken from Godfrey, 2008)

THE VICTIM–OFFENDER OVERLAP

The idea that 'victims are conceptualized as individuals who have no experience of crime as offenders' (as first critiqued by Newburn and Stanko, 1994: 153) has been overturned by recent research on modern victimization (see, for example, Fagan et al., 1987; Lauritsen et al., 1991; Singer, 1981). Many offenders have experienced victimization, and many victims have committed offences. The Crewe data has also been used to investigate the extent of the historical victim–offender overlap. An almost complete 60-year run of petty sessions data revealed many examples of a given person sometimes appearing in court as a victim and at other times as an offender. Godfrey and colleagues (2007) compared 300 persistent offenders and a roughly equal number of one-off offenders who appeared before Crewe magistrates between 1880 and 1940.

Persistent offenders were found to be more likely than one-off offenders to have experienced victimization. For some, this was because they were often involved in fights, where they sometimes prosecuted those who hit them, and at other times were prosecuted by those they had hit. The local newspaper was keen to report these regular incidents: 'it was one of those family rows which sometime happened in Crewe streets, and especially Lockitt Street, which seemed to be a famous resort for pugilists' (*Crewe Chronicle*, 3 December 1892). Walter Green who, during a 15-year period, was charged with seven assaults, also charged seven others with eight counts of assaulting him. For others, it was family problems at the root of their offending and victimization, and Godfrey et al. (2007: 159–60) gave the example of Adam Toshack:

> Adam was born in Crewe in 1866 and married Aurelia Paisley in 1885. Their marriage was not a happy one, and in 1886 she took him to court for aggravated assault, for which he was found guilty and fined 30s. (at that time he was earning 26s. a week at the railway works as a painter). In 1889, Adam took his wife and a local bricklayer (Graeme Rowley, another of our persistent offenders) to court for theft following Aurelia's elopement with Graeme Rowley. Aurelia accused Graeme Rowley of compelling her to pawn the things, saying that he had threatened to act 'Jack the Ripper' on her, but the case was dismissed due to lack of evidence. In the same year Aurelia in turn took Adam to court for assault (also dismissed). An already rocky relationship went from bad to worse in 1890, when Adam took his father in law, James Paisley, and brother in law Casper Low to court for attempted murder. Casper Low (born 1866) was married to Adam's wife's sister (Molly). Casper Low was committed to trial and found guilty and sentenced to imprisonment, part of which he served in Knutsford Prison. Adam and Aurelia's marriage stumbled on despite these setbacks until 1896 when Aurelia died. Adam followed her in 1914.

In keeping with contemporary analyses (Farrall and Calverley, 2006), Godfrey et al. (2007) found that episodes of victimization outlasted offending – even when a person stopped committing crimes, they were still likely to be victims of crime. Some of this was the result of the ageing process, making offenders more likely to cease offending and simultaneously more vulnerable to assault. The explanations are not easy to uncover. Further research on the victim–offender overlap is necessary.

Indeed, despite all of the interesting data which these projects have produced, there are still a number of questions that remain. How did the outcomes for female and male victims of crimes change over time? Were some people multiply victimized? Has there always been a victim–offender overlap? How did the introduction of formal police services change the number and type of victims? We know that victims disappeared from magistrates' courts (like Crewe) because minor assaults were downplayed by the police who refused to take them to court, but was that why more serious offences were not prosecuted in the higher courts (like the Old Bailey)? How would our research findings change if we had access to a bigger sample, to some historical 'Big Data'?

FUTURE RESEARCH DIRECTIONS

As indicated, the kinds of questions that can be answered about the history of victims are dependent on the historical sources that we have had to hand. In the past, crime historians spent numerous months of their lives with pencil in hand transcribing court registers and other court-generated data. There was a considerable step forward in using data with the creation of the Old Bailey Online. As we have seen, this has given us some limited search abilities in order to track the gender (and, to a much smaller extent, the age) of victims of crime since 1674. Now we are entering the age of 'Big Data', and, in this penultimate section, we would like to imagine some different projects which use Big Data to advance our historical knowledge of victims in new and interesting ways.

If we had access to all of the digitized data contained in the Old Bailey Online, for example, what could we do? When the Old Bailey records were digitized, some of the information was 'tagged' so that it could be separated and counted. The gender of victims was 'tagged', for example. However, their occupations, addresses and the nature of any 'legal support' offered or taken up were not, and nor was any previous experience of victimization or offending.

Let us imagine for a moment that we had this kind of data available to us: what kinds of research questions could we now ask? Maybe, with questions of class and social stratification in mind, we would ask: how did the demographic characteristics and socio-economic profile of victims change over time? What correlations were there between the social status of the complainant, their type(s) of victimization (or offending) and the outcome of their trial? Thinking about place and spatiality, we might want to know: Where did victims live? Where were people victimized, in what kinds of places – the streets, their homes – and did this alter if they were male or female? How close did offenders live to their victims? Were they living in the same street, or house? Were they neighbours, family members, workmates or (former) friends? We would examine connections between 'where people lived, where they spent time and with whom they associated' (Gottfredson, 1984: 17), and whether 'entrapment in averse neighbourhoods' was a major determinant of victim–offender overlap (Farrall and Calverley, 2006). With process in mind, we could ask: How did the growing professionalization of criminal justice actors (Langbein, 2003), such as solicitors and sentencers (stipendiary and district judges, for example), change outcomes for victims? What contribution was made by the growing use of medical experts, and forensic evidence? Lastly, how did the formal recording in court records of victim/complainants' details change over time and how might this relate to shifting public perceptions of victims?

How would a future 'imagined' project like this go about answering these questions? To start with, we would want the project to chart the broad infrastructural factors shaping public access to justice in criminal trials across the eighteenth, nineteenth and twentieth centuries. Using historical and legal research methods, we would track the introduction (as well as reform and withdrawal) of rights, resources and services upon which victims could draw prior to, during and after a prosecution. We would also want to track shifts in, for example, the statutory rights of victims to defend themselves, to hire (subsidised) legal representation, to bring charges, to make witness statements and to conduct cross-examination. Relevant resources and services here include: the rise of prosecution associations and prosecution lawyers

(1730s); the police (1830s); the creation of a new public prosecution mechanism (1870s); the Poor Man's Lawyers movement (1880s); the expansion of private insurance schemes (1890s); the removal of victims from court processes (1920s); legal aid (1940s); criminal injuries compensation schemes (1960s); victim support groups (1970s); Crown Prosecution Service and victim surveys (1980s); and victim personal impact statements (2010s).

The project would therefore need to analyse the socio-economic profiles of, resources available to and outcomes for victims of a wide range of crimes prosecuted over the last three centuries in one of the nation's most important courts. The project would assemble a new evidence base to establish who they were, what relationship (if any) they had with offender(s), how they came to be complainants, prosecutors or witnesses, how they made use (if at all) of available resources, how they were viewed by others, and, crucially, in what ways their cases were 'resolved' and their citizenship rights asserted. In this way, this future project would provide a new and much-needed historical angle on established debates around repeat victimization and the 'victim–offender overlap'.

This is quite a project we have dreamt up. What kind of research design and methodology would be required to achieve its aims?

First, we could take all of the existing digitized records of 202,791 Old Bailey trials from 1674 to 1913 (using the existing resource, Old Bailey Online). Because, so far, only certain data has been 'tagged up', we would 'tag' all available data appearing in these records about individual victims and thereby establish a large data set containing, for each victim, their age, gender, ethnicity (where possible), place of residence, occupation, place of work, the nature of the alleged crime(s) against them, relationship (if any) to the accused, the nature of the prosecution process and the outcome of that process. Through multivariate quantitative analysis, we would be able to reveal broad patterns of primary, secondary and repeat victimization from the eighteenth to the twentieth centuries. Although necessarily constrained by archival selection and survival (like all historical research), this kind of analysis would allow us to explore historical parallels (or divergences) with the findings of key contemporary studies.

Second, we could create a database of a number of victims of crime and combine the information we have collected for them (gender, age, and so on) with other digitized data. We would search for the individual victims of crime in the digitized census records (1841, 1851, 1861, 1871, 1881, 1891, 1901 and 1911) and thereby record details about their place of birth, place of residence, neighbourhood, occupation and (in some cases) their relationship to the accused. In order to capture biographical data that is not contained in the criminal justice records or the other available digitized civil records, we will also utilize the online digital newspaper reports. These may help us to 'fill in the gaps' about our victims. They might also help us to carry out some other forms of analysis on victims. Using digital corpus linguistic methods, we will assemble and analyse the descriptive terms used in newspapers from the 1700s to the present (via online archives of *The Times*,

The Guardian and other digitized online newspapers available from Gale Cengage and ProQuest – most university libraries have a subscription to these holdings). Emergent patterns across the whole data set could then be analysed, visualized, mapped and disseminated.

The newspapers offer yet more opportunities. We could use them to analyse the changing descriptions of victims of crime. The textual constructions of victims could tell us a lot about the way victims were perceived (if not by society as a whole, at least by the press?). We could simply count the number of times crimes against women, or children, or a particular occupational group, were reported in the press, compared to the actual number dealt with at the Old Bailey – were there any media biases that we can detect?

This project is imaginary, so can we push our imagination still further.

Taking a prosopographical approach, we could study the lives of victims. We already have the digital material to reveal the lives of victims, just as Godfrey et al. (2007) did for offenders. We could then investigate whether some people were repeat victims, and if they were, speculate why. We could see whether victimization affected future life – did victims of violent sexual assault in their youth go on to form relationships? Did shopkeepers who were regularly victims of theft change their occupation? Did victims of robbery in one area move to another part of town, or a different town? That might take some work, a lot of time, and we still might not have all of the data we would need, so this might not be feasible. Indeed, our imagination is still, it seems, limited by the sources we know exist, even if we cannot process them, and analyse them as we would wish. It is possible that historians of the future discover sources, or find new ways of using them, which we do not yet know. Then, further data will produce (and answer) new questions about victims.

SUMMARY AND REVIEW

This chapter has explored how the history of victims has been studied – how researchers 'did' that; and by following the research journey through some key findings, the chapter has finished by suggesting how we can now 'do' more research. The local court registers that provided the source material for some of the research on victims in the early 2000s have benefited historians considerably. By transcribing cases recorded in original documents and held in local archives and libraries, we have now revealed changes in the number, and gender, over time. We have seen the extent of the victim–offender overlap, and we have seen how the police takeover of prosecutions has affected recorded crime levels (for violence especially). However, the limitations are clear. This kind of work is time-consuming, the geographical range is limited and only a limited number of years can be collected. Digital resources, such as the Old Bailey Online, have speeded up research, but the information they reveal about victims is minimal.

As more digital resources become available, it will be possible to carry out larger 'Big Data' research on victims. If the data on victims from court-generated records can be tied together with contemporary newspaper reports, as well as personal and biographical records (in the way that the Digital Panopticon does for offenders), then it would be possible to produce very wide but detailed histories of victims in the eighteenth and nineteenth centuries. That kind of research would then allow researchers to answer, with confidence, the question posed by pioneering crime historian George Rudé nearly 50 years ago: 'What do we know about victims?'

STUDY QUESTIONS AND ACTIVITIES FOR STUDENTS

1. Do historical records show a gender imbalance in the profile of victims in your local court? Go to your nearest County Records Office and access a magistrates' court register. Pick an offence, and a range of years, and simply count the number of female and male complainants. If you have time, pick a violent offence (say assault) and a property offence (say simple larceny or theft).

2. Did the number of victims of violence increase or decrease in the nineteenth century? Using the statistics tool on the Old Bailey Online website, calculate the number of victims of assault, and of indecent assault, for each of the years between 1800 and 1900.

3. How has the language used to describe victims changed over the last 100 years? Look at some historic newspapers (either digital or paper copies kept in the local library) and compare how victims of, say, indecent assault, were described in the 1900s and the 2000s.

SUGGESTIONS FOR FURTHER READING

Godfrey, B. (2008) 'Changing prosecution practices and their impact on crime figures, 1857–1940', *British Journal of Criminology*, 48(2): 171–90. This article suggests that individual victims of violence were gradually replaced as prosecutors by the police, with the result that violent crime appeared to fall in the 1880 to 1914 period.

Godfrey, B. (2015) 'Setting the scene: the history of victims', in S. Walklate (ed.), *The Handbook of Victims and Victimology*, 2nd edition. London: Routledge. This book chapter examines the changing historical role of victims of crime, and their increasing symbolic power.

Godfrey, B., Cox, D. and Farrall, S. (2007) *Criminal Lives: Family, Employment and Offending*. Clarendon Series in Criminology. Oxford: Oxford University Press. Chapter 6 describes the historiography of victims, then outlines the concept of the victim–offender overlap and gives some examples from a historical study of Crewe in 1880–1940.

Jackson, L. (2000) *Child Sexual Abuse in Victorian England*. London: Routledge. This very well-researched book analyses an under-researched group of victims, children. It reveals the historical context for child sexual abuse today.

Rock, P. (2004) 'Victims, prosecutors and the state in nineteenth-century England and Wales', *Criminal Justice*, 4(4): 331–54. This is a sweeping and extremely good overview of the role of victims, and their relationship with the state in a key period of history.

REFERENCES

Beattie, J. (1986) *Crime and the Courts in England 1660–1800*. Oxford: Clarendon Press.

Brooke, H. (2016) *The History of Legal Aid*, 1945–97. Available at: https://sirhenrybrooke. me/2016/06/16/the-history-of-legal-aid-1945-to-1997 (accessed May 2018).

Clarke, A. (1987) *Women's Silence, Men's Violence: Sexual Assault in England, 1770–1845*. London: Pandora.

Clarke, A. (1997) *The Struggle for the Breeches: Gender and the Making of the British Working Class*. Berkeley, CA: University of California Press.

Conklin, W. (2001) 'Whither justice: the common problematic of five models of "access to justice"', *Windsor Yearbook of Access to Justice*, 19: 297–316.

Conley, C. (1991) *The Unwritten Law: Criminal Justice in Victorian Kent*. New York: Oxford University Press.

Cooper, P. (2009) *No Access to Justice*. Pittsburg, PA: Dorrace Publishing Company.

D'Cruze, S. (1998) *Crimes of Outrage: Sex, Violence and Victorian Working Women*. London: London University College Press.

D'Cruze, S. and Jackson, L. (2009) *Women, Crime and Justice in England since 1660*. London: Palgrave Macmillan.

Emsley, C. (2007) *The English and Violence since 1750*. London: A&C Black.

Emsley, C. (2013) *Crime and Society in England, 1750–1900*, 4th edition. London: Routledge.

Fagan, J., Piper, E. and Cheng, Y.-T. (1987) 'Contributions of victimisation to delinquency in inner cities', *Journal of Criminal Law and Criminology*, 78(3): 586–613.

Farrall, S. and Calverley, A. (2006) *Understanding Desistance from Crime*. Crime and Justice Series. Buckingham: Open University Press.

Godfrey, B. (2008) 'Changing prosecution practices and their impact on crime figures, 1857–1940', *British Journal of Criminology*, 48(2): 171–90.

Godfrey, B. (2015) 'Setting the scene: the history of victims', in S. Walklate (ed.), *The Handbook of Victims and Victimology*, 2nd edition. London: Routledge.

Godfrey, B., Cox, D. and D'Cruze, S. (2009) '"The most troublesome woman in Crewe": crime, gender and sentencing, 1880–1940', in S. D'Cruze, E. Avdela and J. Rowbotham (eds), *Crime, Violence and the Nation State*. New York: Edwin Mellen, pp. 249–92.

Godfrey, B., Cox, D. and Farrall, S. (2007) *Criminal Lives: Family, Employment and Offending*. Clarendon Series in Criminology. Oxford: Oxford University Press.

Godfrey, B., Farrall, S. and Karstedt, S. (2005) 'Explaining gendered sentencing patterns for violent men and women in the late Victorian and Edwardian period', *British Journal of Criminology*, 45(5): 696–720.

Goodey, J. (2004) *Victims and Victimology: Research, Policy and Practice*. London: Longman.

Gottfredson, M. (1984) *Victims of Crime: Dimensions of Risk*. Home Office Research Study No. 81. London: HMSO.

Gray, D. (2016) *Crime, Policing and Punishment in England, 1660–1914*. London: Bloomsbury.

Hay, D. (1975) 'Property, authority and the criminal law', in D. Hay, P. Linebaugh, J. Rule, E.P. Thompson and C. Winslow (eds), *Albion's Fatal Tree: Crime and Society in Eighteenth-Century England*. London: Allen Lane, pp. 17–63.

Hay, D. (1989) 'Using the criminal law, 1750–1850: policing, private prosecution, and the state', in D. Hay and F. Snyder (eds), *Policing and Prosecution in Britain, 1750–1850*. Oxford: Clarendon Press.

Hitchcock, T. and Shoemaker, R. (2007) *Tales from the Hanging Court*. London: Bloomsbury.

Jackson, L. (1999) 'The child's word in court: cases of sexual abuse in London 1870–1914', in C. Usborne and M. Arnot (eds), *Gender and Crime in Modern Europe*. London: UCL Press, pp. 222–37.

Jackson, L. (2000) *Child Sexual Abuse in Victorian England*. London: Routledge.

Kearon, T. and Godfrey, B. (2007) 'Setting the scene: the history of victims', in S. Walklate (ed.), *The Handbook of Victims and Victimology*. Cullompton: Willan Publications.

King, P. (1984) 'Decision-makers and decision-making in the English criminal law, 1750–1800', *Historical Journal*, 27: 25–58.

King, P. (1989) 'Prosecution associations and their impact in eighteenth-century Essex', in D. Hay and F. Snyder (eds), *Policing and Prosecution in Britain, 1750–1850*. Oxford: Clarendon Press.

King, P. (2000) *Crime, Justice and Discretion in England, 1740–1820*. Oxford: Oxford University Press.

King, P. (2004) 'The summary courts and social relations in eighteenth-century England', *Past and Present*, 183: 125–72.

Kirchengast, T. (2006) *The Victim in Criminal Law and Justice*. London: Palgrave Macmillan.

Langbein, J. (2003) *The Origins of the Adversary Criminal Trial*. Oxford: Oxford University Press.

Lauritsen, J., Sampson, R. and Laub, J. (1991) 'The link between offending and victimisation among adolescents', *Criminology*, 29(2): 265–92.

Law Society (Great Britain) (1992) *Access to Justice: The Law Society Manifesto*. London: The Law Society.

Linebaugh, P. (1991) *The London Hanged: Crime and Civil Society in the Eighteenth Century*. Cambridge: Cambridge University Press.

Maguire, J.M. (1928) *The Lance of Justice: A Semi-Centennial History of the Legal Aid Society, 1876–1926*. Littleton, CO: Fred B. Rothman.

Mayo, M., Koessl, G. and Scott, L. (2014) *Access to Justice for Disadvantaged Communities*. London: Policy Press.

Morgan, R.I. (1994) 'The introduction of civil legal aid in England and Wales, 1914–1949', *Twentieth Century British History*, 5(1): 38–76.

Newburn, T. (1993) *The Long-term Needs of Victims: A Review of the Literature*. Home Office Research and Planning Unit Paper No. 80. London: Home Office.

Newburn, T. and Stanko, E. (1994) 'When men are victims', in T. Newburn and E. Stanko (eds), *Just Boys Doing Business?* London: Routledge.

Palmer, E., Cornford, T., Marique, Y. and Guinchard, A. (2015) *Access to Justice: Beyond the Policies and Politics of Austerity*. London: Hart Publishing.

Rock, P. (2004) 'Victims, prosecutors and the state in nineteenth-century England and Wales', *Criminal Justice*, 4(4): 331–54.

Rudé, G. (1985) *Criminal and Victim Crime and Society in Early Nineteenth-Century England*. Oxford: Clarendon Press.

Sandefur, R. (ed.) (2009) *Access to Justice*. Vol. 12 of Sociology of Crime, Law and Deviance. Bingley: Emerald Group.

Singer, S. (1981) 'Homogeneous victim–offender populations: a review and some research implications', *Journal of Criminal Law and Criminology*, 72(2): 779–88.

Tomes, N. (1978) 'A torrent of abuse: crimes of violence between working-class men and women in London, 1840–1875', *Journal of Social History*, 11: 328–45.

CHAPTER CONTENTS

GLOSSARY TERMS

survey research
survey questionnaire
sensitive research
hard-to-reach groups
questionnaires
quantitative research
pilot study
piloting

9

USING SOCIAL SURVEYS IN CRIMINOLOGICAL RESEARCH

JO DEAKIN AND JON SPENCER

INTRODUCTION

In the run-up to the 2016 UK EU referendum, a team of researchers meet to develop a research proposal. Several tabloid newspapers have been running stories about an increase in crime committed by migrants, positioning these alongside calls to leave the EU. The research team is keen to discover the truth behind the criminal migrants' stories: are these headlines merely propaganda designed to feed into these two highly politicized debates? The researchers' aim is to devise a suitable method to investigate the 'extent' of criminal activity and criminal justice contact amongst young migrant men. Clearly, this is a sensitive issue that, if approached insensitively, could potentially be harmful for respondents: adding fuel to an already toxic debate, resulting in legal ramifications for individuals, or posing wider implications for the reputation and treatment of young migrant men.

After weighing up the different approaches, the researchers decide on a large national sample of young migrant men and agree that the survey method will generate the 'extent' of data required. However, a key point of concern is whether a survey-questionnaire will allow the researchers to treat this difficult subject sensitively. The key question is whether it is possible to gather sensitive research data through a large-scale survey. Quantitative survey research has been maligned for failing to deal sensitively with research topics and respondents and, in particular, for employing pre-defined terms and a static agenda (Fox Keller, 1980; Oakley, 1981; Reinharz, 1979). These criticisms are especially problematic where sensitive issues and vulnerable populations are concerned.

It would appear, on first impression, that the survey is not a suitable choice of method for a sensitive research topic, or for use with vulnerable respondents, such as the one described above. However, in this chapter we explore the ways in which surveys *can* be an appropriate method to gather data on sensitive issues. We review the literature on survey methodology and conducting sensitive research with vulnerable populations, provide examples of survey research on sensitive topics and with hard-to-reach groups and present a brief guide to devising and administering a survey on a sensitive issue. We begin with a discussion of the definitions of both sensitive research and hard-to-reach groups and provide a working definition of survey research.

WHAT IS A SENSITIVE TOPIC?

The term 'sensitive research' has been used to describe a range of different types of research that pose ethical and/or methodological dilemmas for the researcher. These include: topics that may be difficult to discuss, socially controversial or taboo; topics that pose a level of risk or involve potential costs to the respondent;

or research that elicits the views of vulnerable or 'powerless' groups such as children (see Box 9.1).

In criminology and victimology, many of the central research questions are of a 'sensitive' nature because the topics may be difficult for respondents to discuss, have potential to cause distress and may elicit information that can be damaging to the respondent, with serious implications for them, their communities and, on occasions, the researcher.

BOX 9.1   A FOCUS ON RESEARCH WITH CHILDREN

Research with children presents specific ethical and methodological issues (Hood et al., 1996; Mahon et al., 1996; Morrow and Richards, 1996). The British Society of Criminology's (2006) guidelines, *Code of Ethics for Researchers in the Field of Criminology*, reinforce the need for caution to be exercised with research concerning children:

> Researchers should consider carefully the possibility that the research experience may be a disturbing one, particularly for those who are vulnerable by virtue of factors such as age, social status, or powerlessness and should seek to minimise such disturbances. (BSC, 2006: 4.1)

Morrow and Richards (1996) argue that the difference between research with children and that with adults can be reduced to two perceptions that adults hold of children: first, that children are vulnerable and adults should take responsibility for them; and second, that children are not as competent as adults. Further, they argue that these perceptions are reinforced by legal notions of the child as powerless and irresponsible. These perceptions have implications for gaining consent for research, the choice of methods and the interpretation of data.

Children are potentially vulnerable in two respects: first, because of their comparative physical weakness and lack of experience and knowledge; and second, 'because of their total lack of political and economic power and their lack of civil rights' (Lansdown, 1994: 35). According to Lansdown, it is children's lack of civil status that has not been adequately addressed as a factor that produces vulnerability.

Some researchers have assumed that children lack the competence to provide valid sociological data (see Morrow and Richards, 1996). American researchers, Fine and Sandstorm (1988), for example, have likened the knowledge gained from children during participant observation to that gained from kittens, and fear that an adult interpretation of the data may be inaccurate. A further question of competence is raised around children's informed consent to the research (Kinaird, 1985).

(Continued)

(Continued)

This requires a respondent to 'voluntarily agree to participate in a research project, based on a full disclosure of pertinent information' (Tymchuk, 1992: 128). However, in the case of research with children (who are usually not seen as competent enough to give consent) consent must come from a parent, teacher or guardian:

> In the UK, consent is usually taken to mean consent from parents or those 'in loco parentis', and in this respect children are to a large extent seen as their parents' property, devoid of the right to say no to the research. (Morrow and Richards, 1996: 94)

Research with children must address the fundamental problem associated with gaining informed consent: can children be informed enough of the implications of the research to give informed consent?

Lee (1993) argues that sensitive research should be understood as that 'which potentially poses a substantial threat to those who are or have been involved in it' (Lee, 1993: 4). Lee defines the threat in three ways:

> The first is where the research poses as an 'intrusive threat', dealing with areas which are private, stressful or sacred. The second relates to the study of deviance and social control and involves the possibility that information may be revealed which is stigmatising or discriminating in some way. Finally, research is often problematic when it impinges on political alignments, if 'political' is taken in its widest sense to refer to the vested interests of powerful persons or institutions, or the exercise of coercion or domination. In these situations, researchers often trespass into areas which are controversial or involve social conflict. (Lee, 1993: 4)

Lee's definition of the three threats posed by sensitive research highlights an additional set of considerations for the researcher: how to access and engage with respondents on sensitive topics. Many respondents of sensitive research are known as 'hard-to-reach' groups; indeed, one could consider them hard to reach simply by virtue of the sensitive topic of the research, as well as by social or situational vulnerabilities. (See Box 9.2 for the Home Office definition and examples of hard-to-reach groups.)

Within criminological research, hard-to-reach respondents are not readily available or able, or willing to be 'the researched', and so have been under-represented. Engaging positively with hard-to-reach groups in order to give them 'a voice' in research requires a particular set of methodological skills. The latter part of this chapter brings together advice, experience and insights into conducting research with hard-to-reach groups on sensitive topics.

A hard-to-reach group can be any group which is difficult to access for any reason, such as:

- physical inaccessibility (e.g. older frail people)
- language (e.g. first-generation immigrants to the UK)
- cultural perceptions and traditions (e.g. disadvantaged young people)
- social expectations (e.g. children and young people who are often not considered an appropriate consultee and whom often also do not consider themselves as likely to be taken seriously). (Home Office crime reduction website)

Hard-to-reach groups could include:

- homeless people
- children and young people
- drug users
- gay men, lesbian women, transsexual and transgendered people
- minority ethnic communities (particular sections of)
- victims of domestic abuse
- older people (especially older frail people, and isolated older people)
- travelers
- asylum seekers
- people with learning difficulties
- people with disabilities
- people with mental health problems
- faith communities
- people who travel or commute into the area
- small businesses
- rural communities
- tourists.

Source: www.crimereduction.homeoffice.gov.uk/toolkits/p03110701.htm referenced in Davies et al. (2007)

SURVEY RESEARCH

Survey research involves the systematic collection of large quantities of data, by means of questionnaires and/or interviews, from a broad sample of a target population. A range of complex issues are involved, including sampling methods, developing meaningful research instruments (questionnaires, interviews), administering the survey, maximizing response rates, and a variety of ethical considerations (protection of respondents, confidentiality, etc.) (see, for example, Bachman and Schutt, 2008; Fowler, 2009, 2014; Nardi, 2014; Seale, 2004). We cannot cover all of these issues in this chapter (suggestions for further reading are offered at the end of this chapter); instead, we provide an overview of survey research, signpost key areas for further reading, and focus more closely on the use of surveys in the area of sensitive topics and with hard-to-reach groups (see Box 9.2).

Survey questionnaires are an important tool of the social scientist in collecting, categorizing and quantifying data. They allow the researcher to frame a research problem using a structured set of questions. Surveys are most commonly used to answer questions about the extent of beliefs or experience and can be used with a whole population or a sample of a population to provide data that can be generalized across a larger group. For this purpose, the sample or cross-section must accurately reflect the complexity and heterogeneity of the population to be studied. A cross-section of the prison population, for example, may be surveyed to gain information that can be applied to the whole of the prison population: a prison-based sample must reflect the characteristics of the whole prison population as closely as possible, including gender, black and minority ethnic populations, those serving different sentence lengths for different types of crime, and so on. A prison-based survey must also take account of differing levels of literacy (a self-completion questionnaire would not be suitable for those who cannot read and write) and should be translated where necessary. An example of such a survey is *Measuring the Quality of Prison Life* (MQPL) which surveys a sample of prisoners in each prison in relation to a number of key elements of prison life, including trust, respect, fairness, order and safety (see Ross et al., 2008).

The aim of survey research may be to generate statistics to describe the characteristics of a population – descriptive statistics (e.g. the extent of physical violence suffered by children); or to explore the correlation between two variables – analytic statistics (e.g. the relationship between the extent of physical violence suffered and the level of fear of violence experienced by children). The statistics generated are often used to inform policy and decision making.

CRITICISMS OF SURVEYS

The disadvantages of a quantitative survey methodology largely centre around five claims:

1. That the complexities of social data cannot reasonably be measured or recorded using an intrinsically positivistic method (Cicourel, 1964)

2. That the survey method assumes respondents understand and interpret the world around them in the same way, as if one were measuring a natural, unthinking phenomenon (Schutz, 1962)
3. That the meanings and definitions people assign to their experiences are ignored through the use of a structured method (Cicourel, 1982; Oakley, 1981), creating a 'static' image of social experience (Blumer, 1956)
4. That they present an obstacle to open discussion and prevent flexibility and spontaneity (Fox Keller, 1980; Oakley, 1981; Reinharz, 1979)
5. That where surveys involve interviews, the influence of the interviewer and the location of the interview significantly distort responses (Phillips, 1971).

Marsh (1982) counters these claims by arguing that, when surveys are well designed and properly administered, they make a key contribution to our understanding of the social world. She suggests that it is a particular style of survey research, known as *smash 'n' grab*, which has resulted in the bad press associated with this method. For Marsh, *smash 'n' grab* refers to the process whereby researchers design research instruments, undertake fieldwork and analyse data within a very short time frame, literally 'smashing' into the field, 'grabbing' data and exiting quickly. The result is a hastily developed, carelessly designed and poorly implemented survey that is well deserving of criticism.

The questionnaire is the most heavily criticized element of survey research. Questionnaires conducted in interview form are accused of failing to acknowledge the respondents' or the researchers' experiences. It is argued that such an approach objectifies the respondent as data, while their subjective experiences and personal meanings become lost in the process (Oakley, 1981). Self-completion questionnaires that do not require direct contact between the researcher and the respondents are viewed as generating detached, stilted data and preventing 'an interactive process' (Kennedy Bergen, 1993: 203).

However, problems with questionnaires, and the survey method more generally, are not insurmountable as Kelly (1990) demonstrates with the use of questionnaires in her research on child sexual assault. With a background in *qualitative research*, Kelly's transition towards quantitative research came as a result of experimenting with different approaches suitable for answering particularly sensitive research questions. She recognized the significance of collecting quantitative data from large groups of respondents to answer questions about the *extent* of personal experience, and began to explore the survey method. However, for a survey to deal with sensitive issues ethically, it must allow for subjective definitions and experience, and create space for views to be expressed (Kelly, 1990). Since most surveys work on pre-defined categories and tick-box style answers, Kelly needed to rethink the traditional survey style to fit her sensitive topic. Kelly's questionnaire, in addressing these problems, allowed respondents to define their own experiences and provided support for participants as required, thereby minimizing distress.

Perhaps most importantly, the research team spent several days, prior to administering the questionnaire, working in the participating institutions to facilitate links and develop relationships. This type of participatory approach to research allows researchers to begin to understand the research environment and become known to potential respondents. Through participation, researchers can gain the respondents' trust, provide appropriate support and have an active role in facilitating change. Even when self-completion questionnaires are the chosen method, the process doesn't have to be detached and stilted. Engaging with the participants in the research environment before and after collecting the data can encourage an interactive process that values the meanings people assign to their experiences and provides support.

The value of the survey method lies in its ability to gather large amounts of data to reveal the extent of a phenomenon. In so doing, it does *not* have to adhere to the stilted, bullish image it has so often been associated with. For the most part, the charges levelled at the survey are failings of the smash 'n' grab method; they are not failings of *all* surveys. Perhaps questionnaires will always have elements of inflexibility in their stable agenda and pre-defined categories, but, in sensitive research, these elements have probably been derived from a qualitative pilot study conducted to explore the area.

LARGE-SCALE SURVEYS: THE CRIME SURVEY FOR ENGLAND AND WALES (FORMERLY THE BRITISH CRIME SURVEY) AND ITS APPROACH TO SENSITIVE TOPICS

The Crime Survey for England and Wales (CSEW) (formerly The British Crime Survey (BCS)) provides annual data about the nature and extent of crime and victimization. The survey collects data about individual experiences of victimization and the information gathered informs government policy. In terms of sensitive research, the CSEW has it all: sensitive topics (such as sexual assault and domestic violence); vulnerable populations (children); a responsibility to include hard-to-reach groups; and the potential to reveal incriminating information. The survey consists of a set of core 'modules' that are asked of all respondents in face-to-face interviews, a set of secondary modules asked of sub-samples of respondents in the interview, and a final set of self-completion modules for all respondents. The self-completion modules deal with the most sensitive issues addressed in the survey. So, how does the CSEW approach questions on topics that may be considered particularly sensitive, such as intimate personal violence including partner abuse, family abuse, sexual assault, coercive and controlling behaviour and stalking?

The BCS and CSEW have included questions on intimate personal violence since 2001. The questions are consulted on, updated and developed regularly (cf. Campbell-Hall et al., 2010; Hall and Smith, 2011; Home Office, 2012) in line with changing definitions and legislation, most recently for the 2012/13 CSEW as part of an Intimate Personal Violence split-sample experiment (CSEW 2012/12). The questions are located in a separate self-completion module entitled 'Intimate Personal Violence (IPV)'. This separation of the module was prompted by concerns raised in earlier waves of the survey that the explicit nature of the questions affected responses to subsequent questions (ONS, 2015). All respondents aged 16–59 are asked to complete this section. The module comprises over 20 pages of questions covering aspects of the respondents' experiences of and attitudes to domestic violence and sexual assault, and because of their sensitive nature they are completed on a laptop. This approach is intended to minimize embarrassment to the respondent and improve the reporting rate. The questions are carefully phrased, free from jargon and easily understood by respondents of all ages (see Box 9.3), and the module reiterates that the respondent does not have to answer the questions: 'Remember, if the questions upset you in any way you can just pass by them by pressing "Don't wish to answer". However, we hope you will continue to the end' (Hall and Smith, 2011: 34).

In addition, a number of procedural safeguards have been put in place to ensure an ethical approach. For example, new researchers are required to attend full briefing sessions and further refresher courses are compulsorily attended by the more experienced researchers. Confidentiality of data is ensured, and advice on how to obtain further help is offered to respondents as necessary.

BOX 9.3 ONS METHODOLOGICAL NOTE (2015)

1. **NIPV1 [ASK ALL AGE 16–59 MODULE C AND D RESPONDENTS IF NONRESP = 1 OR NONRESP2 = 1]**

   a. Since you were 16 has a **partner or ex-partner** ever done any of the things listed below? By partner we mean a boyfriend, girlfriend, husband, wife or civil partner.

   - Prevented you from having your fair share of the household money?
   - Stopped you from seeing friends and relatives?
   - Repeatedly belittled you to the extent that you felt worthless?

   1. Yes
   2. No
   3. Never had a partner/been in a relationship
   4. Don't know/can't remember
   5. Don't wish to answer

2. **NIPV3 [ASK ALL AGE 16–59 MODULE C AND D RESPONDENTS IF (NONRESP = 1 OR NONRESP2 = 1) AND NIPV1 NE 3]**

   a. Since you were 16 has a **partner or ex-partner** ever frightened or threatened you in any way? For example, they may ha**ve threatened to hurt** you, to kill you, to use a weapon on you, or to hurt someone close to you [such as your children]?

      1. Yes
      2. No
      3. Don't know/can't remember
      4. Don't wish to answer

3. **NIPV5 [ASK ALL AGE 16–59 MODULE C AND D RESPONDENTS IF (NONRESP = 1 OR NONRESP2 = 1) AND NIPV3 NE 3]**

   a. Since you were 16 has a **partner or ex-partner** ever used force on you? For example, they may ha**ve pushed you, slapped** you, hit, punched or kicked you, choked you or used a weapon against you.

      1. Yes
      2. No
      3. Don't know/can't remember
      4. Don't wish to answer

4. **NIPV533 [ASK ALL AGE 16–59 MODULE C AND D RESPONDENTS IF NONRESP = 1 OR NONRESP2 = 1]**

   a. Since the age of 16 has **anyone** ever sent you more than one unwanted letter, text message or card that was either obscene or threatening and which caused you fear, alarm or distress? This may have been a partner, a family member, a friend or work colleague, someone you knew casually, or a stranger.

      1. Yes
      2. No
      3. Don't know/can't remember
      4. Don't wish to answer

GENERATING SURVEY DATA ON SENSITIVE TOPICS AND WITH VULNERABLE GROUPS

In this second part of the chapter, we consider how to use surveys and questionnaires to produce ethically sound data on sensitive topics and with hard-to-reach groups. Here, we outline key points for consideration before undertaking sensitive survey research and show how these work in action by providing two examples of surveys that we have worked on. One of our examples, 'The Children and Young People's Safety Survey' (Gallagher et al., 1998), involves a vulnerable population and a sensitive topic, and the other, Public attitudes to sex offenders (Brown et al., 2007), concerns a particularly emotive and sensitive topic. The design and implementation of the survey methods affect the quality, validity and reliability of the data. When the topic or the population to be researched are defined as sensitive, a further level of complexity is added as sensitivity affects almost every stage of the research process (Lee, 1993; Lee and Renzetti, 1990) and should be considered in the conceptualization, piloting, implementation and dissemination processes.

To provide a valid method of gathering attitudes and experiences, surveys should be constructed to be ethically sound, discreet and anonymous.

BOX 9.4   KEY QUESTIONS THAT ALL RESEARCHERS SHOULD ASK WHEN UNDERTAKING ANY PROJECT

- Who will benefit from this research?
- What is the cost (emotional and financial) to respondents?
- What are the barriers to this research and how can we address them? For example, legal barriers, ethical barriers, political barriers, and practical barriers such as access.
- Ultimately, the researcher needs to ask 'can the research be justified?' If the answer is no, the researcher should withdraw from the research; if the answer is yes, then even though there will be problems along the way it is appropriate to proceed.

IDENTIFYING AND DESIGNING SUITABLE RESEARCH QUESTIONS

Surveys are frequently associated with studies of prevalence and incidence, and research on sensitive topics is often concerned with estimating the extent of phenomena that are hidden. Uncovering the extent or frequency of a particular type of deviant behaviour, the size of a hidden deviant population, or the extent of experiences of victimization can all be researched appropriately using the survey method – see, for example, Gfroerer and Kennet's (2014) survey on the nature and extent of substance use, from which they conclude that a tailored approach to survey design, that considers the advantages and disadvantages of varied design options, can produce the most efficient surveys. Furthermore, survey methods can be used to research attitudes and opinions – see, for example, De Cao and Lutz's (2014) survey measuring attitudes towards female genital mutilation in which a 'list experiment' asks respondents to express levels of agreement with a range of statements comprising a mix of sensitive and non-sensitive items. De Cao and Lutz found that respondents were more likely to share their real attitudes concerning the sensitive issue of FGM using a simple list technique. Finally, the survey has been shown to be a useful tool in exploring perceptions and definitions around sensitive topics: in our own research, in surveying public attitudes towards sex offenders (Brown et al., 2007), vignettes were used to ask sensitive attitudinal questions in an indirect way (see Survey Example 2, later in this chapter). Box 9.5 gives examples of different types of questions used in survey research that can help explore attitudes, definitions, values and perceptions.

BOX 9.5   SOME TYPICAL SURVEY QUESTIONS

CLOSED QUESTION TYPES

Dichotomous
Are you male/female?

Ordinal scale
How old are you?
0–20, 20–40, 40–60, 60–80, over 80

Rating scale
How satisfied are you with the response of the police following the crime you reported?
Very satisfied, Moderately satisfied, Neutral, Moderately dissatisfied, Very dissatisfied, Don't know/don't want to say

Likert scale
Please indicate the extent to which you agree or disagree with the following statement:
A person found guilty of a serious sexual offence should always be imprisoned.
Strongly agree, Agree, Neither agree nor disagree, Disagree, Strongly disagree, Don't know

OPEN QUESTION TYPES

Unstructured
How do you see your role as a prison officer in a prison today?

> *Focused semi-structured response*
> What do you think is an appropriate sentence (if any) for a first-time offence of stealing a car?
>
> *Specific, factual response*
> Who would you initially seek help from if you'd been burgled?
>
> *Response to stimulus or hypothetical situation*
> The government has recently proposed to prosecute men who are caught kerb-crawling. What do you think of this proposal?
> (Also see vignette below.)

Designing a survey so that it is accessible to the respondent group seems obvious but can be surprisingly difficult. For example, for each question the researcher needs to think: how are respondents going to understand and answer this question? Have I used appropriate terminology and language? The researcher needs to put themselves in the respondents' shoes and stay there throughout the design and piloting phases. This ensures that the presentation and phrasing of questions are appropriate, engaging, interesting and as unthreatening as possible. The role of the survey researcher is to minimize the feeling of threat so as to gain detailed, accurate and reliable data in an ethical manner. There are a number of threat-reducing techniques that can be used, such as leading gently up to sensitive questions and using computers for self-completion questions. But by far the most significant factor in de-sensitizing a topic is the choice of suitable questions. Here, we provide an overview of the different types of questions developed and discuss the potential advantages and pitfalls of question design.

Open and closed questions

Closed questions containing pre-coded or 'fixed-choice' responses are useful to gather factual data such as personal background information, or data about events or behaviours. This data is often complete and easy to analyse. However, where sensitive topics are involved, closed questions can inhibit accurate reporting as respondents may avoid ticking the outermost response categories (Lee, 1993). Such problems can be circumvented by ensuring that response categories cover all possible behaviours and incorporate the extremes. To achieve the most appropriate closed questions, it can be helpful to take data from a small sample of respondents answering open questions and use this knowledge to design closed-response questions for a larger sample (Gomm, 2004). This technique is called a pilot study and typically involves conducting a number of qualitative interviews from which quantitative, fixed-choice questions may be generated.

Open questions can be more difficult to answer as respondents are required to write down a few words rather than tick one of a number of pre-given answers. However, open questions have the advantage of allowing the respondent to answer freely without being confined by a set of answers. This is particularly valuable in research focused on people's experiences and perceptions. For example, it is more useful to ask someone to describe what it felt like to be sentenced to prison rather than to provide them with a list of emotions to tick. Both open and closed questions have a central place in survey research and are used effectively to draw out different types of information.

BOX 9.6 EXAMPLES OF OPEN AND CLOSED QUESTIONS

Closed questions requiring a simple tick-box answer:

'Has anyone ever deliberately hit you with their fist?'

'When you have been out, has a stranger … done anything else to you, or frightened you, or hurt you in any way?'

Open questions requiring longer responses:

'What sorts of things do you worry about happening to you when you are out?'

'Is it a good time to be a young person in the UK at the moment?'

'What sorts of things do you like to do when you're not at school?'

Long questions

Sensitive research provides the exception to the rule about question length. It is commonly believed that lengthy questions are detrimental on surveys, confusing the respondent and leading to hasty responses (Bryman, 2001). Longer questions allow the researcher to talk around the issue before asking the question so, with sensitive research, this may help to desensitize the topic (Lee, 1993) and a longer question may aid recall (Sudman and Bradburn, 1982). A word of warning: use them sparingly and only where necessary as respondents can become tired of reading or listening to lengthy questions.

Loaded questions

The tone of a question can have an effect on the response of respondents. Loaded questions are accused of leading the respondent towards a particular response

(Bryman, 2001); however, loaded questions can help a respondent feel more comfortable when talking about an uncomfortable subject and provide a forum in which taboo behaviour can be revealed. Sudman and Bradburn (1982) describe four ways to load a sensitive question to achieve more accurate reporting of behaviour. The examples they provide are intended to encourage parents to discuss taboo feelings of anger towards their children (see Box 9.7).

BOX 9.7   SUDMAN AND BRADBURN'S LOADED QUESTIONS

Type of approach	Loaded question
Everybody does it	Even the calmest parents get mad at their children sometimes. Did your children do anything in the past week to make you angry?
Assume the behaviour	How many times during the last week did your child do something that made you angry?
Use expert opinion	Many psychologists believe it is important for parents to express their pent-up frustrations. Did your children do anything in the past week to make you angry?
Explain the behaviour	Parents become angry when they're tired or distracted or when their children are unusually naughty. Did your children do anything in the past week to make you angry?

Source: Adapted from Sudman and Bradburn (1982)

Vignettes

Vignettes are an alternative to traditional questions and are used in surveys to reveal attitudes and behaviour. The main element of a vignette is a description of a scenario involving a number of key factors. However, there are different ways of using them in a survey. For example, Alexander and Becker (1978) describe the use of vignettes in a study concerned with rape victimization attitudes among police and nurses. The vignette described the attack but varied factors relating to the victim, for example marital status, relationship to the attacker, injuries sustained, and so on. In total, the variations produced 64 possible combinations that were distributed randomly across the sample of 680 respondents. Differences in attitudes between the two groups could then be measured by looking at the average response to each version of the vignette (Alexander and Becker, 1978).

Finch (1987) used vignettes in a qualitative study to establish family obligations. The vignettes follow a story that is presented in several stages, adding further information and with questions asking what the protagonists should do after each stage. The questions were designed to allow the respondent to define a situation, and to reveal norms of behaviour. While she notes some problems with this method, particularly around recall of details as the story develops, Finch argues that using stages within a vignette allows the respondent to imagine how a story evolves (Finch, 1987).

Another approach to vignettes involves devising a set of different scenarios linked under a common theme that are distributed to each respondent. This thematic approach can be useful as part of a pilot study or an exploratory investigation into a topic, particularly where definitions or perceptions of a particular term or activity are required. In our nationwide study of public attitudes towards sex offenders (see Survey Example 2, later in this chapter), we developed thematic vignettes to reveal opinions about the classification and severity of a range of offences (Brown et al., 2007). The vignettes provided respondents with an opportunity to explore their thoughts on this sensitive topic whilst retaining an 'outsider' perspective (Box 9.8).

BOX 9.8   VIGNETTES USED IN PUBLIC ATTITUDES TO SEX OFFENDER RESEARCH (BROWN ET AL, 2007)

ACCOUNT 1

Ted rents his house to a group of young professionals. Unknown to any of the tenants, Ted routinely records their bedrooms and bathroom via a digital camera system. He collects hours of footage per day and has videos dating back a number of years.

1. Do you think that Ted is a sex offender? Why?
2. How serious do you consider his actions?

Very serious	☐ 1
Serious	☐ 2
Not that serious	☐ 3
Trivial	☐ 4

ACCOUNT 2

Jim lends his computer to Sarah for a couple of weeks while he is on holiday. Sarah finds a folder containing general pornographic material downloaded from the internet, and one of the pictures is of someone in their early teens.

---

1. Do you think that Jim is a sex offender? Why?
2. How serious do you consider his actions?

Very serious	☐ 1
Serious	☐ 2
Not that serious	☐ 3
Trivial	☐ 4

ACCOUNT 3

Karen and Robert attend a party together. Robert encourages Karen to drink spirits. Karen says that after a few hours of flirting with Robert she went into a bedroom to sleep off some alcohol. The next morning she claims to have been sexually assaulted by Robert. Karen says that no consent was given. Robert states that Karen had implied consent throughout the night.

1. Do you think that Robert is a sex offender? Why?
2. How serious do you consider his actions?

Very serious	☐ 1
Serious	☐ 2
Not that serious	☐ 3
Trivial	☐ 4

ACCOUNT 4

From a window inside his own home, Brian intentionally exposes himself to a passerby. The passerby laughs at first, but becomes concerned for others who might be offended and reports the incident to the police. The police question Brian. Brian states that the person who he flashed laughed at him and did not seem to find his behaviour upsetting.

1. Do you think that Brian is a sex offender? Why?
2. How serious do you consider his actions?

Very serious	☐ 1
Serious	☐ 2
Not that serious	☐ 3
Trivial	☐ 4

These different approaches to the use of vignettes allow for the simulation of a situation. This has the advantage of 'desensitizing' the topic and allowing the respondent to remain detached. However, one problem is that the use of a simulated scenario may produce simulated responses that do not match up with what a respondent would do or think in a real situation. For this reason, Lee (1993) concludes that vignettes are best used to reveal 'normative patterns' (or how respondents think things ought to be), rather than actual behaviours. Despite the drawbacks, the vignette method is a popular tool of the survey researcher. It allows for creativity in the design process, can be shaped to fit sensitive issues very effectively and encourages respondent engagement in the survey.

Once the questionnaire has been devised, it should be 'piloted' to check that it operates effectively. Piloting involves testing the questionnaire with a small set of respondents that are comparable to the target respondents. As Bryman notes, piloting 'may be particularly crucial in relation to research based on the self-completion questionnaire, since there will not be an interviewer present to clear up any confusion' (2001: 155). Problems with questionnaires and survey interview schedules can be identified through this process and alterations to the research instruments can be made.

Confidentiality

While ensuring confidentiality with participants is imperative in any research, reassurance of water-tight confidentiality is arguably the make or break of sensitive research. For respondents, the thought of disclosing personally sensitive information in an interview or on a questionnaire can be daunting and assurances of confidentiality may be essential for their participation. It is imperative that respondents enter into the research process with the knowledge that the data gathered will be collected, handled and stored without fear of leakage or loss. One way to reassure respondents of confidentiality is, where possible, to spend time in the research environment before and after the data collection.

A range of methods can be used to ensure data collected remains confidential. Collecting anonymized data is the most secure method but is obviously a problem if a follow-up interview is required in a longitudinal study. Alternatively, data could be anonymized at a variety of stages during the fieldwork or analysis phases, using separately stored codes to identify respondents for follow-up.

EXAMPLES OF SURVEY RESEARCH

We now discuss our own experiences of survey research on sensitive topics with hard-to-reach groups. The following section presents two examples of surveys that we have been involved with. Both focus on sensitive topics and involve vulnerable or hard-to-reach groups, and each presents specific methodological problems.

Survey example 1: Children and victimization

The Children and Young People's Safety Survey (CYPSS) (Gallagher et al., 1998) is an ESRC-sponsored survey that was conducted between 1996 and 1998. The survey was carried out in 26 primary and secondary schools in the north-west of England by a sizeable multi-disciplinary group and the data produced has provided various analyses of children's fears and experiences of victimization (Deakin, 2006; Gallagher et al., 1998, 2008). We were able to explore these sensitive issues through questionnaires and follow-up interviews, generating quantitative data about the prevalence of victimization and providing a forum for discussion on how victimization and fear are recognized, defined and dealt with by children. We administered questionnaires to 2,420 children and young people between the ages of 9 and 16 from four types of area: the inner city, peripheral council estates, suburban and rural locations. Questionnaires were completed during class-time, and follow-up interviews were conducted with a sub-sample of 52 victims and 52 non-victims in their homes. Our method highlights the importance of the children's subjective experiences by allowing them to define victimization and fear, and it provided support and advice to children and their parents about the issue of abuse (Deakin, 2006).

Questions around the confidentiality of data or disclosure of children's experiences either to parents or to child protection agencies were perhaps our greatest concern during the fieldwork. The National Children's Bureau argues that complete confidentiality can never be guaranteed to children because the researcher has a duty to pass on relevant information to professional agencies as appropriate (Mahon et al., 1996). The children involved in the study were informed that their answers would, for the most part, be confidential, but that, in certain circumstances, they might be encouraged to disclose information to an appropriate professional (Gallagher et al., 2008).

Design

The questionnaire was designed to provide children with a forum to describe their feelings and experiences. It included straightforward language, graphics and colour to appeal to children and feel informal. The number of questions was kept to a minimum whilst as much information as possible was gathered about victimization, safety and fears using closed-response options as much as possible and avoiding loaded questions. The more sensitive questions exploring victimization were carefully worded to reflect the range of experiences, to avoid causing distress, and to be acceptable to schools and parents. Sensitive parts of the questionnaire were introduced after less sensitive questions and followed by a discussion about safety measures intended to leave the child in a positive frame of mind (Gallagher et al., 2002).

Access and piloting

Schools were selected as the most representative of each area and letters were sent to each school explaining the nature of the study, the proposed uses of the research and requesting participation. Most of the schools contacted agreed to take part in the study after a period of consultation with parents, and none of these research sites would typically be considered hard to reach. However, children as a respondent group, and in particular younger children, are often protected from research by a series of gatekeepers (including parents, teachers, youth workers) and so could be considered hard to reach. For the follow-up interviews, consent was sought from both children and parents. Piloting of the questionnaire and the interview schedule were extensive due to the sensitive nature of the study, and, as a result, a number of changes were made including order and wording of questions. For example, a question designed to reveal experiences of unwanted sexual touching was changed from 'Has anyone touched you in a way you didn't like?' to 'Has anyone touched you on a private part of your body in a way you didn't like?' after some children misunderstood the question.

Implementation

Before handing out the questionnaires, the children were briefed on its content and purposes in an age-appropriate manner. We gave the children examples of the types of questions and explained the structure of the questionnaire. We also explained to the children that everything they wrote down was confidential and would be anonymized, and told them they could ask for help, or stop answering the questions at any time. After the questionnaire had been completed, the children were offered the opportunity to talk to the researcher privately and given information about further sources of help and advice (Gallagher et al., 2002).

From our questionnaires, we were able to gather detailed, robust and subtle data in relation to children's fears and experiences of victimization. This study demonstrated that questionnaires can tackle sensitive topics with a vulnerable population. They can use questions that leave definitions open to the respondent and they can be administered ethically, providing advice and support where needed.

Survey example 2: Public attitudes to sex offenders in the community

Our second example of sensitive survey research details a project we conducted in 2004/5 aimed at revealing public perceptions of sexual offences and attitudes towards the sentencing and potential reintegration of those convicted (Brown et al., 2007). Two distinct problems were raised by this research. These were:

1. How to approach the emotive topic of sex offender reintegration sensitively.
2. Ensuring that the sample of the general public is representative, and includes some respondents from hard-to-reach groups.

Just under 1,000 responses were gathered using a range of techniques, including a targeted postal questionnaire, a web-based questionnaire promoted via various Usenet newsgroups, and a community-based questionnaire delivered to community groups, local meetings, health services and local businesses (Brown et al., 2007).

Previous research has shown that gauging public attitudes to offenders and sentencing, in general, is fraught with problems (Stalans, 2002). Results have been varied (often contradicting the common perception that people are generally punitive). Stalans argues that this variance is caused by methodological issues: 'researchers have measured attitudes in a variety of ways and the public's response often depends on the manner in which the question is asked and the context in which it is located' (Stalans, 2002: 16). Stalans (2002) goes on to argue that research considering public attitudes to sentencing tends to be relatively superficial without fully exploring the depth of public opinion. Clearly, attempting to unravel the layers of attitudes to offenders, sentencing and their management in the community is no easy task.

In our study of public attitudes towards sex offenders, the task was further complicated by the highly sensitive and diverse nature of offences that have been termed 'sex crime' and the emotive response they provoke. Our decision to conduct a survey of the general public about this sensitive and controversial topic resulted in a range of challenges to be met and problems to be overcome.

Sample selection and data gathering

Our first problem was in ensuring that we constructed a representative sample. The sample needed to include people from different social, demographic, ethnic and geographic groupings, and include those that could be considered 'hard to reach' (see Box 9.2). In order to take account of these differences within the sample, we used several different sampling methods.

First, using social and demographic research data accessed via the Office of National Statistics we identified a range of socio-economic locations. We were then able to select postal areas from within our larger, targeted, geographic area. We included two areas that had high levels of deprivation, two areas with 'average' levels of economic activity and one area that was 'affluent'; we also included one area that was defined as multicultural. Two of the areas identified were rural areas and the remaining geographic locations were close to city centres. Once we had decided on the geographic locations, we began to negotiate access with local community-based groups and health centres; these were across a spectrum of pursuits and concerns so that we could ensure variations of age and interests. We were available to explain the purpose of the questionnaire, to be on hand while respondents completed the questionnaire and to administer the questionnaire verbally or translate it if necessary. Through this method, we were able to include some respondents within the 'hard to reach' category, and we were able to offer advice and support to this group. However, this is a very time-consuming method of data gathering. Spending time at each of the community groups was a highly labour-intensive means of data gathering and, at times, the questionnaire return was small due to the number of people attending the meetings. We collected 98 questionnaires from community groups and health centres.

At the same time, we mailed out a total of 5,000 questionnaires. The questionnaires were split across our geographic areas to named respondents, which was an attempt to embed an element of control in the structure of the sample. We also mailed the questionnaire to large workplaces. In total, we received a 15% response rate to our postal questionnaire: an average response for an unsolicited postal questionnaire.

Additionally, we placed a web-based questionnaire on a newsgroup site which consisted of mainly open questions. This was intended to supplement the data gathered through the other, more targeted, sampling methods. The problem with the web-based method is that while you can gain rich data you have no control over the structure of the sample (see also Chapter 18 by Yar in this volume). The very nature of the respondents using newsgroups meant that the data could have been skewed towards those with a greater interest in, and knowledge of, current or topical issues. Additionally, people likely to respond to web-linked questionnaires are often those with the most extreme views. There were 72 web questionnaires returned, which we used separately from the postal and community responses as additional, illustrative data to support (and sometimes confound) the rest of our results (Brown et al., 2007).

Making sense of the data

In total, we had 979 responses to our questionnaire. We had attempted to elicit a range and depth of information from respondents and so had used a number of survey data-gathering methods; for example, we included a range of open questions and vignettes to create space for attitudes to be expressed and definitions to be explored (see Box 9.6). We asked a number of questions in relation to definitions of sex crime, attitudes towards sex offender sentencing and rehabilitation, views on the effectiveness of current resettlement strategies and the sex offenders register. All respondents were provided with an information sheet about the project that included the contact details of relevant help and support organizations (for a more detailed report of this research, see Brown et al., 2007).

The data generated from the various survey methods was rich and allowed us to analyse attitudes to sex offenders against the variables of gender, age, socio-economic status and type of area of residence, for example urban or rural. The responses were varied and in sufficient volume to enable us to complete a range of statistical tests on the data. In general, our results were consistent with those of previous research studies and highlighted that attitudes towards sex offenders were much more nuanced and complex than the claims made by the tabloid press. Our survey method had effectively uncovered these complexities through a combination of vignettes and open and closed questions directed at revealing attitudes.

The research highlighted the problem that policy-makers face in continually having to reproduce high levels of trust in the criminal justice system, in order to ensure that the public retain confidence not only in the delivery of justice but also in the management of offenders in the community (Brown et al., 2007). Our research suggests that the level of public trust in the criminal justice system and in criminal justice professionals is essentially very fragile. We were able to discover the fragility of public trust through the use of a survey in what is a very sensitive area.

SUMMARY AND REVIEW

Sensitive survey research is not an oxymoron, providing that care is taken throughout each stage of the process. Clearly, sensitive research poses unique ethical and methodological challenges whatever the chosen method. We have demonstrated in this chapter that it is possible to undertake ethically sound and appropriate survey research in relation to sensitive topics. Through the careful and thoughtful construction and administration of a questionnaire, extensive piloting, participation in the research environment, and by structuring the sample to take account of difference, it is possible to give respondents, some of whom have little voice in research, a forum to share their experiences and thoughts with safety and without threat or coercion. This highlights one of the core principles of any research: that the respondent is never a means to an end but rather an end in themselves. Above all else, criminological research should value the experiences and thoughts of those who agree to participate in our projects.

So, when you are thinking about undertaking research, you should consider the following questions carefully:

- **Is my proposed research sensitive?** Think about the types of questions you are going to be asking respondents and remember to put yourself in their shoes. If the question feels sensitive to you, then by and large it probably is and it therefore needs to be treated with respect and care.
- **What are the key criticisms of my survey research?** In other words, can you justify what you are doing? If you can't, then you probably should not proceed with the research.
- **What are the advantages and disadvantages of using different methodological techniques in my survey?** Think about the various ways you could gather data and judge which would be the most appropriate research instruments to develop.
- **How can I engage with the respondents?** Can you spend time in the research environment before the survey is administered? What support can you provide after the fieldwork has finished? How will you disseminate the findings?
- **What ethical issues does this research pose?** Be alert to the variety of ethical issues posed by sensitive research and the specific ethical issues when research

respondents are under 18. You need to be able to satisfy rigorous ethical scrutiny in order to justify your project.

Clearly, sensitive topics require a sensitive approach. The survey method can be a blunt tool, but, as we hope we have demonstrated, when it is approached in a creative, flexible and thoughtful way, the survey can be fine-tuned into an effective and ethical instrument. From our initial example of researching criminal activity amongst young migrant men, to uncovering experiences of intimate personal violence and victimization amongst children, the much maligned survey can be a valuable and effective tool.

STUDY QUESTIONS AND ACTIVITIES FOR STUDENTS

1. What are the main criticisms of survey research?

2. What issues are included under the umbrella term 'sensitive'?

3. What is a 'hard-to-reach' group?

4. Are surveys ever an appropriate method to use when considering sensitive issues?

5. What ethical issues would you need to consider when conducting survey research with children?

6. Using one of the vignette types described in Box 9.6, design a series of vignettes to explore one of the following topics:

   a. Employees' understanding of workplace bullying
   b. Attitudes of the general public to methods used by the police in the prevention of terrorism.

7. You are directing a research project to reveal employers' attitudes towards employing ex-problem drug users (PDUs). Devise a briefing note to the research team with what you think may be the problems with gathering data from employers and how these may be avoided in the questionnaire design.

8. You are designing a survey to find out the experiences of foreign national (FN) women in prisons in the UK. In particular, you want to know how they experience their relationships with prison staff. Design some questions to be part of a survey using each of the following question types: ordinal, open, interval, yes/no.

9. You are thinking about conducting a survey with children between the ages of 11 and 16 to investigate the relationship between truancy and offending:

a. Make a list of the key factors you would want to ask your respondents about.
b. Make a list of the key ethical considerations and how you would approach them.

10. Using Sudman and Bradburn's examples of loaded questions (Box 9.5), what questions could you use to research the following topics? Try loading your questions using the four different approaches:

a. the extent of promiscuity amongst college students
b. the nature of anti-social behaviour engaged in by 16–18-year-olds
c. the extent of feelings of insecurity experienced by residents of a high-crime estate.

SUGGESTIONS FOR FURTHER READING

Specifically on researching sensitive issues, Lee (1993) provides a full and timeless account of the issues and how to manage them. Chapter 5 is dedicated to conducting survey research sensitively. You can also find excellent guidance on the issues of sensitive research throughout the qualitative research methods books – see, for example, the following texts:

Hollway, W. and Jefferson, T. (2000) *Doing Qualitative Research Differently: Free Association, Narrative and the Interview Method*. London: Sage.

Lee, R.M. (1993) *Doing Research on Sensitive Topics*. London: Sage. Chapter 5 discusses sensitive survey research.

Lee, R.M. and Renzetti, C.M. (1990) The problems of researching sensitive topics: An overview and introduction.

Silverman, D. (ed.) (2016) *Qualitative Research*. London: Sage. There is a plethora of literature dedicated to the art of survey research. The following (chapters in) texts provide discussions of the design and implementation of surveys in social research, including sampling methods, developing research instruments (questionnaires, interviews), administering the survey, maximizing response rates, and a variety of ethical considerations:

Bachman, R. and Schutt, R. (2008) *Fundamentals of Research in Criminology and Criminal Justice*. Thousand Oaks, CA: Sage. Especially Chapter 6.

Bryman, A. (2001) *Social Research Methods*. Oxford: Oxford University Press. Especially Chapters 4–7.

Fowler, F.J. (2014) *Survey Research Methods*, 5th edition. Los Angeles, CA: Sage.

Gomm, R. (2004) *Social Research Methodology: A Critical Introduction*. Basingstoke: Palgrave Macmillan. Especially Chapters 4 and 8.

Groves, R.M., Fowler, F.J., Couper, M.P., Lepkowski, J.M., Singer, E. and Tourangeau, R. (2004) *Survey Methodology*. Hoboken, NJ: Wiley.

Marsh, C. (1982) *The Survey Method: The Contribution of Surveys to Sociological Explanation*. London: Allen and Unwin.

Seale, C. (ed.) (2004) *Social Research Methods: A Reader*. London: Routledge.

REFERENCES

Alexander, C.S. and Becker, H.J. (1978) 'The use of vignettes in survey research', *Public Opinion Quarterly, 42*: 93–104.

Bachman, R. and Schutt, R. (2008) *Fundamentals of Research in Criminology and Criminal Justice*. London: Sage.

Blumer, H. (1956) 'Sociological analysis and the variable', *American Sociological Review, 21*: 683–90.

Bolling, K., Grant, C. and Donovan, J. (2008) 2007–08 British Crime Survey (England and Wales) Technical Report: Volume I. Available at: www.data-archive.ac.uk/doc/6066/mrdoc/pdf/6066techreport1.pdf (accessed 5 April 2018).

British Society of Criminology (2006) *Code of Ethics for Researchers in the Field of Criminology*. Available at: www.britsoccrim.org/docs/CodeofEthics.pdf (accessed 5 April 2018).

Brown, S., Deakin, J. and Spencer, J. (2007) 'Public attitudes towards sex offenders', *Howard Journal of Criminal Justice, 47*(3): 259–74.

Bryman, A. (2001) *Social Research Methods*. Oxford: Oxford University Press.

Campbell-Hall, V., Clegg, S., de Guzman, V. and Bolling, K. (2010) *British Crime Survey: Interpersonal Violence Question Development*. London: TNS-BMRB.

Cicourel, A.V. (1964) *Method and Measurement in Sociology*. New York: Free Press.

Cicourel, A.V. (1982) 'Interviews, surveys and the problem of ecological validity', *American Sociologist, 17*: 11–20.

Davies, P., Francis, P. and Greer, C. (eds) (2007) *Victims, Crime and Society*. London: Sage.

De Cao, E. and Lutz, C. (2014) *Sensitive Survey Questions: Measuring attitudes regarding female circumcision through a list experiment* (SOM Research Reports, Vol. 14017-EEF). Groningen: University of Groningen, SOM Research School.

Deakin, J. (2006) 'Dangerous people, dangerous places: the nature and location of young people's victimisation and fear', *Children and Society, 20*: 376–90.

Finch, J. (1987) 'The vignette technique in survey research', *Sociology, 21*: 105–14.

Fine, G.A. and Sandstrom, K.L. (1988) 'Knowing children: participant observation with minors', *Qualitative Research Methods Series*, No. 15. Newbury Park, CA: Sage.

Fowler, F.J. (2009) *Survey Research Methods*, 4th edition. Los Angeles, CA: Sage.

Fowler, F.J. (2014) *Survey Research Methods*, 5th edition. Los Angeles, CA: Sage.

Fox Keller, E. (1980) 'Feminist critique of science: a forward or backward move?', *Fundamenta Scientiae*, *1*: 341–9.

Gallagher, B., Bradford, M. and Pease, K. (1998) *The Nature, Prevalence and Distribution of Sexual and Physical Abuse of Children by Strangers*. Final Report to the ESRC, No. R000235996. Manchester: University of Manchester.

Gallagher, B., Bradford, M. and Pease, K. (2002) 'The sexual abuse of children by strangers: its extent, nature and victims' characteristics', *Children and Society*, *16*: 356–9.

Gallagher, B., Bradford, M. and Pease, K. (2008) 'Attempted and completed incidents of stranger perpetrated child sexual abuse and abduction', *Child Abuse and Neglect*, *32*: 517–28.

Gfroerer, J. and Kennet, J. (2014) 'Collecting survey data on sensitive topics: substance use', in T.P. Johnson (ed.), *Health Survey Methods*. Hoboken, NJ: Wiley.

Gomm, R. (2004) *Social Research Methodology: A Critical Introduction*. Basingstoke: Palgrave Macmillan.

Hall, P. and Smith, K. (eds) (2011) *Analysis of the 2010/11 British Crime Survey Intimate Personal Violence Split Sample Experiment*. London: Home Office.

Home Office (2012) *Consultation on the British Crime Survey Intimate Personal Violence Questionnaire: Response from Home Office Statistics*. London: Home Office.

Hood, S., Kelley, P. and Mayall, B. (1996) 'Children as research subjects: a risky enterprise', *Children and Society*, *10*: 117–28.

Kelly, L. (1990) 'Journeying in reverse: possibilities and problems in feminist research on sexual violence', in L. Gelsthorpe and A. Morris (eds), *Feminist Perspectives in Criminology*. Milton Keynes: Open University Press, pp. 107–14.

Kennedy Bergen, R. (1993) 'Interviewing survivors of marital rape', in C.M. Renzetti and R.M. Lee (eds), *Researching Sensitive Topics*. Newbury Park, CA: Sage.

Kinaird, E.M. (1985) 'Ethical issues in research with abused children', *Child Abuse and Neglect*, *9*: 301–11.

Lansdown, G. (1994) 'Children's rights', in B. Mayall (ed.), *Children's Childhoods: Observed and Experienced*. London: Falmer Press.

Lee, R.M. (1993) *Doing Research on Sensitive Topics*. London: Sage.

Lee, R.M. and Renzetti, C.M. (1990) 'The problems of researching sensitive topics: an overview and introduction', *American Behavioral Scientist*, *33*: 510–28.

Mahon, A., Glendinning, C., Clarke, K. and Craig, G. (1996) 'Researching children: methods and ethics', *Children and Society*, *10*: 145–54.

Marsh, C. (1982) *The Survey Method: The Contribution of Surveys to Sociological Explanation*. London: Allen and Unwin.

Morrow, V. and Richards, M. (1996) 'The ethics of social research with children: an overview', *Children and Society*, *10*: 90–105.

Nardi, P.M. (2014) *Doing Survey Research: A Guide to Quantitative Methods*, 3rd edition. London: Routledge.

Oakley, A. (1981) 'Interviewing women: a contradiction in terms', in H. Roberts (ed.), *Doing Feminist Research*. London: Routledge & Kegan Paul.

Office for National Statistics (ONS) (2015) Methodological Note: Intimate Personal Violence Split Sample Experiment, CSEW 2012/13. Available at: http://webarchive.national-archives.gov.uk/20160105160709/http://www.ons.gov.uk/ons/guide-method/method-quality/specific/crime-statistics-methodology/methodological-notes/index.html (accessed 31 March 2017).

Phillips, D.L. (1971) *Knowledge from What? Theories and Methods in Social Research*. Chicago: Rand McNally.

Reinharz, S. (1979) *On Becoming a Social Scientist*. San Francisco: Jossey-Bass.

Ross, M.W., Diamond, P.M., Liebling, A. and Saylor, W.G. (2008) 'Measurement of prison social climate: a comparison of an inmate measure in England and the USA', *Punishment Society*, 10(4): 447–74.

Schutz, A. (1962) *Collected Papers I: The Problem of Social Reality*. The Hague: Martinus Nijhof.

Seale, C. (ed.) (2004) *Social Research Methods: A Reader*. London: Routledge.

Stalans, L. (2002) 'Measuring attitudes to sentencing', in J. Roberts and M. Hough (eds), *Changing Attitudes to Punishment: Public Opinion, Crime and Justice*. Cullompton: Willan.

Sudman, S. and Bradburn, N.M. (1982) *Asking Questions: A Practical Guide to Questionnaire Design*. San Francisco: Jossey Bass.

Tymchuk, A.J. (1992) 'Assent processes', in B. Stanley and J.E. Sieber (eds), *Social Research on Children and Adolescents: Ethical Issues*. London: Sage.

CHAPTER CONTENTS

GLOSSARY TERMS

methodological tools   crime concentration
hypothesis testing   natural experiment
clean/dirty data   data signatures
prevalence rates   inverse trend
incidence rates   causal relationship
repeat crime rates

10

DOING QUANTITATIVE DATA ANALYSIS IN CRIMINOLOGICAL RESEARCH

NICK TILLEY, GRAHAM FARRELL AND ANDROMACHI TSELONI

INTRODUCTION

This chapter is about quantitative analysis to test hypotheses in criminology. The specific programme of research described addresses a major puzzle in criminology. Against expectations and following a long period of crime increase, why have many types of crime in many jurisdictions fallen steeply?

We describe the data and analytic methods we used to document and try to explain the international crime drop. The chapter begins by introducing the crime drop, ways in which it can be disaggregated, and the hypotheses we developed to try to explain its patterns. Our hypotheses conjectured that security improvements have been both a direct and indirect source of the falls. Next, we say how and why we have used multiple sweeps of large-scale victimization surveys as our main (but not exclusive) data source to test our hypotheses. We then turn to our findings. We show that specific patterns in the crime drop accord with expectations derived from our hypotheses. We describe some analytic tools we developed specifically for our research, notably the Security Impact Assessment Tool, which generates Security Protection Factors. We show how the specific expected detailed data 'signatures' within the crime drop correspond to our theoretical expectations, in particular as these relate to vehicle theft and domestic burglary. We go on to discuss what we have done and plan to do to test hypotheses relating to falls in violence and criminality, some of which require greater use of other data sources.

The chapter concludes by noting that competing explanations for the crime drop have so far failed to account for detailed patterns within the crime drop, but that there is a rich agenda for future research on the crime drop.

THE CRIME DROP: BACKGROUND CONTEXT

During the roughly 50 years following the Second World War, the best evidence we have from recorded crimes and victimization surveys suggests that the level and rate of crime rose in almost all countries for which data are available. The increases seemed to be inexorable. Then, first in the USA and, after that, in many other countries and against expectations, crime began to fall and to do so precipitously. Moreover, the falls were more than temporary blips: they have been sustained. Since the early 1990s (with variations in specific details), crimes of several types have fallen by more than a half in North America, Europe and Australasia. The changes in direction in crime trajectories took almost all by surprise. They had not been expected by policy-makers, journalists, the general public or, for that matter, criminologists. It seemed to us that the international crime drop poses perhaps the most pressing questions for criminology: what exactly was happening to crime rates and why had they begun to fall?

At the time of writing, we have spent close to a decade working on the crime drop, trying both to describe it more precisely and to explain it.

There are various ways of describing and disaggregating the crime drop and these are detailed in Box 10.1.

BOX 10.1 WAYS OF DESCRIBING AND DISAGGREGATING THE CRIME DROP

They include, for example, the following:

- Overall falls in crime
- The timing of the crime drops
- Drops in specific types of crime
- Crimes that increased in number and rate amongst those that fell
- The order in which crime types fell
- The order of locations where crime fell
- The types of victim where crime fell, or fell more or less, or did not fall at all
- Changes in numbers of offenders
- Changes in rates of offending amongst active offenders
- Changes in age of onset in offending
- Changes in age of desistance in offending
- Changes in patterns of offending amongst active offenders
- Changes in the targets for offending associated with the crime drop.

Ideally, any explanation of the crime drop would make sense of or predict the disaggregated form taken by the crime drop. Indeed, any proposed explanation that is inconsistent with the observed patterns within the overall crime drops thereby becomes suspect. This requirement is akin to that which faced cosmologists looking at the history of the universe and biologists interested in the changing patterns of flora and fauna. In both cases, satisfactory explanations need to be adequate both for the gross observed patterns and for the more detailed expression of those patterns.

The linked set of six hypotheses that has animated the explanatory side of our own work is as follows:

1. The main cause of the crime drop has been increases in security, which have occurred in many countries, and reduced crime opportunities.
2. The improvements in security began with debut crimes, notably theft of cars (which also removed a resource used for many other crimes).

3. The improvements in security in relation to typical debut crimes inhibited the recruitment of newcomers into criminal careers.
4. The inhibition of the onset in criminal careers has led to widespread drops in diverse crime types.
5. The initial drop in crime has been reinforced by changes in routine activities which have contributed, in particular, to reduced youth crime.
6. Where new opportunities for crime have emerged and where new routine activities have led to encounters with new crime opportunities, numbers of crimes have increased.

We have sought the best data we can find to describe trends as accurately and in as much detail as we can, to evaluate alternative explanations for the crime drop and to test our own hypotheses. This is a huge endeavour, with much remaining to be done. What follows is an account of the methodological approach and tools we have adopted and the forms of analysis we have developed.

In addition to our explanatory interests in relation to the crime drop, we have been committed to teasing out any policy and practice implications of our findings. From the start of our efforts, we took the view that if we could find what was producing the welcome but unexpected crime drops, that ought to be useful in working out what might be needed to maintain or extend them. The security hypothesis, if corroborated in our empirical research, has clear potential significance for policy.

DATA SOURCES, METHODS AND METHODOLOGY

Victimization surveys

All data are more or less dirty (clean/dirty data). As with hygiene, we may aspire to perfect cleanliness, but there always remain germs. Official crime records are, however, notoriously dirty as a source of data on relative crime rates and on crime trends. The definition of crime changes and varies; reporting rates for crime events vary and fluctuate; and recording practices likewise differ from place to place and from time to time (Tseloni and Tilley, 2016). We have drawn on quite a wide range of available data, trying in all cases to use the best that we could find. We have drawn especially heavily on victimization surveys.

In response to the well-known and widely acknowledged limitations in official crime records, victimization surveys have been developed which attempt to estimate crime rates by asking detailed questions of those who may have experienced crimes to uncover whether they have suffered crimes of different sorts and, if so, how many. The questions relate to a reference period, most often a year, to enable annual prevalence rates (proportion of the population experiencing a given crime) and incidence rates (typically the number of crimes per 1,000 or 100,000 population or potential targets) to be calculated, within specified confidence limits. Incidence rates are normally (and controversially) calculated with a 'cap' on the number of incidents that count for any victim experiencing multiple incidents (see Farrell and Pease, 2007). Applying a 'cap' is controversial because it affects repeat crime rates (the proportion of crimes which occurred against the same victim or target) and crime concentration (the number of crimes experienced by each victim on average). For this reason, criminologists often study the 'uncapped' crime figures captured in victimization surveys (Chenery et al., 1996; Osborn and Tseloni, 1998). Victimization surveys also ask follow-up questions on details of at least some of the criminal incidents victims have suffered. In addition, surveys often include additional 'modules' for subsets of respondents, asking a raft of supplementary questions, for example on security measures in place, cars owned, lifestyles and attitudes to the police and criminal justice system.

Many countries, such as England and Wales, the USA, Mexico and Chile, administer their own victimization surveys. In addition, there is an International Crime Victimization Survey (ICVS) that asks standard questions to respondents in participant countries, to enable valid comparisons to be made of rates in different jurisdictions as well as the identification of international trends (van Dijk and Tseloni, 2012).

Victimization surveys are imperfect, of course, as sources on crime trends. Limited sample sizes (especially in relation to relatively rare crimes), non-response, omitted victim populations (such as the very young, the homeless and many collective entities such as schools or hospitals) and memory failure all put limits on what can be said and with what confidence. Victimization surveys, nevertheless, by common consent, provide more robust estimates of relative rates and trends, especially for high-volume crimes, than recorded crime figures. It is for this reason that the data we have used to track trends in crime and to try to test many of our security hypotheses have come from high-quality victimization surveys. We have, however, as will become clear, drawn on other sources – the best we can find – where necessary.

We made use of the five sweeps of the ICVS (in 1989, 1992, 1996, 2000 and 2005) to determine whether there had, indeed, been an international crime drop. This task is more complex than might at first sight be apparent. Not all countries participate in each sweep of the ICVS because of the monetary cost of conducting the survey. We were able to identify a subset of countries that had participated in enough sweeps to analyse overall trends. We found 26 that had taken part in at least three sweeps and used these to model the crime trajectories. We were able to extend existing analysis by the ICVS team (van Dijk et al., 2007) to confirm that there had been a rise followed by a fall in the main crime categories included in the ICVS (Tseloni et al., 2010). The most important crimes in individual countries followed similar trends: they tended to go up at around the same time and down at around the same time.

In addition, we were also able to identify the timing of the fall across different crime types: as shown in Figure 10.1, not all offence types fell at the same time. Burglary and car theft fell from the late 1980s onwards. Then it was theft from cars and theft from people, which began to fall in the mid-1990s. And, finally, assaults started declining around the turn of the century. Another finding was that, since 1995, theft from cars and thefts from people fell the most. Theft from cars fell massively – by over three-quarters! Personal theft also fell by 60%. The smallest declines were in assaults but even these went down by one in five.

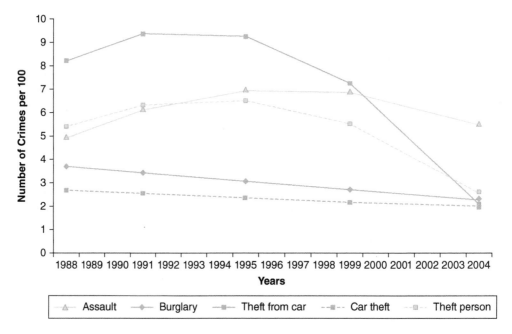

FIGURE 10.1   International Trends in Crime Incidence, ICVS 1988–2004

Source: Tseloni et al. (2010): 383.

We made extensive use of the Crime Survey of England and Wales (CSEW, previously known as the British Crime Survey or 'BCS') to begin to test our security hypotheses about the cause of the crime drop. We chose the CSEW because it was familiar to members of the research team (we had used it in previous studies), because it is recognized as a high-quality survey, because its supplementary questions spoke to various aspects of the security hypothesis and because it spans quite a long time – 35 years at the time of writing.

Rather than attempting to understand the overall crime trend, we decided to focus on individual crime types, notably those that had fallen most substantially, to determine whether findings support or contradict the security hypothesis.

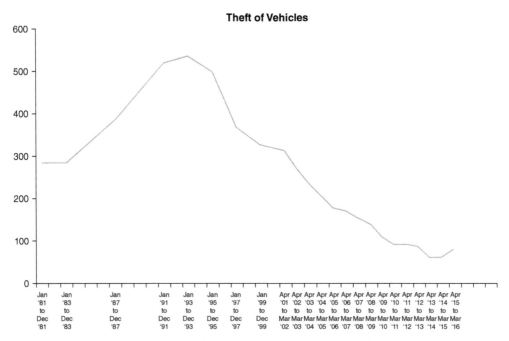

FIGURE 10.2   Trend in numbers of thefts of motor vehicles CSEW 1981–2016

Source: Crime Survey of England and Wales, Office for National Statistics

Security and the drop in car theft

We began with theft of motor vehicles, which increased rapidly for decades before the 1990s but has since dropped by over 80%. Figure 10.2 shows the trend, as found in the CSEW.

The CSEW asks some questions that allowed us to see whether the changing patterns of car theft accorded with what would be expected were improvements in vehicle security to be playing a significant role (Farrell et al., 2011a). It asked about the security to the cars that respondents drove. If there were, indeed, no security improvements, then that would put paid to the security hypothesis. However, successive sweeps of the survey showed increasing levels of security. The survey also asked how the thief gained entry. If security were important, we reasoned that the fall would be felt most acutely in relation to methods that required that security be overcome and least where methods did not require that security be overcome. This is, indeed, what the series of CSEW sweeps showed. Security improvements to vehicles do not make vehicles impossible to steal, albeit they may make their theft more difficult (improved door locks, better window locks, electronic immobilisers), more risky (alarms), and also make the use of security more routine (central locking). Given this circumstance, we thought that younger, less experienced offenders would be more easily stopped by security. Consistent with this, the CSEW showed that temporary theft – where the car is returned because it was used for joyriding or transportation by young people – fell much more initially than did permanent theft (by more experienced offenders stealing to sell parts or re-sell the car). We also know that there was continual improvement to security devices, particularly the electronic immobiliser, and consistent with this there was also a major reduction in permanent theft over time. At the time of writing, joyriding is largely extinct and more organized theft has fallen by three quarters. However, a recent uptake in thefts of high-end vehicles such as Range Rovers suggests manufacturers need to continue to improve security to stay ahead of thieves (Brown, 2017).

We looked to a different, Australian data set, to explore our hunch that electronic immobilisers had played an especially important part in producing the fall in car theft that had been observed in many countries. The Comprehensive Auto-theft Research System (CARS) data set collects details of every car theft reported to the Australian police (and it is worth remembering that rates of reporting car theft are especially high, given insurance requirements). In Australia, a 'natural experiment' occurred in relation to immobilisers and car thefts. Western Australia, one of the six Australian states, legally required electronic immobilisers to be fitted some years before the rest of the country. We found that the decline in car theft began earlier in Western Australia than the rest of the country but that both declines corresponded with the timing of the immobiliser legislation, corroborating our security hypothesis (Farrell et al., 2011a).

Our applied interest led us to ask exactly what it was about security that was rendering vehicles less vulnerable to theft. For this, we devised the 'Security Impact Assessment Tool' (SIAT) with which we calculated the Security Protection Factor (SPF) (see Box 10.2).

Our findings corroborated the importance of electronic immobilisers in protecting against the theft of vehicles. We found that having a suite of security devices was the most effective – combinations of devices had larger SPFs than would be expected by simply summing the scores of each on its own. So, there is added value in producing vehicles that are generally inhospitable to the prospective offender (Farrell et al., 2011b). We also found, for both car crime and burglary (discussed below), that attempted crimes continued at a higher level for two to four years after completed crimes began to fall, suggesting offenders continued to try before being deterred by improved security (Farrell, 2016).

The core set of quantitative data signatures that we have identified relating to vehicle-related theft and the role of security are summarized in Table 10.1. All of the signatures are consistent with security being the cause of the decline in vehicle-related theft.

TABLE 10.1 **Quantitative data signatures consistent with security having reduced vehicle-related theft**

- The timing and spread of security fits with the trajectory of declines in vehicle-related theft in different countries
- Different security devices impact differently against different crime types, consistent with their preventive mechanisms
- Preventive effects are much stronger when multiple security devices are in place
- The average age of stolen vehicles increased over time when crime fell, because new vehicles have better security
- There were quicker and larger effect on temporary theft (joyriding, transportation) than on permanent theft (for re-sale or chopping)
- Offenders' modus operandi changed, with door lock forcing declining disproportionately, consistent with better quality deadlocks.
- Vehicle theft fell somewhat more quickly among higher income groups, consistent with the more rapid replacement of older insecure vehicles
- The rate of attempted theft fell later than completed theft, consistent with offenders continuing to try before quitting in the face of improved security
- There was a disproportionate decline in adolescent crime, consistent with novices being more easily deterred by improved security
- In Australia and Canada, car theft fell earlier in regions that introduced electronic immobilisers earlier, then fell nationally in line with their broader spread.

Of course, security increases in relation to vehicles are not confined to the vehicles themselves. The vehicles have to be stolen from somewhere, and security at parking places is important. In particular, car parks can be more or less secure. There is some evidence that closed circuit television (CCTV) in car parks reduces the rate at which cars are stolen from them (Tilley, 1993; Welsh and Farrington, 2008). Other features of car parks may make them less or more secure, including lighting, barriers and openness to surveillance by businesses based in them. However, while we know car park security is important, to date we have not identified a data source and way of gauging whether or not improved security at car parks contributed significantly to the drop in vehicle-related theft.

We published our findings on security and car theft and they have been corroborated by other researchers studying in other countries (Bässmann, 2011; Brown, 2015; Fujita and Maxfield, 2012; van Ours and Vollaard, 2016). The methodologies applied in these studies varied widely: triangulation of different US data and simple correlation of time series (Fujita and Maxfield, 2012); a mixed methods approach, involving quantitative descriptive trends analyses (with year-on-year changes) and findings from expert interviews in Germany (Bässmann, 2011); (log-linear) regression of over 15 years' data on specific car makes to estimate the overall effect size of the EU-wide intervention on car immobilisers, accounting for age and other car characteristics as well as displacement; and meta-analysis of a number of studies from four countries (the UK, Germany, Australia and the USA) on the impact of electronic immobilisation on vehicle theft. Including our own initial study, three in total employed triangulation investigating the data signatures on any effect of immobilisers on car crime reduction (Bässmann, 2011; Farrell et al., 2011b; Fujita and Maxfield, 2012); one also employed qualitative methodology; another advanced statistical modeling; and a third examined all the above via meta-analysis.

Security and the Drop in Domestic Burglary

Our next focus was on domestic burglary. This has also dropped steeply and the drop has been sustained, as shown in Figure 10.3.

Our approach to domestic burglary was broadly similar to that for car theft: analyse successive sweeps of the CSEW to track changes in security levels; assess the SFPs of security devices and combinations of devices; and look at the changing means of entry to households (modus operandi) (Tseloni et al., 2017). Findings again corroborated the security hypothesis: levels of most forms of security have increased; modus operandi indicate that falls were disproportionate in methods requiring that security be overcome (as against, for example, walk-in burglaries); and the most effective combinations have tended to increase more than others.

Again, we were limited to what the CSEW covered in the questions asked. The survey was not designed to test the security hypothesis. In particular, we noted that there is a matching inverse trend in the proportion of properties with double glazing

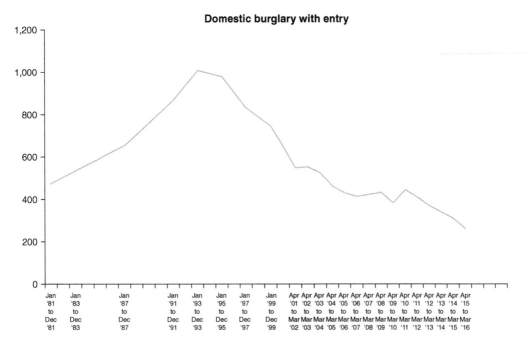

Domestic burglary with entry

FIGURE 10.3 Trend in numbers of domestic burglaries with entry CSEW 1981-2016

Source: Crime Survey of England and Wales, Office for National Statistics

and the levels of domestic burglary with entry. Data on double glazing was not obtained from the CSEW but from other sources. We have been able, thus, to note the broad association and the plausibility of a causal relationship (it is more difficult to break into houses with double glazing), but we have been unable to examine it in detail (Farrell et al., 2014).

One unexpected and paradoxical finding that emerged from the analysis of multiple sweeps of the CSEW relates to burglar alarms (Tilley et al., 2015). We noted that the SPF for burglar alarms in the later sweeps was less than one. In other words, dwellings with a burglar alarm as their sole security device were at slightly greater risk of burglary than dwellings with no security device at all! We wondered if this occasional observation was spurious – perhaps a function of a sampling error. We therefore devised a marginal SPF (MSPF) that would compare the SPFs of any given combination with and without a burglar alarm. Figure 10.4 shows our findings, which compare the MSPFs for earlier and later suites of sweeps of the CSEW.

The overall findings are clear. In the earlier sweeps, the addition of a burglar alarm tended to reduce risk, in some cases substantially. In later sweeps, this effect was reversed. The addition of a burglar alarm increased risk. This suggests that security devices may not unequivocally and under all circumstances reduce crime risk.

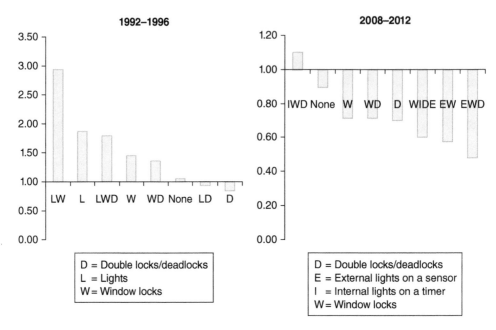

FIGURE 10.4   Marginal SPFs for burglar alarms, burglary with entry

Source: Tilley et al. (2015).

TABLE 10.2   Quantitative data signatures consistent with security having reduced domestic burglary

---

- A steep decline in households without security coincided with burglary's decline
- Variation in the effectiveness of different security devices are consistent with their preventive mechanisms
- Preventive effects are much stronger when multiple security devices are in place
- The drop was mainly a decline in forced entry through doors and windows, consistent with improved security
- Unforced entries (push-pasts, keys used, deception) increased when forced entries and all burglary decreased, consistent with partial short-term displacement as a result of effective security
- Door-forcing at the rear of properties fell first and fastest, consistent with security at the previously most vulnerable entry point
- There was a disproportionate decline in adolescent crime, consistent with novices being more easily deterred by improved security
- The rate of attempted burglary fell later than completed burglary, consistent with offenders continuing to try before quitting in the face of improved security
- Burglary fell slightly faster among more affluent households, consistent with more rapid upgrading

---

We proposed various conjectures, but were unable to test any of them. We suspect that, as burglary has declined, the pool of burglars has become, on average, slightly older and more experienced, and these offenders are unlikely to be deterred by an alarm because they know the chances of the police arriving quickly are small.

The core set of quantitative data signatures that we have identified relating to household burglary and the role of security are summarized in Table 10.2. All of the signatures are consistent with security being the cause of the decline in burglary.

Security and the Drop in Violence between Acquaintances and Strangers

Our current research again draws on the CSEW. For some types of violence, the potential significance of security improvements is obvious. Armed robbery, for example, is likely to have been reduced by improved security (banks are the clearest example), but the CSEW is no help here. There may also have been improvements in security in some traditional violence hotspots, such as city centres and bars, but again the CSEW is limited in what it can tell us. What can be examined through the CSEW are patterns of relatively risky behaviours and their precautionary counterparts that may explain the falls in violence amongst affected groups. Going out less, drinking less and avoiding certain risky behaviours or lifestyles can be measured using the CSEW. While quite significant changes to lifestyle and routine activities appear to have occurred, it is possible that this was after crime began its major decline, which would suggest that their effect was to consolidate the effects of security. Further research is needed to uncover how changes to lifestyle and routine activities may have helped to reduce violence.

Part of our security hypothesis suggested that general falls in crime (including violent crime) followed from the effects of the reduction in debut crimes that mark the onset of criminal careers, which typically include a wide range of offending including violence. These indirect effects of security on criminal careers are discussed next.

FROM REDUCTIONS IN CRIME EVENTS TO REDUCTIONS IN CRIMINALITY

The security hypothesis outlined above proposes that improvements in security have had a knock-on effect on criminal careers. As the term 'debut crimes' suggests, this expectation is rooted in previous research that identified the types of crime that tend to mark the start of criminal careers (Svensson, 2002). Theft of motor vehicles was found to be especially significant. Previous research has also found that prolific offenders tend to be generalists rather than specialists (Piquero et al.,

2014). Hence, if 'debut crimes' are inhibited by making them more difficult, as in the case of vehicle theft, this would stifle further criminal activities. If security improvements were reducing crime by inhibiting the onset of criminal careers, we would expect a greater effect among younger adolescents who are new to offending, and for the effect to be less among older offenders. This could be measured by looking at rates of onset and continuance of offending in different age groups.

CSEW data, which relate to victimization patterns, are not of much use in tracking changes in criminal involvement. We therefore looked to other sources and turned to data from the criminal justice system and found a set of data on arrests in the USA that spanned several decades (making it easier to access and use for this purpose than criminal statistics for England and Wales). Arrest data are not perfect but are preferable to data on prosecutions or convictions, where decisions about how to process those arrested may change over time and influence patterns independently of changes in actual criminal behaviour. The patterns we found in US arrest data accorded with our expectations, as shown in Figure 10.5 (see Farrell et al., 2015, 2016).

CONTEXTS, MECHANISMS, SECURITY, CRIME DROPS AND DATA SIGNATURES

In conducting detailed analyses of our data, we have attempted to specify the precise mechanisms through which particular outcome patterns would be produced in the contexts in which the security upgrades have been introduced. For example, in looking at car security devices we have distinguished which crimes electronic immobilisers might reduce (theft *of* cars, with no direct effect on theft *from* cars). We have looked for specific 'data signatures' that would be expected were our security hypotheses to be warranted (Farrell et al., 2016). We find, indeed, that immobilisers reduce the theft of vehicles but not theft from them (Farrell et al., 2011a, b).

In relation to domestic burglary, we have looked to see whether changing patterns of modus operandi are those that would be expected were security to be reducing the rate of burglary. Such changes include much greater reductions in forced entry as against entry that does not require security to be overcome (for instance, where a door or window has been left open). Figure 10.6 shows that there has indeed been a much greater fall in burglaries requiring forced entry in England and Wales, as measured by the CSEW, when compared to burglaries that did not require forced entry (Farrell et al., 2016).

We have sometimes been surprised where patterns have not accorded with expectations and this has led us to further theory development, which should then be open to test, as in the example of household alarms mentioned earlier.

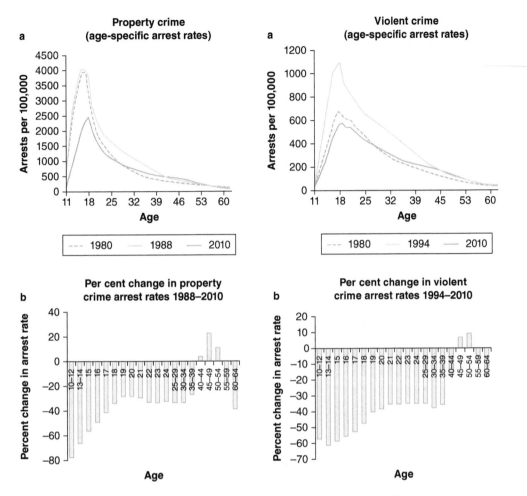

FIGURE 10.5 Changing arrest patterns associated with the crime drop, US

Source: Farrell et al (2015).

Data signatures and alternative explanations of the crime drop

A range of explanations has been proposed for the international crime drop. These have included, for example, changes in policing, increased imprisonment, legislation making abortion easier, changes in the economy, changing drug-taking patterns, immigration, removal of lead from the atmosphere, and processes of civilization (Farrell, 2013; Farrell et al., 2014). In looking at these critically, we have asked

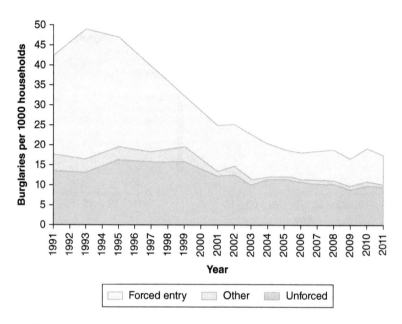

FIGURE 10.6   Forced and unforced entry for burglary with entry, CSEW 1992-2011/12

Source: Farrell et al. (2016).

whether they are consistent with the known data signatures of crime trends and the international crime drop. Several quickly fell by the wayside, given their failure to accord with the varying times of the crime drop, their failure to make sense of the prior crime rise, their failure to explain the property as well as violent crime drop, their failure to explain the specific crime rises that have occurred alongside the crime drops and their failure to make sense of the international range of the crime drops. Although in these cases we have not reconstructed the theories to work through their specific predictions, we have asked whether the explanations are consistent with the patterns associated with the crime drop. We have repeatedly found that the security hypothesis outperforms other explanations in explaining known features of the crime drop. Of course, disproving other hypotheses does not make the security hypothesis correct, but we think it is important to rule out other plausible alternative explanations.

Describing and deconstructing the crime drop

Although we have produced a substantial volume of research exploring data relating to the security hypothesis (some 33 papers at the time of writing), we acknowledge that there are many remaining gaps in evidence relating to the crime drop and its explanation.

The following research remains to be done:

a. testing the security hypothesis in more jurisdictions where the crime drop has occurred
b. testing the security hypothesis in jurisdictions where there has been no crime drop
c. testing the security hypothesis as it relates to a broad range of offences, for example shop theft, robbery, child sexual abuse and homicide
d. describing the changing patterns of criminal involvement associated with the crime drop across jurisdictions where the crime drop has occurred
e. describing the crime drop in terms of prevalence and incidence rate changes, using capped and uncapped estimates of incidence by crime type
f. describing the sequencing of crime drops by crime type within jurisdictions and between jurisdictions.

SUMMARY AND REVIEW

The international crime drop, as indicated from both victimization survey data and recorded crime data, came as a surprise to criminologists as well as the general public. Understanding it poses a major puzzle for criminology. Its explanation clearly has major potential to inform public policy: if we can understand what produced the crime drop, we may learn better how to maintain or extend it where drops have not yet occurred, and how to reduce crimes that are rising. Conducting research on the scale (how much crime has dropped), extent (the range of jurisdictions and crime types), nature (timing, prevalence, incidence, offender involvement, locations, etc.) and possible explanations for the crime drop requires the use of the best data available. In this chapter, we show how we have made extensive, although not exclusive, use of victimization surveys to test the 'security hypothesis', according to which a major cause of the falls in crime lies in widespread improvements in security. We conclude that our quantitative data 'signatures' of the crime drop are consistent with the effects of security but not with other explanations.

We have shown, in this chapter, how and why repeated, large-scale and high-quality victimization surveys provide an invaluable resource for identifying crime patterns and testing hypotheses that might explain them. Research using victimization surveys is not easy. Moreover, the data are imperfect (as is always the case). Victimization surveys provide, however, by far the most robust data source available for identifying crime patterns and trends. With some imagination and quite a lot of effort, we were able to make secondary use of the data systematically to test the hypotheses in which we were interested. We were able to analyse the data in ways not envisaged by the survey's architects. We think that large-scale victimization surveys that are professionally undertaken at public expense provide quantitative material that is fundamental for identifying and analysing crime patterns. We also think that victimization survey data are underused (see Tseloni and Tilley, 2016). Because of some limitations in victimization survey data, where possible, of course, we also made use of other sources to corroborate out findings.

There is scope for further research on the international crime drop. This could take any of several forms. One could be that of trying to develop alternative explanations that improve on or refine those offered so far. Another could be that of testing existing explanations, including that relating to security, more fully in jurisdictions where there are the required data and where research has not yet been undertaken. A third could include more detailed descriptions of the crime drop in terms of offending, victimization, location and crime type patterns, in particular in jurisdictions where no such research has yet been undertaken. A fourth could be the identification of crime rises occurring amongst the crime falls in an effort to work out what is leading those crimes to increase and to determine whether similar offenders to those associated with crimes that have fallen are or are not involved in them. Although there may be scope for some qualitative research in understanding the crime drops, it is clear that quantitative work will be crucial.

STUDY QUESTIONS AND ACTIVITIES FOR STUDENTS

1. Compare the crime trends in recorded crime and crime as measured using victimization survey data. What do you think explains the differences? How might you test your explanations?

2. Search for statistical sources in trends in criminality. What are their strengths and weaknesses? What can we learn with what confidence about trends over the past 20 years?

3. Find crime survey data on trends in incidence and in prevalence. What do they tell us about repeat victimization and about trends in repeats as an explanation for incidence pattern trends?

4. Find some crime trends that are rising, using either recorded crime data or victimization survey data. Develop some hypotheses that explain the rises. How could you robustly test your explanation?

5. How could qualitative research complement quantitative research in helping to understand rising and falling crime trends?

SUGGESTIONS FOR FURTHER READING

There is a growing literature describing the international crime drop, and attempting to explain it. Two important recent edited collections are:

Tonry, M. (2014) *Why Crime Rates Fall and Why they Don't. Crime and Justice* 43. Chicago: University of Chicago Press; and van Dijk, J., Tseloni, A. and Farrell, G. (2012) *The International Crime Drop*. Basingstoke: Palgrave. The chapter by Farrell, Tilley and Tseloni ('Why the crime drop?', pp. 421–90) in Tonry's collection critically examines proposed explanations for the crime drop and argues that all but the security hypothesis fail crucial tests.

The use of data signatures in testing hypotheses is explained and exemplified in: Farrell, G., Tseloni, A. and Tilley, N. (2016) 'Signature dish: triangulation from data signatures to examine the role of security in falling crime', *Methodological Innovations*, 9: 1–11.

A detailed account of and rationale for the Security Impact Assessment Tool is presented in: Farrell, G., Tseloni, A. and Tilley, N. (2011) 'The effectiveness of vehicle security devices and their role in the crime drop', *Criminology and Criminal Justice*, 11(1): 21–35.

A step-by-step example of how to calculate victimization rates (prevalence, incidence, repeat victims, repeat crimes and crime concentration) is given in:

Tseloni, A. (2014) 'Understanding victimization frequency', Chapter 127 in G. Bruinsma and D. Weisburd (eds), *Encyclopaedia of Criminology and Criminal Justice (ECCJ)*. New York: Springer-Verlag, pp. 5370–82.

REFERENCES

Bässmann, J. (2011) 'Vehicle theft reduction in Germany: the long-term effectiveness of electronic immobilisation', *European Journal of Criminal Policy Research*, 17: 221–46.

Brown, R. (2015) 'Reviewing the effectiveness of electronic vehicle immobilisation: evidence from four countries', *Security Journal*, 28(4): 329–51.

Brown, R. (2017) 'Vehicle crime prevention and the co-evolutionary arms race: recent offender countermoves using immobiliser bypass technology', *Security Journal*, 30(1): 60–73.

Chenery, S., Ellingworth, D., Tseloni, A. and Pease, K. (1996) 'Crimes which repeat: undigested evidence from the British Crime Survey 1992', *International Journal of Risk, Security and Crime Prevention*, 1: 207–16.

Farrell, G. (2013) 'Five tests for a theory of the crime drop', *Crime Science, 2*(5): 1–8.

Farrell, G. (2016) 'Attempted crime and the crime drop', *International Criminal Justice Review, 26*(1): 21–30.

Farrell, G. and Pease, K. (2007) 'The sting in the tail of the British Crime Survey', in M. Hough and M. Maxfield (eds), *Surveying Crime in the 21st Century*. Crime Prevention Studies, Vol. 22. Monsey, NY: Criminal Justice Press, pp. 33–53.

Farrell, G., Laycock, G. and Tilley, N. (2015) 'Debuts and legacies: the crime drop and the role of adolescence-limited and persistent offending', *Crime Science, 4*(16): 1–10.

Farrell, G., Tseloni, A., Mailley, J. and Tilley, N. (2011a) 'The crime drop and the security hypothesis', *Journal of Research in Crime and Delinquency, 48*(2): 147–75.

Farrell, G., Tseloni, A. and Tilley, N. (2011b) 'The effectiveness of vehicle security devices and their role in the crime drop', *Criminology and Criminal Justice, 11*(1): 21–35.

Farrell, G., Tseloni, A. and Tilley, N. (2016) 'Signature dish: triangulation from data signatures to examine the role of security in falling crime', *Methodological Innovations, 9*: 1–11.

Farrell, G., Tilley, N. and Tseloni, A. (2014) 'Why the crime drop?', in M. Tonry (ed.), *Why Crime Rates Fall and Why they Don't. Crime and Justice 43*. Chicago: University of Chicago Press, pp. 421–90.

Fujita, S. and Maxfield, M. (2012) 'Security and the drop in car theft in the United States', in J.J.M. van Dijk, A. Tseloni and G. Farrell (eds), *The International Crime Drop: New Directions in Research*. London: Palgrave Macmillan.

Osborn, D.R. and Tseloni, A. (1998) 'The distribution of household property crimes', *Journal of Quantitative Criminology, 14*: 307–30.

Piquero, A.R., Hawkins, D., Kazemian, L. and Petechuk, D. (2014) *Bulletin 2: Criminal Career Patterns*. Washington, DC: Office of Juvenile Justice and Delinquency Prevention.

Svensson, R. (2002) 'Strategic offences in the criminal career context', *British Journal of Criminology, 42*(2): 395–411.

Tilley, N. (1993) *Understanding Car Parks, Crime and CCTV: Evaluation Lessons from Safer Cities*. Crime Prevention Unit Paper No. 42. London: Home Office.

Tilley, N., Farrell, G., Grove, L., Thompson, R. and Tseloni, A. (2015) 'Do burglar alarms increase burglary risk? A counterintuitive finding and possible explanations', *Crime Prevention and Community Safety, 17*(1): 1–19.

Tseloni, A. and Tilley, N. (2016) 'Choosing and using statistical sources in criminology: what can the Crime Survey for England and Wales tell us?', *Legal Information Management, 16*: 78–90.

Tseloni, A., Mailley, J., Farrell, G. and Tilley, N. (2010) 'The cross-national crime and repeat victimization trend for main crime categories: multilevel modeling of the International Crime Victims Survey', *European Journal of Criminology, 7*(5): 375–94.

Tseloni, A., Thompson, R., Grove, L., Tilley, N. and Farrell, G. (2017) 'The effectiveness of burglary security devices', *Security Journal, 30*(2): 646–64.

van Dijk, J. and Tseloni, A. (2012) 'Global overview: international trends in victimisation and recorded crime', in J. van Dijk, A. Tseloni and G. Farrell (eds), *The International Crime Drop: New Directions in Research*. Basingstoke: Palgrave Macmillan, pp. 11–36.

van Dijk, J.J.M., Manchin, R., van Kesteren, J., Nevala, S. and Hideg, G. (2007) 'The burden of crime in the EU', in *Research Report: A Comparative Analysis of the European Survey of Crime and Safety*. EU ICS, 2005. Brussels: Gallup Europe.

van Ours, J.C. and Vollaard, B. (2016) 'The engine immobilizer: a non-starter for car thieves', *Economic Journal*, 126(593): 1264–91.

Welsh, B. and Farrington, D. (2008) 'Effects of closed circuit television surveillance on crime', *Campbell Systematic Reviews*, 4(17). Available at: www.campbellcollaboration. org/library/effects-of-closed-circuit-television-surveillance-on-crime.html (accessed 5 April 2018).

Acknowledgement

Most of the work reported here has been funded by the Economic and Social Research Council, especially under the Secondary Data Analysis Initiative (Grants ES/F015186/1, ES/K003771/1& 2 and ES/L014971/1 & 2).

CHAPTER CONTENTS

GLOSSARY TERMS

Big Data
prediction
intelligence led policing
predictive policing
hot spots
offender risk assessment

machine learning
algorithm
training set
data analytics
correlation

11

USING BIG DATA AND DATA ANALYTICS IN CRIMINOLOGICAL RESEARCH

LYRIA BENNETT MOSES AND JANET CHAN

INTRODUCTION

This chapter explains and critiques approaches to policing and crime prediction based on Big Data and data analytics, particularly predictive policing and offender risk assessment. While limitations of these approaches are discussed, this chapter does not take a position on the comparative question, namely whether these approaches are better or worse than alternatives. Rather, it focuses on understanding the kinds of tools and techniques used, the ways in which they are used and the limitations inherent in their use.

 The chapter begins by explaining what 'Big Data' is and how it is used in criminological research. It then examines two uses of data analytics for crime prediction. The first, predictive policing, is a tool used by police to target particular locations and times, or occasionally individuals, where the likelihood of criminal activity is heightened. The second, offender risk assessment, attempts to quantify the risk that a person charged with or convicted of a crime will commit an offence while on bail, comply with bail conditions, re-offend once released on bail or parole, and/or commit a violent offence while on bail or parole. These assessments can be carried out in order to assess a bail application, during sentencing or in an application for parole. Similar tools are also used in prisoner management.

In the following section, the tools and their current uses are described. After that, the limitations of these kinds of techniques are described at a general level. Because of the diversity of tools available, and the variety of data on which they operate, it is not possible to explain the advantages and disadvantages of each different technique, or compare one to another. However, there are some general matters that need to be considered when assessing predictive accuracy, effectiveness and negative impacts of data-analytic tools in policing and criminal justice. Finally, the chapter describes some difficulties that researchers face in assessing and evaluating these kinds of tools. In particular, we discuss the lack of transparency and the difficulties in obtaining data as well as difficulties in conducting a proper evaluation of effectiveness and impact.

WHAT IS 'BIG DATA' AND HOW IS IT USED IN RESEARCH?

Much has been written about the advent of 'Big Data' and how this new technology will transform how 'we live, work and think' (Mayer-Schönberger and Cukier, 2013). The term Big Data can have a range of meanings, ranging from the volume, velocity and variety of data systems, through the analytic capability or value, or a marketing label, to a sociocultural phenomenon (see boyd and Crawford, 2012; Chan and Bennett Moses, 2017; Kitchin, 2014). The use of Big

Data in social science in general and in criminology in particular is a relatively new trend. As Chan and Bennett Moses (2016) observe, there are two main areas where Big Data has been used for researching crime and justice: first, the use of Big Data such as social media streams as *data* in criminological research (e.g. Procter et al., 2013; Traunmueller et al., 2014; Watters and Phair, 2012: Williams and Burnap, 2016; Williams et al., 2017); and, second, the use of Big Data for real-time monitoring or to make predictions that can be used for law enforcement or criminal justice purposes, such as increasing situational awareness, preventing crime and enhancing efficiency (e.g. Berk and Bleich, 2013; Williams et al., 2013). These categories obviously overlap, and research in the first category may be applied in the second.

USES OF DATA ANALYTICS IN CRIME PREDICTION

Predictions about future crimes are considered useful primarily for making decisions about the deployment of police officers and resources, intelligence led policing (predictive policing) and making decisions about whether a person who has been charged or convicted of an offence ought to be granted bail or parole (offender risk management).

Predictive policing

Predictive policing has been used in at least 48 jurisdictions in the USA as well as in the UK and Europe and some other jurisdictions including Delhi, India and Sao Paolo, Brazil. The term 'predictive policing' has been applied to a range of policing practices linked by their claimed ability to 'forecast where and when the next crime or series of crimes will take place' (Uchida, 2014: 3871), or which individuals are likely to become offenders or victims in order to 'change outcomes' (Beck and McCue, 2009). These predictions can be about 'places and times with an increased risk of crime', 'individuals at risk of offending in the future', creating 'profiles that accurately match likely offenders with specific past crimes' or identifying groups or individuals at risk of becoming victims of crime (Perry et al., 2013: 8–9). Most current predictive policing programs focus on places and times with an increased risk of crime rather than individuals. Predictive policing is a prediction-led business process consisting of a cycle of activities and decision points: data collection, analysis, police operations, criminal response and back to data collection (Perry et al., 2013: 128; see Figure 11.1).

Predictive policing can involve a variety of tools and techniques, including basic tools such as Excel, off-the-shelf software and adapted or tailored software, which vary in terms of complexity, comprehensibility and transparency. Prediction models

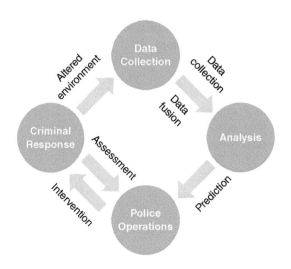

FIGURE 11.1 The prediction-led policing business process. Copyright RAND included with permission

Source: Perry et al. (2013, p. 128, Figure 5.4)

might be based entirely or in part on qualitative rather than quantitative methods, including interviews with offenders (e.g. Johnson and Bowers, 2004). Tools usually incorporate geographic information systems so that patterns in the location of crimes over time, as well as relevant geographical features (including the location of licensed venues), can be recorded and tracked. Approaches can be based on classical statistical techniques, on simple methods such as checklists and indices, on complex applications involving Big Data, and/or on tailored methods and data visualization (Perry et al., 2013: 19). In some contexts, automated linguistic analysis of geo-located social media data is used in predictive models (e.g. Gerber, 2014). Commercial products include those provided by organizations such as Motorola, LexisNexis, Esri, Intrado, PredPol, IBM, Information Builders, Azavea, SPADAC, Accenture and Hitachi.

The model on which one product, PredPol, is based is described in Mohler et al. (2011), although the precise model used currently is not publicly available. Like an earthquake prediction model, PredPol assumes that crimes operate as a self-excited point process, with the probability of an event at a particular location being a combination of background risk and 'near repeat' aftershocks related to recent local events. The variables in the model are calculated through an iterative process.

Figure 11.2 shows an example of a crime map that was used for predicting crime in Washington, DC.

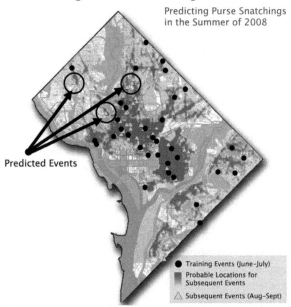

Forecasting Crime in Washington DC

Predicting Purse Snatchings
in the Summer of 2008

Predicted Events

● Training Events (June–July)
■ Probable Locations for
Subsequent Events
△ Subsequent Events (Aug–Sept)

FIGURE 11.2   Peter Borissov, Forecasting Crime in Washington DC, public domain image
on Wikimedia Commons

The focus on the locations of crime makes predictive policing similar to hot spot
policing, the difference being the attempt to predict and account for how hot spots
will change over short periods of time. There is extensive research supporting
location-based approaches for some categories of crime, particularly burglary (e.g.
Bowers et al., 2004). However, not all crime types follow location-based patterns or
trends (Hart and Zandbergen, 2012: 58). Thus, a product such as PredPol, based on
a 'near repeat' model, will be more accurate when predicting some types of crime
(such as burglary) than others (such as kidnapping).

Offender risk assessment

Risk assessment tools that predict the likelihood of an individual committing an
offence (or a particular type of offence) based on Big Data include Correctional
Offender Management Profiling for Alternative Sanctions (COMPAS). Greater
use of these tools in bail, parole or sentencing has been advocated by the
Conference of Chief Justices Conference of State Court Administrators
(National Center for State Courts, 2007) and the Arnold Foundation (2013).

Reasons for promoting these tools include public safety, reduction in recidivism and cost savings through the release of 'low risk' offenders. The data used in making predictions may be based on information from a person's police record as well as on interviews.

The use of risk assessment tools in particular jurisdictions will depend on the laws of that jurisdiction. In some jurisdictions, these tools are expressly permitted or mandated by legislation. For example, in Ohio, the Department of Rehabilitation and Correction is required to select a single validated risk assessment tool for adult offenders to be used by various entities including the parole board and sentencing courts (Ohio Rev Code Ann § 5120.114 (2016)). In *State v Loomis* (2016), the Supreme Court of Wisconsin held that risk assessments tools could be used in sentencing provided that they were not the only factor taken into account, that they were not used in decisions about the *severity* of a sentence, and that reports were accompanied by appropriate warnings.

In many cases, offender risk assessment tools are designed to optimise predictive accuracy rather than assist with explanation or focus on the kinds of variables that might generally be considered appropriate in making decisions about bail and parole. As Berk and Bleich (2013: 517) argue, any variable that can operate as a good predictor should be used even if, like shoe size, it is not obvious why this variable might be important or whether it is something that would have traditionally been taken into account. Offender risk assessment tools are not just concerned with more accurate weighting of traditionally relevant factors (such as number of prior offences and type of offences committed in the past), but also with identifying new variables that correlate with recidivism.

As in the case of predictive policing, there are diverse tools that can be used. One example is the random forest approach used in Berk (2012: 65–6). This involves machine learning from historic data concerning recidivism in order to predict whether a particular person should be flagged as a recidivism risk (the output is thus binary, in that individuals are classified as either high risk or low risk). A random forest is an ensemble of classification trees. A classification tree is essentially a decision tree that, at each branch, requires the user to decide which is the relevant branch based on the value of a particular variable. An example of a (hypothetical) classification tree is shown in Figure 11.3.

In a random forest algorithm, multiple classification trees are constructed based on different data sets drawn from the training set. In particular, random samples of size N are drawn with replacement from a training data set comprising N observations. Each sample is used to construct a classification tree. First, a small random sample of predictors is drawn. The tree is then constructed through a series of partitions of the data, each time selecting the predictor (from the random sample) that most reduces the heterogeneity of outcomes at each node. At each terminal node, the Bayes classifier is used to assign a class to that node, so that the class assigned (e.g. high or low risk) is the most probable class for that node. The Bayes classifier can be determined mathematically by choosing the class that

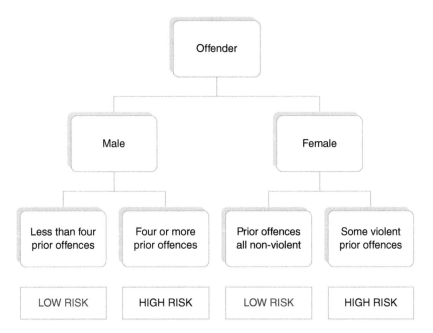

FIGURE 11.3 **Example of a hypothetical classification tree**

minimizes the expected prediction error (for a formal explanation, see Berk (2012: 43–7)). The training data that was not used to construct that particular tree is then dropped down the tree (according to the partition criteria) and is then assigned the class associated with the relevant terminal node (in this case, either high risk or low risk). For each observation in the training data set, classification (in this case, as high risk or low risk) is by vote over those classification trees that it was dropped down (that is, where it was not used to build the tree). Once one has a number of classification trees, one can record actual against predicted classifications, because for training data it is already known whether the person did or did not re-offend within the relevant period of time. Given a new offender, one then works out the terminal node for each classification tree, notes the various classifications as high risk or low risk and votes over the trees to determine the class into which the individual falls.

What is interesting about this technique, and many similar techniques, is that they do not provide an explanation for *why* an individual is high or low risk. Each new classification will be the result of multiple classifications according to many variables, some of which may have no obvious relevance. At most, one can determine the contribution that a particular predictor makes to forecasting accuracy or the extent to which a particular predictor influenced the classification given to a particular individual (Berk, 2012: 66–9). There is a random element to the construction of the random forest which means that, even with access to the same data, one might construct a random forest that makes different predictions for the same person. Nevertheless, it has been claimed that these techniques are often more effective at predicting risk than those that might be easier to explain (Berk and Bleich, 2013).

LIMITATIONS OF THESE TECHNIQUES

Predictive policing and risk assessment tools rely, to varying extents, on flawed data, criminological assumptions and human choices (Bennett Moses and Chan, 2018). An example of choice is the need to decide whether to have more false positives (where a person or location is flagged as high risk despite actually representing a low risk) or more false negatives (which is the inverse), since it is impossible to completely eliminate error. Further, these tools create probabilistic inferences as to what is likely to occur, not perfect predictions of the future. In other words, these tools have limitations. Some of these are specific to particular techniques: for example, linear regression performs poorly where the relationship between variables is non-linear, while more flexible, non-linear techniques have a tendency to over-fit the training set data. Comparison of different techniques, and the circumstances in which each performs well or poorly, requires a more detailed grounding in machine learning (see, for example, Mitchell, 1997) and thus cannot be covered in this chapter. Instead, what we describe here are some general issues that need to be addressed in relation to the use of data analytics for crime prediction.

Limitations in data

Some of the limitations to techniques such as predictive policing and offender risk assessment are inherent in the data on which they draw. Data may be inaccurate for various reasons. Data will often be an unrepresentative sample of a larger whole, as where crime data is used as a proxy for criminal activity or social media data for community opinion. There may be systemic bias in the collection of data, as where police are more likely to record crime events in locations where they are deployed or in places where they are trusted by the local community (Harcourt, 2007). Crime data for some types of offence are more likely to be complete than for others, whether due to underreporting or allocation of police resources. There may be differences in how crimes are recorded, both between particular police officers and between different precincts. There may be quirks in particular data sets, as where devices with unidentified internet protocol (IP) addresses are recorded as located in a 'default' location. Where there are small, random inaccuracies in Big Data, and analysis focuses on drawing out trends rather than identifying outliers, this may not be important. However, where the inaccuracies are systemic or where the goal is to identify individual outliers as potential suspects, errors can have important consequences.

Where data is drawn from more than a single source, there are further issues. Links will be drawn between particular entities based on the probability that the entities are the same. Further, terms may have different meanings or interpretations when data is collected by different individuals or agencies; this interpretive diversity can be lost when data sets are merged. Data collected or held by different organizations may also vary in terms of reliability and completeness. These issues can be minimized when the data analytics conducted is able to preserve information about provenance, being the source and reliability of the underlying data. Where provenance information is retained, it is possible for an analyst to not only see the inferences drawn but also relevant information about the underlying data on which those inferences were based.

Limitations of approaches based on correlation

An important limitation of many data-analytic techniques is that the information or inferences drawn from them are based on correlation rather than causation. For example, in the context of a risk assessment tool, the data may indicate that people with particular characteristics (such as poor educational outcomes) or relationships (such as family members who have been convicted of offences in the past) are more likely to re-offend. These inferences are deduced from patterns in the available data, based on the conduct of different individuals at different times. As explained above, in the case of predictive policing and offender risk assessment tools, many techniques are not concerned with understanding these patterns, finding causal explanations or understanding mechanisms.

Where *correlations* are relied on, without building a causal model, there is a risk that an intervention (such as changing police deployments) will not have the predicted effect (Pearl, 2009). This is because the correlation may be spurious or the two variables may be related in a different way (such as common cause or reverse causation). For example, the assumption behind predictive policing is that having more police in a particular area will deter crime. However, other effects are possible depending on a full causal understanding of the situation. If the cause of high crime in an area is associated with stigmatization and hostility towards police, then increasing police deployments may have the effect of increasing crime in that area. If the cause of high crime rates is a lack of suitable activities for young people, then a youth centre might be a more effective use of resources. A causal model is thus helpful when planning an intervention, such as changing the deployment of police officers, and yet is rarely produced by most predictive policing tools and techniques.

Reliance on correlation rather than causation is not only problematic when contemplating an intervention. In the context of research, an important driver is understanding as well as merely observing or predicting (Chan and Bennett Moses, 2016). In criminology, Big Data techniques can yield important insights but will only answer particular kinds of research questions. In particular, most such techniques tell very little about *why* (causation) or *how* (mechanisms).

Where inferences are drawn from correlations, and used as the basis for an intervention (such as changes in police deployment), there is also a possibility of feedback loops. For example, if police spend more time in particular locations due to predictions that crime is more likely to take place in those locations than elsewhere, then they will also *observe* more crime in those locations than elsewhere (Harcourt, 2007). Their presence may also encourage a greater reporting of crime. Because predictive policing software generally draws data from police databases, future predictions may be based on the assumption that more crime is taking place at the same locations as previously, even where this is no longer the case. Another example is where criminals change behaviour in order to avoid getting caught in circumstances where the basis for police deployment driven by an algorithm itself becomes predictable. Similar problems arise for risk assessment tools, particularly since many tools rely on responses given by offenders in interviews.

Ultimately, the effectiveness of interventions based on these kinds of tools can only be demonstrated through evaluation (Bennett Moses and Chan, 2018).

Assumptions embedded in techniques

Any technique used to analyse data involves assumptions. In machine learning, all approaches involve inductive bias in the sense that they will favour some types of solutions over others (Mitchell, 1997: 39–45). For example, they may prefer simpler to more complex solutions, include or exclude particular variables, give more or less weight to outliers, or they may assume a particular model or theory of crime. An example of the latter is PredPol. PredPol assumes that the likelihood that a crime will take place at a particular location depends on a combination of a static background crime rate at that location combined with an increased risk connected to recent local events. Similarly, in deploying risk assessment tools, a decision must be made as to the extent of any preference for false positives or false negatives. The point here is that an understanding of the particular tool, and in particular the assumptions and choices embedded within it, will affect how well it performs according to any chosen metric. It is also important to bear in mind that different approaches, relying on different data sources and variables, will often produce different results. In this sense, there is no purely 'objective' prediction or inference, but rather one based on choices made in the process of collecting and accessing data, selecting an analytic approach or technique, and determining the metrics on which it will be judged (and on the basis of which its performance will be optimised).

Differential impact and discrimination

When used in predictive policing and risk profiling, Big Data analytics can have a differential impact on particular subpopulations. There are three kinds of potential discrimination that may occur (Schauer, 2003).

First, the discrimination may be due to bias in the data (as where police record a higher proportion of crimes committed by one group relative to another) or the way in which the data is analysed. In this case, the discrimination is a result of finding a correlation that does not really exist.

Second, the discrimination may be due to overly coarse generalization. Data is analysed to find correlations among *selected* variables. If relevant variables are omitted, then the process may identify proxy variables that are less well correlated. Insurance companies do this when they require higher insurance premiums for young people, rather than for those who drive dangerously. The former variable is a rough approximation of the latter, but data on the latter variable is significantly harder to procure. As a result, insurance companies discriminate against young drivers rather than the more accurate category of dangerous drivers. In this case, the correlation exists, but it is not the best variable on which to base a prediction. And it is potentially unfair to young drivers who are not dangerous drivers.

The third type of discrimination occurs where a correlation not only exists (in the world as well as in the data) but is also a strong predictor. Even in this case, there remain controversial questions as to whether it is unjust to target or profile an individual or neighbourhood based on the factor concerned, particularly where it involves a sensitive attribute such as race or religion such that discrimination may be stigmatising or produce excessive separation (Schauer, 2003: 147–51, 189–90). In other words, just as it may be unacceptable to discriminate in employment, even where this could be statistically justified, so too it can be argued that it is unjust to discriminate in the context of law enforcement and criminal justice on the basis of predictive tools, at least where this would negatively impact traditionally stigmatized groups. Predictive power may not be the only relevant factor in determining the appropriateness of using a particular tool. One may also be concerned, for example, about negative social impacts and, in particular, differential impacts on particular subpopulations.

If one is concerned about these impacts, it is insufficient simply to remove particular variables. The alleged differential impact of the COMPAS tool on African Americans (Angwin et al., 2016) is said to occur despite the fact that the company, Northpointe Inc. (now equivant), claimed not to use race as a variable. This is because if A correlates with both B and C, then the omission of A from the data does not prevent the identification of a correlation between B and C. So, if race is omitted but correlates with both education levels and entries in a crime database (say), then the algorithm may identify that those with low education are more likely to commit crimes. This may have a differential impact on the relevant racial group. Indeed, in some circumstances, omitting race as a variable makes the problem worse. For example, if a minority racial group has poor educational outcomes but (for that group) this does not correlate with re-offending, while in the majority racial group there is such a correlation, then the minority group may be assessed as higher risk if race is omitted as a variable.

There are no simple answers to how to manage the issue of discrimination in the use of these kinds of tools. There is, however, work being done to develop discrimination-sensitive approaches to prediction (for example, Kamiran et al., 2013). However, as explained in Verwer and Calders (2013: 255), without a causal model explaining why a particular correlation occurs, the techniques will result in a reduction in accuracy, positive discrimination (which may itself be controversial), or both.

Individual harm

A final limitation of these kinds of tools relates to the way they link with decisions made, either by law enforcement agencies or in the criminal justice system. Being based on correlation, the analysis can suggest high-risk individuals or locations, but is generally unable to explain *why*. There are important questions of fairness, particularly in approaching criminal justice decisions around questions of the similarity between a particular individual and others who have behaved badly in the past. This is particularly so when the analytic tools themselves are not transparent (an issue discussed below), or where it is difficult for individuals to challenge inferences drawn against them (O'Neill, 2016).

CHALLENGES FOR RESEARCHERS

Being aware of the limitations of particular tools is an important first step for researchers considering employing or critiquing data-analytic tools in criminological research. This section discusses two additional matters that will need to be borne in mind: non-transparency of some of the underlying approaches and difficulties in designing and implementing a proper evaluation.

Non-transparency

The most significant barrier for researchers interested in understanding data-driven approaches to predictive policing and offender risk assessment is lack of access to both the algorithms/models employed and the underlying data on which predictions are based. Most commercial software tools keep their methods commercial-in-confidence. While the model underlying PredPol was published in Mohler et al. (2011), the extent to which the original model remains in use is unknown. Even less is known about the models, approaches and algorithms deployed in other commercial software tools.

An additional transparency challenge is obtaining access to data, including data employed in training machine learning algorithms or statistical analysis, and crime data over time (as a proxy for the change in crime based on use of a particular approach to police deployment).

Evaluation

There are two kinds of evaluation that can be conducted on predictive policing and offender risk assessment tools. The first is to test the accuracy of the prediction itself. In the case of offender risk management, this can be done by comparing risk scores with whether the offender is known to have engaged in relevant conduct (offending, breaking bail conditions, violence) over a fixed period of time. For predictive policing, this can be done by comparing the locations of predicted crime to actual events (noting the precision in location and timing). The challenge here is that an evaluation is ideally conducted if one is using the tool (recording the predictions) but not actually intervening – in other words, not using risk scores to make decisions or not focusing police patrols on forecasted hot spot locations. For this kind of evaluation, which assesses predictive accuracy, interventions would introduce bias into the data.

This is easy to see in the context of offender risk management tools. There can be no data on non-compliance with bail conditions of those held in custody pending trial. There can be no data on re-offending rates during periods where people remain in custody. Even though there may be data on whether these people re-offend after they are released, such data does not necessarily reflect the counterfactual of what would have occurred had they been released sooner. For example, a longer period in custody provides greater opportunities for criminal associations to develop. This creates difficulty in evaluating the accuracy of offender risk assessment tools.

The second type of evaluation is to measure the effectiveness of the tool in achieving its purpose (such as reduction in crime, cost savings or reducing recidivism). This requires the evaluation to be done on a programme as implemented. For example, predictive policing software can be operationalized in a sample of locations to test whether it performs better at reducing crime than traditional approaches adopted elsewhere.

A significant challenge for those seeking to evaluate predictive policing programs *as operationalized* is ensuring high levels of implementation. Police resistance can be a barrier to predictive policing (Perry et al., 2013: 129). Indeed, one attempt to evaluate a predictive policing programme noted the challenge of implementation across multiple districts over a period of time (Hunt et al., 2014: xiii).

There are also ethical issues with both forms of evaluation, similar in many ways to the ethical issues inherent in testing new medical treatments. While the test is under way, the person conducting the test has a 'treatment' that is not being deployed to (in this case) prevent crime. In the case of the first type of evaluation, no intervention at all is permitted (despite the knowledge gained from the tool). In the case of the second type of evaluation, operationalization is limited to a sample so that there is a control group or location against which the treated group or location can be compared. Despite these concerns, evaluations are nevertheless necessary, for similar reasons, for clinical tests in medicine – there needs to be proof that a treatment is safe and effective before it is widely adopted.

SUMMARY AND REVIEW

There are many potential applications for Big Data analytics in criminology research. This chapter has focused on two predictive techniques used in law enforcement and criminal justice – predictive policing and offender risk assessment. Big Data techniques allow researchers to gain insights from larger volumes of data than could be analysed without them, possibly discovering patterns that might otherwise remain hidden. However, it is important to understand both the limitations of these techniques and their potential, when used as the basis for intervention, to yield unanticipated or undesirable results. They will be more useful in answering some kinds of research questions (exploratory and descriptive research) than others (understanding causal mechanisms). They should thus be used only with an understanding of their limitations and biases, and their use (particularly where there is an impact on individuals) should be carefully evaluated.

This chapter has detailed in relation to the following:

Defining Big Data:

- The most common definition focuses on data having high volume, high velocity (speed of production and processing) and high variety (of data types and sources), although there is a range of other definitions.

Uses of Big Data in crime prediction:

- Predictive policing is used by police to target particular locations and times, or occasionally individuals, where the likelihood of criminal activity is heightened.
- Offender risk management attempts to quantify risk for the purposes of bail, parole or sentencing decisions. One technique that can be used is the random forest algorithm.

Limitations:

- accuracy and representativeness of data
- challenges in data linking and tracking provenance of data
- based on correlation rather than causation
- inductive bias
- differential impact on subpopulations and the potential for discrimination
- fairness of use, particularly in criminal justice decision making.

Challenges for researchers:

- access to algorithm or analytic technique used
- access to data employed by the algorithm or technique as a basis for future predictions
- evaluation of predictive accuracy distinguished from evaluation of effectiveness.

STUDY QUESTIONS AND ACTIVITIES FOR STUDENTS

1. Consider one of the techniques described above. What kinds of information or inferences does this technique produce about future criminal activity? What assumptions are inherent in the approach?

2. Give an example of a research question that can be answered exclusively by reference to Big Data analytics. Give an example of a research question that cannot be answered in this way. In what ways could Big Data analytics nevertheless provide important insights?

3. How important is it that police officers, those working in the criminal justice system and criminologists understand particular analytic tools such as those used in predictive policing and offender risk assessment?

SUGGESTIONS FOR FURTHER READING

Various books and articles provide critical commentary on the use of Big Data techniques, either generally or particularly in the context of criminal justice.

While somewhat dated as to particular tools being used, Harcourt, B.E. (2007) *Against Prediction: Profiling, Policing and Punishing in an Actuarial Age*. Chicago, IL: University of Chicago Press remains an excellent source for a review of concerns around data-driven approaches in this area.

Chan, J. and Bennett Moses, L. (2016) 'Is Big Data challenging criminology?', *Theoretical Criminology, 20*: 21–39 provides an overview of the use of Big Data in criminology. In the particular context of predictive policing, see Bennett Moses, L. and Chan, J. (2018) 'Algorithmic prediction in policing: assumptions, evaluation, and accountability', *Policing and Society, 28*(7): 806-822. doi: 10.1080/10439463.2016.1253695.

For a student-friendly technical account of some of the techniques used in offender risk assessment, see Berk, R. (2012) *Criminal Justice Forecasts of Risk: A Machine Learning Approach*. New York: Springer.

For a more technical account of discrimination-aware techniques, see Custers, B., Calders, T., Schermer, B. and Zarsky, T. (eds) (2013) *Discrimination and Privacy in the Information Society: Data Mining and Profiling in Large Databases*. Heidelberg: Springer.

For a broader account of Big Data as a 'cultural, technological and scholarly phenomenon', see boyd, d. and Crawford, K. (2012) 'Critical questions for Big Data: provocations for a cultural, technological, and scholarly phenomenon', *Information, Communication and Society*, 15: 662–79.

REFERENCES

Angwin, J., Larson, J., Mattu, S. and Kirchner, L. (2016) 'Machine bias', *ProPublica*, 23 May. Available at: www.propublica.org/article/machine-bias-risk-assessments-in-criminal-sentencing (accessed 2 May 2018).

Arnold Foundation (2013) Developing a National Model for Pre-trial Risk Assessment (November). Available at: www./wp-content/uploads/2014/02 arnoldfoundation.org/ LJAF-research-summary_PSACourt_4_1.pdf (accessed 10 July 2018).

Beck, C. and McCue, C. (2009) 'Predictive policing: what can we learn from WalMart and Amazon about fighting crime in a recession?', *The Police Chief*, 76(11): 20–9.

Bennett Moses, L. and Chan, J. (2018) 'Algorithmic prediction in policing: assumptions, evaluation, and accountability', *Policing and Society*, 28(7): 806-822. doi: 10.1080/10439463. 2016.1253695.

Berk, R. (2012) *Criminal Justice Forecasts of Risk: A Machine Learning Approach*. New York: Springer.

Berk, R. and Bleich, J. (2013) 'Statistical procedures for forecasting criminal behavior', *Criminology & Public Policy*, 12(3): 513–44.

Bowers, K.J., Johnson, S.D. and Pease, K. (2004) 'Prospective hot-spotting: the future of crime mapping?', *British Journal of Criminology*, 44(5): 641–58.

boyd, d. and Crawford, K. (2012) 'Critical questions for Big Data: provocations for a cultural, technological, and scholarly phenomenon', *Information, Communication and Society*, 15: 662–79.

Chan, J. and Bennett Moses, L. (2016) 'Is Big Data challenging criminology?', *Theoretical Criminology*, 20: 21–39.

Chan, J. and Bennett Moses, L. (2017) 'Making sense of Big Data for security', *British Journal of Criminology*, 57(2): 299–319.

Gerber M.S. (2014) 'Predicting crime using Twitter and kernel density estimation', *Decision Support Systems*, 61: 115–25.

Harcourt, B.E. (2007) *Against Prediction: Profiling, Policing and Punishing in an Actuarial Age*. Chicago, IL: University of Chicago Press.

Hart, T.C. and Zandbergen, P.A. (2012) *Effects of Data Quality on Predictive Hotspot Mapping: Final Technical Report*. Washington, DC: National Institute of Justice, 239861.

Hunt, P., Saunders, J. and Hollywood, J.S. (2014) *Evaluation of the Shreveport Predictive Policing Experiment*. Santa Monica, CA: RAND.

Johnson, S.D. and Bowers, K.J. (2004) 'The stability of space–time clusters of burglary', *British Journal of Criminology*, *44*(1): 55–65.

Kamiran, F., Calders, T. and Pechenizkiy, M. (2013) 'Techniques for discrimination-free predictive models', in B. Custers, T. Calders, B. Schermer, and T. Zarsky (eds), *Discrimination and Privacy in the Information Society: Data Mining and Profiling in Large Databases*. Heidelberg: Springer, pp. 223–40.

Kitchin, R. (2014) 'Big Data, new epistemologies and paradigm shifts', *Big Data and Society*, *1*: 1–12.

Mayer-Schönberger, V. and Cukier, K. (2013) *Big Data: A Revolution That Will Transform How We Live, Work and Think*. London: John Murray.

Mitchell, T.M. (1997) *Machine Learning*. New York: McGraw-Hill.

Mohler, G.O., Short, M.B., Brantingham, P.J., Schoenberg, F.P. and Tita, G.E. (2011) 'Self-exciting point process modeling of crime', *Journal of the American Statistical Association*, *106*(493): 100–8.

National Center for State Courts (2007) Conference of Chief Justices and Conference of State Court Administrators, Resolution 12: In Support of Sentencing Practices that Promote Public Safety and Reduce Recidivism (1 August). Available at: http://ncsc.con tentdm.oclc.org/cdm/ref/collection/ctcomm/id/139 (accessed 2 May 2018).

O'Neil, C. (2016) *Weapons of Math Destruction: How Big Data Increases Inequality and Threatens Democracy*. New York: Crown.

Pearl, J. (2009) *Causality: Models, Reasoning, and Inference*, 2nd edition. New York: Cambridge University Press.

Perry, W.L., McInnis, B., Price, C.C., Smith, S.C. and Hollywood, J.S. (2013) *Predictive Policing: The Role of Crime Forecasting in Law Enforcement Operations*. Santa Monica, CA: RAND.

Procter, R., Vis, F. and Voss, A. (2013) 'Reading the riots on Twitter: methodological innovation for the analysis of Big Data', *International Journal of Social Research Methodology*, *16*(3): 197–214.

Schauer, F. (2003) *Profiles, Probabilities and Stereotypes*. Cambridge, MA: Harvard University Press.

State v Loomis (2016) 881 N.W.2d 749 (Wis. 2016).

Traunmueller, M., Quattrone, G. and Capra, L. (2014) 'Mining mobile phone data to investigate urban crime theories at scale', in L.M. Aiello and D. McFarland (eds), *Social Informatics: Lecture Notes in Computer Science*. Dordrecht: Springer, pp. 396–411.

Uchida, C. (2014) 'Predictive policing', in G. Bruinsma and D. Weisburd (eds), *Encyclopedia of Criminology and Criminal Justice*. New York: Springer, pp. 3871–80.

Verwer, S. and Calders, T. (2013) 'Introducing positive discrimination in predictive models', in B. Custers, T. Calders, B. Schermer and T. Zarsky (eds), *Discrimination and Privacy in the Information Society: Data Mining and Profiling in Large Databases*. Heidelberg: Springer, pp. 255–72.

Watters, P.A. and Phair, N. (2012) 'Detecting illicit drugs on social media using Automated Social Media Intelligence Analysis', in Y. Xiang, J. Lopez, C.-C.J. Kuo, et al. (eds), *Cyberspace Safety and Security Lecture Notes in Computer Science*. Heidelberg: Springer, pp. 66–76.

Williams, M.L. and Burnap, P. (2016) 'Cyberhate on social media in the aftermath of Woolwich: a case study in computational criminology and Big Data', *British Journal of Criminology*, 56: 211–38.

Williams, M.L., Burnap, P. and Sloan, L. (2017) 'Crime sensing with Big Data: the affordances and limitations of using open-source communications to estimate crime patterns', *British Journal of Criminology*, 57(2): 320–40.

Williams, M.L., Edwards, A., Housely, W., et al. (2013) 'Policing cyber-neighbourhoods: tension monitoring and social media networks'. *Policing and Society*, 23(4): 461–81.

CHAPTER CONTENTS

GLOSSARY TERMS

interviews

hypothesis testing

grounded theory

secondary analysis

perspective

reflexivity

conceptual themes

praxis

12

DOING QUALITATIVE DATA ANALYSIS IN CRIMINOLOGICAL RESEARCH

PAMELA DAVIES

INTRODUCTION

This chapter focuses on doing analysis using data derived from qualitative research. In broad terms, the chapter addresses connectivities between real-world victimization, evidence-based knowledge and how an advanced stage of analysis can lead to theoretical developments. The examples draw on my own efforts to do qualitative analysis in the context of research on the sensitive and emotive topic of child sexual abuse. I also draw on research conducted by others on the same topic. After a general contextual discussion of child sexual abuse (CSA), an outline of my own research project is provided. Analysing qualitative data in general is then briefly discussed before drilling into an analysis which dovetails documentary and interview data in the context of child sexual abuse. Types and levels of analysis are explored. First, conceptual themes are considered and illustrated before considering analysis that leads to theory building. Hypothesis testing and data analysis are illustrated before a further dimension to the analysis of findings is discussed. Reflexive analysis from a particular perspective and ontological position adds a further dimension to doing analysis of qualitative research.

CONTEXT AND FOCUS: CHILD SEXUAL ABUSE

The main focus of the chapter is on doing qualitative analysis in the context of research on the topic of child sexual abuse and exploitation (CSA/CSE). Both historical abuse and contemporary abuse are presently highly topical and newsworthy subjects. In the British context, the Cleveland Inquiry 1988 was the first major inquiry into child sexual abuse. Reactions to it put into context the difficulties and complexities of understanding and researching CSA/CSE. In the decades that followed, there were several significant changes, including 'Working Together' statutory guidance (1991, 1999, 2006, 2010, 2013, 2015 and 2018); Sexual Offences Acts (1993, 1997); Every Child Matters (Green Paper, 2003); the Munro Review of Child Protection (2011); the Children Act 1989 and Children Act 2004; and The Children and Families Act 2014. All of these documents/guidelines and legislation were designed to ensure the delivery of a child-centred approach to safeguarding. Following a Metropolitan Police investigation – Operation Yewtree – that commenced in late 2012 into the alleged abuse of young people by Jimmy Savile, findings revealed sexual abuse on an unprecedented scale (Gray and Watt, 2013). Since then, many more have felt able to speak out about their experiences and other celebrities have been accused and some convicted of CSA since. At the time of writing, there are widespread reports emerging of historical abuse of the young in connection with sporting activities, and the widespread media broadcasting of these cases has been a key factor in rendering such cases more visible in the public eye. In 2014 the Jay Report into child sexual exploitation in

Rotherham, South Yorkshire, UK described at least 1400 cases of CSE (1997–2013) and highlighted the failures of agencies in that area to act effectively. In the UK, a growing number of large-scale inquiries into the institutional abuse of children culminated in an 'Independent Inquiry into Child Sexual Abuse', though this lengthy ongoing inquiry has been fraught with leadership problems. In the meantime, police operations such as Operation Sanctuary in the north-east of England continue to tackle the sexual exploitation of women and girls, with notable success in securing convictions.

Child sexual abuse has also been catapulted into the foreground of media reports in New Zealand, Australia and Canada, where responses to such abuse and research on this have recently been published. As noted by Stanley in Chapter 14 of this volume, the official response to the violence and harms suffered by those held as children within state institutions in New Zealand has been to silence, deny or minimize testimonies in response to ongoing attempts to secure redress (see also Stanley, 2016). Daly's research in Australia and Canada sought to historicize the emergence of institutional abuse as a social problem, compare responses by authorities and determine whether there was an optimal redress response from victim-surivivors' perspectives (see Chapter 21 in this volume and Daly, 2014).

The emergence of historical abuse alongside contemporary experiences of CSA/ CSE has seen a number of inquiries into child sexual exploitation, trafficking and child sexual abuse being launched in various parts of the world. Despite significant changes to promote children's safety and protection, child sexual abuse is a stubbornly problematic, complex and emotive social problem. Current strategies and interventions leave many unprotected, with opportunities to intervene being missed. In other cases, interventions have been criticized for being over-zealous. In both scenarios, there is a wake of damage and harm to families affected by CSA.

Having contextualized the subject of child sexual abuse, it is clear that researching the problem is likely to involve many obstacles, including definition of terms, different contexts, time periods and places where abuse occurs, the emotive nature of the subject, gender and age dimensions to the problem and changing legislation, policy and practice. I now introduce the research project which I draw on to illustrate my analytical points. My experience of analysing and making sense of qualitative data relates to a research project that explored the needs of, and support for, families affected by child sexual abuse. A brief outline of the aims, methodology and guiding questions is given in Box 12.1.

ANALYSIS OF QUALITATIVE DATA

Data analysis is an activity that students are likely to attend to towards the latter phase of their research project. Students doing independent research projects and dissertations will often engage in proposal work with their supervisors at the start of their research journey, and, in my experience, there is a tendency to omit any clear

BOX 12.1   THE NEEDS OF AND SUPPORT FOR FAMILIES
AFFECTED BY CHILD SEXUAL ABUSE

This research focused on the wider impact that child sexual abuse has on non-abusers (conceptualized as indirect victims) affected by this type of crime and victimization. In order to explore these issues, the research involved collecting information from two main sources: public documents and semi-structured in-depth interviews with key personnel connected to such cases. Interviews were conducted with a range of professionals engaged in investigating and supporting victims of child sexual abuse and other key lay personnel. I gathered perceptions of the wider impact on families and their members. The following questions steered the semi-structured interview conversations:

1. Who is affected by child sexual abuse?
2. How are these people affected? What is the impact?
3. What are their needs?
4. What services/support are available?

Funded by The British Academy RP JO0889

articulation of the proposed approach to how the analysis might be done and what type and level of analysis best fit with the remainder of the research design. A robust research plan will think forward and part of this forward planning will contemplate whether the research questions and research methodology lend themselves to a largely deductive approach or a constructed/constructivist approach that is interpretivist and inductive. Deductive research tends to be associated with theory or hypothesis-testing inquiries, whereas inductive research has clearer links to 'grounded theorizing'. Grounded theory is associated originally with Glaser and Strauss (1967) and refers to an approach which starts with data collection, and, as data emerge, constant comparisons are made between data and theory (Davies, 2011).

Thus, depending on the nature of the research being undertaken, some of the pointers towards how the analysis will be affected are already built into the chosen methodological approach. You may be using documents or other people's data such as crime and victimization data as part of your research. In criminological research, this is most likely to be original data sets – raw data – collected by agencies such as the police or the courts and which belongs to a government department, a criminal justice agency or an academic researcher (Semmens, 2011). Examples of secondary sources include census data and recorded crime statistics (see also Chapter 1). Secondary analysis can be done using data from these sources. Such data will have been collected for some other purpose than your own. You may, however, be gathering primary data through questioning people via surveys, interviews, focus groups and listening, or through life histories, observations and ethnographic research, and each of these methods will determine, to a greater or lesser extent, the manner in which you will be analysing your data. Documents can be analysed via content and discourse analysis as can interview data from transcripts of interviews. Interviews can also be analysed by making summaries and comparisons, by coding and categorizing to identify themes, commonalities and differences in data sets (see Boxes 12.3 and 12.4).

In the literature, there are different definitions of analysis but most definitions capture how qualitative analysis entails disassembling or segmenting and reassembling or synthesizing your data. Boeije (2010) offers the following definition:

> Qualitative analysis is the segmenting of data into relevant categories and the naming of these categories with codes while simultaneously generating the categories from the data. In the reassembling phase the categories are related to one another to generate theoretical understanding of the social phenomena under study in terms of the research questions. (Boeije, 2010: 76)

This definition emphasizes the emerging character of analysis where a stream of several 'thinking and doing' activities, such as sorting, naming and categorizing, go hand in hand. Critically for Boeije (2010), the disassembling part of the analysis enables the researcher to specify which building blocks their research contains, thereby allowing for the emergence of theoretical concepts.

Analysis allows us to discover findings. The analysis we engage in must allow for the accurate representation of the perceptions, views and experiences of our respondents. How you plan to analyse data should, therefore, not be an afterthought but a fundamental part of your initial project plan and, as noted above, within your research proposal there ought to be consideration of how you will approach the analysis. Even these early plans for analysis will ensure that the proposed approach allows for you to attend to meaning. Paying attention to social meanings ensures the research does not become divorced from social reality. Prioritizing social meaning will safeguard the producing of conclusions which are grounded in such meanings and expressed in terms which would be used by the respondents themselves (Davies, 2011: 50). Again, this reminds us of the importance of the interplay between inductive and deductive approaches, where one approach is often tempered by the other in effective and rigorous criminological inquiry. It is important ethically that your choice and use of analytical devices and tools is capable of capturing the essence of the original data you have collected. At the same time, it is important that your analysis is capable of shedding light on the research objectives and research questions. Decisions made at each stage of your analysis should be made transparent. Analysis is therefore a critical component of research and how it is accomplished can impact on the quality of the entire research project. There are few texts that get behind the pure abstract principles of doing quantitative and qualitative data analysis (see Bryman, 2016; Creswell, 2014; and Neuman, 2014, for example). The third section of Jennifer Mason's (2002) book *Qualitative Researching* provides some useful guidance on organizing and indexing and making convincing arguments with qualitative data. Below, I illustrate how there are various different *levels* of analysis that can be achieved from qualitative research and how analysis is guided by your epistemological position (see Chapter 6 in this volume) and your perspective on the problem under consideration. These factors underlie the importance of being reflexive. First however, let us focus on my own continuing efforts to grapple with the problems of how to analyse data arising out of a qualitative research inquiry into a very sensitive area of victimization.

Analysing documents

In the context of this chapter, it might be useful to think about two broad ways in which documentation is used in criminological research. One relates to doing a literature review where you might search out and collate an array of material which you might 'read' (analyse) for a specific purpose (for more on the purpose and types of literature review, see Chapters 1 and 3 in this volume). Another way in which documents are used is as a research resource to be excavated. Documentary analysis is a research term which masks, and can invite, different methods for analysing documents, including content analysis, discourse analysis (also called narrative or semiotic analysis) and critical discourse analysis (for examples of how media texts can be analysed, see Mawby, 2010). Documents come in many different forms, none of which are value-free or 'objective', thus content, discourse or critical discourse analysis can be used to question a document's authenticity, credibility and representativeness.

Criminologists analysing media news stories find that certain combinations of news values guarantee a story as more or less newsworthy (see Jewkes, 2015). Children as victims of sexual abuse and perpetrators of it tend to be highly newsworthy (see Greer, 2017; Jewkes, 2010; Mawby, 2010). Systematic literature reviews are another way in which analysis can be affected – see Box 12.2 which outlines how a citation network analysis was applied to a literature review, and from this a framework model was developed.

In my own research project on child sexual abuse, I used literature to familiarise myself with the nature and impact of child sexual abuse and the existing debates surrounding it. My initial trawl for this purpose included a search and read of official inquiry documentation – initially in the UK: the publications emanating from the Cleveland Inquiry 1988 and subsequent inquiries up to the Jay Report (2014), media reports, local and regional safeguarding and inspection reports of children's services, for example those by Casey (2015a and b) for the Department for Communities and Local Government inquiring into child sexual exploitation in Rotherham. I also scrutinized police and non-governmental organization reports, for example the joint

BOX 12.2 SYSTEMATIC LITERATURE REVIEWS AND
ANALYSIS – AN EXAMPLE

Long Weatherred, J. (2015) 'Child sexual abuse and the media: a literature review', *Journal of Child Sexual Abuse*, *24*(1): 16–34.

ABSTRACT

The media play an important role in practice, policy and public perception of child sexual abuse, in part by the way in which news stories are framed. Child sexual abuse media coverage over the past 50 years can be divided into five time periods based on the types of stories that garnered news coverage and the ways in which public policy was changed. This systematic literature review of research on child sexual abuse media coverage across disciplines and geographic boundaries examines 16 studies published in the English language from 1995 to 2012. A seminal work is identified, citation network analysis is applied and a framework model is developed.

THE AUTHOR REPORTS ON HOW TERMS ARE DEFINED:

Psychologists define CSA as contact between a child and an adult or other person significantly older or in a position of power or control over the child in which the child is being used for sexual gratification for the adult or other.

The law defines CSA as a criminal and civil offence in which an adult engages in sexual activity with a minor or exploits a minor for the purpose of sexual gratification.

The term *media* applies to CSA news stories appearing in newspapers, magazines, tabloid newspapers and television news reports. *Media advocacy* is the strategic use of the media to encourage social and public policy changes.

THE METHODOLOGY IS DESCRIBED:

A search was performed through EBSCO, JSTOR, MEDLINE, Google Scholar, Google and the Web of Social Sciences for English-language articles that (a) included 'child sexual abuse' and 'media' in the title, abstract or keywords; (b) focused its research on CSA and the media; and (c) used qualitative, quantitative or both methods to collect or analyse data about CSA and the media. Research across disciplines and geographic boundaries was included; however, research papers that did not utilize qualitative or quantitative methods and articles from non-peer-reviewed sources (e.g. mainstream media) were excluded.

report by Gray and Watt (2013) for the Metropolitan Police and the National Society for the Prevention of Cruelty to Children (NSPCC) into sexual allegations made against Jimmy Savile. Academic publications and scholarly work encompassed the work of Daly (2014) and Stanley (2016) on institutional abuse and work from outside of the discipline of criminology that contributes to knowledge, for example social psychology and child and family social work.

My gathering together of literature was largely unrestricted in terms of the rules I adopted. In this respect, it was very different from the systematic review example provided in Box 12.2. My research questions were such that I was exploring an avenue of inquiry that presupposed there would be a diffuse effect of victimization emanating from child sexual abuse. I wanted to keep the parameters of my sources as open as possible and was reluctant to close off any potentially useful directions that I might be guided towards. In this sense, even my initial trawl of the literature was 'grounded' in nature and has leanings towards an inductive rather than deductive approach to analysis. This initial search produced a bibliography that was typically eclectic in nature. 'Typically' because in the early stages of most inductive criminological research, the reference list produced in support of your inquiry will be relatively unfocused, limited only perhaps by time periods, crime types and other fairly loose inclusion/exclusion criteria.

This initial analysis of official and grey literatures ensured that I familiarized myself with the language, protocols, provisions and personnel involved in supporting children and their families affected by child sexual abuse, and grasp the nature and focus of the debates that academic colleagues were foregrounding as well as the issues that faded into the background. My analysis involved returning to these publications, incorporating new literatures amassed during the course of the research and interrogating them to determine whether or not any of them made sense of what I had uncovered in my findings from the in-depth interviews. This part of my analysis also involved a more rigorous scrutiny of the provenance of the resources and a thematic review. This re-use and interrogation of the literature involved using both established and new concepts and conceptual themes as emergent from the interview data.

Analysing interviews

As explored elsewhere (see Chapter 14 in this volume and Davies, 2011), interviews can vary in style and format. I had adopted an approach that used semi-structured interviews to allow for a naturalistic discussion that could be steered at times largely by the respondent. This method of interview can lead to lengthy discussions and conversations that lean towards storytelling. In interviews of this nature, respondents slip into a narrative that is guided by their own recollection and experience. The interview elicits responses that are grounded in their own language, or, as in my own interviews, the recollection of language as used by others. Thus, the strength of interviews is their flexibility and their potential for prompting interviewees to speak freely. My respondents relayed their perceptions of who is affected by child sexual abuse, how they are affected and what their needs are, and what services/support were available. I thus gained insight into the wider impact of CSA on non-abusing family members.

I was the principal investigator (PI), the author and owner of the project. I also conducted the research myself. I searched for and gathered the literature and documents myself, negotiated and secured ethical permissions and access and carried out the interviews in person. By doing the interviews myself, I had a significant head start in terms of knowing my data. In other research projects, I had been only one of those engaged in fieldwork. Reading transcriptions of interviews as conducted by others and listening to audio-recordings of interviews carried out by members of your research team give you less of a first-hand feel for the data. Grasping the content and potential themes is rendered a more distanced exercise. Whilst some might argue this demands a greater level of transparency about how analysis is conducted because there has to be a clearly articulated strategy for team members to follow, which provides for a more objective analysis, for others it introduces a mere veneer of objectivity, greater distance from the rich data and greater likelihood of 'meaning' being diluted, misinterpreted or lost. Though there are ways of safeguarding against the latter tendencies, for example by the use of memos, diary or field notes which allow you to capture impressions, thoughts and ideas, such notes also need to be understood by your fellow research team members and they too are susceptible to different interpretations. In qualitative research, these aide memoires are perhaps best adapted for the purpose of recording reflections that may be helpful in ensuring the transparency of how the analysis unfolded in a way that is intimately connected to the raw data (see the section below on reflexivity and critical reflection). In Box 12.3, an example is provided of a research project that involved several researchers and where data analysis included several inductive phases.

BOX 12.3 RESEARCH TEAMS AND ANALYSIS – AN EXAMPLE

Gruenfeld, E., Willis, D.G. and Easton, S.D. (2017) '"A very steep climb": therapists' perspectives on barriers to disclosure of child sexual abuse experiences for men', *Journal of Child Sexual Abuse*, 26(6): 731–51.

Using conventional content analysis, this study examined the perceptions of nine therapists who specialize in the treatment of men who were sexually abused in childhood. The research question was: *What do therapists who specialize in treating men*

(Continued)

(Continued)

with CSA histories perceive as barriers to disclosure? The analysis focused on data related to disclosure barriers. Conventional content analysis took place over a nine-month period. This approach is appropriate when research domains (such as barriers to disclosure of CSA for men) lack an extensive body of literature or substantial theory development. Throughout the process, descriptive codes were developed that represented the main ideas pertinent to the research question. The analysis included several inductive phases:

1. Multiple readings (immersion) and initial coding of four transcripts to allow the researchers to develop an overall sense of participants' perspectives. Independent line-by-line analysis and weekly meetings where researchers read and analysed transcriptions aloud, compared notes and emergent codes (disclosure barriers, disclosure facilitators, treatment strategies, help-seeking resources, mental health impacts) in order to reach a consensus.
2. First-author coding of the remaining transcripts. Revisions of code list (new additions, collapsing of codes, refinement of definitions). Validity checks by the team, review of analytic decisions, development of codebook (4 categories, 12 codes, 25 subcodes).
3. Researchers independently reapplied the same code set to all data. Coding revised to nine and categorization decisions resulted in three categories being identified and defined:

Category 1	Category 2	Category 3
Intrapersonal Experience	**Social Milieu**	**Health Care Environment**
Difficult feelings	Internalized social stigma	Structural barriers
Lack of language and self-engagement	Negative responses	Relational challenges with therapists
	Social loss or judgement	Unhelpful therapeutic strategies
	Masculine identity dissonance	

There are also, of course, several computer-assisted qualitative data analysis (CAQDAS) packages and specialist software and programs, such as Atlas.ti and NVivo, which can aid analysis of your data. The analysis described in Box 12.3 used in vivo coding to stay close to the participants' language and to help ensure the credibility and dependability of analysis. Several chapters in this book refer to and exemplify the use of such computer-assisted analytic technologies which may involve arranging codes in hierarchies or 'trees' (see Chapter 11 in this volume), for example. CAQDAS may assist with the disassembling and reassembling of your data and indeed with the presentation of your findings, but it cannot do the thinking for you. See Box 12.4 for an example of a research project where data analysis involved thematic content analysis using NVivo 10 software. The examples provided emphasize the importance of thinking through the rules that govern your analysis and the importance of articulating what the rules or values are that guide your coding, for example, and inform the different levels of analysis you undertake.

BOX 12.4   THEMATIC CONTENT ANALYSIS USING NVIVO 10 SOFTWARE

Hohendorff, J.V., Habigzang, L.F. and Koller, S.H. (2017) '"A boy, being a victim, nobody really buys that, you know?" Dynamics of sexual violence against boys', *Child Abuse & Neglect, 70*: 53–64.

Using NVivo 10 software, eight interview transcripts were submitted to thematic content analysis (four interviews with boys and four with practitioners). The deductive, or theoretical, analysis of the interviews was guided by six themes (drawn from the integrative module of sexual violence against children proposed by one of the authors), referring to the different stages of sexual abuse against children and adolescents: Preparation, Episodes, Silencing, Narrative, Suppression and Overcoming. The themes, sub-themes and examples drawn from the interviews with the boys are illustrated in Table 12.1.

TABLE 12.1   Themes, Sub-themes and Examples Drawn from the Interviews with the Boys

Themes	Sub-themes	Examples
Preparation	Proximity to the offender	*He would get into my house, then my mother would leave, so he would babysit;* *My friend, when I was playing videogame at his house*
	Relational asymmetry Play activities	*I was really little and didn't understand anything* *He* (i.e. the offender) *is nice sometimes… He even plays with me;* *He was really cool, he used to play with me, then later he raped me*

(Continued)

TABLE 12.1   (Continued)

Themes	Sub-themes	Examples
Episodes	Victim vulnerability	*I slept on his bed by accident, I was passed out (…) I didn't understand it, really. I didn't understand it, really*
	Type/frequency of sexual violence	*Almost every day, when he went to my house and I went to his house, he raped me; He went and put that wiener all the way in my butt (…) Before it was maybe three times; Just once. Just once.*
	Use of physical force by the offender	*He took me (…) When I opened the door like this, he came over really quickly and got me; Then he held me like this, and tied my hand like that*
	Victim reactions	*I was disgusted (…) Then I ran home; After he did that to me I tried to stop him, but I couldn't*
Silencing	Fear	*I was really scared of telling everyone, anyone*
	Disbelief by others	*But then my mom didn't believe me, so I said it was all a lie*
Narrative	Repeated reports	*Then after (telling my mom) my neighbor started to ask about it, because she heard everything (…) So then I told her everything, and she told everything to my mom*
	Facilitators	*Later I began to figure out what he did, because I saw it on TV, right? On the news … Then I began to figure it out, and I talked*
	Victim feelings	*When I talk I feel kind of stressed (…) I feel angry, kind of nervous, I feel so angry I might explode*
	Family reactions	*Then she (sister) told my mom, my mom cried, my dad called the doctor, then took us there*
Repression	Discreditation	*Then my mom told her and she (the mother of the perpetrator) didn't believe it*
	Avoidance by the victim	*So I told her (mother) that I felt like doing it (the same as they did to him) whenever they talked to me about it, but that was a lie, just so she wouldn't talk about it anymore. I don't like it (talking about the abuse)*

Themes	Sub-themes	Examples
Overcoming	Distance from the offender	*She* (mother) *told me not to go to his house anymore* (offender)
	Family support	*And my brother is spending more time with me, because he used to go out, and would only be at home sometimes, but now he talks to me, plays with me sometimes*
	System intervention	*When I talk about it I feel kind of stressed, but not right now, because I'm talking to a specialist! Thankfully the doctor solved what happened…*

Source: Adapted from Hohendorrff et al. (2017: 57)

TYPES AND LEVELS OF ANALYSIS

First, identifying and using conceptual themes in analysis are considered. The additional level of analysis we will explore is the more ambitious level of analysis that is theory building.

Concepts and conceptual themes

An emerging concept can be an idea or a model which, in turn, might represent the beginnings of an emergent perspective or theory. Alternatively, an already established concept might be a signifier of a perspective or theoretical position and epistemological standpoint. Documents can be interrogated and re-visited for already established concepts that they variously draw upon. Concepts that might be expected, yet are omitted or neglected, might be noted. This can produce findings. Similarly, established concepts might emerge out of your interview data or there may be a specific search for such key concepts. This mode of analysis is most suited to unstructured or loosely/semi-structured interviews where respondents were not led towards predetermined responses. Additionally, new concepts might present themselves and these are the sorts of findings that might have import for theory building or theoretical development, especially if theorizing on your subject is less than adequate.

When analysing qualitative data, a concept may be thought of as an underlying idea that is not necessarily referred to directly by respondents, whereas a theme is an idea that can be seen running through several responses (Harding, 2013: 6). Conceptual themes are therefore themes that represent underlying ideas or principles emerging from your data. Conceptual themes are findings in their own right because they are commonalities. As already illustrated, coding frames can be used to analyse a conceptual theme. Conceptual themes may help to explain relationships between different elements of your data. Though the characteristics of conceptual themes vary substantially, Harding (2013) nevertheless presents five characteristics of conceptual themes, each of which are summarized in Box 12.5.

BOX 12.5   FIVE CHARACTERISTICS OF CONCEPTUAL THEMES

1. They are likely to be drawn from different sections of the interview transcripts and to use codes taken from the analysis of different illustrative issues.
2. The conceptual theme may not be referred to directly. Few respondents will refer specifically to any selected theme or themes; however, the conceptual theme is likely to underlie much of what is said.
3. The conceptual theme may not be spotted on the first reading of the transcript.
4. The use of conceptual themes aids examination of the relationship between different elements of the data and understanding patterns of relationships. In this respect, a conceptual theme is an explanatory tool that can help us to understand relationships between other themes and issues.
5. Identifying conceptual themes enables the researcher to move beyond identifying findings to building theory.

Source: Adapted from Harding (2013: 108–9)

In my own research, respondents discussed their experiences, opinions, perceptions and feelings. In some instances, detailed illustrative examples were provided. The analysis was approached as a creative activity, co-produced by myself (already immersed in the topic via an initial review of documentation and steeped in a feminist-influenced victimological epistemology – see critical reflection below) and my respondents. As the principal investigator and the interviewer, I was immediately aware of the nature of the data being collected and the analysis began to take shape whilst I was still in the field. The point at which I was *doing analysis* rather than *doing data collection* was when I had reached saturation point. It was clear that new concepts and themes were no longer being discovered. It was nearing time to exit the field.

Interviews were transcribed verbatim and I used an analytic-inductive process, including data reduction – or the technique of identifying themes – to organize the data. The concepts that were emerging included existing concepts (though these were not predetermined) that were also evident in the initial documentary review, as well as newly emergent conceptual themes. These are illustrated in Box 12.6. My analysis had to find a way of illuminating the key narratives, yet reproducing these in a way that nevertheless allowed for outlying nuances to be retained. By drawing on concepts and conceptual themes, there was added value in terms of findings and the promise of another level of analysis began to present itself. Underlying assumptions, prejudices, stereotypes, values and principles were emerging from the interview data that sometimes resonated with ideas and sentiments evident in the documentary resources I had already explored but sometimes did not. Some of the concepts and conceptual themes had strong affinities with my own epistemological position and there were commonalities emerging between the disconnects. By approaching the analysis in this way, I began to connect different elements of the data together.

BOX 12.6   CHILD SEXUAL ABUSE AND CONCEPTUAL THEMES

- Blame → Parental blaming → Mother blaming
- Guilt/Blame/Fault finding/Neglect/Culpability
- Guilt → Self-blame
- Anger/Shock/Outrage/Disbelief → Traumatization
- Collateral damage, Consequential impacts, Indirect harm, Ripple effect
- Victimization → Injustice
- Secondary victimization → Injustice

Theory building

The fifth characteristic of conceptual themes noted by Harding and listed in Box 12.5 is that they enable the researcher to move beyond identifying findings to building theory. If a theory is a supposition or a system of ideas that are intended to explain something, then a social scientific theory might comprise a set of tested and general propositions that can be expected to be of use as guiding principles that explain and predict certain phenomena.

Citing Grbich (2007), Harding (2013: 109) discusses three levels of theory:

1. *Microtheory*, which uses concepts to identify common aspects of phenomena.
2. *Middle-range theory*, which combines concepts with variables and propositions to form explanations with a focus on a particular academic discipline.

3. *Grand theory*, which combines concepts, propositions and statements that can be applied to a range of academic disciplines.

In terms of criminological theorizing, and according to Akers (2013), there are at least five key features to a good theory. These features can be used as a way of testing out whether or not a particular criminological theory holds good. Akers suggests that to be used for maximum effectiveness, theories must make sense (logical consistency), explain as much crime as possible (scope) and be as concise as possible (parsimony). Most important, the theory must be true or correct (validity). Having met these basic goals, the theory must have some real-world applications and policy implications (Akers, 2013: 6–12).

Given the conceptual themes I was finding, and the inconsistencies and disconnects that appeared to be evident in different elements of the data and in particular between the dominant theoretical framework and policy and practice, it seemed appropriate for me to explore a further level of analysis. I began to ask further questions during my first-level analysis about whether extant theory was adequate. One particular article encouraged me to pursue this avenue of analytical inquiry. Whilst I had used concepts and conceptual themes to identify common aspects of non-abusing family members' response to, and experiences of, child sexual abuse, and this was interesting at the microtheory level, there were indications that a middle-range theory for understanding child sexual abuse might be worth exploring. The hallmarks of my journey towards this level of theoretical analysis and theory building are outlined in Box 12.7.

BOX 12.7 ANALYSIS FOR THEORY BUILDING

My analysis of the needs of, and support for, families affected by child sexual abuse provoked further questions and I began to query the 'fit' between policy, practice and theory. A key article, discovered during my extended literature review (rather than my original trawl), prompted me to explore these analytical hunches:

> Whittier, N. (2015) 'Where are the children? Theorizing the missing piece in gendered sexual violence', *Gender & Society*, 30(1): 95–108.

In this article, Nancy Whittier pointed out the disappearance of CSA from gendered theorizing and feminist sociological work. Her search using the subjects 'incest' and 'child sexual abuse' found few articles in the past 20 years: 14 in four key feminist journals, eight of which were social-psychological in nature, none in the major sociology and criminology journals with an analytical focus on gender, the latter also a feature of the journals whose focus is on CSA. She concludes that a focus on the

child in sexual violence and abuse is virtually non-existent in social science disciplines (Whittier, 2015).

I began to apply the criminological 'good theory' test to the theorizing of CSA. In
terms of theorizing child sexual abuse, from a feminist-influenced victimological
perspective, I asked:

- Does theorizing make logical and consistent sense?
- Does existing theorizing have empirical validity?
- Is current theory supported by research evidence? Is it testable?
- Do the solutions work? Are they adequate?
- Is the scope of theorizing comprehensive?
- Does current theorizing theory explain how things are?
- Are there grounds for middle-range theory building?

Having amassed my own findings on the impact of child sexual abuse on non-abusing
families, I returned to the existing literature surrounding child sexual abuse. Much of
this literature hail from disciplinary areas that criminology rarely expands into.
Whittier had already found theorizing from a feminist perspective wanting and my
own approach was bringing a criminological-cum-victimological perspective to bear on
the problem. Insights from a feminist-inspired victimological perspective were showing
that avenues for theoretical development were opening up. How theory connects to
practice takes us into the area of praxis. I found holes in some of the crucial elements
of theorizing in relation to child sexual abuse. My own assessment is such that:

- theorizing does not have logical consistency in relation to gender and age
- theorizing no longer appears to explain all manifestations of, and contexts for,
  child sexual abuse
- theorizing in light of the above is therefore not entirely true or correct
- current theorizing is failing in several real-world applications and there may be
  new directions as regards policy implications.

The final point is about research having the potential to be transformative and to
effect change in policy and practice.

HYPOTHESIS TESTING AND DATA ANALYSIS

Where a research study is set up such that hypotheses are tested, the data analysis may take
a rather different form, especially where the data collected involves a large sample. An
example of data analysis where two hypotheses are being tested is provided in Box 12.8.

Ullman, S.E. and Filipas, H.H. (2005) 'Gender differences in social reactions to abuse disclosures, post-abuse coping and PTSD of child sexual abuse survivors', *Child Abuse & Neglect*, *29*: 767–82.

Hypothesis:

1. Females would have greater abuse prevalence, more severe abuse, greater self-blame, more use of all coping strategies (both positive and negative), greater PTSD symptom severity, and be more likely to disclose abuse and receive more negative and positive reactions.
2. That negative social reactions would contribute to PTSD symptoms controlling for gender, abuse characteristics, coping and attributions.

Method:

Data were collected on a cross-sectional convenience sample of 733 college students completing a confidential survey about their demographic characteristics, sexual abuse experiences, disclosure characteristics, post-abuse coping and social reactions from others.

Data analytic plan:

To test hypothesis 1, cross-tabs and *t* tests were performed for each study variable, depending on level of measurement.

To test hypothesis 2, multiple regression was conducted.

Factors related to the number of positive and negative social reactions victims received when disclosing CSA were explored with multiple regressions.

Gender was the only demographic variable included (age was restricted due to the college student sample and race was not significantly related to the dependent variable). Abuse characteristics examined were sexual abuse severity, abuse duration, victim–offender relationship familiarity, timing of disclosure, extent of disclosure, post-abuse victim self-blame, and coping.

Source: Adapted from Ullman and Filipas (2005: 773–4)

CRITICAL REFLECTION

My approach to doing qualitative analysis was a creative endeavour stimulated by my own victimological imagination and epistemological standpoint. Here, I briefly explain what I mean by this and why it is important to be self-consciously reflexive and transparent about these positionings when doing analysis of qualitative criminological research. My own interests in gender, crime and victimization and my background in teaching and research as a criminologist-cum-victimologist undoubtedly informed how the analysis unfolded. The analysis was clearly shaped by my interest in the experiences of those suffering both criminal and non-criminal victimization, and, in these respects, a victimological as well as a harms-based perspective is evident. A feminist-informed approach sits alongside this. As Scott has explained in Chapter 6, as a theoretical perspective abolitionism is informed by an ethical and political critique of the violence and harm of the prison. As a strategy, it calls for the end of the use of imprisonment and the building of communities and societies shaped by the principles of social justice. As a social movement, abolitionism is a collective organization working directly through research, policy interventions and direct action for progressive social change. As a theoretical perspective, feminism is a slippery and amorphous perspective to define. Rather, several 'feminisms' or feminist perspectives are apparent, rather than a single unified feminist theory, strategy and social movement (see below). Thus, feminist analysis of the same topic can lead to very different conclusions and feminist analysis of a topic can differ from analysis that is conducted from other perspectives. We touch on this in Chapter 1 (also see the further reading you are guided towards at the end of this chapter).

Feminist ideologies

Various strands of feminism have impacted differently on both victimology and criminology (Walklate, 2004: 94). In many respects, feminism challenges the very heart of the conventional victimological agenda. Feminist research practice has been explored by various writers (Gelsthorpe and Morris, 1994; Maynard and Purvis, 1994; Naffine, 1997; Stanley and Wise, 1993) and many others have brought their own feminist perspective to bear on their fieldwork and analysis of different areas of sociology. This work demonstrates that there is no single feminist viewpoint or perspective. Nevertheless, as Naffine (1997: 51) has argued:

> Many feminists are of the view that the angle from which the dominant class views the world, is one which provides a poor field of vision. Subjugation, and reflection upon that status, makes for a better appreciation of the world.

A variety of feminist positions and feminisms are now evident, including liberal feminism, radical feminism, socialist feminism, cultural feminism, women-of-colour feminism/womanism and post-modern feminisms. There are some common features across feminist positions. They all tend to have the so-called 'woman question' in common and, in terms of doing feminist research, this means doing research, for example, *for* rather than *on* women (Smith and Wincup, 2000).

Thus, we can see that several feminist approaches to the study of crime and victims, rather than a unified 'sisterhood', can now be identified. For liberal feminists, the woman question might include the investigation of sexism; to radical feminists, it includes analysis of men's power over women; to socialist feminists, the compounding of social class and patriarchy are crucial to understanding social justice and victimization; whilst post-modern feminists problematize the notion of 'the other' and celebrate difference (Walklate, 2003, 2004), acknowledging that different women have different needs. Different feminist ideologies offer different preferences in terms of political and policy strategies. Thus, we find that it is generally the case that in the context of policy issues gender neutrality is wedded to the equality-based feminist positions whilst gender-specific policy advocates are wedded to difference-based perspectives (Daly, 1994). Philosophically, feminists have warned that gender neutrality simply equates to the male standard where masculinity and maleness are the yardsticks against which judgements of others are made (MacKinnon, 1987). Daly pointed out many years ago: 'The equality-difference debate has haunted women activists for more than a century' (Daly, 1994: 9), and when it comes to gender-wise policy, transcending such dichotomies remains problematic.

For the most part, the examples and illustrations drawn on throughout this chapter have been taken from those engaged in psychological research including cognitive and therapeutic approaches and research on trauma. My use of a feminist-influenced and theory-sensitive approach to the analysis of those affected by CSA leads me to agree with Whittier's assessment that a focus on the child in sexual violence and abuse is virtually non-existent in social science disciplines.

Reflexivity

As stressed throughout this chapter, when analysing qualitative data there is constant movement between the data and analysis, and simultaneous data collection and analysis help in gaining more insight into the problem being researched. They aid in deciphering core categories and phenomena, concepts and conceptual themes. As I engaged in this toing and froing, I became aware that I was gathering very different experiences of CSA. Patterns were emerging according to the context of abuse, and commonalities between experiences in different contexts were presenting themselves. This was prompting me to deconstruct the broad term CSA and reconstruct it to accommodate the patterns of experiences that were emerging. This is in part what I mean by becoming self-consciously reflexive. Being aware that you are meddling with your raw data is not always immediately apparent and this can be even less apparent when research is written up, reported on and disseminated.

In previous editions of this volume (Davies, 2000, 2010), I have written about my own experiences of doing research, and elsewhere about the pains of writing in the first person (Davies, 2012), following highly reflective and reflexive pieces of writing where I have written about my own experiences of family misfortune (Davies, 2011, 2014, 2017).

In each of these publications, I have laid bare emotions and have made an effort to be authentic about the state I was in. Stanley (in this volume, drawing on Cohen, 2001) has observed that once we 'know' about harms, there is a level of expectation that we will also act to make things better. In the same way that Stanley shows that her research has revealed 'the mundane realities of state violence' that have been 'deeply damaging over victims' lifetimes', the research I have drawn on in this chapter has revealed the mundane realities of child sexual abuse and the deeply damaging effects on direct victims and their non-abusing family members. The ripple effect of child sexual abuse was repeatedly shown. For researchers who are wedded to a particular ontological position, this level of reflexivity creates a strong ethical impulse for progressive social change. Research conducted with rigorous and thoughtful analysis can produce a clear agenda for real-world applications and policy implications. Such research will not only be theoretically sensitive (Glaser, 1978) but also theory building.

SUMMARY AND REVIEW

In this chapter, I have drawn on my own efforts to do qualitative analysis in the context of research around child sexual abuse. I have explored some general issues related to analysing qualitative data and have provided some detail about my own efforts to dovetail analysis of documentary and interview data in the context of child sexual abuse. Concepts and conceptual themes have been illustrated whilst some key qualitative features, including grounded theory, theoretical perspectives, praxis and reflexivity, have been drawn on, all as a segway into a different level of analysis that has contemplated theory building. I have explained how my own approach to analysis has been done through the lens of critical reflection and the use of feminist and victimological perspectives. In these ways, the chapter has attempted to explore the connectivities between real-world victimization, evidence-based knowledge and how an advanced stage of analysis can lead to theoretical developments.

STUDY QUESTIONS AND ACTIVITIES FOR STUDENTS

1. In the context of doing criminological research, what do the terms disassembling and reassembling mean?

2. How would you ensure that your qualitative analysis achieves constant comparison between your data and theorizing?

(Continued)

(Continued)

3. What methodological tools and devices might you use to help you segment your data?

4. In what ways can criminological research help identify a good criminological theory?

5. Explain in your own words how reflexivity is a vital part of demonstrating the factors which have contributed to the social production of knowledge.

SUGGESTIONS FOR FURTHER READING

In a rather different subject area – that of green crime and victimisation – two key articles and a rejoinder piece, written by Davies and Lynch, provide a useful illustration of how different analyses of the same event and phenomenon can be produced:

Davies, P. (2014) 'Green crime and victimisation: tensions between social and environmental justice', *Theoretical Criminology*, *18*(3): 300–16.

Lynch, M.J. (2017) 'Green criminology and social justice: a reexamination of the Lynemouth plant closing and the political economic causes of environmental and social injustice', *Critical Sociology*, *43*(3): 449–64.

Davies, P. (2017) 'Green crime, victimisation and justice: a rejoinder', *Critical Sociology*, *43*(3): 465–71.

These readings also show different styles of writing and how scholarly research can be a very contentious occupation!

REFERENCES

Akers, R.L. (2013) *Criminological Theories: Introduction and Evaluation*, 2nd edition. London: Routledge.

Boeije, H. (2010) *Analysis in Qualitative Research*. London: Sage.

Bryman, A. (2016) *Social Research Methods*, 5th edition. Oxford: Oxford University Press.

Casey, L. (2015a) *Reflections on Child Sexual Exploitation*. London: Department for Communities and Local Government.

Casey, L. (2015b) *Report of Inspection of Rotherham Metropolitan Borough Council*. London: Department for Communities and Local Government.

Cm 5860 (2003) *Every Child Matters*. London: TSO.

Cohen, S. (2001) *State of Denial: Knowing about Atrocities and Suffering*. Cambridge: Polity Press.

Creswell, J.W. (2014) *Educational Research: Planning, Conducting, and Evaluating Quantitative and Qualitative Research*, 4th edition. Harlow: Pearson.

Daly, K. (1994) *Gender, Crime, and Punishment*. London: Yale University Press.

Daly, K. (2014) *Redressing Institutional Abuse of Children*. Basingstoke: Palgrave Macmillan.

Davies, P. (2000) 'Doing interviews with female offenders', in V. Jupp, P. Davies and P. Francis (eds), *Doing Criminological Research*. London: Sage, pp. 82–96.

Davies, P. (2010) 'Doing interviews in prison', in P. Davies, P. Francis and V. Jupp (eds), *Doing Criminological Research*, 2nd edition. London: Sage, pp. 161–78.

Davies, P. (2011) 'The impact of a child protection investigation: a personal reflective account', *Child & Family Social Work, 16*: 201–9.

Davies, P. (2012) '"Me", "me", "me": the use of the first person in academic writing and some reflections on subjective analyses of personal experiences', *Sociology, 46*(4): 744–52.

Davies, P. (2014) 'Green crime and victimisation: tensions between social and environmental justice', *Theoretical Criminology, 18*(3): 300–16.

Davies, P. (2017) 'Green crime, victimisation and justice', *Critical Sociology, 43*(3): 465–71.

Davies, P., Francis, P. and Jupp, V. (eds) (2011) *Doing Criminological Research*, 2nd edition. London: Sage.

Gelsthorpe, L. and Morris, A. (1994) *Feminist Perspectives in Criminology*. Milton Keynes: Open University Press.

Glaser, B. (1978) *Theoretical Sensitivity*. Mill Valley, CA: Sociology Press.

Glaser, B. and Strauss, A. (1967) *The Discovery of Grounded Theory: Strategies for Qualitative Research*. Chicago, IL: Aldine.

Gray, D. and Watt, P. (2013) *Giving Victims a Voice: Joint Report into Sexual Allegations made against Jimmy Savile*. London: MPS/NSPCC.

Grbich, C. (2007) *Qualitative Data Analysis: An Introduction*. London: Sage.

Greer, C. (2017) 'News media, victims and crime', in P. Davies, P. Francis and C. Greer (eds), *Victims, Crime and Society: An Introduction*, 2nd edition. London: Sage, pp. 48–65.

Gruenfeld, E., Willis, D.G. and Easton, S.D. (2017) '"A very steep climb": therapists' perspectives on barriers to disclosure of child sexual abuse experiences for men', *Journal of Child Sexual Abuse, 26*(6): 731–51.

Harding, J. (2013) *Qualitative Data Analysis: From Start to Finish*. London: Sage.

HM Government (2018) *Working Together to Safeguard Children*. London: Department for Education.

Hohendorff, J.V., Habigzang, L.F. and Koller, S.H. (2017) '"A boy, being a victim, nobody really buys that, you know?" Dynamics of sexual violence against boys', *Child Abuse & Neglect*, *70*: 53–64.

Jay, A. (2014) *Independent Inquiry into Child Sexual Exploitation in Rotherham 1997–2013*. London: Office of the Children's Commissioner.

Jewkes, Y. (2010) 'The media and criminological research', in P. Davies, P. Francis and V. Jupp (eds), *Doing Criminological Research*, 2nd edition. London: Sage, pp. 245–61.

Jewkes, Y. (2015) *Media and Crime*, 3rd edition. London: Sage.

Long Weatherred, J. (2015) 'Child sexual abuse and the media: a literature review', *Journal of Child Sexual Abuse*, *24*(1): 16–34.

MacKinnon, C. (1987) *Feminism Unmodified: Discourses on Life and Law*. Cambridge, MA: Harvard University Press.

Mason, J. (2002) *Qualitative Researching*, 2nd edition. London: Sage.

Mawby, R.C. (2010) 'Using the media to understand crime and criminal justice', in P. Davies, P. Francis and V. Jupp (eds), *Doing Criminological Research*, 2nd edition. London: Sage, pp. 223–44.

Maynard, M. and Purvis, J. (eds) (1994) *Researching Women's Lives from a Feminist Perspective*. London: Taylor & Francis.

Munro, E. (2011) *The Munro Review of Child Protection: Final Report. A Child-Centred System*. Cm 8062. London: TSO.

Naffine, N. (1997) *Feminism and Criminology*. Cambridge: Polity Press.

Neuman, W.L. (2014) *Social Research Methods: Qualitative and Quantitative Approaches*, 7th edition. Harlow: Pearson.

Semmens, N. (2011) 'Methodological approaches to criminological research', in P. Davies, P. Francis and V. Jupp (eds), *Doing Criminological Research*. London: Sage.

Smith, C. and Wincup, E. (2000) 'Breaking in: researching criminal justice institutions for women', in R.D. King and E. Wincup (eds), *Doing Research on Crime and Justice*. Oxford: Oxford University Press.

Stanley, E. (2016) *The Road to Hell: State Violence against Children in Postwar New Zealand*. Auckland: Auckland University Press.

Stanley, L. and Wise, S. (1993) *Breaking Out Again: Feminist Ontology and Epistemology*. London: Routledge.

Ullman, S.E. and Filipas, H.H. (2005) 'Gender differences in social reactions to abuse disclosures, post-abuse coping, and PTSD of child sexual abuse survivors', *Child Abuse & Neglect*, *29*: 767–82.

Walklate, S. (2003) 'Can there be a feminist victimology?' in P. Davies, P. Franics and V. Jupp (eds), *Understanding Victimisation*. Newcastle: Northumbria Social Science Press, pp. 14–29.

Walklate, S. (2004) *Gender, Crime and Criminal Justice*, 2nd edition. Cullompton: Willan.

Whittier, N. (2015) 'Where are the children? Theorizing the missing piece in gendered sexual violence', *Gender & Society*, *30*(1): 95–108.

CHAPTER CONTENTS

GLOSSARY TERMS

longitudinal study
life-course study
cross-sectional
longitudinal research
developmental and life-
    course criminology
cross sectional studies
    methodology

prospective design
retrospective design
persistence and desistance
    in crime
operationalization

13 DOING LONGITUDINAL AND LIFE-COURSE CRIMINOLOGICAL RESEARCH[1]

JERZY SARNECKI AND CHRISTOFFER CARLSSON

---

[1] A longer version of this chapter appears as Chapter 4 in *An Introduction to Life-Course Criminology* (Carlsson and Sarnecki, 2015).

INTRODUCTION

What follows is a brief introduction to the field of longitudinal Study and life-course Study research in criminology. Initially, we outline the justification for the time- and money-consuming enterprise of life-course research. Having done so, in the second section we distinguish between two broad forms of life-course research designs – *prospective* and *retrospective* approaches. This is followed by a discussion of quantitative and qualitative methods. We then turn to the question of mixing methods. In criminology, life-course researchers are perhaps more prone than others to combine quantitative and qualitative data to best answer a research question. Finally, our chapter revisits the longitudinal life-course approach and contrasts it with its opposite, the cross-sectional approach, to help the reader more sharply distinguish between the two. We end with a summary and review. Throughout the text, we illustrate and explain the main methodological issues we address with well-known criminological studies, such as the Cambridge Study in Delinquent Development and the Glueck Study.

Time is a funny thing. It can move so slowly, while at other times it flies. We structure our lives according to it and invent ways to keep track of its stream: we use the shadow of the sun, or construct clocks. Time is, in that sense, a constant. It is always there.

When we conduct research, time is also one of our greatest challenges. A number of research questions are not bound by the issue of time, but many are. Think about it: as soon as you start asking questions about a 'before' and an 'after', or a 'now' and a 'then' – for example, 'was the individual's risk of criminal recidivism higher *before* he left the gang, compared to his risk of recidivism *after* he left the gang?' or 'are there any significant differences in the outcomes of the treatment group and the control group *after* treatment, compared to *before* treatment?' – you are perceiving your research topic temporally.

Longitudinal research has traditionally been conducted on individuals, and it is to research on individuals that we devote much of this chapter. However, we should note, today criminological longitudinal research is also conducted where communities and cities, rather than individuals, constitute the unit of analysis (e.g. Sampson, 2013). They all have one thing in common: this mysterious, constant, seemingly banal but deeply challenging issue of time.

Longitudinal research rose to fame as a method and mode of working, within the field commonly known as criminal career research (Blumstein et al., 1986) and, later, developmental and life-course criminology (Sampson and Laub, 1993). As this field has blossomed, the methodology behind this branch of research has developed and become increasingly sophisticated. Several important methodological works have been published in the form of books and articles, mostly on quantitative methods. Our purpose here is not to conduct an exhaustive review of these methods; such a review can, for example, be found in the great work by Biljeveld and van der Kamp (1998).

Here, instead, we concern ourselves with a number of basic core issues. Our aim is quite simple, and practical: to provide you, the reader, with enough knowledge of longitudinal and life-course methodology to enable you to understand the main methodological problems, opportunities and possibilities in this kind of research.

WHY STUDY THE LIFE COURSE?

For researchers, money matters, and life-course research is usually expensive. It takes a lot of time, meaning more work and more research hours, and often creates (even) more methodological issues than most other forms of research in social science. It is therefore highly reasonable to pose the question and demand an answer from its advocates: why do this form of research at all, and why has it become so prominent over the last three decades?

Because, using this methodology, we can answer important research questions which other methods have trouble addressing. The foremost questions in this regard concern the issue of *continuity and change in behaviour over time*.

To contrast life-course research, consider so-called cross-section methodology. Here, researchers study a sample or a population at a single, specific moment in time. The resulting data gives us the possibility to study individuals or groups of individuals when it comes to a whole range of variables (such as crime, peer relations, health, employment, and so on), and how these are related to each other. We commonly call these *between-individual similarities and differences*. Using longitudinal methodology, we study the *same individual at repeated points in time*. Since we can study the relationship between the different variables as we go through time, we can also see whether the relationship between them is constant or changes over time. It is likely, for example, that as long as the individual engages in repeated, serious crime, he or she will have a relatively unstable form of conventional work (if he or she has a job at all), have turbulent relationships with other people, have increasing problems with mental and physical health, etc. Whether or not this is the case becomes impossible to study using cross-sectional research design – it would have to be inferred by theory.

We can also study what happens when change occurs in one of the variables: is there a change in a person's criminal offending when he or she gets a more stable job, starts a romantic relationship or becomes ill? Crucially, we can also – sometimes – study which change occurs before the other, i.e. does a person's criminal offending change as a result of them getting a job etc., as Sampson and Laub (1993) argue, or is it the other way around – a person begins to decrease their criminal offending *and then* gets a job or starts a romantic relationship? This suggests two different causal processes, and thus two different answers to the question of what makes people cease their criminal offending, with important implications for policy and practice.

Thus, we can begin to approach the difficult question of cause and effect, that is, the question of causality.

According to de Lange (2005: 18), four criteria in research in the social sciences should be fulfilled if we are to be able to draw causal conclusions:

> This research should i) demonstrate that the cause variable precedes the outcome variable in time, ii) show a significant statistical relationship between the presumed cause and outcome, iii) exclude possible alternative explanations, and iv) provide a professional theoretical interpretation of the relationship(s) under study.

As you can imagine, criteria ii, iii and iv usually give rise to a number of challenges. But unless you are using longitudinal methodology, it can be extremely hard – in fact, often impossible – to have control over the factor of time, i.e. the first criteria. Life-course research and the longitudinal method provide you with this possibility – when done right.

LIFE–COURSE RESEARCH AND THE LONGITUDINAL METHOD

Life-course research and longitudinal research are not necessarily synonyms. To state it simply, *life course* suggests a distinct research perspective, whereas *longitudinal* suggests a specific methodology which follows from the life-course perspective.

The aim of life-course studies is to study, understand and explain one or more individuals' lives over a short or long time span; some may focus on a specific stage of the life-course (e.g. 'What effect does the transition to adulthood have on the individual's future criminal career?'), whereas others take a more holistic approach ('How does criminal offending wax and wane across the life course?'). The life-course perspective assumes that what happens at one time in life, is contingent on – but not necessarily determined by – what happened at an earlier point in life. This theoretical assumption leads to methodological consequences, where life-course research must be carried out using longitudinal methodology.

Prospective and retrospective designs

Longitudinal research can be of two kinds: prospective and retrospective (Blumstein et al., 1986). Prospective longitudinal designs are forward-looking. You take a sample of individuals, usually defined by age (a whole cohort, or a sample defined by some other criteria), and then follow that sample repeatedly over their life course, or some part of it. As you go along, you make repeated measurements of the same factors or variables that you are interested in. So, say, you take a sample of 8-year-old children and follow them to the age of 38, making new data collections every second year.

The primary advantage of the prospective design is obvious: you collect data on events relatively soon after they have occurred, and this way you manage to avoid the memory problem: it is likely that an 18-year-old can provide a better picture of what her high school experience is like than she would if she was interviewed at the age of 26, since what she experienced during her high school years may be affected by later life events. By using a prospective design, you also have better control over the crucial dimension of *time*. You can identify what comes first: does drug use precede low attachment to the labour market in adulthood, or does low attachment to the labour market precede drug use? The Cambridge Study of Delinquent Development is an example of this prospective approach (Box 13.1).

BOX 13.1 THE CAMBRIDGE STUDY OF DELINQUENT DEVELOPMENT

A sample of 411 South London boys, mostly born in 1953, were enrolled in the study. The sample consisted of all the boys aged 8–9 who were listed on the registers of six primary schools within a 1-mile radius of a research office that the group, headed by the late Donald West, had established. The study's original aims sought to trace and understand the development of delinquent and criminal behaviour in inner-city males, explore the possibilities of predicting such behaviours in advance, and to explain the waxing and waning of crime across the life course. Rather than aim to test any specific theory, the research group wanted to test many different hypotheses about the causes and correlates of crime.

The research group collected extensive data on each male, including surveys and interviews, psychological tests, and interviews with the males' parents and teachers. Part of the reason for casting a wide net at the beginning of the study, in terms of variables and measurements, was that criminology is a changing discipline, in terms of perspectives, theory and method.

Since the start, the 411 males had then been continuously followed up roughly every other year, using register data and interviews, beyond age 50. The study follows up the boys' development with respect to many different life areas from children to adult men, and inter alia studies of how these factors affect their crime, addiction and other criminologically relevant factors. Eventually, the study also included the children of the investigated persons.

The primary disadvantage of the prospective design is obvious: if you want to explore the life courses of a sample from age 8 to 38, it takes 30 years. If you want to make repeated measurements every other, or every third or fourth year, it consumes a lot of resources, both in terms of personnel and money. And not only that – by the time you have followed the sample to age 38, 30 years have passed, and that amount of time can do a lot to a society, and to the sciences – what if the results you now have are no longer relevant? Not to mention the fact that you yourself get old!

The other design is retrospective, a design that looks backwards rather than forward. Typically, a sample is selected based on some criteria or other, such as adult inmates who serve time in a prison in a given year. Having done so, the researcher traces their backgrounds and past experiences, using register data and/or interviews. This was the design Wolfgang, Figlio and Sellin (1972) used in their famous *Delinquency in a Birth Cohort*.

BOX 13.2   DELINQUENCY IN A BIRTH COHORT

In this study, the researchers chose all boys born in 1945 who were living in Philadelphia between 10 and 18 years of age, and then traced their criminal histories and backgrounds using register data. The purpose was to investigate the history of delinquency in a cohort; in particular, the age of onset of delinquent behaviour and the progression and/or cessation of delinquency. Data in the study includes the demographic characteristics of the individuals studied, academic performance, offence information, the demographic characteristics of victims of offences, and criminal incident information.

The main advantage of this design is that it avoids the time-consuming step-by-step exploration of the unfolding of the lives of the sample, as they have to do in the Cambridge study. It is thus much more economical. There is, of course, a problematic issue here as well, constituting the main disadvantage of the retrospective design. It once again has to do with the issue of time, in two ways.

Some studies only include official register data. This is perhaps more common in the Nordic and some other European countries, because the quality of their official records tends to be good and such data is available to the researchers (Skardhamar and Lyngstad, 2011). However, the longer we go back in time, the more unstable the records usually become. In addition, the way data is collected, and the content of what is collected, can change: some data series cease, others start. There may be problems with the different data series' compatibility.

To give just one example, in a research project we, the authors, conducted the Stockholm Life-Course Project (see Carlsson and Sarnecki, 2015), we wanted to understand and explain the criminal histories of a Swedish sample born in the 1940s and 1950s, and the possibilities and problems of predicting future criminal careers from early risk factors and indicators of antisocial behaviour. In this study, we therefore combined register data, interviews, different types of medical and psychological tests and questionnaires. Interviews were both structured and semi-structured and included not only the individuals studied but, in some parts, also their parents and teachers.

In Swedish crime registers, we not only had to handle the problem of using two different sets of crime registers – police records, which are available until the 1980s, and conviction records, which are available from the mid-1970s. We also had to take into account the sorting-out process that takes place within these police records, where individuals once recorded for crimes were sorted out if they were not recorded for a new offence, as the authorities only had the right to keep them for a certain amount of time. These records still exist, at the Swedish National Archive, but must then be added to the 'original' records to provide a full picture of their criminal histories. Other records – such as those kept by the Social Services – also change over time, with new variables replacing older ones, and so on. This makes a longitudinal analysis difficult, because at different points in time we may in fact capture, or measure, partly different things.

Second, if we do not – or not only – rely on register data, we are likely to rely on interviews in some way (we elaborate on life history interviews below). If we do these retrospectively, we sometimes ask the interview participant to recall events and experiences which occurred a long time ago, making the crucial *sequencing of life events* difficult to pin down. Recalling what came first – starting to smoke marihuana or skipping school at the age of 15 – may be very difficult 30, 40 or 50 years later. In retrospective interviews, we also, of course, miss all the people who cannot be interviewed, since they may be dead or, for other reasons, impossible to reach.

BOX 13.3   THE STOCKHOLM LIFE–COURSE PROJECT (SLCP)

The main purpose of the SLCP is to study and explain the different dimensions of the criminal career, e.g. the onset of crime, why offenders persist, and why they desist. It has a relatively long history and consists of two research samples: the 1956 Clientele Study of Juvenile Delinquents (287 males born between 1943 and 1951) and the §12 Youth Group (298 males and 122 females born between 1969 and 1974).

THE CLIENTELE STUDY

In total, 287 boys born in Stockholm between 1943 and 1951 were enrolled in the study; 192 of the boys had been recorded for at least one non-trivial offence (almost

(Continued)

(Continued)

exclusively theft) prior to the age of 15, and constituted the delinquent group. The remaining 95 boys constituted a matched control group. They were matched on age, social group, family type and neighbourhood type, but had no known criminal history.

The low number of cases was compensated for by the extensive and interdisciplinary studies conducted on each boy. The original study comprised around 2,000 variables. Different teams (medical, psychiatric, psychological and sociological) collected a variety of data using an array of methods. For example, the sociological study included interviews with the boys' parents, teachers, the Clientele boys themselves, as well as register data, whereas the data in the psychiatric and psychological parts was obtained almost exclusively through judgements of the research personnel and different kinds of tests. The boys' recorded and self-reported delinquency was also included.

Sarnecki conducted a follow-up study of the Clientele boys, who were by then approaching middle age. The delinquent group was divided into two groups: D1 (n = 131) and D2 (n = 61). In the D1 group, every boy was known by the police to have committed one crime prior to age 15. In the D2 group, the boys were known by the police to have committed two or more crimes prior to age 15. Sarnecki collected register data on the 287 men's health (including mortality), education and employment history, criminal history, drug use and household status, among other things.

THE §12 YOUTH GROUP

The study was originally based on a Stockholm sample of women and men (n = 420) born between 1969 and 1974. Of these, 298 were male and 122 were female. From 1990 to 1994 they were subject to interventions by the Swedish Social Services under the Care of Young Persons (Special Provisions Act) for residential treatment in so-called youth homes, or §12 homes then operated by Stockholm County Council.

THE 2010 STUDY

In 2010, we launched a new follow-up of the two samples. We had access not only to data from the original studies, but also to the data Sarnecki collected on the Clientele boys in the 1980s. In our follow-up, we collected new, extensive register data on both samples, including criminal records, health and medical records, employment history, relationship history and many other things.

We also conducted new, long, life history interviews with a subset of the samples, aiming for depth rather than breadth, setting our goal to 30 Clientele interviews, that is, slightly more than 10% of the total original sample. In total, we conducted interviews with 30 men, drawing cases from the D1, D2 and control groups to get variation.

For the §12 Youth Group, we contacted 118 of the 132 who were interviewed in the previous follow-up. The remaining 14 had either died or could not be located even after extensive searches. In total, life history interviews were conducted with 45 of the 118 (37%). Their structure followed the interviews we did with the Clientele men. In total, 25 men and 20 women were interviewed.

QUANTITATIVE AND QUALITATIVE METHODS

Within the social sciences, a never-ending discussion and debate is centred on this issue of method. Should the social world be explored and explained quantitatively (e.g. using numbers and statistics), or qualitatively (e.g. using words and narratives, in the wide sense), or both?

This question has a partly philosophical basis concerning the fundamental features of the world (what the world 'is', or what exists) and how we can study those features, and what the researcher's task consists of. Quantitative methodology is historically tied to the philosophical branch of positivism and post-positivism, where the (somewhat simplified) stance is that the world exists independently of us and our understanding of it. The essential features can be counted in numbers (e.g. how high is the risk that a given individual re-offends after x years of abstinence?) and thus be studied with the help of statistical methods.

Qualitative methodology, on the other hand, is commonly associated with the traditions of constructivism and symbolic interactionism. This tradition stresses the basically constructed nature of the social world where nothing (not very much, at least) is natural or static, but the result of a specific social and historical context. How people perceive, interpret and understand the world is a big part of what *actually shapes* that world.

This relatively stiff dichotomy of quantitative and qualitative methodology (also discussed in Chapters 1 and 3 of this volume), and their associated philosophical underpinnings, is becoming less and less distinct, however – most prominently within life-course research. The dichotomy is being replaced by a kind of methodological pragmatism where the researcher simply chooses the method(s) that suit(s) the research question and that it is possible to use, given the various practical boundaries of a given project. Maruna (2010: 127f.) expresses this point clearly:

Qualitative methods involve 'deep' immersion into a social scene that allows for awareness of situational and contextual factors that are often missed in [quantitative] research. They produce 'rich', 'holistic' data, as opposed to the focus on 'variables' …
In its published form, qualitative analysis provides vivid illustration of phenomena, bringing social processes 'to life' for readers. Quantitative research does little of this,

but has considerable strengths precisely where qualitative research is weak. Quantitative methods are transparent and do not rely on a 'take my word for it' approach. This work is therefore more replicable, precise (some would say 'objective'), and generalizable than qualitative research. Additionally, statistical techniques allow for the eliminating of confounding influences and better assess cause and effect relationships among variables. In published form, they produce findings that are notable for their clarity, succinctness, exactitude, and parsimony.

Criminal career research and life-course criminology in the 1970s and 1980s was dominated by influential, quantitatively driven studies. This is evident from several of the traditional key concepts: prevalence, offending frequency, duration, intensity, etc. (see Blumstein et al., 1986). Much of the most prominent work within the field has been done with quantitative data, including the pioneering studies of Wolfgang, Figlio and Sellin (1972), Blumstein et al. (1986) and later studies such as that by Piquero, Farrington and Blumstein (2007), to mention just a few.

Two forms of quantitative data

There are, you could say, two forms of quantitative data: official records (i.e. those that are collected and kept by the various authorities of a society) and specific quantitative data collected by the researcher within the frame of a given project – for example, your official employment history, health history and whether you at some point in time have lived in a single household or not, which exists in many countries' official records.

Register data is therefore an amazing research resource. In most countries of the world, but particularly in welfare states such as Sweden and some other European countries, governmental and municipal agencies collect huge amounts of high-quality data on their citizens. Collecting and using these records is made simple by the fact that every person has a unique personal identification number. After getting ethical approval, researchers can be allowed access to these records.

Now, importantly, this data is collected for administrative purposes, which can entail a problem for the researcher: the purpose of the agency is not always compatible with the specific problem the researcher is interested in. Here, then, is a prime example of those compromises the researcher has to make when it comes to the research design and the content of the data. The researcher is often forced to use variables and scales which constitute far from optimal operationalizations of the various constructs the researcher is interested in. However, often the only option to access data is to use data with certain types of restrictions. If the researcher is aware of these limitations and takes them into account in the interpretation of the results, they can still be used.

At the same time, the agencies' administrative records have one huge advantage: data are *dated* and usually entered into the register in a chronological order.

This means that official register data has an *inherently longitudinal character*, even if it is collected by the researcher at a single point in time.

We noted above that whether or not you have lived in a single household often exists in official register data. But, for life-course criminology, it is a crucial question whether you experience that you had a 'good upbringing' or not. You can get indicators of 'good upbringing' by combining a large number of registry variables regarding the individual's early years and possibly even parents, but, in general, that kind of data is better quality if it is gathered through more or less structured interviews, surveys and/or tests specifically constructed for the study, and the validity of the measurement will be better. The great value in doing this is that it can usually provide a much richer description of the people you study and in a much better way covers the research questions and theoretical points of departure than mere official records can.

One possible issue with this, which is very relevant in studies with a prospective design, is that what is considered a 'good' measurement of something can change over time. So, for example, in the research project we worked on (the Stockholm Life-Course Project; SLCP) 287 Stockholm boys born in the 1940s and 1950s were enrolled in a study and underwent a large number of tests, including IQ tests (Terman-Merrill) and Rorschach tests. Today, the first of these measurements is considered an acceptable but not very good indicator of a person's intelligence (and who knows how it will be considered in the future?). The second form of test, Rorschach, is far too unreliable and imprecise to be used. This dilemma – what time does to a data set – is unsolvable but important to keep in mind when it comes to longitudinal studies with long follow-up periods.

Similarly, when researchers construct indicators of important theoretical constructs, they do so from a set of raw variables. The variables we need to use to construct something change over time, as society changes. Stop and think about this: What did it mean to have 'good economic standards' economically in the 1980s? One such study tried to capture this by asking a whole bunch of specific questions, and then adding the answers to those questions together, forming an 'index'. Among other things, that battery of questions included a question about whether or not the respondent owned a VHS player (Sarnecki, 1985). Today, such a question is highly outdated, and if we were to conduct the same measurement of having 'good economic standards' today, we would need to include other questions. The researcher, in other words, must continuously be conscious of the temporal dimension of their study, and how the relevance of certain questions, measurements and variables may change as society changes.

Qualitative data: process, life history and context

Qualitative studies of criminal careers have always been important: consider, for example, Meisenhelder's interview study (1977), which, based on interviews with a small number of property offenders, outlined the process of exiting a criminal career using social control theory. Still, it took until Sampson and Laub's (1993) first book on the Glueck data until qualitative analyses of criminal careers really took off. In life-course criminology, the life history interview has become a particularly important method. Among other things, this interview form reveals 'in the offenders' own words the personal-situational context of their behaviour and their views of the larger social and historical circumstances in which their behavior is embedded' (Laub and Sampson, 2003: 58). This is something quantitative data can never achieve.

Consider the benefits Laub and Sampson (2003: 58f.) see in life history interviews (we believe several of these benefits are valid for qualitative data in general):

- Life-history method uniquely captures the process of both becoming involved in and disengaging from crime and other antisocial behaviour.
- They can uncover complex patters of continuity and change in individual behaviour over time.
- Life histories reveal the complexity of criminal behaviour.
- They are grounded in social and historical context.
- Life-history method shows us the human side of offenders.

Consider the example of desistance. We know that a person ceasing their criminal career in the vast majority takes the form of a process, in which the individual gradually leaves crime behind (Carlsson, 2014). It can also be a very dramatic, static event occurring at a single point in time (e.g. Cusson and Pinsonneault, 1986), but that seems to only rarely be the case. So, when studying desistance, it is a challenge for the researcher who uses quantitative data to conceptualize it as a process. It is not impossible (e.g. Bushway et al., 2001), but very often quantitative studies end up with a static view of desistance, because it must be understood as the *absence of an observation* – when the individual's criminal offending (often measured by official records) is no longer present. There might, of course, be some indications of a desistance process at work in quantitative data: maybe the time between recorded offences becomes longer? Still, the *meaning* of that observation is usually unclear.

Here is where qualitative data, particularly life history interviews, are at their best. By interviewing (ex-) offenders in depth about their lives in and out of crime, going beyond the structured survey-like interview form, something like a story or *narrative* emerges. The idea underlying this perspective on the social world is the notion that we 'understand the occurrence of events by learning the steps in the process by which they came to happen' (Becker, 1998: 61). So, in understanding the meaning of something – such as the processes of cumulative continuity, cumulative disadvantage, or the turning points of employment, military service, marriage and residential change – we use qualitative life-history interviews to study and understand them in the context of the surrounding processes of which they are a part. That is, we see how they are contingent on social context, how the turning point emerges and how change is made possible. When we do these interpretations, we must however be aware that it concerns individuals' subjective experiences that are interpreted by this individual with the aim, consciously or unconsciously, to give the interviewer a certain image of herself.

MIXING METHODS

The reader may have asked him/herself a question: there are obvious strengths and weaknesses to both quantitative and qualitative methods – so why not use both? That is a good question (further explored in Chapters 1 and 3 of this volume). Mixing methods – i.e. using both quantitative and qualitative data to arrive at a deeper, fuller understanding of a given research problem – is becoming more and more common within life-course criminology, and some of the most prominent and well-known studies in the field (e.g. Giordano et al., 2002; Laub and Sampson, 2003; Maruna, 2001) have done so. The strategy of mixing methods goes back to the Chicago School of Sociology, where very quantitatively driven studies (e.g. Shaw and McKay, 1942) were complemented by life histories such as the one by Shaw (1930) about 'Stanley', the famous jack-roller. It has, however, been a controversial area:

> Because of the methodological paradigm struggles that arose in the last three decades and the lingering prejudices that resulted, the idea of combining qualitative and quantitative work has an aura of the exotic or even forbidden among criminologists today. (Maruna, 2010: 124)

The underlying issue here is one concerning the philosophical assumptions that different methods are supposedly attached to. To repeat: quantitative analysis, it is said, assumes an objective reality that it is possible to measure in numbers; qualitative analysis is said to assume a subjective reality that is constructed and made 'real' through people's perceptions and interpretations, a reality thus only possible to access by analysing those interpretations. However, this harsh division between the methods is becoming more and more loose, being replaced by a form of methodological pragmatism where the researcher – as we mentioned above – chooses a method that (1) can provide data that answers the research question, and (2) is possible given the practical circumstances of the research project.

Several research projects adopt a mixed method strategy, and here we only illustrate the strategy with one famous example: Laub and Sampson's (2003) study, where they conduct a follow-up of the Gluecks' (1950) *Unraveling Juvenile Delinquency* study, tracing the men up to age 70 (see Box 13.4).

In the 1940s, Sheldon and Eleanor Glueck at Harvard University designed and conducted one of the most impressive longitudinal studies to date, published as *Unraveling Juvenile Delinquency* (1950). In the 1980s, two researchers, Sampson and Laub stumbled upon the original data and research material in a basement at Harvard. They first re-analysed the material, collected new crime record and mortality data, and published it as *Crime in the Making: Pathways and Turning Points through Life* (1993). Having collected this new data, Laub and Sampson conduct a quantitative analysis and explore the men's recorded criminal careers all the way up to the present day. Having done so, they use this data to select 52 cases from five groups of offenders: (1) those who persistently engaged in violence and theft across the life course; (2) non-violent juvenile offenders who desisted in adulthood; (3) violent juvenile offenders who desisted in adulthood; (4) intermittent offenders with an onset of violence in adulthood; and (5) intermittent offenders with an onset of violence in young adulthood.

Then, through close analyses of these 52 life histories, they delve deeper into the lived experiences of the men in the various groups. By doing so, they find the underlying processes and mechanisms at work in their age-graded theory of informal social control, but also realize the importance of human agency. Indeed, they go so far as to term it the missing link in understanding both persistence and desistance, and as such human agency provides a crucial piece of the puzzle of continuity and change in crime across the life course. This piece would not have been discovered were it not for Laub and Sampson's qualitative data analysis (in traditional, quantitative analysis, human agency may have constituted the portion of the variance in the data that cannot be explained).

Let us leave you with an additional example. Let us say we find a quantitative, statistical relationship between being diagnosed with some form of cancer and desistance from crime. That is, cancer diagnosis is a predictor of desistance; when people get the diagnosis, they are more likely to desist than before. This can be a simple co-variation between the two variables, so we have to create additional statistical tests where we control for various factors – such as age – to make sure that the two changes (in health and criminal offending) indeed are connected to each other. Now, depending on what kind of quantitative data we have access to, we might not be able to say much more than this: other things controlled for (or 'held constant'), cancer diagnosis is a predictor of desistance from crime.

But *why* is cancer diagnosis a predictor of desistance? It could be due to a number of things. First, it could be that the simple 'shock' of the diagnosis makes the individual turn his life around. Or, it could be that the cancer diagnosis is an indicator of the individual's health problems, and people who have severe health problems are often not capable of committing crimes simply because their bodies are not up to the task. Or, third, it could be that the everyday life of the offender now changes in important ways: s/he must go through treatment, counselling sessions, and so on. These things can entail a strengthening social control which inhibits future criminal offending. Any of these three explanations – or a combination of all three and possibly additional ones! – are possible, but they all have one thing in common: the only way to find out is to undertake a qualitative analysis. You take a sub-sample of those you have studied quantitatively and ask to interview them, and ask them about it.

CROSS-SECTIONAL AND LONGITUDINAL RESEARCH: THE MAIN DIFFERENCES

A cross-sectional study usually has two dimensions: individuals and variables. In a longitudinal study, as you now know, a *third* dimension is added: time. In practice, this means that for every individual, not only do we collect data on traits, circumstances and events, but also data on *when* these occur. This three-dimensionality in longitudinal data is described by Biljeveld and van der Kamp (1998) as a data box where every dimension is an axle: the box has the axles people, variables, and moment or time.

People

Every study that strives towards making generalizable conclusions has to handle the question about the representativity of the material. In quantitative studies, the sample is usually drawn from a well-defined sample population. Additionally, the sample must have a certain size for us to be able to get stable, statistically significant findings (the larger the sample, the better, for larger samples give us stronger, statistical power, which, in turn, is necessary for statistical significance).

In so-called cohort studies, such as the Swedish Stockholm Birth Cohort (Stenberg, 2013), you choose to study a whole population of people, in this case every person born in Stockholm in 1953, and who resided in the city in 1963 (when the project was launched). In such cases, given that the attrition and missing data in the study are relatively small and random, it is possible to make claims about the studied population.

Now, a problem here is the issue of time: a cohort born in 1953 turned 60 in 2013 and only then could the researchers get a sense of how the cohort members' lives unfolded. To answer questions regarding, for example, the connection between juvenile delinquency and the risk of dying from different kinds of diseases, you may have to wait even longer. Thus, after many years of research, we may finally have an answer to our question about the relationship between crime and morbidity but do these findings apply to today's youth, or are they by now no more than historical documents?

When it comes to research about relatively rare phenomena, such as serious and persistent criminal offending, you either have to work with very large samples, or stratify your sample, so that those individuals who are especially interesting to the researcher (in our case, those with serious criminal offending) are overrepresented. The Pittsburgh Youth Study (e.g. Loeber et al., 1998) is an example of such a study (Box 13.5).

BOX 13.5   THE PITTSBURGH YOUTH STUDY

Launched by the late, great Rolf Loeber and his life partner Magda Stouthamer-Loeber, these studies initially comprised 2,426 Pittsburgh school boys from grades 1, 4 and 7. However, a follow-up sample was selected using a screening risk score that measured each boy's antisocial behaviour using parent, teacher and self-report instruments. Boys identified as the top 30% on the screening risk measure, for each age cohort, as well as an equal number of boys randomly selected from the remainder, were selected for follow-up.

These assessments and waves of data collection were initially done semi-annually, but later annually, through to the age of 25. The main task of the study was to document and understand the development of antisocial and criminal behaviour from childhood to adulthood, and the risk and protective factors which contribute to that development. Later, a Pittsburgh Girls Study was launched as well.

A difficulty for those of us engaged in prospective longitudinal studies is that serious and persistent criminal offending distinguishes itself relatively late in life (e.g. after the age of 20). If we want to initiate our study before that, we have to over-sample the group of individuals who we believe will have a high risk of developing serious and criminal offending. It is not certain either that our choice of risk variables will be adequate in the long run.

Another problem is the question of attrition. Attrition is a problem for every type of research that, in one way or another, is dependent on the respondents' consent. The whole idea with longitudinal studies is that we, in some way, study individuals through time and place. We thus repeatedly measure the same respondents. So, a respondent may answer our questions at one time, but may change his/her mind (or tire, or die, leave the country, or move to an address we for some reason cannot find) the second or third time. We must remember that, for ethical reasons, we should not attempt to contact those who have already declined to participate. Thus, in longitudinal studies, the problem with attrition is usually larger than in cross-sectional ones, and, at the same time, many of the longitudinal analyses we want to make are sensitive to attrition and missing data (Biljeveld and van der Kamp, 1998). There are, however, various methodological and statistical techniques for handling this issue.

Variables

A big problem in social science research is outlining the manifest variables so that they, in an adequate way, measure the latent ones, that is, the theoretical constructs that our study uses. How do we, for example, turn *antisocial potential, self-control,* or *informal social control* into something we can actually measure? After all, there exist no such universal variables, nor any universal agreement on how such a variable should be constructed and/or what it should include. So, how do we do it?

We usually call this *the problem of* operationalization, and while we almost always encounter it, *why* we do so differs from study to study. If we conduct a self-report study, one reason why this problem occurs could simply be ethical: we cannot always ask what we want. However, much more common is the fact that we have to use data where the existing variables do not fully mirror the theoretical dimensions we want to include. One reason for this, of course, is that we often have to rely on data which is quite old, or in the case of register data, has been collected for a purpose other than the researcher's. At any rate, such issues lead to the inevitable fact of compromise when it comes to validity – for example, 'Do we really measure self-control? Maybe we have to settle for studying one dimension, or simply one or a few *indicators* of the phenomenon we are after?'

The problem of operationalization is likely to increase if the study has a longitudinal character: the same phenomenon (such as social adjustment, for example) must be operationalized differently at different ages. In the case of social adjustment, it is highly logical and relevant to include questions such as 'do you work and, if so, how many hours a week?' To ask the same question to a 13-year-old (or a 5-year-old!) would be somewhat strange. However, we still want to know how socially adjusted our sample was at the age of 13, so the problem does not go away. Thus, as we go through our study, we have to be sensitive to the social process of ageing and the flow of the life course, and re-operationalize many of our theoretical constructs to capture what is actually going on in our participants' lives. Another problem concerns those contextual, social changes that we also have to consider: the times are changing. So, within our measure of social adjustment, we may want to include something that captures economic status. One way to capture this in 1985 or 1990 would be to ask whether or not the respondent has a mobile phone. Today, that question is essentially meaningless for any measure of status.

Additionally, the way we choose to formulate our questions and our interests in certain theoretical constructs and not others, may give rise to issues for long-term studies: what the researchers may have wanted to know when they initiated their research project, when the respondents were children or teenagers; when they are adults and time has passed, the questions we can now answer may not be considered relevant or interesting (although such words are *highly* loaded with value judgements) by the science community or policy makers. The reverse is also true, of course, that new research questions emerge, due to a new social and political climate, that nobody considered relevant when we initiated our study. In our own study, violence is a striking example of this. In Sweden, at the beginning of the 1960s, violence was considered a 'natural way' for young boys and men to solve conflicts. Theft, however, was a very serious crime and an indicator of a highly problematic background and high-risk life circumstances. Thus, among the older samples in the Stockholm Life Course Project, we have practically no variables that capture the use of violence in youth, but a large number of variables that attempt to capture theft. Since the 1960s, of course, there has been a change in how society in general, and the criminal justice system in particular, perceives teenage violence. Today, it is a serious social problem and, at the individual level, an indicator of future problem behaviours.

There is no simple solution to this problem of operationalization (nor indeed to many other, related problems). However, a broad and encompassing data collection in the initial stage of the research project, where one also collects data that does not feel immediately relevant, could make future analyses possible. At the same time, that kind of data collection may not be recommended for other reasons: first of all, data, in many ways, costs money and, second, the need for data always has to be weighed against individuals' personal integrity.

Time

Finally, the dimension of time is what distinguishes longitudinal and life-course studies from other branches of research. Above, we mentioned that our measure of time can be retrospective or prospective, and that the number of 'waves' can range from one alone (and, thus, fully retrospective) to five, 10, 15 or more follow-ups. Here, we must decide how many follow-up waves we should carry out, and when we should do so. Ideally, of course, this should be decided based on the project's research questions. If we are only interested in understanding continuity and change in crime during the pathway from adolescence to young adulthood, for example, it seems pointless to conduct a follow-up study beyond age 30. Instead, we should direct all our resources to get as close and detailed a study as we can of the years between, say, 15 and 25. As always, however, and just as in the case with the other dimensions of the research project, we are likely to have to make a compromise between our ambitions and theoretical ideals, and our economic and other, practical conditions and requirements.

When studying criminal careers, observing teenagers and young adults every year or every second year may be particularly useful, since criminal activity is relatively common during these years. If we want to study, say, their self-reported criminal offending, as often as once a year would be ideal. Using longer time frames between observations when it comes to self-reported offending is possible but not desirable, due to the problems of memory recollection. The same goes for studying other facets of the criminal career, which often demand many observation periods, with short time lapses in between. One such issue concerns the onset of crime, another desistance, and intermittency, where the individual temporarily ceases offending before recidivating.

In our own research project, the SLCP, the number of observation periods was relatively few: three or four, depending on which sample we were referring to. The use of register data offered no problems here, but interviewing them did: at every observation period, we had to rely on the interview participants' retrospective accounts of longer periods of their lives, during which we had had no contact with them. The problem with this, of course, is that much of what interview participants say about their past may be affected by what has happened later in life. The past is, in a sense, always seen and narrated from the perspective of the present. In our interviews (which were conducted on a smaller, strategically chosen subset of the sample), we asked the interview participants to talk about their whole life course. This made it possible for us to compare their life histories as told at age 35 or 40, with the life histories collected from them when they were in their 60s. We also had the possibility of comparing their interviews to the more reliable register data (reliable in the sense that registers do not forget or mix up the timing of events).

One obvious advantage of not having too many observation periods where the sample is actively involved in the data collection (such as interviews or various forms of tests), is that they do not get tired of being examined and leave the study, which increases the attrition rate. Additionally, and importantly, the various observation periods can be assumed to be relatively independent of each other: it is unlikely that the interview participant or respondent remembers what s/he has said during the previous observation period, and, thus, feels no need to stick to a given life history or anything along those lines. However, in studies where the observation periods are many and occur frequently, studies have shown that there tends to develop a relationship between the researcher and the interview participant, which, in turn, may decrease the number of incidences of attrition and missing data.

SUMMARY AND REVIEW

In this chapter, we have outlined the nature, developments, strands, advantages and disadvantages of longitudinal research, and a life-course perspective on criminological topics. At one level, life-course studies are concerned with the 'age-graded sequence of roles, opportunities, constraints and events that shape the biography from birth to death' (Shanahan and MacMillan, 2008: 40). Recently, however, life-course studies have in a way moved beyond this final stage of the life course, by asking partly new research questions. For example, we know that 'crime runs in families' – one of the oldest findings in criminology. But what is *the extent* of this intergenerational transmission, and do children follow similar offending trajectories as their parents? If so, to what extent? These questions are only just now beginning to be investigated (e.g. Besemer and Farrington, 2012; Besemer et al., 2016) and, once again, this puts the spotlight on core criminological questions about the causes of crime: are they predominantly social, genetic, epi-genetic – or a combination of these? Only time, and continued criminological research, will tell.

Life-course criminology is a research enterprise where longitudinal methodology is utilized in various ways: some use only quantitative data and try to uncover continuity and change in criminal careers by studying official records, specifically made tests, assessments and/or self-report surveys. Others use qualitative life history interviews to explore the complexity and processual nature of human life. Some studies combine both quantitative and qualitative methods.

Every method has its strengths, but also its weaknesses. The basic question any potential life-course researcher should start with is: what do I want to know? Beginning with the research question is the scientific ideal and it gets you a long way. The next issue to pursue is whether a method or set of data already exists – or is possible to collect – to answer that question for you. If not, you need to rethink the research question somewhat.

If already at the outset you are faced with a given set of data, whether quantitative and qualitative, a good starting point is to explore the data: what are the characteristics of the sample? What information does it include? Has the information been collected prospectively or retrospectively? Answering these questions simultaneously provides you with the limits and possibilities inherent in the data.

Being pragmatic is not always desirable, but in social research, and life-course and longitudinal research in particular, it is often the only possible way forward.

STUDY QUESTIONS AND ACTIVITIES FOR STUDENTS

1. Describe the main difference between cross-sectional and longitudinal methodology.

2. Can longitudinal methodology help us answer questions of causality in social research? How?

3. Compare and contrast prospective and retrospective research designs: how are they similar? How are they different?

4. What are the main differences between quantitative and qualitative methods when it comes to longitudinal research?

5. The chapter highlights several benefits of mixing methods. What are they?

6. The chapter does not, however, discuss any possible drawbacks or issues with combining methods. Can you think of any?

7. In the chapter, several well-known longitudinal studies are mentioned. What similarities do they all share, and which differences do you find between them?

SUGGESTIONS FOR FURTHER READING

Atkinson, P. (1998) *The Life Story Interview*. London: Sage. A small but immensely useful book. Atkinson's guide to the life story interview is essential reading for the student interested in qualitative longitudinal analysis.

Biljeveld, C.J.H. and van der Kamp, L.J.T. (1998) *Longitudinal Data Analysis: Designs, Models, and Methods*. London: Sage. This book gives a crucial insight, guide and understanding to the student who wishes to undertake a quantitative longitudinal study.

Carlsson, C. and Sarnecki, J. (2015) *An Introduction to Life-Course Criminology*. London: Sage. In this book, we introduce the field of life-course criminology to the reader. We situate the field in its historical context, introduce its main research questions, and review and discuss the field's main theories, methods and findings on the development of crime.

REFERENCES

Atkinson, P. (1998) *The Life Story Interview*. London: Sage.

Becker, H.S. (1998) *Tricks of the Trade*. Chicago: University of Chicago Press.

Besemer, S. and Farrington, D.P. (2012) 'Intergenerational transmission of criminal behavior: conviction, trajectories of fathers and their children', *European Journal of Criminology*, 9: 120–41.

Besemer, S., Axelsson, J. and Sarnecki, J. (2016) 'Intergenerational transmission of trajectories of offending over three generations', *Journal of Developmental and Life-Course Criminology*, 2: 417–41.

Biljeveld, C.J.H. and van der Kamp, L.J.T. (1998) *Longitudinal Data Analysis: Designs, Models, and Methods*. London: Sage.

Blumstein, A., Cohen, J., Roth, J.A. and Visher, C.A. (eds) (1986) *Criminal Careers and Career Criminals*. Washington, DC: National Academy Press.

Bushway, S.D., Piquero, A.R., Broiday, L.M., Cauffman, E. and Mazzerolle, P. (2001) 'An empirical framework for studying desistance as a process', *Criminology*, *39*: 491–515.

Carlsson, C. (2014) *'Continuities and Changes in Criminal Careers'*, Dissertation, Stockholm University, Department of Criminology.

Carlsson, C. and Sarnecki, J. (2015) *An Introduction to Life-Course Criminology*. London: Sage.

Cusson, M. and Pinsonneault, P. (1986) 'The decision to give up crime', in D. Cornish and R.V. Clarke (eds), *The Reasoning Criminal: Rational Choice Perspectives on Offending*. New York: Springer-Verlag.

de Lange, A. (2005) *What about Causality? Examining Longitudinal Relations between Work Characteristics and Mental health'*, Dissertation, University of Amsterdam.

Farrington, D.P., Piquero, A.R. and Jennings, W.G. (2013) *Offending from Childhood to Late Middle Age: Recent Results from the Cambridge Study in Delinquent Development*. New York: Springer.

Giordano, P.C., Cernkovich, S.A. and Rudolph, J.L. (2002) 'Gender, crime, and desistance: toward a theory of cognitive transformation', *American Journal of Sociology*, *107*: 990–1064.

Glueck, S. and Glueck, E. (1950) *Unraveling Juvenile Delinquency*. New York: Commonwealth Fund.

Laub, J.H. and Sampson, R.J. (2003) *Shared Beginnings, Divergent Lives: Delinquent Boys to Age 70*. Cambridge, MA: Harvard University Press.

Loeber, R., Farrington, D.P., Stouthamer-Loeber, M., Moffitt, T.E. and Caspi, A. (1998) 'The development of male offending: key findings from the first decade of The Pittsburgh Youth Study', *Studies on Crime and Crime Prevention*, *7*: 141–71.

Maruna, S. (2001) *Making Good: How Ex-Convicts Reform and Rebuild their Lives*. Washington, DC: American Psychological Association.

Maruna, S. (2010) 'Mixed method research in criminology: why not go both ways?' In A.R. Piquero and D. Weisburd (eds), *Handbook of Quantitative Criminology*. New York: Springer.

Meisenhelder, T. (1977) 'An exploratory study of exiting from criminal careers', *Criminology*, *15*: 319–34.

Piquero, A.R., Farrington, D.P. and Blumstein, A. (2007) *Key Issues in Criminal Career Research*. Cambridge: Cambridge University Press.

Sampson, R.J. (2013) 'The place of context: a theory and strategy for criminology's hard problems', *Criminology*, *51*: 1–31.

Sampson, R.J. and Laub, J.H. (1993) *Crime in the Making: Pathways and Turning Points through Life*. Cambridge, MA: Harvard University Press.

Sarnecki, J. (1985) *Predicting Social Maladjustment: Stockholm Boys Grown Up I*. Stockholm: Esselte Tryck.

Shanahan, M.J. and MacMillan, R. (2008) *Biography and the Sociological Imagination*. New York: Norton.

Shaw, C.R. (1930) *The Jack-Roller: A Delinquent Boy's Own Story*. Chicago: University of Chicago Press.

Shaw, C.R. and McKay, H.D. (1942) *Juvenile Delinquency and Urban Areas*. Chicago: University of Chicago Press.

Skardhamar, T. and Lyngstad, T.H. (2011) 'Nordic register data and their untapped potential for criminological knowledge', in M. Tonry and T. Lappi-Seppälä (eds), *Crime and Justice in Scandinavia. Crime and Justice: A Review of Research*, Vol. 40. Chicago: University of Chicago Press.

Stenberg, S.-Å. (2013) *Född 1953. Folkhemsbarn i Forskarfokus*. Umeå: Boréa.

Wolfgang, M.E., Figlio, R.M. and Sellin, T. (1972) *Delinquency in a Birth Cohort*. Chicago: University of Chicago Press.

CHAPTER CONTENTS

GLOSSARY TERMS

storytelling
structured interviews
critical research
reflexivity
emotionality
praxis

14

USING INTERVIEWS AS STORYTELLING IN CRIMINOLOGICAL RESEARCH

ELIZABETH STANLEY

INTRODUCTION

Some of the most interesting and useful criminological research has interviews at its core (see, for example, Kelly, 1988; Lasslett, 2014; Scraton, 1999). The narratives in these works have changed the way many of us think about crime, harm and criminal justice. A significant part of this education has been that we connect with interviewees' narratives on a deep, human level. Testimonies allow us to move beyond numbers, percentages or 'facts' to consider experiences, perspectives and understandings. For social researchers, interviews are a main route to original findings.

Interviewing also often holds appeal among fledgling researchers – after all, there is a sense of safety in just having a conversation with someone else. However, as this chapter demonstrates, doing interviews does not equate to just 'having a chat'. Further, deciding to interview cannot be taken lightly, particularly when a researcher wishes to explore aspects of violence or harm by powerful individuals or organizations.

This chapter considers 'doing interviews' with victims of state violence – in this case, individuals who were harmed within state-run children's homes in New Zealand. Following an initial overview of interviews, and the storytelling approach that I have pursued, the chapter reflects on why interviews were so necessary for this study. I then consider the sometimes turbulent process of doing interviews with victims, charting the issues of access, building trust, the difficulties in speaking out and the emotional impacts of the research on all involved. Finally, the chapter reflects on the personal, social and political implications of collecting and using this interview data.

INTERVIEWS

Interviews vary enormously – from highly structured meetings in which a researcher asks prescribed questions through to unstructured conversations that involve deeper interactions between the researcher and interviewee (Davies, 2000). Structured interviews are easily replicable and their resultant data can be quickly compared; however, they also produce results that might be ascertained through other methods such as questionnaires. The real strength of interviews comes from unstructured or semi-structured encounters during which interviewees can speak more freely about their understandings, experiences or perspectives of the social world (Kvale, 2007).

Social research is produced through interactions. It is established through verbal exchange, but also through other elements that are often overlooked – such as vocal intonation, body language or preconceived assumptions of what should be said. There is a power dynamic in every interview situation, and both parties have the capacity to fundamentally change the research outcomes as a result (see Kvale, 2007), as outlined in Box 14.1.

BOX 14.1 POWER WITHIN INTERVIEWS

The power of the interviewer:

- Establishes the meeting
- Sets the boundaries of the topic
- Asks or does not ask certain questions
- Interprets the interview
- Creates a final 'truth' of collated data.

The power of the interviewee:

- Accepts the meeting
- Shifts the discussion of the topic
- Emphasizes certain answers
- Withholds information
- Questions the interviewer
- Withdraws from the interview.

As Box 14.1 implies, most of the power within interviews is held by the interviewer. Many researchers, especially those interested in critical, feminist or decolonizing methodologies, are subsequently keen to explore how research can be conducted in ways that reduce power imbalances (Clough and Nutbrown, 2002; Hesse-Biber and Leavy, 2013; Smith, 2003). One way that this might be done is by avoiding traditional 'question-and-answer' interviews (in which the interviewer sets the order of questions in their particular language) and, instead, taking a narrative approach that allows the interviewee to tell their story in their own words (Hollway and Jefferson, 2000). As Box 14.2 illustrates, a storytelling approach changes the dynamics of how research is done and, in so doing, brings rich data.

BOX 14.2 INTERVIEWS AS STORYTELLING

Taking a storytelling approach to research has many benefits. It can:

- allow participants to make sense of situations, and to build or regain control over definitions, experiences and perspectives
- rewrite social life by revealing truths that have previously been silenced, denied or hidden
- reflect the past, present and potential future of narrators' lives
- demonstrate multiple values, beliefs or aspirations
- give an opportunity for the narrator to receive respect or validation from another, as part of a fundamental human interaction
- illustrate hidden experiences of pain or trauma as well as those of coping, survival or resistance
- expose expectations and experiences of emotional, political, legal, moral or social change.

Individual stories will always be mediated and they can lack impartiality. Yet, by collating personal narratives, researchers demonstrate shared experiences and identities, and may subsequently create new social truths.

Notwithstanding the benefits of this approach, the storytelling approach requires researcher sensitivity, particularly in terms of how stories are subsequently represented and used. The stories 'belong' to interviewees and, if used carelessly, researchers can increase exclusion, alienation or damage for tellers. Further, the power of researchers to rewrite stories for our own ends illustrates privilege. There is a question, then, of how we can make interview data accessible, a point intensified by the unequal access to academic journals and resources (Skeggs, 2002; Stanley, 2012).

INTERVIEWING VICTIMS OF STATE VIOLENCE

This chapter considers my experience of interviewing those victimized by state workers and their representatives. As a critical criminologist, I want my research to expose experiential accounts of state violence, ones that might challenge our common-sense assumptions about who commits violence and who is victimized by it. In this chapter, state violence relates to the violence and harm suffered by those held as children within state institutions. I also hope to challenge state denials and impunity, by exposing state harms and calling for redress as well as shifts in the treatment of victims. Box 14.3 identifies the benefits of taking a critical approach in this area.

BOX 14.3 CRITICAL RESEARCH ON STATE VIOLENCE

Taking a critical framework, researchers can:

- ground their work in historical, political, social, economic and cultural analyses
- reflect on how state violence connects to forms of structural violence; structural contexts – such as those linked to class, 'race', gender, sexuality, age, ability or political status – underpin violations, making some groups more likely to be victimized
- examine how mainstream political and ideological factors conceal the reality of state violence, and lead to its legitimization (for example, by depicting victims of state violence as dangerous threats)
- emphasize the 'voices' of those who are commonly silenced, ignored, obscured or misinterpreted

- be self-conscious about their own values and status, and the political purposes of their research
- engage in strategies of resistance, such as to direct their research to struggles of prevention, acknowledgement, redress or accountability.

Source: Adapted from Stanley (2012)

As shown in Box 14.3, a critical approach allows a researcher to uncover how state violence is employed, discussed, experienced and challenged. It brings an opportunity to expose alternative voices on issues that are commonly silenced.

In recent years, over a thousand New Zealanders have approached legal firms and official agencies with complaints about their abuse in 'state care', mainly from the 1950s to the late 1980s. My project connected with 105 claimants. Most (n = 91) had been removed from families due to their experiences of abuse or neglect, while under half (n = 47) had begun to get into trouble, such as by truanting or engaging in petty theft. Removed at an average age of 10 years, most claimants spent many years in state care. Box 14.4 contains a summary of the abuse and its impact on claimants.

BOX 14.4 INSTITUTIONAL ABUSE AND ITS LEGACIES

Of 105 research participants:

- 91 suffered physical violence at the hands of staff members (being whipped, strapped, beaten, kicked and punched)
- 48 reported being sexually assaulted by another child, while 57 were sexually victimized by an adult in the institution (sometimes suffering multiple assaults over prolonged periods)
- 70 endured harsh physical punishments; four were given electroconvulsive therapy as punishment for 'acting up'
- 86 faced more than three days in a secure cell, with just a toilet or bucket, basin and metal bed
- All suffered within institutional cultures of stigmatization and denigration.

Impacts:

- multiple psychological difficulties, including intimacy problems, emotional detachment, hyper-vigilance, flashbacks, nightmares, anxiety and depression

(Continued)

- strong feelings of loss, despair, grief, shame, guilt, fear and anger that have sustained over decades
- loss of cultural connection, particularly for Māori and Pasifika claimants
- high levels of substance abuse, self-harm, homelessness, unemployment, imprisonment and mental health institutionalization.

Choosing interviews

Given the contemporary context in which victims' testimonies have been silenced in New Zealand, I quickly decided to centralize interviews within primary research. Through interviews, I hoped to expose realities that were hidden from view and to allow those most affected by state violence to speak for themselves. Interviews provided a chance for me to question victims about their experiences over their lifetimes – from being removed from their families, through their time in state 'care' institutions, to the long-term legacy of violence on their lives and their ongoing attempts to secure redress.

I dovetailed interviews with an extensive analysis of official documents. With the assistance of a local law firm that had accessed material as part of discovery for taking legal cases, I gained consent from 105 victims to examine their official files. I worked through hundreds of boxes of material, including reports from social welfare workers, boys' and girls' homes, police, corrections, counsellors, psychiatrists, health professionals, finance bodies, lawyers, among others. My approach was to analyse a victim's documentation before interviewing them.

Working through the documents, it soon became clear that I had to allow victims the space to guide the interviews as much as possible. The main reason for this was that victims' voices were squeezed out by official writers who filed reports in line with pre-established agendas. This was apparent in every form of documentation. For example, institutional workers recorded a child's delinquencies and dysfunctions in minute detail, but they noted almost nothing of children's skills, interests or positive personality traits. Administrative reports upheld the common stigmatization and criminalization of children in care. This continued into other domains – so, for example, probation and correctional officers focused almost exclusively on the 'risk' characteristics of those they encountered. Moreover, officials rarely recorded state violations. For instance, social welfare institutions retained remarkably 'clean' files that did not register harmful punishments, or violence by staff members. Official disclosures were rare, as institutions wished to avoid public scrutiny or official intervention. This skewed reporting took on its own 'magical administration' authority, as a lack of recording – under conditions where we expect events will be recorded – meant that abuse just 'did not happen' (Cohen, 2001).

Institutional interests could also be observed within documents led by victims' advocates. For example, victims' lawyers produced statements that viewed state institutions and their workers in almost entirely negative terms. In a bid to propel claims, they logically focused on victims' negative experiences. While necessary, in terms of taking claims through an adversarial legal system, it presented another distorted source from a research perspective.

Following this analysis, and over a period of two years, I interviewed 45 victims from the larger 105 cohort. I chose a storytelling approach, with the intention that victims would have the freedom to fully guide our discussions and would not, once more, be subsumed under another's agenda, albeit well-meaning. In doing so, victims challenged the state's silencing of violence and harm. Yet, beyond this, they gave a more nuanced account of themselves, their time in care, their victimization and claims. For example, they presented a 'fuller' account of themselves, not just as 'abuse claimants' or 'delinquents' but as parents, siblings, children, employees, community workers, artists, gardeners, and so on. Further, they regularly remarked on how physical and sexual violence (that is often seen) entwined with psychological violence or social disadvantage (that often goes unseen). They spoke of the ways in which they perpetrated harms against other children, while also being victimized themselves. They also noted complicated relationships with residential workers as they received love and care from some while enduring abuse from others. They vented anger and despair at their ongoing treatment by official agencies but they also relied on state officials to recognize their histories and to assist in repairing harms. Overall, these unstructured encounters allowed interviewees to say what they felt was important and, in turn, they exposed multiple complexities. In gaining some control over what could be told, many interviewees related events that they had never told anyone else (see Stanley, 2016, for a fuller account).

Doing interviews

Given the social and political nature of criminological topics, it is important to take a reflexive approach to research. Reflexivity allows us to consider the 'ways in which knowledge is produced' – for instance, it interrogates 'hidden biases, conflicts of interest and assumptions' and it permeates 'all aspects of the research' from how we decide what to research right through to how we disseminate findings (Lumsden and Winter, 2014: 2). Certainly, the process of doing interviews brought many challenges that ultimately had an impact on the nature of produced knowledge in this project. Here, I consider four elements – access, building trust, speaking out and emotionality – that influenced how I undertook interviews, analysed data and disseminated findings.

Victims of institutional violence are a relatively difficult group to access. When I began the research, there was no 'survivor' group that I might contact, and government agencies maintained the privacy of claimants. However, this research developed after my contact with a lawyer who represented hundreds of claimants. After several discussions, she agreed to include a note from me – requesting consent to look at claimants' legal files and to register their interest in being interviewed – in her firm's newsletter. Having assumed that I might attract 20 or 30 claimants, I was overwhelmed by the 105 who quickly replied.

As shown in Table 14.1, research participants reflect a broad range of ages, with most born in the 1960s. While different ethnicities are represented, there are few Pasifika in the study. Māori are also under-represented given that (neo)colonial discrimination had ensured that this indigenous group was readily institutionalized from the 1970s (often accounting for over 80% of residents). Further, it is a significantly male cohort. We know that girls were victimized within state institutions; however, few women have chosen to make a legal case. There are many theories on why this has occurred: perhaps women do not want to face adversarial court cases or to publicly expose their story. Invariably, these issues mean that the resulting data is male focused.

TABLE 14.1 **The 105 respondents**

Gender	Male	97 respondents
	Female	8
Ethnicity	European/Pākehā	55 respondents
	Māori	47
	Pasifika	2
	Asian	1
Birth years	1940–49	7 respondents
	1950–59	21
	1960–69	46
	1970–79	21
	1980–89	10

Interviewing 45 respondents, I travelled around New Zealand, from the far north down to Otago in the south. I covered thousands of kilometres. Interviewees welcomed me warmly into their homes and I often spent whole days with them and their families. Nineteen of these respondents were in prison, and had revolved through correctional institutions since leaving state care. Out of all the interviews, these were the most difficult.

Taking the mantle of 'legal visitor', many prison officers helpfully assisted me to establish interview times. With administration in place, I then wrote to prisoners to reconfirm our arrangement and provide them with a clear time for our meeting. My troubles began, however, when I arrived at the gates. Among other things, officers did not always provide reasonably private spaces for the interviews, and I regularly argued with officers who interrupted interviews as it was now 'lock-down' time and the interviewee had to return to his cell. On one occasion, I flew from Wellington to Dunedin (1.5 hours), hired a car and drove 45km to the prison, only to be informed that the interview should end after 25 minutes.

Further, notwithstanding common assumptions that prisoners are a 'captive audience', I could also struggle to access them. Trying to interview one man became particularly tiresome. Having previously established an interview time, I arrived at Auckland prison (after travelling 2.5 hours) to be told that the interviewee had been taken to court. I arranged another visit and returned home. A few days before this new interview time, I rang the prison to reconfirm and was told that the man had transferred to Whanganui. From here, I rearranged the interview with Whanganui prison and arrived (after a three-hour car journey) to be told that he had been re-transferred to Auckland that morning. I finally reached him in Auckland, six weeks later. While this example was frustrating, in terms of my own costs and time, it also clarified an interesting research point. Within state care, children were subject to constant placement changes, a situation that left them isolated, disconnected and ever-fearful. It was not unusual for children to be moved a dozen times over a few years. And, for claimants who remain within institutions, it seems that little has changed. Institutional logistics continue to be prioritized over the wellbeing of those detained by the state.

Building trust

A vital element of this project has been developing trust with interviewees. I often spent hours with people – talking about life, cooing over children, making cups of tea or gardening. I regularly did things that people would not class as research but these actions have been absolutely vital to gaining data. During these periods of connection, interviewees and their loved ones could take measure of me, ask questions about my career or life, and confirm my research intentions. They had a chance to 'suss' me out.

Part of the process of building trust relates to how researchers acknowledge difference. Trust is more easily secured when researchers have empathy with interviewees; however, it is consolidated when researchers reflect on their place within the research, and acknowledge the difference and distance between research parties (Agger and Buus Jensen, 1996).

In many respects, I benefited from attributes that are difficult to change: I'm small in stature and high voiced, so I do not appear as imposing or intimidating. Further, many men who had been sexually assaulted commented that they could never talk to a male researcher. Thus, my female attributes impacted on my ability to access interviewees and gain their trust (see Green, 2003; Huggins and Glebbeek, 2003). At the same time, as a Pākehā, I regularly reflected on my cultural difference and my lack of te reo (language) that would enable a fuller connection with Māori respondents.

My status – as a university lecturer and author – garnered a more mixed response. For the most part, interviewees considered that I held a trustworthy position and they felt optimistic that their stories would be published. But I often had to minimize expectations of what I might achieve. I also had to be aware that my academic status could be a barrier. After replying to one interviewee's questions about my career, he immediately noted the differences in our lives, particularly as we were born just a few months apart. It was an uncomfortable acknowledgement of our unequal positions, and gave me a firm reminder of my ability to 'study, rather than endure' (Farmer, 2003: 224; Skeggs, 2002). For some minutes afterwards, the interviewee gave clipped responses to my questions. In short, my status could also close doors.

Still, my academic background was absolutely preferable to that of others who took an interest in their lives. Many interviewees had some distrust of professionals – including social workers or lawyers – who they felt operated with their own agendas. This issue was particularly emphasized in one of my later visits at a local prison. As was often the case, I was already sitting in an interview room when a prison officer arrived with the interviewee. The officer quickly left and the man sat down across the table. He glowered, arms crossed. I gave my name, but he looked away, saying nothing. I had never experienced such coldness during these interviews, and so I again gave my name and explained why I was there. At this point, his whole demeanour changed as he jumped up, shook my hand and apologized profusely for his rudeness. He had forgotten the date, expected me the following day and had thought I was a Corrections' psychologist, to whom he does not speak. He, alongside others, was wary of psychologists who acted 'for the department' rather than solely in the interests of individual clients. Compared to others, then, my academic role provided a stamp of trustworthy approval.

Speaking out

The purpose of building trust is to create conditions in which interviewees feel that they can open up. Of course, the ability of victims of state violence to speak out is determined by multiple factors beyond any researcher's control. For instance, many interviewees discussed how, for many years, they did not talk about their childhood experiences to anyone. Struggling against psychological harms – including anxiety, depression, suicidal feelings, sleeping difficulties, low self-esteem, isolation or hypervigilance – they often felt shame, guilt, fear, stress and despair about their past (Middleton et al., 2014; Stanley, 2016). It was too painful to talk, and many victims subsequently tried to silence the past or cover it through substance abuse. Within this research, interviewees had addressed many of these 'intrapersonal barriers' to disclosure (Tener and Murphy, 2015) – after all, they had chosen to speak with me – however, remnants of these stresses remained. As a researcher, I had to be attentive to make sure that I did not push against their defence barriers (Stanley, 2012).

Even when interviewees took a strident approach to relating their histories, we often found that language could not really cover their trauma (Laub, 1992). Their '[w]ords slipped and fell about ... [because] we did not have shared meanings built from shared histories' (Lambert et al., 2003: 42). Several interviewees said they found it difficult to describe their feelings of horror, isolation, terror or self-loathing that developed through childhood and that continued, in different forms, into the present. Similarly, interviewees' attempts to relate stories in a linear way often failed as the past so often intruded into the present, and insights from the present imposed on the past.

Moreover, these victims also felt nervous about how their stories would be received, especially as their claims had previously faced official challenge. Speaking about past abuse or state violence has risks. Bystanders can disbelieve victims, condemn them, blame them, or tarnish them with false memories (Tener and Murphy, 2015). In the wake of disclosure, onlookers can regard victims with 'new eyes'. They wonder what other secrets they have, they question whether their sexual abuse has led them to paedophilia, and frequently assume that a care placement meant they were 'trouble'. They can also question why victims can't just 'get over it', seeing ongoing despair as another indication of personal dysfunction (Stringer, 2014; Walklate, 2011). Under these circumstances, many victims made claims when they felt safe in being 'one amongst many'. And, even now, several interviewees had not even spoken to their family members about their past, and a significant number requested a pseudonym. As a researcher, I had to be deeply attentive to the social consequences of speaking out during the interviews and, later, through my analysis, discussion and writing.

Emotionality

It is impossible to do interviews that address what state harms mean and 'feel like' to victims without bringing 'unpleasant emotions' to the fore (Huggins and Glebbeek, 2003: 378). Emotionality took a constant presence over this research. It emerged during interviews and it continued for many years for me.

In the first place, recounting violent pasts is a struggle. Many interviewees said that although they appreciated the opportunity to speak, it also brought up negative emotions. They felt scared, sad, angry, ashamed, embarrassed and pained to discuss past abuse. On many occasions, interviewees also had to juggle interviews while presenting another 'face' to others. For example, one female interviewee sent her son for a day in the local city as she didn't want him to know about her past. In other circumstances, imprisoned interviewees spoke of the significant difficulties in returning to times of vulnerability and harm within a closed environment. The 'face' required to open up on these issues directly challenges the staunch, non-emotional, hard face necessary to survive prison life (Jewkes, 2008; Medlicott, 2001).

Further, while I hoped that interviewees could finish our discussions by talking about good, secure areas of life (Rosenthal, 2003), this was not always possible. Many interviewees found life difficult, and they often reflected on how their childhood experiences had led to substance abuse, difficulties in personal relationships, illiteracy, poverty or unemployment. Although all interviewees demonstrated resilience and humour 'in spades', they still lived with the legacy of victimization. Sometimes their sense of loss was palpable. Nonetheless, most also remarked on the soothing power of the interview, as it gave a rare opportunity to talk freely about their experiences and perceptions. Moreover, they appreciated that I believed their stories, listened without judgement, acknowledged them, and wanted to create change in how the state responded to their claims.

Through the research, I also struggled with my own emotions. During interviews, I felt anger, horror, sadness and outrage at what victims endured (Pickering, 2001). Sometimes, interviewees would check 'are you OK?' before carrying on with their testimony of the most brutal victimization. Often, they helped me along with tea, cake, biscuits and, later, hugs. They cared for and looked after me. Beyond the content of the interviews, the most challenging elements emerged from the institutions I encountered. For example, at one prison, three officers took me aside before an interview to argue against highlighting prisoners' victimization. At another prison, officers placed me and the interviewee in a windowless, dank room that still had water all over the floor from a burst pipe. On another occasion, in moving from one part of a prison to another, I was locked in a corridor for over quarter of an hour while officers ignored my persistent 'buzzers' to open the door (strangely, when an officer arrived in the space, waved at the camera and pressed the buzzer once, the door opened instantly). In sum, then, I felt more challenged by the lack of care within prisons and I often emerged from these interviews feeling upset or annoyed at a system that continued to harm.

The emotional impact of interviewing also developed, in different ways, over a period of years. This was most apparent in the fact that having completed and transcribed all the interviews, I found that I was unable to write anything. This continued for well over a year, during which I felt incapacitated by the sheer volume and intensity of victims' experiences. I struggled, too, with the sense of responsibility to 'get the story right' while victims waited for 'their book' to emerge. In some way, I felt ashamed of these reactions – on paper, I'm supposed to be an efficient, objective and non-emotional 'expert' (Pickering, 2001). Over the years, many interviewees have given me consoling and encouraging words. My only solace is that I believe that my basic 'human' responses have meant that my resulting work is stronger in its capture of the emotional and political impacts of state violence.

Reflections

Interviewing victims of state violence brings responsibilities. Once we 'know' about harms, there is a level of expectation that we will also act to make things better

(Cohen, 2001). As a critical criminologist, this is also a fundamental element of doing research. The creation of knowledge is not just a library exercise; instead, it is directed to progressive change in perceptions, relationships, laws, policies, official practices, societal conditions, and so on.

My research led to several useful outcomes in terms of shifting our knowledge about state violence. For instance, the interviews have unearthed a level of harm against children that has, thus far, been silenced. Unlike other countries where there have been large-scale public inquiries into the institutional abuse of children, the official response to claimants in New Zealand has operated to deny or minimize testimonies (see Stanley, 2015).

By collectivizing individual interviews, a social truth about institutional life and harms has emerged that demonstrates the continuities of experiences, across institutions at different times. Victims' testimonies are consistent in identifying who abused children, where and how. Unknown to each other, victims remarked upon the same violators, the same extreme punishments, the same methods of abuse, the same disregard for humanity and the same limits of accountability. They witnessed the physical, sexual or psychological abuse of others; they name the victims and the violators, and provide new detail on specific events. The extent of corroboration in these testimonies is compelling and it's important as it challenges the official claim (particularly in the court rooms) that those bringing claims are vindictive or delusional. In short, the interviews have affirmed victims *as* victims.

Further, interviewees have also highlighted the problems of viewing state harms in terms of physical or sexual violence, as most official responses have tended to do (Stanley, 2015). Instead, their accounts demonstrate the need to take a more nuanced account that considers the extensive implications of social and cultural harms. For example, interviewees discussed how violence within state residences continued over into foster care, mental health institutions and other community placements. They reflected, too, on how degrading institutional cultures, poor educational provisions, constant placement changes, lack of association with old friends or siblings, loss of cultural connections, or inadequate supports on release from care all contributed to a deep sense of loss as well as long-term economic, social, cultural and personal harms. These experiences, that reveal the mundane realities of state violence, have been deeply damaging over victims' lifetimes. Among other things, they created conditions in which victims were far more likely to experience long-term disadvantages and to progress into offending. By highlighting these wider 'non-criminal' harms, interviewees could also show how their past experiences have continued into present conditions for children in care. There is a continuum of victimization, which includes an 'everydayness of brutality' that permeates social and institutional practices (Stanley, 2012).

Interviewees' accounts challenge common perceptions about state harms, by commission or omission, and in doing so they simultaneously confront myths about who victims are or what they want. For example, victims highlighted that, contrary to common assumptions, they are rarely motivated by compensation. Rather, almost all interviewees focused on their desire for recognition. Above all else, they wanted public disclosure of state violence, so that more New Zealanders would understand the limited protection of children by authorities. Further, opening up discussions would allow them to more easily explain their life journeys to loved ones (sometimes for the first time). The vast majority of interviewees also wanted to hear a public apology for state violence, from the highest levels of government. Most wanted access to social support – such as counselling – while a small group aspired to meet their abusers within a restorative justice setting. Others requested prosecution, but a far more significant desire was to address the poverty and violence currently inflicted on children.

In exposing victims' accounts, this research aimed to show how identities, events and discourses on violence are 'derived and reproduced, historically and contemporaneously, in the structural relations of inequality and oppression that characterize established social orders' (Chadwick and Scraton, 2001: 72). It has demonstrated, for example, how state violence was directed at Māori children in ways that reiterated the power structures of colonization, patriarchy and advanced global capitalism. Yet, in doing so, I also wanted to 'instigate a transformation' (Butler, 2004: 44) and to foster an understanding that we are left with no choice but to act to make things better. As a critical researcher, I am interested in research praxis: how theory connects to practice 'and the struggle that exists in all intellectual movements to transform existing (oppressive or marginalizing) societal conditions into meaningful reflection, action and change' (Arrigo, 2001: 219). While I write *against* state violence, I also want to write *for* change.

To that end, I have argued that official agencies should respond to victims and their accounts through approaches that reflect the needs of recognition, repair and the prevention of future harms (Stanley, 2015, 2016). I have encouraged interviewees' histories to be more widely discussed. Together with others (such as lawyers, judges and human rights commissioners), I have regularly discussed findings with anyone who might listen. I have presented many public lectures, written media commentaries, participated in radio and television programmes, and featured across newspapers, magazines and websites (see, for example, Smale, 2016). And, as journalistic and public interest has grown, the issue has developed. More victims have come forward and are publicly sharing their experiences. Concerns of abuse are also now being connected to other 'care' sites, including residential schools for those with disabilities, psychiatric hospitals, wilderness 'youth justice' camps and foster care. The Human Rights Commission has developed a campaign for a Commission of Inquiry, and the Waitangi Tribunal has received a claim to address the issue of the differential treatment and impact of state care on the lives of Māori. At the time of writing, the new Labour government has announced a commitment to implement an inquiry into abuse in state care. The research has had significant impact and contributed to a developing social history about state care and harms against children more broadly.

The 'burden' of a critical approach to research entails 'high expectations' to progress social, political and economic change (Sim, 2003: 248; see also Cohen, 2001; Giroux, 2002). These steps are not always easy. For example, in writing up,

I struggled with a sense of responsibility in 'getting the story right', so that all respondents would see their own history within the collective. I worried about creating publications that would commodify victims' stories without developing real action (Plummer, 2001). And I was challenged by the onus on me to do research in a way that moved beyond good analysis (Stanley, 2012) – so much so that after completing the book, the publishers asked me to rewrite the whole thing (almost 300 pages!) to ensure that it would reach the largest public audience. I managed this task but, on more than one occasion, I wondered why I hadn't become an aromatherapist. Still, I retain hope and optimism that, by charting these experiences, I have maintained a role of critic and conscience of society and that the research, in turn, might spread 'the values of human rights, the rule of law, and social justice' (Giroux, 2002: 160).

SUMMARY AND REVIEW

Interviewing is a qualitative method that has to be undertaken with a certain degree of foresight and care. For this author, interviewing is an academic endeavour but it also reflects a personal, social and political need to recognize violence in its many forms, to demonstrate empathy for others, and to call for change in the treatment of those made less powerful by state actions (Cohen, 2001).

As this chapter has illustrated, interviewing around these topics is not particularly quick or simple; however, it has the potential to rewrite histories in a way that is individually and socially meaningful. Doing interviews with those whose stories are generally overlooked allowed me to present a startling account of state 'care', and it demonstrated the clear links between state harms against children and long-term negative legacies for victims, their families and communities (Stanley, 2016).

As a critical criminologist, the opportunity to analyse state power in a way that can shift perceptions or actions is a key driver for pursuing research. Yet, these activities bring personal costs and responsibilities. For instance, among other things, I had to face the emotional, social and political impacts of the work, and acknowledge some of the project's weaknesses, such as its inability to secure more stories from women, Māori and other minorities.

In short, there are always implications of requesting interviews. As criminological researchers, those we interview will almost invariably speak about events or issues that bring tension, confusion, pain or trauma. We have a duty to ensure that we respectfully establish, hear and use these stories. This chapter has detailed that:

- There are significant differences between the types of interviews conducted by social researchers.
- Interviewers always have to be attentive to the power differentials between interviewer and interviewee.

- Storytelling allows interviewees to guide the narrative on particular issues or situations. This diminishes the control of interviewers in setting the boundaries of debate.
- Interviews are particularly useful to researchers who wish to expose perceptions and experiences of violence, inequality, discrimination or marginalization – for this reason, interviews are often undertaken by critical, feminist and decolonizing criminologists.
- Doing interviews brings a responsibility to use the resulting data in a respectful way.
- Interviews can often be undertaken as one part of 'multi-method' research projects.
- The practice of 'doing interviews' can bring multiple challenges of access, trust building, language, emotionality and research dissemination. There are both short- and long-term implications of doing interviews, for the interviewer and the interviewee, among others.
- Interviews can generate significant 'truths' about social life that cannot be secured through other primary research practices. Interviews expose the myths, complexities, nuances and commonalities of experiencing harm and violence. Interviews also 'work' for diverse groups of people, especially for those from whom we do not commonly hear.

STUDY QUESTIONS AND ACTIVITIES FOR STUDENTS

1. What is your favourite book that uses research data from interviews? How does the author use this interview material? Which excerpts do you particularly like, and why?

2. Name a group connected with state crime (as victims or perpetrators) that you would like to interview. Why do you want to interview this group? How would interviews be particularly useful (over other methods)? And what factors might make interviews difficult with this group?

3. Your group has decided to conduct research that charts the detention experiences of children held in a local asylum seeker centre. In preparation for this research, you have five tasks to think through:

   a. Preparing access: What difficulties might you face in accessing this population, and how could each obstacle be successfully managed?

   b. Pre-empting harms: What potential harms might these interviews bring – to the child interviewees and their families, to the interviewer, or to others? How might these harms be lessened?

c. Easing communications: this research will be undertaken with children from many different countries, so language and cultural barriers require attention:

   i. You will need to employ interpreters for each interview. What might be some of the drawbacks in using interpreters? How will you manage this?
   ii. How will you ensure that your interviews are culturally sensitive?
   iii. How might you conduct this research to be child-centred?

d. Constructing a schedule: construct an interview schedule of 12–15 questions – with so few questions, each question has to count! In building the schedule, think about:

   i. how you can add to our established knowledge on child asylum seeker experiences of detention
   ii. when you might use 'open' or 'closed' questions
   iii. how your questions will build trust and a sense of safety for interviewees.

e. Potential outcomes: What outcomes do you hope to emerge from this research? How will you use the interview data, in particular, to have maximum impact?

SUGGESTIONS FOR FURTHER READING

Brinkmann and Kvale's (2015) comprehensive book *InterViews* provides clarity on the preparation, design, conduct and analysis of interviews. Hesse-Biber's (2013) edited book *Feminist Research Practice* is, generally, a valuable text, and her chapter on 'in-depth interviewing' is particularly useful. The first and last chapters of Phil Scraton's (2007) *Power, Conflict and Criminalisation* consider the values of critical research and its potential to transform societies. Finally, Ken Plummer's (2001) *Documents of Life 2* examines the political and ethical implications of life story research and encourages critical, humanistic storytelling.

REFERENCES

Agger, I. and Buus Jensen, S. (1996) *Trauma and Healing under State Terrorism*. London: Zed Books.

Arrigo, B. (2001) 'Praxis', in E. McLaughlin and J. Muncie (eds), *The Sage Dictionary of Criminology*. London: Sage.

Brinkmann, S. and Kvale, S. (2015) *InterViews: Learning the Craft of Qualitative Research Interviewing*, 3rd edition. Los Angeles, CA: Sage.

Butler, J. (2004) *Precarious Life: The Powers of Mourning and Violence*. New York: Verso.

Chadwick, K. and Scraton, P. (2001) 'Critical research', in E. McLaughlin and J. Muncie (eds), *The Sage Dictionary of Criminology*. London: Sage.

Clough, P. and Nutbrown, C. (2002) *A Student's Guide to Methodology*. London: Sage.

Cohen, S. (2001) *State of Denial: Knowing about Atrocities and Suffering*. Cambridge: Polity Press.

Davies, P. (2000) 'Doing interviews with female offenders', in V. Jupp, P. Davies and P. Francis (eds), *Doing Criminological Research*. London: Sage.

Farmer, P. (2003) *Pathologies of Power: Health, Human Rights and the New War on the Poor*. Berkeley, CA: University of California Press.

Giroux, H.A. (2002) 'Global capitalism and the return of the garrison state', *Arena Journal*, 19: 141–60.

Green, P. (2003) 'Researching the Turkish state', in S. Tombs and D. Whyte (eds), *Unmasking the Crimes of the Powerful: Scrutinizing States and Corporations*. New York: Peter Lang.

Hesse-Biber, S.N. and Leavy, P.L. (2013) *Feminist Research Practice: A Primer*, 2nd edition. London: Sage.

Hollway, W. and Jefferson, T. (2000) *Doing Qualitative Research Differently*. London: Sage.

Huggins, M.K. and Glebbeek, M. (2003) 'Women studying violent male institutions: cross-gendered dynamics in police research on secrecy and danger', *Theoretical Criminology*, 7(3): 363–87.

Jewkes, Y. (2008) 'Men behind bars', in Y. Jewkes (ed.), *Prisons and Punishment: Punishment, Controversial Issues and Emerging Debates*, Vol. 3. London: Sage.

Kelly, L. (1988) *Surviving Sexual Violence*. London: Polity Press.

Kvale, S. (2007) *Doing Interviews*. London: Sage.

Lambert, C., Pickering, S. and Alder, C. (2003) *Critical Chatter: Women and Human Rights in South East Asia*. Durham, NC: Carolina Academic Press.

Lasslett, K. (2014) *State Crime on the Margins of Empire*. London: Pluto Press.

Laub, D. (1992) 'An event without a witness: truth, testimony and survival', in S. Felman and D. Laub (eds), *Testimony: Crises of Witnessing in Literature, Psychoanalysis, and History*. London: Routledge.

Lumsden, K. and Winter, A. (2014) 'Reflexivity in criminological research', in K. Lumsden and A. Winter (eds), *Reflexivity in Criminological Research: Experiences with the Powerful and the Powerless*. London: Palgrave.

Medlicott, D. (2001) *Surviving the Prison Place: Narratives of Suicidal Prisoners*. Aldershot: Ashgate.

Middleton, W., Stavropoulos, P., Dorahy, M., Kruger, C., Lewis-Fernandez, R., Martinez-Taboas, A., et al. (2014) 'The Australian Royal Commission into Institutional Responses to Child Sexual Abuse', *Australian and New Zealand Journal of Psychiatry*, 48(1): 17–21.

Pickering, S. (2001) 'Undermining the sanitized account: violence and emotionality in the field in Northern Ireland', *British Journal of Criminology*, *41*: 485–501.

Plummer, K. (2001) *Documents of Life 2: An Invitation to a Critical Humanism*. London: Sage.

Rosenthal, G. (2003) 'The healing effects of storytelling: on the conditions of curative storytelling in the context of research and counseling', *Qualitative Inquiry*, *9*(6): 915–33.

Scraton, P. (1999) *Hillsborough: The Truth*. Edinburgh: Mainstream Publishing.

Scraton, P. (2007) *Power, Conflict and Criminalisation*. London: Routledge.

Sim, J. (2003) 'Whose side are we not on? Researching medical power in prisons', in S. Tombs and D. Whyte (eds), *Unmasking the Crimes of the Powerful: Scrutinizing States and Corporations*. New York: Peter Lang.

Skeggs, B. (2002) 'Techniques for telling the reflexive self', in T. May (ed.), *Qualitative Research in Action*. London: Sage.

Smale, A. (2016) 'Justice delayed, justice denied', *Radio NZ*, 9 December. Available at: www.radionz.co.nz/stories/201825742/justice-delayed-justice-denied (accessed 17 August 2017).

Smith, L.T. (2003) *Decolonizing Methodologies: Research and Indigenous Peoples*. London: Zed Books.

Stanley, E. (2012) 'Interviewing victims of state violence', in D. Gadd, S. Karstedt and S.F. Messner (eds), *The Sage Handbook of Criminological Research Methods*. London: Sage.

Stanley, E. (2015) 'Responding to state institutional violence', *British Journal of Criminology*, *55*(6): 1149–67.

Stanley, E. (2016) *The Road to Hell: State Violence against Children in Postwar New Zealand*. Auckland: Auckland University Press.

Stringer, R. (2014) *Knowing Victims: Feminism, Agency and Victim Politics in Neoliberal Times*. London: Routledge.

Tener, D. and Murphy, S. (2015) 'Adult disclosure of child sexual abuse: a literature review', *Trauma, Violence and Abuse*, *16*(4): 391–400.

Walklate, S. (2011) 'Reframing criminal victimization: finding a place for vulnerability and resilience', *Theoretical Criminology*, *15*(2): 179–94.

CHAPTER CONTENTS

GLOSSARY TERMS

qualitative research
research design
semi-structured interviews
discourse analysis

15

USING IN-DEPTH INTERVIEWING AND DOCUMENTARY ANALYSIS IN CRIMINOLOGICAL RESEARCH

MARIE SEGRAVE AND SANJA MILIVOJEVIC

INTRODUCTION

Human trafficking is an issue that encapsulates a broad range of exploitative practices. It is a hugely complex, morally charged and politicized phenomenon. It is an area of interest to researchers from many disciplines including but not limited to criminology, victimology, sociology, psychology, migration studies international relations, politics, refugee studies, gender studies, critical race studies and anthropology. Work published across these fields interrogates how we understand and define human trafficking (Dragiewicz, 2015), the extent and the nature of human trafficking (Andreas and Greenhill, 2010), the implementation of law and policy (Outshoorn, 2015), the strategies to prevent human trafficking and their impact/s (Doezema, 2010), and the connections between human mobility, migration law and regulation, and exploitation (Segrave et al., 2017; see also Segrave, 2013 for a review of work across the field). We situate this chapter and our own research in this area, as a critical criminological account of human trafficking research. This means that, as you read, we encourage you to consider ways to interrogate what is known and reported about this issue via conducting well-designed, rigorous and transparent research.

Human trafficking refers to all forms of exploitation that involve three elements: the act (recruit, transport, transfer, harbour or receive persons), the means (threat or use of force, coercion, abduction, fraud, deception, abuse of power or vulnerability, or giving payments or benefits to a person in control of the victim) and the purpose (i.e. for exploitation, which includes sexual exploitation, forced labour, slavery or similar practices and the removal of organs) (see UNODC, 2016). In the early 2000s, much of the focus was on sex trafficking which referred to one form of human trafficking, where women (and children) are trafficked into the sex industry or into sexual servitude. As outlined in the chapter, the utility of this distinction is questionable and reflects the legacy of the original debates around sex work versus prostitution that underpinned the international recognition of human trafficking. More recently, there has been attention paid to the issue of labour trafficking, which is used as a point of difference from sex trafficking. The distinction is based on the recognition of exploitation connected to labour other than sex work and/or exploitation other than sexual servitude.

In this chapter, we refer to human trafficking and begin by outlining how human trafficking has been defined at the international level. We offer a brief synopsis of the politics related to the development of the Trafficking Protocol, as this provides an understanding of the definition and the prioritization of particular elements of contemporary counter-trafficking strategies. We then outline methodological challenges in researching human trafficking – where potential participants in research include authorities such as law enforcement and other government agencies, NGOs, employers, other stakeholders and migrant men, women and children, some of whom will have the status of unlawful non-citizen. We also point to critical areas of qualitative research that are essential to further understand the debates and impact surrounding the various international responses implemented to counter human trafficking.

HUMAN TRAFFICKING DEFINED

Human trafficking at the international level is now referred to interchangeably as 'modern day slavery' and in some cases as 'forced labour'. We choose not to use these terms. For clarity and consistency of meaning, we focus here on human trafficking as per the *Protocol to Prevent, Suppress and Punish Trafficking in Persons, Especially Women and Children, supplementing the United Nations Convention against Transnational Organized Crime* [hereinafter the Trafficking Protocol]. The Trafficking Protocol offers both a definition of human trafficking and a framework for responding. Article 2 is focused on the purpose of the Protocol. There are three key roles or intentions stated:

- **To prevent and combat** trafficking in persons, paying particular attention to women and children;
- To **protect and assist the victims** of such trafficking, with full respect for their human rights; and
- To **promote cooperation among States Parties** in order to meet those objectives. (UN, 2000: 2)

Human trafficking is defined in Article 3 (see also Box 15.1):

- 'Trafficking in persons' shall mean the recruitment, transportation, transfer, harbouring or receipt of persons, by means of the threat or use of force or other forms of coercion, of abduction, of fraud, of deception, of the abuse of power or of a position of vulnerability or of the giving or receiving of payments or benefits to achieve the consent of a person having control over another person, for the purpose of exploitation. Exploitation shall include, at a minimum, the exploitation of the prostitution of others or other forms of sexual exploitation, forced labour or services, slavery or practices similar to slavery, servitude or the removal of organs. (Article 3, Trafficking Protocol) (UN, 2000: 3)

It is important to recognize that the Trafficking Protocol is one of three supplementary protocols to the *Convention Against Transnational Organised Crime*. All three Protocols (the other two are: *The Protocol against the Smuggling of Migrants by Land, Sea and Air*, and *The Protocol against the Illicit Manufacturing and Trafficking in Firearms, Their Parts and Components and Ammunition*) are focused on these offences as *transnational crimes* that necessarily involve organized crime. State's Party to the Trafficking Protocol (those who have signed and ratified the Protocol) are *required* to implement legislation to criminalize trafficking and to pursue prosecutions against those who perform, participate in or organize trafficking offences (see Article 5). With regard to supporting victims and redressing

> ## BOX 15.1 DEFINITION OF HUMAN TRAFFICKING
>
> For a situation of exploitation to be identified as human trafficking, there are three interrelated elements that must be present:
>
> 1. opportunity to **access** a person ('recruitment, transportation, transfer, harbouring or receipt of persons')
> 2. via **means** ('threat or use of force or other forms of coercion, of abduction, of fraud, of deception, of the abuse of power or of a position of vulnerability or of the giving or receiving of payments or benefits to achieve the consent of a person having control over another person')
> 3. for the **purpose** of exploitation (sexual or other, as defined in Article 3a).
>
> Article 3b–d clarifies that consent is not relevant if the *means* identified above are present and further clarify that for any child (person aged under 18 years) trafficking can occur even in the absence of the elements related to *access* (see Article 3a–d, Trafficking Protocol).

policy and law that might create or sustain vulnerability to exploitation, these measures are recommended or 'encouraged' (see Articles 9–13). The impact is that the focus and emphasis is on a criminal justice response in the first instance.

As we have outlined in detail elsewhere (Segrave et al., 2017), this means that counter-trafficking efforts have been designed around the goals of identifying victims, providing them with welfare-oriented support while an investigation takes place, with a view to determining which cases can be prosecuted. We and others have argued that there are significant consequences for responding to human trafficking as a law and order issue, in which the priority is on prosecution and punishment of traffickers (see Anderson and Andrijasevic, 2008; Milivojevic and Segrave, 2012). Our main concern is that the consequence of such an approach is the focus on prosecutions as an 'outcome'; however, we argue, there is no direct impact from prosecutions on the broader practice of exploitation. While the US Trafficking in Persons report [TIP report] produces data on prosecution statistics related to human trafficking, as researchers we understand that laws in every country are different and such data tells us very little. Instead, we need to ask how 'success' is defined, and how we can measure 'effectiveness' and 'impact'. We identify some ways to achieve this below.

Background to the development of the Protocol

It has been well canvassed by various authors (see Doezema, 2005; Outshoorn, 2015) that what underpinned the development of the Protocol was a specific concern around sex trafficking, which was heavily influenced by the ongoing debate between feminist activists regarding prostitution as violence against women versus advocates for sex work as a legitimate form of labour. We recommend reading further into this, not least because it offers an explanation for the division, particularly in the first decade of human trafficking research and counter-trafficking strategies that focused almost exclusively on sex trafficking. We are researchers who recognize migrant sex workers as labourers, and who adopt a critical approach to the gendered moralizing that occurred in the early responses to sex trafficking (for more, see Segrave et al., 2009).

The impact of the Trafficking Protocol

It is important to recognize that only nations that sign and ratify have obligations under the Protocol. We emphasize this because understanding the obligations of nations and their engagement with the Trafficking Protocol is important to undertaking research that seeks to understand and assess both how and why (and if at all) they have implemented particular counter-trafficking strategies. It is also important to note that there are very limited mechanisms of review at the international level and that these mechanisms are weak (Milivojevic and Segrave, 2012). This highlights the necessity for well-designed, independent research. In relation to the Trafficking Protocol, the Working Group on Trafficking in Persons (WGTIP) was established in 2005 to oversee the implementation of the Protocol and to identify weaknesses and gaps; however, there has been no commitment to rigorous evaluation of counter-trafficking efforts to determine their impact in its reports (see, for example, WGTIP, 2015). While they make recommendations, they cannot enforce sanctions or other measures to ensure that states party to the Protocol comply with their recommendations.

Parallel to the development of the Trafficking Protocol, the US introduced legislation in 2000 to implement a range of domestic counter-trafficking bodies and policies. Included within this was the direction to the US Department of State to produce an annual TIP report, to review US and other selected nations' efforts to address human trafficking. This has been in place since 2001. It has expanded the number of nations included over time, and it reviews counter-trafficking efforts based on US-defined criteria. It judges nations by placing them on a Tier level, with Tier One being the highest standard, and Tier Three being the lowest. It has been subject to ongoing criticism (Chuang, 2006; Gallagher, 2011); however, it has also been recognized as a strong diplomatic tool, particularly for nations dependent on US funding, as sanctions are the currency of poor TIP report results and failure to proactively respond and redress the specific concerns outlined in the TIP report. This reporting mechanism plays an influential role globally in the counter-trafficking agenda, and is relied on as an evidence base for its effectiveness. However, the TIP report assessment is not an 'impact' measure. For example, there is no contact with victims to make assessments of the quality of the services provided, there is no way to indicate whether these efforts reduce exploitation and there is a reliance on process outcomes as indicators of 'success'. The consequence, as many have argued (Feingold, 2010; Goodey, 2008, 2011; Milivojevic, 2012; Steinfatt, 2011; Wylie, 2016), is a reliance on the reproduction of numbers (such as estimates of the scope and breadth of human trafficking and criminal justice data, e.g. the number of prosecutions).

What we know about human trafficking

In the two decades (almost) since the introduction of the Trafficking Protocol, the concept of human trafficking has become mainstream in the international community. In some ways, this has potentially positive consequences: such as better recognition of victims/survivors, strategies in place to support gatekeepers and authorities to make more informed decisions and, significantly, more funding for research and counter-trafficking efforts. The downside, especially for an issue as broad and debated as human trafficking, is that there is a swathe of experts and committed practitioners all working towards different ends and competing for resources, whilst seeking to claim success and expertise. The evidence base, however, is replete with studies that begin with 'the proviso that data on the extent of the problem are unreliable' (Wylie, 2016: 3). This poses a problem in relation to the fast-moving policy context – there are no reliable measures of impact and there is no agreed definition of success. Consequently, it becomes appealing for any successful criminal justice outcome, such as a criminal conviction, to be heralded as a 'success'. Our concern is that little attention is paid to the needs of victims, who are often constructed within very narrow terms (see Doezema, 2010; O'Connell-Davidson, 2015), and the broader context within which trafficking occurs. We think a beginning point is to recognize the complexity of 'the problem' of human trafficking in the first instance, and the resulting complexity of what is required to reduce this form of exploitation.

Once definitions have been established, identifying and quantifying the problem in all research is important. Articulating what we know, including the size and scope of the problem, is part of the researcher's task. However, a significant issue in the field of human trafficking research is reliable empirical data. How prevalent is human trafficking? This question is extremely difficult to answer, and, given the nature of human trafficking, as a clandestine practice that involves (often) unlawful non-citizens (see Box 15.2) who for various reasons avoid any engagement with authorities (and upon contact may simply be deported), we will always be approximating the nature and extent of the problem. There are numbers promoted globally and often repeated, for example the International Labour Organisation (ILO) claims that there are 'nearly 21 million people around the world in forced labour' (www.ilo.org/global/topics/forced-labour/policy-areas/statistics/lang--en/index.htm). However, the ILO includes human trafficking as a subset of the forced labour figure, and consequently the percentage of human trafficking within the 21 million figure is not specified. More recently, the Walkfree Foundation produced a 'global estimate' of slavery, and asserts that today 40.3 million people are enslaved (www.globalslaveryindex.org – accessed 3 August 2018). Close scrutiny of the methodology that leads to the identification of numbers is recommended. Commentators writing in 2005 and 2014 attest to the problem of knowing the numbers. The Global Slavery Index is a laudable attempt to go some way towards this, but it uses a broad definition of modern slavery (which extends beyond human trafficking) and its definition and the methodology utilised to access and extrapolate data do limit the accuracy of the Index (see Box 15.2).

BOX 15.2   DEFINITIONAL ISSUES

Modern Slavery tends to be a term that 'includes the crimes of human trafficking, slavery and slavery like practices such as servitude, forced labour, forced or servile marriage, the sale and exploitation of children, and debt bondage.' (see www.walkfreefoundation.org/understand/). This is a broad range of practices and there are significant challenges in accessing accurate data relating to all or any of these practices. So too, specific and different responses are required to respond to these practices. It is important to be careful when using such data and extrapolating to human trafficking, specifically.

Unlawful non-citizen = unlawfully in the country (e.g. entered the country without a valid visa, or on false documents) or in breach of visa conditions, for example working when their visa does not allow paid employment (rendering their lawful status unlawful). Other terms may be used in the popular media and by politicians and others, such as 'illegal' or undocumented. We do not use that terminology because we adopt the position that no person is illegal, and we recognize that some unlawful non-citizens are documented.

The challenge in estimating the extent to which human trafficking occurs is an ongoing problem given the consequences of inaccuracy, as Tyldum and Brunovskis (2005: 18) have argued:

> overestimating the extent of a phenomenon can have equally negative consequences as underestimating it. Uncritically using or publishing findings not based on sound methodologies may result in misinformation and hinder the creation of relevant policies and appropriate programmes.

The limitations of the data (see Segrave et al., 2009: 12–15 and Gozdziak, 2015) are worth exploring. The work of Andreas and Greenhill (2010) on the broad interrogation of global crime data is useful in this respect, as is that of Goodey (2008) and Weitzer (2014) regarding the production of global human trafficking trend data.

RESEARCH ON HUMAN TRAFFICKING

Human trafficking research is a very broad field with a diverse range of research designs and research approaches. In many ways, this also reflects the diverse disciplinary backgrounds of researchers contributing to the knowledge base. Here, we focus on two broad areas of research: qualitative research via in-depth interviewing and documentary analysis. For the first part, we focus less on the process of doing interviews and instead seek to highlight the complexities and challenges of undertaking qualitative research in this field. In the second part, we draw attention to some key examples of diverse documentary (by which we mean a variety of texts) analyses in the field, and offer some explanation of the types of research tools being applied. We focus on this because, as indicated above, research on human trafficking is more than just about the 'crime' itself and includes, but is not limited to:

- decision making by immigration and criminal justice authorities
- supply chains and issues of responsibilities of corporations to labourers at the resource harvesting and assembly end all the way through to consumers
- the production of data, testing empirical methods for identifying prevalence
- the production of narratives of human trafficking via fictional media (film, books, etc.)
- the examination of reports on 'success' in counter-trafficking strategies
- the interrogation of criminal justice and prosecution data to better understand the attrition of cases from identification to prosecution and to examine which cases are being prosecuted and why.

For undergraduate and postgraduate students, there are significant challenges to undertaking research in this area. Access is difficult due to reaching participants (which requires time to build relationships and rapport with key people and agencies). Ethics approval to undertake research in this area can be difficult, depending on your focus and your intended participant group (for example, victims are perceived to be a vulnerable population often requiring more rigorous ethical safety nets to be put in place, and working with police can require additional ethics approval from within their agency). There are also, often, issues of timeliness, as it is difficult to overcome these research hurdles and still have time to undertake research and produce a high-quality analysis.

An alternative approach might be that you think more broadly about how we understand and respond to human trafficking at the local, national, regional and international levels, and the consequences of this. This too requires careful, rigorous qualitative research that examines, for example, policy, news media and/or art (in forms including cinema, written fiction, visual art), but due to the accessibility of the primary data it may be more practicable for the novice and early career researcher.

Research design

Two points regarding research design. First, we bear in mind one goal of research: to examine policy and practice with independence and rigour. The process should be transparent and replicable. Second, regardless of the type of research being undertaken, it is essential to identify the research focus. Previous research on human trafficking has explored a range of issues, adopting various approaches, as detailed in Box 15.3.

BOX 15.3   RESEARCH ON HUMAN TRAFFICKING

- Migration and border control and how these controls impact individuals (see Segrave, 2015)
- Debates regarding abolition and focused more specifically on sex work and/or prostitution laws and policies (see Doezema, 2010)
- The experiences of those implementing border control and the decision-making processes of those making discretionary decisions (see Pickering and Ham, 2014)
- Migration journeys and routes and/or the trafficking process through documenting these experiences (see Ford et al., 2012)
- Narratives of human trafficking (see Andrijasevic and Mai, 2016).

Researching by talking: interview-based research

There are a range of approaches to doing interview-based research. We focus here on semi-structured interviews. This form of interview enables the researcher to have a consistent set of themes or questions that guide each interview and allow for consistency across the interviews, so that key issues are addressed to some extent in every interview. However, this style of interview allows the researcher and the participant to also follow the flow of conversation, to explore in detail issues or ideas that arise in the course of the interview that may diverge from the research focus. Effectively, this style of interview allows the original research questions to be addressed whilst also enabling unanticipated ideas and issues to arise. As other chapters in this book deal more specifically with interviews, we focus on issues that arise in preparing for fieldwork, and pursuing participants who are victims/survivors of human trafficking.

For our research, which spans multiple projects that inform this chapter, our broad aims and objectives have generally been around the implementation and impact of counter-trafficking policies and border and labour enforcement practices. Across these projects, our aim is to document implementation practices (this includes the attitudes and understanding of key stakeholders, such as police implementing counter-trafficking efforts) with a focus on challenges that arise largely due to the interaction of unlawful migration status and exploitation. Our work has also sought to document the impact of counter-trafficking efforts via talking to migrant workers who have not been recognized as victims, and those who have. We view their experience as critical both to making sense of the impact of the official response, and offering a more complex understanding of how exploitation is experienced and managed by individuals. Given these objectives, interview and documentary research is well suited to achieving this.

Ethics: being prepared

Within every university setting, there is a formal ethics body that governs proposed research and determines whether the design and the various aspects of mitigating risk and harm to participants, the community and the researcher are met.

In the field of human trafficking research, there are additional sensitivities to consider. Those who have been victims of human trafficking may, at the time of the research, be unlawful non-citizens, and this poses a number of challenges. Careful thought and ethical strategizing will be required. Your ethical position will need to articulate how you plan to:

- respond to a situation where the participant becomes upset or traumatized
- support a participant if they are upset or traumatized *after* the interview
- respond to being informed of criminal activity
- respond to a participant asking you directly for assistance (e.g. money, a letter of support, migration advice).

Our own efforts to mitigate these issues are detailed in Box 15.4.

BOX 15.4   RISK MITIGATION IN THE DESIGN AND CONDUCTING OF RESEARCH RELATED TO HUMAN TRAFFICKING

We can mitigate risk by:

- ensuring that we are connected to NGOs that are equipped to provide trauma support
- ensuring that we offer information about free telephone lines (which have translation options) that can be contacted at any time
- ensuring that we are speaking to participants who are very clear on the research we are undertaking and the purpose of that research
- giving participants the option to bring a support person to the interview
- clarifying our role as researchers

- reaffirming that the participant has no obligation to the research: they can stop/pause/leave/withdraw at any time
- if there is a payment/gift to participants, giving this at the start of the interview and not at the end (in our early research, we were not able to do this, due to financial constraints, but we now build this into research grant applications)
- ensuring we have identified criminal justice and other support persons/organizations to connect participants to if participants are seeking this.

As researchers, we have primarily been interested in the policing of the border and the implementation of counter-trafficking strategies, and this has been an important standpoint for us. We have specifically undertaken research that is not seeking to explore every aspect of exploitation any person has endured, but to focus on men and women's experiences as migrants, as (at times) unlawful migrants and/or unlawful labourers, and their interactions with authorities. This has influenced the extent to which the issues identified above have arisen, but they have arisen. We urge researchers to be prepared for such research 'problems'. One of the most important aspects of being prepared is having a clear communication process with your supervisors, and ensuring that before, during and after the research is undertaken, there is constant communication regarding the progress of the research. This is important both for the sharing of ideas as new issues and important data emerge in your fieldwork, and to ensure that timely and well-supported solutions can be made to attend to research 'problems'. This can be achieved whilst upholding your ethical and anonymity/confidentiality commitments. Both of us can recall instances of being asked for migration advice, and sitting with participants who cried as they recalled with bitterness the process through which they were deceived into travelling overseas for an employment opportunity that did not eventuate (and which resulted, instead, in various forms of exploitation), and other situations where the invisible line between the researcher and participants was crossed. As feminist researchers who seek to build rapport with participants and to encourage those we interview to speak with us on their own terms, such requests and situations can be confronting. The decision about where you would like to draw a line and how you will manage these situations is informed by the approach you adopt and is always in negotiation. This highlights the delicate balance of ensuring the needs of the respondent are paramount whilst attending to the well-being of the researcher and their needs. In light of this, we also strongly recommend mitigating your own experience by doing this with the support of your supervision team. Semi-structured interviews take significant energy and can have an emotional impact. The planning for this must include how you will manage your own experience, and establishing a plan for regular debriefing and a pathway to counselling and other support for you as a researcher, as well as a clear process for accessing professional support services such as counselling, migration agents or services, legal services and labour rights advocates for participants.

BOX 15.5   MAKING SENSE OF THE RESEARCH EXPERIENCE – PROMOTING WELL-BEING

For both of us, our PhD research involved international travel and months away from our supervisors and support networks. How did we manage this time?

Both of us established a formal arrangement with our supervision team. We determined a regular email and telephone update routine. We committed to writing lengthy update reports about what we'd been doing but also our broader observations of the issues that were the focus of the research, and our own understandings of the complexities of the issues surrounding migration, trafficking, exploitation and criminalization. The PhD reflexive diary is crucial for this. These early reckonings were the beginning stage of the analysis, where we were trying to reflect on the broader themes and issues.

However, the routine also ensured that our supervisors knew we were safe, and it offered us a chance to talk more broadly about the difficulties we were facing. These were not just research difficulties, but also the inevitable loneliness of travelling for months to undertake interviews nearly every day and the lack of company and relief from the issues we focused on. These are not incredible hardships. They can, however, impact different people in different ways. Good research should not require the researcher to be scarred, traumatized or otherwise negatively impacted in order for it to be 'worthy'. The mental and physical health and wellbeing of researchers is foremost: we are better able to listen and be open to new ideas and issues that arise if we are physically and psychologically well, so too the timely analysis and finalization of our work depends on our ability to perform at our best.

Accessing participants

In the field of human trafficking, there is a myriad of politics around victims that results in many outsider researchers (i.e. university-based researchers who are not directly connected to an NGO) being denied access to victims of trafficking (see Bosworth et al., 2011 regarding access and politics). This is at once understandable and a source of frustration. It impacts research in the area if we cannot have independent researchers speaking with those who have been identified as victims of trafficking about their experience, but also about their experience of criminal justice and immigration processes and, of course, of the specific processes and provisions offered to them via victim support packages implemented by NGOs.

That said, it is also necessary to ensure that researchers are not constantly knocking on the door asking for those who have been identified as victims to 'tell us your story'. NGOs are dependent on government and/or private funding. This necessarily results in restricting access. We recommend, first, developing a very clear outline of the research and your expertise in this area when you approach NGOs. We also recommend offering to work together: that is, to pursue any opportunity to produce something useful for that agency whilst also undertaking your own work. This might be separate to your research or connected. NGOs have limited resources and the least researchers can do is offer to support those NGOs that enable our research to be undertaken.

That said, some NGOs will say no. When the answer is no, the project needs to be revised. It is possible and important to interview others (or to go beyond interviews, as we develop in the next section). It is important when writing about your research design and findings that you acknowledge those avenues that were not available to you, in a way that ensures that it is clear you sought to pursue them, but not in a way that is critical of the NGO as such conduct is not useful in the broader pursuit of encouraging high-quality, independent research. Our work always involves practitioners and policy makers, as we are particularly interested in the assumptions that underpin law and policy, the practical realities of the implementation of law and the extent to which the intention of protection measures realizes that intention (see Segrave et al., 2017). That said, in the same way but for different reasons, these state actors and institutions can also say no. There is little that can be done if this happens. We can interview those who have interactions with authorities, those who have witnessed their actions, but the research must shift in focus. Again, it is as important to acknowledge when writing the analysis who said no as it is to identify your participants; this allows the reader to understand that some of the limitations of the research, and the final scope of the project, were not of your original design, but in part due to the refusal of engagement. A significant challenge across criminological research on issues of victimization and exploitation, that is perhaps a more generalized comment regarding interview processes, is that there is an inherent assumption that proximity to victims equals authority in the data produced. We challenge this and we urge students and researchers in criminology to also challenge this. In the area of human trafficking, this can be refuted in many ways, including the following:

1. Focusing on victims is dependent on victims being identified as such. Absent from this are all the unlawful migrant workers who have been exploited who have not been recognized as victims of human trafficking (see Segrave, 2017; Segrave et al., 2009) – to what extent are their voices and experience counted?
2. Focusing on victim experiences, in an interview setting, is inherently limited by the capacity of this type of research. We can only know *their* experiences. It tells us about experiences of migration and exploitation, and potentially about the ways authorities and NGOs conduct themselves, but that is its limit.

3. At times, there is an expectation that we should ask victims what should be done. However, victims, even those who have been through the criminal justice system, are not necessarily well placed to know how we can, for example, improve the way in which prosecutions are conducted.

There are specific areas of individual experience that are critical to understanding human trafficking and to critically engaging with responses at every jurisdictional level. However, it is possible to do important and groundbreaking work in this area that does not rely on interview data. We focus on that in the next section.

DOCUMENTARY ANALYSIS

Human trafficking has captured the imagination of policy makers, news media, fictional media creators and the general community in diverse ways. Here we focus on two areas: policy and law, and fictional media. Within each, we provide an overview of one or two examples of research, and highlight the methodological and/or analytical approach adopted.

Policy and law

There is a growing body of research that seeks to interrogate the assumptions and ideologies that underpin policy and legislation. Research has examined the application of law, for example via examining prosecutions (see *Anti-Trafficking Review*, Issue 6, Special Issue on Prosecuting Human Trafficking, May 2016).

BOX 15.6   DISCOURSE ANALYSIS

Discourse analysis, unlike content analysis which focuses specifically on words, sentences and the quantification of patterns, is focused more broadly on the ideas, values and meanings articulated directly or indirectly in a text (see Burton and Carlen, 2013, for a foundation text on discourse analysis, and Fairclough, 1995, for an explanation of critical discourse analysis). It is more interpretive than scientific, as it identifies meaning, values and assumptions. Through applying a transparent and rigorous approach, this analysis can reveal much that is of value. In the case of human trafficking, for example, it can focus on how expectations and assumptions about victims are produced, or the central pillars of narratives related to unlawful migrant labourers and their experiences of exploitation (via a study of policy, news

---

reporting or via fiction). Such analysis enables extrapolation regarding how knowledge and meaning are produced, as well as the ways in which different policy and legal responses are justified or explained.

An example of this is Erin O'Brien and Michael Wilson's (2015) qualitative study of the US TIP report over 12 years to chart changing policy and rhetoric in response to changes of presidential leadership and administration.

Their review adopted a discourse analysis (see Box 15.6) of these reports. Findings mapped significant changes between the Clinton, Bush and Obama administrations. These changes pertained particularly to the identified causes of trafficking, the articulation of victim identification and the definition of protection, and the emphasis/focus on and reference to the link between prostitution and sex trafficking. O'Brien and Wilson noted that such an analysis brought to the fore the link between various ideological standpoints and the resulting differences in the policy and agenda focus on human trafficking over these periods of time, whilst also allowing the researchers to identify a consistent reliance on criminal justice responses as a priority, regardless of the administration in power.

Media: fictional accounts of human trafficking

Human trafficking captures media attention everywhere. It is the subject of significant news reporting, as some researchers have noted and explored (see Denton, 2010; Gulati, 2012). Human trafficking is also the subject of a significant body of fictional and creative non-fictional works. This ranges from films and television series, through novels, to photographs and documentaries. There is much to be gained by students and researchers in criminology bringing the practices of film and media studies together with criminological examinations of these representations. We know in many fields, such as rape and sexual assault, that changing cultural expectations and understandings of what a crime is (or is not), who a victim is (or is not) and narratives of blame and justice are important in the development of progressive law and policy to address a crime. In the field of human trafficking, there is an emotive and persuasive victim narrative and this is evident throughout fiction generally. Examining the various accounts and representations of human trafficking, as well as considering the implications of these narratives, is an important area of research. Rather than choosing one example, we point readers to a 2016 Special Issue of *Anti-Trafficking Review* (see Andrijasevic and Mai 2016) focused on representations of human trafficking (offering examples of research into historical and contemporary representations of trafficking and slavery from Australia, Cambodia, Nigeria, Serbia, Denmark, the UK and the USA).

SUMMARY AND REVIEW

We have outlined some of the existing approaches to the study of human trafficking. We are keen to encourage researchers to be aware of the key authors in the field, to be alert to cutting-edge debates and to be up front about their own perspective in relation to these. While we may disagree with researchers who adopt an abolitionist perspective, for example, we appreciate that such a position does not automatically compromise the quality of the research. We have also been at pains to suggest that interviews are not the only way to the 'truth' of human trafficking. Rather, some of the most important research at the moment is the work that seeks to pay careful attention to popular discourse and to dismantle the myths and assumptions that underpin it, as one way to create more informed and nuanced understandings of the complexities of human trafficking. It is also critical that the production of data across the full spectrum of the human trafficking industry – from criminal justice data through non-governmental organization reports to TIP reports and assessments of support programmes – is subject to scrutiny. Scrutiny of the research methodologies employed can be a very worthwhile exercise that produces new avenues for inquiry as well as signposting useful research strategies and tools.

The study of human trafficking is a diverse field, attracting interdisciplinary researchers. This chapter has outlined the background to the international response to human trafficking in order to have an understanding of how and why trafficking in persons has become a global issue. We have identified some of the significant gaps in knowledge around human trafficking, the absence of any formal mechanism for evaluation and the need for ongoing independent examinations of all aspects of human trafficking. We have outlined that research in the area of human trafficking is not just about understanding a crime, but also about examining the broader social, political and moral narratives that surround this phenomenon. We need to interrogate the hyperbole that surrounds human trafficking as much as, if not more than, we need to understand the experiences of victims. Finally, we have indicated two key areas of research: interviews and documentary research, and we have mapped some key possibilities in both areas, and some limitations and challenges.

STUDY QUESTIONS AND ACTIVITIES FOR STUDENTS

1. What are three key elements that constitute the definition of human trafficking?

2. Why is it important to broaden our focus beyond sex trafficking in criminological research?

3. What role does the US TIP report play in international engagements with human trafficking? What is the impact of the TIP report on how nation states respond to human trafficking?

4. What are the upsides and downsides of focusing on human trafficking? How can we address the downsides through criminological research?

5. Which measures are the states required to implement, and which ones are only encouraged by the Protocol? Why is this important/problematic and how can criminological research address this issue?

6. What are key contributions of criminological research to our knowledge on human trafficking? What are the key gaps and how can we address them in the future?

7. How can we overcome the challenges in researching human trafficking? What type of research design can assist us in achieving this goal?

8. Why is it important to think beyond the 'victim perspective' in human trafficking research?

9. Review media reports on human trafficking, slavery and labour exploitation over a period of time or in different jurisdictions. How is the exploitation described and understood in these reports, i.e. who is responsible and what is the solution to the problem, if presented?

10. Watch three films on human trafficking (for example, *Lilya 4-ever* (2002), *The Jammed* (2017) and *The Storm Makers* (2014)) and consider the way in which they offer an understanding of why human trafficking occurs, who the victims are and what the solutions to trafficking should be.

11. Undertake a review of common understandings of human trafficking by surveying friends, fellow students and family about how they would define and describe this phenomenon. Review their responses.

12. Look at the reported number of victims of human trafficking in the country you live in and the number of prosecutions over the past 5–10 years. What are the reasons given for these differences by the agencies and authorities responsible for counter-trafficking efforts? What gaps in knowledge can you identify?

13. Identify the agency or agencies responsible for providing support to victims of trafficking in your country. What kinds of support do victims receive and what, if any, restrictions are placed on victims while accessing support? How are these support provisions evaluated? Are these published and/or publicly available? Can you identify key questions that need to be asked about support provisions that would enable us to better understand whether the support provided to victims meets their needs?

SUGGESTIONS FOR FURTHER READING

The sources provided below are primarily places to begin in order to find out about the Trafficking Protocol and the latest developments in relation to this (see UNODC and USDOS) and international developments more broadly (ILO). *The Anti-Trafficking Review* and the *Journal of Human Trafficking* are good sources for academic literature as they are dedicated journals to this area. However, they are issue-based rather than discipline-based journals. So, for students of criminology, it is important to also look at other criminology journals (such as *British Journal of Criminology, Theoretical Criminology, Feminist Criminology*) where research on human trafficking that is criminological in nature is also published.

1. *Anti-Trafficking Review*: www.antitraffickingreview.org/index.php/atrjournal
2. *International Labour Organisation (ILO)*: www.ilo.org/global/topics/forced-labour/policy-areas/statistics/lang--en/index.htm (NB: the ILO is soon to introduce the Global Slavery Observatory and this will be an important resource)
3. *Journal of Human Trafficking*: www.tandfonline.com/loi/uhmt20
4. United Nations Office of Drugs and Crime (UNODC), Convention against Transnational Organized Crime: www.unodc.org/unodc/en/organized-crime/intro/UNTOC.html
5. United States Department of State (UNOS), Trafficking in Persons Reports from 2001 onwards: www.state.gov/j/tip/rls/tiprpt

REFERENCES

Anderson, B. and Andrijasevic, R. (2008) 'Sex, slaves and citizens: the politics of anti-trafficking', *Soundings, 40*: 135–57.

Andreas, P. and Greenhill, K. (eds) (2010) *Sex, Drugs and Body Counts: The Politics of Numbers in Global Crime and Conflict*. Ithaca, NY: Cornell University Press.

Andrijasevic, R. and Mai, N. (2016) 'Editorial: Trafficking (in) representations – Understanding the recurring appeal of victimhood and slavery in neoliberal times', *Anti-Trafficking Review, 7*: 1–10.

Bosworth, M., Hoyle, C. and Dempsey, M. (2011) 'Researching trafficked women: some thoughts on methodology', *Qualitative Inquiry, 17*(9): 769–79.

Burton, F. and Carlen, P. (2013) *Official Discourse: On Discourse Analysis, Government Publications, Ideology and the State*. Oxon: Routledge Revivals Series.

Chuang, J. (2006) 'The United States as global sheriff: using unilateral sanctions to combat human trafficking', *Michigan Journal of International Law, 27*(2): 437–94.

Denton, E. (2010) 'International news coverage of human trafficking arrests and prosecutions: a content analysis', *Women and Criminal Justice*, 20(1–2): 10–26.

Doezema, J. (2005) '"Now you see her, now you don't": sex workers at the UN Trafficking Protocol negotiation', *Social and Legal Studies*, *14*: 61–89.

Doezema, J. (2010) *Sex Slaves and Discourse Masters: The Construction of Trafficking*. London: Zed Books.

Dragiewicz, M. (ed.) (2015) *Global Human Trafficking: Critical Issues and Contexts*. Oxon: Routledge.

Fairclough, N. (1995) *Critical Discourse Analysis: The Critical Study of Language*. Harlow: Longman.

Feingold, D.A. (2010) 'Trafficking in numbers: the social construction of human trafficking data', in P. Andreas (ed.), *Sex, Drugs, and Body Counts: The Politics of Numbers in Global Crime and Conflict*, Ithaca, NY: Cornell University Press, pp. 46–74.

Ford, M., Lyons, L. and van Schendel, W. (eds) (2012) *Labour Migration and Human Trafficking*. Oxon: Routledge.

Gallagher, A. (2011) 'Improving the effectiveness of the international law of human trafficking: a vision for the future of the US Trafficking in Persons reports', *Human Rights Review*, *12*(3): 381–400.

Gallagher, A. (2014) 'The global slavery index is based on flawed data: why does no one say so?', *The Guardian* (online), 29 November. Available at: www.theguardian.com/global-development/poverty-matters/2014/nov/28/global-slavery-index-walk-free-human-trafficking-anne-gallagher (accessed May 2018).

Goodey, J. (2008) 'Human trafficking: sketchy data and policy responses', *Criminology & Criminal Justice*, 8(4): 421–42.

Goodey, J. (2011) 'Data on human trafficking', in J. Winterdyk, B. Perrin and P. Reichel (eds), *Human Trafficking: Exploring the International Nature, Concerns, and Complexities*. Boca Raton, FL: CRC Press, pp. 39–56.

Gozdziak, E. (2015) 'Data matters: issues and challenges for research on trafficking', in M. Dragiewicz (ed.), *Global Human Trafficking: Critical Issues and Contexts*. Oxon: Routledge.

Gulati, G. (2012) 'Representing trafficking: media in the United States, Great Britain, and Canada', in A. Brysk and A. Choi-Fitzpatrick (eds), *From Human Trafficking to Human Rights: Reframing Contemporary Slavery*. Philadelphia, PA: University of Pennsylvania Press.

Lilya 4-ever (2002) Memfis Film et al., release date 23 August 2002.

Milivojevic, S. (2012) 'The state, virtual borders and e-trafficking: between fact and fiction', in J. McCulloch and S. Pickering (eds), *Borders and Crime*. London: Palgrave Macmillan, pp.72–89.

Milivojevic, S. and Segrave, M. (2012) 'Evaluating responses to human trafficking: a review of international, regional and national counter-trafficking mechanisms', in J. Winterdyk, B. Perrin and P. Reichel (eds), *Human Trafficking: Exploring the International Nature, Concerns, and Complexities*. Boca Raton, FL: CRC Press, pp. 233–63.

O'Brien, E. and Wilson, M. (2015) 'Clinton, Bush and Obama: changing policy and rhetoric in the United States Annual Trafficking in Persons report', in M. Dragiewicz (ed.), *Global Human Trafficking: Critical Issues and Contexts*. Oxon: Routledge.

O'Connell-Davidson, J. (2015) *Modern Slavery: The Margins of Freedom*. London: Palgrave Macmillan.

Outshoorn, J. (2015) 'The trafficking policy debates', in M. Dragiewicz (ed.), *Global Human Trafficking: Critical Issues and Contexts*. Oxon: Routledge.

Pickering, S. and Ham, J. (2014) 'Hot pants at the border: sorting sex work from sex trafficking', *British Journal of Criminology, 54*(1): 2–19.

Segrave, M. (ed.) (2013) *Human Trafficking*. Series of the Library of Essays on Transnational Crime. Farnham: Ashgate.

Segrave, M. (2015) 'Labour trafficking and illegal markets', in S. Pickering and J. Ham (eds), *The Routledge Handbook on Crime and International Migration*. Abingdon, Oxon: Routledge, pp. 302–15.

Segrave, M. (2017) *Exploited and Illegal: Unlawful migrant workers in Australia, Melbourne*: Monash University.

Segrave, M. and Milivojevic, S. (2010) 'Auditing the Australian response to trafficking', *Current Issues in Criminal Justice, 22*(1): 63–81.

Segrave, M., Milivojevic, S. and Pickering, S. (2009) *Sex Trafficking: International Context and Response*. Oxon: Routledge.

Segrave, M., Milivojevic, S. and Pickering, S. (2017) *Sex Trafficking and Modern Slavery: The Absence of Evidence* (Vol. 2 of *Sex Trafficking: International Context and Response*). Oxon: Routledge.

Steinfatt, T.M. (2011) 'Sex trafficking in Cambodia: fabricated numbers versus empirical evidence', *Crime, Law and Social Change, 56*(5): 443–62.

Tyldum, G. and Brunovskis, A. (2005) 'Describing the unobserved: methodological challenges in empirical studies on human trafficking', *International Migration, 43*(1/2): 17–34.

United Nations Office on Drugs and Crime (2000) 'United Nations Convention Against Transnational Organized Crime and the Protocols Thereto', available at https://www.ohchr.org/en/profesionalinterest/pages/protocoltraffickinginpersons.aspxe.pdf (accessed 3 August 2018).

United Nations Office on Drugs and Crime (2004) 'United Nations Convention Against Transnational Organized Crime and the Protocols Thereto', available at https://www.unodc.org/documents/treaties/UNTOC/Publications/TOC%20Convention/TOCebook-e.pdf (accessed 3 August 2018).

UNODC (2016) Human Trafficking. Available at: www.unodc.org/unodc/en/human-trafficking/what-is-human-trafficking.html?ref=menuside (accessed 10 May 2018).

Weitzer, R. (2014) 'New directions in research on human trafficking', *The Annals of the American Academy of Political and Social Science, 653*(1): 6–24.

Working Group on Trafficking in Persons (WGTIP) (2015) Action Plan, Valletta Summit, 11–12, 16–18 November. Available at: www.unodc.org/documents/treaties/organized_crime/2015_CTOC_COP_WG4/CTOC_COP_WG4_2015_CRP2.pdf (accessed 10 May 2018).

Wylie, G. (2016) *The International Politics of Human Trafficking*. Dublin: Springer.

CHAPTER CONTENTS

GLOSSARY TERMS

biography
autobiography
life history
interview
life-course study

16

USING BIOGRAPHY AND AUTOBIOGRAPHY IN CRIMINOLOGICAL (AND VICTIMOLOGICAL) RESEARCH

ROSS MCGARRY AND ZOE ALKER

INTRODUCTION

The aim of this chapter is to explore the theoretical and methodological uses of biography and autobiography as a means of critical social inquiry within criminology. First, this chapter explicates the influences of biography within criminological work as a way of emphasizing the juxtaposition between its usefulness and marginal practice. Second, the method of biography is demonstrated in one specific example of the life story of an individual 'criminal' drawn from historical documentary data to reconstruct the personal life of 'others'. Third, within our discussion we reflect on the value of using this method as a mode of social inquiry (i.e. what can we learn from individual life stories?) and offer some critical observations as to what remains absent within criminological work of this nature. We conclude by advocating for the continued use and development of biographical methods as valuable avenues of criminological *and* victimological inquiry.

PLACING BIOGRAPHY AS A METHOD WITHIN CRIMINOLOGY

The Chicago School of Sociology was influential in the development of criminological research into crime and delinquency. In particular, it had a strong proclivity for conducting positivistic research concerned with studying the city of Chicago in relation to social ecology and social disorganization (see Park et al., 1925; Shaw and McKay, 1942). Also developing out of the Chicago School was a strand of research concerned with ethnography and the individual personal lives of marginalized 'others'. Following this influence, Plummer (1983, 2001) informs us that the use of biography (often in concert with ethnography) as a method of social inquiry derives most notably from Thomas and Znaniecki's (1918) study, *The Polish Peasant in America and Europe*. This study is said to have been the first (within Metropolitan social science at least; see Connell, 2007) to have synthesized the 'objective' factors of social life with 'subjective' interpretations of personal experiences (Plummer, 1983, 2001). The purpose of such an approach was to bring meaning to individual personalized accounts of everyday life as relatable to historical and social structures (Plummer, 1983, 2001). From this tradition came a tranche of further sociological studies 'eliciting and analysing the spoken and written words of people who, earlier, had been seen as marginal to history making or to sociological explanation' (Chamberlayne et al., 2000: 3; see also Wengraf et al., 2002). Notable examples include: Thrasher's (1927) *The Gang*, Foote Whyte's (1943) *Street Corner Society*, Anderson's (1923) *The Hobo*, Sutherland's (1937) *The Professional Thief* and Shaw's (1930) *The Jack Roller*. Each of these studies has been influential in various ways for how we now study 'crime' as *sociologically informed* criminologists, with their main methodological commonality focused on the individual lives of others as meaningful sites of sociological and criminological analysis. This brief preliminary discussion offers a situated sense of place for biography as a method within criminological research. However, to unpack this further we need to recognize that the use of biography within sociological research more broadly has had various changes in emphasis over the decades that have made its use and application less popular than this overview might suggest.

THE 'TURN TO BIOGRAPHY' IN SOCIOLOGY AND CRIMINOLOGY

From our contextual discussion above, the latter study mentioned was Clifford Shaw's (1930) *The Jack Roller*. This particular work from Shaw (1930) is highly regarded and popularly known within criminological research. In brief, this study sees the Chicagoan sociologist Clifford Shaw following the experiences of 'Stanley', a delinquent young boy from a deprived background who experienced destitution and imprisonment in his early life. Shaw is said to have met Stanley during his sentencing in the Chicago House of Correction before taking him under his guidance in a bid to understand the circumstances which eventually found him as a 'delinquent', and (less explicitly) rehabilitate him from criminality (Gelsthorpe, 2007). The influences of this principal biographical study have been profound for criminology. As Gelsthorpe (2007: 516) articulates:

> Shaw's sociological and methodological contribution is widely considered to have been hugely significant. Among other things, life history 'illuminated urban institutions and other aspects of behaviour' (Bennett, 1981: 221), it provided a clear depiction of urban pathology, and, critically, it contributed to an understanding of the development of delinquency.

Despite these influential origins, an engagement with biographical research as a common method within criminology has been inconsistent and variously interpreted. Without the time or space to unpack the past 100 years' influence of Chicagoan research in this area, this is perhaps most notable from how biography (and life history) have been addressed in criminological research methods books. For example, within Jupp's (1989: 65) *Methods of Criminological Research* uses of 'life histories' are cited as a means of informal interviews as part of the 'discovery-based ethnographic tradition'. True to its influence on the discipline of criminology, Jupp (1989: 64) informs us that:

> A typical example of a life history from the Chicago School is Shaw's The Jack Roller ... The data took six years to collect and included a number of stages: first, details about

Stanley's arrests were presented to him as signposts around which he could relate his story; second, the verbatim record of this story was presented to Stanley who was asked to expand on it by including greater detail.

Jupp (1989) continues by informing us that 'discovery-based' approaches, which are contingent on long-term interaction with the life (or life story) of another, are instrumental in building theory (such as Shaw's (1930) *The Jack Roller* and Sutherland's (1937) *The Professional Thief*). Maguire (2008) also makes brief comment on the uses of life history as a means of documenting 'criminal lifestyles' in another edited text (see King and Wincup, 2008). Following further acknowledgment of the influences of Shaw (1930) and Sutherland (1937), Maguire (2008: 279) offers some thoughts on the practical pitfalls of 'life history' when applied to the realities of research in the 'field', such as it being contingent on the skills base of the researcher, and finding the 'right person' who is articulate enough to engage with the process as a participant, recall details coherently and not be a 'plausible liar'. Other criminological methods books, however, have had much less to say about biography. For example, in the previous edition of *Doing Criminological Research* (the methods book you are currently reading) some mention of life history was made by Jewkes (2011) in her study of prisoners' preferences for media as a means of discovering more about their identities and feelings of power and powerlessness, while Hudson (2011) had also briefly mentioned life history as a method of interview for critical criminological research. Others, such as Noakes and Wincup's (2004: 116) *Criminological Research*, also acknowledge the influence of Shaw's (1930) work and advocate the use of 'personal accounts of interactions' to illuminate the workings of the criminal justice process. Although they offer no further instruction on how this can be achieved, Wincup's (2017) later edition of this text provided some further insight and encouragement into the uses of autobiography (discussed below) as a way to 'think creatively' when using existing qualitative data. Within Withrow's (2014) *Research Methods in Crime and Justice*, *The Jack Roller* is mentioned passingly as the explanatory material connecting 'case study' and 'ethnography' with no mention of biography or life history. Other texts, such as Crow and Semmens' (2008) *Researching Criminology*, make no reference to the use of life history or biography whatsoever.

All of this is not to castigate the work within these selected texts, each of which has comprehensively covered a myriad of other methodologies and methods. What this observation instead serves to reflect is Goodey's (2000) remark that biographical methods have long been held with some scepticism as a rigorous mode of social inquiry within criminology. This may well be, as Jock Young (2011) noted, due to the 'nomothetic impulse' of what Jupp (1989) had earlier described as the 'criminological enterprise'. In brief, this refers to mainstream criminology's default to quantitative methodologies and preference for survey data as valid sources of generalizable knowledge. The resulting intermittent use of biography as a method within criminological research, and its recent resurgence (evident by its more established presence within this book), has been referred to as the 'narrative turn' (qua Goodey, 2000).

Similar shifts and developments are known as the 'biographical turn' within sociology (see Chamberlayne et al., 2000). The ascendancy of humanistic methods within sociology leading to these eventual 'turns' is highlighted by Plummer (1983: 8; 2001) as a move towards 'the rise of the personal tale' (i.e. the use of textual artefacts, images, film, oral history, life story and autobiography as important sociological sources of 'data'). And as Jupp (1989) further noted, life histories do not necessarily have to pertain to the living; social history has also been employed within criminology to bring attention to the present by using historical documents to resurrect, rebuild and critically reflect on the past. Within the following sections, we aim to demonstrate the use of such approaches to method to help critically explore one particular example of biography concerned with the narrative history of a 'criminal', and the more peripheral autobiography of the 'victim'.

BIOGRAPHICAL CRIMINOLOGICAL INQUIRY

The use of biography within criminological inquiry remains a paradox to researchers. On the one hand, biographies humanize offenders and redirect their lives away from social margins and place them front and centre an authoritative experience. But, as Goodey (2000) has noted, the use of biographical methods within criminology has been treated with scepticism. 'Criminology, as a social science discipline', Goodey (2000: 474) writes, 'has never embraced the idea of research that is based on the study of the individual'. In particular, criminology's scepticism over biography is due to the emphasis these narratives place on the personal aspects of a 'criminal life' which foreground notions of 'criminal' character and ignore the importance of placing such lives within their social and historical contexts. As Stanley (1993) notes of Merton's (1988) appeal for a 'truly sociological autobiography' that explores the interactional connections between social and cultural locales and structural conditions, so too does Goodey (2000: 474) urge scholars to 'synthesize the individual with the social'. Practical examples of how biography can be practised in these ways as a criminological and victimological research method can be found in contributions from Goodey (2000), Holloway and Jefferson (2000), McGarry and Walklate (2015) and McGarry (2016) for example. For the purposes of our current discussion however, we instead look to digitally produced historical data as a means of constructing biographical information.

Biographies of criminal 'others'

Criminal biographies have a long history. From dramatic adaptations of the notorious early eighteenth-century thief and gaol-breaker Jack Sheppard, to the sensationalist twentieth-century accounts of 'The Krays', criminal biographies have always generated cultural interest. But it is essential to remember that these popular narratives work to mythologize criminal individuals and events (Rogers, 2016). From the 'Ordinary of Newgate' to dramatic retellings of the Confessions of the Condemned (see Box 16.1), these sensationalist accounts were repackaged for an audience eager to glance at the lives of the criminal 'other', and written with the purpose of instructing its readership on how to avoid lives of moral depravity. These accounts then hold more value to researchers as examples of morally didactic reform literature than as authentic retellings of life stories.

Often developed for the popular market, such accounts sensationalize aspects of individual biographies rather than focus on their broader social contexts, including, for example, structural inequalities such as poverty, institutionalized discrimination such as and police bias that inevitably played a part in offending trajectories (Godfrey, 2016).

BOX 16.1   THE ORDINARY OF NEWGATE'S ACCOUNT OF THE BEHAVIOUR, CONFESSION AND DYING WORDS OF CONDEMNED CRIMINALS

The Ordinary of Newgate, as the chaplain of Newgate prison, published accounts of prisoners' last dying speeches and their behaviour on the gallows at Tyburn, as well as details of their lives and crimes. These accounts sold thousands, 'earning [the Chaplain] up to £200 per year' and 'over 400 editions were published, containing biographies of approximately 2,500 executed criminals' (www.oldbaileyonline.org/static/Ordinarys-accounts.jsp). Historian Peter Linebaugh argues that the Ordinary's accounts of the condemned were reliable in his accounting of their birth, occupation, religion and crimes committed (Linebaugh, 1977), and it can be argued that the dying speeches provided a space for criminals to tell their stories and repair their reputations (www.oldbaileyonline.org/static/Ordinarys-accounts.jsp).

Biography and life-course criminology

Biographies differ from life-course approaches in myriad ways, but two reasons are especially significant: first, biographies and autobiographies are subjective accounts of the individual. By contrast, life-course approaches view the individual's life trajectory through a series of interconnected lenses: context, linked lives, agency and timing. Thus, scholars of life-course inquiries present individuals' lives as a product of shifting and interlocking social, economic and political values, structures and contexts (Barnwell, 2017). Popular criminal biographies often emphasize, if not glamorize, criminal activity. Works which divorce an individual's 'criminal career'

from the context/s in which such lives were lived, should be treated with scepticism by social science researchers. 'Criminal' biographies, however, can hold merit when treated in critically sensitive ways. As Goodey (2000) argues, if deployed within criminology it allows us to place individuals central to our analysis and permits a reassessment of their social, structural, cultural and political situations by examining 'turning points' in their lives. Goodey (2000) focuses on Denzin's (1989: 70) 'epiphany' moments, arguing that 'turning points' in one's life can be a useful framework for interpreting an individual's relationship to crime within a broader social context. Such notions that life events – schooling, marriage, employment, and so on – are related to crime and desistance, have been the foundation of life-course criminology since the 1930s.

Defined as 'the study of life-course events, transitions and trajectories and their relation to stability and change in crime involvement' (McLaughlin and Muncie, 2013: 254), 'life course' studies have a long trajectory within criminology (Farrington and Ttofi, 2015; Farrington et al., 2006, 2013; Glueck and Glueck, 1930, 1934, 1950, 1968; Sampson and Laub, 1993, 1997, 2003, 2006. See also J. Sarnecki and C. Carlsson in this volume). Life-course criminologists (see, for example, Benson, 2013) collate individual biographies of offenders and explore the relationships between crime pathways and life-course transitions (i.e. marriage, employment, family formation, other life events) as a means of understanding change at both the personal and the collective level. Placing individual lives and their transitional moments (i.e. entry into school, marriage, family formation, experience of the criminal justice system) – within their social, political, economic and cultural contexts invites criminologists to examine how these transitions contribute to crime and desistance (see Goodey, 2000, for example). Furthermore, by adding each individual life history into a database of several hundred or more lives enables a deeper understanding of the pathways into, and out of, offending. This type of criminological research is driven by two broad – but key – questions: first, are there social factors which make some people more prone to criminality? Second, what social factors make offenders more likely to either persist in or desist from offending? An early and highly influential example of life-course research emerged in America during the 1930s through Sheldon and Eleanor Glueck's infamous study of young offenders (see Box 16.2 and Box 13.4 on page 308).

BOX 16.2   THE GLUECKS' INFAMOUS STUDY OF YOUNG OFFENDERS

Sheldon and Eleanor Glueck charted the 'criminal careers' of 500 young male offenders committed to Massachusetts reform schools and compared them with a control group of 500 non-offending peers, in order to identify the social factors

(Continued)

---

that triggered the onset and persistence of offending (Glueck and Glueck, 1930, 1934, 1950, 1968). The Gluecks' study inspired a wealth of life-course criminological research, including the Cambridge study of Delinquent Development which followed the lives of 400 young male offenders from South London (Farrington et al., 2006, 2013), the Pittsburgh Youth Study which followed 1500 men up to the age of 35 (Jennings et al., 2015) and the Dunedin Longitudinal Study which traced 1000 people born in early 1970s New Zealand. These studies demonstrate the potential that biographies hold when they are collated as a large quantitative sample. These studies applied multivariate analysis to identify key patterns across criminals' lives, including marriage, employment and military service, to assess which social, personal and legal factors impinged on or encouraged their desistance.

History, digitization and biography

Over the past decade, historians of crime have adopted life-course methodology to reconstruct the lives of offenders whose lives would otherwise be forgotten or ignored: 'This approach is holistic and takes in all of the features of a person's life, not just their criminal careers, and does so from the time they were born till the time they died' (Godfrey, 2016: 145). As Godfrey (2016: 146) contends, the life-course approach, with its focus on the personal as well as legal experiences of offenders, 'forces historians to see periods of offending as unusual and secondary in the lives of most offenders'. He continues: 'It emphasizes the humanity of the subject under study – the criminal – and encourages a sympathetic and empathetic response' (Godfrey, 2016: 146. See also P. Cox, H. Shaw and B. Godfrey, Chapter 8).

Contemporarily, the digitization of historical data sets, including the criminal registers, census, and birth, marriage and death records, has enabled researchers to piece together the social, personal and legal worlds of Victorian offenders (see Box 16.3 for further details). Using this data, it is possible to reconstruct a criminal life from the cradle to the grave and examine a chronological series of events, including marriage, family formation, divorce, military service, their employment and residential patterns, alongside records of their offending and punishments by searching for them through genealogical sites (including Ancestry and Findmypast, amongst others). These sources facilitate an understanding of how personal circumstances, legal and socio-economic policies and events impacted on the lives of individuals. And, when we look at a large sample of individuals via such data, it is possible to examine patterns of recidivism and desistance. In doing so, the collation and synthesis of multiple individual lives encourage historians to ask contemporary 'what works?' questions of criminal justice practices in the past and the present. This has been made more possible through the Digital Panopticon project which synthesizes criminal, legal and social records from London and Australia.

> ## BOX 16.3 CRIMINAL LIVES (2007) AND SERIOUS OFFENDERS (2010)
>
> Lucy Frost and Hamish Maxwell-Stewart (1997) examined the lives of habitual offenders who were transported to Australia in the nineteenth century. Godfrey, Cox and Farrall (2007, 2010) combined archival and digital resources to reconstruct the lives of persistent offenders who were sentenced at Crewe magistrate courts in the nineteenth century. The studies, *Criminal Lives* (2007) and *Serious Offenders* (2010), used historical evidence to explore the impact of Victorian justice measures introduced to quell recidivism, including the Habitual Criminals Act 1869. These studies demonstrated that desistance tended to take place away from the criminal justice system and argued that marriage and employment were often stabilizing factors. Criminal Lives and Serious Offenders inspired research into different 'types' of offenders, including women (Turner and Johnston, 2016; Williams, 2014) and young people (Godfrey et al., 2017).

THE DIGITAL PANOPTICON: FROM 'STANLEY' TO 'SCANNELL'

The Digital Panopticon project investigates the effectiveness of punishments, including imprisonment and transportation, in reducing or exacerbating offending by comparing the life experiences of 90,000 criminals sentenced at the Old Bailey between 1790 and 1925. This resource represents the next stage in the 'industrial production' of criminal lives. It is, as Godfrey (2016: 150) argues, 'biographical research on an industrial scale'. The Digital Panopticon is a public, searchable website, aimed at a wide range of users. It weaves together hitherto disparate fragments of the lives of those convicted of criminal offences and follows their journeys from the cradle to the grave. This resource allows users to search for individuals across multiple data sets, examine and compare the lives of offenders sentenced to imprisonment and transportation, and interrogate and develop new research questions for understanding and exploiting vast and complex bodies of social, personal and criminal data. As Godfrey (2016: 150) argues, 'That this data "recovers" and pieces together the lives of the most dispossessed and criminalised in society is remarkable', and, due to data restrictions on contemporary crime data, 'We will know more about eighteenth- and nineteenth-century prisoners serving time today'.

Life through a (biographical) lens

The Digital Panopticon resource usefully does the work of the historian or criminologist. Previously, researchers utilizing historic data for life-course studies had to reconstruct offenders' lives by trawling through archives and online sites such as Ancestry, Findmypast, and birth, marriage and death records, for example. But the Digital Panopticon has synthesized social, criminal and legal data sets from Hanoverian and Victorian London, and Australia. The site then allows students and researchers to put an individual criminal life 'under the microscope', or researchers can use the site as a 'macroscope' and explore thousands of criminal lives.

Having extolled the uses of historical digital data to understand the criminal lives of 'others', we now put this into practice by drawing on a case study of a Victorian offender: Peter Scannell. This particular offender features on the Digital Panopticon website, and we employ his case here to illustrate the potential of using biography as a 'lens' through which to examine the complex dynamics of crime and punishment when experienced as part of the life course (see Box 16.4). What we encourage you to consider when reading through this example is not only what is included within the outlined biography, but also what is missing or unseen.

BOX 16.4   PETER SCANNELL

Peter Scannell was born in London in 1851 to his father Daniel, a brick labourer, and his mother, Catherine. In 1861, Peter lived with his parents who rented out a room in their apartment in Kensington to a family of three. In 1870, Peter, then 19, was charged at Southwark magistrate court for violently robbing William Westwood of a watch, along with co-defendants John Mason, 20, and William Grant, 21. All three of the defendants were described by *Lloyd's Weekly News* as 'well-known thieves'. Scannell wasn't convicted for this offence as 'unfortunately the evidence as to their identities was not sufficient for a jury to convict them, therefore it was his [the judge's] duty to discharge them'. However, official bias on behalf of the courts and police clearly impacted on Peter's future intersections with the criminal justice system. The judge remarked that, 'They were well known, and [had] a very strong suspicion attached to them'. Police inspector Bull corroborated and claimed that 'since the prisoners had been locked up there had been no street robberies in the vicinity of the Waterloo Road' (*Lloyd's Weekly News*, 20 June 1869: 4). Six months later, in January 1870, Peter appeared at the Old Bailey where he was convicted of feloniously receiving stolen goods and was sentenced to seven years' imprisonment in Millbank prison. Repeated periods of incarceration appeared to hinder rather than aid Scannell's desistance. His prison licence notes Peter's height, appearance, including tattoos and scars, his occupation, marital

---

status, previous character, as well as his behaviour in prison. These details, such as Scannell's tattoos, for example, are crucial for examining prisoners' identities, and inform us about how their identities were often socially constructed. Conversely, biometric data can tell us about the impact of imprisonment and poverty on health, for example. And when related to broader social patterns, they reveal significant information about crime and punishment. Following his release in 1877, Peter didn't appear to re-offend. He married at the age of 41, and later died age 47 in 1898.

Source: The Digital Panopticon (www.digitalpanopticon.org)

Biographies like Peter's hold significant value when attempting to examine patterns of offending and desistance. They also pre-date the famous Chicagoan example of the 'jack roller', Stanley, by a considerable historical margin. At an individual level, these biographies emphasize the importance of employment, residential stability and marriage in encouraging desistance from crime. Conversely, these narratives also reveal the trigger factors which encouraged the onset and persistence of offending, such as the poverty experienced by men in casual labouring occupations which encouraged a variety of Peter's life experiences as an offender, including: his onset into theft; the policing of working-class 'rough' masculinities; the regulation of street life through his robbery prosecution; as well as the impact of institutionalization through his repeated spells of imprisonment. When biographies like Peter's are constituted as part of a much larger sample, such as those linked together through the Digital Panopticon, it will be possible to examine patterns of recidivism and desistance on a larger, and potentially global, scale.

When placed within their social, political, legal, economic and cultural contexts, the narrative of biographies can therefore be a 'lens' through which to examine broader structural factors which promote desistance and recidivism. Indeed:

> The lives of the poor can then be contextualized; their 'moral failings' and hereditary weaknesses' revealed as prejudicial labels for people with low financial and social capital who were unable to respond to the inequalities of the prevailing socio-economic system. (Godfrey, 2016: 143)

Historians of crime have long sought to recover the lives of the forgotten as part of the drive to reconstruct 'history from below'. Initially inspired by E.P. Thompson's survey of the working classes, crime historians have sought to explore the social, spatial and legal worlds of offenders in the eighteenth and nineteenth centuries, whilst not condemning their lives to 'the condescension of posterity' (Thompson, 1963: 12). As Godfrey (2016: 149) concludes:

The analysis of the whole life-course of individuals and the representation of those lives in ways which humanize the poor and disadvantaged and make visible the challenges which shaped their lives, is, in essence, an attempt to retrospectively 'rescue' lives.

With the historical and contemporary contexts of biographical methods within criminology now outlined, we now turn our attention to ways in which these approaches to 'doing criminological research' can be considered critically.

THINKING CRITICALLY ABOUT BIOGRAPHICAL METHODS WITHIN CRIMINOLOGY

Returning to our starting points in this chapter, and the work of Clifford Shaw and *The Jack Roller*, there are methodological questions that even this most revered and fundamental study raise for the more general use of biography as a method within criminology. One such question includes: what relationship existed between Shaw (the researcher) and Stanley (the 'subject')? We learn about this from Gelsthorpe (2007), who argues that biographical methods have the ability to transgress the iterative interaction between subjective experiences and objective social circumstances (as was facilitated by Thomas and Znaniecki (1918) in *The Polish Peasant*). By focusing on the relationship between the researcher and the 'subject', a variety of methodological questions are brought to the fore – for example, questions about:

- the extent of Shaw's influence on the authenticity of Stanley's account of his own experiences (i.e. it was perhaps too logically structured)
- the overall paternal influence Shaw *may* have had across Stanley's life course beyond the research project of *The Jack Roller*
- the origins of the rich descriptive insights of delinquency and social disorganization in Chicago within Shaw's other work (i.e. the Chicago Area Project)
- the nomothetic influences of the Chicago School of Sociology at the time of writing and the holding back of any account of the psychological influence that either (researcher or 'subject') had on the other (Gelsthorpe, 2007).

By drawing on historical documentary data (such as the Digital Panopticon, as we have above), some of these methodological issues are circumnavigated; problems inherent to symbolic interactionist studies, such as *The Jack Roller*, are unlikely to be encountered when using historical data. In other words, the arrangement of biographies via historical documentary analysis by criminological historians paints its own picture by allowing the documentary evidence to 'speak for itself' (as it were). Nevertheless, if we take both Stanley and Scannell's lives as exemplars of criminological biography, we can raise a unifying conceptual problem that underpins the theoretical and methodological practices at work in the use of criminological biography both past and present.

To help explore this critical line of inquiry, another methodological question we want to pose is: 'Where is William'? At this point, you might be better first asking yourself, '*who*' rather than '*where*' he is. If you didn't quite catch this, it is not particularly surprising. We suggest a great many 'Williams' have been missed in studies of crime and deviance. In answer to the question of *who* William is: from Box 16.4 above, William Westwood is Peter Scannell's (purported) *victim* of theft. Therefore, in answer to the question of *where* William is: despite his centrality to the history being reconstructed, his own experiences and life story are nowhere to be found in this biographical account. Having made this observation, we urge you to think about what issues this raises for criminological research and biographical methods.

If the uses of biography within sociology and criminology have been subject to certain 'turns' or 'rises' over the decades, within victimology (i.e. the empirical and theoretical study of 'victims') its uses have been almost non-existent (see McGarry, 2016 for an extended discussion). The reasons for this are akin to those noted earlier in this chapter with regard to criminology. In brief, 'conventional victimology' (qua Walklate, 1989) – similar to that of the 'criminological enterprise' (qua Jupp, 1989) – has historically been dominated by a disposition for the scientific measurement of criminal victimization, with a particular emphasis on victimization that takes place in public (i.e. on the 'street') rather than in private (i.e. at home). Positivist victimology (see Miers, 1989) juxtaposes the 'criminal' and the 'victim' in a linear relationship with one another and assumes a 'principle of differentiation', whereby to be a non-victim equates to being 'normal', rendering those who experience *criminal* victimization as 'abnormal' (Walklate, 2006). Preferred ways of documenting and analysing such 'abnormality' then come through the use of large-scale surveys which reduce the complex experiences of criminal victimization to statistical data sets from which patterns and comparisons can indeed be made, but the depth and nuance of the lived experience of victimization is disconnected. Challenges to the reductionism of such experiences were made by writers in the critical victimology tradition (see Mawby and Walklate, 1994). As Francis (2017) outlines, a critical victimological perspective draws on theoretical aspects of socialist feminism and left realism, and mobilizes victim survey data differently by asking critical questions of structure, agency, gender and vulnerability, for example, in relation to victimization – the purpose of which is to unpack the social and cultural contexts of how victimization is experienced, and identify how the abstraction of such experiences is used for politically divisive purposes and policy formation. One way of developing this critical strand of victimological inquiry is through the use of autobiography (see Stanley, 1992, 1993). The entry point into using autobiography as proposed within the context of this discussion derives from the advancement of what is coming to be established as cultural victimology, 'a victimology attuned to human agency, symbolic display, and shared emotion' (Mythen, 2007: 464). This has been variously developed in relation to the theoretical and policy implications of representation as derived from visual artefacts (i.e. images) via 'visual victimology' (see Walklate et al., 2014), the centring of autobiographical reflection, personal testimony, and the role of the 'victimologist as witness' (see McGarry and Walklate, 2015).

To explore this popularized appetite for autobiographical reflection, we encourage you to browse the shelves of bookshops and supermarkets and pay attention to the number of books there that are written by those who have experienced trauma, harm or victimization. Then, once you have found one that takes your interest, make an attempt at the following activity (see Box 16.5), the purpose of which is to use written autobiography as textual data in order to encourage you to think critically about an experience of 'victimization' far removed from the confines of criminological biography. An analysis from the view of a 'victim' will provide quite a different conceptual insight into the depiction of crime, harm and violence.

BOX 16.5   ACTIVITY – 'VICTIM' AUTOBIOGRAPHY

Select a written autobiography of someone who has experienced trauma, victimization, violence or harm of some sort. Once selected, use the 'biographical continuum' within the article from Goodey (2000) (and later developed by McGarry, 2016) to arrange their life story in a chronological order, identifying significant points throughout the person's narrative (i.e. 'epiphany') that you consider may have influenced the trajectory of their life. Next, attempt to apply victimological concepts (i.e. primary, secondary, direct, tertiary victimization, etc.) to the ways in which their experiences can be accounted for analytically, whilst being attentive and sensitive to their own points of reference to themselves as victims, survivors or otherwise. Finally, try to make connections from their experiences to their structural environment (i.e. social, political, cultural and historical) as influencing, or being influenced by, their experience of victimization, violence or harm, and aim to connect this with how the experience of 'victimization' is frequently politicized and a deeply complex issue, as per critical victimology.

A biographical 'malestream view'

In observing the (alleged) victimization of 'William' in Box 16.4, we also come face to face with a fundamental problem of criminology and victimology that urgently needs to be at the forefront of our imaginations when thinking about the 'victim'.

As reflected in the relationship between Scannell and William, young men are frequently the most likely not only to perpetrate violent crime, but – as Walklate (2007) reminds us, and as found consistently in past and present data from the Crime Survey of England and Wales – it is also young men between the ages of 17 and 25 who are more likely to experience 'violent crime' as constituted by 'street' crime. This normative way of considering crime and victimization alone is what is understood as a 'malestream' view of the social (read victimizing) world (Walklate, 2004: 14).

In recognizing this as a fundamental issue of how the 'problem of crime' and criminal victimization are constructed within the political, policy *and* popular imagination, we encourage you to think about what further issues this now raises for *victimological* research. We suggest that criminological students and researchers should be sensitive towards, and willing to consistently challenge, such normatively depicted and commonly held assumptions relating to the experience of victimization; that which are simply assumed to be perpetrated by 'men' against other 'men', and disproportionately experienced by 'men' in public. To be clear, this is not to diminish nor subjugate such experiences of harm, but to instead put 'gender on the agenda' within biographical and autobiographical research (qua Davies, 2011). If we take, for example, the Crime Survey of England and Wales, we learn from Walby et al. (2014) that what this tells us about the experience of victimization from violent crime is not only misleading, but also understates the extent of gender-based violence against women. For Walby et al. (2014), the cap placed on the reporting of violent offences, and the definitional separation of sexual offences from 'violent crimes', has rendered the issue of domestic and sexual violence against women dramatically underreported in official statistics. By challenging legal and methodological definitions of violent crime as gender-based violence, our normative assumptions relating to young men (i.e. 'William') being the most likely victims of violent crime are quickly reimagined. Instead, we would find that women disproportionately experience all violent crime (including interpersonal and sexual violence) by a considerable margin (Walby et al., 2014). This observation may well become more obvious when browsing for an autobiography relating to trauma, harm and victimization, as we have suggested. You will most likely find that a considerable proportion of them are written by women, relating to experiences of violent (often sexual) victimization perpetrated by men, frequently in the private domain. Therefore, a key value of the biographical and autobiographical use of textual artefacts of 'victims' should help facilitate a shift in our attention from the public domain of male interpersonal violence (as overrepresented in democratic recording practices such as the Crime Survey of England and Wales) to the private and often unseen domain of gender-based violence against women. We suggest that such a conceptual approach is a useful starting point, rather than apex, of thinking critically with regard to biographical and autobiographical methods within criminological and victimological research.

SUMMARY AND REVIEW

The aim of this chapter has been to highlight the theoretical and methodological potential of biography and autobiography when studying 'criminals' *and* 'victims'. We have chosen to present the demonstration of these methods within criminological and victimological research by first placing the uses of biography as a method within criminological research to provide a contextual insight with which to develop our discussion. Next, we outlined the methodological approaches with which to develop sociological and criminological research more broadly, drawing particular attention to the importance of the Chicago School of Sociology and Clifford Shaw's influential book *The Jack Roller*. With this scene set, we then sought to illustrate some of the practical and more common uses of biography as a method through exploring how this has been used by criminological historians to reconstruct the lives of criminal 'others' for the purposes of critical inquiry. Then, taking the biography of Peter Scannell from the Digital Panopticon project as a working example of a criminological biography, we problematized the use of biography and encouraged critical ways of thinking about this approach when used as a method of social inquiry. Our key observation in this regard is that within criminological research utilizing biography past and present, the 'victims' of crime are often conspicuous by their absence. You must also remain conscious of gendered constructions of victimization that should be problematized and challenged by victimological research informed by political influences and cultural practices (qua McGarry and Walklate, 2015). To conclude, we advocate for the continued use and development of biography and autobiography as valuable outlets for critical criminological and victimological inquiry.

STUDY QUESTIONS AND ACTIVITIES FOR STUDENTS

1. Select one 'criminal life' from the Digital Panopticon resource (www.digitalpano pticon.org). What can this individual's biography tell us about criminality, desistance and nineteenth-century society?

2. Select one popular autobiographical text recounting the personal experience of harm, trauma and/or victimization (criminal or otherwise). In what ways does this experience offer insights into past and present criminal justice and/or political practices; present critiques of victim policy; or provide detailed commentary on social injustices?

3. Outline three limitations each of biographical and autobiographical research method.

4. What value (if any) is the use of textual data, such as biography and autobiography, to doing criminological and/or victimological research?

SUGGESTIONS FOR FURTHER READING

Useful further literature relating to the methodological nuances and practicalities of biographical research include the following: for sociological perspectives, see Plummer (1983, 2001), Stanley (1993) and Chamberlayne et al. (2000); criminological work covering this area can be found in Goodey (2000) and the special issue of *Theoretical Criminology* edited by Gelsthorpe (2007); for victimological research using autobiography, see McGarry (2016) and McGarry and Walklate (2015). For practical critical insight into 'using existing qualitative data', such as biographical and autobiographical materials from digital and textual sources (as discussed within this chapter), Wincup's (2017) second edition of *Criminological Research: Understanding Qualitative Methods* offers comprehensive guidance.

REFERENCES

Anderson, N. (1923) *The Hobo: The Sociology of the Homeless Man*. Chicago: University of Chicago Press.

Barnwell, A. (2017) 'Life writing and the life course', *Auto/Biography Studies*, 32(2): 387–8.

Benson, M.L. (2013) *Crime and the Life Course: an Introduction*. Oxon: Routledge.

Chamberlayne, P. Bornat, J. and Wengraf, T. (2000) 'Introduction: the biographical turn', in P. Chamberlayne, J. Bornat and T. Wengraf (eds), *The Turn to Biographical Methods in Social Science: Comparative Issues and Examples*. Oxon: Routledge.

Connell, R. (2007) *Southern Theory: The Global Dynamics of Knowledge in Social Science*. Cambridge: Polity Press.

Crow, I. and Semmens, N. (2008) *Researching Criminology*. Maidenhead: Open University Press.

Davies, P. (2011) *Gender, Crime and Victimisation*. London: Sage.

Denzin, N. (1989) *Interpretive Biography*. London: Sage.

Farrington, D.P. and Ttofi, M.M. (2015) 'Developmental and life-course theories of offending', in J. Morizot and L. Kasemian (eds), *The Development of Criminal and Antisocial Behaviour*. Dordrecht: Springer.

Farrington, D.P., Coid, J.W., Harnett, L., Jolliffe, D., Soteriou, N., Turner, R. and West, D.J. (2006) *Criminal Careers and Life Success: New Findings from the Cambridge Study in Delinquent Development*. London: Home Office (Research Findings No. 281). Available at: www.crim.cam.ac.uk/people/academic_research/david_farrington/hofind281.pdf (accessed May 2018).

Farrington, D.P., Piquero, A.R. and Jennings, W.G. (2013) *Offending from Childhood to Late Middle Age: Recent Results from the Cambridge Study in Delinquent Development*. New York: Springer.

Foote Whyte, W. (1943) *Street Corner Society: The Social Structure of the Italian Slum.* Chicago: University of Chicago Press.

Francis, P. (2017) 'Theoretical perspectives in victimology', in P. Davies, P. Francis and C. Greer (eds), *Victims, Crime & Society*, 2nd edition. London: Sage.

Frost, L. and Maxwell-Stewart, H. (1997) *Chain Letters: Narrating Convict Lives.* Melbourne: Melbourne University Press.

Gelsthorpe, L. (2007) 'The Jack-Roller: Telling a story?', *Theoretical Criminology*, 11(4): 515–42.

Glueck, S. and Glueck, E.T. (1930) *500 Criminal Careers.* New York: Alfred A. Knopf.

Glueck, S. and Glueck, E.T. (1934) *One Thousand Juvenile Delinquents.* Cambridge, MA: Harvard University Press.

Glueck, S. and Glueck, E.T. (1950) *Unravelling Juvenile Delinquency.* Cambridge, MA: Harvard University Press.

Glueck, S. and Glueck, E.T. (1968) *Delinquents and Non-delinquents in Perspective.* Cambridge, MA: Harvard University Press.

Godfrey, B. (2016) 'Liquid crime history: digital entrepreneurs and the industrial production of "ruined" lives', in M.H. Jacobsen and S. Walklate (eds), *Liquid Criminology: Doing Imaginative Criminological Research.* London: Routledge.

Godfrey, B., Alker, Z., Cox, P. and Shore, H. (2017) *Young Criminal Lives: Youth Justice and its Impacts, 1855–1925.* Oxford: Oxford University Press.

Godfrey, B., Cox, D. and Farrall, S. (2007) *Criminal Lives: Family, Employment and Offending.* Clarendon Series in Criminology. Oxford: Oxford University Press.

Godfrey, B., Cox, D. and Farrall, S. (2010) *Serious Offenders.* Clarendon Series in Criminology. Oxford: Oxford University Press.

Goodey, J. (2000) 'Biographical lessons for criminology', *Theoretical Criminology*, 4(4): 473–98.

Holloway, W. and Jefferson, T. (2000) 'Biography, anxiety and the experience of locality', in P. Chamberlayne, J. Bornat and T. Wengraf (eds), *The Turn to Biographical Methods in Social Science: Comparative Issues and Examples.* Oxon: Routledge.

Hudson, B. (2011) 'Critical reflection as research methodology', in P. Davies, P. Francis and V. Jupp (eds), *Doing Criminological Research.* London: Sage.

Jennings, W.G., Loeber, R., Pardini, D.A., Piquero, A. and Farrington, D.P. (2015) *Offending from Childhood to Young Adulthood: Recent Results from the Pittsburgh Youth Study.* New York: Springer.

Jewkes, Y. (2011) 'The media and criminological research', in P. Davies, P. Francis and V. Jupp (eds), *Doing Criminological Research.* London: Sage.

Jupp, V. (1989) *Methods of Criminological Research.* Oxon: Routledge.

King, R.D. and Wincup, E. (eds) (2008) *Doing Crime and Justice Research*, 2nd edition. Oxford: Oxford University Press.

Maguire, M. (2008) 'Researching street criminals in the field', in R.D. King and E. Wincup (eds), *Doing Crime and Justice Research*, 2nd edition. Oxford: Oxford University Press.

Mawby, R.I. and Walklate, S. (1994) *Critical Victimology: International Perspectives.* London: Sage.

McGarry, R. (2016) 'The "typical victim": no story to tell, and no one to tell it to', in M.H. Jacobsen and S. Walklate (eds), *Liquid Criminology: Doing Imaginative Criminological Research*. Oxon: Routledge.

McGarry, R. and Walklate, S. (2015) *Victims: Trauma, Testimony and Justice*. Oxon: Routledge.

McLaughlin, E. and Muncie, J. (2013) (eds) *The SAGE Dictionary of Criminology*, 3rd edition. London: Sage.

Merton, R. (1988) 'Some thoughts on the concept of sociological autobiography', in M.W. Riley (ed.) *Sociological Lives*. Newbury Park, CA: Sage.

Miers, D. (1989) 'Positivist victimology: a critique, Part 1', *International Review of Victimology*, 1(1): 1–29.

Mythen, G. (2007) 'Cultural victimology: are we all victims now?', in S. Walklate (ed.), *Handbook of Victims and Victimology*. Cullompton: Willan Publishing.

Noakes, L. and Wincup, E. (2004) *Criminological Research: Understanding Qualitative Methods*. London: Sage.

Park, R.E., Burgess, E.W. and McKenzie, R.D. (1925) *The City*. Chicago: Chicago University Press.

Plummer, K. (1983) *Documents of Life: An Introduction to the Problems and Literature of a Humanistic Method*. London: George Allen & Unwin.

Plummer, K. (2001) *Documents of Life 2: An Invitation to a Critical Humanism*. London: Sage.

Rogers, H. (2016) 'Making their mark: young offenders' life histories and social networks', in A.M. Kilday and D. Nash (eds), *True Crime Histories: Micro-Studies in Law, Crime and Deviance since 1700*. London: Bloomsbury.

Sampson, R.J. and Laub, J.H. (1993) *Crime in the Making: Pathways and Turning Points through Life*. Cambridge, MA: Harvard University Press.

Sampson, R.J. and Laub, J.H. (1997) 'A life-course theory of cumulative disadvantage and the stability of delinquency', in T. Thornberry (ed.), *Developmental Theories of Crime and Deviance: Advances in Criminological Theory*, vol. 7. New Brunswick, NJ: Transaction Publishers.

Sampson, R.J. and Laub, J.H. (2003) 'Life-course desisters? Trajectories of crime among delinquent boys followed to age 70', *Criminology*, 41(3): 555–92.

Sampson, R.J. and Laub, J.H. (2006) *Shared Beginnings, Divergent Lives: Delinquent Boys to Age 70*. Cambridge, MA: Harvard University Press.

Shaw, C.R. (1930) *The Jack Roller: A Delinquent Boy's own Story*. Chicago: University of Chicago Press.

Shaw, C.R. and McKay, H.D. (1942) *Juvenile Delinquency in Urban Areas: A Study of Rates of Delinquency in Relation to Differential Characteristics of Local Communities in American Cities*. Chicago: University of Chicago Press.

Stanley, L. (1992) *The Auto/biographical I*. Manchester: Manchester University Press.

Stanley, L. (1993) 'On auto/biography in sociology', *Sociology*, 27(1): 41–52.

Sutherland, E.H. (1937) *The Professional Thief, by a Professional Thief*. Chicago: University of Chicago Press.

Thomas, W.I. and Znaniecki, F. (1918) *The Polish Peasant in America and Europe: Monograph of an Immigrant Group, Volume I – Primary Group Organization*. Boston: The Gorham Press.

Thompson, E.P. (1963) *The Making of the English Working Class*. London: Vintage.

Thrasher, F. (1927) *The Gang: A Study of 1,313 Gangs in Chicago*. Chicago: University of Chicago Press.

Turner, J. and Johnston, H. (2016) 'Female prisoners, aftercare and release: residential provision and support in late nineteenth century England', *British Journal of Community Justice*, 13(3): 35–50.

Walby, S., Towers, J. and Francis, B. (2014) 'Mainstreaming domestic violence into sociology and the criminology of violence', *The Sociological Review*, 62(2): 187–214.

Walklate, S. (1989) *Victimology: the Victim and the Criminal Justice Process*. London: Unwin Hyman/Oxon: Routledge.

Walklate, S. (2004) *Gender, Crime and Criminal Justice*. Cullompton: Willan Publishing.

Walklate, S. (2006) 'Changing the boundaries of the "victim" in restorative justice: so who is the victim now?', in D. Sullivan and L. Tifft (eds), *Handbook of Restorative Justice: A Global Perspective*. Oxon: Routledge.

Walklate, S. (2007) *Imagining the Victim of Crime*. Maidenhead: Open University Press.

Walklate, S., McGarry, R. and Mythen, G. (2014) 'Trauma, visual victimology, and the poetics of justice', in M.H. Jacobsen (ed.), *The Poetics of Crime: Excursions into Creative Criminologies*. Aldershot: Ashgate.

Wengraf, T., Chamberlayne, P. and Bornat, J. (2002) 'A biographical turn in the social sciences? A British-European view', *Cultural Studies/Critical Methodologies*, 2(2): 245–69.

Williams, L. (2014) 'At Large': Women's Lives and Offending in Victorian Liverpool and London. Unpublished PhD thesis, University of Liverpool.

Wincup, E. (2017) *Criminological Research: Understanding Qualitative Methods*, 2nd edition. London: Sage.

Withrow, B.L. (2014) *Research Methods in Crime and Justice*. London: Routledge.

Young, J. (2011) *The Criminological Imagination*. Cambridge: Polity Press.

CHAPTER CONTENTS

GLOSSARY TERMS

participant observation
fieldwork
observation(s)
covert research
overt research
transcription
realism

interpretivism
generalizability
research ethics
inductive research
non-participant
   observation
symbolic interactionism

17

DOING ETHNOGRAPHIC RESEARCH IN CRIMINOLOGY

STEVE HALL

INTRODUCTION

This chapter provides a brief introduction to the ethnographic approach in criminological research. The next section discusses the tension within the criminological discipline between quantitative and qualitative approaches, and stresses the important role that qualitative research and the ethnographic approach should play in a rebalanced discipline. The third section offers a brief history of the ethnographic approach, its various positions and its role in the development of Western social science. This is followed by a discussion of some of the principal methods and research stages, which also highlights some of the methodological and practical problems ethnographers encounter. We then examine the use of ethnographic methods in criminological research. The discussion focuses on the specific and sometimes extreme methodological, practical and ethical difficulties researchers encounter when they use the ethnographic approach and its principal methods to research hard-to-reach groups involved in crime or its control. The final section discusses the way contemporary ethnographers have collaborated with theorists to draw inspiration and learn lessons from modern criminological classics to develop new, advanced ethnographic methods and theoretical frameworks that will hopefully enhance criminology's explanatory power in a changing world.

DISCIPLINARY TENSION

Respected scientist and mathematician Warren Weaver once distinguished between *simple systems, disorganized complex systems* and *organized complex systems* (1948). The two former types of system consist of variables that are active but predictable and therefore amenable to quantitative analysis. The latter type of system consists of active, unpredictable and relatively autonomous constituents such as individuals, cities, social institutions, cultural values and global markets, which create both complexity and unpredictability. Social science deals with the latter type of system, therefore mathematically based quantitative models are of limited use. This problem has reached a critical point in economics. The orthodox mathematically based neoclassical model has, time after time, proved incapable of predicting the capricious behaviour of actors in markets. For instance, only a handful of economists who were working outside the neoclassical orthodoxy predicted the recent financial crash in 2008 (Keen, 2011).

Yet quantitative methods are still dominant throughout the social sciences. This problem is particularly acute in criminology. A study in 2005 suggested that 94% of articles in the top five criminology journals are based on research that used quantitative methods (Tewksbury et al., 2005). Their more recent study showed that even in journals more receptive to qualitative work, it constitutes only about 30% of published articles (Tewksbury et al., 2010). Today's academics are under intense pressure to publish their research. Researchers' own evaluations of the chances of getting their research published affect their choice of methods, and so the striking bias towards quantitative research continues to be reproduced. Criminology students who opt for qualitative research should be aware that they are not only entering a struggle to explain crime and evaluate systems of justice, but also a struggle for credibility within the discipline itself.

Criminology has neglected both mixed methods and the qualitative approach. Yet, in a calamity that rivals that of the economists, quantitative criminologists failed to predict or explain the so-called 'crime decline' in the 1990s. More recently, they also failed to predict or explain the recent refutation of the 'crime decline', which came to light when cybercrimes were belatedly added to the official figures in the UK. This addition might well prove to be the tip of a larger iceberg consisting of shadowy unresearched criminal markets operating online and in the real world (see Hall and Antonopoulos, 2016). If we accept the basic wisdom that we should have a fairly clear idea of what exists out there to be counted before we start counting it, such elusive phenomena require sophisticated qualitative research and theoretical work before the initial stages of quantification even become possible. This would suggest that qualitative research should have primacy in any mixed methods approach. Some argue that qualitative research is best for theory development whilst quantitative research is best for theory testing (Jacques, 2014), whereas others argue that qualitative research is better all round (Young, 2004). However, until there is a marked change in the discipline's culture and some sort of balance is achieved, qualitative research will be left to continue its struggle for credibility or perhaps even survival.

THE ETHNOGRAPHIC APPROACH IN SOCIAL SCIENCE

If qualitative research is important, it must be conducted with rigour. The ethnographic approach that resides at the heart of qualitative research today consists of a set of methods that have undergone development since modern anthropologists first studied traditional societies and cultures in the mid-nineteenth century. Sociology borrowed this approach and modified its methods for application in the study of urban industrial societies. From the 1920s, the Chicago School of Sociology applied the approach systematically to its research into the social worlds of cities. Accounts of the famous studies conducted by this group of sociologists, whose successors still carry on the tradition today, can be found in most general criminology textbooks. Notable examples include Park et al. (1925), Thrasher (1927), Wirth (1928), Reckless (1933), Whyte (1943) and Becker (1973). However, this book is about *doing* criminological research, so the main focus will be on the methods that constitute the ethnographic approach itself. The principal aim of ethnographic research is to gain insights into the everyday meanings and practices that allow individuals to live together in specific local contexts. This requires the researcher to have sustained contact with humans in their everyday locales. Sustained contact can often produce data so rich, detailed and nuanced that the ethnographic approach has become crucial to qualitative research.

Ethnography's principal method is participant observation. The time-limited method of data collection is usually called fieldwork. Participant observation involves sustained immersion in the research setting to allow the researcher to experience and observe first hand the interactions, behaviours, events and practices that occur in it. To do this effectively, the researcher must develop skills in observing, participating, interviewing, listening, forging relationships, communicating and adopting a role and identity within the research setting. Each one of these craft skills carries with it a host of problems and finely tuned requirements that are beyond the scope of this single chapter. Suffice it to say that participant observation is a complex craft in itself that must first be studied in detail with reference to relevant texts (see Atkinson et al., 2001; Mason, 2002; O'Reilly, 2009) and then honed by the researcher in the field. Participant observation was of course initially developed for small groups. Observation of larger groups, such as the inhabitants of a housing estate or the workers in a large hospital, which comprise different sub-groups, is significantly more difficult. Solutions to this problem include employing multiple research associates, setting up a multi-site project and spending longer in the field. However, these solutions can be expensive. More cost-effective solutions include the use of communal gathering spaces, such as canteens, pubs, clubs, community centres and schools, and the selection of representatives from different sub-groups as key informants and participants in follow-up interviews or focus groups.

The ethnographic process

If participant observation is the ethnographer's principal method, the ethnographic process that surrounds it comprises a number of stages. In the first stage, once the research question has been formulated the relationship between the proposed research setting and its broader context must be established. Some anthropologists have regarded the unique cultural meanings and practices in the research setting as the inhabitants' whole world, but the majority of contemporary ethnographers would accept that most of today's small groups are not isolated from broader economic, political and social contexts (see Ellis, 2016; Horsley, 2015). For instance, if the research question is focused on some aspect of the gender gap in exam success in science subjects, the researcher must develop an initial understanding of the broad social context, in this instance intersectional social relations, and the broad institutional context, in this instance the secondary education system. Then the researcher can make an informed choice of the research setting(s), in this instance a specific school or schools. The researcher would do well to become familiar with the history of the institutional context and the research setting(s) with preliminary reading, document collection and analysis. In a sense, all ethnographies are specific 'case studies' of something broader (O'Reilly, 2009). Case studies can be intrinsic (interesting in themselves, e.g. a single institution in government), instrumental (where the case is secondary and used as an example of a broader structural situation) or comparative (where researchers look at differences between groups, which would usually require a multi-site project).

In the next stage, the researcher must make initial decisions about specific methods, all the time weighing up the advantages and disadvantages. For instance, should the ethnography be overt or covert? Covert research has obvious advantages, such as the increased authenticity of the practices that can be observed. However, a major disadvantage is that it must be justified to satisfy ethics committees or institutional review boards because it is a form of deception. In a covert ethnography, it is also impossible to validate the presence of the researcher, who might not have actually been in the research setting and could literally be fabricating data (Herrera, 2003). In his well-known covert study of occupational police culture, Holdaway's (1984) observation of techniques used to extract confessions of guilt placed him in a difficult ethical situation. This study might not have satisfied today's ethics committees because of problems associated with deception and the duty to report malpractice. If overt research is chosen, all participants know they are being researched and they are usually provided with written information about the research and consent forms to sign. Participants may act naturally, but it often takes a long time to build trust, there is no guarantee they will do it consistently and the assumption that they are actually being authentic can never be established beyond doubt. Duneier's (1994) celebrated study of the 'respectable' black male culture in Chicago is an example of an overt study in which the researcher's presence might well have affected behaviour and disclosure amongst some of the participants. Fielding's (1981) study of the National Front (NF) presents us with an interesting overt–covert hybrid. The NF members knew they were being researched, but Fielding kept his anti-fascist feelings to himself to allow honest disclosure from his informants. In her study of drug dealers, Adler (1985) shifted from covert to overt as trust was gained. However, a contemporary ethics committee would quite possibly point out that these tactics are still forms of deception that, in research fields such as these, might also put the researcher in danger.

The next stage is to negotiate access to the research setting during periods when its participants are going about their everyday social or occupational lives. The recruitment of appropriate research associates, gatekeepers and key informants is essential. This is sometimes problematic. Unsuitable choices – particularly in such cases where research associates and key informants fail to strike up productive relationships – can hinder the research process, in rare cases to the extent that the research has to be abandoned. Informed consent must be sought from all participants, informants and interviewees, usually in written form that explains the purpose and methods of the research in brief but clear detail. This might seem rather formal, but many textbooks warn ethnographers to avoid 'going native' because, should they do so, they can end up exploiting participants and losing all sense of distance and objectivity.

BOX 17.2   'GOING NATIVE'

A classic example of 'going native' is Simon Winlow's (2001) research into the link between violent criminals and night-club doormen. Winlow worked alongside door-men for nine months in a club known for outbreaks of violence and associated with violent criminals. The experience of immersion in this culture furnished Winlow with insights into complex cultural codes and regular patterns of events which could not have been accessed any other way. Although he deceived participants, he did not feel that he had exploited them. However, avoiding the ethically charged issue of participation in violence required a finely detailed knowledge of localized behavioural codes and techniques of neutralizing clients' violence without using violence as a means of restraint, breaking the law or revealing his role as a researcher. Rather than lose all sense of objectivity, Winlow's observation of patterns of regular violent incidents that were largely unreported and unrecorded by police or victim surveys actually increased objectivity.

However, this is hotly disputed, as we will see in the next section. Others question whether over-rapport can be possible, or whether it is simply a complaint lodged by envious ethnographers who failed to develop a rapport (see O'Reilly, 2009). Objectivity can also be threatened by the personal ideology of the researcher, which, if it is allowed to influence data generation and analysis without some degree of reflexive self-questioning, can make the question of formality or informality rather redundant.

Once access is successfully negotiated, the researcher can enter the field to conduct the fieldwork. Fieldwork entails gathering data that are sufficiently rich, nuanced and comprehensive to produce a detailed 'thick description' of everyday meanings and practices. During this process, it is important that the researcher produce good, clear field notes. These are usually written records or recordings ready for transcription. Throughout the process, the researcher must be as rigorous and careful as possible, and in particular must be prepared to focus on the fine details of important events that occur as powerful examples of meaning and practice. It is also essential that the researcher carve out time to reflect on fieldwork through the process, because feelings, insights and ideas that crop up in the moment can be quite easily forgotten if too much time is allowed to elapse. Field notes can be contextualized and enhanced by collecting relevant newspaper cuttings, news items from TV, radio or the internet, reports, memos, etc. that are contemporary with the researcher's time in the field.

In the field, significant events can come and go very quickly; therefore some ethnographers find it helpful to write field notes in stages of progressive complexity that allow for expanding reflection, starting with head notes for quickness and moving through scratch notes to full notes for further reflection before the event becomes hazy in the memory and initial impressions are lost. Transcribing recorded data in the moment is also important. However, some find transcription to be very time-consuming and, out of practical necessity, wait until the fieldwork is finished, but doing it this way the recorded data can go 'cold' and difficult to integrate with insights that crop up during the fieldwork. During his covert fieldwork with bouncers, Winlow (2001) found a useful compromise by writing up his field notes the following day when the context and insights were still fresh in his mind. Reflections on initial analysis and theory can unfold from observation and interview data during the fieldwork, but the researcher's political inclinations, cultural prejudices, theoretical preferences and personal interpretations are present in the ethnographic process from the very beginning, so we could settle on the principle that in the field it is on balance better to focus a little more on data collection. Except in cases where a specific hypothesis is to be tested, ethnographic knowledge production tends to be inductive, and this applies to analysis and theory too. Even the research design, although clear in its purpose and broad methodology at the beginning, tends to be developed inductively because the methods will almost invariably need to be modified as problems crop up during the fieldwork.

The next stage is analysis of the data. As we have seen, even though fieldwork should be inclined towards data collection, it helps if the researcher can conduct some initial analysis during fieldwork rather than leave it all to the end. This helps the research to be a reflexive rather than linear process. Ongoing analysis can help the researcher to come up with modified and/or additional questions, and to develop clearer initial understandings of significant events and cultural practices, which will lead to the collection of richer data and the construction of more sophisticated analysis and theory. PhD students, who tend to gather data and analyse them themselves, are at an advantage in this reflexive process. At the heart of analysis is the technique of coding, which requires the researcher to discern patterns and changes in significant events and everyday meanings and practices in the context of the research setting. Therefore, to achieve this, coding involves the close examination of minute details in the data. Technology can help in the process of coding, but some argue that it encourages a lazy, mechanistic approach in which details vital to the eventual analysis and theory can be missed; therefore it is perhaps best used as an aid rather than a replacement (O'Reilly, 2009).

Coding is often done in two stages: first, open coding, which involves looking at the whole data set for broad emergent themes; and, second, focused coding, where specific emergent themes are thought to be especially significant and require interpretation. As vital as this process is, and as rewarding as the results can be, it is also where the researcher's values and preconceived assumptions and prejudices can assert themselves, and therefore where confirmation bias can become established at the empirical heart of the research. Researchers should be aware that when their research is published it receives institutional validation, and thus it needs to be conducted reflexively and with great honesty. Ideally, all qualitative researchers should engage in an internal dialectic throughout the research process, weighing up different points of view and evaluating possibilities of interpretation and analysis as the eventual grounded theory is constructed. However, the ideal is rarely achieved, which suggests that researchers should at least compromise by being open about the preferred position to which their assumptions belong. When the data, analysis and initial theorization seem to be in good shape, the researcher can begin writing up, which allows for the further development of analysis and theory (see Hall, Chapter 7, this volume).

Challenges: ontology and generalizability

However, what at first glance looks like a fairly straightforward process is replete with challenges. The most fundamental is the choice of the ontological and epistemological framework: in other words, the set of ideas used to conceptualize what exists in the world at the most basic level and how we can produce knowledge about it. This choice will not only influence the final analysis and theorization but also the way the research is carried out. In qualitative research, this usually boils down to whether the researcher chooses a naturalist/realist or interpretivist framework. The ontological issue is at the heart of this choice: is the human world constituted by structures, forces and processes external to individuals and their cultures, or simply a set of cultural meanings and practices? The former, realist position suggests that human experience is underpinned and shaped by more fundamental influences external to culture. For instance, in his study of young people's experiences of the holiday industry in Ibiza, Briggs (2013) firmly connects what seems like compulsory excessive hedonism to the demands of the industry and the circulation of capital. The latter, interpretivist assumption, which suggests that culture is the bedrock of society with nothing below it, and that human experience cannot be reduced to external influences, is also common in ethnography. For instance, Katz (1988) focuses principally on cultural meanings and social micro-interactions in his study of the moral and sensual attractions of doing crime. However, interpretivism tends to ignore or downplay external forces such as the natural environment, economy, politics, ideology and history (see Gilmore, 1990), or even common biological drives and conditions of insecurity and anxiety (see Hall et al., 2008). Or, as yet another alternative, were early French structuralist ethnographers correct in their assumption that meanings and practices are themselves ordered in universal structures of language external to the individual yet mirrored in internal patterns of thought (Lévi-Strauss, 1973)? Can the researcher employ moral and epistemological certainty to make clear judgements about what they experience, or should s/he be completely flexible, celebrate moral pluralism and epistemological uncertainty, make no clear judgements at all and leave interpretation to the reader? The obvious way out of these tough choices is to take account of all these possibilities, but assembling a compound position can be difficult. O'Reilly (2009) argues that a *reflexive-realist position* helps to overcome the rigidity of realism and the defeatism and relativism of endless interpretivism.

Another fundamental problem is the generalizability of knowledge, analysis and theory. Can the researcher's account of what occurs in the chosen research setting be transferred to other research settings that might be different? Do Wakeman's (2016) 'moral economy' of drug users, Ellis's (2016) violent males or Smith's (2014) hedonistic night-time consumers, which these researchers found in their respective research settings, also exist in the same forms in similar research settings in similar structural locations elsewhere? Williams (2000) argues for *moderatum generalization*, which can offer tentative generalizations that leave room for future reformulation. His solution is to offer each analysis and theorization together as a tentative hypothesis to be confirmed or modified as alternative research settings are explored, which adds a deductive element to the otherwise inductive ethnographic approach. The politics of research becomes very influential here. Ethnographies are expensive, funds are extremely limited and quantitative studies soak up most funding; therefore ethnographic explorations of further research settings might never materialise. In this case, early explorations, if the accounts they produce are attuned to the dominant or subdominant cultural and political values of their time and thus achieve initial popularity (see Hall and Winlow, 2015), might remain immune from refutation and establish themselves in the discipline as received wisdom for decades.

THE ETHNOGRAPHIC APPROACH IN CRIMINOLOGY

Ethnographic research in criminology shares basic principles and techniques with sociology and anthropology. However, there is a growing tension between traditional sociological values and emerging criminological research. The research settings and cultural groups investigated by sociologists are diverse and often quite benign, whereas criminologists are more often compelled to address issues and practices that can profoundly diminish the quality of life for victims, perpetrators and their communities. Having said this, because criminology is still in its developmental stages as a distinct social scientific discipline, most well-known ethnographies of criminal activity and the control system have been conducted by sociologists (Bourgois, 1995; Hobbs, 1988). Whereas the traditional rule in sociology and anthropology is to show an appreciation and understanding of human motivations and practices, criminology consistently operates on and beyond the boundary of legality and at the forefront of potential moral condemnation. In some settings, for instance where violence is causing palpable harm to others, it is very difficult for the criminological researcher to respect confidentiality or suspend moral judgement and personal intervention. Criminological ethnographers have encountered significant hostility from sociologists and some other criminologists, who accuse them of sensationalizing, thrill-seeking or giving violent thugs and fascists too much publicity. On the other hand, they have been accused of pathologizing and labelling the poor by revealing too much of their harmful criminal activity. Other sociologists, following Gouldner's (1971) accusation that ethnographers are merely the 'zookeepers of deviance', argue in a rather dismissive tone that ethnographic research tells us little about substantive structural issues such as political economy, power, poverty and the forces of exclusion.

Most sociologists and criminologists followed Sutherland's (1939) cultural pragmatism and switched from theorizing criminality as pathological to appreciating it as practice appearing in the different forms of ethical and social organization that emerged in difficult circumstances. There was a further switch to a more structural approach in the 1970s as the concept of the offender as social predator was replaced by the victimized actor, and in some cases crime and deviance were conceptualized as a form of 'resistance' to capitalist authority, norms and values (see Taylor et al., 1973). Yet, even if criminology rejects the biological metaphor of pathology, which misleadingly implies that crime is some sort of 'disease' in a social body that is otherwise healthy, time after time researchers encounter palpably harmful crimes that are difficult to appreciate, even though some of the reasons why individuals feel motivated to commit these crimes can, to some extent, be understood. Sociology's unwavering command to appreciate has created a one-dimensional, sanitised theoretical approach and restricted research into the darker side of human life, which leaves it hostage to condemnatory right-wing theories and political solutions (Hall and Winlow, 2007). However, in the early 1980s the feminist and left-realist approaches used mixed methods to reveal the extent of harmful intra-class crime after it had been systematically understated for over four decades (Matthews, 2014). This placed a more realistic approach back on the agenda. Simon Winlow's classic ethnographic study of nightclub door staff and violent criminals in an English town (2001) was one of the first to move beyond both the condemnatory and naïve appreciative approaches to present an advanced, reflexive account of reality.

If theory is to be grounded, inductive and reflexive-realist rather than imposed on researchers by dominant disciplinary figures and their preferred politics, and if we are to resist the latest atheoretical quantitative move to 'Big Data', ethnography is still a valuable method. Ethnographic research remains useful for revealing the fine details of the socioeconomic reality and the webs of human meanings, motivations, experiences and practices on which future theory should be built (see Hall and Winlow, 2015).

BOX 17.3 'BIG DATA'

'Big Data' is a buzzword for the analysis of very large data sets that are so unwieldy they require new analytical processes and software. The ambition is to detect large-scale behavioural trends in society, business and the economy. If this is indeed the direction in which sociology and criminology are headed, the ethnographic method would become even more marginalized and its numerous advantages would be lost. Ethnography reveals the nuances, subtleties and ever-changing micro-processes that make up everyday social interaction, which must be connected to social structures and macro-processes with rigorous and reflexive theory (Hall and Winlow, 2015). If ethnography and theory are displaced, the behavioural categories analysed by 'Big Data' social scientists will remain very crude and static.

Research ethics: deception, safety and confidentiality

 Although criminological ethnographers enjoyed a measure of freedom until the early twenty-first century, now they are compelled to negotiate ethical problems under the guidance of university institutions that specialize in research ethics (see Murphy and Dingwall, 2001). Perhaps the most difficult amongst these problems are deception, safety and confidentiality.

BOX 17.4   DECEPTION, SAFETY AND CONFIDENTIALITY

Deception: it is commonly regarded as unethical to deceive participants. Informed consent, preferably in written form, must be obtained.

Safety: it is also regarded as unethical to put anyone involved – researcher, participant or third party – at risk of psychological or physical harm.

Confidentiality: researchers must never disclose any confidential information to any third party. This ethical imperative can put criminological researchers in very difficult situations regarding their knowledge of unreported crimes. All data and supporting information must be kept in secure locations.

These issues can be extremely difficult for a criminological researcher. For instance, it is illegal to withhold information concerning crimes from the police. Where research proposals have been regarded as too risky or impossible to resolve, they have been refused permission by Ethics Committees (UK), Institutional Review Boards (USA) or Human Research Ethics Committees (Australia). Some ethnographers have had no choice but to take unpaid leave and go it alone (see, for example, Nordstrom, 2007). At the political level, institutionalized ethics can serve the interests of incumbent ideological power by preventing the type of research projects that might reveal uncomfortable truths. Winlow and Hall (2012; see also Israel, 2014) identified Ethics Committees as bureaucratic substitutes for what should be an organic culture of ethics reproduced by the researchers themselves. These committees have little to do with ethics but operate as a form of 'risk management', confiscating ethics and politics from researchers to minimize risks and maintain the image of the corporate university.

BOX 17.5 WHAT IS AN ETHICS COMMITTEE?

ABSTRACT

We want to make one very simple claim that we hope might contribute to the developing discourse on the disciplinary and institutional governance of academic criminology: the Ethics Committee is one of a growing number of little others that attempt to compensate for the loss of the traditional symbolic order. While our focus is on the Ethics Committee and criminology, we believe that much of what we have to say is also applicable to other forms of academic governance that characterize the social sciences in the contemporary university. We will take a rather circuitous route to this conclusion in the hope that we might encourage criminological researchers to think seriously about the ways in which Slavoj Žižek's philosophical framework can be used to theorize criminology's position in the current post-political social order. (Winlow and Hall, 2012: 1)

Guillemin and Gillam (2004) distinguish between procedural ethics and ethics in practice. The former are formal and restrictive whereas the latter are flexible and improvised. They argue that most situations in research settings are too complex and ambivalent for formal ethics; therefore the responsibility to remain faithful to ethical values should be returned to the researcher. Sandberg and Copes (2012) offer a compromise. After interviewing 15 researchers in the drug field to discern common ethical problems, they acknowledged that the researcher must make ethical and practical decisions on the ground as the research progresses, but the research community itself needs to establish its own 'standing decisions', based on forethought and common knowledge, as guidance. Yet many funders, university committees and even researchers themselves remain uncomfortable with such autonomy and moral flexibility on the ground and out of constant regulatory reach (Yates, 2004).

Insiders/Outsiders

Standard sociological ethnographies tend to be conducted in communities that are quite open and welcoming, and which can often benefit from the research, but, for criminologists, suspicion and secrecy are perennial problems. Individuals involved in crime or violence, and those policing offenders or supervising them in prisons, generally have little to gain from researchers, therefore they tend to be cautious about granting access to the research field, striking up relationships, allowing participant observation, acting as key informants or offering detailed and truthful information. This issue often invokes the crucial question of whether 'outsiders' or 'insiders' are the most effective researchers. The standard arguments about the advantages and disadvantages of using outsiders or insiders tend to be overwhelmed by the banal but crucial issue that crimes carry penalties; therefore unless a very high level of trust is established participants will conceal the true extent of their activities from outsiders. Even where trust seems to have been established, the researcher can never be quite sure that all motivations, practices and consequences are being revealed. Some argue that, in many cases, the insider is often the only researcher capable of accessing, revealing and understanding the concealed but rich and nuanced cultural practices that pervade those communities involved in crime, criminal markets or crime control (Ancrum, 2013; Ho, 2009).

Insiders will usually already have more complete and intimate knowledge of the field, but of course the insider must be a true active insider rather than a passive inhabitant of the field whose knowledge claims might be hearsay, exaggerations or fabrications. A true insider might be over-familiar with the setting and suffer from 'over-rapport' with its inhabitants and a subsequent tendency to dismiss the subtle nuances of meaning and practice that the outsider might recognize as significant (Hammersley and Atkinson, 1995). However, accusations of 'over-rapport' are possibly based on worries that insiders, benefiting from more access, trust and understanding, might reveal realities that will disrupt the cosy paradigms that social scientists rely on to theorize their data (Ancrum, 2013). Paradoxically, because the long-running moral injunction to appreciate others weighs heavily on outsiders, particularly if they are from a more privileged background, insiders can achieve more critical distance because they are not hampered by this moral injunction – one has to know something intimately to be truly and incisively critical of it. An insider can be trained to recognize the important in the familiar, whereas denial of access to the outsider is more fundamentally problematic, but then again outsiders can overcome this with good key informants and sheer persistence. The debate goes on with no obvious closure in sight, but it tends to omit the fact that there is rarely one researcher. An outsider and an insider working together, either both active in the field or with the outsider as director and interlocutor, can often make a useful combination, balancing the critiques and teasing out the commonalities that are essential to eventual theory building. This merger of two horizons can introduce an active and ongoing dialectic into the research process.

The most serious problem for the criminological ethnographer is that the duty to disclose criminal activity often precludes ethnography's most fundamental method – participant observation. This method was once possible as researchers accompanied minor criminals as they committed non-violent crimes, but institutional control has rendered it virtually extinct. Although Winlow's (2001) study was one of the first to present a truly reflexive-realist account of violent crime, it was, ironically, also one of the last ethnographic research projects to involve direct and enduring participant observation of violent crime. Insider researchers and key informants can help with access to limited participant observation in the vicinity of crimes but never with the act of committing or planning a crime, because this would automatically trigger the ethical imperative to disclose. This applies to actors in criminal markets as well as institutional settings such as police stations or prisons. Criminological ethnographers, forced to find a substitute for direct participant observation, have come to rely on the retrospective narratives of those who have already witnessed criminal activity as associates, onlookers or victims, or on the reminiscences of ex-offenders whose convictions are already spent. To some, this type of criminological ethnography is not a proper ethnography at all, but a series of interviews carried out by researchers who can operate in the locale where crimes are committed, and therefore get a flavour of the research setting and its broader social, economic and cultural contexts, but never actually observe them as significant social events. To enrich this second-hand data, criminological ethnographers must develop their skills in accessing research settings, gaining trust, finding key informants, expanding the informant group by means of snowball sampling, and conducting sequences of interviews in progressively more depth.

Anonymity and confidentiality

However, even key informants often feel the need to conceal many activities and motivations because any suspicion of 'grassing' carries harsh summary penalties in many communities where criminal activities are to be found. The taboo placed on grassing is in direct conflict with the ethical imperative to disclose crimes (Yates, 2004). To overcome this problem, anonymity and confidentiality are of the utmost importance; the only legitimate way of reconciling the ethical imperative to disclose information about crime with the taboo on grassing is for the informants to totally anonymise all discussions from the very beginning. The anonymity of the research setting, the actors and the actions can guarantee confidentiality without hampering the gathering of data and the construction of a narrative. However, to remain ethical the anonymity of actors and actions must be established by the informants and not retrospectively by the researcher, even though the researcher can suggest this general rule at the beginning of the project, because the researcher cannot disclose incriminating details that s/he has never known.

Covert research

Powerful actors associated with white-collar, corporate or governmental crime are able to close rank and construct a wall of silence and non-cooperation that is often impenetrable to the researcher. In such settings, covert research would appear to be the only possibility, but this method is unlikely to achieve ethical approval. Because access is so difficult, ethnographic work on the crimes of the powerful is very rare. Ho's (2009) and Luyendijk's (2015) serialised studies of investment bankers are two of a small number of exceptions. Ho was an insider working in investment banking, while Luyendijk was an outsider who had to arrange access to the social periphery of the research setting and use the techniques of retrospective interviewing and snowball sampling. Despite numerous disappointments, he managed, by sheer persistence, to persuade his slowly expanding group of informants to almost become informers by anonymously disclosing corporate crime and malpractice and describing in fine detail the characters of the criminals and their actions whilst retaining the anonymity of both themselves and the perpetrators.

Semi-structured interviews

Today's criminological ethnographers often use semi-structured interviews during participant observation of the non-criminal periphery of the research setting. Some of these interviews might last a few seconds and produce rather glib responses (Smith, 2014), but they can be followed up with longer semi-structured interviews conducted with key informants and former criminal perpetrators as they emerge during the research (see Ellis, 2016; Hall et al., 2008; Winlow, 2001). Interviews with groups are useful for overcoming the problem that actors will invariably have different interpretations of their actions and motivations (see Alasuutari, 1995). Semi-structured interviews with key informants or informal focus groups might last hours or even continue in sequence for days (see Treadwell et al., 2013). Essential to these methods is the establishment of trust between researcher and informants. Once trust is gained, the interviewing researcher can initially engage in dialogue that taps into broad issues to allow themes to emerge before gently nudging the interviewees towards focusing down in greater depth and clarity on significant events, meanings and practices as the conversations develop. Collecting rich and reliable data in criminological research is difficult, but with persistence and effective techniques it is certainly not impossible.

ADVANCED ETHNOGRAPHIC APPROACHES IN CRIMINOLOGY

'Classic' ethnographies are always worth reading for glimpses into the past and a flavour of the historical development of methods. However, it is probably more important to read 'modern classics' which have tried to overcome some of these problems. Unfortunately, academics have different ideas of what constitutes a 'classic'. Most social scientists are either middle-class individuals or working-class individuals under pressure to conform to middle-class values and understandings (Dews and Law, 1995). The optimism of the middle-class progressive liberal, based on the ontological assumption that people are basically pragmatic problem-solvers who usually mean well, has become the norm. Consequently, there is a tendency throughout the social sciences to understate serious structural socioeconomic problems and overstate the ability of individuals and their cultural codes and practices to overcome them (see, for instance, Anderson, 2001). Since the 1980s, various new types of ethnographic research have been introduced into the discipline in an attempt to overcome the shortcomings of the 'classics' and move forward.

Critical ethnography

The critical ethnographic approach openly encourages researchers to dig underneath everyday meanings and look for significant events that reveal underlying structures of power and control. For instance, researchers could look for the details in significant meanings and events that might indicate the motivations for and the responses to everyday instances of classism, racism, sexism and other forms of domination. Researchers are encouraged to discover precisely how people are subjugated – in the sense of their rights, life chances and expressions of their own culture – by dominant social groups. Classic critical ethnographies, such as Willis's (1981) exploration of class in school and work and Street's (1992) exploration of how daily conflicts related to structural power bear down on nurses' autonomy, focus on underdogs to expose power relations, methods of subjugation and structural imbalances in social relations. The ensuing ethnographic data and analysis can inform policy and encourage activism amongst the subjugated, with significant reform or social transformation in mind. Problems in this approach include the assumption of the subjugated as passive victims (Fleetwood, 2014) rather than already active resistors, and the possibility that the rhetoric of 'empowerment' gives the subjugated false hope for the resolution of problems that require more fundamental political intervention in economy and society.

Feminist ethnography

This approach is associated with critical ethnography, but researchers are encouraged to discover in fine detail how historical and structural subjugation specifically affects women's lives, an approach that should be distinguished from traditional ethnographies that happen to be conducted by women. For instance, McLintock (1995) examines the experiences of South African women in the structures of race and gender in the context of a declining British imperialism. Some feminist ethnographers argue that there is a natural or perhaps cultural affinity between women and qualitative data, and an orientation to regarding people as humans rather than numbers (see O'Reilly, 2009). Some also suggest that women are notably adept at forging equal and appreciative relationships with participants and conducting all interactions in a warm and receptive rather than an interrogative manner (2009). Like critical ethnographers, feminist ethnographers are open about the theoretical assumptions and cultural identity politics that give purpose to their work (see Scheper-Hughes,

1993). However, because these assumptions and political positions tend to essential-ize women and be resistant to critique, it is questionable whether feminist ethnographic research conforms to the principles of inductive research that some argue should be the norm in the ethnographic approach.

Auto-ethnography

This is quite new to criminology. However, the use of personal experience in the gathering and analysis of data has a fairly long history (Wakeman, 2014), so the term 'auto-ethnography' could be criticized as an unnecessary neologism. Hallsworth's (2013) auto-ethnography uses recollections of his personal experience of life on the streets in the 1970s and 1980s to question the ontological claim behind the 'gangland' thesis. Do 'gangs', he asks, actually exist as positivists and realists describe them? He argues that we see arboreal (static and tree-like) gangs rather than transient and nomadic networks because of our historical tendency to think like that. However, to counter the claim that gangs exist he draws on moral panic theory, which is not really using unaffected personal experience to provide a fresh inductive analysis but simply claiming that the opposing nomadic metaphor is correct because that's the way the theory suggests we should see it. Some argue that this approach is self-indulgent and inappropriate in its over-generalization of limited singular experiences (see O'Reilly, 2009), and that memories are not reliable repre-sentations because they come into operation *after* the experiences they are supposed to represent (Winlow, 2014). There is no way to verify data that exist exclusively in the memory of the researcher, and it could be argued that a third party would be able to evaluate data and theoretical concepts in a more balanced way. However, Wakeman (2014) claims that the researcher's own personal experiences and beliefs have always influenced the researcher; therefore ethnography has always been, to some extent, auto-ethnographic. Because of the difficulty of access that plagues criminological ethnography, auto-ethnography could prove valuable in the future.

Visual ethnography

The visual ethnographic approach is becoming more common in anthropology and sociology. It is often used as an aid to participant observation in realist or interpre-tivist frameworks. Images can be supplied by research participants, or produced in partnership with researchers, allowing self-representation to become part of the research. Films and photographs are useful for eventual theory construction because they are permanently available for reanalysis. Visual ethnography can be enhanced by technological innovations in multimedia, such as small, portable video cameras and sensitive recording equipment. Pink (2007) argues for a multisensory ethnography that incorporates input from all the other senses, which might compensate for the inadequacy of linguistic accounts and descriptive writing. The visual approach could be useful in criminology but at the moment it is hindered by the fact that only a limited number of groups are likely to allow visual access and recording. As in all ethnographic research, access is more readily granted to ethnographers who might be able to help the group express and publicise either its pressing problems or its attractive characteristics. Thus, visual ethnographic work is eminently possible with sex workers seeking to avoid criminalization or victims wishing to express the harm inflicted on them (see Arfman et al., 2016), but the chances of criminals, police officers or prison officers allowing extensive visual recording are very low. The big problem with the visual ethnography is that a single image is almost always a *synecdoche*, a term that means the part that misrepresents the whole (or the whole that misrepresents the part). Media researchers have long warned us about the ideological power of the image, which, with all its possibilities of selective focus, presentation, manipulative editing, and so on, would allow ethnographic researchers to be more persuasive in their presentation of their preferred ideological positions.

Online ethnography

This is a new and useful addition to criminology. Essentially, it is participant observation adapted for cyberspace. Some criminologists have realized that crime has mutated rather than declined and most new crimes or advanced means of committing traditional crimes and operating criminal markets are now associated with the internet (see Hall and Winlow, 2015). The internet accommodates virtual forms of economic, social and cultural interchange; therefore the ethnographer, far less hampered by initial problems of access, must learn the virtual community's protocols to be accepted as a member. The internet hosts many different and specific forms of disembodied 'community' – markets, hobbies, identities, political groups, sexual preferences, and so on – that are in constant flux. As they attempt to join these communities, online ethnographers can use avatars to circumvent the ethical problems of deception, risk of harm, anonymity and confidentiality because in most cases members have already agreed that identities should be hidden in a 'covert community'. Webber and Yip's (2013) research into the online trade in fake credit cards and Davey et al.'s (2012) research into online drug forum communities developed innovative methods for online research into the web and the 'dark net', including non-participant observation or 'lurking', and the collection of screenshots adds visuals and records. Hall and Antonopoulos's (2016) research into legal and illegal online pharmacies innovatively combined advanced online methods with advanced offline methods to research the global market in counterfeit pharmaceuticals. They were able to research the supply side of the market by using online methods whilst simultaneously using traditional participant observation and interviews with consumers to research the demand side. However, the use of 'honeypot websites' and covert research amongst users of pharmaceuticals bought online did involve some deception, but difficulties in ethical clearance were overcome because internet research is low risk and the use of pseudonyms as avatars and the omission of locational details in the analysis and writing up provided 'double anonymity' (2016). This suggests that many ethical problems can be overcome with innovation, careful planning and the regulation of research practice. Today's ubiquitous use of the internet has the potential to open up criminal practices hitherto closed off to researchers, such as paedophile networks, fraud, corruption, state crimes, tax evasion and far-right extremism.

Ultra-realist ethnographic networks

Ultra-realist criminologists reject the notion that plural cultures are the bedrock of society. Following Hammersley (1998) and Fine (1999), ultra-realists argue that ethnographers can communicate with each other to construct plausible accounts of our shared reality contextualized in the underlying political economy. This approach understands that the problems of generalization and researcher bias have limited the effectiveness of the isolated ethnographies that have dominated the field up to now, and that the philosophical and theoretical frameworks the researchers have used – pragmatism, symbolic interactionism, post-structuralism, and so on – are threadbare and overly influenced by traditional political positions (see Hall and Winlow, 2015). To escape these restrictions, ultra-realists advocate contextualized reflexive realism and the establishment of ethnographic and theoretical networks within and between nations. The approach advocates the use of advanced ethnographic methods, collaborative data and new theoretical frameworks, such as zemiology and pseudo-pacification, based on concepts adapted from advanced philosophical positions such as speculative realism and transcendental materialism (see Ellis, 2016). Such data and theorization can provide the degree of generalizability necessary to connect localized meanings and practices to the broad global structures and processes of history, economy and consumer culture (see Hall et al., 2008; Horsley, 2015). For instance, Winlow et al. (2015) used ultra-realist principles to gather data and construct an alternative theoretical perspective on the riots that occurred in England, Spain and Greece after the recent economic crash and austerity programmes. Seeking to throw off the romantic baggage associated with traditional ethnographies, the Deviant Leisure Group (see Smith and Raymen, 2018) consists of networked ethnographers and theorists investigating harms that are integral to current commercialized leisure pursuits in various research settings (see Briggs, 2013; Kindynis, 2017; Raymen and Smith, 2016). The aim is not to produce one 'grand theory', but to develop advanced collaborative research methods and new theoretical frameworks that offer more incisive explanatory power in today's rapidly changing world.

SUMMARY AND REVIEW

This chapter has discussed the ethnographic approach in criminological research. It has outlined the basic research methods and processes used by ethnographic researchers in the general social science field and discussed the ethnographic approach to criminological research. The chapter has shown how new contemporary ethnographic methods are advancing and how they can provide innovative ways of generating rich data in the rapidly changing world of crime, harm and control. It has also investigated the possibility of linking the generalizable data produced by ethnographic networks to new theoretical frameworks based on concepts drawn from contemporary philosophy.

I have suggested that the ethnographic approach should be very important to the general social scientific project, but currently quantitative research is dominant, which means that the finely detailed meanings and practices that constitute human life are relatively marginalized. Although the ethnographic approach to criminological research has to contend with many practical and ethical problems, the rich data it can provide offer a sound empirical platform on which convincing theoretical explanations of criminality and its modes of control can be constructed. However, to perform this task the ethnographic approach requires further funding, a more valued place in the criminological publishing industry, increased rigour and the further development of its methods and theoretical frameworks. Despite the disciplinary marginalization, some contemporary ethnographic methods are advancing at quite a pace and providing innovative ways of understanding the rapidly changing world of crime, harm and control. If these methods can be practised in growing networks to produce generalizable data that can be combined with new theoretical frameworks based on contemporary philosophical concepts and perspectives, the ethnographic approach could become the empirical mainstay of a rejuvenated twenty-first-century criminology.

STUDY QUESTIONS AND ACTIVITIES FOR STUDENTS

1. To what extent have qualitative research and the ethnographic approach been marginalized in the social sciences?

2. Does the principle of reflexivity help the ethnographic researcher to organize the whole research process and produce richer data, analysis and theorization?

(Continued)

(Continued)

3. Discuss the practical and ethical problems that make criminological ethnographies uniquely difficult.

4. Is the interview method conducted with key informants in the field an adequate substitute for participant observation when the latter proves impossible?

5. Discuss the relative merits of using insiders and outsiders to conduct ethnographic research in high-crime areas and control institutions.

6. Discuss the advantages and disadvantages associated with one of the following:

   o critical ethnographies
   o feminist ethnographies
   o visual ethnographies.

7. Discuss the methods and problems emerging in the new method of online ethnography.

8. How do the new ultra-realist ethnographers seek to adapt traditional methods and introduce new philosophical concepts and theoretical frameworks to advance qualitative research?

SUGGESTIONS FOR FURTHER READING

Karen O'Reilly's (2009) book *Key Concepts in Ethnography* is an excellent introductory tour of the world of modern ethnography. To get a flavour of a modern classic ethnography, try Dick Hobbs's (1988) *Doing the Business: Entrepreneurship, the Working Class and Detectives in the East End of London*. Jennifer Fleetwood's (2014) *Drug Mules: Women in the International Cocaine Trade* is an award-winning contemporary feminist ethnography that moves beyond the stereotype of the passive female victim. Simon Winlow's (2001) *Badfellas: Crime, Tradition and New Masculinities* is a classic study in which the researcher achieved the deepest possible immersion in the field of violent crime. Tony Ellis's (2016) *Men, Masculinities and Violence: An Ethnographic Study* is an award-winning contemporary ethnography that also achieves deep immersion and adopts a brand new philosophical framework to move forward the theorization of male violence. Alex Hall and Giorgios Antonopoulos's (2016) book *Fake Meds Online: The Internet and the Transnational Market in Illicit Pharmaceuticals* offers one of the most sophisticated examples of the virtual ethnography. The groundbreaking ultra-realist ethnographic and theoretical work of the Deviant Leisure Group can be found at https://deviantleisure.wordpress.com.

REFERENCES

Adler, P. (1985) *Wheeling and Dealing: An Ethnography of an Upper-Level Drug-Dealing and Smuggling Community*. New York: Columbia University Press.

Alasuutari, P. (1995) *Researching Culture: Qualitative Method and Cultural Studies*. London: Sage.

Ancrum, C. (2013) 'Stalking the margins of legality: ethnography, participant observation and the postmodern "underworld"', in S. Winlow and R. Atkinson (eds), *New Directions in Crime and Deviancy*. London: Routledge.

Anderson, E. (2001) *The Code of the Street: Decency, Violence and the Moral Life of the Inner City*, 2nd edition. New York: W.W. Norton.

Arfman, W., Mutsaers, P., Van der Aa, J. and Hoondert, M. (2016) 'The cultural complexity of victimhood', *Tilburg Papers in Culture Studies*, Paper 163. University of Tilburg.

Atkinson, P., Coffey, A., Delamont, S., Lofland, J. and Lofland, L. (2001) *Handbook of Ethnography*. London: Sage.

Becker, H.S. (1973) *Outsiders: Studies in the Sociology of Deviance*. New York: Free Press.

Bourgois, P. (1995) *In Search of Respect: Selling Crack in El Barrio*. New York: Cambridge University Press.

Briggs, D. (2013) *Deviance and Risk on Holiday: An Ethnography of British Tourists in Ibiza*. Basingstoke: Palgrave Macmillan.

Davey, Z., Schifano, F., Corazza, O. and Deluca, P. (2012) 'e-Psychonauts: conducting research in online drug forum communities', *Journal of Mental Health*, 21: 386–94.

Dews, B. and Law, C. (eds) (1995) *This Fine Place so Far from Home: Voices of Academics from the Working Class*. Philadelphia, PA: Temple University Press.

Duneier, M. (1994) *Slim's Table: Race, Respectability and Masculinity*. Chicago: University of Chicago Press.

Ellis, A. (2016) *Men, Masculinities and Violence: An Ethnographic Study*. London: Routledge.

Fielding, N. (1981) *The National Front*. London: Routledge & Kegan Paul.

Fine, G.A. (1999) 'Field labour and ethnographic reality', *Journal of Contemporary Ethnography*, 28(5): 532–9.

Fleetwood, J. (2014) *Drug Mules Women in the International Cocaine Trade*. Basingstoke: Palgrave Macmillan.

Gilmore, D.D. (1990) *Manhood in the Making: Cultural Concepts of Masculinity*. New Haven, CT: Yale University Press.

Gouldner, A. (1971) *The Coming Crisis of Western Sociology*. London: Heinemann.

Guillemin, M. and Gillam, L. (2004) 'Ethics, reflexivity, and "ethically important moments" in research', *Qualitative Inquiry*, 10(2): 261–80.

Hall, A. and Antonopoulos, G. (2016) *Fake Meds Online: The Internet and the Transnational Market in Illicit Pharmaceuticals*. Basingstoke: Palgrave Macmillan.

Hall, S. and Winlow, S. (2007) 'Cultural criminology and primitive accumulation: a formal introduction for two strangers who should really become more intimate', *Crime, Media, Culture*, 3(1): 82–90.

Hall, S. and Winlow, S. (2015) *Revitalizing Criminological Theory: Towards a New Ultra-Realism*. London: Routledge.

Hall, S., Winlow, S. and Ancrum, A. (2008) *Criminal Identities and Consumer Culture: Crime, Exclusion and the New Culture of Narcissism*. London: Routledge/Willan.

Hallsworth, S. (2013) *The Gang and Beyond: Interpreting Violent Street Worlds*. London: Palgrave MacMillan.

Hammersley, M. (1998) *Reading Ethnographic Research*, 2nd edition. London: Longman.

Hammersley, M. and Atkinson, P. (1995) *Ethnography: Principles in Practice*, 2nd edition. London: Routledge.

Herrera, C.D. (2003) 'A clash of methodology and ethics in "undercover" social science', *Philosophy of the Social Sciences*, 33: 351–62.

Ho, K. (2009) *Liquidated: An Ethnography of Wall Street*. Durham, NC: Duke University Press.

Hobbs, D. (1988) *Doing the Business: Entrepreneurship, the Working Class and Detectives in the East End of London*. Oxford: Oxford University Press.

Holdaway, S. (1984) *Inside the British Police: A Force at Work*. Chichester: Wiley/Blackwell.

Horsley, M. (2015) *The Dark Side of Prosperity: Late Capitalism's Culture of Indebtedness*. Farnham: Ashgate.

Israel, M. (2014) *Research Ethics and Integrity for Social Scientists*. London: Sage.

Jacques, S. (2014) 'The quantitative–qualitative divide in criminology: a theory of ideas' importance, attractiveness, and publication', *Theoretical Criminology*, 18(3): 317–34.

Katz, J. (1988) *The Seductions of Crime: Moral and Sensual Attractions in Doing Evil*. New York: Basic Books.

Keen, S. (2011) *Debunking Economics: The Naked Emperor Dethroned?* London: Zed Books.

Kindynis, T. (2017) 'Urban exploration: from subterranean to spectacle', *British Journal of Criminology*, 57(4): 982–1001.

Lévi-Strauss, C. (1973) *Tristes Tropiques* (trans. J. Weightman and D. Weightman). New York: Atheneum.

Luyendijk, J. (2015) *Swimming with Sharks: My Journey into the World of Bankers*. London: Guardian/Faber.

McLintock, A. (1995) *Imperial Leather: Race, Sexuality and Gender in the Colonial Context*. London: Routledge.

Mason, J. (2002) *Qualitative Researching*, 2nd edition. London: Sage.

Matthews, R. (2014) *Realist Criminology*. Basingstoke: Palgrave Macmillan.

Murphy, E. and Dingwall, R. (2001) 'The ethics of ethnography', in P. Atkinson, A. Coffey, S. Delamont, J. Lofland and L. Lofland (eds), *Handbook of Ethnography*. London: Sage.

Nordstrom, C. (2007) *Global Outlaws: Crime, Power and Money in the Contemporary World*. Oakland, CA: University of California Press.

O'Reilly, K. (2009) *Key Concepts in Ethnography*. London: Sage.

Park, R.E., Burgess, E.W. and McKenzie, R.D. (1925) *The City*. Chicago: University of Chicago Press.

Pink, S. (2007) *Doing Visual Ethnography*, 2nd edition. London: Sage.

Raymen, T. and Smith, O. (2016) 'What's deviance got to do with it? Black Friday sales, violence, and hyper-conformity', *British Journal of Criminology*, 56(2): 389–405.

Reckless, W.C. (1933) *Vice in Chicago*. Chicago: University of Chicago Press.

Sandberg, S. and Copes, C. (2012) 'Speaking with ethnographers: the challenges of researching drug dealers and offenders', *Journal of Drug Issues*, 43(2): 176–97.

Scheper-Hughes, N. (1993) *Death without Weeping: The Violence of Everyday Life in Brazil*. Berkeley, CA: University of California Press.

Smith, O. (2014) *Contemporary Adulthood and the Night Time Economy*. Basingstoke: Palgrave Macmillan.

Smith, O. and Raymen, T. (2018) 'Deviant leisure: a criminological perspective', *Theoretical Criminology*, 22(1): 63–82.

Street, A.F. (1992) *Inside Nursing: A Critical Ethnography of Clinical Nursing Practice*. New York: State University of New York Press.

Sutherland, E. (1939) *Principles of Criminology*, 3rd edition. Philadelphia: J.B. Lippincott.

Taylor, I., Walton, P. and Young, J. (1973) *The New Criminology*. London: Routledge.

Tewksbury, R., Dabney, D.D. and Copes, H. (2010) 'The prominence of qualitative research in criminology and criminal justice scholarship', *Journal of Criminal Justice Education*, 21: 391–411.

Tewksbury, R., DeMichele, M.T. and Miller, J.M. (2005) 'Methodological orientation of articles appearing in criminal justice's top journals: who publishes what and where?', *Journal of Criminal Justice Education*, 16: 265–79.

Thrasher, F.M. (1927) *The Gang: A Study of 1,313 Gangs in Chicago*. Chicago: University of Chicago Press.

Treadwell, J., Briggs, D., Winlow, S. and Hall, S. (2013) 'Shopocalypse Now: consumer culture and the English riots of 2011', *British Journal of Criminology*, 53(1): 1–17.

Wakeman, S. (2014) 'Fieldwork, biography and emotion: doing criminological autoethnography', *British Journal of Criminology*, 54(5): 705–21.

Wakeman, S. (2016) 'The moral economy of heroin in "austerity Britain"', *Critical Criminology*, 24(3): 363–77.

Weaver, W. (1948) 'Science and complexity', *American Scientist*, 36: 536–44.

Webber, C. and Yip, M. (2013) 'Drifting on and off-line: humanising the cybercriminal', in S. Winlow and R. Atkinson (eds), *New Directions in Crime and Deviancy*. London: Routledge, pp. 191–205.

Whyte, W.F. (1943) *Street Corner Society: The Social Structure of an Italian Slum*. Chicago: University of Chicago Press.

Williams, M. (2000) 'Interpretivism and generalization', *Sociology*, 34(2): 209–24.

Willis, P. (1981) *Learning to Labor: How Working Class Kids Get Working Class Jobs*. New York: Columbia University Press.

Winlow, S. (2001) *Badfellas: Crime, Tradition and New Masculinities*. Oxford: Berg.

Winlow, S. (2014) 'Trauma, guilt and the unconscious: some theoretical notes on violent subjectivity', in J. Kilby and L. Ray (eds), *Violence and Society: Toward a New Sociology*. Chichester: Wiley/Blackwell, pp. 13–31.

Winlow, S. and Hall, S. (2012) 'What is an ethics committee? Academic governance in an era of belief and incredulity', *British Journal of Criminology*, 52(2): 400–16.

Winlow, S., Hall, S., Treadwell, J. and Briggs, D. (2015) *Riots and Political Protest: Notes from the Post-Political Present*. London: Routledge.

Wirth, L. (1928) *The Ghetto*. Chicago: University of Chicago Press.

Yates, J. (2004) 'Criminological ethnography: risks, dilemmas and their negotiation', in G. Mesko, M. Pagon and B. Dobovsek (eds), *Policing in Central and Eastern Europe: Dilemmas of Contemporary Criminal Justice*. Maribor: Faculty of Criminal Justice, University of Maribor.

Young, J. (2004) 'Voodoo criminology and the numbers game', in J. Ferrell, K. Hayward, W. Morrison and M. Presdee (eds), *Cultural Criminology Unleashed*. London: The Glasshouse Press.

CHAPTER CONTENTS

GLOSSARY TERMS

ethnography
secondary data
content analysis
purposive sampling
participant observation

non-participant observation
snowball or chain-referral
  sampling
virtual ethnography

18

DOING CRIMINOLOGICAL RESEARCH ONLINE

MAJID YAR

INTRODUCTION

The rapid emergence and global expansion of the internet has had a significant impact on how researchers, including criminologists, go about investigating the social world. The importance of the internet in this regard is centred on three main dimensions. First, there is the number of people who now have access to the web – what media analysts call the 'penetration rate', denoting the proportion of the total global population who are active online. According to recent estimates, the number of internet users now stands at 3.3 billion, comprising some 46.4% of the global population (IWS, 2015). Second, there is the sheer weight of content available via the internet; there are now an estimated one billion distinctive websites in existence (Internet Live Stats, 2016), playing host to unprecedented amounts of content in the form of text, image and sound. Third, there is the range of internet-based activities in which users engage – spanning, for example, business transactions, socialization, community building, political engagement, education, social care and support, leisure and consumption, and the delivery of public services. Across this range of practices, we find those that are sometimes illegal and illicit, breaching as they do established laws and norms that regulate social behaviour. As a consequence, the internet presents researchers with many opportunities both to explore crime and justice issues more effectively, and to study a variety of criminal and deviant behaviours that now take place within this electronically mediated environment.

If we think about 'doing criminological research online', it becomes apparent that this phrase can have a number of distinct, if inevitably interconnected, meanings.

First, the internet presents us with numerous resources and avenues for researching a wide range of familiar crime-related issues, such as patterns of offending and victimization; practices of policing and law enforcement; public attitudes, beliefs and knowledge about crime and justice issues; and popular representations of crime and punishment, to name but some. All of these can be explored by using a range of established research methods (such as literature reviews, survey questionnaires, observation, ethnography and content analysis), appropriately adapted to the structures of the online realm. A number of these will be overviewed in this chapter, including reflections on the opportunities and challenges that they present.

A second sense of 'doing criminological research online' relates to the opportunity presented to criminologists for researching criminal behaviours that occur within and are facilitated by the internet itself – these can include a range of (now familiar) 'cybercrime' issues, such as hacking, e-frauds and cons, stalking and harassment, media piracy, and the distribution of obscene and hateful content. The internet offers researchers the chance to observe and study such behaviours in their 'natural environment' as it were, alongside the experiences and reactions of victims as well as the wider community of online users. Once again, these opportunities need to be balanced against a range of practical and ethical challenges that confront us as we seek to 'do criminological research' in, on and through the internet.

DOING AN ONLINE LITERATURE REVIEW

Pretty much every piece of criminological research – whether it's a student dissertation or a large-scale academic research project – inevitably begins with a literature review, intended to draw upon the existing body of scholarship in order to set the foundations for your own particular study (Jesson et al., 2011). Students nowadays are, of course, used to making internet searches as a typical starting point when seeking to answer a question or learn more about a specific topic, theoretical framework or approach. However, the inevitable problem confronting the researcher is not one of quantity but of quality; there is no shortage of online material covering just about every imaginable criminological topic, but ensuring that the resources you draw on are credible or accurate is a real challenge. One of the internet's great strengths – its ability to allow any and all users to transcend barriers to publication and share content – is also a weakness, insofar as material made available online is often not subject to rigorous evaluation or fact-checking. Nevertheless, the internet offers many valuable instruments for undertaking the literature review stage of your research project. The basis for this stage is twofold – first, you need to *identify* literature that is relevant to your research; and second, you need to be able to *access* it. Universities will offer their staff and students access to searchable electronic databases of scholarly publications, such as the ISI Web of Knowledge and Scopus, which can be used to find journal articles relevant to your research topic. However, accessing the articles themselves is dependent on your university or college paying the required subscription fees for the particular journals in question. Many students and academics will be familiar with the frustration of identifying a key piece of literature, only to find that their institution's portfolio of subscriptions doesn't include the particular one in which the article is published. The good news is that the proliferation of web-based academic content means that students and scholars have a number of other, freely available, avenues for finding and accessing relevant literature. One of the most popular is the Google Scholar search engine, which indexes scholarly literature and enables users to identify similar or related works, as well as directing users to the complete documents in those instances that they are available online. A significant portion of the literature (journal articles, book reviews, discussion documents and conference papers) is made available either by universities in their own institutional repositories, or by individual researchers and writers themselves (Khabsa and Giles, 2014). In the case of the latter, an increasing number of authors make their work available for download on academic social networking platforms such as academia.edu and ResearchGate; the latter, for example, boasts more than 10 million researcher members and hosts many millions of articles which can be searched by author, keyword or topic; membership is free, and open to students. Such web-based search engines and platforms offer criminologists an invaluable resource for undertaking a literature review, and crucially provide access to research on a free basis.

FINDING CRIMINOLOGICAL DATA ONLINE

In addition to accessing material for your literature review, the internet provides a rich variety of crime-related data (both quantitative and qualitative) that you can draw upon and use in your own work. Such secondary data (data that has already been collected by other researchers) can cover a wide range of criminological topics, such as nationwide patterns and trends in offending and victimization; social attitudes towards crime and justice issues; the practice of policing, punishment and rehabilitation; and data related both to particular crime types (such as drug-related offences) and particular social groups (such as young people). UK-related data of this kind is accessible online via the UK Data Archive (www.data-archive.ac.uk), as well as the Office for National Statistics (www.ons.gov.uk). Similar data sources are available for the USA through the likes of the National Institute for Justice, the National Archive for Criminal Justice Data, and the Bureau of Justice Statistics. International and comparative statistics about crime are available online via the United Nations Office on Drugs and Crime (UNODC), spanning topics including organized crime, terrorism, the narcotics trade, fraud, money laundering and human trafficking. Valuable crime-related data is also available in the form of studies conducted by charitable organizations (such as the Joseph Rowntree Foundation and the Howard League for Penal Reform). Private organizations and businesses also collect and compile crime-related data and make it available online, especially in respect of internet-related offences such as the distribution of computer malware, and the hacking and theft of private information; for example, the internet security company Symantec publishes an annual Internet Security Threat Report which supplies criminologists with useful statistical information about trends in computer crime.

One of the major advantages of using resources such as those referred to above in your research is that, in addition to ease of access, it enables you to make use of data that would otherwise be impossible for you to collect due to the barriers of cost, time, expertise or access to the sampled populations. However, as with all such data, secondary resources found online are not without their problems and limitations. First, there may be a lack of transparency about precisely how that data has been collected and organized by the original researcher. Second, it may not be entirely suited to answering your own research questions, if, for example, some key variables (such as say gender, age or ethnicity) are absent. Third, when using a number of such secondary data sources, there are inevitable problems of inconsistency in methodology which make it difficult to compare or aggregate the findings (May, 2011). Data about crime patterns and trends compiled by private actors and business organizations also needs to be handled with care, as it may be decisively shaped by commercial interests that lead to bias (Wall, 2007). One example of such problems relates to the overestimation of the costs incurred through online media 'piracy', with data compiled by bodies representing media companies standing accused of consistently inflating figures for rhetorical purposes (in this instance, pushing the case for harsher criminal sanctions for those committing copyright offences) (Yar, 2005). Consequently, such data must be placed in its appropriate context rather than being accepted at face value by the criminological researcher.

ANALYSING WEB-BASED CONTENT

Thus far, we've considered how the internet can serve as a valuable avenue through which the criminological researcher can access relevant academic literature as well as a variety of data sources that are made available online. In this section, we move on to consider how we can approach the content of websites as an object of analysis in and of itself; the words, images and recorded sounds that comprise internet content themselves become the raw material that we study in order to learn more about crime-related issues. As with many other walks of life, the internet has rapidly become a central site or space in which public discourse about crime and related issues is produced. Online discussions and interventions concerning crime come from numerous constituencies: politicians and policy-makers; political parties and campaigning groups; criminal justice and law-enforcement agencies; journalists and commentators; and 'ordinary' members of the public. Consequently, web-based content can be analysed so as to better understand issues such as the following:

- how 'official' discourses construct crime problems – the kinds of crime risks we face, the characteristics of offenders and their victims, trends and patterns in crime, and so on
- how popular 'folk' criminology explains crime and attributes responsibility to various social, cultural, economic, psychological or other factors
- how responses to crime problems are configured and advocated – the creation of new laws, policing and law enforcement, punishment and rehabilitation.

Analysis of web-based crime discourse can focus in on a wide variety of interventions – everything from the policy pronouncements of government departments to the public expressions of interest, concern or moral outrage evident in postings on social media platforms. A variety of methodologies can be adopted, including quantitative content analysis, such as counting the incidence of various kinds of expression and mention of different issues, or measuring trends in frequency of such expressions over time (Riffe et al., 2014). This kind of analysis has been facilitated by the development of web-analytic tools that enable researchers to scour the internet for particular kinds of content and measure their presence (Herring, 2009; McMillan, 2000). However, while web searches can uncover seemingly vast amounts of content, it is important to recognize that the most commonly used search engines (such as Google) only index a small proportion of the total material hosted online. Information scientists make a distinction between the so-called 'surface web' (indexable by search engines)

and the 'deep web' (containing content that is in principle publicly accessible, but is not indexed) (Bergman, 2001). Only a small percentage of the former is covered by our usual web searches, while the latter remains invisible. As a consequence, a search for online discussions of a particular topic will not deliver all (or even a majority) of the potentially relevant content, and may also be skewed by the ways that search engines prioritize some results over others according to their 'popularity' (Evans, 2007). Such limitations mean that a corpus of web content will inevitably be partial and not necessarily representative of all online discourse on the topic as such. Further issues arise due to the unstable character of content hosted online – the web is a dynamic environment in which content appears and disappears with some rapidity, and undergoes constant updating and revision (Adar et al., 2009).

An alternative approach to amassing web-based content for analysis is through a targeted search (in effect, a form of purposive sampling – Palys, 2008). Through this search-based sampling strategy, you can collect data that encompasses a variety of instances of the particular phenomenon you are interested in. Data collected in this way is particularly suited to qualitative analysis, where concerns about statistical representativeness and generalizability are largely set aside. Online sampling of this kind is not restricted to websites but is also increasingly employed in order to analyse crime-related content appearing on various social media platforms, including social networking sites such as Facebook and micro-blogging platforms like Twitter. Various free online tools for searching and analysing Twitter content are now available, including the likes of Socialbearing (www.socialbearing.com). Criminological analysis of content derived from websites and social media is illustrated in Box 18.1.

BOX 18.1   POLICE IMAGE MAKING ONLINE

For some decades, researchers have been interested in how police forces use the media in order to present themselves to the wider public, and in doing so seek to establish their legitimacy, justify their strategies, defend themselves against criticism and engage citizens as active participants in crime control initiatives (for example, through coming forward to report offences and provide potentially vital witness testimony in ongoing investigations). Traditionally, police have pursued such aims through engagement with journalists in print and broadcast media (Chermak, 1995; Mawby, 2002). However, the advent of the internet and related media channels has had a potentially significant impact on these dynamics, with the police now able to bypass media organs such as newspapers and television news programmes so as to address themselves directly to the public. In order to investigate these developments, Sillince and Brown (2009) examined the official websites of 43 police forces in mainland England and Wales in order to uncover how they construct their organizational identities, legitimacy and moral authority; they found that the sites give prominence to self-representations about issues such as diversity, effectiveness and responsiveness to the communities they serve. In a counterpart to the study by Sillince and Brown, Schneider (2016) used qualitative document analysis to explore how the police service in Toronto, Canada, used Twitter to present itself, especially in terms of cultivating an image of professionalism and an orientation towards community policing. By looking at online content in this way, the researchers have been able to extend our understanding of how law enforcement agencies manage their image and seek to shape public perceptions and attitudes in a favourable direction.

Analysis of online content can address not just representations or constructions of crime-related issues, as outlined above, but can also explore forms of expression that are *in and of themselves criminal acts.* Such offences include, first, so-called 'content' crimes in which users post or share material that breaches laws around obscenity, hateful speech or incitement to violence against particular social groups (Holt et al., 2015; Yar, 2013). Particularly topical in this regard is the use of the internet to disseminate terrorist propaganda and extremist political provocations that target minorities and vulnerable populations (Conway, 2016). Second, they include forms of harassment or abuse targeting particular individuals in online forums such as Facebook and Twitter – so-called 'trolling', which may breach laws in England and Wales such as the Malicious Communications Act 1988, the Communications Act 2003 and the Protection from Harassment Act 1997 (Bishop, 2013). Third, we can identify criminal content related to online fraud, such as so-called 'spoofing' websites that mimic the portals of banks in order to induce victims to unwittingly share their passwords and other access-related information (Dinev, 2006). Insofar as such content is posted on publicly accessible websites and platforms (as opposed to restricted-access forums), it is available for collection, collation and analysis. Box 18.2 offers an overview of such research related to one of the above-mentioned topics, namely the online circulation of hateful political speech.

BOX 18.2 ASSESSING THE EXTENT, CONTENT AND SOCIAL IMPACT OF ONLINE HATE SPEECH

Hate speech can be defined as 'speech that (1) has a message of racial inferiority, (2) is directed against a member of a historically oppressed group, and (3) is persecutory, hateful and degrading' (Nielsen, 2002: 266). The circulation of such speech

(Continued)

(Continued)

online (initially in the form of websites and discussion forums, and latterly also including content on social media platforms and micro-blogging services) has been well documented (Yar, 2013: 99). Initial studies sought to identify and count the number of sites containing such content, typically originating with far-right, ultra-nationalist, white supremacist and neo-Nazi groups and their supporters or sympathisers. However, attaining an accurate measure of their number is difficult, and has largely depended on users reporting their presence to anti-racism organizations, internet service providers and/or the relevant authorities. As a result, such data remains indicative of the range and growth of online hate speech, but cannot provide any definitive measure. More effective have been criminological studies that use purposive sampling to map the different kinds of content appearing on such sites. For example, Gerstenfeld et al. (2003) conducted a content analysis of 157 'extremist websites', including variables such as 'multimedia content', 'content for children', 'mention of economic issues', 'use of racist symbols', 'advocacy of violence', and so on. In this way, the researchers were able to attain a clearer view of just what forms were taken by online hate speech and the prevalence of different types of content. Similar sites were used by Duffy (2003) as the basis of a qualitative analysis focused on the themes, symbols and stories that were deployed so as to generate a rhetorical effect; she found that these included appeals to 'fairness and justice', conspiracies about 'Zionist' control of the USA, and the restoration of a supposedly 'natural order' that dictates a 'separation of the races'. Further studies have sought to use hateful online content in an attempt to assess the impact that exposure to such material may have on the beliefs, attitudes and outlook of those exposed to it. Lee and Leets (2002) used a range of psychological measurement techniques to assess the relative persuasiveness of different kinds of hateful conduct in terms of the attitudes reported by 108 adolescents who were exposed to such material. These studies illustrate how internet-based content can be effectively used as the basis of a variety of criminologically oriented research studies.

REACHING RESEARCH PARTICIPANTS ONLINE

Thus far, we have considered approaches to online criminological inquiry in which the researcher acquires information and data at a remove from the actors who normally comprise the heart of social research. Now we turn to consider how you can use the internet and related communication technologies to directly engage and interact with research subjects. These engagements take a number of forms, adapting 'conventional' research techniques to the online environment, including: one-to-one interviewing, focus groups or collective interviews, forms of participant and non-participant observation (ethnography) and surveys via questionnaires. Each will be outlined and discussed in turn, alongside their benefits and drawbacks when compared to offline research methods.

Doing interviews online

The interview is a key instrument at the disposal of criminologists and other social researchers. It is an effective way of gathering primary data through direct interaction with research subjects, and permits the researcher to draw out fine-grained details about opinion and experience (qualitative data) which are particularly valued in interpretive research (Chamberlain, 2013: 51–2). Online research interviews can be either asynchronous or synchronous (Bryman, 2012: 658). Asynchronous interviewing does not occur in real time, as the research will typically send the subject a list of interview questions (e.g. by email) to which they will respond at some later point, hours, days or weeks later. The researcher may then re-engage the subject with further questions if the initial responses are found to be particularly interesting, or if elaboration or clarification is needed. In this way, the interview can stretch over some considerable period of time and involve numerous 'turns' between the researcher and the respondent. On the plus side, taking time in this way can allow both parties to consider and reflect on their questions and answers, and also allows the respondent to potentially commit more time and effort to the research than might be the case with a single interview session (Meho, 2006: 1288). On the negative side, the time lag between questions and responses can render the interview less spontaneous and make it difficult to establish rapport – something that is particularly important when researching potentially sensitive issues including crime and victimization. Synchronous online interviews, in contrast, occur in real time just like conventional face-to-face interviews, only using electronic communication channels; these may be text-only (with the interviewer and respondent exchanging typed answers via a messaging service), or multi-mediated, as when using video-over-internet services such as Skype. Synchronous interviews of this kind can go a considerable way to replicating the immediacy of face-to-face research encounters, and video-based interviews also have the benefit of enabling the interacting parties to use a range of non-verbal or 'para-linguistic' cues which are central to human communication (Fichten et al., 1992).

Whether synchronous or asynchronous, online research interviews offer a number of distinct advantages over their traditional face-to-face counterparts, alongside some notable limitations. Amongst the advantages, we can include:

- **Time and cost savings.** Meeting research participants to conduct interviews can require both money (such as travel and accommodation costs) and the associated time required. If the interviewees are not local to where you happen to be living, studying and researching, these costs can become prohibitive (unless you are in the enviable situation of having substantial dedicated funds available, such as a research grant). Interviewing online minimizes these difficulties, and allows us to conduct research with populations who might otherwise remain inaccessible for all practical purposes (such as those residing in another country or continent).

- **Reaching targets for sample size.** Online methods such as email interviewing are well suited to snowball or chain-referral sampling, where initial respondents act as contacts through which further participants can be recruited (Biernacki and Waldorf, 1981). Use of participants' existing electronic networks and associations can prove vital for rapidly accumulating a significant number of interviewees, especially where this might otherwise prove difficult, as with some small and hard-to-reach populations.
- **Anonymity and distance.** Generally speaking, researchers view interactional distance as a barrier to effective qualitative data collection; as already noted, it is felt that the absence of face-to-face interaction can undermine attempts to build rapport between interviewer and interviewee, making it less likely that disclosures on sensitive, personal or controversial topics will be forthcoming. However, conversely, the kind of distance associated with some forms of online interviewing (such as asynchronous email interactions) may sometimes make it *easier* for respondents to offer such disclosures, especially if they are accompanied by intense emotional responses such as guilt, embarrassment or shame.

The above kinds of advantages notwithstanding, you will need to bear in mind some limitations that accompany such methods, including:

- **Non-response.** Given the sheer volume of unsolicited emails that computer users commonly receive, it is unsurprising that invitations to participate may be met with very low response rates (Meho, 2006: 1288). For example, prospective interviewees may simply dismiss an invitation as 'spam' or 'junk' and delete it without even reading; alternatively, they may read the communication but decide not to respond due to suspicions about the motives of unknown individuals asking to interact with them (an understandable response given the volume of fraud-related communications that target internet users).
- **Sampling problems.** Unlike quantitative research, qualitative inquiry tends to be far less concerned with assembling a sample that can be taken as representative of the general population, and from which one might be able to make broad inferences about society as a whole. Nevertheless, turning to online tools in order to connect with interviewees does generate some problems. At the start of this chapter, I noted how rapidly the internet has grown over just a couple of decades, and how widely it is now used globally. However, there remain significant gaps and imbalances between those who are 'connected' and those who are not – what new media researchers call the 'digital divide' (Ragnedda and Muschert, 2013). Social inequalities based around income, education, age, gender and geography affect the number of people from different social groups who have access to, and regularly make use of, new communication technologies. As a consequence, there will

inevitably be some groups that will prove difficult to recruit and interview using online techniques. For example, given the continuing low levels of internet use amongst older people (those 70+ years of age) (Friemel, 2016), it would be very challenging to use online interviews to study, say, seniors' experiences and perceptions of crime in their neighbourhoods.

Doing criminological surveys online

While interviews are well suited to collecting qualitative data, social researchers generally favour the use of survey questionnaires when seeking to amass large bodies of data that can be used as the raw material for quantitative analysis. Criminologists make frequent use of such surveys when researching topics such as: patterns of criminal victimization (as with the Crime Survey for England & Wales, formerly the British Crime Survey); self-report studies of offending (Thornberry and Krohn, 2000); and fear and anxiety about crime (Hale, 1996). Survey techniques are readily adaptable for online use, and take two main forms – the email survey and the web survey. As the name suggests, email surveys are distributed to respondents via mail (either included in the body of the email itself or included as an attachment) and returned to the researcher by the same means. As with email-based interviewing, there are considerable advantages in terms of cost, efficiency and the ability to reach respondents distributed across significant distances (Andrews et al., 2003). However, email surveys are also limited in terms of low response rates and their inability to reach respondents who are not computer users (something that becomes a particular problem if you are hoping to have a probability sample from which the results of analysis can be generalized to the population as a whole). Also, since respondents return their completed questionnaires using their email accounts, anonymity is potentially undermined as responses can be easily matched to their senders. This latter problem can be side-stepped by using the second type of electronic survey, the web-based survey. Here, the researcher contacts potential respondents through a variety of electronic channels (such as email, social media, blogs and discussion lists), inviting them to complete the questionnaire which is hosted on a website. There are now available a number of such sites that enable the researcher to design their survey, collect data from respondents, and collate and download it for analysis once the survey is complete. While popular sites such as SurveyMonkey (www.surveymonkey.com) charge users for more advanced functions, basic surveys can be conducted for free, making them a popular choice with students conducting research for their dissertations. Amongst the benefits of administering a web-based rather than email-based questionnaire is that the compilation of responses into a downloadable form by the service means that you do not need to manually enter the data into software such as SPSS before analysis, something that reduces the likelihood of errors in data handling (Bryman, 2012: 671). Again, there are limitations insofar as the respondents are unlikely to be demographically representative of the population as a whole (with younger people, better educated people and people with higher levels of income more likely to make themselves available for participation). Nevertheless, bearing this shortcoming in mind, such instruments can be very useful for data collection on a range of criminological topics.

BOX 18.3   PUBLIC PUNITIVENESS TOWARDS SEX OFFENDERS

Pickett, Mancini and Mears (2013) were interested in the fact that public attitudes towards sex offenders in the USA are particularly punitive and hostile; in comparison, the public appears to be willing to embrace more rehabilitative responses to other offender categories. The authors set about exploring the underlying public views and assumptions about sex offenders and their victims that might help explain this pattern of support for 'get tough' laws around sex crimes. They administered an online questionnaire survey to almost 3,000 SurveyMonkey respondents. The respondents comprised volunteer members of SurveyMonkey's online panel. While the sample was non-probablistic, it did achieve a gender balance and included representation from different ethnic groups (white, black and Latino) in broad proportion to the wider US population. Analysis of the survey results revealed that public punitiveness toward sex offenders appeared to be rooted in assumptions such as: (1) victims of sex crimes are particularly vulnerable, being predominantly young and female; (2) sex offending is rooted in moral failings and offenders cannot be rehabilitated; and (3) sex offences are on the rise, thereby creating a heightened sense of risk and feelings of anxiety.

Doing criminological ethnography online

Thus far, we have considered a range of online research tools and techniques (literature searches, mining secondary data, content collection, interviews and surveys) which have in common the maintenance of a separation or a kind of 'scientific detachment' between the researcher and that which they are investigating. Many involve little or no direct contact between the researcher and the researched. Even in the case of interviewing, where varying degrees of interaction take place, the researcher stands apart from the beliefs and behaviours they seek to explore, acting as a 'sympathetic outsider' while seeking insights into the lives of others. We now turn to consider the use of a notably different approach, namely that of online or 'virtual' ethnography. The practice of ethnography originates in the discipline of anthropology, denoting a form of research in which the investigator would immerse themselves in a particular community over an extended period (months, if not years) in order to attain a deep understanding of that group's distinctive 'way of life' (Jones, 2010). While criminologists and sociologists seldom enter into such an intensive and long-drawn-out engagement with their research subjects, they have nevertheless adopted and adapted some core principles from ethnography as the basis of a strategy for doing in-depth qualitative research. These include:

- studying people's actions and interactions in the context or environment in which they naturally occur
- gathering data from ongoing informal interactions and observations as well as more formal or structured questioning in the form of interviews
- focusing on a relatively small number of people in a particular setting, such as a neighbourhood, workplace or other organization
- analysing the data gathered interpretively so as to elicit what actions mean to those who engage in them.

In undertaking ethnographic research, the investigator becomes a participant in the conduct and practices under study rather than simply observing from a distance. It is for this reason that the term 'participant observation' is often used as an alternative to describe ethnographic methods (Hammersley and Atkinson, 2007). Since the early 2000s, social scientists, including criminologists, have sought to adapt the principles of ethnographic research and apply them to the study of online action and interaction, particularly in respect of 'virtual communities' (Hine, 2000). We will consider the use of such methods in criminological research below.

However, before we explore virtual ethnography proper, we need to consider what may be termed a partial or 'quasi-ethnographic' approach to online social research, namely non-participant and/or covert observation. Here, the researcher does not involve him/herself directly in interaction with the community being studied, but simply observes and records the actions and interactions of others. In some cases, the researcher may not make their presence, or activity *as* a researcher, known to those being studied. In the case of online research, such an approach is often referred to as 'lurking' (Elgesem, 2002). Online or offline, it inevitably poses some serious ethical questions, as it breaches some key principles of informed consent: that subjects be aware that research is being conducted; that they be informed as to the nature, purposes and uses of the research and the data gathered; that they be given appropriate assurances about privacy, anonymity and confidentiality; and that they be given the right to withdraw their consent to participate in the research at any time should they wish to do so (Reid, 1996). There are numerous cases where such covert observation has been deemed justifiable, as, for example, when investigating practices that are illegal and/or to which the researcher would likely otherwise be denied access (see, for example, Patrick's (2013) study of violent street gangs in Glasgow, and Pearson's (2009) research on football 'hooligans'). In the online context, we can note Brotsky and Giles' (2007) covert study of a 'pro-ana' (pro-anorexia/pro-eating

disorder) community on the internet. A criminological instance of such online ethnography is provided by Banks' (2013) study of a high-risk internet gambling
sub-culture in which the possibility of criminal victimization is a prominent feature.
However, any student wishing to engage in such research for their own project will
likely face some vigorous questioning from their supervisors and have to justify their
proposal through a process of ethical approval, the result of which would by no
means be assured.

Returning to the more commonplace practice of 'virtual ethnography' or online
participant observation, this is largely based on the idea that internet-based spaces
can be treated as in some sense analogous to offline communities – places that people
inhabit together, and within which they engage in interactions that are bound up
with the formation of shared beliefs, norms and identities. As Williams (2008: 456)
notes, such spaces take diverse forms, including 'web pages, newsgroups, online discussion lists, blogs, wikis, chat rooms, and graphical online communities'. His own
criminological research provides a very good example of ethnographic research
conducted in virtual spaces (Box 18.4).

BOX 18.4   DEVIANCE AND SOCIAL CONTROL IN A VIRTUAL WORLD

Williams (2006, 2008) chose to centre his research on a 'virtual reality online social
space', rendered graphically in 3D and within which participants could interact with
each other, via their online 'avatars', in real time. He observed inhabitants' behaviours in this 'cyberworld' as well as interacting with them as a fellow participant.
Williams explored how such spaces become host to 'unprecedented acts of online
deviance' as participants experience 'disinhibition' and a loosening of the constraints to which they are accustomed in offline interaction. These transgressive acts
included harassment, sexual harassment, racial harassment, vandalism and obscenity. Borrowing from Hirschi's (1969) 'control theory', he linked the levels and kinds of
offending behaviour to the degrees of attachment, commitment and involvement
that offenders had with the online community as well as their commitment to a
shared set of values and beliefs. However, he also found that, over time, there developed norms for regulating and controlling such offending behaviour through the
reactions of condemnation and disapproval on the part of members (Williams, 2006,
2008: 458–9).

As with other forms of internet-based criminological research, virtual ethnography
provides valuable opportunities to investigate a rich variety of groups and communities, from all over the world, who might otherwise be very difficult to observe and

interact with – after all, very few people have the time and resources needed to spend extended periods of time in a distant location for the purposes of research. Moreover, it has been argued that online ethnography needs to be included in our attempts to understand contemporary society (including issues of crime and deviance) simply because an increasing proportion of social action and interaction takes place in such virtual settings (Garcia et al., 2009); online existence is an ever more significant part of people's everyday lives, and no account of those lives can in a sense be complete without exploring how they unfold in computer-mediated settings. However, there are also a number of challenges the researcher must address if attempting to undertake a successful online ethnography, including:

- gaining access and permission from those whose online lives are being studied
- establishing rapport and trust via interactions that lack a physical co-presence and that may take place largely through text-based exchanges
- acquiring the skills necessary to analyse and interpret interactions that can comprise not only written communication, but also a variety of audio and visual data (such as photographs and video recordings).

These challenges notwithstanding, virtual ethnography offers some exciting opportunities for broadening the scope of criminological research, enabling us to generate new insights into the dynamics of crime, deviance and social control in a multimedia age.

SUMMARY AND REVIEW

This chapter has overviewed a variety of ways that the internet may prove useful for those doing criminological research. First, it provides a valuable range of freely accessible resources including articles that can serve as the basis of your literature review and secondary data that you can use as the basis for answering your own research questions. Second, it considered how web-based content can provide the basis for a criminological study, including, for example, crime-related discourse and criminal behaviour found on websites and social media platforms. Third, it examined how you might use the internet to find and engage research participants, by adapting familiar research techniques (interviews, surveys) to the online setting. Fourth, it introduced the practice of virtual ethnography, where the researcher engages in participant observation of online groups and communities. A number of case studies and examples have been offered to illustrate how these techniques have been put to practical use by social and criminological researchers. All of the above approaches offer important new avenues for the researcher to explore criminological topics, but they also have some drawbacks and limitations as well as advantages and benefits, and these have been noted so that you can take them into account when planning and executing your own research project.

Consider the following questions about doing criminological research online:

1. How can you ensure that, as far as possible, the literature and resources you locate online are of sufficient quality and rigour?

2. Do you need to collect your own (primary) data in order to answer your research question, or do online repositories offer data that has already been collected by others which can be 'repurposed'? If so, what are the limitations of relying on secondary data of this kind?

3. What kinds of criminological topics are well suited to research that focuses in on web-based content as the object of analysis?

4. What are the practical and ethical challenges you need to overcome in order to successfully find and engage with research participants online, and what are the relative costs and benefits of using different online techniques such as interviews, surveys, covert observation and participant observation?

SUGGESTIONS FOR FURTHER READING

Elgesem's (2002) article from *Ethics and Information Technology* offers a clear and careful overview of the distinctive ethical issues that arise when conducting online social research. Macmillan's article, 'The microscope and the moving target' considers how content analysis techniques can be adapted for online research, as well as identifying some of the challenges that you are likely to encounter when attempting to do so. Meho's (2006) article examines a range of studies that used email surveys as research tools, and comes up with a useful model that combines online and offline approaches so as to generate the best possible results. Finally, Williams' (2008) chapter on 'Cybercrime and online methodologies' focuses on how online methods can be effectively used to study crimes that themselves take place on the internet.

REFERENCES

Adar, E., Teevan, J., Dumais, S.T. and Elsas, J.L. (2009) 'The web changes everything: understanding the dynamics of web content', in *Proceedings of the Second ACM International Conference on Web Search and Data Mining*. Barcelona, February.

Andrews, D., Nonnecke, B. and Preece, J. (2003) 'Electronic survey methodology: a case study in reaching hard-to-involve internet users', *International Journal of Human-Computer Interaction*, 16(2): 185–210.

Banks, J. (2013) 'Edging your bets: advantage play, gambling, crime and victimisation', *Crime, Media, Culture*, 9(2): 171–87.

Bergman, M.K. (2001) 'White paper: the deep web – surfacing hidden value', *Journal of Electronic Publishing*, 7(1): 1–17.

Biernacki, P. and Waldorf, D. (1981) 'Snowball sampling: problems and techniques of chain referral sampling', *Sociological Methods & Research*, 10(2): 141–63.

Bishop, J. (2013) 'The art of trolling law enforcement: a review and model for implementing "flame trolling" legislation enacted in Great Britain (1981–2012)', *International Review of Law, Computers & Technology*, 27(3): 301–18.

Brotsky, S.R. and Giles, D. (2007) 'Inside the "pro-ana" community: a covert online participant observation', *Eating Disorders*, 15(2): 93–109.

Bryman, A. (2012) *Social Research Methods*, 4th edition. Oxford: Oxford University Press.

Chamberlain, J.M. (2013) *Understanding Criminological Research: A Guide to Data Analysis*. London: Sage.

Chermak, S. (1995) 'Image control: how police affect the presentation of crime news', *American Journal of Police*, 14(2): 21–43.

Conway, M. (2016) 'Determining the role of the internet in violent extremism and terrorism: six suggestions for progressing research', *Studies in Conflict & Terrorism*, 40(1): 77–98.

Dinev, T. (2006) 'Why spoofing is serious internet fraud', *Communications of the ACM*, 49(10): 76–82.

Duffy, M.E. (2003) 'Web of hate: a fantasy theme analysis of the rhetorical vision of hate groups online', *Journal of Communication Inquiry*, 27(3): 291–312.

Elgesem, D. (2002) 'What is special about the ethical issues in online research?', *Ethics and Information Technology*, 4(3): 195–203.

Evans, M.P. (2007) 'Analysing Google rankings through search engine optimization data', *Internet Research*, 17(1): 21–37.

Fichten, C.S., Tagalakis, V., Judd, D., Wright, J. and Amsel, R. (1992) 'Verbal and nonverbal communication cues in daily conversations and dating', *The Journal of Social Psychology*, 132(6): 751–69.

Friemel, T.N. (2016) 'The digital divide has grown old: determinants of a digital divide among seniors', *New Media & Society*, 18(2): 313–31.

Garcia, A.C., Standlee, A.I., Bechkoff, J. and Cui, Y. (2009) 'Ethnographic approaches to the internet and computer-mediated communication', *Journal of Contemporary Ethnography*, 38(1): 52–84.

Gerstenfeld, P.B., Grant, D.R. and Chiang, C.P. (2003) 'Hate online: a content analysis of extremist internet sites', *Analyses of Social Issues and Public Policy*, 3(1): 29–44.

Hale, C. (1996) 'Fear of crime: a review of the literature', *International Review of Victimology*, 4(2): 79–150.

Hammersley, M. and Atkinson, P. (2007) *Ethnography: Principles in Practice*. London: Routledge.

Herring, S.C. (2009) 'Web content analysis: expanding the paradigm', in J. Hunsinger, M. Allen and L. Klastrup (eds), *International Handbook of Internet Research*. Dordrecht: Springer.

Hine, C. (2000) *Virtual Ethnography*. London: Sage.

Hirschi, T. (1969) 'A control theory of delinquency', in F.P. Williams III and M.D. McShane (eds), *Criminology Theory: Selected Classic Readings*. Cincinnati, OH: Elsevier.

Holt, T.J., Bossler, A.M. and Seigfried-Spellar, K.C. (2015) *Cybercrime and Digital Forensics: An Introduction*. Abingdon and New York: Routledge.

Internet Live Stats (2016) Total Number of Websites. Available at: www.internetlivestats.com/total-number-of-websites (accessed May 2018).

Internet World Statistics (IWS) (2015) World Internet Users and 2015 Population Stats. Available at: www.internetworldstats.com/stats.htm (accessed May 2018).

Jesson, J., Matheson, L. and Lacey, F.M. (2011) *Doing Your Literature Review: Traditional and Systematic Techniques*. London: Sage.

Jones, J.S. (2010) 'Origins and ancestors: a brief history of ethnography', in J.S. Jones and S. Watt (eds), *Ethnography in Social Science Practice*. London and New York: Routledge.

Khabsa, M. and Giles, C.L. (2014) 'The number of scholarly documents on the public web', *PloS One*, 9(5): e93949.

Lee, E. and Leets, L. (2002) 'Persuasive storytelling by hate groups online: examining its effects on adolescents', *American Behavioral Scientist*, 45(6): 927–57.

McMillan, S.J. (2000) 'The microscope and the moving target: the challenge of applying content analysis to the World Wide Web', *Journalism & Mass Communication Quarterly*, 77(1): 80–98.

Mawby, R.C. (2002) 'Continuity and change, convergence and divergence: the policy and practice of police–media relations', *Criminology and Criminal Justice*, 2(3): 303–24.

May, T. (2011) *Social Research: Issues, Methods and Process*, 4th edition. Maidenhead: Open University Press/McGraw-Hill.

Meho, L.I. (2006) 'E-mail interviewing in qualitative research: a methodological discussion', *Journal of the American Society for Information Science and Technology*, 57(10): 1284–95.

Nielsen, L.B. (2002) 'Subtle, pervasive, harmful: racist and sexist remarks in public as hate speech', *Journal of Social Issues*, 58(2): 265–80.

Palys, T. (2008) 'Purposive sampling', in L. Given (ed.), *The Sage Encyclopedia of Qualitative Research Methods*, Vol. 2. Thousand Oaks, CA: Sage.

Patrick, J. (2013) *A Glasgow Gang Observed*. London: Neil Wilson Publishing.

Pearson, G. (2009) 'The researcher as hooligan: where "participant" observation means breaking the law', *International Journal of Social Research Methodology*, 12(3): 243–55.

Pickett, J.T., Mancini, C. and Mears, D.P. (2013) 'Vulnerable victims, monstrous offenders, and unmanageable risk: explaining public opinion on the social control of sex crime', *Criminology*, 51(3): 729–59.

Ragnedda, M. and Muschert, G.W. (2013) *The Digital Divide: The Internet and Social Inequality in International Perspective*. Abingdon and New York: Routledge.

Reid, E. (1996) 'Informed consent in the study of on-line communities: a reflection on the effects of computer-mediated social research', *The Information Society*, 12(2): 169–74.

Riffe, D., Lacy, S. and Fico, F. (2014) *Analyzing Media Messages: Using Quantitative Content Analysis in Research*. London and New York: Routledge.

Schneider, C.J. (2016) 'Police presentational strategies on Twitter in Canada', *Policing and Society*, 26(2): 129–47.

Sillince, J.A. and Brown, A.D. (2009) 'Multiple organizational identities and legitimacy: the rhetoric of police websites', *Human Relations*, 62(12): 1829–56.

Thornberry, T.P. and Krohn, M.D. (2000) 'The self-report method for measuring delinquency and crime', *Criminal Justice*, 4(1): 33–83.

Wall, D.S. (2007) *Cybercrime: The Transformation of Crime in the Information Age*. Cambridge: Polity Press.

Williams, M. (2006) *Virtually Criminal*. London: Routledge.

Williams, M. (2008) 'Cybercrime and online methodologies', in R.D. King and E. Wincup (eds), *Doing Research on Crime and Justice*, 2nd edition. Oxford: Oxford University Press.

Yar, M. (2005) 'The global "epidemic" of movie "piracy": crime-wave or social construction?', *Media, Culture & Society*, 27(5): 677–96.

Yar, M. (2013) *Cybercrime and Society*, 2nd edition. London: Sage.

CHAPTER CONTENTS

GLOSSARY TERMS

visual turn
experience
visual criminology
semiotics

19 USING VISUAL METHODS IN CRIMINOLOGICAL RESEARCH

RONNIE LIPPENS

INTRODUCTION

This chapter commences with a discussion about a painting. This is used as a segue into explaining why 'the visual' has emerged, during the last few decades, as one of the more salient themes in the social sciences, including criminology. The main body of the chapter explores how criminologists and criminological research have been impacted by this 'visual turn', leading to the formation of what has become known as *visual criminology*. Reflections on visual methodology and on the importance of 'experience' in visual research are threaded throughout. In the final sections, the chapter will focus on the importance of images of, broadly speaking, justice, law and order in criminology and in criminological research.

CONTEXTUALIZING VISUAL CRIMINOLOGICAL RESEARCH

The Koestler Trust is a charity that supports prisoners who wish to engage in the arts, including visual arts such as painting. The Trust has a website at www.koestlertrust.org.uk. Funded by a variety of national arts councils and offender rehabilitation organizations, the Trust uses artistic mentoring of prisoners and detainees broadly as a rehabilitative strategy. The Trust regularly organizes artistic exhibitions and awards prizes for outstanding work. The overall idea and guiding principle is that by being creative, and by transforming his outlook onto the world in an artistic way, the prisoner will also create himself (or herself, of course; henceforth one or the other) anew and transform or, indeed, reform his own self in the process, and therefore also, at least potentially, the character of his future life choices. On one such an award occasion, a prisoner submitted the painting pictured in Figure 19.1.

The artist himself said that the painting represents Tom Daley, the Olympian, and that he painted it because he sympathised with the diver at a time when he (i.e. Daley) had to endure constant slurs on social media following his 'coming out' about his sexuality.

It is, however, hard not to sense (the use of this word is significant, as we shall see) that there might be more to the picture than just the representation of a well-known Olympic diver. Notice, for example, that the painter chose to paint Daley at the point when he had already broken the surface of the water and not, as one would perhaps have expected of a painting of a diver, during the full free fall of the dive itself. This is quite significant. What happens under water is the one thing that we, as spectators, can only guess at. During the fall itself, the diver's destination is, all his movements notwithstanding, fixed. Gravity will make certain that the only way for the diver to go is downwards. The diver, during the fall, is at the complete mercy of the law of physics and is, ultimately, incapable of doing anything about this.

FIGURE 19.1 'Coming up for Air'

Source: HMP Whitemoor, Koestler Awards 2013, Ariadne Bimberg Highly Commended Award for Oil or Acrylic. Courtesy of the Koestler Trust

Once in the water though, the diver gradually gains more freedom of movement. At first, movements are still hampered by what it seems is the memory of the gravity that came with the fall (do note how the painter has captured this 'memory' with the whitish expanse of air bubbles in Daley's wake). But soon there will be a point when the diver will be able to get a grip, so to speak, and regain a measure of control not just over his own movements, but also over the direction of travel (upwards!) and the path to take. It is worth noting that the painting was given the title *Coming up for Air.* See how the glimmering light at the surface (in the top-left corner of the painting) seems to be beckoning the diver. Of all the moments in a dive this is the exact one that was chosen by the painter. You could now ask yourself, why did the painter choose this moment? What went through the painter's mind when he was staring at the blank canvas? What was he visualizing in his mind's eye? Why? Would this have been a completely deliberate, conscious decision? Or would there have been subconscious motivations at play as well?

The painter himself may not necessarily know the answer to this question. It could very well be that the choice was made, by the painter, at a subconscious level.

He may just have woken up one day saying to himself 'I'll just paint Tom when he's in the water', and that could have been that. But that choice, however subconsciously made, is a significant one. It could, for example, have been the case that the painter actually wanted to express something about what it is like to be in prison, or better, what it *feels* like to be in prison. One 'falls' into prison on what often seems to be a linear, downwards trajectory. Once there – after the plunge into the new environment – it will take a while to get accustomed to your new life as a prisoner. You will need time to find your feet. At some point, you will start thinking about life after prison, and you may even come to realize that, ultimately, there is hope and there is the possibility of redemption. There is light at the end of the tunnel (or in this case: at the surface) but you yourself will have to work your way towards it. You cannot leave it to others to do this for you. Perhaps this painter is, possibly without really consciously realizing it, artistically expressing how he felt, or where he saw himself, in his own process of rehabilitation and reform. Might it not be the case that the painter saw himself at exactly the point where, like the diver, away from the gaze of those in the outside world and quite sheltered in a way, he is wresting himself free from the determinations of his past, gradually preparing to take his life in his own hands, and embarking upon a road which criminologists tend to call the process of desistance from crime? It may have been the case that his artistic endeavours and accomplishments have indeed, as the Koestler Trust hopes, contributed to this painter's rehabilitative 'moment'.

But a picture is worth a lot *more* than a thousand words. We (the painter himself, and us, the criminologists looking at his work) can say all kinds of things about the painting, but none of our words or statements will be able to capture the whole image. Highly metaphorical language, or poetry, or language with very high 'imagery' content, can go some way (see e.g. Bachelard, 1964), but not too far. You could do the following experiment. Just look at the painting for a while, and try to forget all the words and ideas that are now bubbling up in your mind. Try to *sense* what it feels like to fall into a swimming pool from a height of about 15 meters, and to arrive at the point where you are just about finding something like a balance. Well, *that*, the painter seems to be suggesting, is what it feels like to arrive at a turning point in your life, in prison. The point that is made here is that images have something really physical, something really bodily about them. Yes, we can use language to talk about them. Yes, we can use concepts (e.g. 'rehabilitation', 'reform', 'determination', 'desistance', and so on) to think about them. But, in the end, images will always elude the grasp of anything in the way of conceptual language that we can throw at them. They are, first and foremost, *sensory* phenomena. As philosophers (e.g. Gendlin, 1962; Merleau-Ponty, 1968) and neurobiologists (e.g. Damasio, 2003) alike have argued, images are, first and foremost, about the senses, about feeling and about emotion. Realizing this, and acquiring an attitude that takes account of this, could be the first methodological step that researchers of the image may wish to take (see also Young, 2014, for a related argument).

We will explore these issues in some depth below. In the next section, you will find explanations as to why 'the visual' has emerged as one of the more salient themes in criminology.

THE VISUAL TURN IN THE SOCIAL SCIENCES

The visual turn in the social sciences – both in theory and research – is a fairly recent phenomenon. The visual turn gained quite some momentum during the 1990s and today, well into the twenty-first century, it has become part of the mainstream in theoretical exploration and empirical research (for an overview of the theoretical literature on the visual, and the interest in images in particular, see the anthology in Manghani et al., 2006). It could of course be argued that the history of the interest in the visual in the social sciences goes further back in time. Let's take criminology, for example. Was it not the case that nineteenth-century researchers such as Cesare Lombroso were already very much interested in images (in Lombroso's case: photographs of convicted offenders from whose facial and cranial characteristics he tried to infer the presence, or absence, of 'atavistic' criminality)? This is true (see on this Rafter, 1997 and 2014), but Lombroso's basic assumption was that ultimate objective truth could be read from the surface of images and bodies. The visual turn that emerged at the end of the twentieth century, as we shall see, started from radically opposed premises.

It could also be argued that already during the 1970s we had theorists and scholars who were preoccupied with the visual, or with vision. Michel Foucault's well-known work (1977) on Jeremy Bentham's eighteenth-century idea of the *Panopticon* prison-house, and its broader social and governmental implications, focused a lot on the importance of vision, or the gaze, in problems and practices of social control (see again Rafter, 2014). The idea here was that the gaze of the controllers has an impact on the behaviour of those that are thus controlled, and vice versa. Again, this is true. But authors such as Michel Foucault, or his followers (e.g. Edward Said, 1978, who worked on how the West has historically tended to look upon the Orient), did not focus on images as such. They were much more interested in what they called 'discourse', or 'discourses', i.e. collections of ways of thinking and speaking about the world that shape and somehow pre-structure the ways that those who share them indeed think and speak about the world. This is an important point though. If it is indeed the case that we, as criminological researchers, or just as individuals, tend to think and speak about the world in ways that are somehow, at least to some extent, pre-structured by the 'discourses' which, in the course of our life, we have come across, and that surround us, and that we may have adopted without really realizing it, then the likelihood of there being an ultimate, objective truth 'out there' for us to access, becomes very remote indeed. It is this insight (or better: awareness) that prompted a considerable number of social scientists, including criminologists, to change tack and leave their longstanding fixation on language behind.

Language comes in different forms. You have everyday colloquial speech, but there is also scientific, academic or philosophical language which is highly abstract and conceptual. Concepts are language-based instruments that help scientists and researchers to think about the world, or about particular topics in that world (say, 'crime', or 'punishment', 'justice' and 'order'). No amount of language though is able to really 'get to grips' with the world. Depending on where we are standing, and where we are thinking and speaking from, or to rephrase this, depending on our 'perspective', or our 'discursive' positioning, we will think and say this or that about the world, using this or that concept. But the world itself will always elude our language. However many conceptual instruments, and however much language we generate in an attempt to reach the real, objective essence of the world (or the problem under consideration therein), the world itself will remain out of our linguistic grasp. Language cannot 'grasp', although it can have an impact on the world: if I tell you, out of the blue, that I think you are untrustworthy, a 'criminal' even, then this will have an impact on you and on our relationship.

 But here we are already entering the realm of 'experience'. If language is too weak an instrument for 'grasping' the world, and life in it, then perhaps 'experience' is more useful. A focus on 'experience' in social sciences research is as such not new. You know that much ethnographic research is very much about gathering insights in 'experience' and, indeed, about 'experiencing' itself. In criminology, this has been the case since the days of the Chicago School of Urban Sociology in the 1920s and 1930s. During the visual turn of the final decades of the twentieth century though, the focus came to rest on explorations of sensory experience, visual experience in particular, and the role and importance of images in how people, in different cultural contexts, make sense (read again: make *sense*) of their world and their life experiences (see e.g. the collection in Hayward and Presdee, 2010). In the quotation in Box 19.1, one of the editors of *Framing Crime: Cultural Criminology and the Image* (2010) points to the importance of research that is focused on studying images.

BOX 19.1   RESEARCH FOCUSED ON
STUDYING IMAGES

'It is no longer sufficient just to count or codify images, or even to strive to unearth spurious *causal linkages* between media representation and subsequent human behaviour. Instead we must approach our subject matter as a person studies an album of photographs, or as a visitor approaches a painting in a gallery – from various angles and from different perspectives. If images are creatively constructed, then we must study not just the image itself, but also the process of construction and the subsequent processes of production, framing and interpretation.' (Hayward and Presdee, 2010: 13–14)

But more is to be said here. In the dying decades of the twentieth century, life had changed considerably, particularly in Western democracies. In an extremely intensive consumer culture, or a 'society of the spectacle', as French cultural theorist Guy

Debord (1967) once called it, there are of course a lot more images ('spectacles') around. But the changes referred to above are more complicated than that. For a variety of reasons, life became a lot less structured and ordered than it used to be. Just think of the collapse of what we used to call 'the welfare state', with its pre-structured and *institutionalized* life trajectories and provisions. Life today, in this age of what sociologists call *de-institutionalization*, has become a lot more uncertain and insecure, *unhinged* even, some might say. Individual life trajectories have become highly dependent on chance and opportunity. This process has come with considerable levels of anxiety. In a world where we are now forced to forge our own path in life, many of us have become quite wary, obsessed with 'risk' and its 'control', and highly emotional. The institutions that used to keep high levels of emotionality in check are no longer there. Emotionality now runs almost unhindered through the veins of our lives. This, in turn, has added to a sharpening interest, in social science research, in the emotional dimension of life experiences, and in related themes such as bodily and sensory experience, including visual experience. Sensory, and therefore also visual experience, is imbued with 'feeling', and with emotion. It is this feeling and this emotion that researchers of the visual and the image often explore in an attempt to 'get to grips' with life and life experiences.

VISUAL CRIMINOLOGY

This emerging field of visual criminology is quite varied and many criminologists have their own ideas about what it should comprise. The *state of the art* overview volume edited by Brown and Carrabine (2017) illustrates the variety of ideas and themes in the field of visual criminology. The volume, in the field of legal visual culture, edited by Wagner and Sherwin (2014) provides us with even more illustrations. Some authors would include the analysis and study of visual media (film, theatre, television, the press, and so on), or social media. Others, such as the author of this chapter, are more interested in images themselves, that is, in that which is almost purely sensory in media exchanges. A Hollywood movie, for example, is, granted, largely visual, but in reality it is highly language-based; indeed, it is the result of highly structured, pre-planned, conceptual thinking and script-writing. They also include visual images though, and it is the images in films *qua images* that these authors would tend to focus on. It should be noted here that the nature of the study and analysis of images will depend on the type and the purpose of the images under consideration. This point is explored in more depth in the remainder of this chapter.

Images are often studied by visual criminologists as such, as images. But visual criminologists also use images during their very research activities. Indeed, images are often used as research tools in a variety of ways. We shall explore that point in the next section. Before we do that, we will say a little more about the study, by visual criminologists, of images as such. In general, it may be safe to say that the field of visual criminology includes a number of areas or themes where the study of images could find a place. Let us list those by using *artistic* images as illustrations (the following list is not exhaustive):

1. Images as conduits for criminalization or accusation

Images are sometimes made, used or otherwise mobilized, in order to accuse particular groups, or to criminalize or otherwise censure particular behaviours and actions. Think of the painting by Goya, *The Third of May 1808* (you should be able to find this painting, and any other images mentioned below, on the internet), which was painted during the Napoleonic Wars in Spain. One would have trouble to think of a painting that did a better job of accusing or indeed criminalizing brutal power. The theme is Napoleon Bonaparte's siege of Madrid and its aftermath. But look at the colours. Look at the forms in this painting. On the right, you'll see the machine-like force of the firing squad; on the left, the Christ-like features of the rebels.

2. The criminalization of images, or: the image standing accused itself

A number of years ago, the artist Andres Serrano made a photograph which he gave the title 'Piss Christ'. The artist took a picture of a crucifix immersed in what he claimed was his own urine. This picture caused quite a stir and the artist was accused, among other things, of blasphemy. The artwork itself was vandalized on a number of occasions. Or take Marcus Harvey's 'Myra', which he painted in 1995. Harvey used casts of an infant's hand to daub the paint on the canvas, thus producing the face of Myra Hindley, one of the 1960s Moors murderers. This painting too was vandalized on a number of occasions. How to explain the almost obsessive reactions to such paintings? Which are the social and emotional chords that these paintings seem to strike? (On these artworks, see Young, 2000.)

3. The spatial travel of images deemed 'deviant'

Think of graffiti art. Recently, a number of 'bigger than life' graffiti artworks mysteriously materialized in the heart of Brussels. One of them represented a woman masturbating. It appeared on one of the gables in the Avenue Louise, one of Brussels' shopping streets. The picture itself didn't really shock the public. We seem to have arrived at a point in our consumer culture where shoppers in top-end shopping streets take such images in their stride. But the artwork could have been a clever comment on exactly the nature of contemporary consumerism. Graffiti tends to travel through urban spaces, colonizing some, and popping up unannounced in others, as if the artists are trying to say (as they sometimes do using words) that they, and their desires, are uncontrollable, or ungovernable (Halsey and Young, 2006).

4. Images of spaces, and populations therein, deemed 'deviant'

Do Google 'Edward Hopper'. Click on his 'Approaching a City' painting. Hopper painted this in 1946. The city is looming darkly. The tunnel in front of us looks like what seems to be the gates of hell. The city itself is the 'deviant' space here. This probably tells us something about Hopper, or about others, whether artist or not, who think of big cities as Gotham-like dens of hellish vice. The work of British geographer David Sibley (1995) on *spaces of exclusion* has been quite seminal in this area of study and research. Others, such as visual criminologists Keith Hayward and Majid Yar (2006), have researched and theorized how the visual appearance of particular groups (e.g. the dress code of 'chavs') often exacerbates levels of contempt towards them.

5. Images that attempt to explain or comment on crime or deviance

Edward Hopper knew many of the painters who were members of an early twentieth-century artistic group, i.e. the so-called Ashcan group, a group of realist painters. One of those painters was Everett Shinn. He would paint street fights and so on. But he also painted 'Eviction' in 1904 (you may wish to Google this painting). This painting does a lot of explaining. It explains what life was like in the slums of New York around the turn of the twentieth century, and suggests why this was the case.

6. The use of images in crime control and criminal justice

Images have their uses in all stages of the criminal justice process. This is of course well known. One of the emerging phenomena in criminal justice is the introduction, during trial proceedings, of FMRI imaging (brain scans, to you and me). In some trial proceedings, evidence will include visual materials such as photographs, or CCTV footage, and so on. The use of images during court proceedings tends to have a very significant impact on those present (Feigenson, 2016).

7. Images of crime control and criminal justice

Throughout history, artists have produced images of court proceedings, punishment, execution, as well as images of torture and cruel and unusual forms of punishment and treatment (see recent theoretical work on such topics by visual criminologists such as Carrabine (2011a, 2011b) or Morrison (2004)). One topic that has been ignored somewhat is art by prisoners and detainees themselves. Prisoners themselves have of course lots to say about crime and justice. Some of them 'say' it through visual art. Let us remind ourselves that we started this chapter by analysing one such work of art. Let us now move on to some methodological considerations.

EXPERIENCING AND USING IMAGES

It should come as no surprise that roughly since the turn of the century a considerable number of textbooks on visual methodology have seen the light (e.g. Rose, 2016). In what follows, we will be able to highlight only a number of crucially important issues in visual research and methods.

In all the areas or themes listed in the previous sections, images may appear on the researcher's radar in at least two ways. We shall consider both of these separately, although it should be stressed that some research designs may of course include elements of both. First, there are images which the researcher will have stumbled across during her research, such as a photograph taken in a neighbourhood that has a reputation for being 'rough', or a video clip that purports to depict or document police brutality, or the dress, tattoos and jewellery that, gang members tell us, symbolize what they stand for, or perhaps a painting made by a 'lifer' in prison, or a series of photographs taken by political revolutionaries (see e.g. Lippens, 2003a), or by business marketing executives (see e.g. Lippens, 2003b). These images were already there. The researcher was not involved in their fabrication, and now she has to 'make sense' of them, for example in a bid to understand how the images shed light on what life is like within the cultural context (within the 'sub-culture', we would once have said) where it was produced or whence it emerged. Here, the work of the researcher is largely about 'making sense' of the images within their particular social and historical context.

But there is at least one other way through which images may enter a particular research project. Here the researcher uses the image as a tool to get things done, to achieve particular goals. The researcher may wish, for example, to use the image to connect with her research subjects on a more emotional level, thus going beyond the standard interview and observation formats. This certainly 'makes sense' in light of what we have said above. Or the researcher may decide to invite her research subjects, during the very research process itself, to produce their own visual materials and imagery to express, at a sensory level, what their life is like, and what their life experiences 'feel' like. For example, researchers could ask offenders to take photographs or make pictures or artworks that express something of their experience, for instance their experience of imprisonment, or their experience as a supervisee on probation (see e.g. Fitzgibbon et al., 2017). Other researchers have asked asylum seekers and refugees to go on walks in the urban environment and to produce art-work based on their experience as refugees, and their experience of the walk as a refugee (see e.g. O'Neill, 2017).

Making sense of images

Let us first consider the situation whereby the researcher comes across an image. The type of image is important here. Are we talking about a photograph? Is it a painting? Or is it a still from a film? Each of these types has to be considered appropriately. Photographs, for example, as the cultural critic Susan Sontag has argued and demon-strated some time ago (1977), are surprisingly deceptive. They have something 'real' about them (who could deny that the figures on this or that photograph were actually there doing the things they obviously were doing there and then?) but, once taken, the photograph very often ends up in the hands of people who don't have a clue whatsoever about the circumstances in which the photograph was taken, and the purposes or, indeed, the hidden agendas with which this was done. Was the scene in the photograph staged? Was it meant to discredit something? Accuse someone? Is it, for all its apparent 'realness', a blunt lie? The researcher should be very wary of this, particularly where photographic material is concerned. The French philosopher and semiotician Roland Barthes (1977) – semiotics is the discipline and study of signs – adds that photographs have their own 'rhetoric', that is, they evoke a whole series of connotations which the researcher may have the background, or not, as the case may be, to detect. But there will always be a remainder of meaning in the visual dimension of the photographic image that, although very important, the researcher will be unable to put his finger on, explain or interpret. This remainder, or excess of mean-ing, Barthes says, is the image's 'obtuse meaning', i.e. that which cannot really be captured by textual and conceptual explanation, but which, nevertheless, has a serious impact – *sensory* impact – on the beholder. The same applies to stills from films. The complication with stills is that they are actually snapshots taken out of a particular context. By this is meant that stills are 'frozen' images extracted from what, basically, is a story and a more or less structured narrative that has its own often deliberate purpose and contemplated structure. Without any information on the latter, the researcher will often find himself in the dark of the still's 'obtuse meaning'.

The image on the researcher's desk, however, could be a painting, or a drawing, or a work of art. Artworks are a different kind of image. Here, a whole number of questions about the context of its production arise. With historical paintings in par-ticular, the researcher has to be aware of the fact that paintings were often commissioned by public, governmental or individual patrons of the art. That which the researcher believes they are able to 'sense' on the canvas, could, to some extent at least, be the result of what those who commissioned the artwork had in mind. Such artworks would not necessarily be able to 'tell' us (or better: 'show' us) a lot about the particular social or cultural conditions in which they were produced.

On the other hand, works of art, such as paintings for example, that were not commissioned, but that, on the contrary, were the fruit of the artist's creative and expressive imagination, are much more interesting as indicators of the 'feel' of the context of the particular age, or culture, in which they emerged. That said though, the painter, or the visual artist, even those that produce commissioned work, is bound to express something of herself, and her conditions of life, or her life experiences, in her works of art. The work of art, after all, is and remains a work of *art*, and, as art theorists such as Hillis Miller (1992) have argued, the 'artistic' aspect of the work, on the one hand, holds and betrays something of the world that produced it (and that is certainly of interest to us as researchers), whilst, at the same time, it also announces, at least potentially so, what is yet to come. In the next section, we shall discuss illustrations of this. For now, let us stress that, when confronted with artistic images, the researcher could do worse than ponder the extent to which the artwork (an etching of war crime atrocities, for example, or an artistic impression of life on the streets of a drugs-ridden neighbourhood in London) is an expression not just of what is, but also, though perhaps less obviously so, a harbinger of what is to come, or what is in the process of emerging. Artists, as some art historians (e.g. Haskell, 1993) have intimated, tend to be slightly more sensitive about emerging trends than most of us. Even before new social and cultural developments will have found their way into linguistic expressions or conceptual abstraction (i.e. in thought, speech and writing by journalists, academics, and so on), they will often have appeared in works of art by artists who were sensitive enough to pick up ('sense') early manifestations of those emerging trends, and who may have worked them into their paintings, drawings, etchings or installations. To put this somewhat cheekily: if, as a criminologist, you want to be ahead of the game of social and cultural interpretation, maybe you want to become an art historian or an art theorist first?

Let us now return to the researcher's desk and to the image on it. Let us suppose that the researcher has established that the image is a painting by a local community worker who tried to express what life 'feels' like in his local community. In this case, for example, the local community is a seriously deprived neighbourhood in a completely de-industrialized area, marked by high levels of unemployment, drug abuse and organized street crime (do Google, once more, the 'Ashcan' group; see also above). The researcher must now ask himself a number of questions:

- Did the community worker paint this himself?
- Was this work commissioned? If so, who commissioned it? Was it the local council, or a particular political party, or a charity, or an offender rehabilitation volunteering organization, or was it someone else altogether?

In any case, the researcher will then have to find out about, and think through, the artist's 'brief and charge', as the art theorist Michael Baxandall (1985) called it. In other words, what did the artist think he had to do when he was working on the painting? In commissioned work, this may be slightly easier as there may be information available (less so in older works) about the aims, restrictions and instructions that were given to the artist. In non-commissioned work, the artist herself usually invents or imagines her own 'brief and charge', taking clues from her everyday life experience, her surroundings, local and global conditions and trends, media reports, personal ambitions, aspirations, disappointments, and resulting emotions such as affection, anger, thirst for vengeance, or (why not) forgiveness, and so on, and on. Even in commissioned work, such elements will almost inevitably 'slip in'. It is, of course, impossible to completely lay bare the 'patterns of intention' (dixit Baxandall) that underpin the whole 'brief and charge' of a particular artistic image. Nearly always there will be, simply put, too many gaps in our understanding. Sometimes the artist, or the maker of the image, is able to say something that sheds some light on their *patterns of intention*, but this is not always the case, and whatever the artist or image maker says about it should never be taken at face value. The community worker in our example may claim that he painted the work because he felt he needed to give members of the local community hope, and a 'voice' in local policy decisions. He may mean what he says, and it may therefore at some level be 'true'. But in his brief and charge there may also be hidden motivations and unspoken, subconscious ambitions (e.g. his desire to achieve 'heroic' status locally by attacking the local council's policies) which the community worker would rather not talk about, or which he may actually not be fully conscious of. It should come as no surprise that it is often impossible to attain this level of detailed insight and understanding, although it should also be said that in art history this is often attempted. Mary Gedo (1994), for example, has been able to show how subconscious traces of events in the biography of the famous Belgian surrealist painter René Magritte had an impact on his work, and are actually indispensable for a good understanding of his paintings.

Once the brief and charge, or the patterns of intention surrounding the work, have been researched and analysed – always partially, always incompletely – the researcher will then have to 'make sense' of the image. Clues may of course, as said, be found in what the artist himself says or writes about the work. Such material should certainly not be ignored. But we already know that the artist, or the image maker, may not really be, or have been, aware himself of much of his own patterns of intention, or the social and cultural conditions in which those took shape. The artist may actually sometimes make attempts, whether subconsciously or not, to 'hide' or 'mask' some of these materials from the researcher, and from the world. This is the point – the point of 'making sense' – where the researcher properly enters the scene. Depending on the level of her cultural background and baggage, her insight into social and cultural history and trends, and research skills, she may be able – or not, as the case may be – to shed additional light on the 'sense' of the image, and to complement what the artist or the maker (or others for that matter) have already said about it. But here the researcher needs to be critically self-reflective. Her own 'sense making' will itself be structured by her own *patterns of intention*, and by her own adopted and sometimes cherished *brief and charge*. To evoke British cultural critic John Berger's words here, there will always be different 'ways of seeing' (1972).

How to 'make sense' of an image? Images often include symbolic elements. Symbols are images that refer to particular conventional meanings. You know that the notion of 'justice' is often allegorically represented by an image of a woman holding scales and wearing a blindfold. Justice's blindfold, for example, conventionally signifies, for instance, impartiality. In a way, such symbolic elements are not very interesting. Although symbolic conventionality can and often does change through history and across cultural contexts (see on this, for example, Stolleis (2009) on the changing symbolic meaning of the 'all-seeing eye' of authority in official documents and iconography), ultimately there is always something conventional and static – and possibly dull – about symbols. However, images also have form, colour and composition and it is those that the criminological researcher may wish to focus her attention on. It is in those more formal characteristics, for example, that researchers might be able to detect social and cultural historical change. If a painter suddenly uses a new technique, form or composition to express an idea, then this should prompt visual researchers to sit up and take note. They could be on the trace of a newly emerging social or cultural trend that has not yet manifested itself conceptually in language.

Images as useful research tools

'Making sense' of an image is, as I have tried to explain at the start of this chapter, a matter of 'sensing', really bodily 'sensing', what is going on in it. This bodily, sensory dimension of images is also the point where images (e.g. photographs or paintings) can become 'useful' for the researcher. Visual researchers sometimes use images to gain access to their research subjects (e.g. prisoners, homeless people, residents of a particular neighbourhood, graffiti artists, gang members, police officers, and so on). Images don't just help to establish contact with research subjects at a deeper emotional level than questionnaires or interview schedules, but, because they often achieve this, they also make it easier for research subjects, when invited to express what they think and feel about the images under consideration, to talk about their own life experiences and about the meanings they attach to those.

BOX 19.2   LUIGI GARIGLIO AND PHOTO ELICITATION

A recent example of research that has used photo elicitation is that of Luigi Gariglio who used pictures taken by himself during his ethnographic research in an Italian prison institution. He then invited prisoners and prison staff to discuss those images. You may wish to read his recent article, 'Photo-elicitation in prison ethnography' (2016).

The visual researcher may decide to go beyond mere photo elicitation (and subsequent *photo elucidation*) and encourage her research subjects to actually produce their own images or visual materials (videos, paintings, photographs, etc. – all worth a lot more than a thousand words), in order to, more directly and quite often, more *sensitively* express what it feels like to live such a life in such and such conditions. And finally, the researcher may then decide, for similar reasons, to disseminate the results of her research efforts using visual formats or images (e.g. posters, artwork, or perhaps an exhibition of photographs), instead of, or perhaps complementary to, language-based formats such as scientific articles or books.

IMAGES OF JUSTICE, LAW AND ORDER

Let us now add one more insight. The question here is: What is it that images of justice, law and order can 'tell' us about? Do they just tell us about what we know as 'law' or 'justice' or 'order'? Suppose that during your research into the history of the death penalty you stumble across Gerard David's diptych *The Judgment of Cambyses* (Figures 19.2 and 19.3). The painting was completed in 1498 and was hung in the chambers of the then aldermen's court in the Flemish city of Bruges (it still hangs in Bruges, in a local museum). Do have a look at the first panel (Figure 19.2). Here, a magistrate, or judge, Sisamnes, is arrested by the emperor Cambyses and his officials. In the backdrop you can see the judge's crime: he accepts a bribe. Now move to panel 2 (Figure 19.3). Here the judge is executed for his crime. He is being flayed alive. In the background, there is a scene that takes place shortly after the execution: the judge's son, Otanes, has been appointed the new magistrate by the emperor and is seated on a bench draped with his father's skin. The painter's 'brief and charge' was probably to paint such a scene in order to remind Bruges' magistrates of the need to remain morally virtuous.

Now: is this diptych showing us something about law and justice at the end of the fifteenth century in Flanders? We know from the historical record that public executions could be very gruesome indeed in those days. But the theme of this painting is not particularly interesting to us. The painter only depicted a scene from Antiquity that was well known in the fifteenth century. The judgment of Cambyses was then known from ancient Greek historical sources that situated the story during the even earlier reign of a Persian emperor called Cambyses. This is good to know but that is not what makes the paintings in this diptych 'telling'. There is also a lot of symbolism in the paintings – for example, the white hound symbolizes moral virtue, and both genital-licking mongrels stand for corruption and depravity. But, again, this is not what makes the picture interesting.

FIGURE 19.2 Gerard David, *The Judgment of Cambyses* (1498), Panel 1, *The Arrest of Sisamnes*, Bruges, Groeninghe Museum

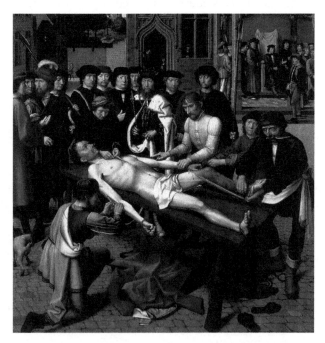

FIGURE 19.3 Gerard David, *The Judgment of Cambyses* (1498), Panel 2, *The Flaying of Sisamnes*, Bruges, Groeninghe Museum

If, however, you look at the form and composition of the panels, then you are bound to notice something. On the first panel, the whole situation has something fixed or 'frozen' about it. The scene on the second panel takes place in the open air, and there is a lot more dynamism to be noted in the market square. The new magistrate, Otanes, governs from what looks like an open and transparent court-house. We are able to see what is going on there. There are no backroom dealings going on in there. All is in the open and citizens seem to be entering and leaving the courthouse freely. This, at the time, was a new way of painting and it could very well be said that the painter, David, must have 'sensed' and picked up the emergence, at the end of the fifteenth century, of new ways of governance, and indeed a whole new way of life and of living together, which philosophers and jurists such as Thomas Moore, Niccolo Machiavelli and Erasmus of Rotterdam were only beginning to theorize about 15 years after the painting was completed (more on this particular painting is to be read in Lippens, 2009). So, here we have a painting that on the surface is about a 'law and justice' theme, but that is actually 'telling' us a lot more about a lot more. It depicts 'social and political change' at the end of the fifteenth century.

The reverse also holds. All images can potentially be useful to the visual crimi-nologist, not just the ones that explicitly depict law and justice related scenes. Think, in art, for example, of Jackson Pollock's signature 'drip technique' paintings which he started roughly from the end of the 1940s onwards. Do Google this painter's name and you will be able to see what is meant here by Pollock's drip technique. This technique, and this 'form' in painting, was, at the time, extremely new. Are these paintings of interest to visual criminologists? They are if you know that Pollock, on one of the very few occasions that he spoke about his art, men-tioned that they are about 'control'. Then you realize that, having gone, like so many others, through the horrible experience of the Second World War, and the authoritarianisms that drove it, Pollock took it as his 'brief and charge' to express a way of life in which no authority, no power, no force would be able to capture and restrict individuals' control over their life conditions or make a dent in their personal sovereignty. Jackson's dripping paint traces, then, represent people's unrelenting attempts to elude the grasp of law and authority. Here again we have an artist who 'sensed' a changing mood which only manifested itself fully in the decades after 1950, and which sociologists and criminologists are still trying to analyse and theorize even now. Pollock had 'sensed' this mood, had 'grasped' it and had very physically – Pollock's painting technique was physically intense – expressed it, all those years ago (on this, see Lippens, 2011).

The point that is made here is that *any image* can, at least potentially, be of inter-est to visual researchers in criminology. Images work on a deeper, sensory level. On this level, linguistic and conceptual boundaries between 'crime' and 'conformity', or 'law' and 'transgression', or 'order' and 'disorder', or 'justice' and 'injustice' make little 'sense'. Images live largely on the pre-conceptual level of *sense* and *experience*.

SUMMARY AND REVIEW

In this chapter, we have, of course, only been able to very briefly touch on a number of issues and problems in the field of visual criminology. Our focus here has largely been on the study and analysis of images and imagery of law, justice and order. The most important lesson, if you wish, that could be taken away from our explorations is that, methodologically speaking, a lot is still undecided in this emerging field of research. That should not worry us. On the contrary, it gives us some leeway to be inventive and to tentatively explore one very important sensory dimension of life experience (the visual) in *imaginative* ways.

In this chapter, the following themes have been explored:

1. The recent emergence of 'visual criminology', and the 'visual turn' in the social sciences and criminology, in an age when 'experience' has, to some extent, taken over from 'language' as the vehicle for communication, knowledge generation and knowledge exchange.
2. Within this context, the study and analysis of images and imagery have become more important than they used to be.
3. Visual criminologists may decide not just to study images as they find them; they may also use them actively during their research as tools to generate and exchange knowledge of, insight in and understanding of life experience.
4. The first and principal methodological step that visual criminologists and visual researchers may wish to take is to acquire an awareness of the specificity of the sensory realm, and the visual therein. This sensory realm of experience cannot be fully grasped by conceptual language. Researchers should, however, not despair.
5. In studying and analysing images of, for example, law, justice and order, researchers should make attempts to situate them within the 'brief and charge' of the image maker(s) and the broader social and cultural contexts within which they emerged.

STUDY QUESTIONS AND ACTIVITIES FOR STUDENTS

1. Read an edition of a newspaper. Locate coverage in which a particular geographical area, or a particular group, is written about in negative terms. Analyse how much of this coverage is based on, or is using, visual clues.

2. Picture yourself a number of youths at the corner of the street, all dressed in similar outfits and all wearing ostentatious jewellery. In small groups, discuss why

these youths may have chosen to dress and adorn themselves in this way, and what their visual appearance might mean to them.

3. Visit the Wikipedia webpage on 'the Abu Ghraib torture and prisoner abuse'. What would have happened if at the time we had known about these events through language-based newspaper coverage only? Could you explain your reasoning?

SUGGESTIONS FOR FURTHER READING

Students may wish to read an introductory textbook on visual methodologies in social sciences research. Gillian Rose's fourth edition (2016) of *Visual Methodologies: An Introduction to Researching with Visual Materials* is a good place to start. Over the course of the years, a number of edited collections and anthologies have appeared on the broader theme of visual criminology. Keith Hayward and the late Mike Presdee's collection (2010) on *Framing Crime: Cultural Criminology and the Image*, for example, includes theoretically informed contributions on the topic of how images are generated and imbued with meaning within particular (sub)-cultures. A state of the art anthology and reference work that includes empirical case-studies in the sphere of visual criminology can be found in Eamonn Carrabine and Michelle Brown's (2017) *Routledge International Handbook of Visual Criminology*. In socio-legal studies more broadly, there is Anne Wagner and Richard K. Sherwin's (2014) *Law, Culture, and Visual Studies*.

REFERENCES

Bachelard, G. (1964) *The Poetics of Space*. Boston: Beacon Press.

Barthes, R. (1977) *Image. Music. Text*. London: Fontana Press.

Baxandall, M. (1985) *Patterns of Intention: On the Historical Explanation of Pictures*. New Haven, CT: Yale University Press.

Berger, J. (1972) *Ways of Seeing*. London: BBC and Penguin.

Brown, M. and Carrabine, E. (eds) (2017) *Routledge International Handbook of Visual Criminology*. London: Routledge.

Carrabine, E. (2011a) 'The iconography of punishment: execution prints and the death penalty', *The Howard Journal of Criminal Justice*, 50(5): 452–64.

Carrabine, E. (2011b) 'Images of torture: culture, politics and power', *Crime, Media, Culture*, 7(1): 5–30.

Damasio, A. (2003) *Looking for Spinoza: Joy, Sorrow and the Feeling Brain*. Orlando, FL: Harcourt.

Debord, G. (1967) *La Société du Spectacle*. Paris: Buchet-Chastel.

Feigenson, N. (2016) *Experiencing Other Minds in the Courtroom*. Chicago: University of Chicago Press.

Fitzgibbon, W., Graebsch, C. and McNeill, F. (2017) 'Pervasive punishment: experiencing supervision', in M. Brown and E. Carrabine (eds), *Routledge International Handbook of Visual Criminology*. London: Routledge, pp. 305–19.

Foucault, M. (1977) *Discipline and Punish: The Birth of the Prison*. New York: Pantheon.

Gariglio, L. (2016) 'Photo-elicitation in prison ethnography: breaking the ice in the field and unpacking prison officers' use of force', *Crime, Media, Culture*, 12(3): 367–79.

Gedo, M.M. (1994) *Looking at Art from the Inside Out: The Psychoiconographic Approach to Modern Art*. Cambridge: Cambridge University Press.

Gendlin, E. (1962) *Experiencing and the Creation of Meaning: A Philosophical and Psychological Approach to the Subjective*. Evanston, IL: Northwestern University Press.

Halsey, M. and Young, A. (2006) 'Our desires are ungovernable: writing graffiti in public spaces', *Theoretical Criminology*, 10(3): 275–306.

Haskell, F. (1993) *History and its Images: Art and the Interpretation of the Past*. New Haven, CT: Yale University Press.

Hayward, K. and Presdee, M. (2010) *Framing Crime: Cultural Criminology and the Image*. London: Routledge.

Hayward, K. and Yar, M. (2006) 'The "chav" phenomenon: consumption, media and the construction of a new underclass', *Crime, Media, Culture*, 2(1): 9–28.

Hillis Miller, J. (1992) *Illustration*. London: Reaktion Books.

Lippens, R. (2003a) 'The imaginary of Zapatista revolutionary punishment and justice: speculations on "the first postmodern revolution"', *Punishment and Society*, 2: 179–95.

Lippens, R. (2003b) 'The imaginary of ethical business practice: contributions to an unobtrusive criminology of organization', *Crime, Law and Social Change*, 4: 323–47.

Lippens, R. (2009) 'Gerard David's *Cambyses* and early modern governance: notes on the geology of skin and the butchery of law', *Law and Humanities*, 3(1): 1–24.

Lippens, R. (2011) 'Jackson Pollock's flight from law and code: theses on responsive choice and the dawn of control society', *International Journal for the Semiotics of Law*, 24(1): 117–38.

Manghani, S., Piper, A. and Simons, J. (eds) (2006) *Images: A Reader*. London: Sage.

Merleau-Ponty, M. (1968) *The Visible and the Invisible*. Evanston, IL: Nothwestern University Press.

Morrison, W. (2004) 'Reflections with memories: everyday photography capturing genocide', *Theoretical Criminology*, 8(3): 341–58.

O'Neill, M. (2017) 'Asylum seekers and moving images: walking, sensorial encounters and visual criminology', in M. Brown and E. Carrabine (eds), *Routledge International Handbook of Visual Criminology*. London: Routledge, pp. 389–403.

Rafter, N.H. (1997) *Creating Born Criminals*. Chicago: University of Illinois Press.

Rafter, N.H. (2014) 'Introduction to the Special issue on Visual Culture and the Iconography of Crime and Punishment', *Theoretical Criminology, 18*(2): 127–33.

Rose, G. (2016) *Visual Methodologies: An Introduction to Researching with Visual Materials*, 4th edition. London: Sage.

Said, E. (1978) *Orientalism: Western Conceptions of the Orient*. London: Penguin.

Sibley, D. (1995) *Geographies of Exclusion*. London: Routledge.

Sontag, S. (1977) *On Photography*. Harmondsworth: Penguin.

Stolleis, M. (2009) *The Eye of the Law: Two Essays on Legal History*. London: Birkbeck Law Press.

Wagner, A. and Sherwin, R.K. (eds) (2014) *Law, Culture, and Visual Studies*. Dordrecht: Springer.

Young, A. (2000) 'Aesthetic vertigo and the jurisprudence of disgust', *Law and Critique, 11*(3): 241–55.

Young, A. (2014) 'From object to encounter: aesthetic politics and visual criminology', *Theoretical Criminology, 18*(2): 159–75.

CHAPTER CONTENTS

GLOSSARY TERMS

comparative methodology
longitudinal studies
cross-sectional studies
sampling error

20

DOING
COMPARATIVE
CRIMINOLOGICAL
RESEARCH

MATTHEW HALL

INTRODUCTION

Increasingly, as the forces of globalization have developed, criminologists have been called upon to examine crime and criminal justice issues in a so-called comparative context – that is to say, gathering information and data from each jurisdiction and comparing such phenomena between countries. Whilst at the outset this may seem a relatively straightforward task, many countries, broadly speaking, experience similar kinds of crime problem and utilize similar kinds of criminal justice responses, and though comparative work has many advantages over limiting research to a single jurisdiction, it can bring particular complications. This chapter will open with some discussion of globalization in relation to criminal justice and how that process has increasingly put the onus on criminologists to consider the criminal justice realms beyond their own national borders. The chapter will then focus on some of the methodological approaches that have been taken to comparative study, drawing on methodological literature from this field and delving into the specifics and the complexities of carrying out comparative research. The following section will then draw on a number of studies as exemplars of comparative research in action: commenting on both the positive aspects of these studies as well as their limitations. The section will draw on issues of policing, crime and victimization as key examples of areas in which comparative study has taken place. The chapter will also look ahead to what has been called the slowing down or even the 'death' of globalization to question what issues this may raise for comparative criminological research in the coming years.

GLOBALIZATION AND CRIMINAL JUSTICE

Up until quite recently, systematic comparison of the approaches taken by different states to crime and criminal justice was relatively uncommon in the mainstream criminological literature (Nelken, 2007). When such comparison did take place, it often involved subjecting different criminal justice systems around the world to blanket categorization into adversarial or inquisitorial models (Nagorcka et al., 2005). The former system is that used in the UK and most of its former territories and is characterized by an evidential contest between prosecution and defence before what are usually lay finders of fact (either juries or magistrates). The process is adjudicated by an impartial judge whose role is restricted to determining questions of law. In the latter model, used principally in mainland Europe, the judge takes a more active role, in most cases determining facts and law based on the collective production of a dossier on a case by prosecution and defence. Over time, however, scholars began to adopt a more sophisticated approach. One pertinent example is the work of Cavadino and Dignan (2007), who drew on comparative analysis of the penal systems across eight jurisdictions in order to categorise those jurisdictions based on the dominant political ideology taken to crime and criminal justice.

In more recent years, an increased focus on comparative work in many areas of social science has frequently been discussed alongside the overarching concept of 'globalization' (see Loader and Sparks, 2007). Most commonly, the term 'globalization' has been used to convey a sense of increasing transnational interconnectedness between processes previously isolated within individual states. Nevertheless, despite broad agreement over the existence and impacts of globalization, the concept itself remains markedly loose: a rhetorical shorthand for a whole collection of macro-social phenomena. Reinicke (1997), for example, criticizes the fact that the term 'globalization' is often used interchangeably with 'interdependence'.

Several commentators have attempted to be more specific about the meaning of globalization. For both Beerkens (2004) and Giddens (1990), for example, the key characteristic of globalization is the decoupling of time and space. Scholte (2000) prefers to think of globalization as 'deterritorialisation' (p. 46) whilst also emphasizing that 'the only consensus about globalisation is that it is contested' (p. 41). Indeed, such is the conceptual confusion surrounding globalization that Wallerstein (2000: 28) expresses doubts as to the overall utility of the term: 'Personally I think it [globalization] is meaningless as an analytical concept and serves primarily as a term of political exhortation.'

In the criminal justice sphere, the influence of globalization tends to be illustrated by reference to a recent emphasis in multiple jurisdictions on the management of risk, a rise in what Bottoms (1995) labelled 'populist punitiveness', and the general swing towards crime control at the expense (it is argued) of due process. This is especially so in relation to certain forms of major transnational crime, which are often conceptualized as a threat to *security*. Examples of such threats include issues of migration, environmental harm, human trafficking, tax evasion and international terrorism.

It is evident then that the forces of globalization have created great synergies between traditionally disparate criminal systems. We can also see that criminal policy in many different countries has coalesced around common issues, driven by both formal international institutions and broader macro-sociological processes. In the latter case, Boutellier (2000) argues that, in our post-modern society of secularized morality, the moral legitimacy of the criminal law is no longer self-evident. For Boutellier, the only public morality to survive this secularization is the awareness people retain for each other's suffering. This leaves us with a *negative* frame of reference for morality and leaves *victims* of *suffering* as the focal point for establishing the moral legitimacy of criminal law. The pain suffered by crime victims becomes a metaphor for wrongful conduct, replacing metaphors of community or collective consciousness. Boutellier calls this the 'victimalization of morality' and it might be taken to explain one of the comparative themes discussed below – the greater attention paid to victims of crime.

Garland (2001) similarly explains the emergence of parallel criminal justice policies in different countries as one aspect of a change in mood concerning criminal justice, reflecting broader social changes witnessed across Western jurisdictions. For Garland, this development is grounded in the collapse of support for penal-welfarism in the 1970s, constituted by a loss of faith in the rehabilitative ideal. This heralded a 'fundamental disenchantment' with the criminal justice system and a loss of faith in its ability to control crime. Consequently, we have seen a shift in focus away from the causes of crime onto its consequences, including victimization. Governments faced with such problems redefine what it means to have a successful criminal justice system, by portraying crime as something the state has little control over. The government therefore focuses on the *management* of criminal justice. In the face of growing concern that little can be done about crime, Garland argues that governments deny their failure by turning to ever more punitive policies.

COMPARATIVE WORK IN CRIME AND CRIMINOLOGY

The preceding discussion of globalization might at first be taken to imply that comparative work has in fact become less worthwhile than might previously have been the case. After all, in a world increasingly interconnected and sharing common solutions and models to all manner of criminal justice problems, it may now make less sense to demarcate strictly between 'British' (say) and other criminal justice systems. As Roux (2002: 430) argues: 'In this day and age, no country can view itself as an island. All countries, great and small, developed or developing, experience the effects of globalisation.' Nevertheless, the danger in this is that it remains a vast oversimplification to approach the globalization of crime and criminal justice simply as being tantamount to 'all' jurisdictions producing identical solutions to given problems. On this point, Nelken (1997) and Muncie (2005) have emphasized that whilst 'blueprint' solutions to the problems presented by crime and disorder are now commonly proliferated internationally, 'the argument that criminal justice is becoming a standardised global product can only be sustained at the very highest level of generality' (Nelken, 1997: 252). As a consequence, such blueprints become adapted to the more local context. Comparative work therefore has a significant role to play in explaining how any given model of criminal justice that works in one social, political or legal context, may work differently in another context and within a different jurisdiction. In an age of evidence-based criminal justice policy, comparative work in fact comes to the fore to help ensure policy makers do not simply employ 'off the shelf' solutions which are unsuitable to their own particular situation. Thus, Box 20.1 provides an example of the practical difficulties in finding common solutions to the relatively well-researched issue of 'burglary' across four European countries.

BOX 20.1   UNDERSTANDING 'BURGLARY' ACROSS
JURISDICTIONS

Mawby (1998) set out to compare the experiences of burglary victims with police services in England, Germany, Poland and Hungary. An initial problem described by the author was that the notion of 'burglary' differed to greater and lesser extents across all these jurisdictions, such that, in England, the definition of burglary of a dwelling included the following:

1. Breaking into a home through door or window.
2. Using other methods (e.g. credit cards) to enter through a locked door or window without causing damage.
3. Entering through an open window.
4. Entering through an open door.
5. Entering without permission, where the offender uses trickery to gain access.

In contrast, in Germany, only the first three examples would be defined by law and statistical classification as burglary ('Einbruch'). Indeed, Mawby notes here that while entry through an open window is *officially* categorized in this way by German lawyers, the crime is commonly referred to as 'einstiegen' ('to break into') rather than burglary. Moreover, examples (iv) and (v) given above are generally defined as simple theft. In Hungary and Poland, Mawby notes that definitions of burglary were rather more like those in Germany than those in England, although they too differed from these in some respects.

One key writer on comparative criminology, David Nelken, notes on this point that:

> An important issue for policy in many societies involves deciding when and how to borrow foreign ideas and practices in criminal justice, which ones are likely to be most appropriate and in what sense punishment practices are 'embedded' in a given context. (Nelken, 2007: 142)

Comparative research is therefore considered to bring a number of distinct advantages, not least of which, first, is its ability to provide an in-depth understanding of how justice systems throughout the world operate. Second, understanding how justice systems evolve and are challenged gives policy makers the basis for helping developing nations advance their justice systems to better cope with internal and transnational crime problems. Third, by conducting comparative research concerning factors related to policy and its implementation, researchers and practitioners can foresee problems and guide the policy to successful implementation. Finally, by studying justice systems worldwide, researchers can begin to collect an inventory of 'best practices' in criminal justice (Bennett, 2009).

(Continued)

Comparative research between jurisdictions is always challenging. The immediate practical issues that may come to mind, such as access to data and language barriers, in fact constitute only a small portion of these issues. More pressing in fact is that the individual researcher is always in danger, when conducting comparative analysis, of failing to appreciate subtle (or even not so subtle) differences in the social, cultural, historical, political and legal contexts between countries which underlie criminal justice culture and practice.

Comparing criminal justice responses between jurisdictions is therefore a complex task, as Box 20.1 details, and care must be taken on the part of both the researcher and indeed the audience of that research to avoid making unfair or sweeping generalizations. Of course, methodologically this is a problem inherent to all transnational or international comparisons and such disadvantages must be viewed in light of the real benefits accrued from comparative research, particularly where it bridges conventional classifications (for example, between common law and civil law countries). If carried out with due care, comparative work can allow 'difference' (in policies, in justifications and in practices) to act as a lens for the understanding of policy and practice development.

Nelken (2007), for his part, offers three possible approaches by which sufficient knowledge from other jurisdictions might be gained in order to overcome some of the difficulties discussed above with comparative work. He characterizes these as involving the researcher being 'virtually there' (i.e. in the foreign jurisdiction being studied), 'researching there' and 'living there'. Each of these approaches does however bring with it its own advantages and disadvantages, as set out in Box 20.2.

BOX 20.2   NELKEN'S TYPOLOGY OF COMPARATIVE METHODOLOGY

1. **Virtually there**: Here the researcher relies on cooperation with foreign experts from the jurisdiction(s) under review to furnish them with an understanding of the local context. In one sense, this is a straightforward collaboration between researchers and requires minimal resources in terms of time and funding. Nelken draws on the discussion by Brants and Field (2000) to emphasize that a very high level of trust is required between the collaborating researchers as well as negotiation over 'mutually acceptable descriptions of legal practice in each of the home countries' (p. 80). Consequently, there is relatively high potential in such

arrangements for misinterpretation and lack of understanding because, fundamentally, the researcher may remain less sensitive to 'broader institutional and ideological contexts' (p. 97).

2. **Researching there**: To address the drawbacks of the first approach, Nelken's second method encompasses short research visits to the countries in question to learn 'on the ground' through fieldwork, interviews and other methods. The key advantages are that 'immersion in another ostial context gives the researcher invaluable opportunities to become more directly involved in the experience of cultural translation' (p. 145). The process also allows for more open-ended inquiry and the discovery of new questions. The disadvantages of this approach, however, revolve around over-reliance on particular actors visited or interviewed in a relatively short time frame as 'representative' of a country in question. It therefore raises the important question (as does the previous method) of who counts as an 'expert' on said country. This is especially the case given that, by definition, such 'experts' will be part of the very culture they are describing.

3. **Living there**: Nelken's 'living there' conceptualization takes the next step of researchers spending considerable time in a foreign jurisdiction, such that they begin to break down the cultural assumptions they bring with them and become aware of, and indeed part of, the taken-for-granted social context experienced by natives. In some ways, however, this is the most difficult method to actually realize given the time, practical and monetary limitations. Indeed, funding for comparative studies is the major roadblock to their undertaking. Any study that involves more than one nation will be costly, whether it employs original archival data, observations, interviews, or the administration of surveys (Bennett, 2009). Overall, Nelken warns that, in practice, pursuing this approach may sometimes *reduce* the quality of the research if it is pursued at the expense of a broader data set which could be gleaned from other methods.

Another typology for categorizing comparative crime and criminal justice studies is offered by Bennett (2009) who characterizes such studies by reference to four essential features: approach, scope, data and design, as explained in Box 20.3.

BOX 20.3 BENNETT'S CONCEPTUALIZATION OF COMPARATIVE STUDIES

Approach: This is determined by whether the purpose of the study is to describe crime problems and/or criminal justice systems or to analyse the causes of crime

(Continued)

or the factors that affect the structure or operations of criminal justice agencies. A leading example of the descriptive approach is Reichel's (2004) multinational treatment of criminal justice systems. A prime example of the analytic approach is Bayley's (1985) work on the structure, role and functioning of police in a sample of nations.

Scope: This refers to the number of nations studied: one or several nations (national) or whether the focus is truly multinational.

Data: The third dimension of the typology is determined by the form of empirical evidence used in a study. Empirical studies can rely on either qualitative or quantitative data, or a mixture of the two.

Design: The final dimension of the typology focuses on the design of the data collection activity and the type of analyses performed: longitudinal or cross-sectional.

Clearly, there is no 'standard' way of approaching internationally comparative work. Indeed, addressing the difficulties and challenges of this work will often require researchers to consider novel solutions to individual challenges arising in different cases. In the next section, this chapter will examine in more detail how some comparative projects in the fields of crime, policing and victimization, have approached such challenges.

COMPARATIVE RESEARCH IN PRACTICE

Having sketched out some of the main contours and methodological questions relating to comparative work, this chapter will next turn to examine how such research methodologies can be utilized in practice. The chapter will look at studies from the three subject areas of victimology, policing and crime as examples, although the purpose of doing so is to illustrate the pitfalls and benefits of comparative study against a backdrop of the much wider bodies of enquiry undertaken by criminologists as a whole.

In the first case, I will draw on work by Brienen and Hoegen (2000) who set out to analyse criminal justice reform agendas ostensibly aimed at victims of crime in 22 European countries. The authors analysed provisions for victims across European jurisdictions based on a combination of survey and interview data carried out across all the countries. In Nelken's terms, this methodology represented a broad mix of being 'virtually there' and 'researching there'. Genuinely comparative research on victim issues is rare (Hall, 2010). The work thus remains a substantial achievement and required reading for any researcher interested in the development of victim initiatives internationally. What is particularly interesting about Brienen and Hoegen's project is that it allows comparisons to be drawn between inquisitorial and adversarial justice systems. There has long been a recurring assertion in the literature in this field that criminal justice systems following the more adversarial, combative model may be inherently less accommodating to victims of crime, especially those who find themselves subject to cross-examination as witnesses (see Ellison, 2001). Thus, by engaging in comparative work the authors of this study were able to shed new light on an old question. In fact, on this point, the authors conclude that neither system has an inherent advantage in terms of victims' experience of the criminal justice system. Instead, they ascribe greater importance to the practical implementation of relevant measures in either system.

Of course, like all comparative (and other) research, the Brienen and Hoegen findings come with health warnings. The research was restricted to Europe, was largely descriptive of legislation and programmes and, although covering a large number of countries, was not focused on the *policy-making* process and context behind victim measures specifically. Work from several jurisdictions implies that a very detailed understanding of the nuances of policy making and policy networks is highly relevant to understanding criminal justice reform (Atkinson and Coleman, 1992), and thus subtleties may well have been missed in each jurisdiction under review. In line with broader notions of governance, policy networks imply horizontal connections between a wide body of relevant stakeholders as contributing to the production of public policy, as opposed to a more top-down 'government-led' understanding of how policies are developed and refined. That said, the literature exemplifies the importance of comparative work in the victimization area: something which is becoming more significant as many jurisdictions are turning more attention to transnational sources of victimization, such as internet crime (Taylor et al., 2014) and people trafficking (Lee, 2007).

Policing is another area that has benefited from comparative study, albeit as Jones and Newburn wrote in 2006: 'Despite the burgeoning academic interest in policing there remains a dearth of rigorous academic international comparative analysis in this field' (2006: 5).

Indeed, although these authors made this assertion in an edited collection entitled *Plural Policing: A Comparative Perspective*, it is notable that even this book mainly relies on individual chapters detailing different jurisdictional contexts of policing positioned 'side by side', with varying degrees of direct comparative analysis within or between each chapter. In practice, this is often how a lot of comparative work is presented, leaving the reader to effectively note the similarities and differences between jurisdictions and to draw their own conclusions. The same criticism could be applied to much of Brienen and Hoegen's (2000) project.

One recent study that tries to take a more directly comparative route is that of Chu and Song (2015) who set out to examine the perceptions Chinese immigrants in New York City (NYC) and in Toronto had of the police. With the assistance of the Chinese Cultural Center of the Taipei Economic and Cultural Office in NYC and Toronto, the authors were able to identify the primary service agencies and community organizations that provided cultural services for Chinese immigrants in both cities. Through such services and organizations, the researchers then conducted a survey of said populations, eliciting 151 respondents from NYC and 293 from Toronto. The researchers appear to have followed what Nelken (2007) would call a 'researching there' method. They describe spending roughly three months focusing on each location, during which time they made several trips to the research sites to visit local community service providers. Both authors were based in the USA: one in Buffalo, New York State and the other in Jonesboro, Arkansas.

The authors spend some time in their paper setting the respective scenes in each jurisdiction: expanding widely on the different demographics of the two research sites, as well as the different factors at play in Canada and the USA which, they argue (based on previous research studies), are predictive of public perceptions of the police in each country. In the USA, the most common such variables are said to be race and age. Citing Mosher (1996: 423), the authors then note that 'in Canada there are comparatively sparse studies regarding public perceptions of the police', but, in that jurisdiction, previous research by O'Connor (2008) found that predictors of public perceptions of the police in Canada were consistent with the findings of most research conducted in the USA. The authors also expand on the different legal and social contexts influencing policing in Canada and the USA. In the latter case, for example, they note 'one of the characteristics that distinguishes Canadians from other people from the world is their tolerance with people with different backgrounds and cultures (Graves, 1997)' (p. 409). The extended comparative points made by the authors here are cited at length in Box 20.4 by way of illustration of how such work can lead to meaningful conclusions.

BOX 20.4   CHU AND SONG'S (2015) COMPARATIVE STUDY

[T]he different political structures [in the USA and Canada] have shaped different police operational policies toward immigrants of similar ethnic backgrounds. Different policing responses may explain different interactions with police in their respective Chinese immigrant communities. The zero tolerance initiatives implemented by NYC Mayor, Giuliani, in the 1990s, were targeted at weeding out social nuances in favor of stricter social order maintenance and crime reduction.

But this sort of aggressive police style can be seen as producing conformity rather than respecting civil liberties (Davis et al., 2004; Human Rights Watch, 1998). Since the passage of the USA PATRIOT Act, the use of counterterrorism tactics and the increase of law enforcement powers have raised concern among liberals, racial/ethnic minorities, and immigrants (Brown, 2007). The multicultural approach to policing in Toronto is also worth mentioning, where an emphasis on community policing might have eased racial tensions inherent in the police–immigrant interactions. (pp. 409–10)

From these comparative points, the authors are able to derive a hypothesis:

In view of the different policing styles in NYC and Toronto, it is reasonable to assume that Chinese immigrants in NYC and Toronto would hold different perceptions of the police. The multiculturalism embraced by the Canadian society and community policing initiatives advocated by the TPD would possibly make immigrants feel more welcome and assimilated to the criminal justice system. However, because of the histories of some incidents of mistreatment of minorities by law enforcement officers in the United States (e.g., the beating of Rodney King by the Los Angeles Police) and the comparatively more aggressive policing approach engaged by the NYPD, immigrants might feel more distant from the police and thus hold less favourable attitudes toward the police. Consequently, we hypothesize that Chinese immigrants in Toronto will hold more positive overall perceptions of the police. (p. 410)

The authors later purport to confirm these hypotheses by multivariate analysis of the two sets of results, which also indicated that Chinese immigrants in New York City were more likely to perceive a slower response from the police to their complaints than those immigrants residing in Toronto. From this analysis, the authors are able to draw the following overall comparative conclusion:

The differential overall perceptions between Toronto and NYC may be attributed to the different policing styles. While the Toronto police have advocated community policing and embraced the philosophy of multiculturalism, immigrants may feel less alienated from the law enforcement officials. However, in response to a high crime rate and the post-9/11 effect, the aggressive policing approach adopted in NYC may somehow affect the police–Chinese community relationship. (p. 420)

This example demonstrates how comparative work can produce meaningful results which help us develop knowledge of different criminal justice solutions and their potential impacts. Of course, the study laid out above can also be criticized in the

(Continued)

sense that its survey methodology and general quantitative design may have led the authors to miss important nuances in each local context. Given that neither author appears to have spent substantial time at each research site, we may question whether they have genuinely reflected the full complexity of these local contexts. Being based in the USA, and indeed one of the authors in New York itself, these are all factors which might influence how they have approached the data. Indeed, one might expect – given the complexities of comparative analysis – for there to be some acknowledgement of these limitations, which is notably absent from the paper. Instead, the paper appears somewhat positivist, which may betray missed nuances given that the nature of the subject matter is surely bound up with a more constructivist, socially derived, impression of policing in both jurisdictional contexts. As with all comparative work, therefore, the results must be treated with an extra degree of caution.

In terms of understanding crime itself and comparing crime rates between jurisdictions, another major comparative project has been the establishment of the International Crime Victimisation Survey (ICVS), which has been carried out in some 54 countries (van Dijk et al., 2007). The ICVS began in 1989 and grew out of a perceived need for reliable crime statistics that could be used for international comparisons. Police-recorded crime statistics are notoriously under-representative of the so-called 'dark figure' of crime in all jurisdictions owing to low reporting rates. At the level of international comparisons, such figures become even more problematic to work with given that reporting rates can differ for different crimes between countries, depending on local cultural sensitivities, practicalities and basic trust in the local police (as confirmed by the Chu and Song (2015) study discussed above). Furthermore, police statistics cannot be used easily for comparative purposes because, as we have already noted above in the work of Mawby (1998), the legal definitions of crimes differ across countries to greater and lesser extents. Recording practices and counting rules of the police also vary greatly.

Certainly, results from nation-specific crime victim surveys have become the preferred source of information on levels of crime in many developed countries in recent years; however, surveys such as the National Crime Victim Survey in the USA and the Crime Survey for England & Wales differ greatly in terms of their questions and methodology. By contrast, the International Crime Victim Survey (ICVS) employs standardized questionnaires and other design elements. Nevertheless, the limits of the ICVS must also be recognized. Full standardization of all design aspects has proven to be unattainable, especially if surveys in developing countries are included. Although there are no reasons to assume that comparability has in any way been systematically compromised, divergent design features such as the mode of interviewing and the period in which the fieldwork was done, may have affected the results of individual countries in unknown ways. Also, since the samples interviewed are relatively small (2000 in most countries and 800 in most cities), all estimates are subject to sampling error. Nevertheless, the ICVS not only adds greatly to our comparative knowledge of crime figures, but is also used as a tool of victimology to ascertain international trends on issues such as victim satisfaction with the criminal justice system, access to information, and so on, in the same way that national criminal victimization surveys do.

COMPARATIVE WORK 'POST'–GLOBALIZATION?

In more recent years, several commentators have spoken of the 'end of globalization' and/or the end of 'internalization' (see Rugman, 2012). The detailed debates behind these statements are beyond the scope of the present chapter, but, in essence, such contentions are usually based on the perceived economic failure of global market-based capitalism in the context of the 2008 global financial crisis and the notion that so-called global markets have in fact resulted in a high degree of regionalization and the transfer of wealth from the global south to the global north. Politically, an apparent shift in support towards more nationalistic political ideals, evidenced by developments such as the population of the UK voting to leave the European Union in the referendum of June 2016 and the election of Donald Trump as president of the USA later that year on the back of considerable anti-international rhetoric, has recently cemented this impression of a slowdown in the degree to which the world is becoming integrated. Further, commentators such as Hirst and Thompson (2002) argue that there may be inherent limits to some of the fundamental processes that create the level of 'interconnectedness' on which the concept of globalization rests. In particular, they speak about the limits of international trade and argue that the degree of economic activity required to sustain it may be waning in a recurring cycle of boom and bust:

> Thus the world may be experiencing the final years of one of those periodic explosions in internationalization that throw so much into confusion and seem to herald the complete transformation in the way societies are organized. A serious questioning of the ability of the global economic system to sustain its seemingly rapid integrationist trajectory is beginning to emerge. (2002: 255)

This cycle has been exaggerated both by the extremes of what many have called 'hyperglobalization' since the 1990s (see Ravenhill, 2017) and, they argue, by the growth of more protectionist policies by a number of jurisdictions. One key example is the USA pulling out of the Trans-Pacific Partnership agreement (the largest international trade agreement in history, between 11 jurisdictions) in 2016.

For the purposes of this chapter, it is relevant to briefly reflect on what impact this alleged anti-globalization trend process of decline might have on comparative work in the criminological field.

In some respects, it might be argued that comparative work takes on added dimensions in a world where the sharing of standardized 'blueprint models' of criminal justice reform, discussed by Nelken (1997) above, is less forthcoming. Indeed, one might argue that the wholesale, ill-considered export of such models is partly to blame for the anti-international feeling taking hold in many jurisdictions. Take, for example, the development of private finance initiative (PFI) contract models to build prisons in the UK, and the subsequent 'export' of that model around the world (see Grout, 1997). Developed by the Australian and UK governments in the 1990s, PFI is an economic model whereby the private sector is approached to fund public infrastructure projects with private capital, thus creating so-called public–private partnerships (PPPs).

Whilst such contracts have arguably brought savings (as well as many disadvantages) in developed countries including the UK itself and the USA, Goyer (2001) argues that this model of the penal state was close to bankrupting the South African prison estate. A reduction in globalization certainly implies still less ability (or perhaps appetite) to transpose 'ready-made' models of criminal justice into different jurisdictional, political, legal and social contexts. Therein, however, may lie an argument for a more considered form of comparative study, one concentrated on establishing how different solutions to given criminal justice issues work in these increasingly pluralized contexts around the world. In other words, a slowdown in globalization might switch the emphasis currently discernible in a lot of comparative work from a search for ready-made solutions to criminal justice problems to an understanding of what particular issues are at play in influencing these different criminal justice contexts. Key examples for further study in this regard might include the different contexts in which so-called 'terrorist attacks' occur in different countries. Recent years have seen what is described as a wave of 'new terrorism' (Tsui, 2016) atrocities committed in urban areas across Europe. Examples include the Brussels bombing of March 2016, the Manchester Arena bombing in May 2017 and the Barcelona attack of August 2017. What appear to be highly similar models of crime, however, each take place in the specific cultural and political context of each state and, thus, in line with the above discussion, require very different means of addressing and preventing these kinds of activities. The danger, of course, is that another impact of reduced global interaction will be that, practically, such work becomes more difficult to arrange – in terms of establishing contacts as well as the academic and financial arrangements required – precisely at a time when such comparisons may take on increased significance to the work of criminologists.

SUMMARY AND REVIEW

Comparative work in the field of criminology has developed markedly in recent years although it is still underutilized. In many cases, work can purport to be comparative whereas in fact it presents more of a 'side-by-side' discussion of two jurisdictions and their responses to criminal justice problems. We have seen above that going beyond this is challenging and requires careful thought given to the social, cultural, political and legal contexts in which two (or more) jurisdictions operate: the subtleties of which can be extremely difficult for the outsider to fully appreciate, let alone compare. This of course reflects much wider concessions made in the methodological literature across the social sciences that genuine 'objectivity' in any research may be impossible to achieve given the inevitable impact of a researcher's training, background and cultural assumptions. We have noted above several proposed methods for addressing these concerns in comparative work, whilst also acknowledging that none of these 'solutions' are without their own limitations. Nevertheless, we have also seen how, when approached with care and due regard to the potential hurdles, comparative work has produced some extremely detailed and important insights into fundamental questions of interest to criminologists and victimologists, including the extent of crime, the impact of policing strategies and the position of victims of crime in the criminal justice system. Comparative work is therefore reaching a level of maturity where it is beginning to show its real value, a value which, I have argued, will persevere – and perhaps in some sense only increase – even in the context of generally anti-global sentiments in the political and social spheres.

STUDY QUESTIONS AND ACTIVITIES FOR STUDENTS

Globalization and criminal justice

1. What is 'globalization' and in what ways could it be said to pre-empt a focus on comparative work?

2. What common challenges can we identify for criminal justice actors across different jurisdictions in the twenty-first century?

3. Is globalization simply a case of all criminal justice systems adopting similar solutions to the problems presented by crime?

(Continued)

(Continued)

Comparative work in crime and criminology

1. What are the key advantages and disadvantages of comparative work?

2. What practical pitfalls exist in attempting to carry out such work and how can researchers attempt to minimize these?

3. In what sense might comparative researchers achieve a genuinely 'objective' view of either their home jurisdiction or those with which they are attempting to draw comparisons?

Comparative research in practice

1. What other areas of criminal justice study can you think of that might benefit from comparative study? How would such study add to existing knowledge in this area?

2. Consider the Chu and Song (2015) piece discussed above again. In what ways might the researchers' position, based in the USA, have influenced their approach and their interpretation of the data?

3. What steps can be taken to try and harmonize crime statistics in a way that makes them genuinely comparable between different countries?

Comparative work 'post'-globalization

1. What extra challenges to comparative work may surface as a result of any slow-down in globalization?

2. How can we adapt comparative methodologies and strategies to combat such potential problems?

3. Does the use of comparative data rely on globalization?

SUGGESTIONS FOR FURTHER READING

Students wishing to learn more about all aspects of comparative research are strongly advised to read Nelken's (2010) *Comparative Criminal Justice: Making Sense of Difference*. Nelken's writings have been extremely influential in the development of comparative methodologies in crime and criminal justice areas and in this volume he expands on many of the issues outlined in the above overview in great detail, drawing on many examples of comparative work in practice. Similarly, Garland's (2001) book *The Culture of Control: Crime and Social Order in Contemporary Society* (OUP) is considered by many the definitive starting point for understanding the role of globalization in the development of criminal justice across the developed world (especially in the UK and the USA). Another extremely illuminating discussion on the wider issues, specifically related to comparative research around sentencing reform, is to be found in Bottoms' (1995) article 'The philosophy and politics of punishment and sentencing'. Here, Bottoms conceptualizes criminal justice in late modernity as being dominated by a quest for populist punitiveness; his paper has become a core reference for those seeking to understand the development of criminal justice at a wide socio-political level.

REFERENCES

Atkinson, M. and Coleman, W. (1992) 'Policy networks, policy communities and the problems of governance', *Governance*, 5(2): 154–80.

Bayley, D. (1985) *Patterns of Policing: A Comparative International Analysis*. New Brunswick, NJ: Rutgers University Press.

Beerkens, E. (2004) *Global Opportunities and Institutional Embeddedness: Higher Education Consortia in Europe and Southeast Asia*. Enschede: CHEPS.

Bennett, R. (2009) 'Comparative criminological and criminal justice research and the data that drive', *International Journal of Comparative and Applied Criminal Justice*, 33(2): 171–92.

Bottoms, A. (1995) 'The philosophy and politics of punishment and sentencing', in C. Clark and R. Morgan (eds), *The Politics of Sentencing Reform*. Oxford: Clarendon Press, pp. 17–50.

Boutellier, H. (2000) *Crime and Morality: The Significance of Criminal Justice in Post-Modern Culture*. Dordrecht: Kluwer.

Brants, C. and Field, S. (2000) 'Legal culture, political cultures and procedural traditions: towards a comparative interpretation of covert and proactive policing in England and Wales and the Netherlands', in D. Nelken (ed.), *Contrasting Criminal Justice*. Aldershot: Dartmouth, pp. 77–116.

Brienen, M. and Hoegen, H. (2000) *Victims of Crime in 22 European Criminal Justice Systems: The Implementation of Recommendation (85) 11 of the Council of Europe on the Position of the Victim in the Framework of Criminal Law and Procedure*. Niemegen: Wolf Legal Productions.

Brown, B. (2007) 'Community policing in post-September 11 America: a comment on the concept of community-oriented counterterrorism', *Police Practice and Research*, 8: 239–51.

Cavadino, M. and Dignan, J. (2007) *The Penal System: An Introduction*. London: Sage.

Chu, D. and Song, J. (2015) 'A comparison of Chinese immigrants' perceptions of the police in New York City and Toronto', *Crime and Delinquency*, 61(3): 402–27.

Davis, R., Ortiz, C., Gilinskiy, Y., Ylesseva, I. and Briller, V. (2004) 'A crossnational comparison of the police in New York City and St Petersburg, Russia', *Policing: An International Journal of Police Strategies and Management*, 27: 22–36.

Ellison, L. (2001) *The Adversarial Process and the Vulnerable Witness*. Oxford: Oxford University Press.

Garland, D. (2001) *The Culture of Control: Crime and Social Order in Contemporary Society*. Oxford: Oxford University Press.

Giddens, A. (1990) *The Consequences of Modernity*. Cambridge: Polity.

Goyer, K. (2001) 'A price worth paying? The cost of South Africa's private prisons', *Nedbank ISS Crime Index*, 5(6): 1–2.

Graves, R. (1997) '"Dear friends": culture and genre in American and Canadian direct marketing letters', *Journal of Business Communication*, 34(1): 235–52.

Grout, P. (1997) 'The economics of the private finance initiative', *Oxford Review of Economic Policy*, 13(4): 53–66.

Hall, M. (2010) *Victims and Policy Making: A Comparative Perspective*. Cullompton: Willan.

Hirst, P. and Thompson, G. (2002) 'The future of globalization', *Cooperation and Conflict*, 37(3): 247–65.

Human Rights Watch (1998) *Shielded from Justice: Police Brutality and Accountability in the United States*. New York: Human Rights Watch.

Jones, T. and Newburn, T. (2006) 'Understanding plural policing', in T. Jones and T. Newburn (eds), *Plural Policing: A Comparative Perspective*. New York: Routledge, pp. 1–12.

Lee, M. (2007) *Human Trafficking*. Cullompton: Willan.

Loader, I. and Sparks, R. (2007) 'Contemporary landscapes of crime, order and control: governance, risk and globalization', in M. Maguire, R. Morgan and R. Reiner (eds), *The Oxford Handbook of Criminology*, 3rd edition. Oxford: Oxford University Press, pp. 78–101.

Mawby, R. (1998) 'Victims' perceptions of police services in east and west Europe', in V. Ruggiero, N. South and I. Taylor (eds), *The New European Criminology: Crime and Social Order in Europe*. New York: Routledge, pp. 180–200.

Mosher, C. (1996) 'Racism and criminal justice', *Canadian Journal of Criminology*, 38: 413–38.

Muncie, J. (2005) 'The globalization of crime control: the case of youth and juvenile justice – neo-liberalism, policy convergence and international conventions', *Theoretical Criminology*, 9(1): 35–64.

Nagorcka, F., Stanton, M. and Wilson, M. (2005) 'Stranded between partisanship and the truth: a comparative analysis of legal ethics in the adversarial and inquisitorial systems of justice', *Melbourne University Law Review*, 29(2): 448–77.

Nelken, D. (1997) 'The globalization of crime and criminal justice: prospects and problems', *Current Legal Problems*, 50: 251–77.

Nelken, D. (2007) 'Comparing criminal justice', in M. Maguire, R. Morgan and R. Reiner (eds), *The Oxford Handbook of Criminology*, 4th edition. Oxford: Oxford University Press, pp. 139–58.

Nelken, D. (2010) *Comparative Criminal Justice: Making Sense of Difference*. London: Sage.

O'Connor, C. (2008) 'Citizen attitudes toward the police in Canada', *Policing: An International Journal of Police Strategies and Management*, 31: 578–95.

Ravenhill, J. (2017) *Global Political Economy*. Oxford: Oxford University Press.

Reichel, P. (2004) *Comparative Criminal Justice Systems: A Topical Approach*. Upper Saddle River, NJ: Prentice Hall.

Reinicke, W. (1997) 'Global public policy', *Foreign Affairs*, 76: 127–51.

Roux, N. (2002) 'Public policy-making and policy analysis in South Africa amidst transformation, change and globalisation: views on participants and role players in the policy analytic procedure', *Journal of Public Administration*, 37: 418–37.

Rugman, A. (2012) *The End of Globalization*. New York: Random House.

Scholte, J. (2000) *Globalization: A Critical Introduction*. London: Macmillan.

Taylor, R., Fritsch, E. and Liederbach, J. (2014) *Digital Crime and Digital Terrorism*. Upper Saddle River, NJ: Prentice Hall.

Tsui, C.-K. (2016) *Clinton, New Terrorism and the Origins of the War on Terror*. London: Routledge.

van Dijk, J., van Kesteren, J. and Smit, P. (2007) *Criminal Victimisation in International Perspective: Key Findings from the 2004–2005 ICVS and EU ICS*. The Hague Haag: Boom Legal Publishers.

Wallerstein, I. (2000) 'From sociology to historical social science: prospects and obstacles', *British Journal of Sociology*, 51: 25–35.

CHAPTER CONTENTS

GLOSSARY TERMS

case study

deductive

observation(s)

variable

spatial variation

temporal variation

synchronic

diachronic

21 USING CASE STUDY METHODS IN CRIMINOLOGICAL RESEARCH

KATHLEEN DALY

INTRODUCTION

 Case studies – broadly defined – have featured in human society for millennia, although the term 'case study' was first used in a scientific sense in the early twentieth century (Gerring, 2017: xvii–viii, and see pp. 17–19 for a survey of the history of case study research). Case study research was common in the US sociological literature until the 1940s when survey research became more popular (Platt, 1992). Interest in case study research re-emerged in the 1980s as researchers recognized that statistical analyses alone could not explain the complexity and context-dependent qualities of social phenomena, and that case study research could do it better. Despite its current popularity, case study research is not well understood by social science practitioners, and it is given superficial treatment in introductory texts for university students.

This chapter gives prominence to Chicago School sociology because it shaped the formative years of criminology during the first half of the twentieth century. However, we must bear in mind that as an interdisciplinary field of knowledge, criminology has been influenced by other disciplines and key texts in developing case study research. Case study research is used throughout the social sciences, and in law, business and medicine. I illustrate the differing ways it has been used in criminology and related fields. The chapter will compare different approaches to case study research, sketch its historical development in US sociology, and define key terms. A potential point of confusion, which I clarify, is how case study research relates to comparative case study research and to comparative criminology.

APPROACHES TO CASE STUDY RESEARCH AND A BRIEF HISTORY

Elman, Gerring and Mahoney (2016: 376) size up the literature on case study research well: '[it] is so abundant and diverse that it defies description'. This poses problems for those new to the area. There is no single authoritative text in the social sciences to rely on as a 'go to' source. The major texts do not speak with one voice, a problem amplified by differing disciplinary concerns and preferred approaches to knowledge building. It is important to address knowledge-building preferences at the start because all else flows from them, and, in particular, how to define and carry out case study research.

These preferences are apparent in Yazan's (2015) comparison of three case study texts: Yin (1984/1994/2014), Merriam (1998) and Stake (1995). I sketch Yazan's argument, relate it to the formative years of case study research in sociology, and demonstrate how the early ideas have threaded their way into contemporary criminology.

Of the three authors in Yazan's analysis, Yin is the most well known and cited. In 1984, he published a highly influential text, which put forth a method for case study research (a fifth edition was published in 2014). His approach to case study research is positivist; he recommends a well-prepared design at the start of the research, which focuses on testing a theory or hypothesis. Yin's largely deductive approach to case study research is well suited to programme or policy evaluation, which is his area of expertise.

By comparison, the texts by Merriam and Stake view knowledge as 'constructed rather than discovered' and 'constructed by individuals acting within their social worlds' (Yazan, 2015: 137). They take a constructivist or interpretivist approach to knowledge and problematize precisely what Yin takes for granted. Furthermore, Merriam and Stake prefer a flexible design that may change as the research evolves. Yazan compares the authors on other dimensions, but my summary is sufficient to show that case study researchers have different assumptions about how best to study the social world and build knowledge.

Several points can be drawn for case study research historically and in its use today. First, Yin was a pioneer in the 1980s in advancing a systematic method for case study research, and many continue to cite him as an authority in criminology. However, his advice may have 'come at the expense' of a more pluralistic understanding of what case studies can offer: contextualized explanations and divergent meanings that actors may have of a situation or case (Piekkari et al., 2010: 3). Moreover, case studies can be used not only to test theories and hypotheses, but also to generate them. At a minimum, researchers may need to be explicit about their approach to knowledge building and the different 'quality criteria by which to judge it' (2010: 3).

Second, Yin's method embodies a narrower meaning of case study research, compared to the way it was practised in the 1920s and 1930s by researchers associated with the University of Chicago. As elucidated by Becker (1999), the founders were Albion Small, W.I. Thomas and George Herbert Mead, with the next generation being Robert E. Park, E.W. Burgess, Everett C. Hughes and Herbert Blumer. What came to be called the Chicago School was eclectic, not unified (Becker, 1999), but, in general, case studies of individuals, groups and neighbourhoods focused on social contexts and actors' life worlds in their own words. For example, W. Lloyd Warner, who was trained as a social anthropologist and had carried out ethnographic research in an Australian Indigenous community, and then later, US communities and cities, was a significant presence for Chicago School students. He guided William Foote Whyte (then a PhD student), whose research on a Boston Italian neighbourhood became a case study classic in sociology and criminology (Whyte, 1943/1981). Research by Warner, Whyte and others associated with the Chicago School centred on 'personal meanings' and knowledge gained by inductive reasoning, methods not recommended by Yin (Platt, 1992: 45–6). At the same time and closer to Yin's concerns, many Chicago School researchers grappled with two problems: how to describe and compare case studies in an 'objective way' and how to 'generalize from case studies to a wider population' (Platt, 1992: 22).

In the 1950s, what came to be called the Second Chicago School emerged, which blended field research (case studies) with social constructivism. Among its practitioners was Howard Becker, who became a leading scholar in social deviance, art and culture (Plummer, 2003). In the late 1980s, Becker and Charles Ragin ran a workshop to discuss the question, 'what is a case?'. Ragin hoped the group would come to agreement on an answer, but he said that Becker 'persistently pulled the rug out from any possible consensus' (Ragin, 1992: 5). Instead, 'Becker wanted to make researchers continually ask the question, "What is this a case *of*?"' (1992: 4). This is a crucial question for case study researchers. From Becker's perspective, the answer may not be known until the conclusion of the research when writing up the findings. He believed that 'the less sure that researchers are of their answers [at the outset of the research], the better their research may be' (p. 6).

Third, the legacy of the Chicago School of the 1920s and 1930s is more multi-faceted than what is conveyed in introductory texts. Although its members launched the 'case study method' in sociology, in fact there was no discernible method per se. Instead, case study research was loosely related to types of evidence: 'life history data ... personal documents, unstructured interviews ... any attempt at holistic study, and non-quantitative data analysis', which Platt (1992: 37) concluded had 'neither a necessary logical nor a regular empirical connection with each other'. Moreover, few of the exemplary texts hewed to the ideal type of case study. In addition, although 'the "case study method" was often contrasted with "statistical method" [by members of the Chicago School] ... many argued that both were useful and acceptable' (Platt, 1992: 38). Thus, in practice, the 'distinction between case study and statistical method ... blurred' (Platt, 1992: 26) because Chicago School texts drew upon both. However, a shift occurred in the 1940s when an increasing number of sociologists, including those associated with the Chicago School, began to rely on surveys and statistical analyses of social phenomena (Gerring, 2007; Platt, 1992).

In the 1980s, a new generation of case study researchers emerged. They sought to sharpen the scientific value of case study research and give it standing as a substantial method in the social sciences. It is striking to see that many of the major methods texts – George and Bennett (2005), Gerring (2007/2017), Ragin (1987/2014) and Yin (1984/1994/2014) – challenge the qualitative–quantitative dichotomy in the social sciences and seek ways to move past it.

KEY TERMS

It is difficult to provide a single definition of a case or case study because case study research is used in many fields of knowledge and there is no agreed-upon authoritative text. After reviewing a number of well-known texts, I chose John Gerring's (2007) *Case Study Methods: Principles and Practices* because it is clear, comprehensive and cross-disciplinary.[1] The next two paragraphs cite from it.

---

[1] A second edition was published in February 2017, which is a substantial re-write of the first. I draw mainly, but not exclusively, from the first edition in this chapter. Gerring is a political scientist and takes a positivist approach to case study research.

A case is a 'spatially and temporally delimited phenomenon' that is 'observed at a single point in time or over some period of time' (2007: 211). In the social sciences, it can be a social or political unit (an individual, family, gang, organization, community, city, state, nation-state); other type of social group (based on age, sex/gender, racial-ethnic, religion, social status, profession); particular type of organization or institution (the police, a court, truth commission, regulatory body); or event (nuclear disaster, terrorist attack, mass shooting, riot, crime). There are myriad potential cases. The only restriction is that a case 'has identifiable boundaries and [is] the primary object of an inference' (p. 19). In other words, a case is bounded in time and space, and it comprises the phenomenon you want to describe and explain.

A case study is 'an intensive study of a single case … to shed light on a larger class of cases (a population)' (p. 20). Case study research has one or several cases. However, as the number of cases increases, it is not possible to study each intensively. 'At the point where the emphasis of a study shifts from the individual case to a sample of cases … a study is cross-case' (p. 20). It is not possible to pinpoint precisely when this shift from case study to cross-case research occurs; rather, it is 'a matter of degree … the fewer cases there are, and the more intensively they are studied', the more we call it case study research (p. 20). Clarifying further, Gerring suggests that case study research is 'usually limited to a dozen cases or fewer … unless the study is extraordinarily long' (p. 22). In the second edition (2017), he considers a medium number of cases (that is, 20 to 30).

Two other terms clarify the relationship of case study research to cross-case research: an observation and a variable. A variable is 'an attribute of an observation or set of observations', which does not 'presume statistical analysis' (Gerring, 2007: 217). I illustrate these two terms by way of an example in Box 21.1.

(Continued)

at your institution to learn more about how it defines and addresses student plagiarism.

Oxford University defines plagiarism this way:

> Plagiarism is presenting someone else's work or ideas as your own, with or without their consent, by incorporating it into your work without full acknowledgement. All published and unpublished material, whether in manuscript, printed or electronic form, is covered under this definition. Plagiarism may be intentional or reckless, or unintentional …

> Forms of plagiarism [are] verbatim (word for word quotation without clear acknowledgement), cutting and pasting from the Internet without clear acknowledgement, paraphrasing [without acknowledgement of the source], collusion, inaccurate citation, failure to acknowledge assistance, use of material written by professional agencies or other persons, and auto-plagiarism [for example, using your work submitted for one course in another course].

Source: www.ox.ac.uk/students/academic/guidance/skills/plagiarism (accessed 14 August 2017)

STUDENT PLAGIARISM IN UNIVERSITY ASSIGNMENTS

For our case study on plagiarism, we select three students and gather in-depth evidence on their experiences and decisions to plagiarize (or not). This would result in many observations over time of each student on variables of interest. We would produce a detailed understanding of each student's experiences and decisions, in their own words, noting variation among them (within-case variation).

For our cross-case study of plagiarism, we survey a sample of 250 students. We have observations of 250 students and create many variables from the survey questions. We produce an analysis of variation among the students, estimating the prevalence of attempted plagiarism with reference to how much time students have been in university, their age and sex/gender, and other variables (cross-case variation).

The difference between case study and cross-case research is the number of cases selected, which is based on the degree to which a case can be studied intensively. Each approach has 'the same [objective] – the explanation of a population of cases – but [each] goes about this task differently' (Gerring, 2007: 21). The two methods can complement one another.

Case study research is often represented as *qualitative* research, but this is not accurate. Case study research is better understood in the following way: it may use qualitative or quantitative methods (or both) in gathering and analysing evidence.

By comparison, cross-case research is *quantitative* because a large number of cases require statistical analysis. The difference between case study research and cross-case research is *not the type of evidence* that is used (which may include statistical surveys, interviews, archival records and the like), but rather that the focus of analysis is on a single case or several cases, with the aim of 'illuminat[ing] features of a broader set of cases' (Gerring, 2007: 29).

Let's return to our case study of plagiarism illustrated in Box 21.1. We may carry out a statistical analysis of the academic records of the three students, or we may conduct a university-wide analysis of the types of courses where plagiarism allegations are more likely to be made. This evidence would be part of our analysis of each student, along with intensive interviews and observations of them. In this way, our analysis would be supplemented with other material that gives a broader context to the three students' experiences. Alternatively, we could carry out a cross-case study of 250 students first, and from that analysis, select three cases for intensive analysis that illustrate which students are likely to plagiarize and why this occurs. This is an example of combining cross-case and case study methods.

Along with other case study analysts (George and Bennett, 2005; Platt, 1992; Ragin, 1987/2014; Yin, 1984/1994/2014) and those in criminology (Karstedt, 2001, 2012), Gerring (2007: 12) argues that viewing case study and cross-case research as 'being in opposition with each other' is wrong. 'Researchers may do both and, arguably, must engage both styles of evidence'. Case study research may need to rely on findings from cross-case research to guide the selection of cases for intensive analysis. Because case study researchers are obliged to answer Becker's question, 'what is this a case *of*?', they need to have in mind a broader set of cases. Likewise, cross-case researchers may be able to predict outcomes or variation in outcomes, but not be able to explain how or why these outcomes came about. To do so, they need to supplement their analysis with case studies. Thus, the primary comparison should be between case study and cross-case research. The types of evidence used – whether qualitative, quantitative, or both – are secondary.

CASE SELECTION

Gerring (2017: Chapter 3) addresses a critical question for case study research: how do we decide which cases to select for intensive study? Like others, he identifies two broad types of case study; these, in turn, relate to the goals of a case study: to describe a case or handful of cases (descriptive) or to explain an outcome (causal). In addition, he identifies a third category, which is applicable to both descriptive and causal goals, in which case selection is guided by practical concerns such as 'intrinsic importance' or whether a researcher has access to relevant evidence (Gerring, 2017: 42).

For a descriptive case study, case selection is of a typical case, or of two or more sub-types of cases (diverse cases). For a causal case study, case selection will depend on which type of causal case study you intend to carry out: exploratory (to generate hypotheses), estimating (to estimate outcomes) or diagnostic (to determine interrelationships among the variables). In Box 21.2, I describe two types of exploratory causal studies. These seek to generate hypotheses on the relationship between one or more variables and an outcome. Common types of exploratory causal studies are *most-similar* and *most-different*. I give examples with reference to our research on plagiarism in Box 21.2.

BOX 21.2   DESCRIPTIVE CASE STUDY AND A CAUSAL (EXPLORATORY) CASE STUDY

Let's assume we have carried out a cross-case study of plagiarism. Using the survey findings, we decide to carry out a descriptive case study and a causal (exploratory) case study. For the former, we identify six student sub-groups, arrayed as a 3 x 2 table, which cross-tabulates their behaviour (never plagiarized, sometimes plagiarized and often plagiarized) and the detection of their behaviour (no, not detected; yes, detected). We then select six students who are typical of that cell for careful examination. This would be a descriptive study of sub-types (diverse).

In the causal case study, we want to understand a surprising finding from our survey: among the subset of students with a high degree of risk-taking behaviour, some of which was illegal, one group was never caught for attempted plagiarism, while another group was. Case selection would be based on a *most-similar* design, which means the case is the same on a background factor that may cause the outcome (risk-taking), but different on the outcome. We decide to select four cases for intensive examination: one male and female each for the two groups. We seek to understand what the mechanisms are that facilitate the ability of one group of students who are similar on risk-taking to evade (or not) detection for plagiarism. For a *most-different* design, we select four cases which are the same on the outcome, but different on the background factor that we think should have caused the outcome.

There are many considerations in selecting cases, but, ultimately, how you decide to select depends on the goals of your research. Case selection should be done with awareness of the relevant rule you are using to select cases, and this, in turn, should be explained in your research. Unfortunately, many researchers do not know the rules and do not report them. Imagine that a survey researcher did not explain the decisions that were made in drawing a sample of cases. This would be unheard of. Thus, case study researchers need to become sophisticated in their knowledge of case selection and how it is reported.

STRENGTHS AND LIMITS OF CASE STUDY RESEARCH: WHAT DO YOU WANT TO KNOW?

All methods of conducting research have strengths and weaknesses. Let us consider what these are by comparing case study and cross-case research. The comparison is not absolute, but reveals 'methodological *affinities*' and a set of 'trade-offs' (Gerring, 2007: 38, emphasis in original; see Chapter 3). In general, case study research is recommended if you seek to:

- *generate* hypotheses, rather than *test* hypotheses
- have *internal* validity (ensure that the interrelationship(s) in your sample are correct) rather than *external* validity (the ability to generalize from a sample to a larger population)
- understand *causal mechanisms* (know how one or more variables relate to the others) rather than predict *causal effects*
- have a *deep*, rather than a *broad*, understanding of phenomena.

Internal validity is typically more relevant for causal than descriptive case studies, and causal mechanisms are more relevant for causal than descriptive case studies.

To understand these terms, let's turn to the second case study (causal exploratory) in our plagiarism research. We are interested to *generate* hypotheses on the surprising finding from the survey of students. We want to be sure we have identified all the relevant variables that are associated with high risk-taking, but with different outcomes in plagiarism detection (*internal validity*). We want to show how the variables are causally related (*causal mechanisms*), and we are able to gain a *deep* understanding of the process. After we complete the case study, and if our survey data permit it, we can test hypotheses generated from the case study. With a large sample size, we will feel more confident in being able to generalize our findings to a larger population (*external validity*) and to have a *broad* understanding of how risk-taking behaviour relates to plagiarism detection for male and female students.

CASE STUDY, COMPARATIVE CASE RESEARCH AND COMPARATIVE CRIMINOLOGY

How does case study research relate to comparative case research and comparative criminology? Table 21.1 is a template, drawn from Gerring (2007: 28), which arrays case study research and cross-case research along two dimensions of spatial variability and temporal variability. Spatial variation normally refers to geographical or political units (such as groups, neighbourhoods, cities, regions, countries) and temporal variation refers to observations over an extended period of time. The term synchronic means at one point in time, whereas diachronic means over time, with a specific focus on historical change. The grey-shaded areas are types of case study research.

TABLE 21.1 **Research design template**

cases	spatial variation	temporal variation **NO**	temporal variation **YES**
ONE	none	1. logically impossible	2. single-case study (diachronic)
	within-case	3. single-case study (synchronic)	4. single-case study (synchronic and diachronic)
SEVERAL	cross-case and within case	5. comparative	6. comparative-historical
MANY	cross-case	7. cross-sectional	8. time-series cross-sectional
	cross-case and within-case	9. hierarchical	10. hierarchical time-series

Source: Gerring (2007: 28), reprinted with permission of the author and Cambridge University Press

One point of confusion is whether a case study has one or several cases. For example, in our study of student plagiarism, we identified three students from a university for intensive case study. Is this one case of plagiarism or three student cases? I believe Gerring would say it is one case of student orientations to plagiarism, with the aim of understanding typicality or diversity in students' behaviours and experiences. When he uses the term several cases, he has in mind the field of comparative politics and research on two or more 'large territorial units' such as nation-states (Gerring, 2007: 27). If we were to apply this logic to our plagiarism study, a comparative study might examine students in two different universities. In general, comparative case research examines large social units such as organisations, cities, states, regions, nation-states, or cultures, not individuals, although there can be exceptions such as in-depth psychoanalytical studies of 'specific individuals' (Gerring, 2017: 4).

When is a case study considered to be 'diachronic'? Virtually all social phenomena travel in time; however, to be diachronic, the research question should be concerned explicitly with the substance and quality of change over time.

Comparative social science can be carried out with case study and cross-case methods, and, by definition, it compares two or more cases. Thus, it falls into cells 5–10. In reviewing Table 21.1, comparative criminology may statistically analyse rates of crime in ten countries at one point in time (cell 7), over time (cell 8), or by using other cross-case methods (cells 9 and 10); or it may focus on one or two countries in depth, using case study methods (cells 3 and 5) or over time (cells 4 and 6). Karstedt's (2012: 373) review of comparative criminology stretches its conventional emphasis on comparing nation-states to comparing cultures, which range from 'sub-cultures to regional and national cultures and to legal cultures'. Her argument suggests a need to re-define spatial boundaries in comparative case study research to include not only political units but also socio-cultural units.

CASE STUDIES IN ACTION: SOME CLASSICS

Let us see case studies in action, first with reference to some classic case studies (Box 21.3). What each of these is 'a case of' is, respectively, total institutions, black families and social groups, and social reaction to youth sub-cultures. All the cases are descriptive and synchronic, but they generated new ways of understanding self and identity, kin and friendship networks, and social responses to deviance.

BOX 21.3   CLASSIC CASE STUDIES

Erving Goffman's (1961) essay 'On the characteristics of total institutions' drew on inmates' experiences in mental hospitals, prisons and other institutions. It is one of four cases in *Asylums*, which examined 'the inmate's situation' from different vantage points: what it is like to live in total institutions, shifts in an inmate's identity, how an inmate relates to and views the institution, and the relationship between medical experts and the body of a client.

Carol Stack's (1974) *All Our Kin: Strategies for Survival in a Black Community* is a case study of poor black families in a US Midwest city in the late 1960s. She shows how kin- and non kin-based networks of cooperation, reciprocity and exploitation operated to sustain survival. This book, together with Eliott Liebow's (1967) *Tally's Corner*, a study of black men in Washington, DC in the 1960s, were among the earliest US case studies of black families and social groups.

Stanley Cohen's (1972) *Folk Devils and Moral Panics* is a case study of the emergence and decline of Mods and Rockers as a social phenomenon in 1960s' England. Cohen showed how the apparent threat of youth sub-cultures materialized as 'folk devils' and the societal processes at play ('moral panics') in defining deviance. He drew upon the ideas of US sociologist Howard Becker in problematizing definitions of crime and deviance.

CASE STUDIES IN ACTION: CONTEMPORARY CRIMINOLOGY

For contemporary examples, I consider case studies of crime and disorder, justice and comparative criminology.

Crime and disorder

Box 21.4 has two case studies. The first describes five sub-types of homicide that target anti-lesbian, gay, bisexual and transgender (LGBT) individuals. Kelley and Gruenewald (2015) theorize homicide as a situated transaction and use the construct of 'doing masculinity' to analyse offenders' motives for targeting a perceived LGBT person. Homicide and other violent offences such as robbery and sexual violence are frequent subjects of case study analysis. Researchers examine the sequence of moves and counter-moves in violent episodes, and they attempt to reach into the subjectivities of offenders and victims, as the violence unfolds.

The second is a case study of a significant political and social event – the riots in England in August 2011 – to determine what groups were involved, why they looted and what legal authorities did during and after the riots. It shows how an event such as social disorder can be studied, using varied evidence sources (interviews, arrests, court prosecutions, social media). It also shows the value of examining what happens after an event, and, in this case, police and court responses to alleged and convicted offenders. Newburn (2015) compared what occurred in 2011 with other urban disorders in post-war England and Wales, and from this he identified a model for carrying out comparative analyses of riots.

BOX 21.4   CASE STUDIES OF CRIME

HOMICIDE

Kristin Kelley and Jeff Gruenewald (2015) analysed five cases from a large database of extremist crimes in the USA. Their selection process had two steps: first, they pared down the database to all potential cases of fatal attacks against lesbian, gay, bisexual and transgender (LGBT) individuals, and then they selected a case from each of five sub-groups. These groups were identified from previous research on anti-LGBT homicide, which focused on mode of victim selection. The authors analyse what occurred before, during and after the violence. Of the five, one sub-group (predatory-instrumental violence, which is an attack with the motive

---

of economic gain) did not fit the general profile of anti-LGBT violence, nor did it explicitly demonstrate masculinity. The research was a single case (anti-LGBT homicide), studied at one point in time; and case selection was descriptive (diverse sub-types).

AUGUST 2011 RIOTS IN ENGLAND

Tim Newburn and Paul Lewis (a journalist from *The Guardian*) teamed up in 2011 to carry out a case study of the August riots, specifically, how and why they came about. The research was unusual because it was undertaken rapidly with a large team of researchers and initial publication in a series of articles in *The Guardian*. Phase 1 examined what happened and why the riots occurred in English cities, mainly in London, from the perspective of those who participated (Lewis et al., 2011). Phase 2 examined the police and criminal justice responses. The project sought to utilize high-quality social science methods, but within an expedited journalistic time frame. The results were published in *The Guardian* in 2011 (December) and 2012 (July); journal articles followed (Newburn, 2015; Newburn et al., 2015), which related the project's findings to academic debates on the character and causes of the riots. The design is a single case study, examined over two years. The case was selected for its political salience and significance; the study design was descriptive and causal (exploratory).

Justice

Justice processes and outcomes lend themselves to case study analysis: legal research is case-based (although it may or may not use social science methods), and criminological research has long focused on police and court responses to crime and victimization. We need to be especially attentive to the question, 'what is this a case *of*?', when designing research on justice. One legal case can be sufficiently significant to be one case study (for example, see Gies, 2017). However, other legal cases such as sentencing decisions may need to be aggregated to form a substantive case for case study. Three examples are given in Box 21.5, one of which draws from my research.

The first examines the dynamics of restorative justice (RJ) practices for intimate partner violence (IPV) cases. Like decisions in youth courts and some specialist courts, restorative justice practices are not open to the public and can be observed only if you have permission. Thus, we require research on what is occurring. For each case, Gaarder (2015) analysed the perspectives of an admitted offender and victim before, during and after the circles; change or relapse in an offender's behaviour; and the impact on a victim. The depth of detail about each person's concerns and circumstances – of drug abuse, unemployment, custody of a child – brought forward the complexities of addressing IPV in a justice process.

The second, of two mothers' experiences supporting their sons in youth court, shows how and why they become increasingly disengaged with court processes. We might have expected that the mothers' differing racial and socio-economic circumstances would have shaped their orientations to the court process. However, the courts' organizational logic, and the roles and responsibilities of court actors, were more determining. Pennington (2015) calls for procedural justice researchers to pay closer attention to context and consider the many points of interaction (not just one) between legal authorities and citizens.

My research (Daly, 2014) examined the ways in which institutions, states and provinces, and two countries (Australia and Canada) responded to the historical institutional abuse of children. It sought to historicize the emergence of institutional abuse as a social problem, compare responses by authorities and determine whether there was an optimal redress response from victim-survivors' perspectives. When carrying out the research, I worked iteratively between two levels of analysis: an in-depth case study of each of the 19 cases and a cross-case analysis of many relevant variables. My design combined case study and cross-case research. Previous research by others had analysed cases in one jurisdiction or one redress mechanism (for example, public inquiries) across cases. I drew inspiration from research on transitional justice, in which authors have compared one or more justice mechanisms (truth commission, criminal prosecution, lustration or purges) for countries in transition (Backer, 2009; Hayner, 2011). Australia and Canada are often considered to be similar in comparative case study research, and I compared the two for some outcomes (thus, a *most similar* design). However, my primary aim was to describe and understand the diversity of redress in the two countries rather than to compare each country.

BOX 21.5 CASE STUDIES OF JUSTICE

RESTORATIVE JUSTICE FOR INTIMATE PARTNER VIOLENCE

Emily Gaarder (2015) examined restorative justice responses to intimate partner violence (IPV) by describing three cases. These were the only cases in a pilot programme in Duluth, Minnesota, which sought to integrate 'RJ values and practices with values and practices from the battered women's movement' (2015: 347). Those targeted for the programme had a history of IPV or were in same-sex relations.

The RJ protocol had separate circles for the victim (the support circle) and the admitted offender (the sentencing circle). With other colleagues, Gaarder spent about 200 hours in participant-observation and carried out interviews with 29 people (victims, offenders, support people, victim advocates, among others). The research focused on what happened during the circles (which often met many times) and afterwards, with follow-up data on re-offending for five years after each offender's last circle. The design was a single case study (with three legal cases) and synchronic, although the cases were followed over time. It was descriptive, and there was no selection from a larger pool of cases.

PARENTAL PERCEPTIONS OF PROCEDURAL JUSTICE IN YOUTH COURT

Liana Pennington (2015) described the experiences of two mothers, Kit and Judy, whose sons were before youth courts in the US north-east. The two were selected from 30 families who had youth in court, of which a high share (24) reported 'dissatisfaction and disengagement in the court process' (2015: 905). Kit and Judy were selected as typical cases of parental disengagement. Kit was African-American, unemployed and lived in an economically disadvantaged part of the city served by Court 1; Judy was white, employed and lived in a more suburban setting served by Court 2. Drawing from the literature on procedural justice and legal consciousness, Pennington explored Kit's and Judy's experiences as parents at three points: before going to court, during the mid-court stages and at the final stages. Her many observations in court and interviews over a 10-month period revealed that Kit's and Judy's initial enthusiasm to participate in a legal process was undermined by the court staff and the court's routines. Despite racial and socio-economic differences, both mothers became more passive and no longer interested in participating in the court activity. The case study used a *most-different* design, in which the mothers' backgrounds and the areas served by the courts differed, but the women experienced the same outcome. It was causal (exploratory) in showing the mechanisms that led to their disengagement.

REDRESS FOR HISTORICAL INSTITUTIONAL ABUSE

My research on historical institutional abuse (Daly, 2014) examined 19 cases of redress activity in Canada and Australia. Some cases were of one organization, and others were large, including redress by a state or country. I sought to explain why institutional abuse emerged as a social problem in the 1980s and to map authorities' responses (criminal prosecution, public inquiries, civil litigation and redress schemes). I created variables to compare who and what were the subjects of redress; how long it took authorities to respond; the structure of

(Continued)

redress schemes (the logic used in deciding monetary payments, other non-monetary elements and the application process); outcomes; and the average time for survivors to achieve a tangible result. Survivors' experiences of redress were analysed with my construct of 'victims' justice interests' (Daly, 2014, 2017). The 19 cases were all the Canadian and Australian cases of abuse in 'total institutions' (Goffman, 1961) to mid-year 2010. The design combined case study and cross-case methods, with some comparative analysis of Canada and Australia. It was descriptive (diverse) and explored some causal mechanisms (exploratory).

COMPARATIVE CRIMINOLOGY

Although my research and that by Pennington had comparative elements, our focus differed from what is commonly featured in comparative social science or comparative criminology. In these areas, the unit of analysis is a nation-state, although as Karstedt (2012) suggests, it may also be useful to focus on socio-cultural units.

In the last decade, there has been an explosion of interest by criminologists in comparative study (for review, see Karstedt, 2012). In part, this reflects an interest in examining the impact of globalization; in part, to better understand crime and justice in the developing world; and in part, to analyse mass atrocities and justice in countries in transition from civil war or state repression to more democratic forms. The example in Box 21.6 reflects the first area of interest, with a comparative analysis of international regulation of bribery. Sáenz (2015) compares Germany, France and Japan to determine why Germany is more compliant than the other two in prosecuting foreign bribery.

BOX 21.6   COMPARING NATION STATES

PROSECUTION OF FOREIGN BRIBERY

Sara Sáenz (2015) examined foreign bribery prosecutions in Germany, France and Japan. Foreign bribery was subject to early US legislation, with passage of the Foreign Corrupt Practices Act (FCPA) in 1977. However, it was not until 1999 that an international convention for bribery prosecution was put into operation by the Organisation for Economic Co-operation and Development. The regulatory expectation was that bribery in international business transactions could be reduced if member states actively prosecuted it. As of 2014, 41 states had signed the Convention, but some are more active than others. The USA is the most active, with prosecutions of 128 bribery schemes; next is Germany with 26; and France and Japan are lower (five and three, respectively). (The US activity reflects a more active stance toward bribery prosecution, not necessarily more bribery cases.) Sáenz asks, what explains the variation for Germany, France and Japan? She analyses the incentives and disincentives of prosecution for each country, and puts forward three explanatory dimensions: economic, cultural and political. The study shows there is specific within-case (within-country) variation in deciding to prosecute or not, which explains the cross-case variation in country prosecution of foreign bribery.

SUMMARY AND REVIEW

This chapter has described the aims and applications of case study research, and compared it with cross-case research. Five points have been advanced. First, case study research may use qualitative and quantitative evidence to describe and explain a case in depth; for that reason, it would be misleading to call case study research qualitative, and more accurate to call it a hybrid form. Second, case study researchers are obliged to address the question, 'what is this a case *of*?' In some research, this may not be certain at the start, but will require continual reflection as the project evolves. Third, how and why cases are selected is a critical decision. Researchers should be cognizant of the selection rule(s) they use, and they should discuss what they did and why in papers that report results. Fourth, approaches to knowledge building in the social sciences – positivist and interpretive, among others – vary. This, along with differing disciplinary concerns, means that there is no one authoritative source for doing case study research. My chapter relied on Gerring's (2007/2017) work for its clarity and comprehensiveness. Fifth, all research methods have strengths and weaknesses, which should be viewed as trade-offs. In general, when you want to know the 'how and why' of social phenomena, case study research would be your choice. When you want to know 'who, what, where, how many, and how much' (Yin, 1994: 6), then cross-case research may be preferable.

Looking to the future, criminology will benefit by an awareness of the value and sophistication of case study research and by seeing it as an equal partner with cross-case research.

1. 'Case study research is qualitative research.' Discuss this claim and illustrate with examples.

2. What is case selection in case study research? Why is it a crucial step in the research process?

3. Becker (1999) says that what a case study is 'a case of' may not be known until the conclusion of the research, and that the less sure a researcher is at the start, the better the research may be. What does he mean?

4. How is case study research related to cross-case research?

5. What is the difference between comparative case study research and comparative criminology?

6. Locate a journal article that uses case study research. Review it with reference to these questions. What is it a case of? Did the author(s) provide a clear and well-defended explanation of *the method* used in case selection? Would you have carried out the study differently? Why or why not?

7. Locate three texts on case study research. Review them with reference to how these terms are defined: a case, a case study, and case selection. What are the points of similarity and difference?

8. Identify a problem in crime and justice that interests you. How would you carry out research on it using a case study method? What would you hope to learn from the case study? How would what you could learn differ from a research design that used a cross-case method?

SUGGESTIONS FOR FURTHER READING

John Gerring's (2007) first edition of *Case Study Research: Principles and Practices* is an accessible and comprehensive introduction to case study research and its relationship to cross-case research in the social sciences. He revised the text substantially in a second edition (2017), in which he considers case selection in greater depth and research with a medium number of cases. I recommend the second edition for those seeking a more sophisticated understanding of case study research. SAGE Publications has produced a two-volume *Encyclopedia of Case Study Research*, edited by Mills, Durepos and Wiebe (2010). The editors' fields are management, business and organizational studies. Their choice of topics and contributors reflect these disciplinary perspectives, not sociology, criminology, history, or law. An edited contemporary collection of case study articles or an analysis of case study research in criminology has yet to be published.

REFERENCES

Backer, D. (2009) 'Cross-national comparative analysis', in H. van der Merwe, V. Baxter and A.R. Chapman (eds), *Assessing the Impact of Transitional Justice*. Washington, DC: United States Institute of Peace Press, pp. 13–89.

Becker, H. (1999) 'The Chicago School, so-called', *Qualitative Sociology*, 22(1): 3–12.

Cohen, S. (1972) *Folk Devils and Moral Panics*. London: Granada Publishing.

Daly, K. (2014) *Redressing Institutional Abuse of Children*. Basingstoke: Palgrave Macmillan.

Daly, K. (2017) 'Sexual violence and victims' justice interests', in E. Zinsstag and M. Keenan (eds), *Sexual Violence and Restorative Justice: Legal, Social and Therapeutic Dimensions*. London: Routledge, pp. 108–39.

Elman, C., Gerring, J. and Mahoney, J. (2016) 'Case study research: putting the quant in the qual', *Sociological Methods & Research*, 45(3): 375–91.

Gaarder, E. (2015) 'Lessons from a restorative circles initiative for intimate partner violence', *Restorative Justice: An International Journal*, 3(3): 342–65.

George, A.L. and Bennett, A. (2005) *Case Studies and Theory Development in the Social Sciences*. Cambridge: The MIT Press.

Gerring, J. (2007/2017) *Case Study Research: Principles and Practices* (1st and 2nd editions). Cambridge: Cambridge University Press.

Gies, L. (2017) 'Miscarriages of justice in the age of social media: the Amanda Knox and Raffaele Sollecito innocence campaign', *British Journal of Criminology*, 57(3): 723–40.

Goffman, E. (1961) *Asylums*. Garden City, NY: Anchor Books.

Hayner, P.B. (2011) *Unspeakable Truths: Transitional Justice and the Challenge of Truth Commissions*, 2nd edition. New York: Routledge.

Karstedt, S. (2001) 'Comparing cultures, comparing crime: challenges, prospects and problems for a global criminology', *Crime, Law and Social Change*, 36: 285–308.

Karstedt, S. (2012) 'Comparing justice and crime across cultures', in D. Gadd, S. Karstedt and S.F. Messner (eds), *The SAGE Handbook of Criminological Research Methods*. London: Sage, pp. 373–89.

Kelley, K. and Gruenewald, J. (2015) 'Accomplishing masculinity through anti-lesbian, gay, bisexual, and transgender homicide: a comparative case study approach', *Men and Masculinities*, 18(1): 3–29.

Lewis, P., Newburn, T., Taylor, M., Mcgillivray, C., Greenhill, A., Frayman, H. and Proctor, R. (2011) *Reading the Riots: Investigating England's Summer of Disorder*. London:

Reading the Riots, The London School of Economics and Political Science (LSE) and The Guardian. Available at: http://eprints.lse.ac.uk/46297 (accessed May 2018).

Liebow, E. (1967) *Tally's Corner: A Study of Negro Streetcorner Men*. Boston: Little, Brown.

Merriam, S.B. (1998) *Qualitative Research and Case Study Applications in Education*. San Francisco: Jossey-Bass.

Mills, A.J., Durepos, G. and Wiebe, E. (eds) (2010) *Encyclopedia of Case Study Research*, Vols I and II. Thousand Oaks, CA: Sage.

Newburn, T. (2015) 'The 2011 English riots in recent historical perspective', *British Journal of Criminology*, *55*(1): 39–64.

Newburn, T., Cooper, K., Deacon, R. and Diski, R. (2015) 'Shopping for free? Looting, consumerism and the 2011 riots', *British Journal of Criminology*, *55*(5): 987–1004.

Pennington, L. (2015) 'A case study approach to procedural justice: parents' views in two juvenile delinquency courts in the United States', *British Journal of Criminology*, *55*(5): 901–20.

Piekkari, R., Welch, C. and Paavilainen, E. (2010) 'Pluralism and case study', in A.J. Mills, G. Durepos and E. Wiebe (eds), *Encyclopedia of Case Study Research*. Thousand Oaks, CA: Sage.

Platt, J. (1992) '"Case study" in American methodological thought', *Current Sociology*, *40*: 17–48.

Plummer, K. (2003) 'Continuity and change in Howard S. Becker's work', *Sociological Perspectives*, *46*(1): 21–39.

Ragin, C.C. (1987/2014) *The Comparative Method: Moving Beyond Qualitative and Quantitative Strategies* (1st and 2nd editions). Oakland, CA: University of California Press.

Ragin, C.C. (1992) 'Introduction: cases of "what is a case?"', in C.C. Ragin and H.S. Becker (eds), *What is a Case? Exploring the Foundations of Social Inquiry*. Cambridge: Cambridge University Press, pp. 1–52.

Sáenz, S.C. (2015) 'Explaining international variance in foreign bribery prosecution: a comparative case study', *Duke Journal of Comparative & International Law*, *26*: 271–98.

Stack, C. (1974) *All Our Kin: Strategies for Survival in a Black Community*. New York: Basic Books.

Stake, R.E. (1995) *The Art of Case Study Research*. Thousand Oaks, CA: Sage.

Whyte, W.F. (1943/1981) *Street Corner Society: The Social Structure of an Italian Slum*. Chicago: University of Chicago Press.

Yazan, B. (2015) 'Three approaches to case study methods in education: Yin, Merriam, and Stake', *The Qualitative Report*, *20*(2): 134–52.

Yin, R.K. (1984/1994/2014) *Case Study Research: Design and Methods* (1st, 2nd and 5th editions). Thousand Oaks, CA: Sage.

CHAPTER CONTENTS

GLOSSARY TERMS

evaluation

performance indicators

performance targets

triangulation

summative evaluation

impact evaluation

formative evaluation

continuous evaluation

benchmarks

22

DOING CRIMINOLOGICAL EVALUATION RESEARCH

ROB WHITE

INTRODUCTION

This chapter will map out some initial considerations essential to the undertaking of criminological evaluation and discuss in greater depth three evaluation projects. These projects were carried out by different teams of evaluators under the lead of myself, and involved various players, agencies and institutions associated with the criminal justice system – prisoners, prison officers, prison managers, political leaders, non-government service providers, academics and practitioners. Each evaluation generated its own particular, and at times even peculiar, 'story', and it is the telling of these that is important from the point of view of acknowledging the real-world toing-and-froing that accompanies this kind of work. But first, we begin with a few preliminary comments about evaluation and the evaluation process.

EVALUATION

Evaluation is basically about assessing what we are doing, valuing why we are doing it, and understanding how we can make improvements in the future. Any project, programme or strategy requires a consideration of the identified 'problem', an understanding of desirable 'outcomes' and a 'theory and method' of how certain interventions can achieve these outcomes. Evaluation research is about determining how an initiative is working, and what might be done to improve its chances of success or, indeed, to stop it altogether (Australian Institute of Criminology, 2003; Shannon and Schaefer, 2014; White, 2013; White and Coventry, 2000).

Criminological evaluation is important as it provides a key indicator as to how some aspect of the criminal justice system, crime prevention measure, or voluntary and third-sector programme or project is working (or not working). It also provides insight into whether and to what extent the goals of justice (and social justice) are being achieved through specific initiatives, social interventions or institutional practices.

The key questions evaluation seeks to address are:

- *what* works, *for whom* and *under what conditions*
- *how* does something work, and for *how long*
- what *consequences*, both intended and unintended, flow from the adoption of certain practices or strategies
- how do we wish to *understand and measure* social progress.

Ideally, evaluation should be both *continuous* (in the sense of monitoring the social processes associated with the conceptualization and implementation of specific initiatives) and *time-specific* (in the sense of providing snapshots of impacts and outcomes at any point in time). The nature of evaluation, however, will be shaped by the specific aims and objectives of an evaluation, the resources and skills available, and the anticipated social purposes for which it will be used (Bowen and Brown, 2012; Crow, 2000; Hough, 2010; Tilley, 2000; Wadsworth, 1991; Wilson and Wright, 1993).

THINKING ABOUT DOING EVALUATION

Criminological evaluation can involve assessing:

- *inputs* (basic resources available to the programme, including staff, facilities, existing networks, and so on)
- *process* (the number and nature of meetings, contacts and collaborations)
- *outputs* (which indicate numbers, of clients, for instance)
- *outcomes* (which indicate meaningful changes in clients, programmes).

Both quantitative and qualitative information are necessary to gauge the effectiveness, efficiency and degree of success of whatever it is that is being assessed (Australian Youth Foundation and Sharp, 1996; Murray et al., 1993; Wadsworth, 1991; White, 2013).

Evaluation involves research that speaks to the applied dimensions of criminology. That is, evaluation seeks to learn about the concrete effects and practical consequences of policies, programmes and projects carried out by government and non-government agencies and organizations. Evaluation projects can be carried out at different times; some are conducted alongside an intervention or an initiative; some are carried out at the end of a defined programme or project; while others involve evaluation on a periodic but continuous basis (for example, once a year or once every three years). When and how evaluation is undertaken reflects the purposes of the evaluation, the resources available and for whom it is being carried out.

Performance indicators

An important step in criminological evaluation is to establish the evaluation criteria or performance indicators (see White, 2013). These are the measures used to evaluate whether something is 'successful' or 'unsuccessful', 'valuable' or 'not valuable', 'working' or 'not working'. Performance indicators refer to concrete ways in which performance is measured, whether in regard to processes or outcomes. They are signs by which we can determine whether a project is doing what its objectives and goals say it is doing. Performance indicators are generally 'descriptive' and 'quantitative' in nature. That is, they refer to actual developments, such as the holding of a meeting to discuss community safety, and quantifiable units of measurement, such as the number of meetings or of participants. Performance indicators indicate present performance in relation to stated goals, such as how far along we are in achieving what we set out to achieve. They should not be confused with performance targets that refer to the end-point goals of a particular programme or project.

Performance indicators can serve different purposes, and reflect the agendas of those involved in the evaluation. They may reflect the immediate concerns of community residents or service-users, who might be interested in how a programme or service is meeting their perceived needs. Alternatively, they may reflect the administrative concerns of government and community agencies, which might be interested in whether or not their programme or service is reaching who it is intended to, or whether it is cost-effective. It is important, therefore, when designing performance indicators that general agreement is reached with the body commissioning the evaluation on both the desired goals and outcomes, and how these will be expressed in objective terms. The emphasis is that the meaning and measurement criteria of performance indicators are clear and agreed upon before the evaluation begins.

The development of performance indicators always takes place in the context of the evaluation's objectives. It is essential to identity the specific need or goal (e.g. to reduce rates of recidivism among prisoners by providing intensive transitional support); the particular meaning of the need or goal (e.g. what is meant by 'reduce', 'recidivism' 'prisoners', 'intensive transitional support'); and the appropriate way to measure whether or not progress is being made relative to the goal (e.g. the number of prisoners recruited to the programme, recidivism rates prior to engagement in the programme, instances of re-offending post-release). As discussed in Box 22.1, performance indicators need to refer to definitions and performance measures suited to the particular goals of a specific project.

BOX 22.1   LINKING PERFORMANCE INDICATORS TO GOALS

If the goal of the project being evaluated is to reduce the number of assaults outside certain licensed establishments, then there is a need to first define (or conceptualize) what is meant by 'reduce', 'assaults', which type of establishment, and also how a reduction is to be measured. In this case, a reduction in the number of arrests, police attendance, or the number of ambulance call-outs may operate as appropriate measurements of a reduction. To take another example, if the goal of a project is to 'increase awareness of safety issues in the local community', then the performance indicators need to, first, describe the *meaning* of each term (i.e. 'increase', 'awareness', 'safety issues', 'local community'), and then to describe the *specific indicators* which best capture this in quantitative terms (e.g. an upwards trend from baseline criteria, whose awareness is being raised; whether the issues relate to crime or injury; whether we are talking about a defined geographical region or specific social groups).

Performance indicators have a number of dimensions. Some of these include:

- *quantity*: measuring performance in terms of 'how many', 'how often' or 'how much' (numbers of, frequency of, rate of)
- *quality*: measuring performance in terms of 'how well' (opinions of, feedback from, continued participation of)
- *time frame*: measuring performance in terms of 'how long' (time taken, changes over time)
- *cost*: measuring performance in terms of 'how expensive' (money spent, equipment purchased, staff wages)
- *resources*: measuring performance in terms of 'how much' and 'what was contributed by whom' (agency contributions, cash and in-kind contributions, use of volunteers, funding base)
- *participation*: measuring performance in terms of 'who was involved' (members of target group, project organizers, funding agency, community residents).

The choice of, and emphasis placed on, different performance indicators is partly a matter of what the evaluation is intended to do. That is, the aims of evaluation will determine the nature of the performance measures to be used.

Methods of data collection

To assess whether or not a programme or project performance is measuring up to what it says it is meant to be doing requires the collection of relevant data. This can be achieved in several different ways (Bartels and Richards, 2011; Queensland Government, 2016; Walter, 2013a). Using multiple sources and a triangulation (Walter, 2013b) or combining of different research methods (that is, using at least two different sources of information or types of data collection) increases the reliability (or consistency) of the findings and reduces the limitations of a single research method.

Quantitative

This type of data collection is basically concerned with *counting* and *measurement*. It provides an indication of broad statistical trends:

- *numbers* of people using a service (a simple numerical count of referrals to the programme, or who uses which specific types of service provision, such as counsellors, doctors, youth workers)

- *extent* of service use in particular geographical area (linking of numbers with particular location, or expressed as a proportion of possible user population, e.g. total prison releases in region)
- *rate* of service use (expressed in relation to time: fluctuations in number of users per week or month or year, and/or expressed in relation to total populations: relative to prison releases in region (which itself can fluctuate over time))
- *trends* in service use (broad changes in rate over specified time periods, downwards or upwards).

This type of method may involve the use of formal pre-set questionnaires (e.g. asking people specific questions which have a limited number of optional answers: yes/no), as well as drawing upon formal records (e.g. the use of official prison statistics). Quantitative method thus lends itself to large-scale studies and statistical collection (Walter, 2013a).

Qualitative

This type of data collection is basically concerned with *understanding*. It is about gaining information about how people feel about things, and what their perceptions are about particular issues. It provides for more in-depth appreciation of how people make sense of their lives, and emphasizes *their* accounts of post-release experiences and service provision.

While the method is generally based on some form of interviewing, the findings may nonetheless be presented in statistical form (e.g. of the 50 people we spoke with, 25 thought that a pre-release plan was a good idea).

Qualitative methods generally involve a combination of description (based on observation) and relatively unstructured interviews (based around certain core questions or themes). The point is to gain information which will enable the researcher/evaluator to better appreciate the social contexts and social processes which inform how people feel about themselves, and their issues of concern. As such, qualitative method tends to be oriented toward small-scale research, involving interactions with small groups and in local contexts (Bartels and Richards, 2011).

Interpretive

This type of data collection is basically concerned with *critical analysis*. It is intended to be a form of reflection on the social meaning of official documents, existing statistical collections, policy statements and media reports.

This form of research/evaluation is concerned with the identification of the perspectives which underlie post-release issues. It is an attempt to expose the assumptions, discourses and ideological propositions which are embodied in post-release studies and policies. The 'data' which is collected is, in effect, the *meanings* assigned to particular forms and kinds of information, and the theories which are implicit in the language used, and concepts employed, in the documentation of an issue or trend.

The contribution of this form of data collection, therefore, is to provide critical appraisal of taken-for-granted assumptions, and thereby to open the door for alternative explanations, programmes for action or suggestions for reform (Hough, 2010; Tilley, 2000).

DOING EVALUATION: WHY AND FOR WHOM?

Different projects have different goals and may be informed by very different values, concepts, intentions and rationales. The main point of any particular intervention may range from trying to foster better processes of community interaction through to providing a substantial change in local crime rates.

Each project will, therefore, have its own focus and rationale. These, in turn, imply the use of evaluation criteria that best suit the purpose and context of the project. The model of evaluation that is used needs to be relevant and useful as it applies to specific types of projects or strategies. Choosing a particular evaluation model is thus inextricably linked to the nature of the project or programme itself.

There is a need to know concretely whether or not something is making a difference. However, the criteria for success (from an evaluation viewpoint) should not be rigidly assumed either. For example, *learning from errors* is often a valuable experience in its own right. It is also a normal part of developing the skills and methods that will enable better work in the future. A 'mistake' is an error that is not fixed.

Also, projects are not static but are in a continual state of flux or change (e.g. changes in personnel or in methods of service delivery). Process or continuous evaluation, therefore, is important to monitor such changes over time.

Who an evaluation is intended for (e.g. a government agency or third-sector organization) and why it is being carried out (e.g. to enhance service provision, or as a requirement for a funding agreement) are important questions, as is who is doing the evaluation (e.g. the agency itself or external evaluators). The intended outcome of the evaluation will also vary, from measuring the administrative competence of a funded agency through to identifying the future strategic goals and objectives of an organization. The values that underpin evaluation may mainly orient toward efficiency and effectiveness or place the greatest stress on social empowerment.

The diverse purposes, values and approaches to evaluation mean that, in practice, there will be considerable variation in how evaluation is carried out, and how it will be received and/or used. Evaluation is, therefore, an inherently political exercise. It can be managerialist and politically conservative in some instances, such as when government bodies demand 'value for money' from funded agencies offering minimalist client servicing. On the other hand, it can be used progressively to extend models of participatory practice amongst social reform-oriented agencies and thereby to enhance existing service provision. Evaluation is not intrinsically 'good' or 'bad'. It all depends on what it is for, who is funding it, who undertakes it and under what conditions, and what the ultimate objective is.

STORIES FROM THE FIELD

The remainder of the chapter provides sketches of three evaluation projects, each of which involved different objectives and methods of assessment, and most instructive, very specific problems and dilemmas arising from each evaluation.

Politics – evaluation of the 'Inside Out' Prison Program

Evaluation is frequently beset by 'politics', and in particular the manipulation of processes and outcomes to achieve certain (sometimes preordained) ends. This can create problems for criminological evaluation that strives to be fair, objective and unbiased. No academic research is ever 'value-free', but good research, including evaluation, demands that the high standards of rigour, validity, transparency and ethical conduct be applied (Australasian Evaluation Society, 1998). This is illustrated in the discussion of an evaluation of the Inside Out Prison Program, the features of which are described in Box 22.2.

BOX 22.2 EVALUATING THE INSIDE OUT PRISON PROGRAM

The Inside Out Prison Program (White and Mason, 2003) was directed at providing material and non-material support to prisoners and their families, with the aim of preventing suicide and self-harm among prisoners. An evaluation of the programme at Risdon Prison was commissioned by Corrective Services, Tasmania in 2003. The terms of reference for the evaluation of the Inside Out Program included its appropriateness, efficiency and effectiveness in regards to reducing re-offending, whether its processes are suited to reducing recidivism, and whether the allocation of resources, including budgets, lines of accountability and authorization are appropriate and effective, and, if not, what changes should be made to increase performance and better measure progress in the future. The evaluation was carried out over a period of several months by a two-person team from the University of Tasmania.

This evaluation was a summative evaluation, that is, one that is basically concerned with results. It takes place after a project or strategy has been in place for some time. The purpose of such evaluation is to monitor performance and outcomes up to a certain point in time. In this sense, it is retrospective (or backward-looking). It is concerned with learning from experience, in order to determine the impact of an initiative.

Two primary questions were central to the evaluation. These were: what are the benefits and strengths of the programme and what are the limitations and shortcomings of the programme? Data collected for the evaluation was derived from two main sources: documentation held by various agencies, such as the Attorney-General's Department, the Department of Justice (Corporate Office), Corrective Services, Care and Communication Concern (CCC) and the Inside Out service; and interviews with major stakeholders, such as prisoners, prison officers, prison managers, support service providers and prisoner family members.

The key findings of the Inside Out Program evaluation were that:

- Prisoners valued the Inside Out Program and thought it provided a useful non-institutional avenue for inmates to reduce/relieve the stresses associated with incarceration by providing someone to talk to and communicate with, and that it enabled them to better liaise with their families and loved ones. It also provided an avenue to release pent-up emotions.
- Prison authorities have mixed attitudes towards the programme, due to (a) problems with how it was introduced and implemented; (b) how funding was established and subsequently allocated for the programme; (c) differing perceptions among prison officials regarding the status and role of a 'lay' worker within the prison environment; and (d) the perceived lack of reporting and accountability of a prison-funded programme.
- From a service provision perspective, while the Inside Out support worker was highly committed and motivated to assist prisoners and their families, there were serious shortcomings in the support available to the worker – both from prison authorities (such as provision of adequate space, or suitable report back/consultative mechanisms) and from the funded organization (in the form of a locally based support network and constructive administrative and supervisory support).
- The support worker himself was inevitably placed in an ambiguous position due to the nature of the work. On the one hand, to do the job effectively requires certain personal qualities and task-related attributes. On the other hand, these very qualities and attributes may be seen as inappropriate in secure punishment facilities. This is a Catch 22 situation that can only be resolved by careful consideration of the philosophical rationale guiding prison management and prison programmes.

A number of recommendations were made about improving communication and consultation, and basically it was found that while the programme provided an invaluable service to prisoners, there were aspects of the programme, particularly relating to reporting mechanisms and procedures, that required attention. Overall, however, the evaluation report stated that the programme represented excellent value for money, given the time, energy and resources put into direct service provision by the key support worker, and the positive response from prisoners and their families to the service.

To understand the politics of criminological evaluation, several things need to be appreciated from the outset. First, evaluation research tends to revolve around specific projects (e.g. a youth project that involves teaching young offenders about car maintenance and safety issues), specific programmes (e.g. a school programme designed to reduce truancy among students), or specific intervention strategies (e.g. use of juvenile conferencing as an alternative to court or to detention).

Second, evaluation research does not usually originate with the researcher. In most cases, evaluation will be commissioned by a state agency (such as an Education Department, Department of Justice, Health Department), a business organization, or a professional body, rather than being initiated by the researcher. This means that the terms of reference – what is being evaluated and how – are frequently predetermined by those funding the evaluation. This can influence the evaluation process in terms of budgets, who is consulted and the potential outcomes of the evaluation.

Third, evaluation research is ultimately about making judgements, and these, in turn, may have significant consequences for the actors involved in the evaluation, and such research also tends to be more overtly politicized than other types of social research. Values and interests are thus always close to the surface in evaluation research. The institutional environment within which agencies or businesses operate will shape how they construct and how they respond to the evaluation. In the light of this, it is vital that evaluators be vigilant in protecting the integrity of their work, and that they be clear about where they stand in the evaluation process (i.e. as independent evaluators rather than employees). From an evaluator's perspective, the success or otherwise of any particular strategy or specific project cannot be taken for granted, no matter how good the intentions of the people involved or how laudable the goals and objectives.

In respect to this particular evaluation, two 'political' aspects stood out. On the one hand, from the very beginning the prison director had been critical of the way in which the programme had been foisted upon the prison by the Attorney General at the time. The Attorney General had unilaterally made the decision to introduce the programme, yet it was paid for out of the prison budget. Thus, there was internal antagonism to this particular programme due to the way in which it had been introduced.

On the other hand, the next Attorney General decided to axe the programme, in part due to overall government budget constraints. In doing so, she explicitly referred to the evaluation of the programme that we had carried out – and which *did not* recommend discontinuation of the programme but only that certain things could be done to enhance a programme that was deemed to be overall beneficial. Fortunately, after previously contacting the Secretary of Justice for permission, we had published the evaluation on the Criminology Research Unit website and printed hard copies for general distribution. Thus, we were able to contradict the Minister's pronouncement that the axing of the programme stemmed from our evaluation. By having publicly available documents, this ensured that, while the programme suffered, our reputation for integrity and independence did not. We did not provide the political justification for its demise and we were able to demonstrate this.

Relationships – evaluation of a prisoner peer support programme

The translation of evaluation methods into practice very often hinges on one key element – the human factor. That is, the success or otherwise depends to a great extent on the human resources available, the quality of the individual contributions to the evaluation, and the level of conflict or cooperation associated with a particular project. Who does what and how can have major implications, not only for the evaluation process but also for longer-term relationships between evaluators and criminal justice officials. This is demonstrated in our second example, which, as summarized in Box 22.3, consisted of an evaluation of a prisoner peer support programme.

BOX 22.3   EVALUATING A PRISONER PEER SUPPORT PROGRAMME

This evaluation was commissioned by the Australian Red Cross and funded through a Community Capacity Grant from the Tasmanian Department of Health and Human Services. The evaluation was conducted by a consultancy team from the Criminology Research Unit at the University of Tasmania, comprising three members (White, 2011). In the early stages of the project, the UTAS consultancy team met with senior management and correctional unit managers from the Tasmania Prison Service (TPS) to explain the evaluation and were guided and assisted by a project steering committee comprising senior managers from the Tasmania Prison Service and the Australian Red Cross. The evaluation took approximately 12 months to complete, and involved several draft reports and regular feedback from the funding agency about their expectations and requirements (e.g. the number of prisoners interviewed about the programme).

A core function of this evaluation was to inform ongoing improvement of the Red Cross peer support programme and its delivery in the Tasmania Prison Service. The evaluation process focused on the way in which the programme approached and met stated outcomes, by examining whether peer support structures and mentoring activities promoted positive change in inmate choices and behaviour. The evaluation was intended to strengthen evidence-based practice and to generate knowledge to inform future funding submissions, social policy positions and advocacy initiatives within Tasmania and more widely across the Australian Red Cross.

A distinguishing characteristic of impact evaluation is the emphasis and priority given to establishing the effect of the initiative (in this case, the Red Cross peer support programme). In addition to considering traditional evaluation criteria such as the context or environment within which the programme is operating, the evaluation examined the effects (positive and negative, intended and unintended) of the programme. Six key questions guided this evaluation:

1. What is the *impact* of the peer support programme on peer supporters, prisoners, correctional officers and ancillary care service providers working within the prison system?
2. Is the peer support programme having a demonstrable *effect*?
3. What is the perceived *quality* of the programme?
4. Is the programme *operating as intended*?
5. What are the comparative *cost benefits* of the programme?
6. How *relevant* are the supporting training manuals, measurement frameworks and policy/procedure materials?

The impact of this programme was measured in a number of different ways and data collected from varying sources. Key documents relating to the programme, collected for analysis from the Australian Red Cross and the Tasmania Prison Service, included such things as prison guidelines and policies, the Red Cross prisoner support programme operations manual, peer support programme implementation policies, peer supporter data collection sheets, and so on. These supporting documents were evaluated in the context of practical activities and shared understandings of purpose.

Interviews were conducted with 23 key stakeholders involved in or associated with the programme in some way. All participants, with the exception of the Red Cross project officer, were recruited with the assistance of the Tasmania Prison Service. Peer supporters and inmates using the service were recruited with the assistance of the Red Cross project officer, who introduced peer supporters to the UTAS evaluation team. The evaluation objectives were explained to potential participants in a joint presentation by the Red Cross project officer and the UTAS evaluator. Following expressions of interest from peer supporters and from other prisoners, separate appointments were made to conduct interviews with participants. Those interviewed included five peer supporters, seven inmates, eight correctional staff, two integrated offender management staff and the Red Cross project officer. A number of 'impromptu' conversations also occurred, particularly with correctional officers, in the course of the evaluator's visits to the prison. Although they declined to be formally interviewed, these officers were more than willing to provide input and opinions about the peer support programme 'off the record'. Their views are not recorded or presented in the final evaluation report; however, they did influence the interpretation of the documents and interviews formally relied on for the evaluation.

A limitation of the evaluation and the programme itself was that, at times, data collection was interrupted by the uncertainty and unpredictability of the prison environment, including lock-downs at short notice. Data collection took place over a period of five months between August and December 2010, and then over a further five-month period between March and August 2011. During these periods, there were occasions when appointments were made, postponed and cancelled due to confusion among correctional officers about the purpose of the visits, due to lock-downs, and due to timetable logistics within the prison. There were in fact a number of different issues associated with the interviewing process. The evaluators and others involved in the evaluation were variously frustrated in their efforts at different times and for diverse reasons.

Overall, the evaluation found that the tenets of the programme are consistent with the Australian Red Cross (ARC) commitment to caring for those on the margins of Australian society; supporting young people; improving opportunities, resilience and positive social connections; and assisting inmates to develop mature coping skills surrounding relationship and family issues, thereby helping families to better cope with having their family member incarcerated. The key evaluation finding was that, by and large, the peer support programme was working well and effectively in what can be, at times, a volatile and chaotic work and living environment. Key strengths of the programme were summarized and a number of areas where specific action could be taken to improve existing performance were recommended.

The issue that arose during the course of this evaluation was one pertaining to damage or potential damage to existing and future relationships – between the evaluation team and the prison, and between the Australian Red Cross and the prison. This was due primarily to the hiring of an interviewer for the evaluation team who, unknown to myself, was actively hostile to prison and those who work within such institutions. Her 'relationship' with those she interviewed, especially among correctional officers, was basically poisonous. This not only skewed the interviews in particularly negative directions, but it also meant that pursuing interviews was made that much more difficult as the evaluation proceeded. One consequence of this was that the evaluation was briefly suspended, and new interviewers, including myself, were thrust into the assessment process. This enabled a friendlier atmosphere to be constructed and reclaimed. It also provided for a number of additional interviews to be carried out – at the evaluator's expense in terms of additional time and money – so that a valid and insightful evaluation could be provided.

One lesson from this is that the ethics of evaluation is about 'trust', 'honesty' and 'reliability'. It means treating people fairly and openly. It implies a commitment to the physical, psychological and emotional well-being of everyone concerned. Ethics is not simply about 'correct procedures' – it is about human relationships. In undertaking criminological evaluation, the evaluators must therefore be conscious of any conflict of interest involving members of the evaluation team, including any especially ideological partiality that impacts on the evaluation process. Knowledge of codes of conduct for members of an evaluation team in relation to participants is important, as is recognition of the responsibilities of evaluators in regards to procedural rules and protocols.

Fortunately, the deficiencies in data collection and quality of data were detected before too much damage was done. Moreover, the funding body (the Australian Red Cross) was acutely aware of the need not only for robust data, but also for positive ongoing relationships at the prison. Extra work put in by the evaluation team, including volunteer labour, ensured that the final evaluation report was of a high standard and was a valuable source of information for the commissioning body. Strong relationships of trust (and forbearance) were also maintained across various communities of interest.

Consequences – evaluation of the Post Release Options Program

Formative evaluation is basically concerned with processes. It takes place at the beginning and during the implementation phase of an initiative. The purpose of such evaluation is to identify needs, clarify rationales and improve implementation. In this sense, it is prospective (or forward-looking). It is concerned with continuous assessment and ongoing feedback as a means to guide further development of the initiative.

If evaluation is continuous, then certain expectations, and assurances, have to be negotiated from the onset of the evaluation project, so that everyone – the funding bodies, the evaluators, the project or programme being evaluated, the client group, the local community – is clear about the role and contribution of evaluation as distinct from the project or intervention itself.

For continuous evaluation, it is essential that time be spent right at the very beginning of the project to have extensive discussions with stakeholders about the evaluation. These preliminary discussions need to be directed at clarifying roles, perspectives and key players, and the specific tasks of the evaluators relative to the overall programme. For instance, who is to collect what data and for what purposes has to be negotiated, and data-sharing procedures have to be put in place. A case study of continuous evaluation is provided in the next example, which is introduced in Box 22.4.

From the point of view of evaluation methodology, it is important to monitor those factors which impact on the evaluation process and which may either enhance or debilitate the evaluation. Building trust relationships is essential, and can be achieved to some extent by ensuring constant and transparent communication among key stakeholders. On the other hand, there is always the danger in continuous evaluation (which requires assessment of progress and regular feedback to projects/ programmes on how best to improve performance or achieve mission objectives) that the evaluators end up becoming *de facto* project managers. Again, clarity of roles and

The third evaluation involved assessment of the Post Release Options Project (PROP) that was run by a non-government organization called Bethlehem House. Its funding was in part contingent on the project being evaluated. As part of the evaluation process, the UTAS evaluation team, comprising three members, met regularly on an informal basis with representatives from Bethlehem House, the Tasmania Prison Service and PROP case managers (White et al., 2011). Data for this evaluation included PROP client records (de-identified) and organizational documents, interviews with prisoners, interviews with members of the Integrated Offender Management team at the local prison, and PROP staff. This evaluation took place over the course of three years.

As a form of 'continuous evaluation', the PROP evaluation involved regular reports on a variety of issues as they arose and as perceived by the evaluators. An evaluation strategy was put in place prior to the implementation of the project, and was consciously designed to foster appropriate and constructive review of the project on a regular basis and in a systematic form. For example, Table 22.1 (with some modifications) provides an illustration of the feedback format.

TABLE 22.1   Matters arising and PROP responses

Matters arising	Responses by PROP team
Defusing suspicion and resistance to collaboration	Some defensiveness still exists surrounding access to PROP clients and their families for interview. This needs to be surfaced and discussed between PROP case workers and the evaluation team and a sensitive approach taken to working with this vulnerable client group.
Educating all referral agencies about what the PROP project is (and is not), to address underlying fears about duplication of roles and services	PROP has successfully delivered a number of information sessions to Community Corrections staff. The sessions familiarized staff with the PROP progject, its objectives, limitations and referral processes, as well as providing good opportunities for networking and consolidating existing relationships.

(Continued)

TABLE 22.1 (Continued)

Matters arising	Responses by PROP team
Ongoing education and dissemination of information about PROP to referral and support agencies	For a detailed listing of networking activities, please refer to the PROP Forums, Conferences and Meetings document attached.
Technical training for PROP case managers in SMART software	The SMART software has been abandoned in favour of a more user-friendly client database in Microsoft Access. Specific training is recommended for the project manager and a back-up person in use of the query/ reporting function of the software to generate monthly reports for the evaluator. The Tasmania Prison Service will provide a resource to assist PROP to achieve this outcome.
Further streamlining of PROP referral processes with primary and secondary referral sources	A collaborative approach between PROP and TPS is required to achieve a common understanding of what constitutes an 'appropriate' referral, together with critique, analysis and documenting of the referral process in both narrative and flow-chart form.
Defining key terms such as recidivism for the purposes of this evaluation	The evaluation has adopted the following definition of recidivism, provided by the policy officer, Community Corrections, at the request of the core working group: 'return to corrective services with a new correctional sanction within 2 years of release, following a term of sentenced imprisonment, or final discharge from community corrections supervision following completion of an order(s) or supervision requirements'. This definition excludes ex-offenders returning to corrective services with remand, bail supervision, fine default or fine option matters only (or any combination thereof). Using the Report on Government Services (ROGS) definition will allow the project to make comparisons to published data for all Australian jurisdictions. It should also be noted that there are very clear rules about exactly how this data should be counted and calculated. *Tasmania Together* defines recidivism as the proportion of adult offenders convicted again within two years. However, performance data is yet to be published and it won't allow one to benchmark as widely as ROGS.

Matters arising	Responses by PROP team
Clearly defining and documenting the eligibility and selection criteria	Since inception, the project eligibility and selection criteria appear to have shifted from high risk to medium and high risk. As mentioned above, there is a need for PROP and TPS to collaborate more effectively in defining and refining this criteria, so that there is a common understanding of who is eligible and who is not.
Developing a flow chart clearly illustrating how clients will move through the PROP progject step by step	The PROP manager has done some work in this regard and will continue to develop this flow chart over the next six months.

purposes is crucial to distinguishing between project management and evaluation assessment, even though inevitably evaluation feedback will shape the evolution of projects over time.

It also needs to be emphasized that evaluators engaged in continuous assessment need to be independent of the project or programme, and to 'play with a straight bat' when it comes to critical observations of process, detailing problems in project management, identifying problems in data collection and more generally acknowledging both the strengths *and* limitations of project development. At a personal level, the relationship between evaluators and evaluatees can sometimes be close and involve individuals who know each other quite well. Negotiating personal relationships is part of the challenge of providing evaluation that is fair, objective and constructive.

Living with the consequences of what one 'sees' and describes is one outcome of such processes. These consequences can be very personal and difficult. For instance, as part of the feedback the evaluation team made the observations in Table 22.2.

TABLE 22.2 **PROP team observations**

Matters arising	Responses by PROP team
Need for dedicated project management	This has been addressed by PROP's recent restructuring which saw [Person Z] assume the role of project manager.
Capacity building and increased management and administrative support for the project manager	The project co-ordinator will need to exhibit strong leadership and organizational skills to successfully juggle the demands of co-ordinating two projects.

(Continued)

TABLE 22.2   (Continued)

Matters arising	Responses by PROP team
	Administrative support for the project has been partly addressed by the transitional support worker assuming some administrative duties, however once he has a full caseload this may become problematic
Record keeping and document management for the project and evaluation	Evaluators need to be provided with substantial evidence on whether project files are now in place, including key documents, policy manual, etc.

What this does not fully indicate is that, as a direct result of our feedback, the original project manager – who was the instigator for the funding grant that financially underpinned the PROP and who was inspirational in selling the idea of a highly sophisticated and supportive prison release programme – was released from his job. As it turned out, while he is a great visionary this person was not really suited to project management. Thankfully, he recognized this himself during the course of our continuous feedback sessions and there was no acrimony associated with his departure. We remain close friends to this day.

SUMMARY AND REVIEW

Doing criminological evaluation involves many different variables. It is usually done in teams, with varying degrees of competence, experience, expertise and understanding. It is frequently undertaken in the context of a 'who pays the piper calls the tune' type of situation that, in turn, demands that evaluators clearly establish their independence and ethical integrity from the very beginning. It is highly politically charged insofar as evaluation outcomes have funding implications as well as providing fodder for claims of 'evidence-based' policy making.

This chapter has provided a basic introduction to some of the key concerns and concepts of criminological evaluation. As part of this, the concept of performance indicators was introduced, and quantitative, qualitative and interpretive approaches were identified as potential methods of data collection. The three stories were used to elaborate on certain themes stemming from actual evaluations: (1) politics, in this case referring to a situation in which the results of an evaluation were misused by the Attorney General to cut a programme's funding; (2) relationships, in which a person hired to do interviews was totally opposed to imprisonment and subsequently very rude to prison staff that she interviewed, thereby putting other relationships in jeopardy; and (3) consequences, in which a good person and nice friend in effect lost his job as project manager as a result of the findings derived from the continuous evaluation model.

Evaluation research has its dilemmas and limitations, but for criminology and criminologists it is an essential part of the trade. For it is through criminological evaluation that we can best measure – to some degree and with some precision – that what happens in criminal justice institutions, and by those contributing in some way to criminal justice processes and outcomes (such as NGOs, volunteers, academics and others), is what we say is happening. 'For better or for worse' is not simply a matter of opinion, basic social values and ideological disposition. It is also determined in the crucible of grounded assessment and honest evaluation.

STUDY QUESTIONS AND ACTIVITIES FOR STUDENTS

1. Evaluation is often seen as threatening rather than empowering. Discuss.

2. What is the difference between a formative and a summative evaluation?

3. What are the resource implications of continuous evaluation as compared to evaluation that focuses solely on outputs and results?

4. There are multiple purposes of evaluation that include the assessment of outcomes, processes, management issues and the identification of current and future needs. Discuss.

5. Why are establishing benchmarks and performance indicators essential to assessing what a specific project, programme or strategy is doing?

6. Evaluating a local post-release prison service

THE ISSUE

Most prisoners do eventually leave prison. However, very often they find difficulty in gaining access to needed social resources such as affordable housing, employment opportunities and health services. Moreover, spending time in prison can carry with it considerable social stigma. For this reason, government and non-government support agencies are important in providing a stepping stone toward social reintegration. However, provision of such support is resource intensive and very demanding, and there are major questions as to whether or not it works and under

(Continued)

(Continued)

what conditions. Among the key questions are: does post-release support reduce recidivism among ex-prisoners, and how does it address the multiple criminogenic factors of the ex-prisoner?

The evaluation is concerned with processes and outcomes directly linked to the post-release process. General questions might include:

- Which services are most useful to ex-prisoners and their families?
- Which processes and practices deliver relevant and timely support?
- Which aspects of the programme/services are most useful in deterring re-offending/recidivism?
- Which collaborative processes and practices are most effective in delivering post-release services?

Describe other general and specific questions that should be asked in undertaking an evaluation of a post-release support programme, project or strategy. [Hint: the evaluation could also use an Appreciative Inquiry approach to evaluation, which draws out moments of excellence/peak experiences; successful processes and outcomes; and feedback and insights for improved outcomes.]

Data would need to be collected that would show:

- a reduction in anti-social behaviour
- multiple criminogenic factors identified, prioritized, targeted and addressed
- increased engagement with families
- increased support for offenders transitioning from prison
- increased access to support services
- the ability to access stable accommodation for the duration of the programme
- increased employment and vocational opportunities
- decreased dependency on transitional support services measured over the duration of participation in the programme.

What methods of data collection and which data could be used as part of this evaluation? [Hint: this can include literature reviews, document analysis, statistical records, media accounts, observation, regular site visits and in-depth interviews.]

SUGGESTIONS FOR FURTHER READING

Bartels, L. and Richards, K. (eds) (2011) *Qualitative Criminology: Stories from the Field*. Sydney: Hawkins Press. This book provides an opportunity for researchers to reflect on the practical, ideological and ethical issues that arise in the course of undertaking qualitative criminology.

Bowen, E. and Brown, S. (eds) (2012) *Perspectives on Evaluating Criminal Justice and Corrections*. Bingley: Emerald Group. This book provides a general introduction and overview of different perspectives and approaches to doing evaluation work involving criminal justice institutions.

Hough, M. (2010) 'Gold standard or fool's gold? The pursuit of certainty in experimental criminology', *Criminology and Criminal Justice*, 10(1): 11–22. This article provides a critical review of the idea that one method – namely, experimental criminology – is the best standard against which to compare other research methods when undertaking criminological research.

Shannon, L. and Schaefer, J. (2014) 'Evaluation research', in *The Encyclopedia of Criminology and Criminal Justice*. Oxford: Blackwell. This entry provides an overview of evaluation research within a criminological context and as applied to criminal justice.

White, R. (2013) 'Doing evaluation research', in M. Walter (ed.), *Social Research Methods*, 3rd edition. Melbourne: Oxford University Press. This book chapter provides an introduction and overview of the ways in which evaluation research is carried out, and includes reference to criminal justice issues and institutions.

REFERENCES

Australasian Evaluation Society (AES) (1998) *Guidelines for the Ethical Conduct of Evaluations*. Canberra: AES.

Australian Institute of Criminology (AIC) (2003) Evaluation in Crime and Justice: Trends and Methods. Available at: www.aic.gov.au/events/aic_upcoming_events/2003/evaluation.html (accessed 2 May 2018).

Australian Youth Foundation (AYF) and Sharp, C. (1996) *START: Do-It-Yourself Evaluation Manual*. Sydney: AYF.

Bartels, L. and Richards, K. (eds) (2011) *Qualitative Criminology: Stories from the Field*. Sydney: Hawkins Press.

Bowen, E. and Brown, S. (eds) (2012) *Perspectives on Evaluating Criminal Justice and Corrections*. Bingley: Emerald Group.

Crow, I. (2000) 'Evaluating initiatives in the community', in V. Jupp, P. Davies and P. Francis (eds), *Doing Criminological Research*. London: Sage.

Hough, M. (2010) 'Gold standard or fool's gold? The pursuit of certainty in experimental criminology', *Criminology and Criminal Justice*, 10(1): 11–22.

Murray, G., Homel, R., Wimshurst, K., Prenzler, T. and O'Connor, I. (1993) *A Framework for Evaluating Community-Based Juvenile Crime Prevention Programs*. Research and Policy Paper No.4, Centre for Crime Policy and Public Safety, Griffith University, Queensland.

Queensland Government (2016) Criminal Justice Evaluation Framework. Available at: www.premiers.qld.gov.au/publications/categories/guides/criminal-justice.aspx (accessed 2 May 2018).

Shannon, L. and Schaefer, J. (2014) 'Evaluation research', in *The Encyclopedia of Criminology and Criminal Justice*. Oxford: Blackwell.

Tilley, N. (2000) 'Doing realistic evaluation of criminal justice', in V. Jupp, P. Davies and P. Francis (eds), *Doing Criminological Research*. London: Sage.

Wadsworth, Y. (1991) *Everyday Evaluation on the Run*. Melbourne: Action Research Issues Association (Inc.).

Walter, M. (ed.) (2013a) *Social Research Methods*. Melbourne: Oxford University Press.

Walter, M. (2013b) 'The nature of social science research', in M. Walter (ed.), *Social Research Methods*. Melbourne: Oxford University Press.

White, R. (2011) *Evaluating the Australian Red Cross Peer Support Program*. Hobart: Criminology Research Unit, School of Sociology and Social Work, University of Tasmania and Australian Red Cross, Canberra.

White, R. (2013) 'Doing evaluation research', in M. Walter (ed.), *Social Research Methods*, 3rd edition. Melbourne: Oxford University Press.

White, R. and Coventry, G. (2000) *Evaluating Community Safety: A Guide*. Melbourne: Crime Prevention Victoria, Department of Justice.

White, R. and Mason, R. (2003) *An Evaluation of the 'Inside Out' Prison Program*. Occasional Paper No. 2, Criminology Research Unit, School of Sociology and Social Work, University of Tasmania.

White, R., Heckenberg, D. and O'Halloran, N. (2011) *Evaluation of the Post Release Options Program*. Hobart: School of Sociology and Social Work, UTAS and Bethlehem House, Hobart.

Wilson, G. and Wright, M. (1993) *Evaluation Framework: Women's Health Services and Centres against Sexual Assault*. Melbourne: Centre for Development and Innovation in Health.

GLOSSARY

Abolitionism: a theory, a strategy and a social movement. As a theoretical perspective, it is informed by an ethical and political critique of the violence and harm of prison. As a strategy, it calls for the end of the use of imprisonment and the building of communities and societies shaped by the principles of social justice. As a social movement, abolitionism is a collective organization working directly through research, policy interventions and direct action for progressive social change.

Algorithm: a finite sequence of instructions, to perform a task, solve a problem or answer a question. For example, long division is an algorithm that converts inputs (the dividend and divisor) into the output (here, quotient). Machine learning relies on algorithms.

Autobiography: an account of one's own personal life as described by the person holding such experience (i.e. the person themselves).

Benchmarks: data that are collected at a particular time and in relation to which future comparisons are made.

Big Data: generally defined as data having high volume, high velocity (speed of production and processing) and high variety (of data types and sources). The term sometimes also incorporates analytic techniques employed to extract information from such data. However, there are different definitions (Chan and Bennett Moses, 2016), including a 'new epistemological approach for making sense of the world' (Kitchin, 2014: 2) and 'a cultural, technological and scholarly phenomenon' involving technology, analysis and mythology (boyd and Crawford, 2012: 663).

Biography: an account of the experiences of another person, as described by someone else (i.e. an author, biographer or social scientist).

'Brief and charge':   the totality of intentions, instructions and restrictions adopted or generated by the maker(s) of images (e.g. artists), whether consciously or subconsciously, before and during the image production process.

Case: a spatially and temporally bounded unit, which is observed at one point in time (synchronic) or over time (diachronic); it is the phenomenon you want to explain.

Case study: an intensive study of one case to understand a larger set of cases.

Category saturation: in qualitative analysis, the point at which your interviews/observations add nothing to what you already know about a category, its properties, and its relationship to the core category. When this occurs you cease coding for that category.

Causal relationship: something that exists when one phenomenon exerts an influence on another.

Chain referral sampling (also known as snowball sampling): a technique by which researchers use existing participants to recruit further respondents from their circle of acquaintances. Since the respondents are recruited solely because they are known to other participants, the sample cannot be probabilistic or taken as representative of the population as a whole.

Clean/dirty data: involves the notion that many data sets contain flaws. Cleaning data involves identifying those flaws and removing them. Like hygiene, we can remove many known flaws but can never know that we have removed all of them.

Coining: an offence that involved the making and passing off of counterfeit coins. The offence was particularly associated with women, who were thought to be able to pass counterfeit currency in shops, although the number of women who were prosecuted at the Old Bailey and elsewhere suggests that this was actually a very risky form of offending for women.

Comparative methodology: widely used to test hypotheses by examining whether similarities and differences between two or more cases accord with theoretical expectations.

Complainant: the person who brings the case to court, not necessarily the victim of the crime. It may be a police officer or a parent who brings a case on behalf of another person.

Complementarity: used in mixed methods research where two or more methods are used to investigate distinct, albeit often overlapping, aspects of a phenomenon in order to produce rich, deep understanding.

Conceptual themes: themes that represent underlying ideas or principles emerging from your data. A conceptual theme or themes are findings in their own right because they are commonalities.

Constructivism: a philosophical notion of science that is critical of positivism's and postpositivism's belief in objective reality, and the proposition that it can be explored using the human senses. Constructivists instead consider that there are people and groups of people who construct images of reality. These are the images that should be the subject of scientific research.

Content analysis: a research method based on the study of documents or other forms of communication. The content of such communications can take the form of text, images, audio and video recordings, animations and even computer games. The aim is to examine such content so as to uncover patterns or tendencies in communications or representations, and it can be undertaken using both quantitative and qualitative techniques.

Continuous evaluation: the efforts by evaluators to generate feedback and improvement in, and as part of, the evaluation process itself.

Correlation: occurs where two variables tend to fluctuate together, either positively or negatively. The demonstration of correlation can be distinguished from the demonstration of causation, the latter implying that a change in one variable is what leads to a change in the other.

Covert observation: a social research method that involves data collection through observation of people's social practices in the natural settings in which they occur, and without those individuals' knowledge that they are being observed and studied.

Covert research: conducted by a researcher in the absence of the participants' knowledge. Once common, it is now regarded by many universities as a form of deception and therefore unethical, especially when it coincides with a high safety risk for the researcher.

Crime concentration: the number of crimes experienced by each victim on average.

Critical research: that which connects personal problems to wider social issues, and exposes how structural relations of power impact on understandings and experiences of violence, harms and justice.

Cross-sectional methodology: involves researchers studying a sample or a population at a single, specific moment in time, in contrast to longitudinal research.

Cross-sectional studies: rely on multiple observations of different cases from the same point in time. Such studies are generally cheaper than longitudinal studies and can often involve more cases or a larger sample size. Nevertheless, they present what is essentially a 'static' snapshot of what may be a dynamic and quickly changing phenomenon.

Data analytics: a general term to describe analysis that is conducted on data in order to extract useful information or inferences, including approaches based on machine learning. Related terms include data analysis, data science and data mining.

Data signature: describes the available evidence patterns that follow from the operation of specific causes in specific contexts. The more detailed the better for testing hypotheses.

Decision making: the process of adjudicating between alternative courses of action and of making choices based on such adjudication. One way of viewing the research process is as a series of decisions taken about the topic of research, the way in which research problems are formulated, the form of case selection, data collection and data analysis. The validity of research conclusions is the outcome of such decisions.

Deductive: refers to the relationship between theory and research, where the research is conducted based on a hypothesis that utilizes existing theory (see inductive for a contrasting approach). In simple terms, deductive is an approach to research that seeks to test a theory or hypothesis with observations or data.

Deductive research: involves the use of qualitative or quantitative research to test the validity of hypotheses derived from existing theories or data sets.

Descriptive research: aims to provide information about the unit of analysis at the centre of the research question. The research can be qualitative (e.g. the physical layout of a courtroom) or quantitative (e.g. the number of offences recorded by the police across police force areas). Although the aim of the research is not to look for causal relationships (see explanatory research), it is possible for descriptive research to be deeply analytic.

Development: a technique of mixed methods research involving the employment of a sequential design, with the inferences drawn from the first component used to help inform the development of the second component. This approach is employed to increase the robustness of the findings and any concepts generated as a result.

Developmental and life-course criminology: in contrast to traditional criminology, has its focus on the similarities and differences in crime *between* or *within* individuals measured at the same point in time or at repeated points in time. The field focuses on understanding the onset, persistence and desistance of crime.

Diachronic: an approach to research that seeks to determine whether there is change over a period of time in the phenomenon of interest.

Digital corpus linguistic methods: put simply, where we take a large amount of text and count the number of times that particular words or phrases appear. This allows the researcher, for example, to count how many times words like 'lawyer' or 'victim' are used each year.

Discourse analysis: a broad term that refers to the analysis of written and spoken communication. It generally focuses on what is being said, and the implicit ideas, assumptions and ideologies that may underpin this. It is concerned with the implications of the construction of knowledge and ideas. In the criminal justice and criminological setting, it may be applied, for example, to seek to know how crime or victimization or responsibility are understood.

Emotionality: involves reflecting on how research processes and practices generate (sometimes challenging) emotional responses, and how these impact on the collection and use of research.

Environment assessment: analysis of the context within which research or evaluation is to occur, such as auditing the human and material resources needed for a project and examining the policies that might affect its development.

Epistemology: the theory of knowledge, concerned with the question of what counts as valid knowledge. Broadly, epistemology is constructive or positivistic. It concerns how we go about evidencing our beliefs and claims to legitimate knowledge. It refers to what and who is included/excluded from our conception of social reality.

Ethnography: a research method that originates in social and cultural anthropology, but which has been widely adopted and adapted across the social sciences. A qualitative approach, ethnography focuses on the cultural practices and interactions that take place in a particular locale, setting or community, and seeks to elicit a detailed and fine-grained understanding of the lives of those studied.

Evaluation: a process of assessing what we are doing, understanding why we are doing it and evaluating how we can make improvements in the future.

Expansion: refers to mixed methods research that provides breadth and depth to the exploration of a particular phenomenon. This approach reflects the philosophically pragmatic notion of selecting the most appropriate tool for the job at hand.

Experience: the sensory awareness of the world during encounters with objects in it. At this sensory level, experience is largely pre-conceptual, pre-language even.

Explanatory research: about looking for patterns and relationships between variables, thus providing a causal explanation for a phenomenon.

Fieldwork: primary data collection done in the field, which is a time-limited and space-limited setting in which a particular ethnographic research project is being conducted. Field notes and audio or visual recordings are the standard methods used in fieldwork.

Formative evaluation: forward-looking evaluation, the purpose of which is to identify needs, clarify rationales and improve implementation in the future.

Generalizability: the extent to which data and analyses produced in one specific research setting can be claimed to be relevant to similar research settings in other places and time periods.

Grounded theory: associated originally with Glaser and Strauss (1967) and is an inductive approach which starts with data collection, and then, as data emerge, constant comparisons are made between data and theory.

Hard to reach: a term which refers to a group of people who are not typically represented in survey data due to their marginalized, isolated, socially excluded or highly mobile nature. Examples include rough sleepers, chaotic drug users and undocumented migrants. They may also be termed 'seldom heard'.

Hot spots: locations where crime rates are relatively high. Hot spot policing focuses police efforts on hot spot locations, for example by increasing police deployments in those areas or focusing problem-solving efforts on those areas.

Hypothesis: a logical conjecture about the possible relationship between two or more variables expressed in the form of a testable statement.

Hypothesis testing: refers to the collection and analysis of data whose patterns are expected in the light of theory. The more specific the expected pattern and the more closely high-quality data patterns accord with it, the better corroborated the theory.

Incidence rates: incidence rates for crime describe the number of incidents in relation to the population at risk. It is often expressed as crimes per 1,000 or per 100,000. The denominator refers to the population at risk, which depends on the crime in question.

Inductive: an orientation to research inquiry that involves reasoning from evidence or 'inference' and often involves generalizing from something that has been studied or observed to other cases that have not.

Inductive research: a broad approach in which researchers start with as few preconceptions as possible and build theory from the ground as they gather and reflexively analyse their data.

Inference quality: the evaluative term used in mixed methods research to judge the value of the conclusions and interpretations that stem from the integration of findings from each component of the research. It is the mixed methods equivalent of the evaluative term 'validity'.

Inferences and meta-inferences: the conclusions and interpretations from each single component (quantitative or qualitative) of a mixed methods research project, whilst meta-inferences are the conclusions and interpretations drawn from across all of the quantitative and qualitative components.

Initiation: mixed methods research where new perspectives or paradoxes emerge. This may not have been the purpose of the mixed methods design, but the inferences generated from each component of the research allow for further analysis to be undertaken to create new knowledge and ideas.

Inquest: a judicial inquiry which is tasked with ascertaining the facts regarding the circumstances of a given incident. When a person dies in prison (or indeed any other form of state custody), an inquest is conducted by a coroner with the assistance of a jury in a specially convened 'coroners court'.

Intelligence-led policing: (which includes predictive policing): a 'strategic, future-oriented and targeted approach to crime control, focusing upon the identification, analysis and "management" of persisting and developing "problems" or "risks" ... rather than on the reactive investigation and detection of individual crime' (Maguire, 2000: 315).

Interviews: a method of data collection, information or opinion gathering that specifically involves asking a series of questions.

Inverse trend: a trend where an increase in one is associated with a fall in another.

Life-course study: in general, focuses on tracing, understanding and explaining within-individual continuity and/or changes in attitudes, thought patterns and/or behaviour over time.

Life history interview: a form of interview where the interviewee narrates their life in a more or less structured form.

Literature review: an evaluative overview, synthesis or survey of the main published work in a given topic or field. It provides an overview of the state of academic knowledge on a research topic and is increasingly known as a narrative literature review.

Longitudinal research: a form of research involving repeated observations (through measures such as surveys, register data, tests or interviews) of the same unit of analysis (such as a variable, person or place) over time.

Longitudinal studies: studies that rely on repeated observations of the same examples/cases over time. They are often time-consuming and costly but bring the advantage of being able to demonstrate the dynamic nature of a given phenomenon – for example, the development of the impact of crime on victims over time.

Machine learning: occurs where a computer optimizes parameters in a model drawing on data in a training set. Examples of machine learning techniques include neural networks, decision trees, random forests and Bayesian learning. Machine learning can be supervised (where a training set with known classifications is employed) or unsupervised (where the algorithm itself identifies clusters or patterns in data).

Method: the tools used to collect data on a particular phenomenon, broadly categorized as quantitative or qualitative.

Methodological tools: the data collection and analysis techniques that are used in research.

Methodology: the principles and ideas on which researchers base their procedures and strategies, shaped by ontological and epistemological positions. Methodology is a process or system.

Mixed methods design: the element of a mixed methods study where decisions on the priority question (is there a dominant component or are the components equal in status?) and the sequence question (do the components occur simultaneously or sequentially?) are made.

Multiple realities: an ontological position often associated with mixed methods research. It suggests that there is no single 'correct' ontological understanding of the social world, and that instead there are multiple understandings of reality and each has some validity.

Narrative literature review: see literature review.

Natural experiment: occurs where changes that can be used to test a hypothesis are made, but not through an experimenter's intervention.

Non-participant observation: a social research method that involves data collection through the observation of people's social practices in the natural settings in which they occur, but in which the researcher him or herself does not participate. The researcher typically maintains a distance from the activities and phenomena being studied.

Observation(s): the basic unit of empirical inquiry; the 'lowest-level units in an analysis' (Gerring, 2017: xxviii).

Offender risk assessment: tools that attempt to quantify the risk that a person charged with or convicted of a crime will commit an offence while on bail, comply with bail conditions, re-offend once released or released on bail, and/or commit a violent offence while on bail or parole. These tools are used in some jurisdictions by those tasked with making decisions about bail, parole and/or sentencing.

Old Bailey (or The 'Bailey'): London's central criminal court which dealt with serious offences, and still does today.

Ontology: a way of conceiving of the social world around us. It reflects certain assumptions about the nature of society and the way in which society is likely to develop in the future. It is the theory of 'reality' – whether reality exists independent of society, or whether it is constructed by people.

Operationalization: this refers to the laying down of rules which stipulate when instances of a concept have occurred. Operational rules link abstract concepts to observations. Such observations are sometimes also known as indicators. The extent to which observations are truly indicating instances of a concept is the extent to which an operationalisation has measurement validity.

Overt research: research conducted openly by a researcher who supplies the participants with full and transparent information about the research project and the purpose and destination of the findings. The information is usually provided in writing and accompanied by consent forms for participants to sign.

Participant observation: ethnography's principal research method. It is a social research method that involves data collection through the observation of people's social practices in the natural settings in which they occur, and in which the researcher is an active participant. It entails the immersion of the researcher in the research setting and the systematic recording of data regarding events, cultural practices, artefacts and symbolic meanings ready for analysis and theorization. Most closely associated with ethnography, participant observation typically involves the researcher in a close and extended interaction with those under study, taking part in the various activities that are the focus of analysis.

Performance indicators: measures designed to indicate present performance in relation to stated goals.

Performance targets: identification of the end point goals of a particular programme or project.

Persistence and desistance in crime: in criminology, *persistence* is used to describe an individual's continuity in crime; *desistance* means the cessation, or ending, of the criminal career.

Perspective: a particular attitude towards or way of regarding something; a dedicated point of view.

Pilot study: is an exploratory investigation that attempts to outline the area of study prior to the development of questionnaires. "If the main study is going to employ mainly closed questions, open questions can be asked in the pilot to generate the fixed-choice answers" (Bryman, 2001: 155).

Piloting: is a term used to describe the process of 'trying-out' or practicing your research instruments (interview/ questionnaire) on a population that matches your target population. Piloting reveals which parts of an interview/questionnaire work and which don't. Research tools can then be adjusted accordingly.

Positivism: the scientific approach to studying human life. It is a philosophical notion of science, where one assumes that an objective reality exists and can be studied systematically and numerically (e.g. using quantitative data) and without interference from the researcher's subjectivity. Positivists believe that the methods and methodologies of the natural sciences can be applied to the study of human societies.

Pragmatism: an epistemological position often adopted in mixed methods research. Pragmatism seeks to bypass the debates around positivism and interpretivism by taking a practical stance that focuses on the research question at hand, utilizing the 'best' research tools available to provide the 'best' outcome.

Praxis: how theory connects to practice, particularly in terms of the research contribution to transforming unequal or oppressive social conditions.

Prediction: refers, in Chapter 11, to statements or inferences as to the probability that particular events will take place in the future, such as statements as to the most likely locations of future crime or statements as to the probability that a particular individual will commit, or be the victim of, an offence.

Predictive policing: a term applied to a range of policing practices linked by their claimed ability to 'forecast where and when the next crime or series of crimes will take place' (Uchida, 2014: 3871) in order to 'change outcomes' (Beck and McCue, 2009). Predictive policing is a prediction-led business process consisting of a cycle of activities and decision points: data collection, analysis, police operations, criminal response and back to data collection (Perry et al., 2013: 128).

Prevalence rates: prevalence rates for crime describe the proportion of a population at risk that has experienced one or more incidents. It is normally expressed as a percentage. The denominator refers to the population at risk, which depends on the crime in question.

Primary data this refers to the data that is derived from a form of inquiry and analysis whereby an investigator collects the data at first hand.

Probability sampling: a method by which all elements of a given population have a chance of being included in the sample studied. Unlike a purposive sample, a probabilistic sample uses random selection so as to generate, as far as possible, a sample that is representative of the broader population. Using probability sampling enables researchers to generalize from their findings, thereby deriving conclusions about a far larger group of people to which the sample belongs.

Process analysis: assessment of progressive changes over time that may include actions directed at a particular result or impact.

Prosopography: collecting key characteristics of the lives of a group of people (e.g. doctors, prisoners, railway train drivers; it can be any group) and aggregating them together to form a group 'pattern' of their lives.

Prospective design: a research design consisting of repeated observations of the same group of individuals through time, as they age. Prospective essentially means 'looking forward'.

Purposive sampling (also known as nonprobability sampling): organized around a non-randomly derived subset of a population. Convenience sampling and Chain referral sampling are commonplace instances of such an approach. Given its non-random nature, a purposively derived sample cannot be taken as representative of the wider population from which it has been drawn.

Qualitative: qualitative methodology is concerned with exploring the behaviour, opinions or perspectives, feelings and experiences of people as individuals or groups. It lies in the *interpretive* approach to social reality: reality does not exist independently of people, but rather is socially constructed and meaning is developed through experience.

Qualitative research: research that investigates aspects of social life which are not amenable to quantitative measurement. Associated with a variety of theoretical perspectives, qualitative research uses a range of methods to focus on meanings and interpretations of social phenomena and social processes in the particular contexts in which they occur. Qualitative data includes words, sounds and images.

Quality assurance: ensuring that what is done is of the highest standard through constructive critical review.

Quantitative: quantitative methodology is concerned with measuring or testing existing ideas or theories (hypotheses) and generally assumes that reality exists independently of human construction and experience. It is associated with *positivism*.

Quantitative research: involves the collection of data in numerical form for quantitative analysis. The numerical data can be durations, scores, counts of incidents, ratings or scales. Quantitative data can be collected in either controlled or naturalistic environments, in laboratories or field studies, from special populations or from samples of the general population. The defining factor is that numbers result from the process, whether the initial data collection produced numerical values, or whether non-numerical values were subsequently converted to numbers as part of the analysis process, as in content analysis (Garwood, 2006).

Questionnaire: a structured set of questions designed to gather comparable information from research respondents. Most of the questions will have a fixed choice of answers.

Reflexivity: a broad concept but essentially encompasses a process whereby the researcher actively engages in self-assessment at all stages of the research process with a view to acknowledging and, where possible, addressing any biases or other shortcomings in their work, especially those deriving from culturally held assumptions. It encourages researchers' recognition and articulation of the research process and their own relationship to the research (including to participants, where relevant), and it offers an ongoing reflection on the development of understanding in the research process. Often, it is identified as a point of distinction from 'hard' science where the research is presumed to be objective; however, there are ongoing debates in this area on the meaning and relevance of reflexivity.

Repeat crime rates: the number of crimes experienced by each victim on average.

Research design: a detailed plan of the procedures for data collection and analysis.

Research ethics: institutionalized means of ensuring that research is carried out in ways that respect the rights of all researchers and participants. The three main issues associated with ethnographic research and governed by research ethics are deception, safety and confidentiality.

Research objectives: the purposes for which the research is being carried out. They can be basic – couched in terms of exploration, description, understanding, explanation or prediction – or they can be of an applied nature, for example to change, to evaluate or to assess social impacts.

Research proposal: a written document which describes the proposed research, including what it aims to do, how it will be undertaken and the anticipated outcome(s). A proposal also outlines why the proposed research is important and justifies the research design, including how it connects the research questions to the data.

Research question: the overarching question that defines the scope, scale and conduct of a research project. It is an initial statement of the territory to be examined in the research inquiry.

Retrospective design: meaning 'looking backward', a research design in which a sample is selected based on some criteria. Having done so, the researcher traces their backgrounds and past experiences through some empirical material (such as register data or life history interviews).

Sampling there are different ways of and approaches to constructing samples in social and criminological research. Sometimes it is not possible, simple or necessary to generate a statistically representative sample (e.g. of all young adults living in a particular locality). Convenience sampling refers to the process of constructing a sample in a way that is convenient to the researcher, given lack of resources such as time (e.g. interviewing relatively easily accessible young adults in a particular locality, such as those attending local colleges). Theoretical sampling refers to the way that a sample is generated that reflects the theoretical concerns and research questions of the study. Random samples are intended to be representative of the population from which they are drawn and therefore the characteristics of the sample are assumed to be generalisable across the whole population. Members of the sample are drawn randomly using a sampling frame and everyone in the population stands the same chance of being included in the sample. Probability sampling is another name given to random sampling. Purposive samples are not intended to be generalisable to the population as a whole. Instead, they are used to focus on specific groups or categories and select units based on pre-defined characteristics (such as gender or victim status). They are particularly useful for populations that are hard to reach. Non probability sampling is another name given to purposive sampling.

Sampling error: essentially refers to false findings from statistical data caused by the use of a sample that is unrepresentative of the full population under study.

Secondary research/analysis is based upon existing sources of information which has been collected by someone other than the researcher and with some purpose other than the current research problem in mind. It can be distinguished from primary research and analysis whereby an investigator collects the data at first hand. Examples of secondary sources include Census data and the Recorded Crime Statistics.

Secondary data: data that has already been collected by someone other than the researcher who is presently analysing it. Such data may well have been collected for a purpose other than that for which it is now being examined or re-used. Commonplace and widely used examples of secondary data include official statistics, large-scale surveys and census returns.

Self-inflicted deaths (SIDs): refer to people who have taken their own life and is a term now used by the prison service to describe all non-natural prisoner deaths. Although the injury or harmful activity that resulted in the death of the prisoner was inflicted by their own hands, the person who died may not necessarily have intended to take their own life. The harmful activity may have been a cry of pain or a cry for help rather than an attempt to kill themselves.

Semiotics: the discipline and study of signs.

Semi-structured interviews: a popular form of interview in the social sciences, which requires the development of an interview schedule. This is not necessarily specified questions but key areas to address in an interview, which can be raised in any order. It is semi-structured because the loose structure allows the interviewer to explore new ideas and diversions or issues that arise in the course of the interview in depth, whilst also ensuring that they consistently address the questions outlined in the schedule.

Sensitive research: used to describe taboo or difficult topics, for example victimization or deviant behaviour. The term may be used where research elicits the views of vulnerable or 'powerless' groups such as children.

Snowball sampling: see chain referral sampling.

Spatial variation: involves differences in the social, geographical or political organization of the phenomenon of interest; in the social sciences, the typical referent is to individuals, small groups, neighbourhoods, cities, regions or countries.

Storytelling: an unstructured interview approach that allows interviewees to guide the narrative on their own terms, in their own language.

Structured interviews: involve the interviewer setting the same questions for all respondents. Standardization means that interviews are easily replicated and analysed. However, the data is deeply influenced by the researcher's values, definitions and perceptions.

Summative evaluation: concerned with results and backward looking; it is used to assess performances and outcomes up to a certain point in time.

Survey questionnaire: a research tool that gathers data from respondents through eliciting answers to an organized series of questions. The questionnaire may be administered in written form, verbally (with the researcher and respondent interacting in real time), face to face or at a distance (e.g. online, via telephone, email or post).

Survey research: involves the systematic collection of large quantities of data, by means of questionnaires and/or interviews, from a broad sample of a target population

Symbolic interactionism: the theory that deals with how an individual builds the image of him/herself through a communication process with other individuals. It is communication that takes place through symbols, mainly language. In criminology, symbolic interactionism is most commonly associated with the works of Howard S. Becker and Erving Goffman, and the perspective known as 'labelling': a process through which the individual is labelled by the social environment as evil, deviant or criminal. Methodologically, symbolic interactionism is associated with qualitative data and fieldwork.

Synchronic: an approach to research that describes a phenomenon at one point in time.

Systematic review: a formulaic and prescriptive form of review that employs transparent and systematic criteria for searching the literature, evaluating the suitability of each source and synthesizing results. Such reviews are favoured for feeding into policy making as they bring together the most directly relevant and rigorous evaluations on a particular topic.

Tagging: where original documents are digitized and certain words are picked out or 'tagged' so that those words, phrases or figures can be searched for and sometimes additional labels can be adopted. For example, if a victim is called 'John Smith', he can be tagged as 'John Smith', so that his name can be searched for, and also tagged as 'male' since we assume that it is a man's name. Hence, the gender of all victims in the Old Bailey can be collected.

Temporal variation: the differences or change over time in the phenomenon of interest.

Training set: the data in a set, often drawn from past experience, used in machine learning in order to discover predictive relationships. This can be contrasted with test or validation data, which is used subsequently to assess the validity and strength of an identified predictive relationship.

Transcription: the method of converting the audio and visual data gathered by the researcher into a written form in preparation for coding and analysis. Naturalized transcription is informed by conversation analysis and takes account of every nuance in speech and bodily movement, whilst denaturalized transcription focuses on the more significant meanings.

Triangulation: used in mixed methods research where two or more methods are used to investigate the same phenomenon to ensure consistency and reduce the limitations of a single method. The aim is to seek a convergence and corroboration of the inferences generated from each research component.

Validity the extent to which one can rely upon and trust the findings and conclusions of a research study. This involves an evaluation of the methodological objections that can be raised. This means looking at internal validity (can we be sure that a causal relationship exists?), external validity (can the results be generalised?) and ecological validity (are the conclusions applicable to everyday situations or have they been drawn from unnatural or unique conditions?). In addition, construct or measurement validity is concerned with whether a measure accurately reflects the concept it is designed to measure.

Variable: an attribute of an observation or set of observations; having a shared meaning with 'factor', it is the name a researcher gives to what is being described or measured.

Victim–offender overlap: the notion that many victims of crime are also perpetrators. There is a considerable overlap between the two, which is often not recognized in debates about victims of crime.

Virtual ethnography: the adaptation of ethnography to the online environment. Unlike traditional ethnography, where the researcher and those being researched are physically co-present in a given spatial location, virtual ethnography takes place in various online forums or spaces such as chatrooms, discussion groups, social media platforms and interactive simulations.

Visual criminology: the field in criminological and criminal justice studies in which the role and importance of visual experience, images and imagery in criminal offending, criminalization and stigmatization, and crime control, as broadly defined, are explored, analysed and studied.

Visual turn: the focus, from about the 1990s onwards, in the humanities and social sciences, on the visual sphere and visual experience as dimensions of study and analysis.

REFERENCES

Beck, C. and McCue, C. (2009) 'Predictive policing: what can we learn from Wal-Mart and Amazon about fighting crime in a recession?', *The Police Chief*, *76*(11): 20–9.

boyd, d. and Crawford, K. (2012) 'Critical questions for Big Data: provocations for a cultural, technological, and scholarly phenomenon', *Information, Communication and Society*, *15*: 662–79.

Chan, J. and Bennett Moses, L. (2016) 'Is Big Data challenging criminology?', *Theoretical Criminology*, *20*: 21–39.

Garwood, J. (2006) 'Quantitative research', in V. Jupp (ed.), *The SAGE Dictionary of Social Research Methods*. London: Sage, pp. 251–2.

Gerring, J. (2017) *Case Study Research: Principles and Practices*, 2nd edition. Cambridge: Cambridge University Press.

Glaser, B.G. and Strauss, A.L. (1967) *The Discovery of Grounded Theory: Strategies for Qualitative Research*. Chicago: Aldine.

Kitchin, R. (2014) 'Big Data, new epistemologies and paradigm shifts', *Big Data and Society*, *1*: 1–12.

Maguire, M. (2000) 'Policing by risks and targets: some dimensions and implications of intelligence-led crime control', *Policing and Society*, *9*: 315–36.

Perry, W.L., McInnis, B., Price, C.C., Smith, S.C. and Hollywood, J.S. (2013) *Predictive Policing: The Role of Crime Forecasting in Law Enforcement Operations*. Santa Monica, CA: RAND.

Uchida, C. (2014) 'Predictive policing', in G. Bruinsma and D. Weisburd (eds), *Encyclopedia of Criminology and Criminal Justice*. New York: Springer, pp. 3871–80.

INDEX

NOTE: Page numbers in *italic* type refer to boxes, figures and tables. Page numbers in bold type refer to glossary entries.

convergent parallel design, 122
Copes, C., 397
copyediting, 168
copyright, 171
Correctional Offender Management Profiling
for Alternative Sanctions (COMPAS),
255, 261
correlation, 259–60, 261, **521**
costs, 329, 421
counter-trafficking efforts, 345, 349–50
court registers, 181–82
covert observation, 425–6, **521**
covert research, 389, *390*, 399–400, 403,
404, **521**
Cox, D., *371*
Cox, P., 179
creative methods, 104–5
Creswell, J.W., 128
crime
case study examples, 486–7
comparative research on, 466–7
data *see* data
desistance from, 308, *310*
disclosure of, 396, 398, 399
crime concentration, 233
crime control, and images, 441–42
crime drop
alternative explanations, 243–4
background, 230–32
data sources, 232–4
future research, 244, 245
and reductions in criminality, 241–42
research methods, 232–3
security and burglary, 238–8, 242–3
security and car theft, 234–8, 242
security and violence, 240–1
Crime in the Making (Sampson and Laub), *310*
crime prediction *see* offender risk assessment;
predictive policing
crime rates
comparative research, 466–7
see also crime drop
Crime Survey for England and Wales (CSEW),
15–17, 19
and crime drop, 234, 235, 239, 240–1
and gender, 377
and sensitive topics, 206–8
criminal biographies, 367–74
criminal careers, 241
criminal justice
case study examples, 487–90
comparative research in practice, 462–4
and globalization, 456–8, 468
historical study *see* history of victims

human trafficking in context of, 343–4, 346
and images, 440–42, 447–9
importance of comparative work, 458–60
international comparisons, 456–7
and researching victims, 180–1
shifting focus of, 457–8
Criminal Lives (Godfrey et al), *371*
criminality, reductions in, 241–42
criminalization, 440
criminological research, golden threads
of, 3–5
criminology
and biography *see* biographical research
and ethnography *see* ethnography
and scientific relevancy, 143–4
critical approach
in evaluation research, 502–3
in victimology, 375–6
critical engagement with literature, 85
critical ethnography, 401
critical reading, 46
critical reflection, 26, 57–8, 288–91, 445
see also reflexivity
critical research, 324–5, 334, **521**
cross-case research, 479–81, 481, 483, 485
cross-cultural research, 8–9
cross-sectional methodology, **521**
compared with longitudinal, 299, 311–15
cross-sectional studies, **521**
CSEW *see* Crime Survey for England and Wales
cybercrime, 414, 419–20
CYPSS (Children and Young People's Safety
Survey), 217

Daley, Tom, 434–6
Daly, K., 475, 488, *489–90*
data
on crime, 14–17
and ethics, *56*
limitations of, 258–9, 302, 303, 306, 346–7,
416–17
qualitative, 49, 307–9
quantitative, 49, 306–7, 501–2
see also Big Data; crime rates; official data/
documents; secondary data
data analysis
in ethnography, 392
qualitative and quantitative, 54, *55–6*
of web-based content, 417–20
see also qualitative data analysis; secondary
analysis
data analytics, **521**
evaluation of, 263–4
limitations of, 258–62

building trust, 329–30
emotionality, 331–32
method choice, 326–7
reflections, 332–5
speaking out, 330–1
intimate partner violence, 487–9
intimate personal violence, 207–8
introductions, 163
inverse trend, **524**

The Jack Roller, 365–6, 374
Jay Report, 272–3
Joliffe, D., 77
Jones, T., 463
journal articles, 415
joyriding, 235–6
The Judgement of Cambyses (David), 447–9
Jupp, V., 41, 48–9, 365–6, 367
justice *see* criminal justice

Kearon, T., 188
Kelley, K., *486*
Kelly, L., 205
Kennet, J., 209
key informants, 389, 398, 400
Khasnabish, A., 154
King, A., 125
Kirchengast, T., 186
Kleck, G., 98
knowledge *see* epistemology; theory building
Koestler Trust, 434
Koller, S.H., *281–83*

labour trafficking, 342
language, 437–8
Laub, J.H., 308, 310
law
  and documentary analysis, 354–5
  see also criminal justice; police and policing
learning from mistakes, 173
Lee, E., 420
Lee, R.M., 202, 216
Leets, L., 420
length of dissertations, 166–7
Lewis, P., 487
library catalogues, 81
life history interviews, 308–9, 315, 365–6, **524**
life-course research
  advantages of, 299–300
  and biography, 368–70
  cross-sectional and longitudinal compared,
    311–15
  definition of, 300, **524**
  mixed methods, 309–11

prospective and retrospective, 300–305
quantitative and qualitative, 305–9
Lippens, R., 433
literature, types of, 69–70
literature reviews, 11–12, **525**
  in dissertation structure, 163
  examples of, 72–3, 77
  narrative reviews, *37–8*, 45, 73–4, 79, 83
  nature of, 44–5, 68–71
  online, 415
  process, 80–5
  purpose of, 12, 71–2, 95
  as research method, 106
  systematic reviews, *37–8*, 45, 75–9, 106,
    276, 277
literature searches, 80–2
literature-based dissertations, *37–8*, 48–52
Lloyd Warner, W., 477
loaded questions, 212–13
location of crime, predicting, 254–5
location of research, 388–9
Loeber, R., 312
Lombroso, C., 437
long questions, 212
Long Weatherred, J., 277
longitudinal research/studies
  compared with cross-sectional, 311–15
  definition, 300, **525**
  mixed methods, 309–11
  prospective and retrospective, 300–305
  quantitative and qualitative, 305–9
Lösel, F., 77
lurking, 425
Lutz, C., 210
Luyendijk, J., 399–400

McCormack, D., 154
McGarry, R., 363
machine learning, 260, **525**
macro theories, 69
Maguire, M., 366
malestream view, 376–7
Mancini, C., *424*
Marsh, C., 205
Maruna, S., 125, 305–6, 309
Mawby, R., *459*
Maxwell-Stewart, H., *371*
May, T., 41, 70
meaning, 275, 443
Mears, D.P., *424*
media, 170, *276, 277*, 355
Meisenhelder, T., 307–8
Merriam, S.B., 477
meso theories, 69

sources *see* digital sources; secondary data
spatial variation, 483–5, **530**
speaking out, victims of state violence, 330–1
Spencer, J., 199
SPF (Security Protection Factor), 236–7, 239
sponsors, 27, *151*
  see also research funding
Stack, C., *485*
Stake, R.E., 477
stakeholders, 27, 507–10
  see also research funding
Stalans, L., 219
standpoint research, 9
Stanford Prison Experiment, 149–50
Stanley, E., 321
Stanley (*The Jack Roller*), 365–6, 374
State, 143, 144, 147, 152
state violence *see* victims of state violence
status (priority) question, 119–20, 122
Stockholm Life-Course Project (SLCP),
  302–5, 315
storytelling, 323–4, 327, **531**
Stouthamer-Loeber, M., 312
stratified samples, *53*
stress management, 173
structural ethnography, 393
structure of dissertations, 163–5
structured interviews, 19, 322, **531**
student plagiarism research, *479–81, 481, 482,*
  483, 484
subject-specific guides, 81
substantive literature, 70
Sudman, S., 213
suicide, 138, 146, 154, **531**
summarising oral presentations, 172
summative evaluations, 505, **531**
supervision, 57, 351, *352*
survey questionnaires, *51*, 98–100, 205–6,
  217–21, **531**
survey questions, 98–9, 209–16, 217, 220
survey research, 18–19, 98–100, 203–4, **531**
  criticisms of, 100, 204–6
  online, 423–4
  and sensitive research, 198, 205–6
    CSEW approach, 206–8
    examples, 216–21
    questions, 209–16, 217, 220
    with vulnerable groups, 19, 200, 208–9,
      217–18
  victimization surveys, 206–8, 232–4, 245, 466–7
  see also Crime Survey for England and Wales
symbolic interactionism, 167, 305, 374, **531**
symbols, 446, 447
synchronic, 484, **531**

synchronous interviews, 421
systematic literature reviews, 37–8, 45, 75–9,
  106, **531**
  and analysis, 276, 277
systematic samples, *53*

tagging, 191, 192, **531**
Tashakkori, A., 124–5, 128, 129
Taylor, L., 145, 146
Teddlie, C., 124–5, 128, 129
telephone interviews, 20
temporal variation, 483–4, **532**
Tewksbury, R., 68
theft *see* burglary; car theft
thematic content analysis, *281–83*
thematically structured literature reviews, 85
theoretical literature, 69–70
theory building, 285–7, 476, 477
The Third of May 1808 (Goya), 441
Thody, A., 165–8
Thomas, W.I., 364
Thompson, G., 467
Tilley, N., 229
time frames
  and interviews, 329, 421
  in longitudinal research, 314–15
time management, 46–7, 166, 172
timing, in oral presentations, 170
title pages, 163
tone, 168
topic *see* research topic
Trafficking Protocol, 343–6
training set, *256*, **532**
transcription, 391, **532**
triangulation, 97, 125, 238, **532**
trust, 329–10, 398, 400, 427, 509–10
  see also rapport
truth, 115, 142–3
  see also authenticity
Tseloni, A., 229
Tyldum, G., 347

Ullman, S.E., *288*
ultra-realism, 167, 168
ultra-realist ethnographic networks, 404
Unraveling Juvenile Delinquency (Glueck), *310*
unstructured interviews, 19, 20, 100,
  322,323–4, 327

validity, 13–14, 22, 28–9, 96, 128, 483
validity 'trade-off', 13
value neutrality, 142
values, 503, 504, 506
variables, 313–14, 479, **532**